The Editors

RICHARD E. FLATHMAN is George Armstrong Kelly Memorial Professor of Political Science at Johns Hopkins University, where he has taught since 1976. His many books include *Thomas Hobbes: Skepticism, Individuality and Chastened Politics; Willful Liberalism: Individuality and Voluntarism in Liberal Theory and Practice; Toward a Liberalism; The Philosophy and Politics of Freedom;* and *The Practice of Political Authority.*

DAVID JOHNSTON is Associate Professor of Political Science at Columbia University, where he has taught since 1986. He is the author of *The Idea of a Liberal Theory: A Critique and Reconstruction* and *The Rhetoric of Leviathan: Thomas Hobbes and the Politics of Cultural Transformation.*

LEVIATHAN

AUTHORITATIVE TEXT
BACKGROUNDS
INTERPRETATIONS

Norton Critical Editions in the History of Ideas

For a complete list of Norton Critical Editions, visit
www.wwnorton.com/college/english/nce/welcome.htm

A NORTON CRITICAL EDITION

Thomas Hobbes
LEVIATHAN

AUTHORITATIVE TEXT

BACKGROUNDS

INTERPRETATIONS

Edited by

RICHARD E.
FLATHMAN

JOHNS HOPKINS UNIVERSITY

DAVID
JOHNSTON

COLUMBIA UNIVERSITY

W • W • NORTON & COMPANY • *New York* • *London*

The text of this book is composed in Electra
with the display set in Bernhard Modern.
Composition by PennSet, Inc.
Manufacturing by Courier.
Book design by Antonina Krass.
Cover illustration: Frontispiece to the 1651 edition of *Leviathan*.

The illustrations on p. 3 and p. 49 are from the 1651 edition of *Leviathan* in the
Seligman collection of the Rare Books Library at Columbia University.

Library of Congress Cataloging-in-Publication Data
Hobbes, Thomas, 1588–1679.
Leviathan : an authoritative text : backgrounds interpretations /
Thomas Hobbes ; edited by Richard E. Flathman, David Johnston.
p.   cm. — (A Norton critical edition)
Includes bibliographical references.
1. Political science — Early works to 1800. 2. State, The.
I. Flathman, Richard E. II. Johnston, David, 1951–   . III. Title.
IV. Series.
JC153.H65   1996b
320.1 — dc20   95-42021
Rev.
ISBN 0-393-96798-0 (pbk.)

W. W. Norton & Company, Inc., 500 Fifth Avenue, New York, N.Y. 10110
W. W. Norton & Company Ltd., Castle House, 75/76 Wells Street,
London W1T 3QT

7 8 9 0

Contents

Preface

Hobbes wrote the bulk of *Leviathan* during the closing phase of a civil war and completed the work soon after the war had come to a decisive end. In many respects the book bears the marks of its origins in the particular circumstances of that war and the long string of events that preceded it. But *Leviathan* is also, and was intended to be, a book for the ages. It deals with themes and topics that have been with us since the beginning of recorded history and are likely to remain significant for as long a time as we can foresee. Moreover, few thinkers in the history of political thought have been Hobbes's equal as a shrewd observer of political events, and none has ever exceeded him in boldness of argument. For these reasons *Leviathan* is widely regarded as the greatest work of political theory ever composed in the English language and one of the greatest in any language.

Leviathan is not, however, an easy book to read, both because Hobbes's arguments are challenging and because his language is sometimes archaic and unfamiliar. The task of grasping Hobbes's argument is one that the reader must accomplish on his or her own, but this edition will ease the burden imposed by Hobbes's seventeenth-century prose by explaining the meanings of words that are unusual or archaic and by identifying references that are likely to be unfamiliar to modern readers. For the most part, these explanations appear in footnotes and only at the first occurrence of an unfamiliar term, but we have also provided a brief glossary that includes terms Hobbes uses repeatedly.

A large part of the text of *Leviathan* consists of arguments from Scripture addressed to a seventeenth-century audience that considered the Bible to be the written Word of God and, hence, to be at least as authoritative as any argument based on reason. These arguments were crucial to the aims that led Hobbes to write and publish *Leviathan*, but they are far less accessible to modern readers than they were to Hobbes's contemporaries. In any case, it is not necessary to read through the whole of Hobbes's Scriptural exegesis to understand the central points he was making. Accordingly, we have deleted from this edition several chapters that are most likely to seem esoteric to modern readers, mainly from Part Three. At the same time, we have retained the chapters from Part Three that are essential to an understanding of Hobbes's argument, particularly chapters thirty-two, thirty-three, thirty-seven, and forty-three.

Our edition is based on the version published by Oxford University Press in 1909, a version in turn based on a "standard paper" copy of the genuine first edition of *Leviathan*, known among scholars as the

"Head" edition (because of the ornament that appears near the bottom of the title page). Various copies of this first edition are not identical, because some incorporated more of Hobbes's corrections than others, but the 1909 edition was made up from one of the most fully corrected copies and, for this reason, is superior to most modern editions, including the edition edited by C. B. Macpherson and published in 1968 by Penguin Books. We have also compared the text on which our edition is based with a "large paper" copy of the genuine first edition — from which both Richard Tuck's 1991 edition (Cambridge University Press) and Edwin Curley's 1994 edition (Hackett Press) are derived — as well as with the manuscript copy of *Leviathan* in the British Museum (cataloged as British Library MS Egerton 1910). Tuck is undoubtedly right to assert that the large paper edition is even more fully corrected than the standard paper copy upon which our edition is ultimately based. But large paper copies were available to very few readers in the seventeenth century; the standard paper version, in one edition or another, is the one to which most readers have, until very recently, had access. For these reasons we have chosen the standard paper version as the basis for our edition. In any case, few of the variations among these versions are significant. Where potentially significant variations occur, however, we have included them in our text. *Additions* to the standard paper copy are enclosed in brackets, with their source (either the large paper edition or the manuscript version) indicated in a footnote. Where *alternative* passages occur, we have enclosed the relevant passage in brackets, and the alternative passage is given in a footnote, together with its source. The numbers enclosed in brackets in the margins of the text give the page numbers of the Head edition of 1651.

The Text of
LEVIATHAN

LEVIATHAN,

OR

The Matter, Forme, & Power

OF A

COMMON-WEALTH

ECCLESIASTICALL

AND

CIVILL.

By THOMAS HOBBES *of* Malmesbury.

LONDON,
Printed for ANDREW CROOKE, at the Green Dragon
in St. *Pauls* Church-yard, 1651.

To My Most Honor'd Friend
Mr Francis Godolphin of *Godolphin*.

Honor'd Sir,

Your most worthy Brother Mr *Sidney Godolphin*,[1] when he lived, was pleas'd to think my studies something, and otherwise to oblige me, as you know, with reall testimonies of his good opinion, great in themselves, and the greater for the worthinesse of his person. For there is not any vertue that disposeth a man, either to the service of God, or to the service of his Country, to Civill Society, or private Friendship, that did not manifestly appear in his conversation,[2] not as acquired by necessity, or affected upon occasion, but inhærent, and shining in a generous constitution of his nature. Therefore in honour and gratitude to him, and with devotion to your selfe, I humbly Dedicate unto you this my discourse of Common-wealth. I know not how the world will receive it, nor how it may reflect on those that shall seem to favour it. For in a way beset with those that contend, on one side for too great Liberty, and on the other side for too much Authority, 'tis hard to passe between the points of both unwounded. But yet, me thinks, the endeavour to advance the Civill Power, should not be by the Civill Power condemned; nor private men, by reprehending it, declare they think that Power too great. Besides, I speak not of the men, but (in the Abstract) of the Seat of Power, (like to those simple and unpartiall creatures in the Roman Capitol, that with their noyse defended those within it, not because they were they, but there,) offending none, I think, but those without, or such within (if there be any such) as favour them. That which perhaps may most offend, are certain Texts of Holy Scripture, alledged by me to other purpose than ordinarily they use to be by others. But I have done it with due submission, and also (in order to my Subject) necessarily; for they are the Outworks of the Enemy, from whence they impugne the Civill Power. If notwithstanding this, you find my labour generally decryed, you may be pleased to excuse your selfe, and say I am a man that love my own opinions, and think all true I say, that I honoured your Brother, and honour you, and have presum'd on that, to assume the Title (without your knowledge) of being, as I am,

SIR

Your most humble, and most

obedient servant,

Paris, *Aprill* $\frac{15}{25}$. 1651.   THO. HOBBES.

---

1. Sidney Godolphin (1610–1643) died in battle fighting for the king. He left Hobbes £200 in his will. His brother Francis (1605–1667) was governor of the Scilly Islands until 1646.
2. Behavior; dealings with others.

5

The Contents of the Chapters*

The first Part,

Of Man.

The second Part,

Of Common-wealth.

* Brackets enclose the titles of chapters omitted from this Norton Critical Edition.

7

The third Part.

Of a Christian Common-wealth.

The fourth Part.

Of The Kingdome Of Darknesse

Nature (the Art whereby God hath made and governes the World) is by the *Art* of man, as in many other things, so in this also imitated, that it can make an Artificial Animal. For seeing life is but a motion of Limbs, the begining whereof is in some principall part within; why may we not say, that all *Automata* (Engines that move themselves by springs and wheels as doth a watch) have an artificiall life? For what is the *Heart*, but a *Spring*; and the *Nerves*, but so many *Strings*; and the *Joynts*, but so many *Wheeles*, giving motion to the whole Body, such as was intended by the Artificer? *Art* goes yet further, imitating that Rationall and most excellent worke of Nature, *Man*. For by Art is created that great LEVIATHAN called a COMMON-WEALTH, or STATE, (in latine CIVITAS) which is but an Artificiall Man; though of greater stature and strength than the Naturall, for whose protection and defence it was intended; and in which, the *Soveraignty* is an Artificiall *Soul*, as giving life and motion to the whole body; The *Magistrates*, and other *Officers* of Judicature and Execution, artificiall *Joynts*; *Reward* and *Punishment* (by which fastned to the seate of the Soveraignty, every joynt and member is moved to perform his duty) are the *Nerves*, that do the same in the Body Naturall; The *Wealth* and *Riches* of all the particular members, are the *Strength*; *Salus Populi* (the *peoples safety*) its *Businesse*; *Counsellors*, by whom all things needfull for it to know, are suggested unto it, are the *Memory*; *Equity* and *Lawes*, an artificiall *Reason* and *Will*; *Concord*, *Health*; *Sedition*, *Sickness*; and *Civill war*, *Death*. Lastly, the *Pacts* and *Covenants*, by which the parts of this Body Politique were at first made, set together, and united, resemble that *Fiat*, or the *Let us make man*, pronounced by God in the Creation.

To describe the Nature of this Artificiall man, I will consider [2]

First, the *Matter* thereof, and the *Artificer*; both which is *Man*.
Secondly, *How*, and by what *Covenants* it is made; what are the *Rights* and just *Power* or *Authority* of a *Soveraigne*; and what it is that *preserveth* and *dissolveth* it.
Thirdly, what is a *Christian Common-wealth*.
Lastly, what is the *Kingdome of Darkness*.

Concerning the first, there is a saying much usurped of late, That *Wisedome* is acquired, not by reading of *Books*, but of *Men*. Consequently whereunto, those persons, that for the most part can give no other proof of being wise, take great delight to shew what they think they have read in men, by uncharitable censures of one another behind

9

their backs. But there is another saying not of late understood, by which they might learn truly to read one another, if they would take the pains; and that is, *Nosce teipsum*, *Read thy self*: which was not meant, as it is now used, to countenance, either the barbarous state of men in power, towards their inferiors; or to encourage men of low degree, to a sawcie behaviour towards their betters; But to teach us, that for the similitude of the thoughts, and Passions of one man, to the thoughts, and Passions of another, whosoever looketh into himself, and considereth what he doth, when he does *think, opine, reason, hope, feare,* &c, and upon what grounds; he shall thereby read and know, what are the thoughts, and Passions of all other men, upon the like occasions. I say the similitude of *Passions*, which are the same in all men, *desire, feare, hope,* &c; not the similitude of the *objects* of the Passions, which are the things *desired, feared, hoped,* &c: for these the constitution individuall, and particular education do so vary, and they are so easie to be kept from our knowledge, that the characters of mans heart, blotted and confounded as they are, with dissembling, lying, counterfeiting, and erroneous doctrines, are legible onely to him that searcheth hearts. And though by mens actions wee do discover their designe sometimes; yet to do it without comparing them with our own, and distinguishing all circumstances, by which the case may come to be altered, is to decypher without a key, and be for the most part deceived, by too much trust, or by too much diffidence; as he that reads, is himself a good or evil man.

But let one man read another by his actions never so perfectly, it serves him onely with his acquaintance, which are but few. He that is to govern a whole Nation, must read in himself, not this, or that particular man; but Man-kind: which though it be hard to do, harder than to learn any Language, or Science; yet, when I shall have set down my own reading orderly, and perspicuously, the pains left another, will be onely to consider, if he also find not the same in himself. For this kind of Doctrine, admitteth no other Demonstration.

Of Man

Chap. I.

Of SENSE.

Concerning the Thoughts of man, I will consider them first *Singly*, and afterwards in *Trayne*, or dependance upon one another. *Singly*, they are every one a *Representation* or *Apparence*, of some quality, or other Accident of a body without us; which is commonly called an *Object*. Which Object worketh on the Eyes, Eares, and other parts of mans body; and by diversity of working, produceth diversity of Apparences.

The Originall of them all, is that which we call SENSE; (For there is no conception in a mans mind, which hath not at first, totally, or by parts, been begotten upon the organs of *Sense*.) The rest are derived from that originall.

To know the naturall cause of Sense, is not very necessary to the business now in hand; and I have elsewhere written of the same at large. Nevertheless, to fill each part of my present method, I will briefly deliver the same in this place.

The cause of Sense, is the Externall Body, or Object, which presseth the organ proper to each Sense, either immediatly, as in the Tast and Touch; or mediately, as in Seeing, Hearing, and Smelling: which pressure, by the mediation of Nerves, and other strings, and membranes of the body, continued inwards to the Brain, and Heart, causeth there a resistance, or counter-pressure, or endeavour of the heart, to deliver it self: which endeavour because *Outward*, seemeth to be some matter without. And this *seeming*, or *fancy*, is that which men call *Sense*; and consisteth, as to the Eye, in a *Light*, or *Colour figured*; To the Eare, in a *Sound*; To the Nostrill, in an *Odour*; To the Tongue and Palat, in a *Savour*; And to the rest of the body, in *Heat, Cold, Hardnesse, Softnesse,* and such other qualities, as we discern by *Feeling*. All which qualities called *Sensible*, are in the object that causeth them, but so many several motions of the matter, by which it presseth our organs diversly. Neither in us that are pressed, are they any thing else, but divers motions; (for motion, produceth nothing but motion.) But their apparence to us is Fancy, the same waking, that dreaming. And as pressing, rubbing, or striking the Eye, makes us fancy a light; and pressing the Eare, produceth a dinne; so do the bodies also we see, or hear, produce the same by their strong, though unobserved action. For if those Colours, and Sounds, were in the Bodies, or Objects that cause them, they could

11

[4] not be severed from them, as by glasses, and in Ecchoes by reflection, wee see they are; where we know the thing we see, is in one place; the apparence, in another. And though at some certain distance, the reall, and very object seem invested with the fancy it begets in us; Yet still the object is one thing, the image or fancy is another. So that Sense in all cases, is nothing els but originall fancy, caused (as I have said) by the pressure, that is, by the motion, of externall things upon our Eyes, Eares, and other organs thereunto ordained.

But the Philosophy-schooles, through all the Universities of Christendome, grounded upon certain Texts of *Aristotle*, teach another doctrine; and say, For the cause of *Vision*, that the thing seen, sendeth forth on every side a *visible species* (in English) a *visible shew, apparition*, or *aspect*, or *a being seen*; the receiving whereof into the Eye, is *Seeing*. And for the cause of *Hearing*, that the thing heard, sendeth forth an *Audible species*, that is, an *Audible aspect*, or *Audible being seen*; which entring at the Eare, maketh *Hearing*. Nay for the cause of *Understanding* also, they say the thing Understood sendeth forth *intelligible species*, that is, an *intelligible being seen*; which comming into the Understanding, makes us Understand. I say not this, as disapproving the use of Universities: but because I am to speak hereafter of their office in a Common-wealth, I must let you see on all occasions by the way, what things would be amended in them; amongst which the frequency of insignificant Speech is one.

Chap. II.

Of IMAGINATION.

That when a thing lies still, unlesse somewhat els stirre it, it will lye still for ever, is a truth that no man doubts of. But that when a thing is in motion, it will eternally be in motion, unless somewhat els stay it, though the reason be the same, (namely, that nothing can change it selfe,) is not so easily assented to. For men measure, not onely other men, but all other things, by themselves: and because they find themselves subject after motion to pain, and lassitude, think every thing els growes weary of motion, and seeks repose of its own accord; little considering, whether it be not some other motion, wherein that desire of rest they find in themselves, consisteth. From hence it is, that the Schooles say, Heavy bodies fall downwards, out of an appetite to rest, and to conserve their nature in that place which is most proper for them; ascribing appetite and Knowledge of what is good for their conservation, (which is more than man has) to things inanimate, absurdly.

When a Body is once in motion, it moveth (unless something els hinder it) eternally; and whatsoever hindreth it, cannot in an instant, but in time, and by degrees quite extinguish it: And as wee see in the water, though the wind cease, the waves give not over rowling for a
[5] long time after; so also it happeneth in that motion, which is made in the internall parts of a man, then, when he Sees, Dreams, &c. For after

the object is removed, or the eye shut, wee still retain an image of the thing seen, though more obscure than when we see it. And this is it, the Latines call *Imagination*, from the image made in seeing; and apply the same, though improperly, to all the other senses. But the Greeks call it *Fancy*; which signifies *apparence*, and is as proper to one sense, as to another. IMAGINATION therefore is nothing but *decaying sense*; and is found in men, and many other living Creatures, aswell sleeping, as waking.

The decay of Sense in men waking, is not the decay of the motion made in sense; but an obscuring of it, in such manner, as the light of the Sun obscureth the light of the Starres; which starrs do no less exercise their vertue by which they are visible, in the day, than in the night. But because amongst many stroaks, which our eyes, eares, and other organs receive from externall bodies, the predominant onely is sensible; therefore the light of the Sun being predominant, we are not affected with the action of the starrs. And any object being removed from our eyes, though the impression it made in us remain; yet other objects more present succeeding, and working on us, the Imagination of the past is obscured, and made weak; as the voyce of a man is in the noyse of the day. From whence it followeth, that the longer the time is, after the sight, or Sense of any object, the weaker is the Imagination. For the continuall change of mans body, destroyes in time the parts which in sense were moved: So that distance of time, and of place, hath one and the same effect in us. For as at a great distance of place, that which wee look at, appears dimme, and without distinction of the smaller parts; and as Voyces grow weak, and inarticulate: so also after great distance of time, our imagination of the Past is weak; and wee lose (for example) of Cities wee have seen, many particular Streets; and of Actions, many particular Circumstances. This *decaying sense*, when wee would express the thing it self, (I mean *fancy* it selfe,) wee call *Imagination*, as I said before: But when we would express the *decay*, and signifie that the Sense is fading, old, and past, it is called *Memory*. So that *Imagination* and *Memory*, are but one thing, which for divers considerations hath divers names. *Memory*.

Much memory, or memory of many things, is called *Experience*. Againe, Imagination being only of those things which have been formerly perceived by Sense, either all at once, or by parts at severall times; The former, (which is the imagining the whole object, as it was presented to the sense) is *simple Imagination*; as when one imagineth a man, or horse, which he hath seen before. The other is *Compounded*; as when from the sight of a man at one time, and of a horse at another, we conceive in our mind a Centaure. So when a man compoundeth the image of his own person, with the image of the actions of an other man; as when a man imagins himselfe a *Hercules*, or an *Alexander*, (which happeneth often to them that are much taken with reading of Romants[1]) it is a compound imagination, and properly but a Fiction of the mind. There be also other Imaginations that rise in men, (though [6]

---

1. Romances.

waking) from the great impression made in sense: As from gazing upon the Sun, the impression leaves an image of the Sun before our eyes a long time after; and from being long and vehemently attent upon[2] Geometricall Figures, a man shall in the dark, (though awake) have the Images of Lines, and Angles before his eyes: which kind of Fancy hath no particular name; as being a thing that doth not commonly fall into mens discourse.

Dreams.   The imaginations of them that sleep, are those we call *Dreams*. And these also (as all other Imaginations) have been before, either totally, or by parcells in the Sense. And because in sense, the Brain, and Nerves, which are the necessary Organs of sense, are so benummed in sleep, as not easily to be moved by the action of Externall Objects, there can happen in sleep, no Imagination; and therefore no Dreame, but what proceeds from the agitation of the inward parts of mans body; which inward parts, for the connexion they have with the Brayn, and other Organs, when they be distempered, do keep the same in motion; whereby the Imaginations there formerly made, appeare as if a man were waking; saving that the Organs of Sense being now benummed, so as there is no new object, which can master and obscure them with a more vigorous impression, a Dreame must needs be more cleare, in this silence of sense, than are our waking thoughts. And hence it cometh to passe, that it is a hard matter, and by many thought impossible to distinguish exactly between Sense and Dreaming. For my part, when I consider, that in Dreames, I do not often, nor constantly think of the same Persons, Places, Objects, and Actions that I do waking; nor remember so long a trayne of coherent thoughts, Dreaming, as at other times; And because waking I often observe the absurdity of Dreames, but never dream of the absurdities of my waking Thoughts; I am well satisfied, that being awake, I know I dreame not; though when I dreame, I think my selfe awake.

And seeing dreames are caused by the distemper of some of the inward parts of the Body; divers distempers must needs cause different Dreams. And hence it is, that lying cold breedeth Dreams of Feare, and raiseth the thought and Image of some fearfull object (the motion from the brain to the inner parts, and from the inner parts to the Brain being reciprocall:) And that as Anger causeth heat in some parts of the Body, when we are awake; so when we sleep, the over heating of the same parts causeth Anger, and raiseth up in the brain the Imagination of an Enemy. In the same manner; as naturall kindness, when we are awake causeth desire; and desire makes heat in certain other parts of the body; so also, too much heat in those parts, while wee sleep, raiseth in the brain an imagination of some kindness shewn. In summe, our Dreams are the reverse of our waking Imaginations; The motion when we are awake, beginning at one end; and when we Dream, at another.

[7]   The most difficult discerning of a mans Dream, from his waking
Apparitions or thoughts, is then, when by some accident we observe not that we have
Visions.   slept: which is easie to happen to a man full of fearfull thoughts; and

2. Attentive to.

whose conscience is much troubled; and that sleepeth, without the circumstances, of going to bed, or putting off his clothes, as one that noddeth in a chayre.[3] For he that taketh pains, and industriously layes himself to sleep, in case any uncouth[4] and exorbitant fancy come unto him, cannot easily think it other than a Dream. We read of *Marcus Brutus*, (one that had his life given him by *Julius Cæsar*, and was also his favorite, and notwithstanding murthered him,) how at *Philippi*, the night before he gave battell to *Augustus Cæsar*, hee saw a fearfull apparition, which is commonly related by Historians as a Vision: but considering the circumstances, one may easily judge to have been but a short Dream. For sitting in his tent, pensive and troubled with the horrour of his rash act, it was not hard for him, slumbering in the cold, to dream of that which most affrighted him; which feare, as by degrees it made him wake; so also it must needs make the Apparition by degrees to vanish: And having no assurance that he slept, he could have no cause to think it a Dream, or any thing but a Vision. And this is no very rare Accident: for even they that be perfectly awake, if they be timorous, and supperstitious, possessed with fearfull tales, and alone in the dark, are subject to the like fancies; and believe they see spirits and dead mens Ghosts walking in Church-yards; whereas it is either their Fancy onely, or els the knavery of such persons, as make use of such superstitious feare, to passe disguised in the night, to places they would not be known to haunt.

From this ignorance of how to distinguish Dreams, and other strong Fancies, from Vision and Sense, did arise the greatest part of the Religion of the Gentiles in time past, that worshipped Satyres, Fawnes, Nymphs, and the like; and now adayes the opinion that rude[5] people have of Fayries, Ghosts, and Goblins; and of the power of Witches. For as for Witches, I think not that their witchcraft is any reall power; but yet that they are justly punished, for the false beliefe they have, that they can do such mischiefe, joyned with their purpose to do it if they can: their trade being neerer to a new Religion, than to a Craft or Science. And for Fayries, and walking Ghosts, the opinion of them has I think been on purpose, either taught, or not confuted, to keep in credit the use of Exorcisme, of Crosses, of holy Water, and other such inventions of Ghostly men. Neverthelesse, there is no doubt, but God can make unnaturall Apparitions: But that he does it so often, as men need to feare such things, more than they feare the stay, or change, of the course of Nature, which he also can stay, and change, is no point of Christian faith. But evill men under pretext that God can do any thing, are so bold as to say any thing when it serves their turn, though they think it untrue; It is the part of a wise man, to believe them no further, than right reason makes that which they say, appear credible. If this superstitious fear of Spirits were taken away, and with it, Prognostiques from Dreams, false Prophecies, and many other things depending thereon, by which, crafty ambitious persons abuse the simple   [8]

3. Chair.
4. Unfamiliar.
5. Uneducated.

people, men would be much more fitted than they are for civill
Obedience.

And this ought to be the work of the Schooles: but they rather nourish such doctrine. For (not knowing what Imagination, or the Senses
are), what they receive, they teach: some saying, that Imaginations rise
of themselves, and have no cause: Others that they rise most commonly
from the Will; and that Good thoughts are blown (inspired) into a man,
by God; and Evill thoughts by the Divell: or that Good thoughts are
powred (infused) into a man, by God, and Evill ones by the Divell.
Some say the Senses receive the Species of things, and deliver them to
the Common-sense; and the Common Sense delivers them over to the
Fancy, and the Fancy to the Memory, and the Memory to the Judgement, like handing of things from one to another, with many words
making nothing understood.

Understand-
ing.
The Imagination that is raysed in man (or any other creature indued
with the faculty of imagining) by words, or other voluntary signes, is
that we generally call *Understanding*; and is common to Man and
Beast. For a dogge by custome will understand the call, or the rating
of his Master; and so will many other Beasts. That Understanding which
is peculiar to man, is the Understanding not onely his will; but his
conceptions and thoughts, by the sequell and contexture of the names
of things into Affirmations, Negations, and other formes of Speech: And
of this kinde of Understanding I shall speak hereafter.

Chap. III.

Of the Consequence or TRAYNE of Imaginations.

By *Consequence*, or TRAYNE of Thoughts, I understand that succession of one Thought to another, which is called (to distinguish it from
Discourse in words) *Mentall Discourse.*

When a man thinketh on any thing whatsoever, His next Thought
after, is not altogether so casuall as it seems to be. Not every Thought
to every Thought succeeds indifferently. But as wee have no Imagination, whereof we have not formerly had Sense, in whole, or in parts;
so we have no Transition from one Imagination to another, whereof
we never had the like before in our Senses. The reason whereof is this.
All Fancies are Motions within us, reliques of those made in the Sense:
And those motions that immediately succeeded one another in the
sense, continue also together after Sense: In so much as the former
comming again to take place, and be prædominant, the later followeth,
by coherence of the matter moved, in such manner, as water upon a
plain Table is drawn which way any one part of it is guided by the
finger. But because in sense, to one and the same thing perceived,
sometimes one thing, sometimes another succeedeth, it comes to passe
[9]   in time, that in the Imagining of any thing, there is no certainty what
we shall Imagine next; Onely this is certain, it shall be something that
succeeded the same before, at one time or another.

This Trayne of Thoughts, or Mentall Discourse, is of two sorts. The first is *Unguided, without Designe,* and inconstant; Wherein there is no Passionate Thought, to govern and direct those that follow, to it self, as the end and scope of some desire, or other passion: In which case the thoughts are said to wander, and seem impertinent[1] one to another, as in a Dream. Such are Commonly the thoughts of men, that are not onely without company, but also without care of any thing; though even then their Thoughts are as busie as at other times, but without harmony; as the sound which a Lute out of tune would yeeld to any man; or in tune, to one that could not play. And yet in this wild ranging of the mind, a man may oft-times perceive the way of it, and the dependance of one thought upon another. For in a Discourse of our present civill warre, what could seem more impertinent, than to ask (as one did) what was the value of a Roman Penny? Yet the Cohærence to me was manifest enough. For the Thought of the warre, introduced the Thought of the delivering up the King to his Enemies; The Thought of that, brought in the Thought of the delivering up of Christ; and that again the Thought of the 30 pence, which was the price of that treason: and thence easily followed that malicious question; and all this in a moment of time; for Thought is quick.

Trayne of Thoughts unguided.

The second is more constant; as being *regulated* by some desire, and designe. For the impression made by such things as wee desire, or feare, is strong, and permanent, or, (if it cease for a time,) of quick return: so strong it is sometimes, as to hinder and break our sleep. From Desire, ariseth the Thought of some means we have seen produce the like of that which we ayme at; and from the thought of that, the thought of means to that mean; and so continually, till we come to some beginning within our own power. And because the End, by the greatnesse of the impression, comes often to mind, in case our thoughts begin to wander, they are quickly again reduced into the way: which observed by one of the seven wise men, made him give men this præcept, which is now worne out, *Respice finem;* this is to say, in all your actions, look often upon what you would have, as the thing that directs all your thoughts in the way to attain it.

Trayne of Thoughts regulated.

The Trayn of regulated Thoughts is of two kinds; One, when of an effect imagined, wee seek the causes, or means that produce it: and this is common to Man and Beast. The other is, when imagining any thing whatsoever, wee seek all the possible effects, that can by it be produced; that is to say, we imagine what we can do with it, when wee have it. Of which I have not at any time seen any signe, but in man onely; for this is a curiosity hardly incident to the nature of any living creature that has no other Passion but sensuall, such as are hunger, thirst, lust, and anger. In summe, the Discourse of the Mind, when it is governed by designe, is nothing but *Seeking,* or the faculty of Invention, which the Latines call *Sagacitas,* and *Solertia;* a hunting out of the causes, of some effect, present or past; or of the effects, of some present or past cause. Sometimes a man seeks what he hath lost; and

[10]

---

1. Unrelated.

from that place, and time, wherein hee misses it, his mind runs back, from place to place, and time to time, to find where, and when he had it; that is to say, to find some certain, and limited time and place, in which to begin a method of seeking. Again, from thence, his thoughts run over the same places and times, to find what action, or other oc-

Remembrance. casion might make him lose it. This we call *Remembrance*, or Calling to mind: the Latines call it *Reminiscentia*, as it were a *Re-conning* of our former actions.

Sometimes a man knows a place determinate, within the compasse whereof he is to seek; and then his thoughts run over all the parts thereof, in the same manner, as one would sweep a room, to find a jewell; or as a Spaniel ranges the field, till he find a sent[2] or as a man should run over the Alphabet, to start a rime.

Prudence. Sometime a man desires to know the event[3] of an action; and then he thinketh of some like action past, and the events thereof one after another; supposing like events will follow like actions. As he that foresees what wil become of a Criminal, re-cons what he has seen follow on the like Crime before; having this order of thoughts, The Crime, the Officer, the Prison, the Judge, and the Gallowes. Which kind of thoughts is called *Foresight*, and *Prudence*, or *Providence*; and sometimes *Wisdome*; though such conjecture, through the difficulty of observing all circumstances, be very fallacious. But this is certain; by how much one man has more experience of things past, than another; by so much also he is more Prudent, and his expectations the seldomer faile him. The *Present* onely has a being in Nature; things *Past* have a being in the Memory onely, but things *to come* have no being at all; the *Future* being but a fiction of the mind, applying the sequels[4] of actions Past, to the actions that are Present; which with most certainty is done by him that has most Experience; but not with certainty enough. And though it be called Prudence, when the Event answereth our Expectation; yet in its own nature, it is but Presumption. For the foresight of things to come, which is Providence, belongs onely to him by whose will they are to come. From him onely, and supernaturally, proceeds Prophecy. The best Prophet naturally is the best guesser; and the best guesser, he that is most versed and studied in the matters he guesses at: for he hath most *Signes* to guesse by.

Signes. A *Signe*, is the Event Antecedent, of the Consequent; and contrarily, the Consequent of the Antecedent, when the like Consequences have been observed, before: And the oftner they have been observed, the lesse uncertain is the Signe. And therefore he that has most experience in any kind of businesse, has most Signes, whereby to guesse at the Future time; and consequently is the most prudent: And so much more prudent than he that is new in that kind of business, as not to be equalled by any advantage of naturall and extemporary wit: though perhaps many young men think the contrary.

[11]   Neverthelesse it is not Prudence that distinguisheth man from beast.

2. Scent.
3. Result.
4. Consequences or projected consequences.

There be beasts, that at a year old observe more, and pursue that which is for their good, more prudently, than a child can do at ten.

As Prudence is a *Præsumtion* of the *Future*, contracted from the *Experience* of time *Past*: So there is a Præsumtion of things Past taken from other things (not future but) past also. For he that hath seen by what courses and degrees, a flourishing State hath first come into civil warre, and then to ruine; upon the sight of the ruines of any other State, will guesse, the like warre, and the like courses have been there also. But this conjecture, has the same incertainty almost with the conjecture of the Future; both being grounded onely upon Experience.

Conjecture of the time past.

There is no other act of mans mind, that I can remember, naturally planted in him, so, as to need no other thing, to the exercise of it, but to be born a man, and live with the use of his five Senses. Those other Faculties, of which I shall speak by and by, and which seem proper to man onely, are acquired, and encreased by study and industry; and of most men learned by instruction, and discipline; and proceed all from the invention of Words, and Speech. For besides Sense, and Thoughts, and the Trayne of thoughts, the mind of man has no other motion; though by the help of Speech, and Method, the same Facultyes may be improved to such a height, as to distinguish men from all other living Creatures.

Whatsoever we imagine, is *Finite*. Therefore there is no Idea, or conception of any thing we call *Infinite*. No man can have in his mind an Image of infinite magnitude; nor conceive infinite swiftness, infinite time, or infinite force, or infinite power. When we say any thing is infinite, we signifie onely, that we are not able to conceive the ends, and bounds of the thing named; having no Conception of the thing, but of our own inability. And therefore the Name of *God* is used, not to make us conceive him; (for he is *Incomprehensible*; and his greatnesse, and power are unconceivable;) but that we may honour him. Also because whatsoever (as I said before,) we conceive, has been perceived first by sense, either all at once, or by parts; a man can have no thought, representing any thing, not subject to sense. No man therefore can conceive any thing, but he must conceive it in some place; and indued with some determinate magnitude; and which may be divided into parts; nor that any thing is all in this place, and all in another place at the same time; nor that two, or more things can be in one, and the same place at once: For none of these things ever have, or can be incident to Sense; but are absurd speeches, taken upon credit (without any signification at all,) from deceived Philosophers, and deceived, or deceiving Schoolemen.

Chap. IV.

[12]

Of SPEECH.

The Invention of *Printing*, though ingenious, compared with the invention of *Letters*, is no great matter. But who was the first that found

Originall of Speech.

the use of Letters, is not known. He that first brought them into *Greece*, men say was *Cadmus*, the sonne of *Agenor*, King of Phænicia. A profitable Invention for continuing the memory of time past, and the conjunction of mankind, dispersed into so many, and distant regions of the Earth; and with all difficult, as proceeding from a watchfull observation of the divers motions of the Tongue, Palat, Lips, and other organs of Speech; whereby to make as many differences of characters, to remember them. But the most noble and profitable invention of all other, was that of SPEECH, consisting of *Names* or *Appellations*, and their Connexion; whereby men register their Thoughts; recall them when they are past; and also declare them one to another for mutuall utility and conversation; without which, there had been amongst men, neither Common-wealth, nor Society, nor Contract, nor Peace, no more than amongst Lyons, Bears, and Wolves. The first author of Speech was *God* himself, that instructed *Adam* how to name such creatures as he presented to his sight; For the Scripture goeth no further in this matter. But this was sufficient to direct him to adde more names, as the experience and use of the creatures should give him occasion; and to joyn them in such manner by degrees, as to make himself understood; and so by succession of time, so much language might be gotten, as he had found use for; though not so copious, as an Orator or Philosopher has need of. For I do not find any thing in the Scripture, out of which, directly or by consequence can be gathered, that *Adam* was taught the names of all Figures, Numbers, Measures, Colours, Sounds, Fancies, Relations; much less the names of Words and Speech, as *Generall, Speciall, Affirmative, Negative, Interrogative, Optative, Infinitive,* all which are usefull; and least of all, of *Entity, Intentionality, Quiddity,* and other insignificant words of the School.

But all this language gotten, and augmented by *Adam* and his posterity, was again lost at the tower of *Babel,* when by the hand of God, every man was stricken for his rebellion, with an oblivion of his former language. And being hereby forced to disperse themselves into severall parts of the world, it must needs be, that the diversity of Tongues that now is, proceeded by degrees from them, in such manner, as need (the mother of all inventions) taught them; and in tract of time grew every where more copious.

The use of   The generall use of Speech, is to transferre our Mentall Discourse,
Speech.   into Verbal; or the Trayne of our Thoughts, into a Trayne of Words; and that for two commodities[1]; whereof one is, the Registring of the
[13]   Consequences of our Thoughts; which being apt to slip out of our memory, and put us to a new labour, may again be recalled, by such words as they were marked by. So that the first use of names, is to serve for *Markes,* or *Notes* of remembrance. Another is, when many use the same words, to signifie (by their connexion and order,) one to another, what they conceive, or think of each matter; and also what they desire, feare, or have any other passion for. And for this use they are called *Signes.* Speciall uses of Speech are these; First, to Register, what by

---

1. Conveniences.

cogitation, wee find to be the cause of any thing, present or past; and what we find things present or past may produce, or effect: which in summe, is acquiring of Arts. Secondly, to shew to others that knowledge which we have attained; which is, to Counsell, and Teach one another. Thirdly, to make known to others our wills, and purposes, that we may have the mutuall help of one another. Fourthly, to please and delight our selves, and others, by playing with our words, for pleasure or ornament, innocently.

To these Uses, there are also foure correspondent Abuses. First, when men register their thoughts wrong, by the inconstancy of the signification of their words; by which they register for their conceptions, that which they never conceived; and so deceive themselves. Secondly, when they use words metaphorically; that is, in other sense than that they are ordained for; and thereby deceive others. Thirdly, when by words they declare that to be their will, which is not. Fourthly, when they use them to grieve one another: for seeing nature hath armed living creatures, some with teeth, some with horns, and some with hands, to grieve an enemy, it is but an abuse of Speech, to grieve him with the tongue, unlesse it be one whom wee are obliged to govern; and then it is not to grieve, but to correct and amend. *Abuses of Speech.*

The manner how Speech serveth to the remembrance of the consequence of causes and effects, consisteth in the imposing of *Names,* and the *Connexion* of them.

Of Names, some are *Proper,* and singular to one onely thing; as *Peter, John, This man, this Tree:* and some are *Common* to many things; as *Man, Horse, Tree;* every of which though but one Name, is nevertheless the name of divers particular things; in respect of all which together, it is called an *Universall;* there being nothing in the world Universall but Names; for the things named, are every one of them Individuall and Singular. *Names Proper & Common.*

Universall.

One Universall name is imposed on many things, for their similitude in some quality, or other accident: And wheras a Proper Name bringeth to mind one thing onely; Universals recall any one of those many.

And of Names Universall, some are of more, and some of lesse extent; the larger comprehending the less large: and some again of equall extent, comprehending each other reciprocally. As for example, the Name *Body* is of larger signification than the word *Man,* and comprehendeth it; and the names *Man* and *Rationall,* are of equall extent, comprehending mutually one another. But here wee must take notice, that by a Name is not always understood, as in Grammar, one onely Word; but sometimes by circumlocution many words together. For all these words, *Hee that in his actions observeth the Lawes of his Country,* make but one Name, equivalent to this one word, *Just.* [14]

By this imposition of Names, some of larger, some of stricter signification, we turn the reckoning of the consequences of things imagined in the mind, into a reckoning of the consequences of Appellations. For example, a man that hath no use of Speech at all, (such, as is born and remains perfectly deafe and dumb,) if he set before his eyes a triangle, and by it two right angles, (such as are the corners of a square figure,) he may by meditation compare and find, that the three angles of that triangle, are equall to those two right angles that stand by it. But if another triangle be shewn him different in shape from the former, he cannot know without a new labour, whether the three angles of that also be equall to the same. But he that hath the use of words, when he observes, that such equality was consequent, not to the length of the sides, nor to any other particular thing in his triangle; but onely to this, that the sides were straight, and the angles three; and that that was all, for which he named it a Triangle; will boldly conclude Universally, that such equality of angles is in all triangles whatsoever; and register his invention[2] in these generall termes, *Every triangle hath its three angles equall to two right angles.* And thus the consequence found in one particular, comes to be registred and remembred, as an Universall rule; and discharges our mentall reckoning, of time and place; and delivers us from all labour of the mind, saving the first; and makes that which was found true *here*, and *now*, to be true in *all times* and *places*.

But the use of words in registring our thoughts, is in nothing so evident as in Numbring. A naturall foole that could never learn by heart the order of numerall words, as *one*, *two*, and *three*, may observe every stroak of the Clock, and nod to it, or say one, one, one; but can never know what houre it strikes. And it seems, there was a time when those names of number were not in use; and men were fayn[3] to apply their fingers of one or both hands, to those things they desired to keep account of; and that thence it proceeded, that now our numerall words are but ten, in any Nation, and in some but five, and then they begin again. And he that can tell ten, if he recite them out of order, will lose himselfe, and not know when he has done: Much lesse will he be able to adde, and substract, and performe all other operations of Arithmetique. So that without words, there is no possibility of reckoning of Numbers; much lesse of Magnitudes, of Swiftnesse, of Force, and other things, the reckonings whereof are necessary to the being, or well-being of man-kind.

When two Names are joyned together into a Consequence, or Affirmation; as thus, A *man is a living creature*; or thus, *if he be a man, he is a living creature*, If the later name *Living creature*, signifie all that the former name *Man* signifieth, then the affirmation, or consequence [15] is *true*; otherwise *false*. For *True* and *False* are attributes of Speech, not of Things. And where Speech is not, there is neither *Truth* nor *Falshood*. *Errour* there may be, as when wee expect that which shall not be; or suspect what has not been: but in neither case can a man be charged with Untruth.

Necessity of Definitions. Seeing then that *truth* consisteth in the right ordering of names in our affirmations, a man that seeketh precise *truth*, had need to remember what every name he uses stands for; and to place it accordingly; or else he will find himselfe entangled in words, as a bird in lime-twiggs; the more he struggles, the more belimed. And therefore in Geometry, (which is the onely Science that it hath pleased God hitherto to bestow on mankind,) men begin at settling the significations of their words;

2. Discovery.
3. Willing.

which settling of significations, they call *Definitions*; and place them in the beginning of their reckoning.

By this it appears how necessary it is for any man that aspires to true Knowledge, to examine the Definitions of former Authors; and either to correct them, where they are negligently set down; or to make them himselfe. For the errours of Definitions multiply themselves, according as the reckoning proceeds; and lead men into absurdities, which at last they see, but cannot avoyd, without reckoning anew from the beginning; in which lyes the foundation of their errours. From whence it happens, that they which trust to books, do as they that cast up many little summs into a greater, without considering whether those little summes were rightly cast up or not; and at last finding the errour visible, and not mistrusting their first grounds, know not which way to cleere themselves; but spend time in fluttering over their bookes; as birds that entring by the chimney, and finding themselves inclosed in a chamber, flutter at the false light of a glasse window, for want of wit to consider which way they came in. So that in the right Definition of Names, lyes the first use of Speech; which is the Acquisition of Science: And in wrong, or no Definitions, lyes the first abuse; from which proceed all false and senslesse Tenets; which make those men that take their instruction from the authority of books, and not from their own meditation, to be as much below the condition of ignorant men, as men endued with true Science are above it. For between true Science, and erroneous Doctrines, Ignorance is in the middle. Naturall sense and imagination, are not subject to absurdity. Nature it selfe cannot erre: and as men abound in copiousnesse of language; so they become more wise, or more mad than ordinary. Nor is it possible without Letters for any man to become either excellently wise, or (unless his memory be hurt by disease, or ill constitution of organs) excellently foolish. For words are wise mens counters, they do but reckon by them: but they are the mony of fooles, that value them by the authority of an *Aristotle*, a *Cicero*, or a *Thomas*, or any other Doctor whatsoever, if but a man.

Subject to Names, is whatsoever can enter into, or be considered in an account; and be added one to another to make a summe; or substracted one from another, and leave a remainder. The Latines called Accounts of mony *Rationes*, and accounting, *Ratiocinatio*: and that which we in bills or books of account call *Items*, they called *Nomina*; that is, *Names*: and thence it seems to proceed, that they extended the word *Ratio*, to the faculty of Reckoning in all other things. The Greeks have but one word λόγος,[4] for both *Speech* and *Reason*; not that they thought there was no Speech without Reason; but no Reasoning without Speech: And the act of reasoning they called *Syllogisme*; which signifieth summing up of the consequences of one saying to another. And because the same things may enter into account for divers accidents; their names are (to shew that diversity) diversly wrested,[5] and diversified. This diversity of names may be reduced to foure generall heads.

First, a thing may enter into account for *Matter*, or *Body*; as *living*,

Subject to Names.

[16]

4. Logos.
5. Twisted.

sensible, rationall, hot, cold, moved, quiet; with all which names the word *Matter*, or *Body* is understood; all such, being names of Matter.

Secondly, it may enter into account, or be considered, for some accident or quality, which we conceive to be in it; as for *being moved*, for *being so long*, for *being hot*, &c; and then, of the name of the thing it selfe, by a little change or wresting, wee make a name for that accident, which we consider; and for *living* put into the account *life*; for *moved, motion*; for *hot, heat*; for *long, length*, and the like: And all such Names, are the names of the accidents and properties, by which one Matter, and Body is distinguished from another. These are called *names Abstract*; because severed (not from Matter, but) from the account of Matter.

Thirdly, we bring into account, the Properties of our own bodies, whereby we make such distinction: as when any thing is *Seen* by us, we reckon not the thing it selfe; but the *sight*, the *Colour*, the *Idea* of it in the fancy: and when any thing is *heard*, wee reckon it not; but the *hearing*, or *sound* onely, which is our fancy or conception of it by the Eare: and such are names of fancies.

Fourthly, we bring into account, consider, and give names, to Names themselves, and to Speeches: For, *generall, universall, speciall, æquivocall*, are names of Names. And *Affirmation, Interrogation, Commandement, Narration, Syllogisme, Sermon, Oration*, and many other such, are names of Speeches. And this is all the variety of Names *Positive*; which are put to mark somewhat which is in Nature, or may be feigned[6] by the mind of man, as Bodies that are, or may be conceived to be; or of bodies, the Properties that are, or may be feigned to be; or Words and Speech.

There be also other Names, called *Negative*; which are notes to signifie that a word is not the name of the thing in question; as these words *Nothing, no man, infinite, indocible*,[7] *three want foure*, and the like; which are nevertheless of use in reckoning, or in correcting of reckoning; and call to mind our past cogitations, though they be not names of any thing; because they make us refuse to admit of Names not rightly used.

All other Names, are but insignificant sounds; and those of two sorts. One, when they are new, and yet their meaning not explained by Definition; whereof there have been aboundance coyned by Schoole-men, and pusled[8] Philosophers.

Another, when men make a name of two Names, whose significations are contradictory and inconsistent; as this name, an *incorporeall body*, or (which is all one) an *incorporeall substance*, and a great number more. For whensoever any affirmation is false, the two names of which it is composed, put together and made one, signifie nothing at all. For example, if it be a false affirmation to say *a quadrangle is round*, the word *round quadrangle* signifies nothing; but is a meere sound. So likewise if it be false, to say that vertue can be powred[9] or blown up

Use of Names Positive.

Negative Names with their Uses.

Words insignificant.

[17]

---

6. Contrived or imagined (but not necessarily with an intent to deceive).
7. Unteachable.
8. Puzzled.
9. Poured.

and down; the words *In-powred vertue, In-blown vertue*, are as absurd and insignificant, as a *round quadrangle*. And therefore you shall hardly meet with a senslesse and insignificant word, that is not made up of some Latin or Greek names. A Frenchman seldome hears our Saviour called by the name of *Parole*, but by the name of *Verbe* often; yet *Verbe* and *Parole* differ no more, but that one is Latin, the other French.

When a man upon the hearing of any Speech, hath those thoughts which the words of that Speech, and their connexion, were ordained and constituted to signifie; Then he is said to understand it: *Understanding* being nothing else, but conception caused by Speech. And therefore if Speech be peculiar to man (as for ought I know it is,) then is Understanding peculiar to him also. And therefore of absurd and false affirmations, in case they be universall, there can be no Understanding; though many think they understand, then, when they do but repeat the words softly, or con[1] them in their mind. *Understanding.*

What kinds of Speeches signifie the Appetites, Aversions, and Passions of mans mind; and of their use and abuse, I shall speak when I have spoken of the Passions.

The names of such things as affect us, that is, which please, and displease us, because all men be not alike affected with the same thing, nor the same man at all times, are in the common discourses of men, of *inconstant* signification. For seeing all names are imposed to signifie our conceptions; and all our affections are but conceptions; when we conceive the same things differently, we can hardly avoyd different naming of them. For though the nature of that we conceive, be the same; yet the diversity of our reception of it, in respect of different constitutions of body, and prejudices of opinion, gives every thing a tincture[2] of our different passions. And therefore in reasoning, a man must take heed of words; which besides the signification of what we imagine of their nature, have a signification also of the nature, disposition, and interest of the speaker; such as are the names of Vertues, and Vices; For one man calleth *Wisdome*, what another calleth *feare*; and one *cruelty*, what another *justice*; one *prodigality*, what another *magnanimity*; and one *gravity*, what another *stupidity*, &c. And therefore such names can never be true grounds of any ratiocination. No more can Metaphors, and Tropes of speech: but these are less dangerous, because they profess their inconstancy; which the other do not. *Inconstant names.*

Chap. V. [18]

Of REASON, *and* SCIENCE.

When a man *Reasoneth*, hee does nothing else but conceive a summe totall, from *Addition* of parcels; or conceive a Remainder, from *Substraction* of one summe from another: which (if it be done by Words,) is conceiving of the consequence of the names of all the parts, to the name of the whole; or from the names of the whole and one *Reason what it is.*

1. Study; pore over.
2. Color, tint, taste, or flavor.

part, to the name of the other part. And though in some things, (as in numbers,) besides *Adding* and *Substracting*, men name other operations, as *Multiplying* and *Dividing*; yet they are the same; for Multiplication, is but Adding together of things equall; and Division, but Substracting of one thing, as often as we can. These operations are not incident to Numbers onely, but to all manner of things that can be added together, and taken one out of another. For as Arithmeticians teach to adde and substract in *numbers*; so the Geometricians teach the same in *lines*, *figures* (solid and superficiall,[1]) *angles*, *proportions*, *times*, degrees of *swiftnesse*, *force*, *power*, and the like; The Logicians teach the same in *Consequences of words*; adding together *two Names*, to make an *Affirmation*; and *two Affirmations*, to make a *Syllogisme*; and *many Syllogismes* to make a *Demonstration*; and from the *summe*, or *Conclusion* of a *Syllogisme*, they substract one *Proposition*, to finde the other. Writers of Politiques, adde together *Pactions*,[2] to find mens *duties*; and Lawyers, *Lawes*, and *facts*, to find what is *right* and *wrong* in the actions of private men. In summe, in what matter soever there is place for *addition* and *substraction*, there also is place for *Reason*; and where these have no place, there *Reason* has nothing at all to do.

Reason defined.

Out of all which we may define, (that is to say determine,) what that is, which is meant by this word *Reason*, when wee reckon it amongst the Faculties of the mind. For Reason, in this sense, is nothing but *Reckoning* (that is, Adding and Substracting) of the Consequences of generall names agreed upon, for the *marking* and *signifying* of our thoughts; I say *marking* them, when we reckon by our selves; and *signifying*, when we demonstrate, or approve our reckonings to other men.

Right Reason where.

And as in Arithmetique, unpractised men must, and Professors themselves may often erre, and cast up false; so also in any other subject of Reasoning, the ablest, most attentive, and most practised men, may deceive themselves, and inferre false Conclusions; Not but that Reason it selfe is alwayes Right Reason, as well as Arithmetique is a certain and infallible Art: But no one mans Reason, nor the Reason of any one number of men, makes the certaintie; no more than an account is therefore well cast up, because a great many men have unanimously approved it. And therfore, as when there is a controversy in an account,

[19]

the parties must by their own accord, set up for right Reason, the Reason of some Arbitrator, or Judge, to whose sentence they will both stand, or their controversie must either come to blowes, or be undecided, for want of a right Reason constituted by Nature; so is it also in all debates of what kind soever: And when men that think themselves wiser than all others, clamor and demand right Reason for judge; yet seek no more, but that things should be determined, by no other mens reason but their own, it is as intolerable in the society of men, as it is in play after trump is turned, to use for trump on every occasion, that suite whereof they have most in their hand. For they do nothing els, that will have every of their passions, as it comes to bear sway in them, to be taken

1. Two-dimensional.
2. Contracts.

for right Reason, and that in their own controversies: bewraying[3] their want of right Reason, by the claym they lay to it.

The Use and End of Reason, is not the finding of the summe, and truth of one, or a few consequences, remote from the first definitions, and settled significations of names; but to begin at these; and proceed from one consequence to another. For there can be no certainty of the last Conclusion, without a certainty of all those Affirmations and Negations, on which it was grounded, and inferred. As when a master of a family, in taking an account, casteth up the summs of all the bills of expence, into one sum; and not regarding how each bill is summed up, by those that give them in account; nor what it is he payes for; he advantages himself no more, than if he allowed the account in grosse, trusting to every of the accountants skill and honesty: so also in Reasoning of all other things, he that takes up conclusions on the trust of Authors, and doth not fetch them from the first Items in every Reckoning, (which are the significations of names settled by definitions), loses his labour; and does not know any thing; but onely beleeveth. *The use of Reason.*

When a man reckons without the use of words, which may be done in particular things, (as when upon the sight of any one thing, wee conjecture what was likely to have preceded, or is likely to follow upon it;) if that which he thought likely to follow, followes not; or that which he thought likely to have preceded it, hath not preceded it, this is called ERROR; to which even the most prudent men are subject. But when we Reason in Words of generall signification, and fall upon a generall inference which is false; though it be commonly called *Error*, it is indeed an ABSURDITY, or senslesse Speech. For Error is but a deception, in presuming that somewhat is past, or to come; of which, though it were not past, or not to come; yet there was no impossibility discoverable. But when we make a generall assertion, unlesse it be a true one, the possibility of it is unconceivable. And words whereby we conceive nothing but the sound, are those we call *Absurd, Insignificant*, and *Nonsense*. And therefore if a man should talk to me of a *round Quadrangle*; or *accidents of Bread in Cheese*; or *Immateriall Substances*; or of *A free Subject*; *A free-Will*; or any *Free*, but free from being hindred by opposition, I should not say he were in an Errour; but that his words were without meaning; that is to say, Absurd. *Of Error and Absurdity.*

I have said before, (in the second chapter,) that a Man did excell all other Animals in this faculty, that when he conceived any thing whatsoever, he was apt to enquire the consequences of it, and what effects he could do with it. And now I adde this other degree of the same excellence, that he can by words reduce the consequences he findes to generall Rules, called *Theoremes*, or *Aphorismes*; that is, he can Reason, or reckon, not onely in number; but in all other things, whereof one may be added unto, or substracted from another. [20]

But this priviledge, is allayed by another; and that is, by the priviledge of Absurdity; to which no living creature is subject, but man onely. And of men, those are of all most subject to it, that professe Philosophy. For

3. Revealing.

it is most true that *Cicero* sayth of them somewhere; that there can be
nothing so absurd, but may be found in the books of Philosophers. And
the reason is manifest. For there is not one of them that begins his
ratiocination from the Definitions, or Explications of the names they
are to use; which is a method that hath been used onely in Geometry;
whose Conclusions have thereby been made indisputable.

Causes of   The first cause of Absurd conclusions I ascribe to the want of
absurditie. Method; in that they begin not their Ratiocination from Definitions;
1.   that is, from settled significations of their words: as if they could cast
account, without knowing the value of the numerall words, *one, two,*
and *three.*

And whereas all bodies enter into account upon divers considerations, (which I have mentioned in the precedent chapter;) these considerations being diversly named, divers absurdities proceed from the
confusion, and unfit connexion of their names into assertions. And
therefore

The second cause of Absurd assertions, I ascribe to the giving of
names of *bodies,* to *accidents;*[4] or of *accidents,* to *bodies;* As they do,
that say, *Faith is infused,* or *inspired;* when nothing can be *powred,* or
breathed into any thing, but body; and that, *extension is body;* that
phantasmes are *spirits,* &c.

3.   The third I ascribe to the giving of the names of the *accidents* of
bodies without us, to the *accidents* of our *own bodies;* as they do that
say, the *colour is in the body; the sound is in the ayre,* &c.

4.   The fourth, to the giving of the names of *bodies,* to *names,* or
speeches; as they do that say, that *there be things universall;* that *a living
creature is Genus,* or *a generall thing,* &c.

5.   The fifth, to the giving of the names of *accidents,* to *names* and
speeches; as they do that say, *the nature of a thing is its definition; a
mans command is his will;* and the like.

6.   The sixth, to the use of Metaphors, Tropes, and other Rhetoricall
figures, in stead of words proper. For though it be lawfull to say, (for
example) in common speech, *the way goeth, or leadeth hither, or
thither, The Proverb sayes this or that* (whereas wayes cannot go, nor
Proverbs speak;) yet in reckoning, and seeking of truth, such speeches
are not to be admitted.

7.   The seventh, to names that signifie nothing; but are taken up, and
[21]   learned by rote from the Schooles, as *hypostatical, transubstantiate,
consubstantiate, eternal-Now,* and the like canting of Schoolemen.

To him that can avoyd these things, it is not easie to fall into any
absurdity, unlesse it be by the length of an account; wherein he may
perhaps forget what went before. For all men by nature reason alike,
and well, when they have good principles. For who is so stupid, as both
to mistake in Geometry, and also to persist in it, when another detects
his error to him?

Science.   By this it appears that Reason is not as Sense, and Memory, borne
with us; nor gotten by Experience onely, as Prudence is; but attayned

4. Qualities or attributes of a thing.

by Industry[5]; first in apt imposing of Names; and secondly by getting a good and orderly Method in proceeding from the Elements, which are Names, to Assertions made by Connexion of one of them to another; and so to Syllogismes, which are the Connexions of one Assertion to another, till we come to a knowledge of all the Consequences of names appertaining to the subject in hand; and that is it, men call SCIENCE. And whereas Sense and Memory are but knowledge of Fact, which is a thing past, and irrevocable; *Science* is the knowledge of Consequences, and dependance of one fact upon another: by which, out of that we can presently do, we know how to do something else when we will, or the like, another time: Because when we see how any thing comes about, upon what causes, and by what manner; when the like causes come into our power, wee see how to make it produce the like effects.

Children therefore are not endued with Reason at all, till they have attained the use of Speech: but are called Reasonable Creatures, for the possibility apparent of having the use of Reason in time to come. And the most part of men, though they have the use of Reasoning a little way, as in numbring to some degree; yet it serves them to little use in common life; in which they govern themselves, some better, some worse, according to their differences of experience, quicknesse of memory, and inclinations to severall ends; but specially according to good or evill fortune, and the errors of one another. For as for *Science*, or certain rules of their actions, they are so farre from it, that they know not what it is. Geometry they have thought Conjuring: But for other Sciences, they who have not been taught the beginnings, and some progresse in them, that they may see how they be acquired and generated, are in this point like children, that having no thought of generation, are made believe by the women, that their brothers and sisters are not born, but found in the garden.

But yet they that have no *Science*, are in better, and nobler condition with their naturall Prudence; than men, that by mis-reasoning, or by trusting them that reason wrong, fall upon false and absurd generall rules. For ignorance of causes, and of rules, does not set men so farre out of their way, as relying on false rules, and taking for causes of what they aspire to, those that are not so, but rather causes of the contrary.

To conclude, The Light of humane minds is Perspicuous Words, but by exact definitions first snuffed,[6] and purged from ambiguity; *Reason* is the *pace*; Encrease of *Science*, the *way*; and the Benefit of mankind, the *end*. And on the contrary, Metaphors, and senslesse and ambiguous words, are like *ignes fatui*;[7] and reasoning upon them, is wandering amongst innumerable absurdities; and their end, contention, and sedition, or contempt.[8]   [22]

As, much Experience, is *Prudence*; so, is much Science, *Sapience*.   *Prudence &*
For though wee usually have one name of Wisedome for them both;   *Sapience, with*
                                                                   their
                                                                   difference.

5. Diligence.
6. Clarified.
7. Fool's fires (something that deludes or misleads).
8. Disgrace.

yet the Latines did alwayes distinguish between *Prudentia* and *Sapientia*; ascribing the former to Experience, the later to Science. But to make their difference appeare more cleerly, let us suppose one man endued with an excellent naturall use, and dexterity in handling his armes; and another to have added to that dexterity, an acquired Science, of where he can offend,[9] or be offended by his adversarie, in every possible posture, or guard: The ability of the former, would be to the ability of the later, as Prudence to Sapience; both usefull; but the later infallible. But they that trusting onely to the authority of books, follow the blind blindly, are like him that trusting to the false rules of a master of Fence, ventures præsumptuously upon an adversary, that either kills, or disgraces him.

Signes of Science. The signes of Science, are some, certain and infallible; some, uncertain. Certain, when he that pretendeth[1] the Science of any thing, can teach the same; that is to say, demonstrate the truth thereof perspicuously to another: Uncertain, when onely some particular events answer to his pretence, and upon many occasions prove so as he sayes they must. Signes of prudence are all uncertain; because to observe by experience, and remember all circumstances that may alter the successe, is impossible. But in any businesse, whereof a man has not infallible Science to proceed by; to forsake his own naturall judgement, and be guided by generall sentences[2] read in Authors, and subject to many exceptions, is a signe of folly, and generally scorned by the name of Pedantry. And even of those men themselves, that in Councells of the Common-wealth, love to shew their reading of Politiques and History, very few do it in their domestique affaires, where their particular interest is concerned; having Prudence enough for their private affaires: but in publique they study more the reputation of their owne wit, than the successe of anothers businesse.

[23]

Chap. VI.

Of the Interiour Beginnings of Voluntary Motions; commonly called the PASSIONS. *And the Speeches by which they are expressed.*

Motion Vitall and Animal. There be in Animals, two sorts of *Motions* peculiar to them: One called *Vitall;* begun in generation, and continued without interruption through their whole life; such as are the *course* of the *Bloud,* the *Pulse,* the *Breathing,* the *Concoction,*[1] *Nutrition, Excretion,* &c; to which Motions there needs no help of Imagination: The other is *Animall motion,* otherwise called *Voluntary motion;* as to *go,* to *speak,* to *move* any of our limbes, in such manner as is first fancied in our minds. That Sense, is Motion in the organs and interiour parts of mans body, caused by the action of the things we See, Heare, &c; And that Fancy is but the

9. Harm.
1. Claims (expertise in).
2. Conclusions, judgments.
1. Digestion.

Reliques of the same Motion, remaining after Sense, has been already sayd in the first and second Chapters. And because *going, speaking,* and the like Voluntary motions, depend alwayes upon a precedent thought of *whither, which way,* and *what;* it is evident, that the Imagination is the first internall beginning of all Voluntary Motion. And although unstudied men, doe not conceive any motion at all to be there, where the thing moved is invisible; or the space it is moved in, is (for the shortnesse of it) insensible; yet that doth not hinder, but that such Motions are. For let a space be never so little, that which is moved over a greater space, whereof that little one is part, must first be moved over that. These small beginnings of Motion, within the body of Man, before they appear in walking, speaking, striking, and other visible actions, are commonly called ENDEAVOUR. *Endeavour.*

This Endeavour, when it is toward something which causes it, is called APPETITE, or DESIRE; the later, being the generall name; and the other, often-times restrayned to signifie the Desire of Food, namely *Hunger* and *Thirst.* And when the Endeavour is fromward something, it is generally called AVERSION. These words *Appetite*, and *Aversion* we have from the *Latines*; and they both of them signifie the motions, one of approaching, the other of retiring. So also do the Greek words for the same, which are ὁρμή,[2] and ἀφορμή.[3] For Nature it selfe does often presse upon men those truths, which afterwards, when they look for somewhat beyond Nature, they stumble at. For the Schooles find in meere Appetite to go, or move, no actuall Motion at all: but because some Motion they must acknowledge, they call it Metaphoricall Motion; which is but an absurd speech: for though Words may be called metaphoricall; Bodies, and Motions cannot. *Appetite.* *Desire.* *Hunger.* *Thirst.* *Aversion.*

That which men Desire, they are also sayd to LOVE: and to HATE those things, for which they have Aversion. So that Desire, and Love, are the same thing; save that by Desire, we alwayes signifie the Absence of the Object; by Love, most commonly the Presence of the same. So also by Aversion, we signifie the Absence; and by Hate, the Presence of the Object. *Love.* *Hate.* [24]

Of Appetites, and Aversions, some are born with men; as Appetite of food, Appetite of excretion, and exoneration,[4] (which may also and more properly be called Aversions, from somewhat they feele in their Bodies;) and some other Appetites, not many. The rest, which are Appetites of particular things, proceed from Experience, and triall of their effects upon themselves, or other men. For of things wee know not at all, or believe not to be, we can have no further Desire, than to tast and try. But Aversion wee have for things, not onely which we know have hurt us; but also that we do not know whether they will hurt us, or not.

Those things which we neither Desire, nor Hate, we are said to *Contemne:* CONTEMPT being nothing else but an immobility, or con- *Contempt.*

2. Horme.
3. Aphorme.
4. Defecation.

tumacy[5] of the Heart, in resisting the action of certain things; and proceeding from that the Heart is already moved otherwise, by other more potent objects; or from want of experience of them.

And because the constitution of a mans Body, is in continuall mutation; it is impossible that all the same things should alwayes cause in him the same Appetites, and Aversions: much lesse can all men consent,[6] in the Desire of almost any one and the same Object.

Good.
Evill.

But whatsoever is the object of any mans Appetite or Desire; that is it, which he for his part calleth *Good*: And the object of his Hate, and Aversion, *Evill*; And of his Contempt, *Vile* and *Inconsiderable*. For these words of Good, Evill, and Contemptible, are ever used with relation to the person that useth them: There being nothing simply and absolutely so; nor any common Rule of Good and Evill, to be taken from the nature of the objects themselves; but from the Person of the man (where there is no Common-wealth;) or, (in a Common-wealth,) from the Person that representeth it; or from an Arbitrator or Judge, whom men disagreeing shall by consent set up, and make his sentence the Rule thereof.

Pulchrum.
Turpe.

The Latine Tongue has two words, whose significations approach to those of Good and Evill; but are not precisely the same; And those are *Pulchrum* and *Turpe*. Whereof the former signifies that, which by some apparent signes promiseth Good; and the later, that, which promiseth Evil. But in our Tongue we have not so generall names to expresse them by. But for *Pulchrum*, we say in some things, *Fayre*; in others, *Beautifull*, or *Handsome*; or *Gallant*, or *Honourable*, or *Comely*, or *Amiable*; and for *Turpe, Foule, Deformed, Ugly, Base, Nauseous,* and the like, as the subject shall require; All which words, in their proper places signifie nothing els, but the *Mine*,[7] or Countenance, that promiseth Good and Evil. So that of Good there be three kinds; Good in the Promise, that is *Pulchrum*; Good in Effect, as the end desired, which is called *Jucundum, Delightfull*; and Good as the Means, which is called *Utile, Profitable*; and as many of Evil: For *Evill*, in Promise, is that they call *Turpe*; Evil in Effect, and End, is *Molestum, Unpleasant, Troublesome*; and Evill in the Means, *Inutile, Unprofitable, Hurtfull*.

Delightfull.
Profitable.

[25]
Unpleasant.
Unprofitable.

Delight.
Displeasure.

As, in Sense, that which is really within us, is (as I have sayd before) onely Motion, caused by the action of externall objects, but in apparence; to the Sight, Light and Colour; to the Eare, Sound; to the Nostrill, Odour, &c: so, when the action of the same object is continued from the Eyes, Eares, and other organs to the Heart; the reall effect there is nothing but Motion, or Endeavour; which consisteth in Appetite, or Aversion, to, or from the object moving. But the apparence, or sense of that motion, is that wee either call DELIGHT, or TROUBLE OF MIND.

This Motion, which is called Appetite, and for the apparence of it

5. Obstinacy.
6. Agree.
7. Mien.

Delight, and *Pleasure,* seemeth to be, a corroboration[8] of Vitall motion, and a help thereunto; and therefore such things as caused Delight, were not improperly called *Jucunda, (a Juvando,)* from helping or fortifying; and the contrary, *Molesta, Offensive,* from hindering, and troubling the motion vitall.

Pleasure.

Offence.

Pleasure therefore, (or *Delight,)* is the apparence, or sense of Good; and *Molestation*[9] or *Displeasure,* the apparence, or sense of Evill. And consequently all Appetite, Desire, and Love, is accompanied with some Delight more or lesse; and all Hatred, and Aversion, with more or lesse Displeasure and Offence.

Of Pleasures, or Delights, some arise from the sense of an object Present; And those may be called *Pleasures of Sense,* (The word *sensuall,* as it is used by those onely that condemn them, having no place till there be Lawes.) Of this kind are all Onerations[1] and Exonerations of the body; as also all that is pleasant, in the *Sight, Hearing, Smell, Tast, or Touch;* Others arise from the Expectation, that proceeds from foresight of the End, or Consequence of things; whether those things in the Sense Please or Displease: And these are *Pleasures of the Mind* of him that draweth those consequences; and are generally called JOY. In the like manner, Displeasures, are some in the Sense, and called PAYNE; others, in the Expectation of consequences, and are called GRIEFE.

Pleasures of sense.

Pleasures of the Mind.
Joy.
Paine.
Griefe.

These simple Passions called *Appetite, Desire, Love, Aversion, Hate, Joy,* and *Griefe,* have their names for divers considerations diversified. As first, when they one succeed another, they are diversly called from the opinion men have of the likelihood of attaining what they desire. Secondly, from the object loved or hated. Thirdly, from the consideration of many of them together. Fourthly, from the Alteration or succession it selfe.

For *Appetite* with an opinion of attaining, is called HOPE.

The same, without such opinion, DESPAIRE.

Aversion, with opinion of *Hurt* from the object, FEARE.

The same, with hope of avoyding that Hurt by resistence, COURAGE.

Sudden *Courage,* ANGER.

Constant *Hope,* CONFIDENCE of our selves.

Constant *Despayre,* DIFFIDENCE of our selves.

Anger for great hurt done to another, when we conceive the same to be done by Injury,[2] INDIGNATION.

Desire of good to another, BENEVOLENCE, GOOD WILL, CHARITY. If to man generally, GOOD NATURE.

Desire of Riches, COVETOUSNESSE: a name used alwayes in signification of blame; because men contending for them are displeased with one anothers attaining them; though the desire in it selfe, be to be blamed, or allowed, according to the means by which those Riches are sought.

Hope.
Despaire.
Feare.
Courage.
Anger.
Confidence.
Diffidence.
[26]
Indignation.

Benevolence.
Good Nature.
Covetousnesse.

8. Strengthening.
9. Annoyance.
1. Burdening or filling (the stomach).
2. Violation of right.

Ambition.   *Desire* of Office, or precedence, AMBITION: a name used also in the worse sense, for the reason before mentioned.

Pusillanimity.   *Desire* of things that conduce but a little to our ends; And fear of things that are but of little hindrance, PUSILLANIMITY.

Magnanimity.   *Contempt* of little helps, and hindrances, MAGNANIMITY.

Valour.   *Magnanimity*, in danger of Death, or Wounds, VALOUR, FORTITUDE.

Liberality.   *Magnanimity*, in the use of Riches, LIBERALITY.

Miserable-nesse.   *Pusillanimity*, in the same WRETCHEDNESSE, MISERABLENESSE; or PARSIMONY; as it is liked, or disliked.

Kindnesse.   *Love* of Persons for society, KINDNESSE.

Naturall Lust.   *Love* of Persons for Pleasing the sense onely, NATURALL LUST.

Luxury.   *Love* of the same, acquired from Rumination, that is, Imagination of Pleasure past, LUXURY.

The Passion of Love.   *Love* of one singularly, with desire to be singularly beloved, THE PASSION OF LOVE. The same, with fear that the love is not mutuall,

Jealousie.   JEALOUSIE.

Revengeful-nesse.   *Desire*, by doing hurt to another, to make him condemn some fact of his own, REVENGEFULNESSE.

Curiosity.   *Desire*, to know why, and how, CURIOSITY; such as is in no living creature but *Man*: so that Man is distinguished, not onely by his Reason; but also by this singular Passion from other *Animals*; in whom the appetite of food, and other pleasures of Sense, by prædominance, take away the care of knowing causes; which is a Lust of the mind, that by a perseverance of delight in the continuall and indefatigable generation of Knowledge, exceedeth the short vehemence of any carnall Pleasure.

Religion.   *Superstition.*   *True Religion.*   *Panique Terrour.*   *Feare* of power invisible, feigned by the mind, or imagined from tales publiquely allowed, RELIGION; not allowed, SUPERSTITION. And when the power imagined, is truly such as we imagine, TRUE RELIGION.

Feare, without the apprehension of why, or what, PANIQUE TERROR; called so from the Fables, that make *Pan* the author of them; whereas in truth there is alwayes in him that so feareth, first, some apprehension of the cause, though the rest run away by Example; every one supposing his fellow to know why. And therefore this Passion happens to none but in a throng, or multitude of people.

Admiration.   *Joy*, from apprehension of novelty, ADMIRATION; proper to Man, because it excites the appetite of knowing the cause.

[27]   *Glory.*   *Joy*, arising from imagination of a mans own power and ability, is that exultation of the mind which is called GLORYING: which if grounded upon the experience of his own former actions, is the same with *Confidence*: but if grounded on the flattery of others; or onely supposed by himself, for delight in the consequences of it, is called

Vain-glory.   VAINE-GLORY: which name is properly given; because a well grounded *Confidence* begetteth Attempt; whereas the supposing of power does not, and is therefore rightly called *Vaine*.

Dejection.   *Griefe*, from opinion of want of power, is called DEJECTION of mind.

The *vain-glory* which consisteth in the feigning or supposing of abilities in our selves, which we know are not, is most incident to young men, and nourished by the Histories, or Fictions of Gallant Persons; and is corrected oftentimes by Age, and Employment.

Sudden Glory, is the passion which maketh those *Grimaces* called LAUGHTER; and is caused either by some sudden act of their own, that pleaseth them; or by the apprehension of some deformed thing in another, by comparison whereof they suddenly applaud themselves. And it is incident most to them, that are conscious of the fewest abilities in themselves; who are forced to keep themselves in their own favour, by observing the imperfections of other men. And therefore much Laughter at the defects of others, is a signe of Pusillanimity. For of great minds, one of the proper workes is, to help and free others from scorn; and compare themselves onely with the most able.

On the contrary, *Sudden Dejection*, is the passion that causeth WEEPING; and is caused by such accidents, as suddenly take away some vehement hope, or some prop of their power: And they are most subject to it, that rely principally on helps externall, such as are Women, and Children. Therefore some Weep for the losse of Friends; Others for their unkindnesse; others for the sudden stop made to their thoughts of revenge, by Reconciliation. But in all cases, both Laughter, and Weeping, are sudden motions; Custome taking them both away. For no man Laughs at old jests; or Weeps for an old calamity.

Griefe, for the discovery of some defect of ability, is SHAME, or the passion that discovereth it selfe in BLUSHING; and consisteth in the apprehension of some thing dishonourable; and in young men, is a signe of the love of good reputation; and commendable: In old men it is a signe of the same; but because it comes too late, not commendable.

The *Contempt* of good Reputation is called IMPUDENCE.

Griefe, for the Calamity of another, is PITTY; and ariseth from the imagination that the like calamity may befall himselfe; and therefore is called also COMPASSION, and in the phrase of this present time a FELLOW-FEELING: And therefore for Calamity arriving from great wickednesse, the best men have the least Pitty; and for the same Calamity, those have least Pitty, that think themselves least obnoxious[3] to the same.

Contempt, or little sense of the calamity of others, is that which men call CRUELTY; proceeding from Security of their own fortune. For, that any man should take pleasure in other mens great harmes, without other end of his own, I do not conceive it possible.

Griefe, for the successe of a Competitor in wealth, honour, or other good, if it be joyned with Endeavour to enforce[4] our own abilities to equall or exceed him, is called EMULATION: But joyned with Endeavour to supplant,[5] or hinder a Competitor, ENVIE.

When in the mind of man, Appetites, and Aversions, Hopes, and Feares, concerning one and the same thing, arise alternately; and divers good and evill consequences of the doing, or omitting the thing propounded, come successively into our thoughts; so that sometimes we have an Appetite to it; sometimes an Aversion from it; sometimes Hope to be able to do it; sometimes Despaire, or Feare to attempt it; the

Sudden Glory.
Laughter.

Sudden Dejection.
Weeping.

Shame.
Blushing.

Impudence.
Pitty.

Cruelty.
[28]

Emulation.
Envy.

3. Liable.
4. Strengthen.
5. Undermine.

Deliberation.

whole summe of Desires, Aversions, Hopes and Fears, continued till the thing be either done, or thought impossible, is that we call DELIBERATION.

Therefore of things past, there is no *Deliberation*; because manifestly impossible to be changed: nor of things known to be impossible, or thought so; because men know, or think such Deliberation vain. But of things impossible, which we think possible, we may Deliberate; not knowing it is in vain. And it is called *Deliberation*; because it is a putting an end to the *Liberty* we had of doing, or omitting, according to our own Appetite, or Aversion.

This alternate Succession of Appetites, Aversions, Hopes and Fears, is no lesse in other living Creatures then in Man: and therefore Beasts also Deliberate.

Every *Deliberation* is then sayd to *End*, when that whereof they Deliberate, is either done, or thought impossible; because till then wee retain the liberty of doing, or omitting, according to our Appetite, or Aversion.

The Will.

In *Deliberation*, the last Appetite, or Aversion, immediately adhæring to the action, or to the omission thereof, is that wee call the WILL; the Act, (not the faculty,) of *Willing*. And Beasts that have *Deliberation*, must necessarily also have *Will*. The Definition of the *Will*, given commonly by the Schooles, that it is a *Rationall Appetite*, is not good. For if it were, then could there be no Voluntary Act against Reason. For a *Voluntary Act* is that, which proceedeth from the *Will*, and no other. But if in stead of a Rationall Appetite, we shall say an Appetite resulting from a precedent Deliberation, then the Definition is the same that I have given here. *Will* therefore *is the last Appetite in Deliberating*. And though we say in common Discourse, a man had a Will once to do a thing, that neverthelese he forbore to do; yet that is properly but an Inclination, which makes no Action Voluntary; because the action depends not of it, but of the last Inclination, or Appetite. For if the intervenient Appetites, make any action Voluntary; then by the same Reason all intervenient Aversions, should make the same action Involuntary; and so one and the same action, should be both Voluntary & Involuntary.

[29]

By this it is manifest, that not onely actions that have their beginning from Covetousnesse, Ambition, Lust, or other Appetites to the thing propounded; but also those that have their beginning from Aversion, or Feare of those consequences that follow the omission, are *voluntary actions*.

Formes of Speech, in Passion.

The formes of Speech by which the Passions are expressed, are partly the same, and partly different from those, by which wee expresse our Thoughts. And first, generally all Passions may be expressed *Indicatively*; as *I love, I feare, I joy, I deliberate, I will, I command*: but some of them have particular expressions by themselves, which neverthelesse are not affirmations, unlesse it be when they serve to make other inferences, besides that of the Passion they proceed from. Deliberation is expressed *Subjunctively*; which is a speech proper to signifie suppositions, with their consequences; as, *If this be done, then this will follow*;

and differs not from the language of Reasoning, save that Reasoning is in generall words; but Deliberation for the most part is of Particulars. The language of Desire, and Aversion, is *Imperative*; as *Do this, forbeare that*; which when the party is obliged to do, or forbeare, is *Command*; otherwise *Prayer*; or els *Counsell*. The language of Vain-Glory, of Indignation, Pitty and Revengefulness, *Optative*: But of the Desire to know, there is a peculiar expression, called *Interrogative*; as, *What is it, when shall it, how is it done*, and *why so?* other language of the Passions I find none: For Cursing, Swearing, Reviling, and the like, do not signifie as Speech; but as the actions of a tongue accustomed.

These formes of Speech, I say, are expressions, or voluntary significations of our Passions: but certain signes they be not; because they may be used arbitrarily,[6] whether they that use them, have such Passions or not. The best signes of Passions present, are either in the countenance, motions of the body, actions, and ends, or aimes, which we otherwise know the man to have.

And because in Deliberation, the Appetites, and Aversions are raised by foresight of the good and evill consequences, and sequels of the action whereof we Deliberate; the good or evill effect thereof dependeth on the foresight of a long chain of consequences, of which very seldome any man is able to see to the end. But for so farre as a man seeth, if the Good in those consequences, be greater than the Evill, the whole chaine is that which Writers call *Apparent*, or *Seeming Good*. And contrarily, when the Evill exceedeth the Good, the whole is *Apparent* or *Seeming Evill*: so that he who hath by Experience, or Reason, the greatest and surest prospect of Consequences, Deliberates best himselfe; and is able when he will, to give the best counsell unto others.

Good and Evill apparent.

Continuall successe in obtaining those things which a man from time to time desireth, that is to say, continuall prospering, is that men call FELICITY; I mean the Felicity of this life. For there is no such thing as perpetuall Tranquillity of mind, while we live here; because Life it selfe is but Motion, and can never be without Desire, nor without Feare, no more than without Sense. What kind of Felicity God hath ordained to them that devoutly honour him, a man shall no sooner know, than enjoy; being joyes, that now are as incomprehensible, as the word of Schoole-men *Beatificall Vision* is unintelligible.

Felicity.

[30]

The forme of Speech whereby men signifie their opinion of the Goodnesse of any thing, is PRAISE. That whereby they signifie the power and greatnesse of any thing, is MAGNIFYING. And that whereby they signifie the opinion they have of a mans Felicity, is by the Greeks called μακαρισός[7] for which wee have no name in our tongue. And thus much is sufficient for the present purpose, to have been said of the PASSIONS.

Praise.

Magnification.

μακαρισμός

6. Discretionarily. Hobbes sometimes calls the authority of a sovereign *arbitrary*. In Hobbes's usage, however, *arbitrary* is not necessarily synonymous with *capricious* (as it usually is in late-twentieth-century usage); it is often used to mean "depending on the discretion of an *arbitrator* or other legally recognized authority."
7. *Makarismos* (a declaration of happiness, a blessing).

Chap. VII.

Of the ENDS, *or* RESOLUTIONS *of* DISCOURSE.

Of all *Discourse*, governed by desire of Knowledge, there is at last an *End*, either by attaining, or by giving over. And in the chain of Discourse, wheresoever it be interrupted, there is an End for that time.

If the Discourse be meerly Mentall, it consisteth of thoughts that the thing will be, and will not be, or that it has been, and has not been, alternately. So that wheresoever you break off the chayn of a mans Discourse, you leave him in a Præsumption of *it will be*, or, *it will not be*; or *it has been*, or, *has not been*. All which is *Opinion*. And that which is alternate Appetite, in Deliberating concerning Good and Evil; the same is alternate Opinion, in the Enquiry of the truth of *Past*, and *Future*. And as the last Appetite in Deliberation, is called the *Will*; so the last Opinion in search of the truth of Past, and Future, is called the JUDGEMENT, or *Resolute* and *Finall Sentence* of him that discourseth. And as the whole chain of Appetites alternate, in the question of Good, or Bad, is called *Deliberation*; so the whole chain of Opinions alternate, in the question of True, or False, is called DOUBT.

Judgement, or Sentence final.

Doubt.

No Discourse whatsoever, can End in absolute knowledge of Fact, past, or to come. For, as for the knowledge of Fact, it is originally, Sense; and ever after, Memory. And for the knowledge of Consequence, which I have said before is called Science, it is not Absolute, but Conditionall. No man can know by Discourse, that this, or that, is, has been, or will be; which is to know absolutely: but onely, that if This be, That is; if This has been, That has been; if This shall be, That shall be: which is to know conditionally; and that not the consequence of one thing to another; but of one name of a thing, to another name of the same thing.

And therefore, when the Discourse is put into Speech, and begins with the Definitions of Words, and proceeds by Connexion of the same into generall Affirmations, and of these again into Syllogismes; the End or last summe is called the Conclusion; and the thought of the mind by it signified, is that conditionall Knowledge, or Knowledge of the consequence of words, which is commonly called SCIENCE. But if the first ground of such Discourse, be not Definitions; or if the Definitions be not rightly joyned together into Syllogismes, then the End or Conclusion, is again OPINION, namely of the truth of somewhat said, though sometimes in absurd and senslesse words, without possibility of being understood. When two, or more men, know of one and the same fact, they are said to be CONSCIOUS of it one to another; which is as much as to know it together. And because such are fittest witnesses of the facts of one another, or of a third; it was, and ever will be reputed a very Evill act, for any man to speak against his *Conscience*; or to corrupt or force another so to do: Insomuch that the plea of Conscience, has been alwayes hearkened unto very diligently in all times. Afterwards, men made use of the same word metaphorically, for the knowledge of their own secret facts, and secret thoughts; and therefore it is Rhetori-

[31]

Science.

Opinion.

Conscience.

cally said, that the Conscience is a thousand witnesses. And last of all, men, vehemently in love with their own new opinions, (though never so absurd,) and obstinately bent to maintain them, gave those their opinions also that reverenced name of Conscience, as if they would have it seem unlawfull, to change or speak against them; and so pretend to know they are true, when they know at most, but that they think so.

When a mans Discourse beginneth not at Definitions, it beginneth either at some other contemplation of his own, and then it is still called Opinion; Or it beginneth at some saying of another, of whose ability to know the truth, and of whose honesty in not deceiving, he doubteth not; and then the Discourse is not so much concerning the Thing, as the Person; And the Resolution is called BELEEFE, and FAITH: *Faith*, in the man; *Beleefe*, both *of* the man, and *of* the truth of what he sayes. So that in Beleefe are two opinions; one of the saying of the man; the other of his vertue. To *have faith in*, or *trust to*, or *beleeve a man*, signifie the same thing; namely, an opinion of the veracity of the man: But to *beleeve what is said*, signifieth onely an opinion of the truth of the saying. But wee are to observe that this Phrase, *I beleeve in*; as also the Latine, *Credo in*; and the Greek, πιστεύω ἐις,[1] are never used but in the writings of Divines. In stead of them, in other writings are put, *I beleeve him*; *I trust him*; *I have faith in him*; *I rely on him*; and in Latin, *Credo illi*; *fido illi*: and in Greek, πιστεύω αὐτῷ:[2] and that this singularity of the Ecclesiastique use of the word hath raised many disputes about the right object of the Christian Faith.

Beliefe.
Faith.

But by *Beleeving in*, as it is in the Creed, is meant, not trust in the Person; but Confession and acknowledgement of the Doctrine. For not onely Christians, but all manner of men do so believe in God, as to hold all for truth they heare him say, whether they understand it, or not; which is all the Faith and trust can possibly be had in any person whatsoever: But they do not all believe the Doctrine of the Creed.

From whence we may inferre, that when wee believe any saying whatsoever it be, to be true, from arguments taken, not from the thing it selfe, or from the principles of naturall Reason, but from the Authority, and good opinion wee have, of him that hath sayd it; then is the speaker, or person we believe in, or trust in, and whose word we take, the object of our Faith; and the Honour done in Believing, is done to him onely. And consequently, when wee Believe that the Scriptures are the word of God, having no immediate revelation from God himselfe, our Beleefe, Faith, and Trust is in the Church; whose word we take, and acquiesce therein. And they that believe that which a Prophet relates unto them in the name of God, take the word of the Prophet, do honour to him, and in him trust, and believe, touching the truth of what he relateth, whether he be a true, or a false Prophet. And so it is also with all other History. For if I should not believe all that is written by Historians, of the glorious acts of *Alexander*, or *Cæsar*; I do not think the Ghost of *Alexander*, or *Cæsar*, had any just cause to be offended; or any body else, but the Historian. If *Livy* say the Gods

[32]

1. *Pisteuo eis.*
2. *Pisteuo auto.*

made once a Cow speak, and we believe it not; wee distrust not God therein, but *Livy*. So that it is evident, that whatsoever we believe, upon no other reason, then what is drawn from authority of men onely, and their writings; whether they be sent from God or not, is Faith in men onely.

Chap. VIII.

Of the VERTUES *commonly called* INTELLECTUALL; *and their contrary* DEFECTS.

Intellectuall Vertue defined. Vertue generally, in all sorts of subjects, is somewhat that is valued for eminence; and consisteth in comparison. For if all things were equally in all men, nothing would be prized. And by *Vertues* INTELLECTUALL, are always understood such abilityes of the mind, as men praise, value, and desire should be in themselves; and go commonly under the name of a *good wit*; though the same word WIT, be used also, to distinguish one certain ability from the rest.

Wit, Naturall, or Acquired. These *Vertues* are of two sorts; *Naturall*, and *Acquired*. By Naturall, I mean not, that which a man hath from his Birth: for that is nothing else but Sense; wherein men differ so little one from another, and from brute Beasts, as it is not to be reckoned amongst Vertues. But I mean, that *Wit*, which is gotten by Use onely, and Experience; without *Naturall Wit.* Method, Culture, or Instruction. This NATURALL WIT, consisteth principally in two things; *Celerity of Imagining*, (that is, swift succession of one thought to another;) and *steddy direction* to some approved end. On the Contrary a slow Imagination, maketh that Defect, or fault of the mind, which is commonly called DULNESSE, *Stupidity*, and sometimes by other names that signifie slownesse of motion, or difficulty to be moved.

[33] And this difference of quicknesse, is caused by the difference of mens passions; that love and dislike, some one thing, some another: and therefore some mens thoughts run one way, some another; and are held to, and observe differently the things that passe through their imagination. And whereas in this succession of mens thoughts, there is nothing to observe in the things they think on, but either in what they be *like one another*, or in what they be *unlike*, or *what they serve for*, or *how they serve to such a purpose*; Those that observe their similitudes, in case they be such as are but rarely observed by others, are sayd to *Good Wit, or* have a *Good Wit*; by which, in this occasion, is meant a *Good Fancy*. *Fancy.* But they that observe their differences, and dissimilitudes; which is called *Distinguishing*, and *Discerning*, and *Judging* between thing and *Good* thing; in case, such discerning be not easie, are said to have a *good Judgement.* *Judgement*: and particularly in matter of conversation and businesse; wherein, times, places, and persons are to be discerned, this Vertue is *Discretion.* called DISCRETION. The former, that is, Fancy, without the help of Judgement, is not commended as a Vertue: but the later which is Judgement, and Discretion, is commended for it selfe, without the help of

Fancy. Besides the Discretion of times, places, and persons, necessary to a good Fancy, there is required also an often application of his thoughts to their End; that is to say, to some use to be made of them. This done; he that hath this Vertue, will be easily fitted with similitudes, that will please, not onely by illustration of his discourse, and adorning it with new and apt metaphors; but also, by the rarity of their invention. But without Steddinesse, and Direction to some End, a great Fancy is one kind of Madnesse; such as they have, that entring into any discourse, are snatched from their purpose, by every thing that comes in their thought, into so many, and so long digressions, and Parentheses, that they utterly lose themselves: Which kind of folly, I know no particular name for: but the cause of it is, sometimes want of experience; whereby that seemeth to a man new and rare, which doth not so to others: sometimes Pusillanimity; by which that seems great to him, which other men think a trifle: and whatsoever is new, or great, and therefore thought fit to be told, withdrawes a man by degrees from the intended way of his discourse.

In a good Poem, whether it be *Epique*, or *Dramatique*; as also in *Sonnets*, *Epigrams*, and other Pieces, both Judgement and Fancy are required: But the Fancy must be more eminent; because they please for the Extravagancy; but ought not to displease by Indiscretion.

In a good History, the Judgement must be eminent; because the goodnesse consisteth, in the Method, in the Truth, and in the Choyse[1] of the actions that are most profitable to be known. Fancy has no place, but onely in adorning the stile.

In Orations of Prayse, and in Invectives, the Fancy is prædominant; because the designe is not truth, but to Honour or Dishonour; which is done by noble, or by vile[2] comparisons. The Judgement does but suggest what circumstances make an action laudable, or culpable.

In Hortatives, and Pleadings, as Truth, or Disguise serveth best to the Designe in hand; so is the Judgement, or the Fancy most required.   [34]

In Demonstration, in Councell, and all rigourous search of Truth, Judgement does all; except sometimes the understanding have need to be opened by some apt similitude; and then there is so much use of Fancy. But for Metaphors, they are in this case utterly excluded. For seeing they openly professe deceipt; to admit them into Councell, or Reasoning, were manifest folly.

And in any Discourse whatsoever, if the defect of Discretion be apparent, how extravagant soever the Fancy be, the whole discourse will be taken for a signe of want of wit; and so will it never when the Discretion is manifest, though the Fancy be never so ordinary.

The secret thoughts of a man run over all things, holy, prophane, clean, obscene, grave, and light, without shame, or blame; which verball discourse cannot do, farther than the Judgement shall approve of the Time, Place, and Persons. An Anatomist, or a Physitian may speak, or write his judgement of unclean things; because it is not to please, but profit: but for another man to write his extravagant, and pleasant

1. Choice.
2. Ignominious.

fancies of the same, is as if a man, from being tumbled into the dirt, should come and present himselfe before good company. And 'tis the want of Discretion that makes the difference. Again, in profest remissnesse of mind, and familiar company, a man may play with the sounds, and æquivocall significations of words; and that many times with encounters[3] of extraordinary Fancy: but in a Sermon, or in publique, or before persons unknown, or whom we ought to reverence, there is no Gingling[4] of words that will not be accounted folly: and the difference is onely in the want of Discretion. So that where Wit is wanting, it is not Fancy that is wanting, but Discretion. Judgement therefore without Fancy is Wit, but Fancy without Judgement not.

Prudence.   When the thoughts of a man, that has a designe in hand, running over a multitude of things, observes how they conduce to that designe; or what designe they may conduce unto; if his observations be such as are not easie, or usuall, This wit of his is called PRUDENCE; and dependeth on much Experience, and Memory of the like things, and their consequences heretofore. In which there is not so much difference of Men, as there is in their Fancies and Judgements; Because the Experience of men equall in age, is not much unequall, as to the quantity; but lyes in different occasions; every one having his private designes. To govern well a family, and a kingdome, are not different degrees of Prudence; but different sorts of businesse; no more then to draw a picture in little, or as great, or greater then the life, are different degrees of Art. A plain husband-man is more Prudent in affaires of his own house, then a Privy Counseller in the affaires of another man.

Craft. [35]   To Prudence, if you adde the use of unjust, or dishonest means, such as usually are prompted to men by Feare, or Want; you have that Crooked Wisdome, which is called CRAFT; which is a signe of Pusillanimity. For Magnanimity is contempt of unjust, or dishonest helps. And that which the Latines call *Versutia,* (translated into English, *Shifting,*) and is a putting off of a present danger or incommodity, by engaging into a greater, as when a man robbs one to pay another, is but a shorter sighted Craft, called *Versutia,* from *Versura,* which signifies taking mony at usurie, for the present payment of interest.

Acquired Wit.   As for *acquired Wit,* (I mean acquired by method and instruction,) there is none but Reason; which is grounded on the right use of Speech; and produceth the Sciences. But of Reason and Science, I have already spoken in the fifth and sixth Chapters.

The causes of this difference of Witts, are in the Passions: and the difference of Passions, proceedeth partly from the different Constitution of the body, and partly from different Education. For if the difference proceeded from the temper of the brain, and the organs of Sense, either exterior or interior, there would be no lesse difference of men in their Sight, Hearing, or other Senses, than in their Fancies, and Discretions. It proceeds therefore from the Passions; which are different, not onely from the difference of mens complexions; but also from their difference of customes, and education.

3. Ideas (especially those that occur to one unexpectedly).
4. Jingling (an arrangement of words intended to produce a striking sound).

The Passions that most of all cause the differences of Wit, are principally, the more or lesse Desire of Power, of Riches, of Knowledge, and of Honour. All which may be reduced to the first, that is Desire of Power. For Riches, Knowledge and Honour are but severall sorts of Power.

And therefore, a man who has no great Passion for any of these things; but is as men terme it indifferent; though he may be so farre a good man, as to be free from giving offence; yet he cannot possibly have either a great Fancy, or much Judgement. For the Thoughts, are to the Desires, as Scouts, and Spies, to range abroad, and find the way to the things Desired: All Stedinesse of the minds motion, and all quicknesse of the same, proceeding from thence. For as to have no Desire, is to be Dead: so to have weak Passions, is Dulnesse; and to have Passions indifferently for everything, GIDDINESSE, and *Distraction*; and to have stronger, and more vehement Passions for any thing, than is ordinarily seen in others, is that which men call MADNESSE.   *Giddinesse.*

Madnesse.

Whereof there be almost as many kinds, as of the Passions themselves. Sometimes the extraordinary and extravagant Passion, proceedeth from the evill constitution of the organs of the Body, or harme done them; and sometimes the hurt, and indisposition of the Organs, is caused by the vehemence, or long continuance of the Passion. But in both cases the Madnesse is of one and the same nature.

The Passion, whose violence, or continuance maketh Madnesse, is either great *vaine-Glory*; which is commonly called *Pride*, and *selfe-conceipt*; or great *Dejection* of mind.

Pride, subjecteth a man to Anger, the excesse whereof, is the Madnesse called RAGE, and FURY. And thus it comes to passe that excessive   *Rage.*
desire of Revenge, when it becomes habituall, hurteth the organs, and   [36]
becomes Rage: That excessive lóve, with jealousie, becomes also Rage: Excessive opinion of a mans own selfe, for divine inspiration, for wisdome, learning, forme,[5] and the like, becomes Distraction, and Giddinesse: The same, joyned with Envy, Rage: Vehement opinion of the truth of any thing, contradicted by others, Rage.

Dejection, subjects a man to causelesse fears; which is a Madnesse commonly called MELANCHOLY, apparent also in divers manners;[6] as   *Melancholy.*
in haunting of solitudes, and graves; in superstitious behaviour; and in fearing some one, some another particular thing. In summe, all Passions that produce strange and unusuall behaviour, are called by the generall name of Madnesse. But of the severall kinds of Madnesse, he that would take the paines, might enrowle a legion. And if the Excesses be madnesse, there is no doubt but the Passions themselves, when they tend to Evill, are degrees of the same.

(For example,) Though the effect of folly, in them that are possessed of an opinion of being inspired, be not visible alwayes in one man, by any very extravagant action, that proceedeth from such Passion; yet when many of them conspire together, the Rage of the whole multitude is visible enough. For what argument of Madnesse can there be greater,

5. Appearance.
6. Ways of conducting oneself.

than to clamour, strike, and throw stones at our best friends? Yet this is somewhat lesse than such a multitude will do. For they will clamour, fight against, and destroy those, by whom all their life-time before, they have been protected, and secured from injury. And if this be Madnesse in the multitude, it is the same in every particular man. For as in the middest of the sea, though a man perceive no sound of that part of the water next him; yet he is well assured, that part contributes as much, to the Roaring of the Sea, as any other part, of the same quantity: so also, though wee perceive no great unquietnesse, in one, or two men; yet we may be well assured, that their singular Passions, are parts of the Seditious roaring of a troubled Nation. And if there were nothing else that bewrayed their madnesse; yet that very arrogating such inspiration to themselves, is argument enough. If some man in Bedlam[7] should entertaine you with sober discourse; and you desire in taking leave, to know what he were, that you might another time requite his civility; and he should tell you, he were God the Father; I think you need expect no extravagant action for argument of his Madnesse.

This opinion of Inspiration, called commonly, Private Spirit, begins very often, from some lucky finding of an Errour generally held by others; and not knowing, or not remembring, by what conduct of reason, they came to so singular a truth, (as they think it, though it be many times an untruth they light on,) they presently admire themselves; as being in the speciall grace of God Almighty, who hath revealed the same to them supernaturally, by his Spirit.

Again, that Madnesse is nothing else, but too much appearing Passion, may be gathered out of the effects of Wine, which are the same with those of the evill disposition of the organs. For the variety of behaviour in men that have drunk too much, is the same with that of Mad-men: some of them Raging, others Loving, others Laughing, all extravagantly, but according to their severall domineering Passions: For the effect of the wine, does but remove Dissimulation; and take from them the sight of the deformity of their Passions. For, (I believe) the most sober men, when they walk alone without care and employment of the mind, would be unwilling the vanity and Extravagance of their thoughts at that time should be publiquely seen: which is a confession, that Passions unguided, are for the most part meere Madnesse.

The opinions of the world, both in antient and later ages, concerning the cause of madnesse, have been two. Some, deriving them from the Passions; some, from Dæmons, or Spirits, either good, or bad, which they thought might enter into a man, possesse him, and move his organs in such strange, and uncouth manner, as mad-men use[8] to do. The former sort therefore, called such men, Mad-men: but the Later, called them sometimes Dæmoniacks, (that is, possessed with spirits;) sometimes Energumeni, (that is, agitated, or moved with spirits;) and now in Italy they are called not onely Pazzi, Mad-men; but also Spiritati, men possest.

There was once a great conflux of people in Abdera, a City of the

[37]

7. A mental asylum in London.
8. Are accustomed.

Greeks, at the acting of the Tragedy of *Andromeda*, upon an extream hot day: whereupon, a great many of the spectators falling into Fevers, had this accident from the heat, and from the Tragedy together, that they did nothing but pronounce Iambiques, with the names of *Perseus* and *Andromeda*; which together with the Fever, was cured, by the comming on of Winter: And this madnesse was thought to proceed from the Passion imprinted by the Tragedy. Likewise there raigned a fit of madnesse in another Græcian City, which seized onely the young Maidens; and caused many of them to hang themselves. This was by most then thought an act of the Divel. But one that suspected, that contempt of life in them, might proceed from some Passion of the mind, and supposing they did not contemne also their honour, gave counsell to the Magistrates, to strip such as so hang'd themselves, and let them hang out naked. This the story sayes cured that madnesse. But on the other side, the same Græcians, did often ascribe madnesse, to the operation of the Eumenides, or Furyes; and sometimes of *Ceres*, *Phœbus*, and other Gods: so much did men attribute to Phantasmes, as to think them aëreal living bodies; and generally to call them Spirits. And as the Romans in this, held the same opinion with the Greeks: so also did the Jewes; For they called mad-men Prophets, or (according as they thought the spirits good or bad) Dæmoniacks; and some of them called both Prophets, and Dæmoniacks, mad-men; and some called the same man both Dæmoniack, and mad-man. But for the Gentiles, 'tis no wonder; because Diseases, and Health; Vices, and Vertues; and many naturall accidents, were with them termed, and worshipped as Dæmons. So that a man was to understand by Dæmon, as well (sometimes) an Ague,[9] as a Divell. But for the Jewes to have such opinion, [38] is somewhat strange. For neither *Moses*, nor *Abraham* pretended to Prophecy by possession of a Spirit; but from the voyce of God; or by a Vision or Dream: Nor is there any thing in his Law, Morall, or Ceremoniall, by which they were taught, there was any such Enthusiasme;[1] or any Possession. When God is sayd, *Numb.* II. 25. to take from the Spirit that was in *Moses*, and give to the 70. Elders, the Spirit of God (taking it for the substance of God) is not divided. The Scriptures by the Spirit of God in man, mean a mans spirit, enclined to Godlinesse. And where it is said *Exod.* 28. 3. *Whom I have filled with the spirit of wisdome to make garments for Aaron*, is not meant a spirit put into them, that can make garments; but the wisdome of their own spirits in that kind of work. In the like sense, the spirit of man, when it produceth unclean actions, is ordinarily called an unclean spirit; and so other spirits, though not alwayes, yet as often as the vertue or vice so stiled, is extraordinary, and Eminent. Neither did the other Prophets of the old Testament pretend Enthusiasme; or, that God spake in them; but to them by Voyce, Vision, or Dream; and the *Burthen of the Lord* was not Possession, but Command. How then could the Jewes fall into this opinion of possession? I can imagine no reason, but that which is common to all men; namely, the want of curiosity to search naturall causes;

9. Fever or shivering fit.
1. Prophetic frenzy.

and their placing Felicity, in the acquisition of the grosse pleasures of the Senses, and the things that most immediately conduce thereto. For they that see any strange, and unusuall ability, or defect in a mans mind; unlesse they see withall, from what cause it may probably proceed, can hardly think it naturall; and if not naturall, they must needs thinke it supernaturall; and then what can it be, but that either God, or the Divell is in him? And hence it came to passe, when our Saviour (*Mark* 3. 21.) was compassed about with the multitude, those of the house doubted[2] he was mad, and went out to hold him: but the Scribes said he had *Belzebub*,[3] and that was it, by which he cast out divels; as if the greater mad-man had awed the lesser. And that (*John* 10. 20.) some said, *He hath a Divell, and is mad*; whereas others holding him for a Prophet, sayd, *These are not the words of one that hath a Divell*. So in the old Testament he that came to anoynt *Jehu*, 2 *Kings* 9. II. was a Prophet; but some of the company asked *Jehu*, *What came that mad-man for*? So that in summe, it is manifest, that whosoever behaved himselfe in extraordinory manner, was thought by the Jewes to be possessed either with a good, or evill spirit; except by the Sadduces, who erred so farre on the other hand, as not to believe there were at all any spirits, (which is very neere to direct Atheisme;) and thereby perhaps the more provoked others, to terme such men Dæmoniacks, rather than mad-men.

But why then does our Saviour proceed in the curing of them, as if they were possest; and not as if they were mad? To which I can give no other kind of answer, but that which is given to those that urge the Scripture in like manner against the opinion of the motion of the Earth. The Scripture was written to shew unto men the kingdome of God,
[39] and to prepare their mindes to become his obedient subjects; leaving the world, and the Philosophy thereof, to the disputation of men, for the exercising of their naturall Reason. Whether the Earths, or Suns motion make the day, and night; or whether the Exorbitant actions of men, proceed from Passion, or from the Divell, (so we worship him not) it is all one, as to our obedience, and subjection to God Almighty; which is the thing for which the Scripture was written. As for that our Saviour speaketh to the disease, as to a person; it is the usuall phrase of all that cure by words onely, as Christ did, (and Inchanters pretend to do, whether they speak to a Divel or not.) For is not Christ also said (*Math.* 8. 26.) to have rebuked the winds? Is not he said also (*Luk.* 4. 39.) to rebuke a Fever? Yet this does not argue that a Fever is a Divel. And whereas many of those Divels are said to confesse Christ; it is not necessary to interpret those places otherwise, than that those mad-men confessed him. And whereas our Saviour (*Math.* 12. 43.) speaketh of an unclean Spirit, that having gone out of a man, wandreth through dry places, seeking rest, and finding none; and returning into the same man, with seven other spirits worse than himselfe;[4] It is manifestly a Parable, alluding to a man, that after a little endeavour to quit his lusts, is vanquished by the strength of them; and becomes seven times worse

2. Suspected.
3. The devil.
4. Hobbes returns to this image toward the end of *Leviathan*. See below, p. 252.

than he was. So that I see nothing at all in the Scripture, that requireth a beliefe, that Dæmoniacks were any other thing but Mad-men.

There is yet another fault in the Discourses of some men; which may also be numbred amongst the sorts of Madnesse; namely, that abuse of words, whereof I have spoken before in the fifth chapter, by the Name of Absurdity. And that is, when men speak such words, as put together, have in them no signification at all; but are fallen upon by some, through misunderstanding of the words they have received, and repeat by rote; by others, from intention to deceive by obscurity. And this is incident to none but those, that converse in questions of matters incomprehensible, as the Schoole-men; or in questions of abstruse Philosophy. The common sort of men seldome speak Insignificantly, and are therefore, by those other Egregious[5] persons counted Idiots. But to be assured their words are without any thing correspondent to them in the mind, there would need some Examples; which if any man require, let him take a Schoole-man into his hands, and see if he can translate any one chapter concerning any difficult point; as the Trinity; the Deity; the nature of Christ; Transubstantiation; Free-will, &c. into any of the moderne tongues, so as to make the same intelligible; or into any tolerable Latine, such as they were acquainted withall, that lived when the Latine tongue was Vulgar.[6] What is the meaning of these words. *The first cause does not necessarily inflow any thing into the second, by force of the Essentiall subordination of the second causes, by Which it may help it to worke?* They are the Translation of the Title of the sixth chapter of *Suarez*[7] first Booke, *Of the Concourse, Motion, and Help of God.* When men write whole volumes of such stuffe, are they not Mad, or intend to make others so? And particularly, in the question of Transubstantiation; where after certain words spoken, they that say, the Whitenesse, Roundnesse, Magnitude, Quality, Corruptibility, all which are incorporeall, &c. go out of the Wafer, into the Body of our blessed Saviour, do they not make those Nesses, Tudes, and Ties, to be so many spirits possessing his body? For by Spirits, they mean always things, that being incorporeall, are neverthelesse moveable from one place to another. So that this kind of Absurdity, may rightly be numbred amongst the many sorts of Madnesse; and all the time that guided by clear Thoughts of their worldly lust,[8] they forbear disputing, or writing thus, but Lucide Intervals. And thus much of the Vertues and Defects Intellectuall.

Insignificant Speech.

[40]

Chap. IX.

Of the Severall SUBJECTS *of* KNOWLEDGE.

There are of KNOWLEDGE two kinds; whereof one is *Knowledge of Fact:* the other *Knowledge of the Consequence of one Affirmation to*

5. Prominent.
6. Common.
7. Francisco de Suarez (1548–1617), a Spanish Jesuit and the leading Scholastic philosopher and theologian of his time.
8. Desires (not necessarily sexual).

another. The former is nothing else, but Sense and Memory, and is *Absolute Knowledge;* as when we see a Fact doing, or remember it done: And this is the Knowledge required in a Witnesse. The later is called *Science;* and is *Conditionall;* as when we know, that, *If the figure showne be a Circle, then any straight line through the Center shall divide it into two equall parts.* And this is the Knowledge required in a Philosopher; that is to say, of him that pretends to Reasoning.

The Register of *Knowledge of Fact* is called *History.* Whereof there be two sorts: one called *Naturall History;* which is the History of such Facts, or Effects of Nature, as have no Dependance on Mans *Will;* Such as are the Histories of *Metalls, Plants, Animals, Regions,* and the like. The other, is *Civill History;* which is the History of the Voluntary Actions of men in Commonwealths.

The Registers of Science, are such *Books* as contain the *Demonstrations* of Consequences of one Affirmation, to another; and are commonly called *Books of Philosophy;* whereof the sorts are many, according to the diversity of the Matter; And may be divided in such manner as I have divided them in the following Table. [*See facing page—Ed.*]

Chap. X.

Of POWER, WORTH, DIGNITY, HONOUR, *and* WORTHINESSE.

Power.   The POWER *of a Man,* (to take it Universally,) is his present means, to obtain some future apparent Good. And is either *Originall,* or *Instrumentall.*

Naturall Power, is the eminence of the Faculties of Body, or Mind: as extraordinary Strength, Forme, Prudence, Arts, Eloquence, Liberality, Nobility. *Instrumentall* are those Powers, which acquired by these, or by fortune, are means and Instruments to acquire more: as Riches, Reputation, Friends, and the secret working of God, which men call Good Luck. For the nature of Power, is in this point, like to Fame, increasing as it proceeds; or like the motion of heavy bodies, which the further they go, make still the more hast.

The Greatest of humane Powers, is that which is compounded of the Powers of most men, united by consent, in one person, Naturall, or Civill, that has the use of all their Powers depending on his will; such as is the Power of a Common-wealth: Or depending on the wills of each particular; such as is the Power of a Faction, or of divers factions leagued. Therefore to have servants, is Power; To have friends, is Power: for they are strengths united.

Also Riches joyned with liberality, is Power; because it procureth friends, and servants: Without liberality, not so; because in this case they defend not; but expose men to Envy, as a Prey.

Reputation of power, is Power; because it draweth with it the adhærence of those that need protection.

So is Reputation of love of a mans Country, (called Popularity,) for the same Reason.

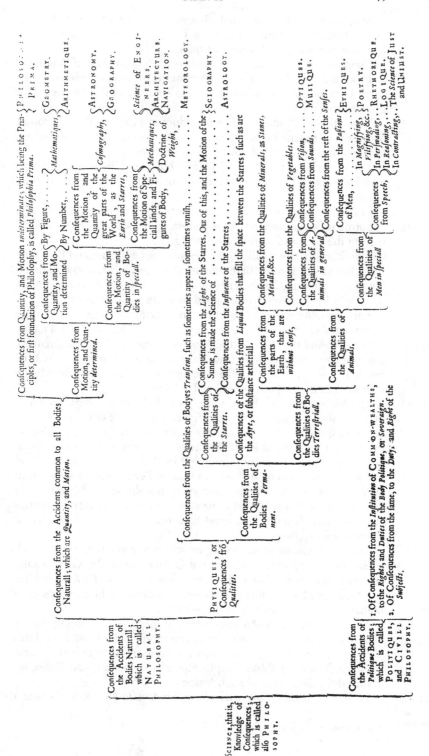

SCIENCE, that is, Knowledge of Consequences; which is called also PHILOSOPHY.

- Consequences from the Accidents of Bodies Naturall; which is called NATURALL PHILOSOPHY.
  - Consequences from the Accidents common to all Bodies Naturall; which are *Quantity*, and *Motion*.
    - Consequences from *Quantity*, and *Motion indeterminate*; which being the Principles or first foundation of Philosophy, is called *Philosophia Prima*. ⟩ PHILOSOPHIA PRIMA.
    - Consequences from Motion, and Quantity *determined*.
      - Consequences from *Quantity*, and *Motion determined* { By Figure, ... ⟩ GEOMETRY. / By Number, ... ⟩ ARITHMETIQUE. } *Mathematiques*, *Quantity, and Motion determined.*
      - Consequences from the Motion, and Quantity of Bodies *in speciall*.
        - Consequences from the Motion, and Quantity of the great parts of the World, as the *Earth* and *Starres*, { ASTRONOMY. / GEOGRAPHY. } *Cosmography*,
        - Consequences from the Motion of Speciall kinds, and Figures of Body, { *Mechaniques*, Doctrine of *Weight*, ⟩ *Science* of ENGINEERS, ARCHITECTURE. NAVIGATION. }
  - PHYSIQUES, or Consequences from Qualities.
    - Consequences from the Qualities of Bodyes *Transient*, such as sometimes appear, sometimes vanish, ... METEOROLOGY.
    - Consequences from the Qualities of Bodies *Permanent*.
      - Consequences from the Qualities of the *Starres*. { Consequences from the *Light* of the Starres. Out of this, and the Motion of the Sunne, is made the Science of .... SCIOGRAPHY. / Consequences from the *Influence* of the Starres, ... ASTROLOGY. }
      - Consequences of the Qualities from *Liquid* Bodies that fill the space between the Starres; such as are the *Ayre*, or substance aetheriall.
      - Consequences from the Qualities of Bodies *Terrestriall*.
        - Consequences from the parts of the Earth, that are *without Sense*, { Consequences from the Qualities of *Minerals*, as *Stones*, *Metalls*, &c. / Consequences from the Qualities of *Vegetables*. }
        - Consequences from the Qualities of *Animals*. { Consequences from the Qualities of *Animals in generall*. { Consequences from *Vision*, ... OPTIQUES. / Consequences from *Sounds*, ... MUSIQUE. / Consequences from the rest of the *Senses*. } / Consequences from the Qualities of *Men in speciall*. { Consequences from the *Passions* of Men, ⟩ ETHIQUES. / Consequences from *Speech*, { In *Magnifying*, *Vilifying*, &c. ⟩ POETRY. / In *Perswading*, ... RHETORIQUE. / In *Reasoning*, ... LOGIQUE. / In *Contracting*, ... The *Science of* JUST and UNJUST. } } }

- Consequences from the Accidents of *Politique* Bodies; which is called POLITIQUES, and CIVILL PHILOSOPHY.
  1. Of Consequences from the *Institution* of COMMON-WEALTHS, to the *Rights*, and *Duties* of the *Body Politique*, or *Soveraign*.
  2. Of Consequences from the same, to the *Duty*, and *Right* of the *Subjects*.

Also, what quality soever maketh a man beloved, or feared of many; or the reputation of such quality, is Power; because it is a means to have the assistance, and service of many.

Good successe is Power; because it maketh reputation of Wisdome, or good fortune; which makes men either feare him, or rely on him.

Affability of men already in power, is encrease of Power; because it gaineth love.

Reputation of Prudence in the conduct of Peace or War, is Power; because to prudent men, we commit the government of our selves, more willingly than to others.

Nobility is Power, not in all places, but onely in those Common-wealths, where it has Priviledges: for in such priviledges consisteth their Power.

Eloquence is power; because it is seeming Prudence.

[42] Forme is Power; because being a promise of Good, it recommendeth men to the favour of women and strangers.

The Sciences, are small Power; because not eminent; and therefore, not acknowledged in any man; nor are at all, but in a few; and in them, but of a few things. For Science is of that nature, as none can understand it to be, but such as in a good measure have attayned it.

Arts of publique use, as Fortification, making of Engines, and other Instruments of War; because they conferre[1] to Defence, and Victory, are Power: And though the true Mother of them, be Science, namely the Mathematiques; yet, because they are brought into the Light, by the hand of the Artificer, they be esteemed (the Midwife passing with the vulgar for the Mother,) as his issue.

Worth. The *Value*, or WORTH of a man, is as of all other things, his Price; that is to say, so much as would be given for the use of his Power: and therefore is not absolute; but a thing dependant on the need and judgement of another. An able conductor of Souldiers, is of great Price in time of War present, or imminent; but in Peace not so. A learned and uncorrupt Judge, is much Worth in time of Peace; but not so much in War. And as in other things, so in men, not the seller, but the buyer determines the Price. For let a man (as most men do,) rate themselves at the highest Value they can; yet their true Value is no more than it is esteemed by others.

The manifestation of the Value we set on one another, is that which is commonly called Honouring, and Dishonouring. To Value a man at a high rate, is to *Honour* him; at a low rate, is to *Dishonour* him. But high, and low, in this case, is to be understood by comparison to the rate that each man setteth on himselfe.

Dignity. The publique worth of a man, which is the Value set on him by the Common-wealth, is that which men commonly call DIGNITY. And this Value of him by the Common-wealth, is understood, by offices of Command, Judicature, publike Employment; or by Names and Titles, introduced for distinction of such Value.

To Honour and Dishonour. To pray to another, for ayde of any kind, is *to* HONOUR; because a

1. Contribute.

signe we have an opinion he has power to help; and the more difficult the ayde is, the more is the Honour.

To obey, is to Honour; because no man obeyes them, whom they think have no power to help, or hurt them. And consequently to disobey, is to *Dishonour.*

To give great gifts to a man, is to Honour him; because 'tis buying of Protection, and acknowledging of Power. To give little gifts, is to Dishonour; because it is but Almes, and signifies an opinion of the need of small helps.

To be sedulous in promoting anothers good; also to flatter, is to Honour; as a signe we seek his protection or ayde. To neglect, is to Dishonour.

To give way, or place to another, in any Commodity, is to Honour; being a confession of greater power. To arrogate, is to Dishonour.

To shew any signe of love, or feare of another, is to Honour; for both [43] to love, and to feare, is to value. To contemne, or lesse to love or feare, then he expects, is to Dishonour; for 'tis undervaluing.

To praise, magnifie, or call happy, is to Honour; because nothing but goodnesse, power, and felicity is valued. To revile, mock, or pitty, is to Dishonour.

To speak to another with consideration, to appear before him with decency, and humility, is to Honour him; as signes of fear to offend. To speak to him rashly, to do any thing before him obscenely, slovenly, impudently, is to Dishonour.

To believe, to trust, to rely on another, is to Honour him; signe of opinion of his vertue and power. To distrust, or not believe, is to Dishonour.

To hearken to a mans counsell, or discourse of what kind soever, is to Honour; as a signe we think him wise, or eloquent, or witty. To sleep, or go forth, or talk the while, is to Dishonour.

To do those things to another, which he takes for signes of Honour, or which the Law or Custome makes so, is to Honour; because in approving the Honour done by others, he acknowledgeth the power which others acknowledge. To refuse to do them, is to Dishonour.

To agree with in opinion, is to Honour; as being a signe of approving his judgement, and wisdome. To dissent, is Dishonour; and an upbraiding of errour; and (if the dissent be in many things) of folly.

To imitate, is to Honour; for it is vehemently to approve. To imitate ones Enemy, is to Dishonour.

To honour those another honours, is to Honour him; as a signe of approbation of his judgement. To honour his Enemies, is to Dishonour him.

To employ in counsell, or in actions of difficulty, is to Honour; as a signe of opinion of his wisdome, or other power. To deny employment in the same cases, to those that seek it, is to Dishonour.

All these wayes of Honouring, are naturall; and as well within, as without Common-wealths. But in Common-wealths, where he, or they that have the supreme Authority, can make whatsoever they please, to stand for signes of Honour, there be other Honours.

A Soveraigne doth Honour a Subject, with whatsoever Title, or Office, or Employment, or Action, that he himselfe will have taken for a
signe of his will to Honour him.

The King of *Persia*, Honoured *Mordecay*, when he appointed[2] he
should be conducted through the streets in the Kings Garment, upon
one of the Kings Horses, with a Crown on his head, and a Prince before
him, proclayming, *Thus shall it be done to him that the King will honour.* And yet another King of *Persia*, or the same another time, to one
that demanded for some great service, to weare one of the Kings robes,
gave him leave so to do; but with this addition, that he should weare
it as the Kings foole; and then it was Dishonour. So that of Civill
Honour, the Fountain is in the person of the Common-wealth, and
dependeth on the Will of the Soveraigne; and is therefore temporary,

[44]   and called *Civill Honour*; such as are Magistracy, Offices, Titles; and
in some places Coats, and Scutchions painted: and men Honour such
as have them, as having so many signes of favour in the Common-
wealth; which favour is Power.

Honourable.   *Honourable* is whatsoever possession, action, or quality, is an argument and signe of Power.

And therefore To be Honoured, loved, or feared of many, is Honourable; as arguments of Power. To be Honoured of few or none,
Dishonourable.

Dishonour-   Dominion,[3] and Victory is Honourable; because acquired by Power;
able.   and Servitude, for need, or feare, is Dishonourable.

Good fortune (if lasting,) Honourable; as a signe of the favour of
God. Ill fortune, and losses, Dishonourable. Riches, are Honourable;
for they are Power. Poverty, Dishonourable. Magnanimity, Liberality,
Hope, Courage, Confidence, are Honourable; for they proceed from
the conscience[4] of Power. Pusillanimity, Parsimony, Fear, Diffidence,
are Dishonourable.

Timely Resolution, or determination of what a man is to do, is Honourable; as being the contempt of small difficulties, and dangers. And
Irresolution, Dishonourable; as a signe of too much valuing of little
impediments, and little advantages: For when a man has weighed things
as long as the time permits, and resolves not, the difference of weight
is but little; and therefore if he resolve not, he overvalues little things,
which is Pusillanimity.

All Actions, and Speeches, that proceed, or seem to proceed from
much Experience, Science, Discretion, or Wit, are Honourable; For
all these are Powers. Actions, or Words that proceed from Errour, Ignorance, or Folly, Dishonourable.

Gravity, as farre forth as it seems to proceed from a mind employed
on some thing else, is Honourable; because employment is a signe of
Power. But if it seem to proceed from a purpose to appear grave, it is
Dishonourable. For the gravity of the former, is like the steddinesse of
a Ship laden with Merchandise; but of the later, like the steddinesse of
a Ship ballasted with Sand, and other trash.

2. Decreed.
3. Right of governing or possession.
4. Consciousness.

To be Conspicuous, that is to say, to be known, for Wealth, Office, great Actions, or any eminent Good, is Honourable; as a signe of the power for which he is conspicuous. On the contrary, Obscurity, is Dishonourable.

To be descended from conspicuous Parents, is Honourable; because they the more easily attain the aydes, and friends of their Ancestors. On the contrary, to be descended from obscure Parentage, is Dishonourable.

Actions proceeding from Equity, joyned with losse, are Honourable; as signes of Magnanimity: for Magnanimity is a signe of Power. On the contrary, Craft, Shifting, neglect of Equity, is Dishonourable.

Covetousnesse of great Riches, and ambition of great Honours, are Honourable; as signes of power to obtain them. Covetousnesse, and ambition, of little gaines, or preferments, is Dishonourable.

Nor does it alter the case of Honour, whether an action (so it be great and difficult, and consequently a signe of much power,) be just [45] or unjust: for Honour consisteth onely in the opinion of Power. Therefore the ancient Heathen did not thinke they Dishonoured, but greatly Honoured the Gods, when they introduced them in their Poems, committing Rapes, Thefts, and other great, but unjust, or unclean acts: In so much as nothing is so much celebrated in *Jupiter*, as his Adulteries; nor in *Mercury*, as his Frauds, and Thefts: of whose praises, in a hymne of *Homer*, the greatest is this, that being born in the morning, he had invented Musique at noon, and before night, stolne away the Cattell of *Apollo*, from his Herdsmen.

Also amongst men, till there were constituted great Commonwealths, it was thought no dishonour to be a Pyrate, or a High-way Theefe; but rather a lawfull Trade, not onely amongst the Greeks, but also amongst all other Nations; as is manifest by the Histories of antient time. And at this day, in this part of the world, private Duels are, and always will be Honourable, though unlawfull, till such time as there shall be Honour ordained for them that refuse, and Ignominy for them that make the Challenge. For Duels also are many times effects of Courage; and the ground of Courage is always Strength or Skill, which are Power; though for the most part they be effects of rash speaking, and of the fear of Dishonour, in one, or both the Combatants; who engaged by rashnesse, are driven into the Lists to avoyd disgrace.

Scutchions, and Coats of Armes hæreditary, where they have any eminent Priviledges, are Honourable; otherwise not: for their Power consisteth either in such Priviledges, or in Riches, or some such thing as is equally honoured in other men. This kind of Honour, commonly called Gentry, has been derived from the Antient Germans. For there never was any such thing known, where the German Customes were unknown. Nor is it now any where in use, where the Germans have not inhabited. The antient Greek Commanders, when they went to war, had their Shields painted with such Devises as they pleased; insomuch as an unpainted Buckler was a signe of Poverty, and of a common Souldier: but they transmitted not the Inheritance of them. The Romans transmitted the Marks of their Families: but they were the Images, not the Devises of their Ancestors. Amongst the people of *Asia*,

Coats of Armes.

Afrique, and *America*, there is not, nor was ever, any such thing. The Germans onely had that custome; from whom it has been derived into *England*, *France*, *Spain* and *Italy*, when in great numbers they either ayded the Romans, or made their own Conquests in these Westerne parts of the world.

For *Germany*, being antiently, as all other Countries, in their beginnings, divided amongst an infinite number of little Lords, or Masters of Families, that continually had wars one with another; those Masters, or Lords, principally to the end they might, when they were Covered with Arms, be known by their followers; and partly for ornament, both painted their Armor, or their Scutchion, or Coat, with the picture of [46] some Beast, or other thing; and also put some eminent and visible mark upon the Crest of their Helmets. And this ornament both of the Armes, and Crest, descended by inheritance to their Children; to the eldest pure, and to the rest with some note of diversity, such as the Old master, that is to say in Dutch, the *Here-alt* thought fit. But when many such Families, joyned together, made a greater Monarchy, this duty of the Herealt,[5] to distinguish Scutchions, was made a private Office a part. And the issue of these Lords, is the great and antient Gentry; which for the most part bear living creatures, noted for courage, and rapine; or Castles, Battlements, Belts, Weapons, Bars, Palisadoes, and other notes of War; nothing being then in honour, but vertue military. Afterwards, not onely Kings, but popular Common-wealths, gave divers manners of Scutchions, to such as went forth to the War, or returned from it, for encouragement, or recompence to their service. All which, by an observing Reader, may be found in such antient Histories, Greek and Latine, as make mention of the German Nation, and Manners, in their times.

Titles of Honour.   Titles of *Honour*, such as are Duke, Count, Marquis, and Baron, are Honourable; as signifying the value set upon them by the Soveraigne Power of the Common-wealth: Which Titles, were in old time titles of Office, and Command, derived some from the Romans, some from the Germans, and French. Dukes, in Latine *Duces*, being Generalls in War: Counts, *Comites*, such as bare the Generall company out of friendship; and were left to govern and defend places conquered, and pacified: Marquises, *Marchiones*, were Counts that governed the Marches, or bounds of the Empire. Which titles of Duke, Count, and Marquis, came into the Empire, about the time of *Constantine* the Great, from the customes of the German *Militia*. But Baron, seems to have been a Title of the Gaules, and signifies a Great man; such as were the Kings, or Princes men, whom they employed in war about their persons; and seems to be derived from *Vir*, to *Ber*, and *Bar*, that signified the same in the Language of the Gaules, that *Vir* in Latine; and thence to *Bero*, and *Baro*: so that such men were called *Berones*, and after *Barones*; and (in Spanish) *Varones*. But he that would know more particularly the originall of Titles of Honour, may find it, as I have done this, in Mr. *Seldens*[6] most excellent Treatise of that subject.

5. Herald.
6. John Selden (1584–1654), a leading English political theorist and author of *Titles of Honour* (1614), to which Hobbes refers here.

In processe of time these offices of Honour, by occasion of trouble, and for reasons of good and peaceable government, were turned into meer Titles; serving for the most part, to distinguish the precedence, place, and order of subjects in the Common-wealth: and men were made Dukes, Counts, Marquises, and Barons of Places, wherein they had neither possession, nor command: and other Titles also, were devised to the same end.

WORTHINESSE, is a thing different from the worth, or value of a man; and also from his merit, or desert; and consisteth in a particular power, or ability for that, whereof he is said to be worthy: which particular ability, is usually named FITNESSE, or *Aptitude*.

Worthinesse. Fitnesse.

For he is Worthiest to be a Commander, to be a Judge, or to have any other charge, that is best fitted, with the qualities required to the well discharging of it; and Worthiest of Riches, that has the qualities most requisite for the well using of them: any of which qualities being absent, one may neverthelesse be a Worthy man, and valuable for some thing else. Again, a man may be Worthy of Riches, Office, and Employment, that neverthelesse, can plead no right to have it before another; and therefore cannot be said to merit or deserve it. For Merit, præsupposeth a right, and that the thing deserved is due by promise: Of which I shall say more hereafter, when I shall speak of Contracts.

[47]

Chap. XI.

Of the difference of MANNERS.

By MANNERS, I mean not here, Decency of behaviour; as how one man should salute another, or how a man should wash his mouth, or pick his teeth before company, and such other points of the *Small Moralls*; But those qualities of man-kind, that concern their living together in Peace, and Unity. To which end we are to consider, that the Felicity of this life, consisteth not in the repose of a mind satisfied. For there is no such *Finis ultimus*, (utmost ayme,) nor *Summum Bonum*, (greatest Good,) as is spoken of in the Books of the old Morall Philosophers. Nor can a man any more live, whose Desires are at an end, than he, whose Senses and Imaginations are at a stand. Felicity is a continuall progresse of the desire, from one object to another; the attaining of the former, being still but the way to the later. The cause whereof is, That the object of mans desire, is not to enjoy once onely, and for one instant of time; but to assure for ever, the way of his future desire. And therefore the voluntary actions, and inclinations of all men, tend, not onely to the procuring, but also to the assuring of a contented life; and differ only in the way: which ariseth partly from the diversity of passions, in divers men; and partly from the difference of the knowledge, or opinion each one has of the causes, which produce the effect desired.

What is here meant by Manners.

So that in the first place, I put for a generall inclination of all mankind, a perpetuall and restlesse desire of Power after power, that ceaseth onely in Death. And the cause of this, is not alwayes that a man hopes

A restlesse desire of Power, in all men.

for a more intensive delight, than he has already attained to; or that he cannot be content with a moderate power: but because he cannot assure the power and means to live well, which he hath present, without the acquisition of more. And from hence it is, that Kings, whose power is greatest, turn their endeavours to the assuring it at home by Lawes, or abroad by Wars: and when that is done, there succeedeth a new desire; in some, of Fame from new Conquest; in others, of ease and sensuall pleasure; in others, of admiration, or being flattered for excellence in some art, or other ability of the mind.

[48]
Love of Contention from Competition.

Competition of Riches, Honour, Command, or other power, enclineth to Contention, Enmity, and War: Because the way of one Competitor, to the attaining of his desire, is to kill, subdue, supplant, or repell the other. Particularly, competition of praise, enclineth to a reverence of Antiquity. For men contend with the living, not with the dead; to these ascribing more than due, that they may obscure the glory of the other.

Civil obedience from love of Ease. From feare of Death, or Wounds.

Desire of Ease, and sensuall Delight, disposeth men to obey a common Power: Because by such Desires, a man doth abandon the protection might be hoped for from his own Industry, and labour. Fear of Death, and Wounds, disposeth to the same; and for the same reason. On the contrary, needy men, and hardy, not contented with their present condition; as also, all men that are ambitious of Military command, are enclined to continue the causes of warre; and to stirre up trouble and sedition: for there is no honour Military but by warre; nor any such hope to mend an ill game, as by causing a new shuffle.

And from love of Arts.

Desire of Knowledge, and Arts of Peace, enclineth men to obey a common Power: For such Desire, containeth a desire of leasure; and consequently protection from some other Power than their own.

Love of Vertue, from love of Praise.

Desire of Praise, disposeth to laudable actions, such as please them whose judgement they value; for of those men whom we contemn, we contemn also the Praises. Desire of Fame after death does the same. And though after death, there be no sense of the praise given us on Earth, as being joyes, that are either swallowed up in the unspeakable joyes of Heaven, or extinguished in the extreme torments of Hell: yet is not such Fame vain; because men have a present delight therein, from the foresight of it, and of the benefit that may redound thereby to their posterity: which though they now see not, yet they imagine; and any thing that is pleasure in the sense, the same also is pleasure in the imagination.

Hate, from difficulty of Requiting great Benefits.

To have received from one, to whom we think our selves equall, greater benefits than there is hope to Requite, disposeth to counterfeit love; but really secret hatred; and puts a man into the estate of a desperate debtor, that in declining the sight of his creditor, tacitely wishes him there, where he might never see him more. For benefits oblige; and obligation is thraldome; and unrequitable obligation, perpetuall thraldome; which is to ones equall, hatefull. But to have received benefits from one, whom we acknowledge for superiour, enclines to love; because the obligation is no new depression[1]: and cheerfull acceptation,

---

1. Humbling experience.

(which men call *Gratitude*,) is such an honour done to the obliger, as is taken generally for retribution. Also to receive benefits, though from an equall, or inferiour, as long as there is hope of requitall, disposeth to love: for in the intention of the receiver, the obligation is of ayd, and service mutuall; from whence proceedeth an Emulation of who shall exceed in benefiting; the most noble and profitable contention possible; wherein the victor is pleased with his victory, and the other revenged by confessing it.

To have done more hurt to a man, than he can, or is willing to expiate, enclineth the doer to hate the sufferer. For he must expect revenge, or forgivenesse; both which are hatefull.

And from Conscience of deserving to be hated.

Feare of oppression, disposeth a man to anticipate, or to seek ayd by society: for there is no other way by which a man can secure his life and liberty.

[49] Promptnesse to hurt, from Fear.

Men that distrust their own subtilty, are in tumult, and sedition, better disposed for victory, than they that suppose themselves wise, or crafty. For these love to consult, the other (fearing to be circumvented,) to strike first. And in sedition, men being alwayes in the procincts of battell, to hold together, and use all advantages of force, is a better stratagem, than any that can proceed from subtilty of Wit.

And from distrust of their own wit.

Vain-glorious men, such as without being conscious to themselves of great sufficiency, delight in supposing themselves gallant men, are enclined onely to ostentation; but not to attempt: Because when danger or difficulty appears, they look for nothing but to have their insufficiency discovered.

Vain under-taking from Vain-glory.

Vain-glorious men, such as estimate their sufficiency by the flattery of other men, or the fortune of some precedent action, without assured ground of hope from the true knowledge of themselves, are enclined to rash engaging; and in the approach of danger, or difficulty, to retire if they can: because not seeing the way of safety, they will rather hazard their honour, which may be salved with an excuse; than their lives, for which no salve is sufficient.

Men that have a strong opinion of their own wisdome in matter of government, are disposed to Ambition. Because without publique Employment in counsell or magistracy, the honour of their wisdome is lost. And therefore Eloquent speakers are enclined to Ambition; for Eloquence seemeth wisedome, both to themselves and others.

Ambition, from opinion of sufficiency.

Pusillanimity disposeth men to Irresolution, and consequently to lose the occasions, and fittest opportunities of action. For after men have been in deliberation till the time of action approach, if it be not then manifest what is best to be done, 'tis a signe, the difference of Motives, the one way and the other, are not great: Therefore not to resolve then, is to lose the occasion by weighing of trifles; which is Pusillanimity.

Irresolution, from too great valuing of small matters.

Frugality, (though in poor men a Vertue,) maketh a man unapt to atchieve such actions, as require the strength of many men at once: For it weakeneth their Endeavour, which is to be nourished and kept in vigor by Reward.

Eloquence, with flattery, disposeth men to confide in[2] them that have

2. Have confidence in.

Confidence in others from Ignorance of the marks of Wisdome and Kindnesse. And from Ignorance of naturall causes.

it; because the former is seeming Wisdome, the later seeming Kindnesse. Adde to them Military reputation, and it disposeth men to adhære, and subject themselves to those men that have them. The two former, having given them caution against danger from him; the later gives them caution against danger from others.

Want of Science, that is, Ignorance of causes, disposeth, or rather constraineth a man to rely on the advise, and authority of others. For all men whom the truth concernes, if they rely not on their own, must rely on the opinion of some other, whom they think wiser than themselves, and see not why he should deceive them.

[50]
And from want of Understanding.

Ignorance of the signification of words; which is, want of understanding, disposeth men to take on trust, not onely the truth they know not; but also the errors; and which is more, the non-sense of them they trust: For neither Error, nor non-sense, can without a perfect understanding of words, be detected.

From the same it proceedeth, that men give different names, to one and the same thing, from the difference of their own passions: As they that approve a private opinion, call it Opinion; but they that mislike it, Hæresie[3]: and yet hæresie signifies no more than private opinion; but has onely a greater tincture of choler.

From the same also it proceedeth, that men cannot distinguish, without study and great understanding, between one action of many men, and many actions of one multitude; as for example, between the one action of all the Senators of *Rome* in killing *Catiline*, and the many actions of a number of Senators in killing *Cæsar*; and therefore are disposed to take for the action of the people, that which is a multitude of actions done by a multitude of men, led perhaps by the perswasion of one.

Adhærence to Custome from Ignorance of the nature of Right and Wrong.

Ignorance of the causes, and originall constitution of Right, Equity, Law, and Justice, disposeth a man to make Custome and Example the rule of his actions; in such manner, as to think that Unjust which it hath been the custome to punish; and that Just, of the impunity and approbation whereof they can produce an Example, or (as the Lawyers which onely use this false measure of Justice barbarously call it) a Precedent; like little children, that have no other rule of good and evill manners, but the correction they receive from their Parents, and Masters; save that children are constant to their rule, whereas men are not so; because grown strong, and stubborn, they appeale from custome to reason, and from reason to custome, as it serves their turn; receding from custome when their interest requires it, and setting themselves against reason, as oft as reason is against them: Which is the cause, that the doctrine of Right and Wrong, is perpetually disputed, both by the Pen and the Sword: Whereas the doctrine of Lines, and Figures, is not so; because men care not, in that subject what be truth, as a thing that crosses no mans ambition, profit, or lust. For I doubt not, but if it had been a thing contrary to any mans right of dominion, or to the interest of men that have dominion, *That the three Angles of a Triangle, should*

---

3. Heresy.

be equall to two Angles of a Square; that doctrine should have been, if
not disputed, yet by the burning of all books of Geometry, suppressed,
as farre as he whom it concerned was able.

Ignorance of remote causes, disposeth men to attribute all events, to
the causes immediate, and Instrumentall: For these are all the causes
they perceive. And hence it comes to passe, that in all places, men that
are grieved with payments to the Publique, discharge their anger upon
the Publicans, that is to say, Farmers,[4] Collectors, and other Officers
of the publique Revenue; and adhære to such as find fault with the
publike Government; and thereby, when they have engaged themselves
beyond hope of justification, fall also upon the Supreme Authority, for
feare of punishment, or shame of receiving pardon.

Adhærence to private men, From Ignorance of the Causes of Peace.

[51]

Ignorance of naturall causes disposeth a man to Credulity, so as to
believe many times impossibilities: For such know nothing to the contrary, but that they may be true; being unable to detect the Impossibility. And Credulity, because men love to be hearkened unto in
company, disposeth them to lying: so that Ignorance it selfe without
Malice, is able to make a man both to believe lyes, and tell them; and
sometimes also to invent them.

Credulity from Ignorance of nature.

Anxiety for the future time, disposeth men to enquire into the causes
of things: because the knowledge of them, maketh men the better able
to order the present to their best advantage.

Curiosity to know, from Care of future time. Naturall Religion, from the same.

Curiosity, or love of the knowledge of causes, draws a man from
consideration of the effect, to seek the cause; and again, the cause of
that cause; till of necessity he must come to this thought at last, that
there is some cause, whereof there is no former cause, but is eternall;
which is it men call God. So that it is impossible to make any profound
enquiry into naturall causes, without being enclined thereby to believe
there is one God Eternall; though they cannot have any Idea of him
in their mind, answerable to his nature. For as a man that is born blind,
hearing men talk of warming themselves by the fire, and being brought
to warm himself by the same, may easily conceive, and assure himselfe,
there is somewhat there, which men call *Fire,* and is the cause of the
heat he feeles; but cannot imagine what it is like; nor have an Idea of
it in his mind, such as they have that see it: so also, by the visible things
of this world, and their admirable order, a man may conceive there is
a cause of them, which men call God; and yet not have an Idea, or
Image of him in his mind.

And they that make little, or no enquiry into the naturall causes of
things, yet from the feare that proceeds from the ignorance it selfe, of
what it is that hath the power to do them much good or harm, are
enclined to suppose, and feign unto themselves, severall kinds of Powers
Invisible; and to stand in awe of their own imaginations; and in time
of distresse to invoke them; as also in the time of [an expected][5] good
successe, to give them thanks; making the creatures of their own fancy,
their Gods. By which means it hath come to passe, that from the innumerable variety of Fancy, men have created in the world innumer-

4. Tax collectors.
5. Manuscript version reads *unexpected.*

able sorts of Gods. And this Feare of things invisible, is the naturall Seed of that, which every one in himself calleth Religion; and in them that worship, or feare that Power otherwise than they do, Superstition.

And this seed of Religion, having been observed by many; some of those that have observed it, have been enclined thereby to nourish, dresse, and forme it into Lawes; and to adde to it of their own invention, any opinion of the causes of future events, by which they thought they should best be able to govern others, and make unto themselves the greatest use of their Powers.

Chap. XII.

OF RELIGION.

Religion, in Man onely.

Seeing there are no signes, nor fruit of *Religion*, but in Man onely; there is no cause to doubt, but that the seed of *Religion*, is also onely in Man; and consisteth in some peculiar quality, or at least in some eminent degree therof, not to be found in other Living creatures.

First, from his desire of knowing Causes.

And first, it is peculiar to the nature of Man, to be inquisitive into the Causes of the Events they see, some more, some lesse; but all men so much, as to be curious in the search of the causes of their own good and evill fortune.

From the consideration of the Beginning of things.
From his observation of the Sequell of things.

Secondly, upon the sight of any thing that hath a Beginning, to think also it had a cause, which determined the same to begin, then when it did, rather than sooner or later.

Thirdly, whereas there is no other Felicity of Beasts, but the enjoying of their quotidian[1] Food, Ease, and Lusts; as having little, or no foresight of the time to come, for want of observation, and memory of the order, consequence, and dependance of the things they see; Man observeth how one Event hath been produced by another; and remembreth in them Antecedence and Consequence; And when he cannot assure himselfe of the true causes of things, (for the causes of good and evill fortune for the most part are invisible), he supposes causes of them, either such as his own fancy suggesteth; or trusteth to the Authority of other men, such as he thinks to be his friends, and wiser than himselfe.

The naturall Cause of Religion, the Anxiety of the time to come.

The two first, make Anxiety. For being assured that there be causes of all things that have arrived hitherto, or shall arrive hereafter; it is impossible for a man, who continually endeavoureth to secure himselfe against the evill he feares, and procure the good he desireth, not to be in a perpetuall solicitude of the time to come; So that every man, especially those that are over provident,[2] are in an estate like to that of *Prometheus*. For as *Prometheus*, (which interpreted, is, *The prudent man*,) was bound to the hill *Caucasus*, a place of large prospect, where, an Eagle feeding on his liver, devoured in the day, as much as was repayred in the night: So that man, which looks too far before him, in the care of future time, hath his heart all the day long, gnawed on by

1. Everyday.
2. Exceptionally foresightful.

feare of death, poverty, or other calamity; and has no repose, nor pause
of his anxiety, but in sleep.

This perpetuall feare, alwayes accompanying mankind in the igno- *Which makes*
rance of causes, as it were in the Dark, must needs have for object *them fear the*
something. And therefore when there is nothing to be seen, there is *Power of Invis-*
nothing to accuse, either of their good, or evill fortune, but some *Power*, *ible things.*
or Agent *Invisible*: In which sense perhaps it was, that some of the old
Poets said, that the Gods were at first created by humane Feare: which [53]
spoken of the Gods, (that is to say, of the many Gods of the Gentiles)
is very true. But the acknowledging of one God Eternall, Infinite, and
Omnipotent, may more easily be derived, from the desire men have to
know the causes of naturall bodies, and their severall vertues, and operations; than from the feare of what was to befall them in time to
come. For he that from any effect hee seeth come to passe, should
reason to the next and immediate cause thereof, and from thence to
the cause of that cause, and plonge himselfe profoundly in the pursuit
of causes; shall at last come to this, that there must be (as even the
Heathen Philosophers confessed) one First Mover; that is, a First, and
an Eternall cause of all things; which is that which men mean by the
name of God: And all this without thought of their fortune; the solicitude whereof, both enclines to fear, and hinders them from the search
of the causes of other things; and thereby gives occasion of feigning of
as many Gods, as there be men that feigne them.

And for the matter, or substance of the Invisible Agents, so fancyed; *And suppose*
they could not by naturall cogitation, fall upon any other conceipt, but *them*
that it was the same with that of the Soule of man; and that the Soule *Incorporeall.*
of man, was of the same substance, with that which appeareth in a
Dream, to one that sleepeth; or in a Looking-glasse, to one that is
awake; which, men not knowing that such apparitions are nothing else
but creatures of the Fancy, think to be reall, and externall Substances;
and therefore call them Ghosts; as the Latines called them *Imagines*,
and *Umbræ*; and thought them Spirits, that is, thin aëreall bodies; and
those Invisible Agents, which they feared, to bee like them; save that
they appear, and vanish when they please. But the opinion that such
Spirits were Incorporeall, or Immateriall, could never enter into the
mind of any man by nature; because, though men may put together
words of contradictory signification, as *Spirit*, and *Incorporeall*; yet they
can never have the imagination of any thing answering to them: And
therefore, men that by their own meditation, arrive to the acknowledgement of one Infinite, Omnipotent, and Eternall God, choose
rather to confesse he is Incomprehensible, and above their understanding; than to define his Nature by *Spirit Incorporeall*, and then confesse
their definition to be unintelligible: or if they give him such a title, it
is not *Dogmatically*, with intention to make the Divine Nature understood; but *Piously*, to honour him with attributes, of significations, as
remote as they can from the grossenesse of Bodies Visible.

Then, for the way by which they think these Invisible Agents wrought *But know not*
their effects; that is to say, what immediate causes they used, in bringing *the way how*
things to passe, men that know not what it is that we call *causing*, (that *they effect any*
thing.

is, almost all men) have no other rule to guesse by, but by observing, and remembering what they have seen to precede the like effect at some other time, or times before, without seeing between the antecedent and subsequent Event, any dependance or connexion at all: And therefore from the like things past, they expect the like things to come; and hope for good or evill luck, superstitiously, from things that have no part at all in the causing of it: As the Athenians did for their war at *Lepanto*, demand another *Phormio*; The Pompeian faction for their warre in *Afrique*, another *Scipio*; and others have done in divers other occasions since. In like manner they attribute their fortune to a stander by, to a lucky or unlucky place, to words spoken, especially if the name of God be amongst them; as Charming, and Conjuring (the Leiturgy of Witches;) insomuch as to believe, they have power to turn a stone into bread, bread into a man, or any thing, into any thing.

[54]

But honour them as they honour men.

Thirdly, for the worship which naturally men exhibite to Powers invisible, it can be no other, but such expressions of their reverence, as they would use towards men; Gifts, Petitions, Thanks, Submission of Body, Considerate Addresses, sober Behaviour, premeditated Words, Swearing (that is, assuring one another of their promises,) by invoking them. Beyond that reason suggesteth nothing; but leaves them either to rest there; or for further ceremonies, to rely on those they believe to be wiser than themselves.

And attribute to them all extraordinary events.

Lastly, concerning how these Invisible Powers declare to men the things which shall hereafter come to passe, especially concerning their good or evill fortune in generall, or good or ill successe in any particular undertaking, men are naturally at a stand; save that using to conjecture of the time to come, by the time past, they are very apt, not onely to take casuall things, after one or two encounters, for Prognostiques of the like encounter ever after, but also to believe the like Prognostiques from other men, of whom they have once conceived a good opinion.

Foure things, Naturall seeds of Religion.

And in these foure things, Opinion of Ghosts, Ignorance of second causes, Devotion towards what men fear, and Taking of things Casuall for Prognostiques, consisteth the Naturall seed of *Religion*; which by reason of the different Fancies, Judgements, and Passions of severall men, hath grown up into ceremonies so different, that those which are used by one man, are for the most part ridiculous to another.

Made different by Culture.

For these seeds have received culture from two sorts of men. One sort have been they, that have nourished, and ordered them, according to their own invention. The other, have done it, by Gods commandement, and direction: but both sorts have done it, with a purpose to make those men that relyed on them, the more apt to Obedience, Lawes, Peace, Charity, and civill Society. So that the Religion of the former sort, is a part of humane Politiques; and teacheth part of the duty which Earthly Kings require of their Subjects. And the Religion of the later sort is Divine Politiques; and containeth Precepts to those that have yeelded themselves subjects in the Kingdome of God. Of the former sort, were all the founders of Common-wealths, and the Law-givers of the Gentiles: Of the later sort, were *Abraham, Moses*, and our *Blessed Saviour*; by whom have been derived unto us the Lawes of the Kingdome of God.

And for that part of Religion, which consisteth in opinions concern- *The absurd*
ing the nature of Powers Invisible, there is almost nothing that has a *opinion of*
name, that has not been esteemed amongst the Gentiles, in one place *Gentilisme.*
or another, a God, or Divell; or by their Poets feigned to be inani- [55]
mated,[3] inhabited, or possessed by some Spirit or other.

The unformed matter of the World, was a God, by the name of
Chaos.

The Heaven, the Ocean, the Planets, the Fire, the Earth, the Winds,
were so many Gods.

Men, Women, a Bird, a Crocodile, a Calf, a Dogge, a Snake, an
Onion, a Leeke, Deified. Besides, that they filled almost all places, with
spirits called *Dæmons*: the plains, with *Pan*, and *Panises*, or Satyres; the
Woods, with *Fawnes*, and *Nymphs*; the Sea, with *Tritons*, and other
Nymphs; every River, and Fountayn, with a Ghost of his name, and
with *Nymphs*; every house, with its *Lares*, or Familiars; every man, with
his *Genius*; Hell, with Ghosts, and spirituall Officers, as *Charon, Cer-
berus*, and the *Furies*; and in the night time, all places with *Larvæ*,[4]
Lemures,[5] Ghosts of men deceased, and a whole kingdome of Fayries,
and Bugbears.[6] They have also ascribed Divinity, and built Temples to
meer Accidents, and Qualities; such as are Time, Night, Day, Peace,
Concord, Love, Contention, Vertue, Honour, Health, Rust, Fever, and
the like; which when they prayed for, or against, they prayed to, as if
there were Ghosts of those names hanging over their heads, and letting
fall, or withholding that Good, or Evill, for, or against which they
prayed. They invoked also their own Wit, by the name of *Muses*; their
own Ignorance, by the name of *Fortune*; their own Lust, by the name
of *Cupid*; their own Rage, by the name *Furies*; their own privy members
by the name of *Priapus*; and attributed their pollutions, to *Incubi*, and
Succubæ: insomuch as there was nothing, which a Poet could introduce
as a person in his Poem, which they did not make either a *God*, or a
Divel.

The same authors of the Religion of the Gentiles, observing the
second ground for Religion, which is mens Ignorance of causes; and
thereby their aptnesse to attribute their fortune to causes, on which
there was no dependance at all apparent, took occasion to obtrude on
their ignorance, in stead of second causes, a kind of second and min-
isteriall Gods; ascribing the cause of Fœcundity, to *Venus*; the cause
of Arts, to *Apollo*; of Subtilty and Craft, to *Mercury*; of Tempests and
stormes, to *Æolus*; and of other effects, to other Gods: insomuch as
there was amongst the Heathen almost as great variety of Gods, as of
businesse.

And to the Worship, which naturally men conceived fit to bee used
towards their Gods, namely Oblations, Prayers, Thanks, and the rest
formerly named; the same Legislators of the Gentiles have added their
Images, both in Picture, and Sculpture; that the more ignorant sort,
(that is to say, the most part, or generality of the people,) thinking the

3. Animated.
4. Disembodied spirits.
5. Spirits of the dead.
6. Hobgoblins.

[56]

Gods for whose representation they were made, were really included, and as it were housed within them, might so much the more stand in feare of them: And endowed them with lands, and houses, and officers, and revenues, set apart from all other humane uses; that is, consecrated, and made holy to those their Idols; as Caverns, Groves, Woods, Mountains, and whole Ilands; and have attributed to them, not onely the shapes, some of Men, some of Beasts, some of Monsters; but also the Faculties, and Passions of men and beasts; as Sense, Speech, Sex, Lust, Generation, (and this not onely by mixing one with another, to propagate the kind of Gods; but also by mixing with men, and women, to beget mongrill Gods, and but inmates of Heaven, as *Bacchus, Hercules*, and others;) besides, Anger, Revenge, and other passions of living creatures, and the actions proceeding from them, as Fraud, Theft, Adultery, Sodomie, and any vice that may be taken for an effect of Power, or a cause of Pleasure; and all such Vices, as amongst men are taken to be against Law, rather than against Honour.

Lastly, to the Prognostiques of time to come; which are naturally, but Conjectures upon the Experience of time past; and supernaturally, divine Revelation; the same authors of the Religion of the Gentiles, partly upon pretended Experience, partly upon pretended Revelation, have added innumerable other superstitious wayes of Divination; and made men believe they should find their fortunes, sometimes in the ambiguous or senslesse answers of the Priests at *Delphi, Delos, Ammon*, and other famous Oracles; which answers, were made ambiguous by designe, to own[7] the event both wayes; or absurd, by the intoxicating vapour of the place, which is very frequent in sulphurous Cavernes: Sometimes in the leaves of the Sibills; of whose Prophecyes (like those perhaps of *Nostradamus*; for the fragments now extant seem to be the invention of later times) there were some books in reputation in the time of the Roman Republique: Sometimes in the insignificant Speeches of Mad-men, supposed to be possessed with a divine Spirit; which Possession they called Enthusiasme; and these kinds of foretelling events, were accounted Theomancy, or Prophecy: Sometimes in the aspect of the Starres at their Nativity; which was called Horoscopy, and esteemed a part of judiciary Astrology: Sometimes in their own hopes and feares, called Thumomancy, or Presage:[8] Sometimes in the Prediction of Witches, that pretended conference with the dead; which is called Necromancy, Conjuring, and Witchcraft; and is but juggling[9] and confederate knavery: Sometimes in the Casuall flight, or feeding of birds; called Augury: Sometimes in the Entrayles of a sacrificed beast; which was *Aruspicina*: Sometimes in Dreams: Sometimes in Croaking of Ravens, or chattering of Birds: Sometimes in the Lineaments of the face; which was called Metoposcopy; or by Palmistry in the lines of the hand; in casuall words, called *Omina*: Sometimes in Monsters, or unusuall accidents; as Ecclipses, Comets, rare Meteors, Earthquakes, Inundations, uncouth Births, and the like, which they called *Portenta*,

7. Claim.
8. Omen, presentiment.
9. Trickery.

and *Ostenta*, because they thought them to portend, or foreshew some great Calamity to come: Somtimes, in meer Lottery, as Crosse and Pile;[1] counting holes in a sive; dipping[2] of Verses in *Homer*, and *Virgil*; and innumerable other such vaine conceipts. So easie are men to be drawn to believe any thing, from such men as have gotten credit with them; and can with gentlenesse, and dexterity, take hold of their fear, and ignorance.

And therefore the first Founders, and Legislators of Common-wealths amongst the Gentiles, whose ends were only to keep the people in obedience, and peace, have in all places taken care; First, to imprint in their minds a beliefe, that those precepts which they gave concerning Religion, might not be thought to proceed from their own device, but from the dictates of some God, or other Spirit; or else that they themselves were of a higher nature than mere mortalls, that their Lawes might the more easily be received: So *Numa Pompilius*[3] pretended to receive the Ceremonies he instituted amongst the Romans, from the Nymph *Egeria*: and the first King and founder of the Kingdome of *Peru*, pretended himselfe and his wife to be the children of the Sunne: and *Mahomet*,[4] to set up his new Religion, pretended to have conferences with the Holy Ghost, in forme of a Dove. Secondly, they have had a care, to make it believed, that the same things were displeasing to the Gods, which were forbidden by the Lawes. Thirdly, to prescribe Ceremonies, Supplications, Sacrifices, and Festivalls, by which they were to believe, the anger of the Gods might be appeased; and that ill success in War, great contagions of Sicknesse, Earthquakes, and each mans private Misery, came from the Anger of the Gods; and their Anger from the Neglect of their Worship, or the forgetting, or mistaking some point of the Ceremonies required. And though amongst the antient Romans, men were not forbidden to deny, that which in the Poets is written of the paines, and pleasures after this life; which divers of great authority, and gravity in that state have in their *Harangues* openly derided; yet that beliefe was alwaies more cherished, than the contrary.

And by these, and such other Institutions, they obtayned in order to their end, (which was the peace of the Commonwealth,) that the common people in their misfortunes, laying the fault on neglect, or errour in their Ceremonies, or on their own disobedience to the lawes, were the lesse apt to mutiny against their Governors. And being entertained with the pomp, and pastime of Festivals, and publike Games, made in honour of the Gods, needed nothing else but bread, to keep them from discontent, murmuring, and commotion against the State. And therefore the Romans, that had conquered the greatest part of the then known World, made no scruple[5] of tollerating any Religion whatsoever in the City of *Rome* it selfe; unlesse it had something in it, that could not consist with their Civill Government; nor do we read, that any

[57]
The designes of the Authors of the Religion of the Heathen.

1. Heads or tails, i.e., a toss of the coin.
2. Reading brief passages selected randomly.
3. According to legend, the second king of Rome, who invented a shared public religion.
4. Mohammed (570–632), the prophet who founded Islam and is believed to be the principal author of the Koran.
5. Did not hesitate.

Religion was there forbidden, but that of the Jewes; who (being the peculiar Kingdome of God) thought it unlawfull to acknowledge subjection to any mortall King or State whatsoever. And thus you see how the Religion of the Gentiles was a part of their Policy.

The true Religion, and the lawes of Gods kingdome the same.

[58]

But where God himselfe, by supernaturall Revelation, planted Religion; there he also made to himselfe a peculiar Kingdome; and gave Lawes, not only of behaviour towards himselfe; but also towards one another; and thereby in the Kingdome of God, the Policy, and lawes Civill, are a part of Religion; and therefore the distinction of Temporall, and Spirituall Domination, hath there no place. It is true, that God is King of all the Earth: Yet may he be King of a peculiar, and chosen Nation. For there is no more incongruity there in, than that he that hath the generall command of the whole Army, should have withall a peculiar Regiment, or Company of his own. God is King of all the Earth by his Power: but of his chosen people, he is King by Covenant. But to speake more largly of the Kingdome of God, both by Nature, and Covenant, I have in the following discourse assigned an other place.

Chap. 35.

The causes of Change in Religion.

From the propagation of Religion, it is not hard to understand the causes of the resolution of the same into its first seeds, or principles; which are only an opinion of a Deity, and Powers invisible, and supernaturall; that can never be so abolished out of humane nature, but that new Religions may againe be made to spring out of them, by the culture of such men, as for such purpose are in reputation.

For seeing all formed[6] Religion, is founded at first, upon the faith which a multitude hath in some one person, whom they believe not only to be a wise man, and to labour to procure their happiness, but also to be a holy man, to whom God himselfe vouchsafeth to declare his will supernaturally; It followeth necessarily, when they that have the Government of Religion, shall come to have either the wisedome of those men, their sincerity, or their love suspected; or that they shall be unable to shew any probable token of Divine Revelation; that the Religion which they desire to uphold, must be suspected likewise; and (without the feare of the Civill Sword) contradicted and rejected.

Injoyning beleefe of Impossibilities.

That which taketh away the reputation of Wisedome, in him that formeth a Religion, or addeth to it when it is allready formed, is the enjoyning of a beliefe of contradictories: For both parts of a contradiction cannot possibly be true: and therefore to enjoyne the beleife of them, is an argument of ignorance; which detects the Author in that; and discredits him in all things else he shall propound as from revelation supernaturall: which revelation a man may indeed have of many things above, but of nothing against naturall reason.

Doing contrary to the Religion they establish.

That which taketh away the reputation of Sincerity, is the doing, or saying of such things, as appeare to be signes, that what they require other men to believe, is not believed by themselves; all which doings, or sayings are therefore called Scandalous, because they be stumbling blocks, that make men to fall in the way of Religion: as Injustice, Cru-

6. Institutionalized; organized.

elty, Prophanesse, Avarice, and Luxury. For who can believe, that he that doth ordinarily such actions, as proceed from any of these rootes, believeth there is any such Invisible Power to be feared, as he affrighteth other men withall, for lesser faults?

That which taketh away the reputation of Love, is the being detected of private ends: as when the beliefe they require of others, conduceth or seemeth to conduce to the acquiring of Dominion, Riches, Dignity, [59] or secure Pleasure, to themselves onely, or specially. For that which men reap benefit by to themselves, they are thought to do for their own sakes, and not for love of others.

Lastly, the testimony that men can render of divine Calling, can be no other, than the operation of Miracles; or true Prophecy, (which also is a Miracle;) or extraordinary Felicity. And therefore, to those points of Religion, which have been received from them that did such Miracles; those that are added by such, as approve not their Calling by some Miracle, obtain no greater beliefe, than what the Custome, and Lawes of the places, in which they be educated, have wrought into them. For as in naturall things, men of judgement require naturall signes, and arguments; so in supernaturall things, they require signes supernaturall, (which are Miracles,) before they consent inwardly, and from their hearts. *Want of the testimony of Miracles.*

All which causes of the weakening of mens faith, do manifestly appear in the Examples following. First, we have the Example of the children of Israel; who when *Moses*, that had approved his Calling to them by Miracles, and by the happy conduct of them out of *Egypt*, was absent but 40.dayes, revolted from the worship of the true God, recommended to them by him; and setting up * a Golden Calfe for their God, relapsed into the Idolatry of the Egyptians; from whom they had been so lately delivered. And again, after *Moses, Aaron, Joshua,* and that generation which had seen the great works of God in Israel, * were dead; another generation arose, and served *Baal.* So that Miracles fayling, Faith also failed. **Exod. 32. 1, 2.* **Judges 2. 11.*

Again, when the sons of *Samuel,* * being constituted by their father Judges in *Bersabee,* received bribes, and judged unjustly, the people of Israel refused any more to have God to be their King, in other manner than he was King of other people; and therefore cryed out to *Samuel,* to choose them a King after the manner of the Nations. So that Justice fayling, Faith also fayled: Insomuch, as they deposed their God, from reigning over them. **I Sam. 8. 3.*

And whereas in the planting of Christian Religion, the Oracles ceased in all parts of the Roman Empire, and the number of Christians encreased wonderfully every day, and in every place, by the preaching of the Apostles, and Evangelists; a great part of that successe, may reasonably be attributed, to the contempt, into which the Priests of the Gentiles of that time, had brought themselves, by their uncleannesse, avarice, and jugling between Princes. Also the Religion of the Church of *Rome*, was partly, for the same cause abolished in *England*, and many other parts of Christendome; insomuch, as the fayling of Vertue in the Pastors, maketh Faith faile in the People: and partly from bringing of the Philosophy, and doctrine of *Aristotle* into Religion, by the Schoole-men; from whence there arose so many contradictions, and absurdities, as brought the Clergy into a reputation both of Ignorance, and of Fraudulent intention; and enclined people to revolt from them, either against the will of their own Princes, as in *France*, and *Holland*; or with their will, as in *England*.

[60]   Lastly, amongst the points by the Church of *Rome* declared necessary for Salvation, there be so many, manifestly to the advantage of the Pope, and of his spirituall subjects, residing in the territories of other Christian Princes, that were it not for the mutuall emulation of those Princes, they might without warre, or trouble, exclude all forraign Authority, as easily as it has been excluded in *England*. For who is there that does not see, to whose benefit it conduceth, to have it believed, that a King hath not his Authority from Christ, unlesse a Bishop crown him? That a King, if he be a Priest, cannot Marry? That whether a Prince be born in lawfull Marriage, or not, must be judged by Authority from *Rome*? That Subjects may be freed from their Alleageance, if by the Court of *Rome*, the King be judged an Heretique? That a King (as *Chilperique of France*) may be deposed by a Pope (as Pope *Zachary*,) for no cause; and his Kingdome given to one of his Subjects? That the Clergy, and Regulars,[7] in what Country soever, shall be exempt from the Jurisdiction of their King, in cases criminall? Or who does not see, to whose profit redound the Fees of private Masses, and Vales[8] of Purgatory; with other signes of private interest, enough to mortifie the most lively Faith, if (as I sayd) the civill Magistrate, and Custome did not more sustain it, than any opinion they have of the Sanctity, Wisdome, or Probity of their Teachers?[9] So that I may attribute all the changes of Religion in the world, to one and the same cause; and that is, unpleasing Priests; and those not onely amongst Catholiques, but even in that Church that hath presumed most of Reformation.

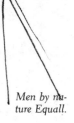

Chap. XIII.

Of the NATURALL CONDITION *of Mankind, as concerning their Felicity, and Misery.*

Men by na-
ture Equall.   Nature hath made men so equall, in the faculties of body, and mind; as that though there bee found one man sometimes manifestly stronger in body, or of quicker mind then another; yet when all is reckoned together, the difference between man, and man, is not so considerable, as that one man can thereupon claim to himselfe any benefit, to which another may not pretend,[1] as well as he. For as to the strength of body, the weakest has strength enough to kill the strongest, either by secret

7. Members of religious orders.
8. Gratuities or payments (usually spelled "vails").
9. See below, ch. 47.
1. Aspire or claim a right to.

machination, or by confederacy with others, that are in the same danger with himselfe.

And as to the faculties of the mind, (setting aside the arts grounded upon words, and especially that skill of proceeding upon generall, and infallible rules, called Science; which very few have, and but in few things; as being not a native faculty, born with us; nor attained, (as Prudence,) while we look after somewhat els,) I find yet a greater equality amongst men, than that of strength. For Prudence, is but Experience; which equall time, equally bestowes on all men, in those things they equally apply themselves unto. That which may perhaps make such equality incredible, is but a vain conceipt of ones owne wisdome, which almost all men think they have in a greater degree, than the Vulgar; that is, than all men but themselves, and a few others, whom by Fame, or for concurring with themselves, they approve. For such is the nature of men, that howsoever they may acknowledge many others to be more witty, or more eloquent, or more learned; Yet they will hardly believe there be many so wise as themselves: For they see their own wit at hand, and other mens at a distance. But this proveth rather that men are in that point equall, than unequall. For there is not ordinarily a greater signe of the equall distribution of any thing, than that every man is contented with his share. [61]

From this equality of ability, ariseth equality of hope in the attaining of our Ends. And therefore if any two men desire the same thing, which neverthelesse they cannot both enjoy, they become enemies; and in the way to their End, (which is principally their owne conservation, and sometimes their delectation[2] only,) endeavour to destroy, or subdue one an other. And from hence it comes to passe, that where an Invader hath no more to feare, than an other mans single power; if one plant, sow, build, or possesse a convenient Seat, others may probably be expected to come prepared with forces united, to dispossesse, and deprive him, not only of the fruit of his labour, but also of his life, or liberty. And the Invader again is in the like danger of another. *From Equality proceeds Diffidence.*

And from this diffidence of one another, there is no way for any man to secure himselfe, so reasonable, as Anticipation; that is, by force, or wiles, to master the persons of all men he can, so long, till he see no other power great enough to endanger him: And this is no more than his own conservation requireth, and is generally allowed. Also because there be some, that taking pleasure in contemplating their own power in the acts of conquest, which they pursue farther than their security requires; if others, that otherwise would be glad to be at ease within modest bounds, should not by invasion increase their power, they would not be able, long time, by standing only on their defence, to subsist. And by consequence, such augmentation of dominion over men, being necessary to a mans conservation, it ought to be allowed him. *From Diffidence Warre.*

Againe, men have no pleasure, (but on the contrary a great deale of griefe) in keeping company, where there is no power able to over-awe

---

2. Delight.

them all. For every man looketh that his companion should value him, at the same rate he sets upon himselfe: And upon all signes of contempt, or undervaluing, naturally endeavours, as far as he dares (which amongst them that have no common power to keep them in quiet, is far enough to make them destroy each other,) to extort a greater value from his contemners, by dommage;[3] and from others, by the example.

So that in the nature of man, we find three principall causes of quarrell. First, Competition; Secondly, Diffidence; Thirdly, Glory.

[62]   The first, maketh men invade for Gain; the second, for Safety; and the third, for Reputation. The first use Violence, to make themselves Masters of other mens persons, wives, children, and cattell; the second, to defend them; the third, for trifles, as a word, a smile, a different opinion, and any other signe of undervalue, either direct in their Persons, or by reflexion in their Kindred, their Friends, their Nation, their Profession, or their Name.

Out of Civil States, there is alwayes Warre *of every one against every one.*   Hereby it is manifest, that during the time men live without a common Power to keep them all in awe, they are in that condition which is called Warre; and such a warre, as is of every man, against every man. For WARRE, consisteth not in Battell onely, or the act of fighting; but in a tract of time, wherein the Will to contend by Battell is sufficiently known: and therefore the notion of *Time*, is to be considered in the nature of Warre; as it is in the nature of Weather. For as the nature of Foule weather, lyeth not in a showre or two of rain; but in an inclination thereto of many dayes together: So the nature of War, consisteth not in actuall fighting; but in the known disposition thereto, during all the time there is no assurance to the contrary. All other time is PEACE.

The Incommodities of such a War.   Whatsoever therefore is consequent to a time of Warre, where every man is Enemy to every man; the same is consequent to the time, wherein men live without other security, than what their own strength, and their own invention shall furnish them withall. In such condition, there is no place for Industry; because the fruit thereof is uncertain: and consequently no Culture of the Earth; no Navigation, nor use of the commodities that may be imported by Sea; no commodious Building; no Instruments of moving, and removing such things as require much force; no Knowledge of the face of the Earth; no account of Time; no Arts; no Letters; no Society; and which is worst of all, continuall feare, and danger of violent death; And the life of man, solitary, poore, nasty, brutish, and short.

It may seem strange to some man, that has not well weighed these things; that Nature should thus dissociate, and render men apt to invade, and destroy one another: and he may therefore, not trusting to this Inference, made from the Passions, desire perhaps to have the same confirmed by Experience. Let him therefore consider with himselfe, when taking a journey, he armes himselfe, and seeks to go well accompanied; when going to sleep, he locks his dores; when even in his house he locks his chests; and this when he knowes there bee Lawes, and

---

3. Damage.

publike Officers, armed, to revenge all injuries shall bee done him; what opinion he has of his fellow subjects, when he rides armed; of his fellow Citizens, when he locks his dores; and of his children, and servants, when he locks his chests. Does he not there as much accuse mankind by his actions, as I do by my words? But neither of us accuse mans nature in it. The Desires, and other Passions of man, are in themselves no Sin. No more are the Actions, that proceed from those Passions, till they know a Law that forbids them: which till Lawes be made they cannot know: nor can any Law be made, till they have agreed upon the Person that shall make it.

It may peradventure[4] be thought, there was never such a time, nor condition of warre as this; and I believe it was never generally so, over all the world: but there are many places, where they live so now. For the savage people in many places of *America*, except the government of small Families, the concord whereof dependeth on naturall lust, have no government at all; and live at this day in that brutish manner, as I said before. Howsoever, it may be perceived what manner of life there would be, where there were no common Power to feare; by the manner of life, which men that have formerly lived under a peacefull government, use to degenerate into, in a civill Warre. [63]

But though there had never been any time, wherein particular men were in a condition of warre one against another; yet in all times, Kings, and Persons of Soveraigne authority, because of their Independency, are in continuall jealousies, and in the state and posture of Gladiators; having their weapons pointing, and their eyes fixed on one another; that is, their Forts, Garrisons, and Guns upon the Frontiers of their Kingdomes; and continuall Spyes upon their neighbours; which is a posture of War. But because they uphold thereby, the Industry of their Subjects; there does not follow from it, that misery, which accompanies the Liberty of particular men.

To this warre of every man against every man, this also is consequent; that nothing can be Unjust. The notions of Right and Wrong, Justice and Injustice have there no place. Where there is no common Power, there is no Law: where no Law, no Injustice. Force, and Fraud, are in warre the two Cardinall vertues. Justice, and Injustice are none of the Faculties neither of the Body, nor Mind. If they were, they might be in a man that were alone in the world, as well as his Senses, and Passions. They are Qualities, that relate to men in Society, not in Solitude. It is consequent also to the same condition, that there be no Propriety,[5] no Dominion, no *Mine* and *Thine* distinct; but onely that to be every mans, that he can get; and for so long, as he can keep it. And thus much for the ill condition, which man by meer Nature is actually placed in; though with a possibility to come out of it, consisting partly in the Passions, partly in his Reason. *In such a Warre, nothing is Unjust.*

The Passions that encline men to Peace, are Feare of Death; Desire of such things as are necessary to commodious[6] living; and a Hope by *The Passions that incline men to Peace.*

4. Perhaps.
5. Property.
6. Comfortable or convenient.

their Industry to obtain them. And Reason suggesteth convenient Articles of Peace, upon which men may be drawn to agreement. These Articles, are they, which otherwise are called the Lawes of Nature: whereof I shall speak more particularly, in the two following Chapters.

Chap. XIV.

Of the first and second NATURALL LAWES, and of CONTRACTS.

Right of Nature what.
THE RIGHT OF NATURE, which Writers commonly call *Jus Naturale*, is the Liberty each man hath, to use his own power, as he will himselfe, for the preservation of his own Nature; that is to say, of his own Life, and consequently, of doing any thing, which in his own Judgement, and Reason, hee shall conceive to be the aptest means thereunto.

Liberty what.
By LIBERTY, is understood, according to the proper signification of the word, the absence of externall Impediments: which Impediments, may oft take away part of a mans power to do what hee would; but cannot hinder him from using the power left him, according as his judgement, and reason shall dictate to him.

A Law of Nature what.
A LAW OF NATURE, (*Lex Naturalis*,) is a Precept, or generall Rule, found out by Reason, by which a man is forbidden to do, that, which is destructive of his life, or taketh away the means of preserving the same; and to omit, that, by which he thinketh it may be best preserved. For though they that speak of this subject, use to confound *Jus*, and *Lex, Right* and *Law*; yet they ought to be distinguished; because RIGHT,

Difference of Right and Law.
consisteth in liberty to do, or to forbeare; Whereas LAW, determineth, and bindeth to one of them: so that Law, and Right, differ as much, as Obligation, and Liberty; which in one and the same matter are inconsistent.

Naturally every man has Right to everything.
And because the condition of Man, (as hath been declared in the precedent Chapter) is a condition of Warre of every one against every one; in which case every one is governed by his own Reason; and there is nothing he can make use of, that may not be a help unto him, in preserving his life against his enemyes; It followeth, that in such a condition, every man has a Right to every thing; even to one anothers body. And therefore, as long as this naturall Right of every man to every thing endureth, there can be no security to any man, (how strong or wise soever he be,) of living out the time, which Nature ordinarily alloweth men to live. And consequently it is a precept, or generall rule

The Fundamentall Law of Nature.
of Reason, *That every man, ought to endeavour Peace, as farre as he has hope of obtaining it; and when he cannot obtain it, that he may seek, and use, all helps, and advantages of Warre.* The first branch of which Rule, containeth the first, and Fundamentall Law of Nature; which is, *to seek Peace, and follow it.* The Second, the summe of the Right of Nature; which is, *By all means we can, to defend our selves.*

The second Law of Nature.
From this Fundamentall Law of Nature, by which men are commanded to endeavour Peace, is derived this second Law; *That a man*

[65] *be willing, when others are so too, as farre-forth, as for Peace, and defence*

of himselfe he shall think it necessary, to lay down this right to all things; and be contented with so much liberty against other men, as he would allow other men against himselfe. For as long as every man holdeth this Right, of doing any thing he liketh; so long are all men in the condition of Warre. But if other men will not lay down their Right, as well as he; then there is no Reason for any one, to devest himselfe of his: For that were to expose himselfe to Prey, (which no man is bound to) rather than to dispose himselfe to Peace. This is that Law of the Gospell; *Whatsoever you require that others should do to you, that do ye to them.* And that Law of all men, *Quod tibi fieri non vis, alteri ne feceris.*[1]

To *lay downe* a mans *Right* to any thing, is to *devest* himselfe of the *Liberty,* of hindring another of the benefit of his own Right to the same. For he that renounceth, or passeth away his Right, giveth not to any other man a Right which he had not before; because there is nothing to which every man had not Right by Nature: but onely standeth out of his way, that he may enjoy his own originall Right, without hindrance from him; not without hindrance from another. So that the effect which redoundeth to one man, by another mans defect[2] of Right, is but so much diminution of impediments to the use of his own Right originall.

What it is to lay down a Right.

Right is layd aside, either by simply Renouncing it; or by Transferring it to another. By *Simply* RENOUNCING; when he cares not to whom the benefit thereof redoundeth. By TRANSFERRING; when he intendeth the benefit thereof to some certain person, or persons. And when a man hath in either manner abandoned, or granted away his Right; then is he said to be OBLIGED, or BOUND, not to hinder those, to whom such Right is granted, or abandoned, from the benefit of it: and that he *Ought,* and it is his DUTY, not to make voyd that voluntary act of his own: and that such hindrance is INJUSTICE, and INJURY, as being *Sine Jure;*[3] the Right being before renounced, or transferred. So that *Injury,* or *Injustice,* in the controversies of the world, is somewhat like to that, which in the disputations of Scholers is called *Absurdity.* For as it is there called an Absurdity, to contradict what one maintained in the Beginning: so in the world, it is called Injustice, and Injury, voluntarily to undo that, which from the beginning he had voluntarily done. The way by which a man either simply Renounceth, or Transferreth his Right, is a Declaration, or Signification, by some voluntary and sufficient signe, or signes, that he doth so Renounce, or Transferre; or hath so Renounced, or Transferred the same, to him that accepteth it. And these Signes are either Words onely, or Actions onely; or (as it happeneth most often) both Words, and Actions. And the same are the BONDS, by which men are bound, and obliged: Bonds, that have their strength, not from their own Nature, (for nothing is more easily broken then a mans word,) but from Feare of some evill consequence upon the rupture.

Renouncing a Right what it is.
Transferring Right what.
Obligation.

Duty.
Injustice.

Whensoever a man Transferreth his Right, or Renounceth it; it is

Not all Rights are alienable.

1. Do not do to others what you do not want done to yourself.
2. Lack.
3. Without right.

[66] either in consideration of some Right reciprocally transferred to him-selfe; or for some other good he hopeth for thereby. For it is a voluntary act: and of the voluntary acts of every man, the object is some *Good to himselfe*. And therefore there be some Rights, which no man can be understood by any words, or other signes, to have abandoned, or trans-ferred. As first a man cannot lay down the right of resisting them, that assault him by force, to take away his life; because he cannot be un-derstood to ayme thereby, at any Good to himselfe. The same may be sayd of Wounds, and Chayns, and Imprisonment; both because there is no benefit consequent to such patience;[4] as there is to the patience of suffering another to be wounded, or imprisoned: as also because a man cannot tell, when he seeth men proceed against him by violence, whether they intend his death or not. And lastly the motive, and end for which this renouncing, and transferring of Right is introduced, is nothing else but the security of a mans person, in his life, and in the means of so preserving life, as not to be weary of it. And therefore if a man by words, or other signes, seem to despoyle himselfe of the End, for which those signes were intended; he is not to be understood as if he meant it, or that it was his will; but that he was ignorant of how such words and actions were to be interpreted.

Contract what. The mutuall transferring of Right, is that which men call CONTRACT.

There is difference, between transferring of Right to the Thing; and transferring, or tradition, that is, delivery of the Thing it selfe. For the Thing may be delivered together with the Translation[5] of the Right; as in buying and selling with ready mony; or exchange of goods, or lands: and it may be delivered some time after.

Again, one of the Contractors, may deliver the Thing contracted for on his part, and leave the other to perform his part at some determinate time after, and in the mean time be trusted; and then the Contract on *Covenant what.* his part, is called PACT, or COVENANT: Or both parts[6] may contract now, to performe hereafter: in which cases, he that is to performe in time to come, being trusted, his performance is called *Keeping of Promise*, or Faith; and the fayling of performance (if it be voluntary) *Violation of Faith*.

When the transferring of Right, is not mutuall; but one of the parties transferreth, in hope to gain thereby friendship, or service from another, or from his friends; or in hope to gain the reputation of Charity, or Magnanimity; or to deliver his mind from the pain of compassion; or in hope of reward in heaven; This is not Contract, but GIFT, FREE-*Free-gift.* GIFT, GRACE: which words signifie one and the same thing.

Signes of Con- Signes of Contract, are either *Expresse*, or *by Inference*. Expresse, are *tract Expresse.* words spoken with understanding of what they signifie: And such words are either of the time *Present*, or *Past*; as, *I Give, I Grant, I have Given, I have Granted, I will that this be yours*: Or of the future; as, *I will Give, I will Grant*: which words of the future, are called PROMISE.

Signes by Inference, are sometimes the consequence of Words; some-

4. Forbearance.
5. Transfer.
6. Parties (to a contract).

times the consequence of Silence; sometimes the consequence of Actions; sometimes the consequence of Forbearing an Action: and generally a signe by Inference, of any Contract, is whatsoever sufficiently argues the will of the Contractor.

[67]
Signes of Contract by Inference.

Words alone, if they be of the time to come, and contain a bare promise, are an insufficient signe of a Free-gift and therefore not obligatory. For if they be of the time to Come, as, *To morrow I will Give*, they are a signe I have not given yet, and consequently that my right is not transferred, but remaineth till I transferre it by some other Act. But if the words be of the time Present, or Past, as, *I have given, or do give to be delivered to morrow*, then is my to morrows Right given away to day; and that by the vertue of the words, though there were no other argument of my will. And there is a great difference in the signification of these words, *Volo hoc tuum esse cras*, and *Cras dabo*; that is, between *I will that this be thine to morrow*, and, *I will give it thee to morrow*: For the word *I will*, in the former manner of speech, signifies an act of the will Present; but in the later, it signifies a promise of an act of the will to Come: and therefore the former words, being of the Present, transferre a future right; the later, that be of the Future, transferre nothing. But if there be other signes of the Will to transferre a Right, besides Words; then, though the gift be Free, yet may the Right be understood to passe by words of the future: as if a man propound a Prize to him that comes first to the end of a race, The gift is Free; and though the words be of the Future, yet the Right passeth: for if he would not have his words so be understood, he should not have let them runne.

Free gift passeth by words of the Present or Past.

In Contracts, the right passeth, not onely where the words are of the time Present, or Past; but also where they are of the Future: because all Contract is mutuall translation, or change of Right; and therefore he that promiseth onely, because he hath already received the benefit for which he promiseth, is to be understood as if he intended the Right should passe: for unlesse he had been content to have his words so understood, the other would not have performed his part first. And for that cause, in buying, and selling, and other acts of Contract, a Promise is equivalent to a Covenant; and therefore obligatory.

Signes of Contract are words both of the Past, Present, and Future.

He that performeth first in the case of a Contract, is said to MERIT that which he is to receive by the performance of the other; and he hath it as *Due*. Also when a Prize is propounded to many, which is to be given to him onely that winneth; or mony is thrown amongst many, to be enjoyed by them that catch it; though this be a Free gift; yet so to Win, or so to Catch, is to *Merit*, and to have it as DUE. For the Right is transferred in the Propounding of the Prize, and in throwing down the mony; though it be not determined to whom, but by the Event of the contention. But there is between these two sorts of Merit, this difference, that In Contract, I Merit by vertue of my own power, and the Contractors need; but in this case of Free gift, I am enabled to Merit onely by the benignity[7] of the Giver: In Contract, I merit at the Contractors hand that hee should depart with[8] his right; In this case

Merit what.

[68]

7. Kindness.
8. Part with, give up.

of Gift, I Merit not that the giver should part with his right; but that when he has parted with it, it should be mine, rather than anothers. And this I think to be the meaning of that distinction of the Schooles, between *Meritum congrui*, and *Meritum condigni*. For God Almighty, having promised Paradise to those men (hoodwinkt[9] with carnall desires,) that can walk through this world according to the Precepts, and Limits prescribed by him; they say, he that shall so walk, shall Merit Paradise *Ex congruo*. But because no man can demand a right to it, by his own Righteousnesse, or any other power in himselfe, but by the Free Grace of God onely; they say, no man can Merit Paradise *ex condigno*. This I say, I think is the meaning of that distinction; but because Disputers do not agree upon the signification of their own termes of Art, longer than it serves their turn; I will not affirme any thing of their meaning: onely this I say; when a gift is given indefinitely, as a prize to be contended for, he that winneth Meriteth, and may claime the Prize as Due.

Covenants of Mutuall trust, when Invalid. If a Covenant be made, wherein neither of the parties performe presently, but trust one another; in the condition of meer Nature, (which is a condition of Warre of every man against every man,) upon any reasonable suspition, it is Voyd: But if there be a common Power set over them both, with right and force sufficient to compell performance; it is not Voyd. For he that performeth first, has no assurance the other will performe after; because the bonds of words are too weak to bridle mens ambition, avarice, anger, and other Passions, without the feare of some coerceive Power; which in the condition of meer Nature, where all men are equall, and judges of the justnesse of their own fears, cannot possibly be supposed. And therfore he which performeth first, does but betray himselfe to his enemy; contrary to the Right (he can never abandon) of defending his life, and means of living.

But in a civill estate, where there is a Power set up to constrain those that would otherwise violate their faith, that feare is no more reasonable; and for that cause, he which by the Covenant is to perform first, is obliged so to do.

The cause of feare, which maketh such a Covenant invalid, must be alwayes something arising after the Covenant made; as some new fact, or other signe of the Will not to performe: else it cannot make the Covenant voyd. For that which could not hinder a man from promising, ought not to be admitted as a hindrance of performing.

Right to the End, Containeth Right to the Means. He that transferreth any Right, transferreth the Means of enjoying it, as farre as lyeth in his power. As he that selleth Land, is understood to transferre the Herbage, and whatsoever growes upon it; Nor can he that sells a Mill turn away the Stream that drives it. And they that give to a man the Right of government in Soveraignty, are understood to give him the right of levying mony to maintain Souldiers; and of appointing Magistrates for the administration of Justice.

No Covenant with Beasts. To make Covenants with bruit Beasts, is impossible; because not understanding our speech, they understand not, nor accept of any trans-

9. Blinded.

lation of Right; nor can translate any Right to another: and without
mutuall acceptation, there is no Covenant. [69]

To make Covenant with God, is impossible, but by Mediation of *Nor with God*
such as God speaketh to, either by Revelation supernaturall, or by his *without*
Lieutenants that govern under him, and in his Name: For otherwise *special*
we know not whether our Covenants be accepted, or not. And therefore *Revelation.*
they that Vow any thing contrary to any law of Nature, Vow in vain;
as being a thing unjust to pay such Vow. And if it be a thing commanded by the Law of Nature, it is not the Vow, but the Law that
binds them.

The matter, or subject of a Covenant, is alwayes something that *No Covenant,*
falleth under deliberation; (For to Covenant, is an act of the Will; that *but of Possible*
is to say an act, and the last act, of deliberation;) and is therefore alwayes *and Future.*
understood to be something to come; and which is judged Possible for
him that Covenanteth, to performe.

And therefore, to promise that which is known to be Impossible, is
no Covenant. But if that prove impossible afterwards, which before was
thought possible, the Covenant is valid, and bindeth, (though not to
the thing it selfe,) yet to the value; or, if that also be impossible, to the
unfeigned endeavour of performing as much as is possible: for to more
no man can be obliged.

Men are freed of their Covenants two wayes; by Performing; or by *Covenants*
being Forgiven. For Performance, is the naturall end of obligation; and *how made*
Forgivenesse, the restitution of liberty; as being a re-transferring of that *voyd.*
Right, in which the obligation consisted.

Covenants entred into by fear, in the condition of meer Nature, are *Covenants ex-*
obligatory. For example, if I Covenant to pay a ransome, or service for *torted by feare*
my life, to an enemy; I am bound by it. For it is a Contract, wherein *are valide.*
one receiveth the benefit of life; the other is to receive mony, or service
for it; and consequently, where no other Law (as in the condition, of
meer Nature) forbiddeth the performance, the Covenant is valid.
Therefore Prisoners of warre, if trusted with the payment of their Ransome, are obliged to pay it: And if a weaker Prince, make a disadvan-
tageous peace with a stronger, for feare; he is bound to keep it; unlesse
(as hath been sayd before) there ariseth some new, and just cause of
feare, to renew the war. And even in Common-wealths, if I be forced
to redeem my selfe from a Theefe by promising him mony, I am bound
to pay it, till the Civill Law discharge me. For whatsoever I may lawfully
do without Obligation, the same I may lawfully Covenant to do through
feare: and what I lawfully Covenant, I cannot lawfully break.

A former Covenant, makes voyd a later. For a man that hath passed *The former*
away his Right to one man to day, hath it not to passe to morrow to *Covenant to*
another: and therefore the later promise passeth no Right, but is null. *one, makes*
A Covenant not to defend my selfe from force, by force, is alwayes *voyd the later*
voyd. For (as I have shewed before) no man can transferre, or lay down *to another. A*
his Right to save himselfe from Death, Wounds, and Imprisonment, *mans Cove-*
(the avoyding whereof is the onely End of laying down any Right,) and *nant not to*
therefore the promise of not resisting force, in no Covenant transferreth *defend him-*
any right; nor is obliging. For though a man may Covenant thus, *Un-* *selfe, is voyd.*
[70]

lesse I do so, or so, kill me; he cannot Covenant thus, *Unlesse I do so, or so, I will not resist you, when you come to kill me.* For man by nature chooseth the lesser evill, which is danger of death in resisting; rather than the greater, which is certain and present death in not resisting. And this is granted to be true by all men, in that they lead Criminals to Execution, and Prison, with armed men, notwithstanding that such Criminals have consented to the Law, by which they are condemned.

No man obliged to accuse himself.   A Covenant to accuse ones selfe, without assurance of pardon, is likewise invalid. For in the condition of Nature, where every man is Judge, there is no place for Accusation: and in the Civill State, the Accusation is followed with Punishment; which being Force, a man is not obliged not to resist. The same is also true, of the Accusation of those, by whose Condemnation a man falls into misery; as of a Father, Wife, or Benefactor.

For the Testimony of such an Accuser, if it be not willingly given, is præsumed to be corrupted by Nature; and therefore not to be received: and where a mans Testimony is not to be credited, he is not bound to give it. Also Accusations upon Torture, are not to be reputed as Testimonies. For Torture is to be used but as means of conjecture, and light, in the further examination, and search of truth: and what is in that case confessed, tendeth to the ease of him that is Tortured; not to the informing of the Torturers: and therefore ought not to have the credit of a sufficient Testimony: for whether he deliver himselfe by true, or false Accusation, he does it by the Right of preserving his own life.

The End of an Oath.   The force of Words, being (as I have formerly noted) too weak to hold men to the performance of their Covenants; there are in mans nature, but two imaginable helps to strengthen it. And those are either a Feare of the consequence of breaking their word; or a Glory, or Pride in appearing not to need to breake it. This later is a Generosity[1] too rarely found to be presumed on, especially in the pursuers of Wealth, Command, or sensuall Pleasure; which are the greatest part of Mankind. The Passion to be reckoned upon, is Fear; whereof there be two very generall Objects: one, The Power of Spirits Invisible; the other, The Power of those men they shall therein Offend. Of these two, though the former be the greater Power, yet the feare of the later is commonly the greater Feare. The Feare of the former is in every man, his own Religion: which hath place in the nature of man before Civill Society. The later hath not so; at least not place enough, to keep men to their promises; because in the condition of meer Nature, the inequality of Power is not discerned, but by the event of Battell. So that before the time of Civill Society, or in the interruption thereof by Warre, there is nothing can strengthen a Covenant of Peace agreed on, against the temptations of Avarice, Ambition, Lust, or other strong desire, but the feare of that Invisible Power, which they every one Worship as God; and Feare as a Revenger of their perfidy. All therefore that can be done between two men not subject to Civill Power, is to put one another to swear by the God he feareth: Which *Swearing*, or OATH, is

[71]
The forme of an Oath.

1. Moral virtuousness.

a *Forme of Speech, added to a Promise; by which he that promiseth, signifieth, that unlesse he performe, he renounceth the mercy of his God, or calleth to him for vengeance on himselfe.* Such was the Heathen Forme, *Let* Jupiter *kill me else, as I kill this Beast.* So is our Forme, *I shall do thus, and thus, so help me God.* And this, with the Rites and Ceremonies, which every one useth in his own Religion, that the feare of breaking faith might be the greater.

By this it appears, that an Oath taken according to any other Forme, or Rite, then his, that sweareth, is in vain; and no Oath: And that there is no Swearing by any thing which the Swearer thinks not God. For though men have sometimes used to swear by their Kings, for feare, or flattery; yet they would have it thereby understood, they attributed to them Divine honour. And that Swearing unnecessarily by God, is but prophaning of his name: and Swearing by other things, as men do in common discourse, is not Swearing, but an impious Custome, gotten by too much vehemence of talking. *No Oath, but by God.*

It appears also, that the Oath addes nothing to the Obligation. For a Covenant, if lawfull, binds in the sight of God, without the Oath, as much as with it: if unlawfull, bindeth not at all; though it be confirmed with an Oath. *An Oath addes nothing to the Obligation.*

Chap. XV.

Of other Lawes of Nature.

FROM that law of Nature, by which we are obliged to transferre to another, such Rights, as being retained, hinder the peace of Mankind, there followeth a Third; which is this, *That men performe their Covenants made:* without which, Covenants are in vain, and but Empty words; and the Right of all men to all things remaining, wee are still in the condition of Warre. *The third Law of Nature, Justice.*

And in this law of Nature, consisteth the Fountain and Originall of JUSTICE. For where no Covenant hath preceded, there hath no Right been transferred, and every man has right to every thing; and consequently, no action can be Unjust. But when a Covenant is made, then to break it is *Unjust:* And the definition of INJUSTICE, is no other than *the not Performance of Covenant.* And whatsoever is not Unjust, is *Just.* *Justice and Injustice what.*

But because Covenants of mutuall trust, where there is a feare of not performance on either part, (as hath been said in the former Chapter,) are invalid; though the Originall of Justice be the making of Covenants; yet Injustice actually there can be none, till the cause of such feare be taken away; which while men are in the naturall condition of Warre, cannot be done. Therefore before the names of Just, and Unjust can have place, there must be some coërcive Power, to compell men equally to the performance of their Covenants, by the terrour of some punishment, greater than the benefit they expect by the breach of their Covenant; and to make good that Propriety, which by mutuall Contract men acquire, in recompence of the universall Right they abandon: and *Justice and Propriety begin with the Constitution of Commonwealth.*

[72]

such power there is none before the erection of a Common-wealth. And this is also to be gathered out of the ordinary definition of Justice in the Schooles: For they say, that *Justice is the constant Will of giving to every man his own.* And therefore where there is no *Own,* that is, no Propriety, there is no Injustice; and where there is no coërceive Power erected, that is, where there is no Common-wealth, there is no Propriety; all men having Right to all things: Therefore where there is no Common-wealth, there nothing is Unjust. So that the nature of Justice, consisteth in keeping of valid Covenants: but the Validity of Covenants begins not but with the Constitution of a Civill Power, sufficient to compell men to keep them: And then it is also that Propriety begins.

Justice not Contrary to Reason.   The Foole hath sayd in his heart, there is no such thing as Justice; and sometimes also with his tongue; seriously alleaging, that every mans conservation, and contentment, being committed to his own care, there could be no reason, why every man might not do what he thought conduced thereunto: and therefore also to make, or not make; keep, or not keep Covenants, was not against Reason, when it conduced to ones benefit. He does not therein deny, that there be Covenants; and that they are sometimes broken, sometimes kept; and that such breach of them may be called Injustice, and the observance of them Justice: but he questioneth, whether Injustice, taking away the feare of God, (for the same Foole hath said in his heart there is no God,) may not sometimes stand with that Reason, which dictateth to every man his own good; and particularly then, when it conduceth to such a benefit, as shall put a man in a condition, to neglect not onely the dispraise, and revilings, but also the power of other men. The Kingdome of God is gotten by violence: but what if it could be gotten by unjust violence? were it against Reason so to get it, when it is impossible to receive hurt by it? and if it be not against Reason, it is not against Justice: or else Justice is not to be approved for good. From such reasoning as this, Succesfull wickednesse hath obtained the name of Vertue: and some that in all other things have disallowed the violation of Faith; yet have allowed it, when it is for the getting of a Kingdome. And the Heathen that believed, that *Saturn* was deposed by his son *Jupiter,* believed neverthelesse the same *Jupiter* to be the avenger of Injustice: Somewhat like to a piece of Law in *Cokes*[1] Commentaries on *Litleton*; where he sayes, If the right Heire of the Crown be attainted[2] of Treason; yet the Crown shall descend to him, and *eo instante*[3] the Atteynder[4] be voyd: From which instances a man will be very prone to inferre; that when the Heire apparent of a Kingdome, shall kill him that is in possession, though his father; you may call it Injustice, or by what other name you will; yet it can never be against Reason, seeing all the voluntary actions of men tend to the benefit of themselves; and those actions are most Reasonable, that conduce most to their ends. This specious reasoning is neverthelesse false.

[73]

1. Sir Edward Coke (1552–1634), a prominent English lawyer and author who was the first person to hold the title of lord chief justice of England.
2. Convicted.
3. Immediately.
4. Conviction or allegation.

For the question is not of promises mutuall, where there is no security of performance on either side; as when there is no Civill Power
erected over the parties promising; for such promises are no Covenants:
But either where one of the parties has performed already; or where
there is a Power to make him performe; there is the question whether
it be against reason, that is, against the benefit of the other to performe,
or not. And I say it is not against reason. For the manifestation whereof,
we are to consider; First, that when a man doth a thing, which notwithstanding any thing can be foreseen, and reckoned on, tendeth to
his own destruction, howsoever some accident which he could not expect, arriving may turne it to his benefit; yet such events do not make
it reasonably or wisely done. Secondly, that in a condition of Warre,
wherein every man to every man, for want of a common Power to keep
them all in awe, is an Enemy, there is no man can hope by his own
strength, or wit, to defend himselfe from destruction, without the help
of Confederates; where every one expects the same defence by the
Confederation, that any one else does: and therefore he which declares
he thinks it reason to deceive those that help him, can in reason expect
no other means of safety, than what can be had from his own single
Power. He therefore that breaketh his Covenant, and consequently declareth that he thinks he may with reason do so, cannot be received
into any Society, that unite themselves for Peace and Defence, but by
the errour of them that receive him; nor when he is received, be retayned in it, without seeing the danger of their errour; which errours a
man cannot reasonably reckon upon as the means of his security: and
therefore if he be left, or cast out of Society, he perisheth; and if he
live in Society, it is by the errours of other men, which he could not
foresee, nor reckon upon; and consequently against the reason of his
preservation; and so, as all men that contribute not to his destruction,
forbear him onely out of ignorance of what is good for themselves.

As for the Instance of gaining the secure and perpetual felicity of
Heaven, by any way; it is frivolous: there being but one way imaginable;
and that is not breaking, but keeping of Covenant.

And for the other Instance of attaining Soveraignty by Rebellion; it
is manifest, that though the event follow, yet because it cannot reasonably be expected, but rather the contrary; and because by gaining it so,
others are taught to gain the same in like manner, the attempt thereof
is against reason. Justice therefore, that is to say, Keeping of Covenant,
is a Rule of Reason, by which we are forbidden to do any thing destructive to our life; and consequently a Law of Nature.

There be some that proceed further; and will not have the Law of
Nature, to be those Rules which conduce to the preservation of mans
life on earth; but to the attaining of an eternall felicity after death; to
which they think the breach of Covenant may conduce; and consequently be just and reasonable; (such are they that think it a work of
merit to kill, or depose, or rebell against, the Soveraigne Power consti- [74]
tuted over them by their own consent.) But because there is no naturall
knowledge of mans estate after death; much lesse of the reward that is
then to be given to breach of Faith; but onely a beliefe grounded upon

other mens saying, that they know it supernaturally, or that they know those, that knew them, that knew others, that knew it supernaturally; Breach of Faith cannot be called a Precept of Reason, or Nature.

Covenants not discharged by the Vice of the Person to whom they are made.

Others, that allow for a Law of Nature, the keeping of Faith, do neverthelesse make exception of certain persons; as Heretiques, and such as use not to performe their Covenant to others: And this also is against reason. For if any fault of a man, be sufficient to discharge our Covenant made; the same ought in reason to have been sufficient to have hindred the making of it.

Justice of Men, & Justice of Actions what.

The names of Just, and Injust, when they are attributed to Men, signifie one thing; and when they are attributed to Actions, another. When they are attributed to Men, they signifie Conformity, or Inconformity of Manners, to Reason. But when they are attributed to Actions, they signifie the Conformity or Inconformity to Reason, not of Manners, or manner of life, but of particular Actions. A Just man therefore, is he that taketh all the care he can, that his Actions may be all Just: and an Unjust man, is he that neglecteth it. And such men are more often in our Language stiled by the names of Righteous, and Unrighteous; then Just, and Unjust; though the meaning be the same. Therefore a Righteous man, does not lose that Title, by one, or a few unjust Actions, that proceed from sudden Passion, or mistake of Things, or Persons: nor does an Unrighteous man, lose his character, for such Actions, as he does, or forbeares to do, for feare: because his Will is not framed by the Justice, but by the apparent benefit of what he is to do. That which gives to humane Actions the relish of Justice, is a certain Noblenesse or Gallantnesse of courage, (rarely found,) by which a man scorns to be beholding for the contentment of his life, to fraud, or breach of promise. This Justice of the Manners, is that which is meant, where Justice is called a Vertue; and Injustice a Vice.

But the Justice of Actions denominates men, not Just, [but][5] *Guiltlesse*: and the Injustice of the same, (which is also called Injury,) gives them but the name of *Guilty*.

Justice of Manners, and Justice of Actions.

Again, the Injustice of Manners, is the disposition, or aptitude to do Injurie; and is Injustice before it proceed to Act; and without supposing any individuall person injured. But the Injustice of an Action, (that is to say Injury,) supposeth an individuall person Injured; namely him, to whom the Covenant was made: And therefore many times the injury is received by one man, when the dammage redoundeth to another. As when the Master commandeth his servant to give mony to a stranger; if it be not done, the Injury is done to the Master, whom he had before Covenanted to obey; but the dammage redoundeth to the stranger, to whom he had no Obligation; and therefore could not Injure him.

[75] And so also in Common-wealths, private men may remit to one another their debts; but not robberies or other violences, whereby they are endammaged;[6] because the detaining[7] of Debt, is an Injury to themselves; but Robbery and Violence, are Injuries to the Person of the Common-wealth.

5. Large paper edition.
6. Damaged.
7. Withholding.

Whatsoever is done to a man, conformable to his own Will signified to the doer, is no Injury to him. For if he that doeth it, hath not passed away his originall right to do what he please, by some Antecedent Covenant, there is no breach of Covenant; and therefore no Injury done him. And if he have; then his Will to have it done being signified, is a release of that Covenant: and so again there is no Injury done him.

Nothing done to a man, by his own consent can be Injury.

Justice of Actions, is by Writers divided into *Commutative*, and *Distributive*: and the former they say consisteth in proportion Arithmeticall; the later in proportion Geometricall. Commutative therefore, they place in the equality of value of the things contracted for; And Distributive, in the distribution of equall benefit, to men of equall merit. As if it were Injustice to sell dearer than we buy; or to give more to a man than he merits. The value of all things contracted for, is measured by the Appetite of the Contractors: and therefore the just value, is that which they be contented to give. And Merit (besides that which is by Covenant, where the performance on one part, meriteth the performance of the other part, and falls under Justice Commutative, not Distributive,) is not due by Justice; but is rewarded of Grace onely. And therefore this distinction, in the sense wherein it useth to be expounded, is not right. To speak properly, Commutative Justice, is the Justice of a Contractor; that is, a Performance of Covenant, in Buying, and Selling; Hiring, and Letting to Hire; Lending, and Borrowing; Exchanging, Bartering, and other acts of Contract.

Justice Commutative, and Distributive.

And Distributive Justice, the Justice of an Arbitrator; that is to say, the act of defining what is Just. Wherein, (being trusted by them that make him Arbitrator,) if he performe his Trust, he is said to distribute to every man his own: and this is indeed Just Distribution, and may be called (though improperly) Distributive Justice; but more properly Equity; which also is a Law of Nature, as shall be shewn in due place.

As Justice dependeth on Antecedent Covenant; so does GRATITUDE depend on Antecedent Grace; that is to say, Antecedent Free-gift: and is the fourth Law of Nature; which may be conceived in this Forme, *That a man which receiveth Benefit from another of meer Grace, Endeavour that he which giveth it, have no reasonable cause to repent him of his good will.* For no man giveth, but with intention of Good to himselfe; because Gift is Voluntary; and of all Voluntary Acts, the Object is to every man his own Good; of which if men see they shall be frustrated, there will be no beginning of benevolence, or trust; nor consequently of mutuall help; nor of reconciliation of one man to another; and therefore they are to remain still in the condition of *War*; which is contrary to the first and Fundamentall Law of Nature, which commandeth men to *Seek Peace*. The breach of this Law, is called *Ingratitude*; and hath the same relation to Grace, that Injustice hath to Obligation by Covenant.

The fourth Law of Nature, Gratitude.

[76]

A fifth Law of Nature, is COMPLEASANCE; that is to say, *That every man strive to accommodate himselfe to the rest.* For the understanding whereof, we may consider, that there is in mens aptnesse to Society, a diversity of Nature, rising from their diversity of Affections; not unlike to that we see in stones brought together for building of an Ædifice. For as that stone which by the asperity, and irregularity of Figure, takes

The fifth, Mutuall accommodation, or Compleasance.

more room from others, than it selfe fills; and for the hardnesse, cannot be easily made plain, and thereby hindereth the building, is by the builders cast away as unprofitable, and troublesome: so also, a man that by asperity of Nature, will strive to retain those things which to himselfe are superfluous, and to others necessary; and for the stubbornness of his Passions, cannot be corrected, is to be left, or cast out of Society, as combersome thereunto. For seeing every man, not onely by Right, but also by necessity of Nature, is supposed to endeavour all he can, to obtain that which is necessary for his conservation; He that shall oppose himselfe against it, for things superfluous, is guilty of the warre that thereupon is to follow; and therefore doth that, which is contrary to the fundamentall Law of Nature, which commandeth *to seek Peace.* The observers of this Law, may be called SOCIABLE, (the Latines call them *Commodi;*) The contrary, *Stubborn, Insociable, Froward,*[8] *Intractable.*

The sixth, Facility to Pardon.   A sixth Law of Nature, is this, *That upon caution of the Future time, a man ought to pardon the offences past of them that repenting, desire it.* For PARDON, is nothing but granting of Peace; which though granted to them that persevere in their hostility, be not Peace, but Feare; yet not granted to them that give caution of the Future time, is signe of an aversion to Peace; and therefore contrary to the Law of Nature.

The seventh, that in Revenges, men respect onely the future good.   A seventh is, *That in Revenges,* (that is, retribution of Evil for Evil,) *Men look not at the greatnesse of the evill past, but the greatnesse of the good to follow.* Whereby we are forbidden to inflict punishment with any other designe, than for correction of the offender, or direction of others. For this Law is consequent to the next before it, that commandeth Pardon, upon security of the Future time. Besides, Revenge without respect to the Example, and profit to come, is a triumph, or glorying in the hurt of another, tending to no end; (for the End is always somewhat to Come;) and glorying to no end, is vain-glory, and contrary to reason; and to hurt without reason, tendeth to the introduction of Warre; which is against the Law of Nature; and is commonly stiled by the name of *Cruelty.*

The eighth, against Contumely.   And because all signes of hatred, or contempt, provoke to fight; insomuch as most men choose rather to hazard their life, than not to be revenged; we may in the eighth place, for a Law of Nature, set down this Precept, *That no man by deed, word, countenance, or gesture, declare Hatred, or Contempt of another.* The breach of which Law, is commonly called *Contumely.*

The ninth, against Pride.

[77]   The question who is the better man, has no place in the condition of meer Nature; where, (as has been shewn before,) all men are equall. The inequallity that now is, has bin introduced by the Lawes civill. I know that *Aristotle* in the first booke of his Politiques, for a foundation of his doctrine, maketh men by Nature, some more worthy to Command, meaning the wiser sort (such as he thought himselfe to be for his Philosophy;) others to Serve, (meaning those that had strong bodies, but were not Philosophers as he;) as if Master and Servant were not

8. Perverse; difficult to deal with.

introduced by consent of men, but by difference of Wit: which is not only against reason; but also against experience. For there are very few so foolish, that had not rather governe themselves, than be governed by others: Nor when the wise in their own conceit, contend by force, with them who distrust their owne wisdome, do they alwaies, or often, or almost at any time, get the Victory. If Nature therefore have made men equall, that equalitie is to be acknowledged: or if Nature have made men unequall; yet because men that think themselves equall, will not enter into conditions of Peace, but upon Equall termes, such equalitie must be admitted. And therefore for the ninth law of Nature, I put this, *That every man acknowledge other for his Equall by Nature.* The breach of this Precept is *Pride.*

On this law, dependeth another, *That at the entrance into conditions of Peace, no man require to reserve to himselfe any Right, which he is not content should be reserved to every one of the rest.* As it is necessary for all men that seek peace, to lay down certaine Rights of Nature; that is to say, not to have libertie to do all they list: so is it necessarie for mans life, to retaine some; as right to governe their owne bodies; enjoy aire, water, motion, waies to go from place to place; and all things else without which a man cannot live, or not live well. If in this case, at the making of Peace, men require for themselves, that which they would not have to be granted to others, they do contrary to the precedent law, that commandeth the acknowledgment of naturall equalitie, and therefore also against the law of Nature. The observers of this law, are those we call *Modest,* and the breakers *Arrogant* men. The Greeks call the violation of this law πλεονεξία;[9] that is, a desire of more than their share. The tenth, against Arrogance.

Also if *a man be trusted to judge between man and man,* it is a precept of the Law of Nature, *that he deale Equally between them.* For without that, the Controversies of men cannot be determined but by Warre. He therefore that is partiall in judgment, doth what in him lies, to deterre men from the use of Judges, and Arbitrators; and consequently, (against the fundamentall Lawe of Nature) is the cause of Warre. The eleventh, Equity.

The observance of this law, from the equall distribution to each man, of that which in reason belongeth to him, is called EQUITY, and (as I have sayd before) distributive Justice: the violation, *Acception of persons,*[1] προσωποληψία.[2]

And from this followeth another law, *That such things as cannot be divided, be enjoyed in Common, if it can be; and if the quantity of the thing permit, without Stint; otherwise Proportionably to the number of them that have Right.* For otherwise the distribution is Unequall, and contrary to Equitie. The twelfth, Equall use of things Common.

But some things there be, that can neither be divided, nor enjoyed in common. Then, The Law of Nature, which prescribeth Equity, requireth, *That the Entire Right; or else, (making the use alternate,) the First Possession, be determined by Lot.* For equall distribution, is of the [78]
The thirteenth, of Lot.

9. *Pleonexia.*
1. *Favoritism.*
2. *Prosopolepsia.*

Law of Nature; and other means of equall distribution cannot be imagined.

The four-teenth, of Pri-mogeniture, and First seising.

Of *Lots* there be two sorts, *Arbitrary*, and *Naturall*. Arbitrary, is that which is agreed on by the Competitors: Naturall, is either *Primogeni-ture*, (which the Greek calls ΚΛηρονομια,[3] which signifies, *Given by Lot;*) or *First Seisure*.

And therefore those things which cannot be enjoyed in common, nor divided, ought to be adjudged to the First Possessor; and in some cases to the First-Borne, as acquired by Lot.

The fifteenth, of Mediators.

It is also a Law of Nature, *That all men that mediate Peace, be allowed safe Conduct*. For the Law that commandeth Peace, as the *End*, commandeth Intercession, as the *Means*; and to Intercession the Means is safe Conduct.

The sixteenth, of Submission to Arbitrement.

And because, though men be never so willing to observe these Lawes, there may neverthelesse arise questions concerning a mans action; First, whether it were done, or not done; Secondly (if done) whether against the Law, or not against the Law; the former whereof, is called a ques-tion *Of Fact*; the later a question *Of Right*; therefore unlesse the parties to the question, Covenant mutually to stand to the sentence of another, they are as farre from Peace as ever. This other, to whose Sentence they submit, is called an Arbitrator. And therefore it is of the Law of Nature, *That they that are at controversie, submit their Right to the judgement of an Arbitrator.*

The seven-teenth, No man is his own Judge.

And seeing every man is presumed to do all things in order to his own benefit, no man is a fit Arbitrator in his own cause: and if he were never so fit; yet Equity allowing to each party equall benefit, if one be admitted to be Judge, the other is to be admitted also; & so the con-troversie, that is, the cause of War, remains, against the Law of Nature.

The eigh-teenth, no man to be Judge, that has in him a natural cause of Partiality.

For the same reason no man in any Cause ought to be received for Arbitrator, to whom greater profit, or honour, or pleasure apparently ariseth out of the victory of one party, than of the other: for hee hath taken (though an unavoydable bribe, yet) a bribe; and no man can be obliged to trust him. And thus also the controversie, and the condition of War remaineth, contrary to the Law of Nature.

The nine-teenth, of Witnesses.

And in a controversie of *Fact*, the Judge being to give no more credit to one, than to the other, (if there be no other Arguments) must give credit to a third; or to a third and fourth; or more: For else the question is undecided, and left to force, contrary to the Law of Nature.

These are the Lawes of Nature, dictating Peace, for a means of the conservation of men in multitudes; and which onely concern the doc-trine of Civill Society. There be other things tending to the destruction of particular men; as Drunkenness, and all other parts of Intemperance; which may therefore also be reckoned amongst those things which the [79] Law of Nature hath forbidden; but are not necessary to be mentioned, nor are pertinent enough to this place.

And though this may seem too subtile a deduction of the Lawes of Nature, to be taken notice of by all men; whereof the most part are too

3. *Kleronomia.*

busie in getting food, and the rest too negligent to understand; yet to leave all men unexcusable, they have been contracted into one easie sum, intelligible, even to the meanest capacity; and that is, *Do not that to another, which thou wouldest not have done to thy selfe*; which shew-eth him, that he has no more to do in learning the Lawes of Nature, but, when weighing the actions of other men with his own, they seem too heavy, to put them into the other part of the ballance, and his own into their place, that his own passions, and selfe-love, may adde nothing to the weight; and then there is none of these Lawes of Nature that will not appear unto him very reasonable.

A Rule, by which the Laws of Nature may easily be examined.

The Lawes of Nature oblige *in foro interno*; that is to say, they bind to a desire they should take place: but *in foro externo*; that is, to the putting them in act, not alwayes. For he that should be modest, and tractable, and performe all he promises, in such time, and place, where no man els should do so, should but make himselfe a prey to others, and procure his own certain ruine, contrary to the ground of all Lawes of Nature, which tend to Natures preservation. And again, he that hav-ing sufficient Security, that others shall observe the same Lawes towards him, observes them not himselfe, seeketh not Peace, but War; & con-sequently the destruction of his Nature by Violence.

The Lawes of Nature oblige in Conscience alwayes, but in Effect then onely when there is Security.

And whatsoever Lawes bind *in foro interno*, may be broken, not onely by a fact contrary to the Law, but also by a fact according to it, in case a man think it contrary. For though his Action in this case, be according to the Law; yet his Purpose was against the Law; which where the Obligation is *in foro interno*, is a breach.

The Lawes of Nature are Immutable and Eternall; For Injustice, Ingratitude, Arrogance, Pride, Iniquity, Acception of persons, and the rest, can never be made lawfull. For it can never be that Warre shall preserve life, and Peace destroy it.

The Laws of Nature are Eternal;

The [same] Lawes, because they oblige onely to a desire, and en-deavour, I mean an unfeigned and constant endeavour, are easie to be observed. For in that they require nothing but endeavour; he that en-deavoureth their performance, fulfilleth them; and he that fulfilleth the Law, is Just.

And yet Easie.

And the Science of them, is the true and onely Moral Philosophy. For Morall Philosophy is nothing else but the Science of what is *Good*, and *Evill*, in the conversation, and Society of man-kind. *Good*, and *Evill*, are names that signifie our Appetites, and Aversions; which in different tempers, customes, and doctrines of men, are different: And divers men, differ not onely in their Judgement, on the senses of what is pleasant, and unpleasant to the tast, smell, hearing, touch, and sight; but also of what is conformable, or disagreeable to Reason, in the ac-tions of common life. Nay, the same man, in divers times, differs from himselfe; and one time praiseth, that is, calleth Good, what another time he dispraiseth, and calleth Evil: From whence arise Disputes, Controversies, and at last War. And therefore so long a man is in the condition of meer Nature, (which is a condition of War,) as private Appetite is the measure of Good, and Evill: And consequently all men agree on this, that Peace is Good, and therefore also the way, or means

The Science of these Lawes, is the true Mor-all Philos-ophy.

[80]

of Peace, which (as I have shewed before) are *Justice, Gratitude, Modesty, Equity, Mercy,* & the rest of the Laws of Nature, are good; that is to say, *Morall Vertues;* and their contrarie *Vices,* Evill. Now the science of Vertue and Vice, is Morall Philosophie; and therfore the true Doctrine of the Lawes of Nature, is the true Morall Philosophie. But the Writers of Morall Philosophie, though they acknowledge the same Vertues and Vices; Yet not seeing wherein consisted their Goodnesse; nor that they come to be praised, as the meanes of peaceable, sociable, and comfortable living; place them in a mediocrity[4] of passions: as if not the Cause, but the Degree of daring, made Fortitude; or not the Cause, but the Quantity of a gift, made Liberality.

These dictates of Reason, men use to call by the name of Lawes; but improperly: for they are but Conclusions, or Theoremes concerning what conduceth to the conservation and defence of themselves; wheras Law, properly is the word of him, that by right hath command over others. But yet if we consider the same Theoremes, as delivered in the word of God, that by right commandeth all things; then are they properly called Lawes.

Chap. XVI.

Of PERSONS, AUTHORS, *and things Personated.*

*A person
what.*

A PERSON, is he, *whose words or actions are considered, either as his own, or as representing the words or actions of an other man, or of any other thing to whom they are attributed, whether Truly or by Fiction.*

*Person Naturall and
Artificiall.*

When they are considered as his owne, then is he called a *Naturall Person*: And when they are considered as representing the words and actions of an other, then is he a *Feigned* or *Artificiall person*.

The word Person, whence.

The word Person is latine: insteed whereof the Greeks have πρόσωπον,[1] which signifies the *Face*, as *Persona* in latine signifies the *disguise*, or *outward appearance* of a man, counterfeited on the Stage; and somtimes more particularly that part of it, which disguiseth the face, as a Mask or Visard[2]: And from the Stage, hath been translated to any Representer of speech and action, as well in Tribunalls, as Theaters. So that a *Person*, is the same that an *Actor* is, both on the Stage and in common Conversation; and to *Personate*, is to *Act*, or *Represent* himselfe, or an other; and he that acteth another, is said to beare his Person, or act in his name; (in which sence *Cicero* useth it where he saies, *Unus sustineo tres Personas; Mei, Adversarii, & Judicis,* I beare three Persons; my own, my Adversaries, and the Judges;) and is called

[81]

in diverse occasions, diversly; as a *Representer*, or *Representative*, a *Lieutenant*, a *Vicar*, an *Attorney*, a *Deputy*, a *Procurator*, an *Actor*, and the like.

Of Persons Artificiall, some have their words and actions *Owned* by

4. Moderation.
1. *Prosopon.*
2. Visor.

those whom they represent. And then the Person is the *Actor*; and he that owneth his words and actions, is the AUTHOR: In which case the Actor acteth by Authority. For that which in speaking of goods and possessions, is called an *Owner*, and in latine *Dominus*, in Greeke κύριοσ;[3] speaking of Actions, is called Author. And as the Right of possession, is called Dominion; so the Right of doing any Action, is called AUTHORITY. So that by Authority, is alwayes understood a Right of doing any act: and *done by Authority*, done by Commission, or Licence from him whose right it is. *Actor, Author,*

Authority.

From hence it followeth, that when the Actor maketh a Covenant by Authority, he bindeth thereby the Author, no lesse than if he had made it himselfe; and no lesse subjecteth him to all the consequences of the same. And therfore all that hath been said formerly, (*Chap.* 14.) of the nature of Covenants between man and man in their naturall capacity, is true also when they are made by their Actors, Representers, or Procurators, that have authority from them, so far-forth as is in their Commission, but no farther. *Covenants by Authority, bind the Author.*

And therefore he that maketh a Covenant with the Actor, or Representer, not knowing the Authority he hath, doth it at his own perill. For no man is obliged by a Covenant, whereof he is not Author; nor consequently by a Covenant made against, or beside the Authority he gave.

When the Actor doth any thing against the Law of Nature by command of the Author, if he be obliged by former Covenant to obey him, not he, but the Author breaketh the Law of Nature: for though the Action be against the Law of Nature; yet it is not his: but contrarily, to refuse to do it, is against the Law of Nature, that forbiddeth breach of Covenant. *But not the Actor.*

And he that maketh a Covenant with the Author, by mediation of the Actor, not knowing what Authority he hath, but onely takes his word; in case such Authority be not made manifest unto him upon demand, is no longer obliged: For the Covenant made with the Author, is not valid, without his Counter-assurance. But if he that so Covenanteth, knew before hand he was to expect no other assurance, than the Actors word; then is the Covenant valid; because the Actor in this case maketh himselfe the Author. And therefore, as when the Authority is evident, the Covenant obligeth the Author, not the Actor; so when the Authority is feigned, it obligeth the Actor onely; there being no Author but himselfe. *The Authority is to be shewne.*

There are few things, that are uncapable of being represented by Fiction. Inanimate things, as a Church, an Hospital, a Bridge, may be personated by a Rector, Master, or Overseer. But things Inanimate, cannot be Authors, nor therefore give Authority to their Actors: Yet the Actors may have Authority to procure their maintenance, given them by those that are Owners, or Governours of those things. And therefore, such things cannot be Personated, before there be some state of Civill Government. *Things personated, Inanimate.*

[82]

3. *Kurios.*

Irrational; Likewise Children, Fooles, and Mad-men that have no use of Reason, may be Personated by Guardians, or Curators; but can be no Authors (during that time) of any action done by them, longer then (when they shall recover the use of Reason) they shall judge the same reasonable. Yet during the Folly, he that hath right of governing them, may give Authority to the Guardian. But this again has no place but in a State Civill, because before such estate, there is no Dominion of Persons.

False Gods; An Idol, or meer Figment of the brain, may be Personated; as were the Gods of the Heathen; which by such Officers as the State appointed, were Personated, and held Possessions, and other Goods, and Rights, which men from time to time dedicated, and consecrated unto them. But Idols cannot be Authors: for an Idol is nothing. The Authority proceeded from the State: and therefore before introduction of Civill Government, the Gods of the Heathen could not be Personated.

The true God. The true God may be Personated. As he was; first, by *Moses;* who governed the Israelites, (that were not his, but Gods people,) not in his own name, with *Hoc dicit Moses;*[4] but in Gods Name, with *Hoc dicit Dominus.*[5] Secondly, by the Son of man, his own Son, our Blessed Saviour *Jesus Christ,* that came to reduce[6] the Jewes, and induce all Nations into the Kingdome of his Father; not as of himselfe, but as sent from his Father. And thirdly, by the Holy Ghost, or Comforter, speaking, and working in the Apostles: which Holy Ghost, was a Comforter that came not of himselfe; but was sent, and proceeded from them both.

A Multitude of men, how one Person. A Multitude of men, are made *One* Person, when they are by one man, or one Person, Represented; so that it be done with the consent of every one of that Multitude in particular. For it is the *Unity* of the Representer, not the *Unity* of the Represented, that maketh the Person *One.* And it is the Representer that beareth the Person, and but one Person: And *Unity,* cannot otherwise be understood in Multitude.

Every one is Author. And because the Multitude naturally is not *One,* but *Many;* they cannot be understood for one; but many Authors, of every thing their Representative saith, or doth in their name; Every man giving their common Representer, Authority from himselfe in particular; and owning all the actions the Representer doth, in case they give him Authority without stint: Otherwise, when they limit him in what, and how farre he shall represent them, none of them owneth more, than they gave him commission to Act.

An Actor may be Many men made One by Plurality of Voyces.
[83] And if the Representative consist of many men, the voyce of the greater number, must be considered as the voyce of them all. For if the lesser number pronounce (for example) in the Affirmative, and the greater in the Negative, there will be Negatives more than enough to destroy the Affirmatives; and thereby the excesse of Negatives, standing uncontradicted, are the onely voyce the Representative hath.

And a Representative of even number, especially when the number

4. Thus says Moses.
5. Thus says the Lord.
6. Bring back; restore (to their covenant with God).

is not great, whereby the contradictory voyces are oftentimes equall, is therefore oftentimes mute, and uncapable of Action. Yet in some cases contradictory voyces equall in number, may determine a question; as in condemning, or absolving, equality of votes, even in that they condemne not, do absolve; but not on the contrary condemne, in that they absolve not. For when a Cause is heard; not to condemne, is to absolve: but on the contrary, to say that not absolving, is condemning, is not true. The like it is in a deliberation of executing presently, or deferring till another time: For when the voyces are equall, the not decreeing Execution, is a decree of Dilation.[7] *Representatives, when the number is even, unprofitable.*

Or if the number be odde, as three, or more, (men, or assemblies;) whereof every one has by a Negative Voice, authority to take away the effect of all the Affirmative Voices of the rest, This number is no Representative; because by the diversity of Opinions, and Interests of men, it becomes oftentimes, and in cases of the greatest consequence, a mute Person, and unapt, as for many things else, so for the government of a Multitude, especially in time of Warre. *Negative voyce.*

Of Authors there be two sorts. The first simply so called; which I have before defined to be him, that owneth the Action of another simply. The second is he, that owneth an Action, or Covenant of another conditionally; that is to say, he undertaketh to do it, if the other doth it not, at, or before a certain time. And these Authors conditionall, are generally called Suretyes, in Latine *Fidejussores*, and *Sponsores*; and particularly for Debt, *Prædes*; and for Appearance before a Judge, or Magistrate, *Vades*.

---

7. Delay.

Of
Common-Wealth

Chap. XVII.

Of the Causes, Generation, and Definition of a COMMON-WEALTH.

The finall Cause, End, or Designe of men, (who naturally love Liberty, and Dominion over others,) in the introduction of that restraint upon themselves, (in which wee see them live in Common-wealths,) is the foresight of their own preservation, and of a more contented life thereby; that is to say, of getting themselves out from that miserable condition of Warre, which is necessarily consequent (as hath been shewn) to the naturall Passions of men, when there is no visible Power to keep them in awe, and tye them by feare of punishment to the performance of their Covenants, and observation of those Lawes of Nature set down in the fourteenth and fifteenth Chapters.

For the Lawes of Nature (as *Justice, Equity, Modesty, Mercy,* and (in summe) *doing to others, as wee would be done to,*) of themselves, without the terrour of some Power, to cause them to be observed, are contrary to our naturall Passions, that carry us to Partiality, Pride, Revenge, and the like. And Covenants, without the Sword, are but Words, and of no strength to secure a man at all. Therefore notwithstanding the Lawes of Nature, (which every one hath then kept, when he has the will to keep them, when he can do it safely,) if there be no Power erected, or not great enough for our security; every man will, and may lawfully rely on his own strength and art, for caution against all other men. And in all places, where men have lived by small Families, to robbe and spoyle one another, has been a Trade, and so farre from being reputed against the Law of Nature, that the greater spoyles they gained, the greater was their honour; and men observed no other Lawes therein, but the Lawes of Honour; that is, to abstain from cruelty, leaving to men their lives, and instruments of husbandry. And as small Familyes did then; so now do Cities and Kingdomes which are but greater Families (for their own security) enlarge their Dominions, upon all pretences of danger, and fear of Invasion, or assistance that may be given to Invaders, endeavour as much as they can, to subdue, or weaken their neighbours, by open force, and secret arts, for want of other Caution, justly; and are remembred for it in after ages with honour.

Nor is it the joyning together of a [small]¹ number of men, that gives

The End of Common-wealth, particular Security:

Chap. 13.

Which is not to be had from the Law of Nature:

Nor from the conjunction of a few men or familyes:

---

1. Large paper edition has *finall.*

93

them this security; because in small numbers, small additions on the
one side or the other, make the advantage of strength so great, as is
sufficient to carry the Victory; and therefore gives encouragement to an
Invasion. The Multitude sufficient to confide in for our Security, is not
determined by any certain number, but by comparison with the Enemy
we feare; and is then sufficient, when the odds[2] of the Enemy is not of
so visible and conspicuous moment,[3] to determine the event of warre,
as to move him to attempt.

Nor from a great Multitude, unlesse directed by one judgement:

And be there never so great a Multitude; yet if their actions be directed according to their particular judgements, and particular appetites, they can expect thereby no defence, nor protection, neither against
a Common enemy, nor against the injuries of one another. For being
distracted[4] in opinions concerning the best use and application of their
strength, they do not help, but hinder one another; and reduce their
strength by mutuall opposition to nothing: whereby they are easily, not
onely subdued by a very few that agree together; but also when there
is no common enemy, they make warre upon each other, for their
particular interests. For if we could suppose a great Multitude of men
to consent in the observation of Justice, and other Lawes of Nature,
without a common Power to keep them all in awe; we might as well
suppose all Man-kind to do the same; and then there neither would
be, nor need to be any Civill Government, or Common-wealth at all;
because there would be Peace without subjection.

And that continually.

Nor is it enough for the security, which men desire should last all
the time of their life, that they be governed, and directed by one judgement, for a limited time; as in one Battell, or one Warre. For though
they obtain a Victory by their unanimous endeavour against a forraign
enemy; yet afterwards, when either they have no common enemy, or
he that by one part is held for an enemy, is by another part held for a
friend, they must needs by the difference of their interests dissolve, and
fall again into a Warre amongst themselves.

Why certain creatures with-out reason, or speech, do neverthelesse live in Society, without any coërcive Power.

It is true, that certain living creatures, as Bees, and Ants, live sociably
one with another, (which are therefore by *Aristotle* numbred amongst
Politicall creatures;) and yet have no other direction, than their particular judgements and appetites; nor speech, whereby one of them can
signifie to another, what he thinks expedient for the common benefit:
and therefore some man may perhaps desire to know, why Man-kind
cannot do the same. To which I answer,

First, that men are continually in competition for Honour and Dignity, which these creatures are not; and consequently amongst men
there ariseth on that ground, Envy and Hatred, and finally Warre; but
amongst these not so.

Secondly, that amongst these creatures, the Common good differeth
not from the Private; and being by nature enclined to their private, they
procure thereby the common benefit. But man, whose Joy consisteth
in comparing himselfe with other men, can relish nothing but what is
eminent.

2. Comparative advantage.
3. Importance.
4. Perplexed (by conflicting thoughts).

Thirdly, that these creatures, having not (as man) the use of reason, do not see, nor think they see any fault, in the administration of their common businesse: whereas amongst men, there are very many, that thinke themselves wiser, and abler to govern the Publique better than the rest; and these strive to reforme and innovate, one this way, another that way; and thereby bring it into Distraction and Civill warre. [87]

Fourthly, that these creatures, though they have some use of voice, in making knowne to one another their desires, and other affections; yet they want that art of words, by which some men can represent to others, that which is Good, in the likenesse of Evill; and Evill, in the likenesse of Good; and augment, or diminish the apparent greatnesse of Good and Evill; discontenting men, and troubling their Peace at their pleasure.

Fiftly, irrationall creatures cannot distinguish betweene *Injury*, and *Dammage*; and therefore as long as they be at ease, they are not offended with their fellowes: whereas Man is then most troublesome, when he is most at ease: for then it is that he loves to shew his Wisdome, and controule[5] the Actions of them that governe the Commonwealth.

Lastly, the agreement of these creatures is Naturall; that of men, is by Covenant only, which is Artificiall: and therefore it is no wonder if there be somwhat else required (besides Covenant) to make their Agreement constant and lasting; which is a Common Power, to keep them in awe, and to direct their actions to the Common Benefit.

The only way to erect such a Common Power, as may be able to defend them from the invasion of Forraigners, and the injuries of one another, and thereby to secure them in such sort, as that by their owne industrie, and by the fruites of the Earth, they may nourish themselves and live contentedly; is, to conferre all their power and strength upon one Man, or upon one Assembly of men, that may reduce all their Wills, by plurality of voices, unto one Will: which is as much as to say, to appoint one Man, or Assembly of men, to beare their Person; and every one to owne, and acknowledge himselfe to be Author of whatsoever he that so beareth their Person, shall Act, or cause to be Acted, in those things which concerne the Common Peace and Safetie; and therein to submit their Wills, every one to his Will, and their Judgements, to his Judgment. This is more than Consent, or Concord; it is a reall Unitie of them all, in one and the same Person, made by Covenant of every man with every man, in such manner, as if every man should say to every man, *I Authorise and give up my Right of Governing my selfe, to this Man, or to this Assembly of men, on this condition, that thou give up thy Right to him, and Authorise all his Actions in like manner.* This done, the Multitude so united in one Person, is called a COMMON-WEALTH, in latine CIVITAS. This is the Generation of that great LEVIATHAN, or rather (to speake more reverently) of that *Mortall God*, to which wee owe under the *Immortall God*, our peace and defence. For by this Authoritie, given him by every particular man in the Common-Wealth, he hath the use of so much Power and Strength

The Generation of a Commonwealth.

[88]

5. Find fault with.

conferred on him, that by terror thereof, he is inabled to [con][6]forme the wills of them all, to Peace at home, and mutuall ayd against their enemies abroad. And in him consisteth the Essence of the Common-wealth; which (to define it,) is *One Person, of whose Acts a great Multitude, by mutuall Covenants one with another, have made themselves every one the Author, to the end he may use the strength and means of them all, as he shall think expedient, for their Peace and Common Defence.*

The Definition of a Common-wealth.

And he that carryeth this Person, is called SOVERAIGNE, and said to have *Soveraigne Power*; and every one besides, his SUBJECT.

Soveraigne, and Subject, what.

The attaining to this Soveraigne Power, is by two wayes. One, by Naturall force; as when a man maketh his children, to submit themselves, and their children to his government, as being able to destroy them if they refuse; or by Warre subdueth his enemies to his will, giving them their lives on that condition. The other, is when men agree amongst themselves, to submit to some Man, or Assembly of men, voluntarily, on confidence to be protected by him against all others. This later, may be called a Politicall Common-wealth, or Common-wealth by *Institution*; and the former, a Common-wealth by *Acquisition*. And first, I shall speak of a Common-wealth by Institution.

Chap. XVIII.

Of the RIGHTS *of Soveraignes by Institution.*

The act of Instituting a Common-wealth, what.

A *Common-wealth* is said to be *Instituted,* when a *Multitude* of men do Agree, and *Covenant, every one, with every one,* that to whatsoever *Man,* or *Assembly of Men,* shall be given by the major part, the *Right* to *Present* the Person of them all, (that is to say, to be their *Representative;*) every one, as well he that *Voted for it,* as he that *Voted against it,* shall *Authorise* all the Actions and Judgements, of that Man, or Assembly of men, in the same manner, as if they were his own, to the end, to live peaceably amongst themselves, and be protected against other men.

The Consequences to such Institution, are I. The Subjects cannot change the forme of government.

From this Institution of a Common-wealth are derived all the *Rights,* and *Facultyes* of him, or them, on whom the Soveraigne Power is conferred by the consent of the People assembled.

First, because they Covenant, it is to be understood, they are not obliged by former Covenant to any thing repugnant hereunto. And Consequently they that have already Instituted a Common-wealth, being thereby bound by Covenant, to own the Actions, and Judgements of one, cannot lawfully make a new Covenant, amongst themselves, to be obedient to any other, in any thing whatsoever, without his permission. And therefore, they that are subjects to a Monarch, cannot without his leave cast off Monarchy, and return to the confusion of a disunited Multitude; nor transferre their Person from him that beareth it, to an-

6. Per large paper edition.

other Man, or other Assembly of men: for they are bound, every man [89]
to every man, to Own, and be reputed Author of all, that he that already
is their Soveraigne, shall do, and judge fit to be done: so that any one
man dissenting, all the rest should break their Covenant made to that
man, which is injustice: and they have also every man given the Soveraignty to him that beareth their Person; and therefore if they depose
him, they take from him that which is his own, and so again it is
injustice. Besides, if he that attempteth to depose his Soveraign, be
killed, or punished by him for such attempt, he is author of his own
punishment, as being by the Institution, Author of all his Soveraign
shall do: And because it is injustice for a man to do any thing, for
which he may be punished by his own authority, he is also upon that
title, unjust. And whereas some men have pretended for their disobedience to their Soveraign, a new Covenant, made, not with men, but
with God; this also is unjust: for there is no Covenant with God, but
by mediation of some body that representeth Gods Person; which none
doth but Gods Lieutenant, who hath the Soveraignty under God. But
this pretence of Covenant with God, is so evident a lye, even in the
pretenders own consciences, that it is not onely an act of an unjust,
but also of a vile, and unmanly disposition.

Secondly, Because the Right of bearing the Person of them all, is
given to him they make Soveraigne, by Covenant onely of one to another, and not of him to any of them; there can happen no breach of
Covenant on the part of the Soveraigne; and consequently none of his
Subjects, by any pretence of forfeiture, can be freed from his Subjection. That he which is made Soveraigne maketh no Covenant with his
Subjects before-hand, is manifest; because either he must make it with
the whole multitude, as one party to the Covenant; or he must make
a severall[1] Covenant with every man. With the whole, as one party, it
is impossible; because as yet they are not one Person: and if he make
so many severall Covenants as there be men, those Covenants after he
hath the Soveraignty are voyd, because what act soever can be pretended by any one of them for breach thereof, is the act both of himselfe, and of all the rest, because done in the Person, and by the Right
of every one of them in particular. Besides, if any one, or more of them,
pretend a breach of the Covenant made by the Soveraigne at his Institution; and others, or one other of his Subjects, or himselfe alone,
pretend there was no such breach, there is in this case, no Judge to
decide the controversie: it returns therefore to the Sword again; and
every man recovereth the right of Protecting himselfe by his own
strength, contrary to the designe they had in the Institution. It is therefore in vain to grant Soveraignty by way of precedent Covenant. The
opinion that any Monarch receiveth his Power by Covenant, that is to
say on Condition, proceedeth from want of understanding this easie
truth, that Covenants being but words, and breath, have no force to
oblige, contain, constrain, or protect any man, but what it has from the
publique Sword; that is, from the untyed hands of that Man, or Assem-

2. Soveraigne
Power cannot
be forfeited.

1. Separate.

[90]

bly of men that hath the Soveraignty, and whose actions are avouched by them all, and performed by the strength of them all, in him united. But when an Assembly of men is made Soveraigne; then no man imagineth any such Covenant to have past in the Institution; for no man is so dull as to say, for example, the People of *Rome*, made a Covenant with the Romans, to hold the Soveraignty on such or such conditions; which not performed, the Romans might lawfully depose the Roman People. That men see not the reason to be alike in a Monarchy, and in a Popular Government, proceedeth from the ambition of some, that are kinder to the government of an Assembly, whereof they may hope to participate, than of Monarchy, which they despair to enjoy.

3. No man can without injustice protest against the Institution of the Soveraigne declared by the major part.

Thirdly, because the major part hath by consenting voices declared a Soveraigne; he that dissented must now consent with the rest; that is, be contented to avow all the actions he shall do, or else justly be destroyed by the rest. For if he voluntarily entered into the Congregation of them that were assembled, he sufficiently declared thereby his will (and therefore tacitely covenanted) to stand to what the major part should ordayne: and therefore if he refuse to stand thereto, or make Protestation against any of their Decrees, he does contrary to his Covenant, and therfore unjustly. And whether he be of the Congregation, or not; and whether his consent be asked, or not, he must either submit to their decrees, or be left in the condition of warre he was in before; wherein he might without injustice be destroyed by any man whatsoever.

4. The Soveraigns Actions cannot be justly accused by the Subject.

Fourthly, because every Subject is by this Institution Author of all the Actions, and Judgments of the Soveraigne Instituted; it followes, that whatsoever he doth, it can be no injury to any of his Subjects; nor ought he to be by any of them accused of Injustice. For he that doth any thing by authority from another, doth therein no injury to him by whose authority he acteth: But by this Institution of a Common-wealth, every particular man is Author of all the Soveraigne doth; and consequently he that complaineth of injury from his Soveraigne, complaineth of that whereof he himselfe is Author; and therefore ought not to accuse any man but himselfe; no nor himselfe of injury; because to do injury to ones selfe, is impossible. It is true that they that have Soveraigne power, may commit Iniquity; but not Injustice, or Injury in the proper signification.

5. What soever the Soveraigne doth, is unpunishable by the Subject.

Fiftly, and consequently to that which was sayd last, no man that hath Soveraigne power can justly be put to death, or otherwise in any manner by his Subjects punished. For seeing every Subject is Author of the actions of his Soveraigne; he punisheth another, for the actions committed by himselfe.

6. The Soveraigne is judge of what is necessary for the Peace and Defence of his Subjects.

And because the End of this Institution, is the Peace and Defence of them all; and whosoever has right to the End, has right to the Means; it belongeth of Right, to whatsoever Man, or Assembly that hath the Soveraignty, to be Judge both of the meanes of Peace and Defence; and also of the hindrances, and disturbances of the same; and to do whatsoever he shall think necessary to be done, both before hand, for the preserving of Peace and Security, by prevention of Discord at home,

[91]

and Hostility from abroad; and, when Peace and Security are lost, for the recovery of the same. And therefore,

Sixtly, it is annexed to the Soveraignty, to be Judge of what Opinions and Doctrines are averse, and what conducing to Peace; and consequently, on what occasions, how farre, and what, men are to be trusted withall, in speaking to Multitudes of people; and who shall examine the Doctrines of all bookes before they be published. For the Actions of men proceed from their Opinions; and in the wel governing of Opinions, consisteth the well governing of mens Actions, in order to their Peace, and Concord. And though in matter of Doctrine, nothing ought to be regarded but the Truth; yet this is not repugnant to regulating of the same by Peace. For Doctrine repugnant to Peace, can no more be True, than Peace and Concord can be against the Law of Nature. It is true, that in a Common-wealth, where by the negligence, or unskilfullnesse of Governours, and Teachers, false Doctrines are by time generally received; the contrary Truths may be generally offensive: Yet the most sudden, and rough busling in of a new Truth, that can be, does never breake the Peace, but only somtimes awake the Warre. For those men that are so remissely governed, that they dare take up Armes, to defend, or introduce an Opinion, are still in Warre; and their condition not Peace, but only a Cessation of Armes for feare of one another; and they live as it were, in the procincts of battaile continually. It belongeth therefore to him that hath the Soveraign Power, to be Judge, or constitute[2] all Judges of Opinions and Doctrines, as a thing necessary to Peace; therby to prevent Discord and Civill Warre.

And Judge of what Doctrines are fit to be taught them.

Seventhly, is annexed to the Soveraigntie, the whole power of prescribing the Rules, whereby every man may know, what Goods he may enjoy, and what Actions he may doe, without being molested by any of his fellow Subjects: And this is it men call *Propriety*. For before constitution of Soveraign Power (as hath already been shewn) all men had right to all things; which necessarily causeth Warre: and therefore this Proprietie, being necessary to Peace, and depending on Soveraign Power, is the Act of that Power, in order to the publique peace. These Rules of Propriety (or *Meum* and *Tuum*) and of *Good, Evill, Lawfull*, and *Unlawfull* in the actions of Subjects, are the Civill Lawes; that is to say, the Lawes of each Commonwealth in particular; though the name of Civill Law be now restrained[3] to the antient Civill Lawes of the City of *Rome*; which being the head of a great part of the World, her Lawes at that time were in these parts the Civill Law.

7. The Right of making Rules, whereby the Subjects may every man know what is so his owne, as no other Subject can without injustice take it from him.

Eightly, is annexed to the Soveraigntie, the Right of Judicature; that is to say, of hearing and deciding all Controversies, which may arise concerning Law, either Civill, or Naturall, or concerning Fact. For without the decision of Controversies, there is no protection of one Subject, against the injuries of another; the Lawes concerning *Meum* and *Tuum* are in vaine; and to every man remaineth, from the naturall and necessary appetite of his own conservation, the right of protecting

8. To him also belongeth the Right of all Judicature and decision of Controversies:

2. Appoint.
3. Restricted.

9. And of
making War,
and Peace, as
he shall think
best:

10. And of
choosing all
Counsellours,
and Ministers,
both of Peace,
and Warre:

11. And of Re-
warding, and
Punishing,
and that
(where no for-
mer Law hath
determined the
measure of it)
arbitrary:
12. And of
Honour and
Order.

These Rights
indivisible.

himselfe by his private strength, which is the condition of Warre; and contrary to the end for which every Common-wealth is instituted.

Ninthly, is annexed to the Soveraignty, the Right of making Warre, and Peace with other Nations, and Common-wealths; that is to say, of Judging when it is for the publique good, and how great forces are to be assembled, armed, and payd for that end; and to levy mony upon the Subjects, to defray the expences thereof. For the Power by which the people are to be defended, consisteth in their Armies; and the strength of an Army, in the union of their strength under one Command; which Command the Soveraign Instituted, therefore hath; because the command of the *Militia*, without other Institution, maketh him that hath it Soveraign. And therefore whosoever is made Generall of an Army, he that hath the Soveraign Power is alwayes Generallissimo.

Tenthly, is annexed to the Soveraignty, the choosing of all Counsellours, Ministers, Magistrates, and Officers, both in Peace, and War. For seeing the Soveraign is charged with the End, which is the common Peace and Defence; he is understood to have Power to use such Means, as he shall think most fit for his discharge.

Eleventhly, to the Soveraign is committed the Power of Rewarding with riches, or honour; and of Punishing with corporall, or pecuniary punishment, or with ignominy every Subject according to the Law he hath formerly made; or if there be no Law made, according as he shall judge most to conduce to the encouraging of men to serve the Common-wealth, or deterring of them from doing dis-service to the same.

Lastly, considering what values men are naturally apt to set upon themselves; what respect they look for from others; and how little they value other men; from whence continually arise amongst them, Emulation,[4] Quarrells, Factions, and at last Warre, to the destroying of one another, and diminution of their strength against a Common Enemy; It is necessary that there be Lawes of Honour, and a publique rate of the worth of such men as have deserved, or are able to deserve well of the Common-wealth; and that there be force in the hands of some or other, to put those Lawes in execution. But it hath already been shewn, that not onely the whole *Militia*, or forces of the Common-wealth; but also the Judicature of all Controversies, is annexed to the Soveraignty. To the Soveraign therefore it belongeth also to give titles of Honour; and to appoint what Order of place, and dignity, each man shall hold; and what signes of respect, in publique or private meetings, they shall give to one another.

These are the Rights, which make the Essence of Soveraignty; and which are the markes, whereby a man may discern in what Man, or Assembly of men, the Soveraign Power is placed, and resideth. For these are incommunicable,[5] and inseparable. The Power to coyn Mony; to dispose of the estate and persons of Infant heires; to have præemption[6] in Markets; and all other Statute Prærogatives, may be transferred

4. Rivalry.
5. Incapable of being shared.
6. Right to purchase before opportunity is offered to others.

by the Soveraign; and yet the Power to protect his Subjects be retained. But if he transferre the *Militia*, he retains the Judicature in vain, for want of execution of the Lawes: Or if he grant away the Power of raising Mony; the *Militia* is in vain: or if he give away the government of Doctrines, men will be frighted into rebellion with the feare of Spirits. And so if we consider any one of the said Rights, we shall presently see, that the holding of all the rest, will produce no effect, in the conservation of Peace and Justice, the end for which all Common-wealths are Instituted. And this division is it, whereof it is said, *a King-dome divided in it selfe cannot stand:* For unlesse this division precede, division into opposite Armies can never happen. If there had not first been an opinion received of the greatest part of *England*, that these Powers were divided between the King, and the Lords, and the House of Commons, the people had never been divided, and fallen into this Civill Warre; first between those that disagreed in Politiques; and after between the Dissenters about the liberty of Religion; which have so instructed men in this point of Soveraign Right, that there be few now (in *England*,) that do not see, that these Rights are inseparable, and will be so generally acknowledged, at the next return of Peace; and so continue, till their miseries are forgotten; and no longer, except the vulgar be better taught than they have hetherto been.

[93]

And because they are essentiall and inseparable Rights, it follows necessarily, that in whatsoever words any of them seem to be granted away, yet if the Soveraign Power it selfe be not in direct termes re-nounced, and the name of Soveraign no more given by the Grantees to him that Grants them, the Grant is voyd: for when he has granted all he can, if we grant back the Soveraignty, all is restored, as insepa-rably annexed thereunto.

And can by no Grant passe away without direct renouncing of the Soveraign Power.

This great Authority being Indivisible, and inseparably annexed to the Soveraignty, there is little ground for the opinion of them, that say of Soveraign Kings, though they be *singulis majores*, of greater Power than every one of their Subjects, yet they be *Universis minores*, of lesse power than them all together. For if by *all together*, they mean not the collective body as one person, then *all together*, and *every one*, signifie the same; and the speech is absurd. But if by *all together*, they under-stand them as one Person (which person the Soveraign bears,) then the power of all together, is the same with the Soveraigns power; and so again the speech is absurd: which absurdity they see well enough, when the Soveraignty is in an Assembly of the people; but in a Monarch they see it not; and yet the power of Soveraignty is the same in whomsoever it be placed.

The Power and Honour of Subjects vanisheth in the presence of the Power Soveraign.

And as the Power, so also the Honour of the Soveraign, ought to be greater, than that of any, or all the Subjects. For in the Soveraignty is the fountain of Honour. The dignities of Lord, Earle, Duke, and Prince are his Creatures. As in the presence of the Master, the Servants are equall, and without any honour at all; So are the Subjects, in the presence of the Soveraign. And though they shine some more, some lesse, when they are out of his sight; yet in his presence, they shine no more than the Starres in presence of the Sun.

[94]
Soveraigne
Power not so
hurtfull as the
want of it,
and the hurt
proceeds for
the greatest
part from not
submitting
readily, to a
lesse.
But a man may here object, that the Condition of Subjects is very miserable; as being obnoxious to the lusts, and other irregular passions of him, or them that have so unlimited a Power in their hands. And commonly they that live under a Monarch, think it the fault of Monarchy; and they that live under the government of Democracy, or other Soveraign Assembly, attribute all the inconvenience to that forme of Common-wealth; whereas the Power in all formes, if they be perfect[7] enough to protect them, is the same; not considering that the estate of Man can never be without some incommodity or other; and that the greatest, that in any forme of Government can possibly happen to the people in generall, is scarce sensible, in respect of[8] the miseries, and horrible calamities, that accompany a Civill Warre; or that dissolute condition of masterlesse men, without subjection to Lawes, and a coërcive Power to tye their hands from rapine, and revenge: nor considering that the greatest pressure[9] of Soveraign Governours, proceedeth not from any delight, or profit they can expect in the dammage, or weakening of their Subjects, in whose vigor, consisteth their own strength and glory; but in the restiveness of themselves, that unwillingly contributing to their own defence, make it necessary for their Governours to draw from them what they can in time of Peace, that they may have means on any emergent occasion, or sudden need, to resist, or take advantage of their Enemies. For all men are by nature provided of notable multiplying[1] glasses, (that is their Passions and Selfe-love,) through which, every little payment appeareth a great grievance; but are destitute of those prospective glasses, (namely Morall and Civill Science,) to see a farre off the miseries that hang over them, and cannot without such payments be avoyded.

Chap. XIX.

Of the severall Kinds of Common-Wealth by Institution, and of Succession to the Soveraigne Power.

The different
Formes of
Common-
wealths but
three.
The difference of Common-wealths, consisteth in the difference of the Soveraign, or the Person representative of all and every one of the Multitude. And because the Soveraignty is either in one Man, or in an Assembly of more than one; and into that Assembly either Every man hath right to enter, or not every one, but Certain men distinguished from the rest; it is manifest, there can be but Three kinds of Common-wealth. For the Representative must needs be One man, or More: and if more, then it is the Assembly of All, or but of a Part. When the Representative is One man, then is the Common-wealth a MONARCHY: when an Assembly of All that will come together, then it is a DEMOC-RACY, or Popular Common-wealth: when an Assembly of a Part onely,

7. Complete.
8. Compared with.
9. Oppression, burden.
1. Magnifying.

then it is called an ARISTOCRACY. Other kind of Common-wealth there can be none: for either One, or More, or All, must have the Soveraign Power (which I have shewn to be indivisible) entire.

There be other names of Government, in the Histories, and books of Policy; as *Tyranny,* and *Oligarchy:* But they are not the names of other Formes of Government, but of the same Formes misliked. For they that are discontented under *Monarchy,* call it *Tyranny;* and they that are displeased with *Aristocracy,* called it *Oligarchy:* So also, they which find themselves grieved under a *Democracy,* call it *Anarchy,* (which signifies want of Government;) and yet I think no man believes, that want of Government, is any new kind of Government: nor by the same reason ought they to believe, that the Government is of one kind, when they like it, and another, when they mislike it, or are oppressed by the Governours.

[95]
Tyranny and Oligarchy, but different names of Monarchy, and Aristocracy.

It is manifest, that men who are in absolute liberty, may, if they please, give Authority to One man, to represent them every one; as well as give such Authority to any Assembly of men whatsoever; and consequently may subject themselves, if they think good, to a Monarch, as absolutely, as to any other Representative. Therefore, where there is already erected a Soveraign Power, there can be no other Representative of the same people, but onely to certain particular ends, by the Soveraign limited. For that were to erect two Soveraigns; and every man to have his person represented by two Actors, that by opposing one another, must needs divide that Power, which (if men will live in Peace) is indivisible; and thereby reduce the Multitude into the condition of Warre, contrary to the end for which all Soveraignty is instituted. And therefore as it is absurd, to think that a Soveraign Assembly, inviting the People of their Dominion, to send up their Deputies, with power to make known their Advise, or Desires, should therefore hold such Deputies, rather than themselves, for the absolute Representative of the people: so it is absurd also, to think the same in a Monarchy. And I know not how this so manifest a truth, should of late be so little observed; that in a Monarchy, he that had the Soveraignty from a descent of 600 years, was alone called Soveraign, had the title of Majesty from every one of his Subjects, and was unquestionably taken by them for their King, was notwithstanding never considered as their Representative; that name without contradiction passing for the title of those men, which at his command were sent up by the people to carry their Petitions, and give him (if he permitted it) their advise. Which may serve as an admonition, for those that are the true, and absolute Representative of a People, to instruct men in the nature of that Office, and to take heed how they admit of any other generall Representation upon any occasion whatsoever, if they mean to discharge the trust committed to them.

Subordinate Representatives dangerous.

The difference between these three kindes of Common-wealth, consisteth not in the difference of Power; but in the difference of Convenience, or Aptitude to produce the Peace, and Security of the people; for which end they were instituted. And to compare Monarchy with the other two, we may observe; First, that whosoever beareth the Person

Comparison of Monarchy, with Soveraign Assemblyes.

of the people, or is one of that Assembly that bears it, beareth also his
[96] own naturall Person. And though he be carefull in his politique Person
to procure the common interest; yet he is more, or no lesse carefull to
procure the private good of himselfe, his family, kindred and friends;
and for the most part, if the publique interest chance to crosse the
private, he preferrs the private: for the Passions of men, are commonly
more potent than their Reason. From whence it follows, that where the
publique and private interest are most closely united, there is the publique most advanced. Now in Monarchy, the private interest is the same
with the publique. The riches, power, and honour of a Monarch arise
onely from the riches, strength and reputation of his Subjects. For no
King can be rich, nor glorious, nor secure; whose Subjects are either
poore, or contemptible, or too weak through want, or dissention, to
maintain a war against their enemies: Whereas in a Democracy, or
Aristocracy, the publique prosperity conferres[1] not so much to the private fortune of one that is corrupt, or ambitious, as doth many times a
perfidious advice, a treacherous action, or a Civill warre.

Secondly, that a Monarch receiveth counsell of whom, when, and
where he pleaseth; and consequently may heare the opinion of men
versed in the matter about which he deliberates, of what rank or quality
soever, and as long before the time of action, and with as much secrecy,
as he will. But when a Soveraigne Assembly has need of Counsell,
none are admitted but such as have a Right thereto from the beginning;
which for the most part are of those who have beene versed more in
the acquisition of Wealth than of Knowledge; and are to give their
advice in long discourses, which may, and do commonly excite men
to action, but not governe them in it. For the *Understanding* is by the
flame of the Passions, never enlightned, but dazled: Nor is there any
place, or time, wherein an Assemblie can receive Counsell with secre-
cie, because of their owne Multitude.

Thirdly, that the Resolutions of a Monarch, are subject to no other
Inconstancy, than that of Humane Nature; but in Assemblies, besides
that of Nature, there ariseth an Inconstancy from the Number. For the
absence of a few, that would have the Resolution once taken, continue
firme, (which may happen by security,[2] negligence, or private impediments,) or the diligent appearance of a few of the contrary opinion,
undoes to day, all that was concluded yesterday.

Fourthly, that a Monarch cannot disagree with himselfe, out of envy,
or interest; but an Assembly may; and that to such a height, as may
produce a Civill Warre.

Fifthly, that in Monarchy there is this inconvenience; that any Subject, by the power of one man, for the enriching of a favourite or
flatterer, may be deprived of all he possesseth; which I confesse is a
great and inevitable inconvenience. But the same may as well happen,
where the Soveraigne Power is in an Assembly: For their power is the
same; and they are as subject to evill Counsell, and to be seduced by
Orators, as a Monarch by Flatterers; and becoming one an others Flat-

1. Contributes.
2. Unfounded confidence.

terers, serve one anothers Covetousnesse and Ambition by turnes. And whereas the Favorites of Monarchs, are few, and they have none els to advance but their owne Kindred; the Favorites of an Assembly, are many; and the Kindred much more numerous, than of any Monarch.   [97] Besides, there is no Favourite of a Monarch, which cannot as well succour his friends, as hurt his enemies: But Orators, that is to say, Favorites of Soveraigne Assemblies, though they have great power to hurt, have little to save. For to accuse, requires lesse Eloquence (such is mans Nature) than to excuse; and condemnation, than absolution more resembles Justice.

Sixtly, that it is an inconvenience in Monarchie, that the Soveraigntie may descend upon an Infant, or one that cannot discerne between Good and Evill: and consisteth in this, that the use of his Power, must be in the hand of another Man, or of some Assembly of men, which are to governe by his right, and in his name; as Curators, and Protectors of his Person, and Authority. But to say there is inconvenience, in putting the use of the Soveraign Power, into the hand of a Man, or an Assembly of men; is to say that all Government is more Inconvenient, than Confusion, and Civill Warre. And therefore all the danger that can be pretended, must arise from the Contention of those, that for an office of so great honour, and profit, may become Competitors. To make it appear, that this inconvenience, proceedeth not from that forme of Government we call Monarchy, we are to consider, that the precedent Monarch, hath appointed who shall have the Tuition[3] of his Infant Successor, either expressely by Testament, or tacitly, by not controlling the Custome in that case received: And then such inconvenience (if it happen) is to be attributed, not to the Monarchy, but to the Ambition, and Injustice of the Subjects; which in all kinds of Government, where the people are not well instructed in their Duty, and the Rights of Soveraignty, is the same. Or else the precedent Monarch, hath not at all taken order for such Tuition; And then the Law of Nature hath provided this sufficient rule, That the Tuition shall be in him, that hath by Nature most interest in the preservation of the Authority of the Infant, and to whom least benefit can accrue by his death, or diminution. For seeing every man by nature seeketh his own benefit, and promotion; to put an Infant into the power of those, that can promote themselves by his destruction, or dammage, is not Tuition, but Trechery. So that sufficient provision being taken, against all just quarrell, about the Government under a Child, if any contention arise to the disturbance of the publique Peace, it is not to be attributed to the forme of Monarchy, but to the ambition of Subjects, and ignorance of their Duty. On the other side, there is no great Common-wealth, the Soveraignty whereof is in a great Assembly, which is not, as to consultations of Peace, and Warre, and making of Lawes, in the same condition, as if the Government were in a Child. For as a Child wants the judgement to dissent from counsell given him, and is thereby necessitated to take the advise of them, or him, to whom he is committed: So

3. Custody.

an Assembly wanteth the liberty, to dissent from the counsell of the major part, be it good, or bad. And as a Child has need of a Tutor, or Protector, to preserve his Person, and Authority: So also (in great Common-wealths,) the Soveraign Assembly, in all great dangers and troubles, have need of *Custodes libertatis*; that is of Dictators, or Protectors of their Authoritie; which are as much as Temporary Monarchs; to whom for a time, they may commit the entire exercise of their Power; and have (at the end of that time) been oftner deprived thereof, than Infant Kings, by their Protectors, Regents, or any other Tutors.

[98]

    Though the Kinds of Soveraigntie be, as I have now shewn, but three; that is to say, Monarchie, where One Man has it; or Democracie, where the generall Assembly of Subjects hath it; or Aristocracie, where it is in an Assembly of certain persons nominated, or otherwise distinguished from the rest: Yet he that shall consider the particular Common-wealthes that have been, and are in the world, will not perhaps easily reduce them to three, and may thereby be inclined to think there be other Formes, arising from these mingled together. As for example, Elective Kingdomes; where Kings have the Soveraigne Power put into their hands for a time; or Kingdomes, wherein the King hath a power limited: which Governments, are nevertheles by most Writers called Monarchie. Likewise if a Popular, or Aristocraticall Common-wealth, subdue an Enemies Countrie, and govern the same, by a President, Procurator, or other Magistrate; this may seeme perhaps at first sight, to be a Democraticall, or Aristocraticall Government. But it is not so. For Elective Kings, are not Soveraignes, but Ministers of the Soveraigne; nor limited Kings Soveraignes, but Ministers of them that have the Soveraigne Power: Nor are those Provinces which are in subjection to a Democracie, or Aristocracie of another Common-wealth, Democratically, or Aristocratically governed, but Monarchically.

    And first, concerning an Elective King, whose power is limited to his life, as it is in many places of Christendome at this day; or to certaine Yeares or Moneths, as the Dictators power amongst the Romans; If he have Right to appoint his Successor, he is no more Elective but Hereditary. But if he have no Power to elect his Successor, then there is some other Man, or Assembly known, which after his decease may elect a new, or else the Common-wealth dieth, and dissolveth with him, and returneth to the condition of Warre. If it be known who have the power to give the Soveraigntie after his death, it is known also that the Soveraigntie was in them before: For none have right to give that which they have not right to possesse, and keep to themselves, if they think good. But if there be none that can give the Soveraigntie, after the decease of him that was first elected; then has he power, nay he is obliged by the Law of Nature, to provide, by establishing his Successor, to keep those that had trusted him with the Government, from relapsing into the miserable condition of Civill warre. And consequently he was, when elected, a Soveraign absolute.

    Secondly, that King whose power is limited, is not superiour to him, or them that have the power to limit it; and he that is not superiour, is not supreme; that is to say not Soveraign. The Soveraignty therefore

was alwaies in that Assembly which had the Right to Limit him; and
by consequence the government not Monarchy, but either Democracy,
or Aristocracy; as of old time in *Sparta*; where the Kings had a priviledge to lead their Armies; but the Soveraignty was in the *Ephori*.

Thirdly, whereas heretofore the Roman People, governed the land
of *Judea* (for example) by a President; yet was not *Judea* therefore a
Democracy; because they were not governed by any Assembly, into the
which, any of them, had right to enter; nor by an Aristocracy; because
they were not governed by any Assembly, into which, any man could
enter by their Election: but they were governed by one Person, which
though as to the people of *Rome* was an Assembly of the people, or
Democracy; yet as to people of *Judea*, which had no right at all of
participating in the government, was a Monarch. For though where the
people are governed by an Assembly, chosen by themselves out of their
own number, the government is called a Democracy, or Aristocracy;
yet when they are governed by an Assembly, not of their own choosing,
'tis a Monarchy; not of *One* man, over another man; but of one people,
over another people.

Of all these Formes of Government, the matter being mortall, so that   *Of the Right*
not onely Monarchs, but also whole Assemblies dy, it is necessary for   *of Succession.*
the conservation of the peace of men, that as there was order taken for
an Artificiall Man, so there be order also taken, for an Artificiall Eternity
of life; without which, men that are governed by an Assembly, should
return into the condition of Warre in every age; and they that are
governed by One man, assoon as their Governour dyeth. This Artificiall
Eternity, is that which men call the Right of *Succession*.

There is no perfect forme of Government, where the disposing of
the Succession is not in the present Soveraign. For if it be in any other
particular Man, or private Assembly, it is in a person subject, and may
be assumed by the Soveraign at his pleasure; and consequently the
Right is in himselfe. And if it be in no particular man, but left to a
new choyce; then is the Common-wealth dissolved; and the Right is in
him that can get it; contrary to the intention of them that did Institute
the Common-wealth, for their perpetuall, and not temporary security.

In a Democracy, the whole Assembly cannot faile, unlesse the Multitude that are to be governed faile. And therefore questions of the right
of Succession, have in that forme of Government no place at all.

In an Aristocracy, when any of the Assembly dyeth, the election of
another into his room[4] belongeth to the Assembly, as the Soveraign, to
whom belongeth the choosing of all Counsellours, and Officers. For
that which the Representative doth, as Actor, every one of the Subjects
doth, as Author. And though the Soveraign Assembly, may give Power
to others, to elect new men, for supply of their court; yet it is still by
their Authority, that the Election is made; and by the same it may
(when the publique shall require it) be recalled.

The greatest difficultie about the right of Succession, is in Monarchy:
And the difficulty ariseth from this, that at first sight, it is not manifest   *The present*
                                                                          Monarch hath
                                                                          Right to

4. To take his place.

dispose of the who is to appoint the Successor; nor many times, who it is whom he
Succession. hath appointed. For in both these cases, there is required a more exact
ratiocination, than every man is accustomed to use. As to the question,
who shall appoint the Successor, of a Monarch that hath the Soveraign
Authority; that is to say, who shall determine of the right of Inheritance,
(for Elective Kings and Princes have not the Soveraign Power in propriety, but in use only,) we are to consider, that either he that is in
possession, has right to dispose of the Succession, or else that right is
again in the dissolved Multitude. For the death of him that hath the
Soveraign power in propriety, leaves the Multitude without any Soveraign at all; that is, without any Representative in whom they should
be united, and be capable of doing any one action at all: And therefore
they are incapable of Election of any new Monarch; every man having
equall right to submit himselfe to such as he thinks best able to protect
him; or if he can, protect himselfe by his owne sword, which is a
returne to Confusion, and to the condition of a War of every man
against every man, contrary to the end for which Monarchy had its first
Institution. Therefore it is manifest, that by the Institution of Monarchy,
the disposing of the Successor, is alwaies left to the Judgment and Will
of the present Possessor.

And for the question (which may arise sometimes) who it is that the
Monarch in possession, hath designed[5] to the succession and inheritance of his power; it is determined by his express Words, and Testament; or by other tacite signes sufficient.

Succession By express Words, or Testament, when it is declared by him in his
passeth by ex- life time, *viva voce,*[6] or by Writing; as the first Emperours of *Rome*
presse Words; declared who should be their Heires. For the word Heire does not of
it selfe imply the Children, or nearest Kindred of a man; but whomsoever a man shall any way declare, he would have to succeed him in
his Estate. If therefore a Monarch declare expresly, that such a man
shall be his Heire, either by Word or Writing, then is that man immediately after the decease of his Predecessor, Invested in the right of
being Monarch.

Or, by not But where Testament, and expresse Words are wanting, other natur-
controlling a all signes of the Will are to be [followed][7]: whereof the one is Custome.
Custome; And therefore where the Custome is, that the next of Kindred absolutely
succeedeth, there also the next of Kindred hath right to the Succession;
for that, if the will of him that was in posession had been otherwise,
he might easily have declared the same in his life time. And likewise
where the Custome is, that the next of the Male Kindred succeedeth,
there also the right of Succession is in the next of the Kindred Male,
for the same reason. And so it is if the Custome were to advance the
Female. For whatsoever Custome a man may by a word controule, and
does not, it is a naturall signe he would have that Custome stand.

But where neither Custome, nor Testament hath preceded, there it
[101] is to be understood, First, that a Monarchs will is, that the government

---

5. Designated.
6. Orally.
7. Large paper edition has *allowed.*

remain Monarchicall; because he hath approved that government in *Or, by pre-* himselfe. Secondly, that a Child of his own, Male, or Female, be pre- *sumption of* ferred before any other; because men are presumed to be more en- *naturall* clined by nature, to advance their own children, than the children of *affection.* other men; and of their own, rather a Male than a Female; because men, are naturally fitter than women, for actions of labour and danger. Thirdly, where his own Issue faileth, rather a Brother than a stranger; and so still the neerer in bloud, rather than the more remote; because it is alwayes presumed that the neerer of kin, is the neerer in affection; and 'tis evident that a man receives alwayes, by reflexion, the most honour from the greatnesse of his neerest kindred.

But if it be lawfull for a Monarch to dispose of the Succession by *To dispose of* words of Contract, or Testament, men may perhaps object a great in- *the Succes-* convenience: for he may sell, or give his Right of governing to a *sion, though* stranger; which, because strangers (that is, men not used to live under *to a King of* the same government, nor speaking the same language) do commonly *another Na-* undervalue one another, may turn to the oppression of his Subjects; *tion, not* which is indeed a great inconvenience: but it proceedeth not necessarily *unlawfull.* from the subjection to a strangers government, but from the unskilful- nesse of the Governours, ignorant of the true rules of Politiques. And therefore the Romans when they had subdued many Nations, to make their Government digestible, were wont to take away that grievance, as much as they thought necessary, by giving sometimes to whole Nations, and sometimes to Principall men of every Nation they conquered, not onely the Privileges, but also the Name of Romans; and took many of them into the Senate, and Offices of charge, even in the Roman City. And this was it our most wise King, King *James*, aymed at, in endeav- ouring the Union of his two Realms of *England* and *Scotland*. Which if he could have obtained, had in all likelihood prevented the Civill warres, which make both those Kingdomes, at this present, miserable. It is not therefore any injury to the people, for a Monarch to dispose of the Succession by Will; though by the fault of many Princes, it hath been sometimes found inconvenient. Of the lawfulnesse of it, this also is an argument, that whatsoever inconvenience can arrive by giving a Kingdome to a stranger, may arrive also by so marrying with strangers, as the Right of Succession may descend upon them: yet this by all men is accounted lawfull.

Chap. XX.

Of Dominion PATERNALL, and DESPOTICALL.

A *Common-wealth by Acquisition*, is that, where the Soveraign Power *A Common-* is acquired by Force; And it is acquired by force, when men singly, or *wealth by* many together by plurality of voyces, for fear of death, or bonds, do *Acquisition.* authorise all the actions of that Man, or Assembly, that hath their lives [102] and liberty in his Power.

And this kind of Dominion, or Soveraignty, differeth from Sover-

Wherein different from a Common-wealth by Institution.

aignty by Institution, onely in this, That men who choose their Soveraign, do it for fear of one another, and not of him whom they Institute: But in this case, they subject themselves, to him they are afraid of. In both cases they do it for fear: which is to be noted by them, that hold all such Covenants, as proceed from fear of death, or violence, voyd: which if it were true, no man, in any kind of Common-wealth, could be obliged to Obedience. It is true, that in a Common-wealth once Instituted, or acquired, Promises proceeding from fear of death, or violence, are no Covenants, nor obliging, when the thing promised is contrary to the Lawes; But the reason is not, because it was made upon fear, but because he that promiseth, hath no right in the thing promised. Also, when he may lawfully performe, and doth not, it is not the Invalidity of the Covenant, that absolveth him, but the Sentence of the Soveraign. Otherwise, whensoever a man lawfully promiseth, he unlawfully breaketh: But when the Soveraign, who is the Actor, acquitteth him, then he is acquitted by him that extorted the promise, as by the Author of such absolution.

The Rights of Soveraignty the same in both.

But the Rights, and Consequences of Soveraignty, are the same in both. His Power cannot, without his consent, be Transferred to another: He cannot Forfeit it: He cannot be Accused by any of his Subjects, of Injury: He cannot be Punished by them: He is Judge of what is necessary for Peace; and Judge of Doctrines: He is Sole Legislator; and Supreme Judge of Controversies; and of the Times, and Occasions of Warre, and Peace: to him it belongeth to choose Magistrates, Counsellours, Commanders, and all other Officers, and Ministers; and to determine of Rewards, and Punishments, Honour, and Order. The reasons whereof, are the same which are alledged in the precedent Chapter, for the same Rights, and Consequences of Soveraignty by Institution.

Dominion Paternall how attained.

Dominion is acquired two wayes; By Generation, and by Conquest. The right of Dominion by Generation, is that, which the Parent hath over his Children; and is called PATERNALL. And is not so derived from the Generation, as if therefore the Parent had Dominion over his Child because he begat him; but from the Childs Consent, either expresse,

Not by Generation, but by Contract;

or by other sufficient arguments declared. For as to the Generation, God hath ordained to man a helper; and there be alwayes two that are equally Parents: the Dominion therefore over the Child, should belong equally to both; and he be equally subject to both, which is impossible; for no man can obey two Masters. And whereas some have attributed the Dominion to the Man onely, as being of the more excellent Sex; they misreckon in it. For there is not alwayes that difference of strength, or prudence between the man and the woman, as that the right can be determined without War. In Common-wealths, this controversie is decided by the Civill Law: and for the most part, (but not alwayes) the

[103]

sentence is in favour of the Father; because for the most part Common-wealths have been erected by the Fathers, not by the Mothers of families. But the question lyeth now in the state of meer Nature; where there are supposed no lawes of Matrimony; no lawes for the Education of Children; but the Law of Nature, and the naturall inclination of the

Sexes, one to another, and to their children. In this condition of meer Nature, either the Parents between themselves dispose of the dominion over the Child by Contract; or do not dispose thereof at all. If they dispose thereof, the right passeth according to the Contract. We find in History that the *Amazons* Contracted with the Men of the neighbouring Countries, to whom they had recourse for issue, that the issue Male should be sent back, but the Female remain with themselves: so that the dominion of the Females was in the Mother.

If there be no Contract, the Dominion is in the Mother. For in the condition of meer Nature, where there are no Matrimoniall lawes, it cannot be known who is the Father, unlesse it be declared by the Mother: and therefore the right of Dominion over the Child dependeth on her will, and is consequently hers. Again, seeing the Infant is first in the power of the Mother, so as she may either nourish, or expose it; if she nourish it, it oweth its life to the Mother; and is therefore obliged to obey her, rather than any other; and by consequence the Dominion over it is hers. But if she expose it, and another find, and nourish it, the Dominion is in him that nourisheth it. For it ought to obey him by whom it is preserved; because preservation of life being the end, for which one man becomes subject to another, every man is supposed to promise obedience, to him, in whose power it is to save, or destroy him. *Or Education;*

If the Mother be the Fathers subject, the Child, is in the Fathers power: and if the Father be the Mothers subject, (as when a Soveraign Queen marrieth one of her subjects,) the Child is subject to the Mother; because the Father also is her subject. *Or Precedent subjection of one of the Parents to the other.*

If a man and a woman, Monarches of two severall Kingdomes, have a Child, and contract concerning who shall have the Dominion of him, the Right of the Dominion passeth by the Contract. If they contract not, the Dominion followeth the Dominion of the place of his residence. For the Soveraign of each Country hath Dominion over all that reside therein.

He that hath the Dominion over the Child, hath Dominion also over the Children of the Child; and over their Childrens Children. For he that hath Dominion over the person of a man, hath Dominion over all that is his; without which, Dominion were but a Title, without the effect.

The Right of Succession to Paternall Dominion, proceedeth in the same manner, as doth the Right of Succession to Monarchy; of which I have already sufficiently spoken in the precedent chapter. *The Right of Succession followeth the Rules of the Right of Possession.*

Dominion acquired by Conquest, or Victory in war, is that which some Writers call DESPOTICALL, from Δεσπότης[1] which signifieth a *Lord*, or *Master*; and is the Dominion of the Master over his Servant. And this Dominion is then acquired to the Victor, when the Vanquished, toavoyd the present stroke of death, covenanteth either in expresse words, or by other sufficient signes of the Will, that so long as his life, and the liberty of his body is allowed him, the Victor shall have the use thereof, at his pleasure. And after such Covenant made, the *[104] Despoticall Dominion how attained.*

1. Despotes.

Vanquished is a SERVANT, and not before: for by the word *Servant* (whether it be derived from *Servire*, to Serve, or from *Servare*, to Save, which I leave to Grammarians to dispute) is not meant a Captive, which is kept in prison, or bonds, till the owner of him that took him, or bought him of one that did, shall consider what to do with him: (for such men, (commonly called Slaves,) have no obligation at all; but may break their bonds, or the prison; and kill, or carry away captive their Master, justly:) but one, that being taken, hath corporall liberty allowed him; and upon promise not to run away, nor to do violence to his Master, is trusted by him.

Not by the Victory, but by the Consent of the Vanquished.

It is not therefore the Victory, that giveth the right of Dominion over the Vanquished, but his own Covenant. Nor is he obliged because he is Conquered; that is to say, beaten, and taken, or put to flight; but because he commeth in, and Submitteth to the Victor; Nor is the Victor obliged by an enemies rendring himselfe, (without promise of life,) to spare him for this his yeelding to discretion;[2] which obliges not the Victor longer, than in his own discretion hee shall think fit.

And that which men do, when they demand (as it is now called) *Quarter*, (which the Greeks called Ζωγρία,[3] *taking alive*,) is to evade the present fury of the Victor, by Submission, and to compound for their life, with Ransome, or Service: and therefore he that hath Quarter hath not his life given, but deferred till farther deliberation; For it is not an yeelding on condition of life, but to discretion. And then onely is his life in security, and his service due, when the Victor hath trusted him with his corporall liberty. For Slaves that work in Prisons, or Fetters, do it not of duty, but to avoyd the cruelty of their task-masters.

The Master of the Servant, is Master also of all he hath; and may exact the use thereof; that is to say, of his goods, of his labour, of his servants, and of his children, as often as he shall think fit. For he holdeth his life of his Master, by the covenant of obedience; that is, of owning, and authorising whatsoever the Master shall do. And in case the Master, if he refuse, kill him, or cast him into bonds, or otherwise punish him for his disobedience, he is himselfe the author of the same; and cannot accuse him of injury.

In summe, the Rights and Consequences of both *Paternall* and *Despoticall* Dominion, are the very same with those of a Soveraign by Institution; and for the same reasons: which reasons are set down in the precedent chapter. So that for a man that is Monarch of divers Nations, whereof he hath, in one the Soveraignty by Institution of the people assembled, and in another by Conquest, that is by the submission of each particular, to avoyd death or bonds; to demand of one Nation more than of the other, from the title of Conquest, as being a Conquered Nation, is an act of ignorance of the Rights of Soveraignty. For the Soveraign is absolute over both alike; or else there is no Soveraignty at all; and so every man may Lawfully protect himselfe, if he can, with his own sword, which is the condition of war.

[105]

By this it appears, that a great Family if it be not part of some

2. Submitting to arbitrary power.
3. *Zogria.*

Common-wealth, is of it self, as to the Rights of Soveraignty, a little | *Difference be-*
Monarchy; whether that Family consist of a man and his children; or | *tween a Fam-*
of a man and his servants; or of a man, and his children, and servants | *ily and a*
together: wherein the Father or Master is the Soveraign. But yet a | *Kingdom.*
Family is not properly a Common-wealth; unlesse it be of that power
by its own number, or by other opportunities, as not to be subdued
without the hazard of war. For where a number of men are manifestly
too weak to defend themselves united, every one may use his own
reason in time of danger, to save his own life, either by flight, or by
submission to the enemy, as hee shall think best; in the same manner
as a very small company of souldiers, surprised by an army, may cast
down their armes, and demand quarter, or run away, rather than be
put to the sword. And thus much shall suffice; concerning what I find
by speculation, and deduction, of Soveraign Rights, from the nature,
need, and designes of men, in erecting of Common-wealths, and putting themselves under Monarchs, or Assemblies, entrusted with power
enough for their protection.

Let us now consider what the Scripture teacheth in the same point. | *The Rights of*
To *Moses*, the children of *Israel* say thus. * *Speak thou to us, and we* | *Monarchy from*
will heare thee; but let not God speak to us, lest we dye. This is absolute | *Scripture.*
obedience to *Moses*. Concerning the Right of Kings, God himself by | **Exod. 20.19.*
the mouth of *Samuel*, saith, * *This shall be the Right of the King you* | **I Sam 8.11,*
will have to reigne over you. He shall take your sons, and set them to | *12, &c.*
drive his Chariots, and to be his horsemen, and to run before his chariots;
and gather in his harvest; and to make his engines of War, and Instru-
ments of his chariots; and shall take your daughters to make perfumes,
to be his Cookes, and Bakers. He shall take your fields, your vine-yards,
and your olive-yards, and give them to his servants. He shall take the
tyth of your corne and wine, and give it to the men of his chamber, and
to his other servants. He shall take your man-servants, and your maid-
servants, and the choice of your youth, and employ them in his businesse.
He shall take the tyth of your flocks; and you shall be his servants. This
is absolute power, and summed up in the last words, *you shall be his*
servants. Againe, when the people heard what power their King was to
have, yet they consented thereto, and say thus, * *We will be as all other* | **Verse. 19,*
nations, and our King shall judge our causes, and goe before us, to | *&c.*
conduct our wars. Here is confirmed the Right that Soveraigns have,
both to the *Militia*, and to all *Judicature*; in which is conteined as
absolute power, as one man can possibly transferre to another. Again,
the prayer of King *Salomon* to God, was this. * *Give to thy servant* | **I Kings 3.9.*
understanding, to judge thy people, and to discerne between Good and
Evill. It belongeth therefore to the Soveraigne to bee *Judge*, and to | [106]
præscribe the Rules of *discerning Good and Evill*: which Rules are
Lawes; and therefore in him is the Legislative Power. *Saul* sought the
life of *David*; yet when it was in his power to slay *Saul*, and his Servants
would have done it, *David* forbad them, saying, * *God forbid I should* | **I Sam. 24.9.*
do such an act against my Lord, the anoynted of God. For obedience
of servants St. *Paul* saith, * *Servants obey your masters in All things*; | **Coll. 3.20.*
and, * *Children obey your Parents in All things.* There is simple obe- | **Verse 22.*

dience in those that are subject to Paternall or Despoticall Dominion.

*Math.
23.2,3. Again, * *The Scribes and Pharisees sit in Moses chayre, and therefore All that they shall bid you observe, that observe and do.* There again is
*Tit. 3.2. simple obedience. And St *Paul,* * *Warn them that they subject themselves to Princes, and to those that are in Authority, & obey them.* This obedience is also simple. Lastly, our Saviour himselfe acknowledges, that men ought to pay such taxes as are by Kings imposed, where he sayes, *Give to Cæsar that which is Cæsars;* and payed such taxes himselfe. And that the Kings word, is sufficient to take any thing from any Subject, when there is need; and that the King is Judge of that need:
*Mat. 21.2, 3. For he himselfe, as King of the Jewes, commanded his Disciples to take the Asse, and Asses Colt to carry him into *Jerusalem,* saying, * *Go into the Village over against you, and you shall find a shee Asse tyed, and her Colt with her, unty them, and bring them to me. And if any man ask you, what you mean by it, Say the Lord hath need of them: And they will let them go.* They will not ask whether his necessity be a sufficient title; nor whether he be judge of that necessity; but acquiesce in the will of the Lord.

*Gen. 3.5. To these places may be added also that of *Genesis,* * *You shall be as Gods, knowing Good and Evill.* And verse II. *Who told thee that thou wast naked? hast thou eaten of the tree, of which I commanded thee thou shouldest not eat?* For the Cognisance or Judicature of *Good* and *Evill,* being forbidden by the name of the fruit of the tree of Knowledge, as a triall of *Adams* obedience; The Divel to enflame the Ambition of the woman, to whom that fruit already seemed beautifull, told her that by tasting it, they should be as Gods, knowing *Good* and *Evill.* Whereupon having both eaten, they did indeed take upon them Gods office, which is Judicature of Good and Evill; but acquired no new ability to distinguish between them aright. And whereas it is sayd, that having eaten, they saw they were naked; no man hath so interpreted that place, as if they had been formerly blind, and saw not their own skins: the meaning is plain, that it was then they first judged their nakednesse (wherein it was Gods will to create them) to be uncomely;[4] and by being ashamed, did tacitely censure God himselfe. And thereupon God saith, *Hast thou eaten, &c.* as if he should say, doest thou that owest me obedience, take upon thee to judge of my Commandements? Whereby it is cleerly, (though Allegorically,) signified, that the Commands of them that have the right to command, are not by their Subjects to be censured, nor disputed.

[107]
*Soveraign
Power ought
in all
Common-
wealths to be
absolute.* So that it appeareth plainly, to my understanding, both from Reason, and Scripture, that the Soveraign Power, whether placed in One Man, as in Monarchy, or in one Assembly of men, as in Popular, and Aristocraticall Common-wealths, is as great, as possibly men can be imagined to make it. And though of so unlimited a Power, men may fancy many evill consequences, yet the consequences of the want of it, which is perpetuall warre of every man against his neighbour, are much worse. The condition of man in this life shall never be without Inconven-

---

4. Improper.

iences; but there happeneth in no Common-wealth any great Inconvenience, but what proceeds from the Subjects disobedience, and
breach of those Covenants, from which the Common-wealth hath its
being. And whosoever thinking Soveraign Power too great, will seek to
make it lesse; must subject himselfe, to the Power, that can limit it;
that is to say, to a greater.

The greatest objection is, that of the Practise; when men ask, where,
and when, such Power has by Subjects been acknowledged. But one
may ask them again, when, or where has there been a Kingdome long
free from Sedition and Civill Warre. In those Nations, whose Common-
wealths have been long-lived, and not been destroyed, but by forraign
warre, the Subjects never did dispute of the Soveraign Power. But howsoever, an argument from the Practise of men, that have not sifted to
the bottom, and with exact reason weighed the causes, and nature of
Common-wealths, and suffer daily those miseries, that proceed from
the ignorance thereof, is invalid. For though in all places of the world,
men should lay the foundation of their houses on the sand, it could
not thence be inferred, that so it ought to be. The skill of making, and
maintaining Common-wealths, consisteth in certain Rules, as doth
Arithmetique and Geometry; not (as Tennis-play) on Practise onely:
which Rules, neither poor men have the leisure, nor men that have
had the leisure, have hitherto had the curiosity, or the method to find
out.

Chap. XXI.

Of the LIBERTY of Subjects.

LIBERTY, or FREEDOME, signifieth (properly) the absence of Oppo-   *Liberty what.*
sition; (by Opposition, I mean externall Impediments of motion;) and
may be applyed no lesse to Irrationall, and Inanimate creatures, than
to Rationall. For whatsoever is so tyed, or environed, as it cannot move,
but within a certain space, which space is determined by the opposition
of some externall body, we say it hath not Liberty to go further. And
so of all living creatures, whilest they are imprisoned, or restrained,
with walls, or chayns; and of the water whilest it is kept in by banks,
or vessels, that otherwise would spread it selfe into a larger space, we
use to say, they are not at Liberty, to move in such manner, as without
those externall impediments they would. But when the impediment of
motion, is in the constitution of the thing it selfe, we use not to say, it
wants the Liberty; but the Power to move; as when a stone lyeth still,
or a man is fastned to his bed by sicknesse.

And according to this proper, and generally received meaning of the   [108]
word, A FREE-MAN, *is he, that in those things, which by his strength*   What it is to
and wit he is able to do, is not hindred to doe what he has a will to.   be Free
But when the words *Free*, and *Liberty*, are applyed to any thing but
Bodies, they are abused; for that which is not subject to Motion, is not
subject to Impediment: And therefore, when 'tis said (for example) The

way is Free, no Liberty of the way is signified, but of those that walk in it without stop. And when we say a Guift is Free, there is not meant any Liberty of the Guift, but of the Giver, that was not bound by any law, or Covenant to give it. So when we *speak Freely*, it is not the Liberty of voice, or pronunciation, but of the man, whom no law hath obliged to speak otherwise then he did. Lastly, from the use of the word *Free-will*, no Liberty can be inferred of the will, desire, or inclination, but the Liberty of the man; which consisteth in this, that he finds no stop, in doing what he has the will, desire, or inclination to doe.

Feare and Liberty consistent.   Feare, and Liberty are consistent; as when a man throweth his goods into the Sea for *feare* the ship should sink, he doth it neverthelesse very willingly, and may refuse to doe it if he will: It is therefore the action, of one that was *free*: so a man sometimes pays his debt, only for *feare* of Imprisonment, which because no body hindred him from detaining,[1] was the action of a man at *liberty*. And generally all actions which men doe in Common-wealths, for *feare* of the law, are actions, which the doers had *liberty* to omit.

Liberty and Necessity consistent.   *Liberty*, and *Necessity* are consistent: As in the water, that hath not only *liberty*, but a *necessity* of descending by the Channel; so likewise in the Actions which men voluntarily doe: which, because they proceed from their will, proceed from *liberty*; and yet, because every act of mans will, and every desire, and inclination proceedeth from some cause, and that from another cause, in a continuall chaine, (whose first link is in the hand of God the first of all causes,) they proceed from *necessity*. So that to him that could see the connexion of those causes, the *necessity* of all mens voluntary actions, would appeare manifest. And therefore God, that seeth, and disposeth all things, seeth also that the *liberty* of man in doing what he will, is accompanied with the *necessity* of doing that which God will, & no more, nor lesse. For though men may do many things, which God does not command, nor is therefore Author of them; yet they can have no passion, nor appetite to any thing, of which appetite Gods will is not the cause. And did not his will assure the *necessity* of mans will, and consequently of all that on mans will dependeth, the *liberty* of men would be a contradiction, and impediment to the omnipotence and *liberty* of God. And this shall suffice, (as to the matter in hand) of that naturall *liberty*, which only is properly called *liberty*.

Artificiall Bonds, or Covenants.   But as men, for the atteyning of peace, and conservation of themselves thereby, have made an Artificiall Man, which we call a Common-wealth; so also have they made Artificiall Chains, called *Civill Lawes*, which they themselves, by mutuall covenants, have fastned

[109]   at one end, to the lips of that Man, or Assembly, to whom they have given the Soveraigne Power; and at the other end to their own Ears. These Bonds in their own nature but weak, may neverthelesse be made to hold, by the danger, though not by the difficulty of breaking them.

Liberty of Subjects con-   In relation to these Bonds only it is, that I am to speak now, of the *Liberty of Subjects*. For seeing there is no Common-wealth in the

---

1. Withholding.

world, wherein there be Rules enough set down, for the regulating of   *sisteth in Lib-*
all the actions, and words of men, (as being a thing impossible:) it   *erty from*
followeth necessarily, that in all kinds of actions, by the laws præter- *covenants.*
mitted,[2] men have the Liberty, of doing what their own reasons shall
suggest, for the most profitable to themselves. For if wee take Liberty
in the proper sense, for corporall Liberty; that is to say, freedome from
chains, and prison, it were very absurd for men to clamor as they doe,
for the Liberty they so manifestly enjoy. Againe, if we take Liberty, for
an exemption from Lawes, it is no lesse absurd, for men to demand as
they doe, that Liberty, by which all other men may be masters of their
lives. And yet as absurd as it is, this is it they demand; not knowing that
the Lawes are of no power to protect them, without a Sword in the
hands of a man, or men, to cause those laws to be put in execution.
The Liberty of a Subject, lyeth therefore only in those things, which
in regulating their actions, the Soveraign hath prætermitted: such as is
the Liberty to buy, and sell, and otherwise contract with one another;
to choose their own aboad, their own diet, their own trade of life, and
institute[3] their children as they themselves think fit; & the like.

Neverthelesse we are not to understand, that by such Liberty, the   *Liberty of the*
Soveraign Power of life, and death, is either abolished, or limited. For   *Subject consis-*
it has been already shewn, that nothing the Soveraign Representative   *tent with the*
can doe to a Subject, on what pretence soever, can properly be called   *unlimited*
Injustice, or Injury; because every Subject is Author of every act the   *power of the*
Soveraign doth; so that he never wanteth Right to any thing, otherwise,   *Soveraign.*
than as he himself is the Subject of God, and bound thereby to observe
the laws of Nature. And therefore it may, and doth often happen in
Common-wealths, that a Subject may be put to death, by the command
of the Soveraign Power; and yet neither doe the other wrong: As when
Jeptha[4] caused his daughter to be sacrificed: In which, and the like
cases, he that so dieth, had Liberty to doe the action, for which he is
neverthelesse, without Injury put to death. And the same holdeth also
in a Soveraign Prince, that putteth to death an Innocent Subject. For
though the action be against the law of Nature, as being contrary to
Equitie, (as was the killing of *Uriah*, by *David*;) yet it was not an Injurie
to *Uriah*; but to God. Not to *Uriah*, because the right to doe what he
pleased, was given him by *Uriah* himself: And yet to *God*, because
David was *Gods* Subject; and prohibited all Iniquitie by the law of
Nature. Which distinction, *David* himself, when he repented the fact,
evidently confirmed, saying, *To thee only have I sinned.* In the same
manner, the people of *Athens*, when they banished the most potent of   [110]
their Common-wealth for ten years, thought they committed no Injustice; and yet they never questioned what crime he had done; but what
hurt he would doe: Nay they commanded the banishment of they knew
not whom; and every Citizen bringing his Oystershell into the market
place, written with the name of him he desired should be banished,

2. Not mentioned, omitted.
3. Educate.
4. A leader of ancient Israel who promised during the invasion of the Ammonites (c. 1100 B.C.)
to sacrifice the first person he saw after the decisive battle. At it happened, that person was
his daughter.

without actuall accusing him, sometimes banished an *Aristides*, for his reputation of Justice; And sometimes a scurrilous Jester, as *Hyperbolus*, to make a Jest of it. And yet a man cannot say, the Soveraign People of *Athens* wanted right to banish them; or an *Athenian* the Libertie to Jest, or to be Just.

The Liberty which writers praise, is the Liberty of Soveraigns; not of Private men.

The Libertie, whereof there is so frequent, and honourable mention, in the Histories, and Philosophy of the Antient Greeks, and Romans, and in the writings, and discourse of those that from them have received all their learning in the Politiques, is not the Libertie of Particular men; but the Libertie of the Common-wealth: which is the same with that, which every man then should have, if there were no Civil Laws, nor Common-wealth at all. And the effects of it also be the same. For as amongst masterlesse men, there is perpetuall war, of every man against his neighbour; no inheritance, to transmit to the Son, nor to expect from the Father; no propriety of Goods, or Lands; no security; but a full and absolute Libertie in every Particular man: So in States, and Common-wealths not dependent on one another, every Common-wealth, (not every man) has an absolute Libertie, to doe what it shall judge (that is to say, what that Man, or Assemblie that representeth it, shall judge) most conducing to their benefit. But withall, they live in the condition of a perpetuall war, and upon the confines of battel, with their frontiers armed, and canons planted against their neighbours round about. The *Athenians,* and *Romanes* were free; that is, free Common-wealths: not that any particular men had the Libertie to resist their own Representative; but that their Representative had the Libertie to resist, or invade other people. There is written on the Turrets of the city of *Luca* in great characters at this day, the word LIBERTAS; yet no man can thence inferre, that a particular man has more Libertie, or Immunitie from the service of the Commonwealth there, than in *Constantinople*. Whether a Common-wealth be Monarchicall, or Popular, the Freedome is still the same.

But it is an easy thing, for men to be deceived, by the specious name of Libertie; and for want of Judgement to distinguish, mistake that for their Private Inheritance, and Birth right, which is the right of the Publique only. And when the same errour is confirmed by the authority of men in reputation for their writings in this subject, it is no wonder if it produce sedition, and change of Government. In these westerne parts of the world, we are made to receive our opinions concerning the Institution, and Rights of Common-wealths, from *Aristotle, Cicero,* and other men, Greeks and Romanes, that living under Popular States, derived those Rights, not from the Principles of Nature, but transcribed them into their books, out of the Practise of their own Common-wealths, which were Popular; as the Grammarians describe the Rules of Language, out of the Practise of the time; or the Rules of Poetry, out of the Poems of *Homer* and *Virgil*. And because the Athenians were taught, (to keep them from desire of changing their Government,) that they were Freemen, and all that lived under Monarchy were slaves; therefore *Aristotle* puts it down in his *Politiques, (lib. 6. cap. 2.) In democracy, Liberty is to be supposed: for 'tis commonly held, that no*

[111]

man is Free *in any other Government.* And as *Aristotle;* so *Cicero,* and other Writers have grounded their Civill doctrine, on the opinions of the Romans, who were taught to hate Monarchy, at first, by them that having deposed their Soveraign, shared amongst them the Soveraignty of *Rome;* and afterwards by their Successors. And by reading of these Greek, and Latine Authors, men from their childhood have gotten a habit (under a false shew of Liberty,) of favouring tumults, and of licentious controlling the actions of their Soveraigns; and again of controlling those controllers, with the effusion of so much blood; as I think I may truly say, there was never any thing so deerly bought, as these Western parts have bought the learning of the Greek and Latine tongues.

To come now to the particulars of the true Liberty of a Subject; that is to say, what are the things, which though commanded by the Soveraign, he may neverthelesse, without Injustice, refuse to do; we are to consider, what Rights we passe away, when we make a Commonwealth; or (which is all one,) what Liberty we deny our selves, by owning all the Actions (without exception) of the Man, or Assembly we make our Soveraign. For in the act of our *Submission,* consisteth both our *Obligation,* and our *Liberty;* which must therefore be inferred by arguments taken from thence; there being no Obligation on any man, which ariseth not from some Act of his own; for all men equally, are by Nature Free. And because such arguments, must either be drawn from the expresse words, *I Authorise all his Actions,* or from the Intention of him that submitteth himselfe to his Power, (which Intention is to be understood by the End for which he so submitteth;) The Obligation, and Liberty of the Subject, is to be derived, either from those Words, (or others equivalent;) or else from the End of the Institution of Soveraignty; namely, the Peace of the Subjects within themselves, and their Defence against a common Enemy.

Liberty of Subjects how to be measured.

First therefore, seeing Soveraignty by Institution, is by Covenant of every one to every one; and Soveraignty by Acquisition, by Covenants of the Vanquished to the Victor, or Child to the Parent; It is manifest, that every Subject has Liberty in all those things, the right whereof cannot by Covenant be transferred. I have shewn before in the 14. Chapter, that Covenants, not to defend a mans own body, are voyd. Therefore,

Subjects have Liberty to defend their own bodies, even against them that lawfully invade them;

If the Soveraign command a man (though justly condemned,) to kill, wound, or mayme himselfe; or not to resist those that assault him; or to abstain from the use of food, ayre, medicine, or any other thing, without which he cannot live; yet hath that man the Liberty to disobey.

[112]

If a man be interrogated by the Soveraign, or his Authority, concerning a crime done by himselfe, he is not bound (without assurance of Pardon) to confesse it; because no man (as I have shewn in the same Chapter) can be obliged by Covenant to accuse himselfe.

Are not bound to hurt themselves;

Again, the Consent of a Subject to Soveraign Power, is contained in these words, *I Authorise, or take upon me, all his actions;* in which there is no restriction at all, of his own former naturall Liberty: For by allowing him to *kill me,* I am not bound to kill my selfe when he commands me. 'Tis one thing to say, *Kill me, or my fellow, if you please*; another thing to say, *I will kill my selfe, or my fellow*. It followeth therefore, that No man is bound by the words themselves, either to kill himselfe, or any other man; And consequently, that the Obligation a man may sometimes have, upon the Command of the Soveraign to execute any dangerous, or dishonourable Office, dependeth not on the Words of our Submission; but on the Intention; which is to be understood by the End thereof. When therefore our refusall to obey, frustrates the End for which the Soveraignty was ordained; then there is no Liberty to refuse: otherwise there is.

Upon this ground, a man that is commanded as a Souldier to fight against the enemy, though his Soveraign have Right enough to punish his refusall with death, may neverthelesse in many cases refuse, without Injustice; as when he substituteth a sufficient Souldier in his place: for in this case he deserteth not the service of the Common-wealth. And there is allowance to be made for naturall timorousnesse, not onely to women, (of whom no such dangerous duty is expected,) but also to men of feminine courage. When Armies fight, there is on one side, or both, a running away; yet when they do it not out of trechery, but fear, they are not esteemed to do it unjustly, but dishonourably. For the same reason, to avoyd battell, is not Injustice, but Cowardise. But he that inrowleth[5] himselfe a Souldier, or taketh imprest mony,[6] taketh away the excuse of a timorous nature; and is obliged, not onely to go to the battell, but also not to run from it, without his Captaines leave. And when the Defence of the Common-wealth, requireth at once the help of all that are able to bear Arms, every one is obliged; because otherwise the Institution of the Common-wealth, which they have not the purpose, or courage to preserve, was in vain.

To resist the Sword of the Common-wealth, in defence of another man, guilty, or innocent, no man hath Liberty; because such Liberty, takes away from the Soveraign, the means of Protecting us; and is therefore destructive of the very essence of Government. But in case a great many men together, have already resisted the Soveraign Power unjustly, or committed some Capitall crime, for which every one of them expecteth death, whether have they not the Liberty then to joyn together, [113] and assist, and defend one another? Certainly they have: For they but defend their lives, which the Guilty man may as well do, as the Innocent. There was indeed injustice in the first breach of their duty; Their bearing of Arms subsequent to it, though it be to maintain what they have done, is no new unjust act. And if it be onely to defend their persons, it is not unjust at all. But the offer of pardon taketh from them, to whom it is offered, the plea of self-defence, and maketh their perseverance in assisting, or defending the rest, unlawfull.

The Greatest Liberty of Subjects, dependeth on the Silence of the Law. As for other Lyberties, they depend on the Silence of the Law. In cases where the Soveraign has prescribed no rule, there the Subject hath the Liberty to do, or forbeare, according to his own discretion. And therefore such Liberty is in some places more, and in some lesse;

5. Enlists.
6. Money paid in advance.

and in some times more, in other times lesse, according as they that have the Soveraignty shall think most convenient. As for Example, there was a time, when in *England* a man might enter in to his own Land, (and dispossesse such as wrongfully possessed it,) by force. But in after-times, that Liberty of Forcible Entry, was taken away by a Statute made (by the King) in Parliament. And in some places of the world, men have the Liberty of many wives: in other places, such Liberty is not allowed.

If a Subject have a controversie with his Soveraigne, of debt, or of right of possession of lands or goods, or concerning any service required at his hands, or concerning any penalty, corporall, or pecuniary, grounded on a precedent Law; he hath the same Liberty to sue for his right, as if it were against a Subject; and before such Judges, as are appointed by the Soveraign. For seeing the Soveraign demandeth by force of a former Law, and not by vertue of his Power; he declareth thereby, that he requireth no more, than shall appear to be due by that Law. The sute therefore is not contrary to the will of the Soveraign; and consequently the Subject hath the Liberty to demand the hearing of his Cause; and sentence, according to that Law. But if he demand, or take any thing by pretence of his Power; there lyeth, in that case, no action of Law: for all that is done by him in Vertue of his Power, is done by the Authority of every Subject, and consequently, he that brings an action against the Soveraign, brings it against himselfe.

If a Monarch, or Soveraign Assembly, grant a Liberty to all, or any of his Subjects, which Grant standing, he is disabled to provide for their safety, the Grant is voyd; unlesse he directly renounce, or transferre the Soveraignty to another. For in that he might openly, (if it had been his will,) and in plain termes, have renounced, or transferred it, and did not; it is to be understood it was not his will; but that the Grant proceeded from ignorance of the repugnancy between such a Liberty and the Soveraign Power: and therefore the Soveraignty is still retayned; and consequently all those Powers, which are necessary to the exercising thereof; such as are the Power of Warre, and Peace, of Judicature, of appointing Officers, and Councellours, of levying Mony, and the rest named in the 18th Chapter.

The Obligation of Subjects to the Soveraign, is understood to last as long, and no longer, than the power lasteth, by which he is able to protect them. For the right men have by Nature to protect themselves, when none else can protect them, can by no Covenant be relinquished. The Soveraignty is the Soule of the Common-wealth; which once departed from the Body, the members doe no more receive their motion from it. The end of Obedience is Protection; which, wheresoever a man seeth it, either in his own, or in anothers sword, Nature applyeth his obedience to it, and his endeavour to maintaine it. And though Soveraignty, in the intention of them that make it, be immortall; yet is it in its own nature, not only subject to violent death, by forreign war; but also through the ignorance, and passions of men, it hath in it, from the very institution, many seeds of a naturall mortality, by Intestine Discord.

[114]

In what Cases Subjects are absolved of their obedience to their Soveraign.

In case of Captivity. If a Subject be taken prisoner in war; or his person, or his means of life be within the Guards of the enemy, and hath his life and corporall Libertie given him, on condition to be Subject to the Victor, he hath Libertie to accept the condition; and having accepted it, is the subject of him that took him; because he had no other way to preserve himself. The case is the same, if he be deteined on the same termes, in a forreign country. But if a man be held in prison, or bonds, or is not trusted with the libertie of his bodie; he cannot be understood to be bound by Covenant to subjection; and therefore may, if he can, make his escape by any means whatsoever.

In case the Soveraign cast off the government from himself and his Heyrs. If a Monarch shall relinquish the Soveraignty, both for himself, and his heires; His Subjects returne to the absolute Libertie of Nature; because, though Nature may declare who are his Sons, and who are the nerest of his Kin; yet it dependeth on his own will, (as hath been said in the precedent chapter,) who shall be his Heyr. If therefore he will have no Heyre, there is no Soveraignty, nor Subjection. The case is the same, if he dye without known Kindred, and without declaration of his Heyre. For then there can no Heire be known, and consequently no Subjection be due.

In case of Banishment. If the Soveraign Banish his Subject; during the Banishment, he is not Subject. But he that is sent on a message, or hath leave to travell, is still Subject; but it is, by Contract between Soveraigns, not by vertue of the covenant of Subjection. For whosoever entreth into anothers dominion, is Subject to all the Laws thereof; unlesse he have a privilege by the amity of the Soveraigns, or by speciall licence.

In case the Soveraign render himself Subject to another. If a Monarch subdued by war, render himself Subject to the Victor; his Subjects are delivered from their former obligation, and become obliged to the Victor. But if he be held prisoner, or have not the liberty of his own Body; he is not understood to have given away the Right of Soveraigntie; and therefore his Subjects are obliged to yield obedience to the Magistrates formerly placed, governing not in their own name, but in his. For, his Right remaining, the question is only of the Administration; that is to say, of the Magistrates and Officers; which, if he have not means to name, he is supposed to approve those, which he himself had formerly appointed.

[115]

* * *

[127]

Chap. XXIV.

Of the NUTRITION, *and* PROCREATION *of a Common-wealth.*

The Nourishment of a Common-wealth consisteth in the Commodities of Sea and Land: THE NUTRITION of a Common-wealth consisteth, in the *Plenty*, and *Distribution* of *Materials* conducing to Life: In *Concoction*, or *Preparation*; and (when concocted) in the *Conveyance* of it, by convenient conduits, to the Publique use.

As for the Plenty of Matter, it is a thing limited by Nature, to those commodities, which from (the two breasts of our common Mother) Land, and Sea, God usually either freely giveth, or for labour selleth to man-kind.

For the Matter of this Nutriment, consisting in Animals, Vegetals, and Minerals, God hath freely layd them before us, in or neer to the face of the Earth; so as there needeth no more but the labour, and industry of receiving them. Insomuch as Plenty dependeth (next to Gods favour) meerly on the labour and industry of men.

This Matter, commonly called Commodities, is partly *Native*, and partly *Forraign*: *Native*, that which is to be had within the Territory of the Common-wealth: *Forraign*, that which is imported from without. And because there is no Territory under the Dominion of one Common-wealth, (except it be of very vast extent,) that produceth all things needfull for the maintenance, and motion of the whole Body; and few that produce not something more than necessary; the superfluous commodities to be had within, become no more superfluous, but supply these wants at home, by importation of that which may be had abroad, either by Exchange, or by just Warre, or by Labour: for a mans Labour also, is a commodity exchangeable for benefit, as well as any other thing: And there have been Common-wealths that having no more Territory, than hath served them for habitation, have neverthelesse, not onely maintained, but also encreased their Power, partly by the labour of trading from one place to another, and partly by selling the Manifactures, whereof the Materials were brought in from other places.

The Distribution of the Materials of this Nourishment, is the constitution of *Mine*, and *Thine*, and *His*; that is to say, in one word *Propriety*; and belongeth in all kinds of Common-wealth to the Soveraign Power. For where there is no Common-wealth, there is (as hath been already shewn) a perpetuall warre of every man against his neighbour; And therefore every thing is his that getteth it, and keepeth it by force; which is neither *Propriety*, nor *Community*; but *Uncertainty*. Which is so evident, that even *Cicero*, (a passionate defender of Liberty,) in a publique pleading, attributeth all Propriety to the Law Civil, *Let the Civill Law*, saith he, *be once abandoned, or but negligently guarded, (not to say oppressed,) and there is nothing, that any man can be sure to receive from his Ancestor, or leave to his Children.* And again; *Take away the Civill Law, and no man knows what is his own, and what another mans.* Seeing therefore the Introduction of *Propriety* is an effect of Common-wealth; which can do nothing but by the Person that Represents it, it is the act onely of the Soveraign; and consisteth in the Lawes, which none can make that have not the Soveraign Power. And this they well knew of old, who called that Νόμος,[1] (that is to say, Distribution,) which we call Law; and defined Justice, by *distributing* to every man *his own*.

In this Distribution, the First Law, is for Division of the Land it selfe: wherein the Soveraign assigneth to every man a portion, according as he, and not according as any Subject, or any number of them, shall judge agreeable to Equity, and the Common Good. The Children of Israel, were a Common-wealth in the Wildernesse; but wanted the commodities of the Earth, till they were masters of the Land of Promise;

And the right Distribution of them.

[128]

All private Estates of land proceed originally from the arbitrary Distribution of the Soveraign.

1. *Nomos.*

which afterward was divided amongst them, not by their own discretion, but by the discretion of *Eleazar* the Priest, and *Joshua* their Generall: who when there were twelve Tribes, making them thirteen by subdivision of the Tribe of *Joseph*; made neverthelesse but twelve portions of the Land; and ordained for the Tribe of *Levi* no land; but assigned them the tenth part of the whole fruits; which division was therefore Arbitrary. And though a People comming into possession of a Land by warre, do not alwaies exterminate the antient Inhabitants, (as did the Jewes,) but leave to many, or most, or all of them their estates; yet it is manifest they hold them afterwards, as of the Victors distribution; as the people of *England* held all theirs of *William* the *Conquerour*.

Propriety of a Subject excludes not the Dominion of the Soveraign, but onely of another Subject. From whence we may collect,[2] that the propriety which a subject hath in his lands, consisteth in a right to exclude all other subjects from the use of them; and not to exclude their Soveraign, be it an Assembly, or a Monarch. For seeing the Soveraign, that is to say, the Common-wealth (whose Person he representeth,) is understood to do nothing but in order to the common Peace and Security, this Distribution of lands, is to be understood as done in order to the same: And consequently, whatsoever Distribution [he][3] shall make in prejudice thereof,[4] is contrary to the will of every subject, that committed his Peace, and safety to his discretion, and conscience; and therefore by the will of every one of them, is to be reputed voyd. It is true, that a Soveraign Monarch, or the greater part of a Soveraign Assembly, may ordain the doing of many things in pursuit of their Passions, contrary to their own consciences, which is a breach of trust, and of the Law of Nature; but this is not enough to authorise any subject, either to make warre upon, or so much as to accuse of Injustice, or any way to speak evill of their Soveraign; because they have authorised all his actions, and in bestowing the Soveraign Power, made them their own. But in what cases the Commands of Soveraigns are contrary to Equity, and the Law of Nature, is to be considered hereafter in another place.

[129]
The Publique is not to be dieted. In the Distribution of land, the Common-wealth it selfe, may be conceived to have a portion, and possesse, and improve the same by their Representative; and that such portion may be made sufficient, to susteine the whole expence to the common Peace, and defence necessarily required: Which were very true, if there could be any Representative conceived free from humane passions, and infirmities. But the nature of men being as it is, the setting forth of Publique Land, or of any certaine Revenue for the Common-wealth, is in vaine; and tendeth to the dissolution of Government, and to the condition of meere Nature, and War, assoon as ever the Soveraign Power falleth into the hands of a Monarch, or of an Assembly, that are either too negligent of mony, or too hazardous in engaging the publique stock, into a long, or costly war. Common-wealths can endure no Diet: For seeing their expence is not limited by their own appetite, but by externall Accidents, and the appetites of their neighbours, the Publique Riches cannot be limited

2. Infer.
3. Manuscript version reads *another*.
4. Detrimental to.

by other limits, than those which the emergent occasions[5] shall require. And whereas in *England*, there were by the Conquerour, divers Lands reserved to his own use, (besides Forrests, and Chases, either for his recreation, or for preservation of Woods,) and divers services reserved on the Land he gave his Subjects; yet it seems they were not reserved for his Maintenance in his Publique, but in his Naturall capacity: For he, and his Successors did for all that, lay Arbitrary Taxes on all Subjects Land, when they judged it necessary. Or if those publique Lands, and Services, were ordained as a sufficient maintenance of the Common-wealth, it was contrary to the scope of the Institution; being (as it appeared by those ensuing Taxes) insufficient, and (as it appeares by the late small Revenue of the Crown) Subject to Alienation, and Diminution. It is therefore in vaine, to assign a portion to the Common-wealth; which may sell, or give it away; and does sell, and give it away when tis done by their Representative.

As the Distribution of Lands at home; so also to assigne in what places, and for what commodities, the Subject shall traffique abroad, belongeth to the Soveraign. For if it did belong to private persons to use their own discretion therein, some of them would bee drawn for gaine, both to furnish the enemy with means to hurt the Common-wealth, and hurt it themselves, by importing such things, as pleasing mens appetites, be neverthelesse noxious, or at least unprofitable to them. And therefore it belongeth to the Common-wealth, (that is, to the Soveraign only,) to approve, or disapprove both of the places, and matter of forraign Traffique. *The Places and matter of Traffique depend, as their Distribution, on the Soveraign.*

Further, seeing it is not enough to the Sustentation[6] of a Common-wealth, that every man have a propriety in a portion of Land, or in some few commodities, or a naturall property in some usefull art, and there is no art in the world, but is necessary either for the being, or well being almost of every particular man; it is necessary, that men distribute that which they can spare, and transferre their propriety therein, mutually one to another, by exchange, and mutuall contract. And therefore it belongeth to the Common-wealth, (that is to say, to the Soveraign,) to appoint in what manner, all kinds of contract between Subjects, (as buying, selling, exchanging, borrowing, lending, letting, and taking to hire,) are to bee made; and by what words, and signes they shall be understood for valid. And for the Matter, and Distribution of the Nourishment, to the severall Members of the Common-wealth, thus much (considering the modell of the whole worke) is sufficient. *The Laws of transferring propriety belong also to the Soveraign.*

[130]

By Concoction, I understand the reducing of all commodities, which are not presently consumed, but reserved for Nourishment in time to come, to some thing of equall value, and withall so portable, as not to hinder the motion of men from place to place; to the end a man may have in what place soever, such Nourishment as the place affordeth. And this is nothing else but Gold, and Silver, and Mony. For Gold and Silver, being (as it happens) almost in all Countries of the world *Mony the Bloud of a Common-wealth.*

5. Circumstances that arise.
6. Sustenance, maintenance.

highly valued, is a commodious measure of the value of all things else between Nations; and Mony (of what matter soever coyned by the Soveraign of a Common-wealth,) is a sufficient measure of the value of all things else, between the Subjects of that Common-wealth. By the means of which measures, all commodities, Moveable, and Immoveable, are made to accompany a man, to all places of his resort, within and without the place of his ordinary residence; and the same passeth from Man to Man, within the Common-wealth; and goes round about, Nourishing (as it passeth) every part thereof; In so much as this Concoction, is as it were the Sanguification of the Common-wealth: For naturall Bloud is in like manner made of the fruits of the Earth; and circulating, nourisheth by the way, every Member of the Body of Man.

And because Silver and Gold, have their value from the matter it self; they have first this priviledge, that the value of them cannot be altered by the power of one, nor of a few Common-wealths; as being a common measure of the commodities of all places. But base[7] Mony, may easily be enhansed, or abased. Secondly, they have the priviledge to make Common-wealths move, and stretch out their armes, when need is, into forraign Countries; and supply, not only private Subjects that travell, but also whole Armies with Provision. But that Coyne, which is not considerable for the Matter, but for the Stamp of the place, being unable to endure change of ayr, hath its effect at home only; where also it is subject to the change of Laws, and thereby to have the value diminished, to the prejudice many times of those that have it.

The Conduits and Way of mony to the Publique use.

The Conduits, and Wayes by which it is conveyed to the Publique use, are of two sorts; One, that Conveyeth it to the Publique Coffers; The other, that Issueth the same out againe for publique payments. Of the first sort, are Collectors, Receivers, and Treasurers; of the second are the Treasurers againe, and the Officers appointed for payment of severall publique or private Ministers. And in this also, the Artificiall Man maintains his resemblance with the Naturall; whose Veins receiv-

[131]

ing the Bloud from the severall Parts of the Body, carry it to the Heart; where being made Vitall, the Heart by the Arteries sends it out again, to enliven, and enable for motion all the Members of the same.

The Children of a Commonwealth Colonies.

The Procreation, or Children of a Common-wealth, are those we call *Plantations*, or *Colonies*; which are numbers of men sent out from the Common-wealth, under a Conductor, or Governour, to inhabit a Forraign Country, either formerly voyd of Inhabitants, or made voyd then, by warre. And when a Colony is setled, they are either a Common-wealth of themselves, discharged of their subjection to their Soveraign that sent them, (as hath been done by many Common-wealths of antient time,) in which case the Common-wealth from which they went, was called their Metropolis, or Mother, and requires no more of them, then Fathers require of the Children, whom they emancipate, and make free from their domestique government, which is Honour, and Friendship; or else they remain united to their Metropolis, as were the Colonies of the people of *Rome*; and then they

7. Ordinary, not intrinsically precious.

are no Common-wealths themselves, but Provinces, and parts of the Common-wealth that sent them. So that the Right of Colonies (saving Honour, and League with their Metropolis,) dependeth wholly on their Licence, or Letters, by which their Soveraign authorised them to Plant.

Chap. XXV.

Of COUNSELL.

How fallacious it is to judge of the nature of things, by the ordinary and inconstant use of words, appeareth in nothing more, than in the confusion of Counsels, and Commands, arising from the Imperative manner of speaking in them both, and in many other occasions besides. For the words *Doe this*, are the words not onely of him that Commandeth; but also of him that giveth Counsell; and of him that Exhorteth; and yet there are but few, that see not, that these are very different things; or that cannot distinguish between them, when they perceive who it is that speaketh, and to whom the Speech is directed, and upon what occasion. But finding those phrases in mens writings, and being not able, or not willing to enter into a consideration of the circumstances, they mistake sometimes the Precepts of Counsellours, for the Precepts of them that Command; and sometimes the contrary; according as it best agreeth with the conclusions they would inferre, or the actions they approve. To avoyd which mistakes, and render to those termes of Commanding, Counselling, and Exhorting, their proper and distinct significations. I define them thus.

COMMAND is where a man saith, *Doe this*, or *Doe not this*, without expecting other reason than the Will of him that sayes it. From this it followeth manifestly, that he that Commandeth, pretendeth thereby his own Benefit: For the reason of his Command is his own Will onely, and the proper object of every mans Will, is some Good to himselfe.

COUNSELL, is where a man saith, *Doe*, or *Doe not this*, and deduceth his reasons from the benefit that arriveth by it to him to whom he saith it. And from this it is evident, that he that giveth Counsell, pretendeth onely (whatsoever he intendeth) the good of him, to whom he giveth it.

Therefore between Counsell and Command, one great difference is, that Command is directed to a mans own benefit; and Counsell to the benefit of another man. And from this ariseth another difference, that a man may be obliged to do what he is Commanded; as when he hath covenanted to obey: But he cannot be obliged to do as he is Counselled, because the hurt of not following it, is his own; or if he should covenant to follow it, then is the Counsell turned into the nature of a Command. A third difference between them is, that no man can pretend a right to be of another mans Counsell;[1] because he is not to pretend benefit by it to himselfe: but to demand right to Counsell

Counsell what.

Differences between command, and Counsell.

[132]

1. I.e., no person can claim a right to be another's counselor.

another, argues a will to know his designes, or to gain some other Good to himselfe; which (as I said before) is of every mans will the proper object.

This also is incident to the nature of Counsell; that whatsoever it be, he that asketh it, cannot in equity accuse, or punish it: For to ask Counsell of another, is to permit him to give such Counsell as he shall think best; And consequently, he that giveth counsell to his Soveraign, (whether a Monarch, or an Assembly) when he asketh it, cannot in equity be punished for it, whether the same be conformable to the opinion of the most, or not, so it be to the Proposition in debate. For if the sense of the Assembly can be taken notice of, before the Debate be ended, they should neither ask, nor take any further Counsell; For the Sense of the Assembly, is the Resolution of the Debate, and End of all Deliberation. And generally he that demandeth Counsell, is Author of it; and therefore cannot punish it; and what the Soveraign cannot, no man else can. But if one Subject giveth Counsell to another, to do any thing contrary to the Lawes, whether that Counsell proceed from evill intention, or from ignorance onely, it is punishable by the Common-wealth; because ignorance of the Law, is no good excuse, where every man is bound to take notice of the Lawes to which he is subject.

Exhortation and Dehortation what.

EXHORTATION, and DEHORTATION, is Counsell, accompanied with signes in him that giveth it, of vehement desire to have it followed; or to say it more briefly, *Counsell vehemently pressed.* For he that Exhorteth, doth not deduce the consequences of what he adviseth to be done, and tye himselfe therein to the rigour of true reasoning; but encourages him he Counselleth, to Action: As he that Dehorteth, deterreth him from it. And therefore they have in their speeches, a regard to the common Passions, and opinions of men, in deducing their reasons; and make use of Similitudes, Metaphors, Examples, and other tooles of Oratory, to perswade their Hearers of the Utility, Honour, or Justice of following their advise.

[133]

From whence may be inferred, First, that Exhortation and Dehortation, is directed to the Good of him that giveth the Counsell, not of him that asketh it, which is contrary to the duty of a Counsellour; who (by the definition of Counsell) ought to regard, not his own benefit, but his whom he adviseth. And that he directeth his Counsell to his own benefit, is manifest enough, by the long and vehement urging, or by the artificiall[2] giving thereof; which being not required of him, and consequently proceeding from his own occasions, is directed principally to his own benefit, and but accidentarily to the good of him that is Counselled, or not at all.

Secondly, that the use of Exhortation and Dehortation lyeth onely, where a man is to speak to a Multitude; because when the Speech is addressed to one, he may interrupt him, and examine his reasons more rigorously, than can be done in a Multitude; which are too many to enter into Dispute, and Dialogue with him that speaketh indifferently[3] to them all at once.

2. Contrived or deceitful.
3. Equally, without partiality.

Thirdly, that they that Exhort and Dehort, where they are required to give Counsell, are corrupt Counsellours, and as it were bribed by their own interest. For though the Counsell they give be never so good; yet he that gives it, is no more a good Counsellour, than he that giveth a Just Sentence for a reward, is a Just Judge. But where a man may lawfully Command, as a Father in his Family, or a Leader in an Army, his Exhortations and Dehortations, are not onely lawfull, but also necessary, and laudable: But then they are no more Counsells, but Commands; which when they are for Execution of soure labour; sometimes necessity, and alwayes humanity requireth to be sweetned in the delivery, by encouragement, and in the tune[4] and phrase of Counsell, rather then in harsher language of Command.

Examples of the difference between Command and Counsell, we may take from the formes of Speech that expresse them in Holy Scripture. *Have no other Gods but me; Make to thy selfe no graven Image; Take not Gods name in vain; Sanctifie the Sabbath; Honour thy Parents; Kill not; Steale not,* &c. are Commands; because the reason for which we are to obey them, is drawn from the will of God our King, whom we are obliged to obey. But these words, *Sell all thou hast; give it to the poore; and follow me,* are Counsell; because the reason for which we are to do so, is drawn from our own benefit; which is this, that we shall have *Treasure in heaven.* These words, *Go into the Village over against you, and you shall find an Asse tyed, and her Colt; loose her, and bring her to me,* are a Command: for the reason of their fact is drawn from the will of their Master: but these words, *Repent, and be Baptized in the Name of Jesus,* are Counsell; because the reason why we should so do, tendeth not to any benefit of God Almighty, who shall still be King in what manner soever we rebell; but of our selves, who have no other means of avoyding the punishment hanging over us for our sins.

As the difference of Counsell from Command, hath been now deduced from the nature of Counsell, consisting in a deducing of the benefit, or hurt that may arise to him that is to be Counselled, by the necessary or probable consequences of the action he propoundeth; so may also the differences between *apt,* and *inept* Counsellours be derived from the same. For Experience, being but Memory of the consequences of like actions formerly observed, and Counsell but the Speech whereby that experience is made known to another; the Vertues, and Defects of Counsell, are the same with the Vertues, and Defects Intellectuall: And to the Person of a Common-wealth, his Counsellours serve him in the place of Memory, and Mentall Discourse. But with this resemblance of the Common-wealth, to a naturall man, there is one dissimilitude joyned, of great importance; which is, that a naturall man receiveth his experience, from the naturall objects of sense, which work upon him without passion, or interest of their own; whereas they that give Counsell to the Representative person of a Common-wealth, may have, and have often their particular ends, and passions, that render their Counsells alwayes suspected, and many times

[134]
Differences of fit and unfit Counsellours.

4. Style or tone.

unfaithfull. And therefore we may set down for the first condition of a good Counsellour, *That his Ends, and Interest, be not inconsistent with the Ends and Interest of him he Counselleth.*

Secondly, Because the office of a Counsellour, when an action comes into deliberation, is to make manifest the consequences of it, in such manner, as he that is Counselled may be truly and evidently informed; he ought to propound his advise, in such forme of speech, as may make the truth most evidently appear; that is to say, with as firme ratiocination, as significant and proper language, and as briefly, as the evidence will permit. And therefore *rash, and unevident Inferences;* (such as are fetched onely from Examples, or authority of Books, and are not arguments of what is good, or evill, but witnesses of fact, or of opinion,) *obscure, confused, and ambiguous Expressions, also all metaphoricall Speeches, tending to the stirring up of Passion,* (because such reasoning, and such expressions, are usefull onely to deceive, or to lead him we Counsell towards other ends than his own) *are repugnant to the Office of a Counsellour.*

Thirdly, Because the Ability of Counselling proceedeth from Experience, and long study; and no man is presumed to have experience in all those things that to the Administration of a great Common-wealth are necessary to be known, *No man is presumed to be a good Counsellour, but in such Businesse, as he hath not onely been much versed in, but hath also much meditated on, and considered.* For seeing the businesse of a Common-wealth is this, to preserve the people in Peace at home, and defend them against forraign Invasion, we shall find, it requires great knowledge of the disposition of Man-kind, of the Rights of Government, and of the nature of Equity, Law, Justice, and Honour, not to be attained without study; And of the Strength, Commodities, Places, both of their own Country, and their Neighbours; as also of the inclinations, and designes of all Nations that may any way annoy them. And this is not attained to, without much experience. Of which things, [135] not onely the whole summe, but every one of the particulars requires the age, and observation of a man in years, and of more than ordinary study. The wit required for Counsel, as I have said before (Chap. 8.) is Judgement. And the differences of men in that point come from different education, of some to one kind of study, or businesse, and of others to another. When for the doing of any thing, there be Infallible rules, (as in Engines, and Edifices, the rules of Geometry,) all the experience of the world cannot equal his Counsell, that has learnt, or found out the Rule. And when there is no such Rule, he that hath most experience in that particular kind of businesse, has therein the best Judgement, and is the best Counsellour.

Fourthly, to be able to give Counsell to a Common-wealth, in a businesse that hath reference to another Common-wealth, *It is necessary to be acquainted with the Intelligences, and Letters* that come from thence, *and with all the records of Treaties, and other transactions of State* between them; which none can doe, but such as the Representative shall think fit. By which we may see, that they who are not called to Counsell, can have no good Counsell in such cases to obtrude.

Fifthly, Supposing the number of Counsellors equall, a man is better Counselled by hearing them apart, then in an Assembly; and that for many causes. First, in hearing them apart, you have the advice of every man; but in an Assembly many of them deliver their advise with *I*, or *No*, or with their hands, or feet, not moved by their own sense, but by the eloquence of another, or for feare of displeasing some that have spoken, or the whole Assembly, by contradiction; or for feare of appearing duller in apprehension, than those that have applauded the contrary opinion. Secondly, in an Assembly of many, there cannot choose but be some whose interests are contrary to that of the Publique; and these their Interests make passionate, and Passion eloquent, and Eloquence drawes others into the same advice. For the Passions of men, which asunder are moderate, as the heat of one brand; in Assembly are like many brands, that enflame one another, (especially when they blow one another with Orations) to the setting of the Common-wealth on fire, under pretence of Counselling it. Thirdly, in hearing every man apart, one may examine (when there is need) the truth, or probability of his reasons, and of the grounds of the advise he gives, by frequent interruptions, and objections; which cannot be done in an Assembly, where (in every difficult question) a man is rather astonied,[5] and dazled with the variety of discourse upon it, than informed of the course he ought to take. Besides, there cannot be an Assembly of many, called together for advice, wherein there be not some, that have the ambition to be thought eloquent, and also learned in the Politiques; and give not their advice with care of the businesse propounded, but of the applause of their motly orations, made of the divers colored threds, or shreds of Authors; which is an Impertinence at least, that takes away the time of serious Consultation, and in the secret way of Counselling apart, is easily avoided. Fourthly, in Deliberations that ought to be kept [136] secret, (whereof there be many occasions in Publique Businesse,) the Counsells of many, and especially in Assemblies, are dangerous; And therefore great Assemblies are necessitated to commit such affaires to lesser numbers, and of such persons as are most versed, and in whose fidelity they have most confidence.

To conclude, who is there that so far approves the taking of Counsell from a great Assembly of Counsellours, that wisheth for, or would accept of their pains,[6] when there is a question of marrying his Children, disposing of his Lands, governing his Household, or managing his private Estate, especially if there be amongst them such as wish not his prosperity? A man that doth his businesse by the help of many and prudent Counsellours, with every one consulting apart in his proper element, does it best, as he that useth able Seconds at Tennis play, placed in their proper stations. He does next best, that useth his own Judgement only; as he that has no Second at all. But he that is carried up and down to his businesse in a framed Counsell, which cannot move but by the plurality of consenting opinions, the execution whereof is commonly (out of envy, or interest) retarded by the part dissenting,

5. Astonished.
6. Efforts.

does it worst of all, and like one that is carried to the ball, though by
good Players, yet in a Wheele-barrough, or other frame, heavy of it self,
and retarded also by the inconcurrent[7] judgements, and endeavours of
them that drive it; and so much the more, as they be more that set
their hands to it; and most of all, when there is one, or more amongst
them, that desire to have him lose. And though it be true, that many
eys see more then one; yet it is not to be understood of many Counsellours; but then only, when the finall Resolution is in one man. Otherwise, because many eyes see the same thing in divers lines, and are
apt to look asquint towards their private benefit; they that desire not to
misse their marke, though they look about with two eyes, yet they never
ayme but with one; And therefore no great Popular Common-wealth
was ever kept up; but either by a forraign Enemy that united them; or
by the reputation of some one eminent Man amongst them; or by the
secret Counsell of a few; or by the mutuall feare of equall factions; and
not by the open Consultations of the Assembly. And as for very little
Common-wealths, be they Popular, or Monarchicall, there is no humane wisdome can uphold them, longer then the Jealousy lasteth of
their potent Neighbours.

Chap. XXVI.

Of CIVILL LAWES.

Civill Law
what.

[137]

By CIVILL LAWES, I understand the Lawes, that men are therefore
bound to observe, because they are Members, not of this, or that
Common-wealth in particular, but of a Common-wealth. For the
knowledge of particular Lawes belongeth to them, that professe the
study of the Lawes of their severall Countries; but the knowledge of
Civill Law in generall, to any man. The antient Law of *Rome* was called
their *Civil Law*, from the word *Civitas*, which signifies a Common-
wealth: And those Countries, which having been under the Roman
Empire, and governed by that Law, retaine still such part thereof as
they think fit, call that part the Civill Law, to distinguish it from the
rest of their own Civill Lawes. But that is not it I intend to speak of
here; my designe being not to shew what is Law here, and there; but
what is Law; as *Plato*, *Aristotle*, *Cicero*, and divers others have done,
without taking upon them the profession of the study of the Law.

And first it is manifest, that Law in generall, is not Counsell, but
Command; nor a Command of any man to any man; but only of him,
whose Command is addressed to one formerly obliged to obey him.
And as for Civill Law, it addeth only the name of the person Commanding, which is *Persona Civitatis*, the Person of the Common-
wealth.

Which considered, I define Civill Law in this manner. CIVILL LAW,
Is to every Subject, those Rules, which the Common-wealth hath Com-

7. Conflicting.

manded him, by Word, Writing, or other sufficient Sign of the Will, to make use of, for the Distinction of Right, and Wrong; that is to say, of what is contrary, and what is not contrary to the Rule.

In which definition, there is nothing that is not at first sight evident. For every man seeth, that some Lawes are addressed to all the Subjects in generall; some to particular Provinces; some to particular Vocations; and some to particular Men; and are therefore Lawes, to every of those to whom the Command is directed; and to none else. As also, that Lawes are the Rules of Just, and Unjust; nothing being reputed Unjust, that is not contrary to some Law. Likewise, that none can make Lawes but the Common-wealth; because our Subjection is to the Common-wealth only: and that Commands, are to be signified by sufficient Signs; because a man knows not otherwise how to obey them. And therefore, whatsoever can from this definition by necessary consequence be deduced, ought to be acknowledged for truth. Now I deduce from it this that followeth.

1. The Legislator in all Common-wealths, is only the Soveraign, be he one Man, as in a Monarchy, or one Assembly of men, as in a Democracy, or Aristocracy. For the Legislator, is he that maketh the Law. And the Common-wealth only, præscribes, and commandeth the observation of those rules, which we call Law: Therefore the Common-wealth is the Legislator. But the Common-wealth is no Person, nor has capacity to doe any thing, but by the Representative, (that is, the Soveraign;) and therefore the Soveraign is the sole Legislator. For the same reason, none can abrogate a Law made, but the Soveraign; because a Law is not abrogated, but by another Law, that forbiddeth it to be put in execution. *The Soveraign is Legislator.*

2. The Soveraign of a Common-wealth, be it an Assembly, or one Man, is not Subject to the Civill Lawes. For having power to make, and repeale Lawes, he may when he pleaseth, free himselfe from that subjection, by repealing those Lawes that trouble him, and making of new; and consequently he was free before. For he is free, that can be free when he will: Nor is it possible for any person to be bound to himselfe; because he that can bind, can release; and therefore he that is bound to himselfe onely, is not bound. *[138] And not Subject to Civill Law.*

3. When long Use obtaineth the authority of a Law, it is not the Length of Time that maketh the Authority, but the Will of the Soveraign signified by his silence, (for Silence is sometimes an argument of Consent;) and it is no longer Law, then the Soveraign shall be silent therein. And therefore if the Soveraign shall have a question of Right grounded, not upon his present Will, but upon the Lawes formerly made; the Length of Time shal bring no prejudice to his Right; but the question shal be judged by Equity. For many unjust Actions, and unjust Sentences, go uncontrolled a longer time, than any man can remember. And our Lawyers account no Customes Law, but such as are reasonable, and that evill Customes are to be abolished: But the Judgement of what is reasonable, and of what is to be abolished, belongeth to him that maketh the Law, which is the Soveraign Assembly, or Monarch. *Use, a Law not by vertue of Time, but of the Soveraigns consent.*

The Law of Nature, and the Civill Law contain each other.

4. The Law of Nature, and the Civill Law, contain each other, and are of equall extent. For the Lawes of Nature, which consist in Equity, Justice, Gratitude, and other morall Vertues on these depending, in the condition of meer Nature (as I have said before in the end of the 15th Chapter,) are not properly Lawes, but qualities that dispose men to peace, and to obedience. When a Common-wealth is once settled,[1] then are they actually Lawes, and not before; as being then the commands of the Common-wealth; and therefore also Civill Lawes: For it is the Soveraign Power that obliges men to obey them. For in the differences of private men, to declare, what is Equity, what is Justice, and what is morall Vertue, and to make them binding, there is need of the Ordinances of Soveraign Power, and Punishments to be ordained for such as shall break them; which Ordinances are therefore part of the Civill Law. The Law of Nature therefore is a part of the Civill Law in all Common-wealths of the world. Reciprocally also, the Civill Law is a part of the Dictates of Nature. For Justice, that is to say, Performance of Covenant, and giving to every man his own, is a Dictate of the Law of Nature. But every subject in a Common-wealth, hath covenanted to obey the Civill Law, (either one with another, as when they assemble to make a common Representative, or with the Representative it selfe one by one, when subdued by the Sword they promise obedience, that they may receive life;) And therefore Obedience to the Civill Law is part also of the Law of Nature. Civill, and Naturall Law are not different kinds, but different parts of Law; whereof one part being written, is called Civill, the other unwritten, Naturall. But the Right of Nature, that is, the naturall Liberty of man, may by the Civill Law be abridged, and restrained: nay, the end of making Lawes, is no other, but such Restraint; without the which there cannot possibly be any

[139]

Peace. And Law was brought into the world for nothing else, but to limit the naturall liberty of particular men, in such manner, as they might not hurt, but assist one another, and joyn together against a common Enemy.

Provinciall Lawes are not made by Custome, but by the Soveraign Power.

5. If the Soveraign of one Common-wealth, subdue a People that have lived under other written Lawes, and afterwards govern them by the same Lawes, by which they were governed before; yet those Lawes are the Civill Lawes of the Victor, and not of the Vanquished Common-wealth. For the Legislator is he, not by whose authority the Lawes were first made, but by whose authority they now continue to be Lawes. And therefore where there be divers Provinces, within the Dominion of a Common-wealth, and in those Provinces diversity of Lawes, which commonly are called the Customes of each severall Province, we are not to understand that such Customes have their force, onely from Length of Time; but that they were antiently Lawes written, or otherwise made known, for the Constitutions,[2] and Statutes of their Soveraigns; and are now Lawes, not by vertue of the Præscription of time,[3] but by the Constitutions of their present Soveraigns. But if an unwritten Law, in all the Provinces of a Dominion, shall be generally

1. Established.
2. Decrees.
3. Legitimacy based on custom.

observed, and no iniquity appear in the use thereof; that Law can be
no other but a Law of Nature, equally obliging all man-kind.

6. Seeing then all Lawes, written, and unwritten, have their Author- *Some foolish*
ity, and force, from the Will of the Common-wealth; that is to say, from *opinions of*
the Will of the Representative; which in a Monarchy is the Monarch, *Lawyers con-*
and in other Common-wealths the Soveraign Assembly; a man may *cerning the making of*
wonder from whence proceed such opinions, as are found in the Books *Lawes.*
of Lawyers of eminence in severall Common-wealths, directly, or by
consequence making the Legislative Power depend on private men, or
subordinate Judges. As for example, *That the Common Law. hath no
Controuler but the Parlament*; which is true onely where a Parlament
has the Soveraign Power, and cannot be assembled, nor dissolved, but
by their own discretion. For if there be a right in any else to dissolve
them, there is a right also to controule them, and consequently to
controule their controulings. And if there be no such right, then the
Controuler of Lawes is not *Parlamentum*, but *Rex in Parlamento*,[4] And
where a Parlament is Soveraign, if it should assemble never so many,
or so wise men, from the Countries subject to them, for whatsoever
cause; yet there is no man will believe, that such an Assembly hath
thereby acquired to themselves a Legislative Power. *Item*, that the two
arms of a Common-wealth, are *Force, and Justice; the first whereof is
in the King; the other deposited in the hands of the Parlament.* As if a
Common-wealth could consist, where the Force were in any hand,
which Justice had not the Authority to command and govern.

7. That Law can never be against Reason, our Lawyers are agreed;
and that not the Letter, (that is, every construction of it,) but that which
is according to the Intention of the Legislator, is the Law. And it is
true: but the doubt[5] is, of whose Reason it is, that shall be received for
Law. It is not meant of any private Reason; for then there would be as
much contradiction in the Lawes, as there is in the Schooles; nor yet, [140]
(as Sr. *Ed. Coke* makes it,) an *Artificiall perfection of Reason, gotten by* Sir Edw.
long study, observation, and experience, (as his was.) For it is possible Coke, *upon*
long study may encrease, and confirm erroneous Sentences: and where Littleton, *Lib.*
men build on false grounds, the more they build, the greater is the 2. *Ch. 6. fol.*
ruine: and of those that study, and observe with equall time, and dili- 97. *b.*
gence, the reasons and resolutions are, and must remain discordant:
and therefore it is not that *Juris prudentia*, or wisedome of subordinate
Judges; but the Reason of this our Artificiall Man the Common-wealth,
and his Command, that maketh Law: And the Common-wealth being
in their Representative but one Person, there cannot easily arise any
contradiction in the Lawes; and when there doth, the same Reason is
able, by interpretation, or alteration, to take it away. In all Courts of
Justice, the Soveraign (which is the Person of the Common-wealth,) is
he that Judgeth: The subordinate Judge, ought to have regard to the
reason, which moved his Soveraign to make such Law, that his Sentence may be according thereunto; which then is his Soveraigns Sentence; otherwise it is his own, and an unjust one. *Law made, if*

8. From this, that the Law is a Command, and a Command consist- *not also made
known, is no
Law.*

4. Not the Parliament, but the King in Parliament.
5. Question.

eth in declaration, or manifestation of the will of him that commandeth, by voyce, writing, or some other sufficient argument of the same,
we may understand, that the Command of the Common-wealth, is Law
onely to those, that have means to take notice of it. Over naturall fooles,
children, or mad-men there is no Law, no more than over brute beasts;
nor are they capable of the title of just, or unjust; because they had
never power to make any covenant, or to understand the consequences
thereof; and consequently never took upon them to authorise the actions of any Soveraign, as they must do that make to themselves a
Common-wealth. And as those from whom Nature, or Accident hath
taken away the notice of all Lawes in generall; so also every man, from
whom any accident, not proceeding from his own default, hath taken
away the means to take notice of any particular Law, is excused, if he
observe it not; And to speak properly, that Law is no Law to him. It is
therefore necessary, to consider in this place, what arguments, and
signes be sufficient for the knowledge of what is the Law; that is to say,
what is the will of the Soveraign, as well in Monarchies, as in other
formes of government.

*Unwritten
Lawes are all
of them Lawes
of Nature.*

And first, if it be a Law that obliges all the Subjects without exception, and is not written, nor otherwise published in such places as they
may take notice thereof, it is a Law of Nature. For whatsoever men are
to take knowledge of for Law, not upon other mens words, but every
one from his own reason, must be such as is agreeable to the reason
of all men; which no Law can be, but the Law of Nature. The Lawes
of Nature therefore need not any publishing, nor Proclamation; as being contained in this one Sentence, approved by all the world, *Do not
that to another, which thou thinkest unreasonable to be done by another
to thy selfe.*

[141]

Secondly, if it be a Law that obliges only some condition of men, or
one particular man, and be not written, nor published by word, then
also it is a Law of Nature; and known by the same arguments, and
signs, that distinguish those in such a condition, from other Subjects.
For whatsoever Law is not written, or some way published by him that
makes it Law, can be known no way, but by the reason of him that is
to obey it; and is therefore also a Law not only Civill, but Naturall. For
Example, if the Soveraign employ a Publique Minister, without written
Instructions what to doe; he is obliged to take for Instructions the Dictates of Reason; As if he make a Judge, The Judge is to take notice,
that his Sentence ought to be according to the reason of his Soveraign,
which being alwaies understood to be Equity, he is bound to it by the
Law of Nature: Or if an Ambassador, he is (in all things not conteined
in his written Instructions) to take for Instruction that which Reason
dictates to be most conducing to his Soveraigns interest; and so of all
other Ministers of the Soveraignty, publique and private. All which
Instructions of naturall Reason may be comprehended under one name
of *Fidelity*; which is a branch of naturall Justice.

The Law of Nature excepted, it belongeth to the essence of all other
Lawes, to be made known, to every man that shall be obliged to obey
them, either by word, or writing, or some other act, known to proceed

from the Soveraign Authority. For the will of another, cannot be understood, but by his own word, or act, or by conjecture taken from his scope and purpose; which in the person of the Common-wealth, is to be supposed alwaies consonant to Equity and Reason. And in antient time, before letters were in common use, the Lawes were many times put into verse; that the rude people taking pleasure in singing, or reciting them, might the more easily reteine them in memory. And for the same reason *Solomon* adviseth a man, to bind the ten Commandements * upon his ten fingers. And for the Law which *Moses* gave to the people of *Israel* at the renewing of the Covenant, * he biddeth them to teach it their Children, by discoursing of it both at home, and upon the way; at going to bed, and at rising from bed; and to write it upon the posts, and dores of their houses; and * to assemble the people, man, woman, and child, to heare it read.

*Prov. 7.3.
*Deut. 11.19.

*Deut. 31.12.

Nor is it enough the Law be written, and published; but also that there be manifest signs, that it proceedeth from the will of the Soveraign. For private men, when they have, or think they have force enough to secure their unjust designes, and convoy[6] them safely to their ambitious ends, may publish for Lawes what they please, without, or against the Legislative Authority. There is therefore requisite, not only a Declaration of the Law, but also sufficient signes of the Author, and Authority. The Author, or Legislator is supposed in every Common-wealth to be evident, because he is the Soveraign, who having been Constituted by the consent of every one, is supposed by every one to be sufficiently known. And though the ignorance, and security of men be such, for the most part, as that when the memory of the first Constitution of their Common-wealth is worn out, they doe not consider, by whose power they use to be defended against their enemies, and to have their industry protected, and to be righted when injury is done them; yet because no man that considers, can make question of it, no excuse can be derived from the ignorance of where the Soveraignty is placed. And it is a Dictate of Naturall Reason, and consequently an evident Law of Nature, that no man ought to weaken that power, the protection whereof he hath himself demanded, or wittingly received against others. Therefore of who is Soveraign, no man, but by his own fault, (whatsoever evill men suggest,) can make any doubt. The difficulty consisteth in the evidence of the Authority derived from him; The removing whereof, dependeth on the knowledge of the publique Registers, publique Counsels, publique Ministers, and publique Seales; by which all Lawes are sufficiently verified; Verifyed, I say, not Authorised: for the Verification, is but the Testimony and Record; not the Authority of the Law; which consisteth in the Command of the Soveraign only.

Nothing is Law where the Legislator cannot be known.

[142]

Difference between Verifying and Authorising.

If therefore a man have a question of Injury, depending on the Law of Nature; that is to say, on common Equity; the Sentence of the Judge, that by Commission hath Authority to take cognisance of such causes, is a sufficient Verification of the Law of Nature in that individuall case. For though the advice of one that professeth the study of the Law, be

The Law Verifyed by the subordinate Judge.

6. Convey, carry.

usefull for the avoyding of contention; yet it is but advice: tis the Judge must tell men what is Law, upon the hearing of the Controversy.

By the Publique Registers. But when the question is of injury, or crime, upon a written Law; every man by recourse to the Registers, by himself, or others, may (if he will) be sufficiently enformed, before he doe such injury, or commit the crime, whither it be an injury, or not: Nay he ought to doe so: For when a man doubts whether the act he goeth about, be just, or injust; and may informe himself, if he will; the doing is unlawfull. In like manner, he that supposeth himself injured, in a case determined by the written Law, which he may by himself, or others see and consider; if he complaine before he consults with the Law, he does unjustly, and bewrayeth a disposition rather to vex other men, than to demand his own right.

By Letters Patent, and Publique Seale. If the question be of Obedience to a publique Officer; To have seen his Commission, with the Publique Seale, and heard it read; or to have had the means to be informed of it, if a man would, is a sufficient Verification of his Authority. For every man is obliged to doe his best endeavour, to informe himself of all written Lawes, that may concerne his own future actions.

The Interpretation of the Law dependeth on the Soveraign Power.

[143]

The Legislator known; and the Lawes, either by writing, or by the light of Nature, sufficiently published; there wanteth yet another very materiall circumstance to make them obligatory. For it is not the Letter, but the Intendment, or Meaning; that is to say, the authentique Interpretation of the Law (which is the sense of the Legislator,) in which the nature of the Law consisteth; And therefore the Interpretation of all Lawes dependeth on the Authority Soveraign; and the Interpreters can be none but those, which the Soveraign, (to whom only the Subject oweth obedience) shall appoint. For else, by the craft of an Interpreter, the Law may be made to beare a sense, contrary to that of the Soveraign; by which means the Interpreter becomes the Legislator.

All Lawes need Interpretation. All Laws, written, and unwritten, have need of Interpretation. The unwritten Law of Nature, though it be easy to such, as without partiality, and passion, make use of their naturall reason, and therefore leaves the violaters thereof without excuse; yet considering there be very few, perhaps none, that in some cases are not blinded by self love, or some other passion, it is now become of all Laws the most obscure; and has consequently the greatest need of able Interpreters. The written Laws, if they be short, are easily mis-interpreted, from the divers significations of a word, or two: if long they be more obscure by the diverse significations of many words: in so much as no written Law, delivered in few, or many words, can be well understood, without a perfect understanding of the finall causes, for which the Law was made; the knowledge of which finall causes is in the Legislator. To him therefore there can not be any knot in the Law, insoluble; either by finding out the ends, to undoe it by; or else by making what ends he will, (as *Alexander* did with his sword in the Gordian knot,) by the Legislative power; which no other Interpreter can doe.

The Authenticall Interpreta- The Interpretation of the Lawes of Nature, in a Common-wealth, dependeth not on the books of Morall Philosophy. The Authority of writers, without the Authority of the Common-wealth, maketh not their opinions Law, be they never so true. That which I have written in this Treatise, concerning the Morall Vertues, and of their necessity, for the procuring, and maintaining peace, though it bee evident Truth, is not therefore presently Law; but because in all Common-wealths in the world, it is part of the Civill Law: For though it be naturally reasonable; yet it is by the Soveraigne Power that it is Law: Otherwise, it were a great errour, to call the Lawes of Nature unwritten Law; whereof wee see so many volumes published, and in them so many contradictions of one another, and of themselves.

tion of Law is not that of writers.

The Interpretation of the Law of Nature, is the Sentence of the Judge constituted by the Soveraign Authority, to heare and determine such controversies, as depend thereon; and consisteth in the application of the Law to the present case. For in the act of Judicature, the Judge doth no more but consider, whither the demand of the party, be con-sonant to naturall reason, and Equity; and the Sentence he giveth, is therefore the Interpretation of the Law of Nature; which Interpretation is Authentique;[7] not because it is his private Sentence; but because he giveth it by Authority of the Soveraign, whereby it becomes the Sov-eraigns Sentence; which is Law for that time, to the parties pleading.

The Interpreter of the Law is the Judge giv-ing sentence vivâ voce *in every particu-lar case.*

But because there is no Judge Subordinate, nor Soveraign, but may erre in a Judgement of Equity; if afterward in another like case he find it more consonant to Equity to give a contrary Sentence, he is obliged to doe it. No mans error becomes his own Law; nor obliges him to persist in it. Neither (for the same reason) becomes it a Law to other Judges, though sworn to follow it. For though a wrong Sentence given by authority of the Soveraign, if he know and allow it, in such Lawes as are mutable, be a constitution of a new Law, in cases, in which every little circumstance is the same; yet in Lawes immutable, such as are the Lawes of Nature, they are no Lawes to the same, or other Judges, in the like cases for ever after. Princes succeed one another; and one Judge passeth, another commeth; nay, Heaven and Earth shall passe; but not one title of the Law of Nature shall passe; for it is the Eternall Law of God. Therefore all the Sentences of precedent Judges that have ever been, cannot all together make a Law contrary to naturall Equity: Nor any Examples of former Judges, can warrant an unreasonable Sen-tence, or discharge the present Judge of the trouble of studying what is Equity (in the case he is to Judge,) from the principles of his own naturall reason. For example sake, 'Tis against the Law of Nature, *To punish the Innocent*; and Innocent is he that acquitteth himselfe Judi-cially, and is acknowledged for Innocent by the Judge. Put the case now, that a man is accused of a capitall crime, and seeing the power and malice of some enemy, and the frequent corruption and partiality of Judges, runneth away for feare of the event, and afterwards is taken, and brought to a legall triall, and maketh it sufficiently appear, he was not guilty of the crime, and being thereof acquitted, is neverthelesse condemned to lose his goods; this is a manifest condemnation of the

[144]
The Sentence of a Judge, does not bind him, or an-other Judge to give like Sen-tence in like Cases ever after.

7. Authoritative.

Innocent. I say therefore, that there is no place in the world, where this can be an interpretation of a Law of Nature, or be made a Law by the Sentences of precedent Judges, that had done the same. For he that judged it first, judged unjustly; and no Injustice can be a pattern of Judgement to succeeding Judges. A written Law may forbid innocent men to fly, and they may be punished for flying: But that flying for feare of injury, should be taken for presumption of guilt, after a man is already absolved of the crime Judicially, is contrary to the nature of a Presumption, which hath no place after Judgement given. Yet this is set down by a great Lawyer for the common Law of *England*. *If a man* (saith he) *that is Innocent, be accused of Felony, and for feare flyeth for the same; albeit he judicially acquitteth himselfe of the Felony; yet if it be found that he fled for the Felony, he shall notwithstanding his Innocency, Forfeit all his goods, chattells, debts, and duties. For as to the Forfeiture of them, the Law will admit no proofe against the Presumption in Law, grounded upon his flight.*[8] Here you see, An Innocent man, Judicially acquitted, notwithstanding his Innocency, (when no written Law forbad him to fly) after his acquitall, *upon a Presumption in Law,* condemned to lose all the goods he hath. If the Law ground upon his [145] flight a Presumption of the fact, (which was Capitall,) the Sentence ought to have been Capitall: if the Presumption were not of the Fact, for what then ought he to lose his goods? This therefore is no Law of *England*; nor is the condemnation grounded upon a Presumption of Law, but upon the Presumption of the Judges. It is also against Law, to say that no Proofe shall be admitted against a Presumption of Law. For all Judges, Soveraign and subordinate, if they refuse to heare Proofe, refuse to do Justice: for though the Sentence be Just, yet the Judges that condemn without hearing the Proofes offered, are Unjust Judges, and their Presumption is but Prejudice; which no man ought to bring with him to the Seat of Justice, whatsoever precedent judgements, or examples he shall pretend to follow. There be other things of this nature, wherein mens Judgements have been perverted, by trusting to Precedents: but this is enough to shew, that though the Sentence of the Judge, be a Law to the party pleading, yet it is no Law to any Judge, that shall succeed him in that Office.

In like manner, when question is of the Meaning of written Lawes, he is not the Interpreter of them, that writeth a Commentary upon them. For Commentaries are commonly more subject to cavill, than the Text; and therefore need other Commentaries; and so there will be no end of such Interpretation. And therefore unlesse there be an Interpreter authorised by the Soveraign, from which the subordinate Judges are not to recede, the Interpreter can be no other than the ordinary Judges, in the same manner, as they are in cases of the unwritten Law; and their Sentences are to be taken by them that plead, for Lawes in that particular case; but not to bind other Judges, in like cases to give like judgements. For a Judge may erre in the Interpretation even of written Lawes; but no errour of a subordinate Judge, can change the Law, which is the generall Sentence of the Soveraigne.

8. A reference to Sir Edward Coke's *The First Part of the Institutes of the Lawes of England* (2nd ed., London, 1629).

In written Lawes, men use to make a difference between the Letter, and the Sentence of the Law: And when by the Letter, is meant whatsoever can be gathered from the bare words, 'tis well distinguished. For the significations of almost all words, are either in themselves, or in the metaphoricall use of them, ambiguous; and may be drawn in argument, to make many senses; but there is onely one sense of the Law. But if by the Letter, be meant the literall sense, then the Letter, and the Sentence or intention of the Law, is all one. For the literall sense is that, which the Legislator intended, should by the letter of the Law be signified. Now the Intention of the Legislator is always supposed to be Equity: For it were a great contumely for a Judge to think otherwise of the Soveraigne. He ought therefore, if the Word of the Law doe not fully authorise a reasonable Sentence, to supply[9] it with the Law of Nature; or if the case be difficult, to respit[1] Judgement till he have received more ample authority. For Example, a written Law ordaineth, that he which is thrust out of his house by force, shall be restored by force: It happens that a man by negligence leaves his house empty, and returning is kept out by force, in which case there is no speciall Law ordained. It is evident, that this case is contained in the same Law: for else there is no remedy for him at all; which is to be supposed against the Intention of the Legislator. Again, the word of the Law, commandeth to Judge according to the Evidence: A man is accused falsly of a fact, which the Judge saw himself done by another; and not by him that is accused. In this case neither shall the Letter of the Law be followed to the condemnation of the Innocent, nor shall the Judge give Sentence against the evidence of the Witnesses; because the Letter of the Law is to the contrary: but procure of the Soveraign that another be made Judge, and himself Witnesse. So that the incommodity that follows the bare words of a written Law, may lead him to the Intention of the Law, whereby to interpret the same the better; though no Incommodity can warrant a Sentence against the Law. For every Judge of Right, and Wrong, is not Judge of what is Commodious, or Incommodious to the Common-wealth.

The difference between the Letter and Sentence of the Law.

[146]

The abilities required in a good Interpreter of the Law, that is to say, in a good Judge, are not the same with those of an Advocate; namely the study of the Lawes. For a Judge, as he ought to take notice of the Fact, from none but the Witnesses; so also he ought to take notice of the Law, from nothing but the Statutes, and Constitutions of the Soveraign, alledged in the pleading, or declared to him by some that have authority from the Soveraign Power to declare them; and need not take care before-hand, what hee shall Judge; for it shall bee given him what hee shall say concerning the Fact, by Witnesses; and what hee shall say in point of Law, from those that shall in their pleadings shew it, and by authority interpret it upon the place. The Lords of Parlament in *England* were Judges, and most difficult causes have been heard and determined by them; yet few of them were much versed in the study of the Lawes, and fewer had made profession of them: and though they consulted with Lawyers, that were appointed to be present there for that

The abilities required in a Judge.

9. Supplement.
1. Reserve.

purpose; yet they alone had the authority of giving Sentence. In like manner, in the ordinary trialls of Right, Twelve men of the common People, are the Judges, and give Sentence, not onely of the Fact, but of the Right; and pronounce simply for the Complaynant, or for the Defendant; that is to say, are Judges not onely of the Fact, but also of the Right: and in a question of crime, not onely determine whether done, or not done; but also whether it be Murder, Homicide, Felony, Assault, and the like, which are determinations of Law: but because they are not supposed to know the Law of themselves, there is one that hath Authority to enforme them of it, in the particular case they are to Judge of. But yet if they judge not according to that he tells them, they are not subject thereby to any penalty; unlesse it be made appear, they did it against their consciences, or had been corrupted by reward.

The things that make a good Judge, or good Interpreter of the Lawes, are, first, A right understanding of that principall Law of Nature called Equity; which depending not on the reading of other mens Writings, [147] but on the goodnesse of a mans own naturall Reason, and Meditation, is presumed to be in those most, that have had most leisure, and had the most inclination to meditate thereon. Secondly, Contempt of unnecessary Riches, and Preferments. Thirdly, To be able in judgement to devest himselfe of all feare, anger, hatred, love, and compassion. Fourthly, and lastly, Patience to heare; diligent attention in hearing; and memory to retain, digest and apply what he hath heard.

Divisions of Law. The difference and division of the Lawes, has been made in divers manners, according to the different methods, of those men that have written of them. For it is a thing that dependeth not on Nature, but on the scope[2] of the Writer; and is subservient to every mans proper method. In the Institutions of Justinian, we find seven sorts of Civill Lawes. 1. The Edicts, Constitutions, and Epistles of the Prince, that is, of the Emperour; because the whole power of the people was in him. Like these, are the Proclamations of the Kings of England.

2. The Decrees of the whole people of Rome (comprehending the Senate,) when they were put to the Question by the Senate. These were Lawes, at first, by the vertue of the Soveraign Power residing in the people; and such of them as by the Emperours were not abrogated, remained Lawes by the Authority Imperiall. For all Lawes that bind, are understood to be Lawes by his authority that has power to repeale them. Somewhat like to these Lawes, are the Acts of Parliament in England.

3. The Decrees of the Common people (excluding the Senate,) when they were put to the question by the Tribune of the people. For such of them as were not abrogated by the Emperours, remained Lawes by the Authority Imperiall. Like to these, were the Orders of the House of Commons in England.

4. Senatûs consulta, the Orders of the Senate; because when the people of Rome grew so numerous, as it was inconvenient to assemble them; it was thought fit by the Emperour, that men should Consult

2. Purpose.

the Senate, in stead of the people: And these have some resemblance with the Acts of Counsell.

5. *The Edicts of Prætors*, and (in some Cases) of the *Ædiles*: such as are the Chiefe Justices in the Courts of *England*.

6. *Responsa Prudentum*; which were the Sentences, and Opinions of those Lawyers, to whom the Emperour gave Authority to interpret the Law, and to give answer to such as in matter of Law demanded their advice; which Answers, the Judges in giving Judgement were obliged by the Constitutions of the Emperour to observe: And should be like the Reports of Cases Judged, if other Judges be by the Law of *England* bound to observe them. For the Judges of the Common Law of *England*, are not properly Judges, but *Juris Consulti*;[3] of whom the Judges, who are either the Lords, or Twelve men of the Country, are in point of Law to ask advice.

7. Also, *Unwritten Customes*, (which in their own nature are an imitation of Law,) by the tacite consent of the Emperour, in case they be not contrary to the Law of Nature, are very Lawes.

Another division of Lawes, is into *Naturall* and *Positive*. *Naturall* are those which have been Lawes from all Eternity; and are called not onely *Naturall*, but also *Morall* Lawes; consisting in the Morall Vertues, as Justice, Equity, and all habits of the mind that conduce to Peace, and Charity; of which I have already spoken in the fourteenth and fifteenth Chapters.   [148]

Positive, are those which have not been from Eternity; but have been made Lawes by the Will of those that have had the Soveraign Power over others; and are either written, or made known to men, by some other argument of the Will of their Legislator.

Again, of Positive Lawes, some are *Humane*, some *Divine*: And of Humane positive lawes, some are *Distributive*, some *Penal*. *Distributive* are those that determine the Rights of the Subjects, declaring to every man what it is, by which he acquireth and holdeth a propriety in lands, or goods, and a right or liberty of action: and these speak to all the Subjects. *Penal* are those, which declare, what Penalty shall be inflicted on those that violate the Law; and speak to the Ministers and Officers ordained for execution. For though every one ought to be informed of the Punishments ordained beforehand for their transgression; neverthelesse the Command is not addressed to the Delinquent, (who cannot be supposed will faithfully punish himselfe,) but to publique Ministers appointed to see the Penalty executed. And these Penal Lawes are for the most part written together with the Lawes Distributive; and are sometimes called Judgements. For all Lawes are generall Judgements, or Sentences of the Legislator; as also every particular Judgement, is a Law to him, whose case is Judged.   *Another Division of Law.*

Divine Positive Lawes (for Naturall Lawes being Eternall, and Universall, are all Divine,) are those, which being the Commandements of God, (not from all Eternity, nor universally addressed to all men, but onely to a certain people, or to certain persons,) are declared for   *Divine Positive Law how made known to be Law.*

3. Legal experts; consultants.

such, by those whom God hath authorised to declare them. But this Authority of man to declare what be these Positive Lawes of God, how can it be known? God may command a man by a supernaturall way, to deliver Lawes to other men. But because it is of the essence of Law, that he who is to be obliged, be assured of the Authority of him that declareth it, which we cannot naturally take notice to be from God, *How can a man without supernaturall Revelation be assured of the Revelation received by the declarer?* and *how can he be bound to obey them?* For the first question, how a man can be assured of the Revelation of another, without a Revelation particularly to himselfe, it is evidently impossible: For though a man may be induced to believe such Revelation, from the Miracles they see him doe, or from seeing the Extraordinary sanctity of his life, or from seeing the Extraordinary wisedome, or Extraordinary felicity of his Actions, all which are marks of God[s] extraordinary favour; yet they are not assured evidences of speciall Revelation. Miracles are Marvellous workes: but that which is marvellous to one, may not be so to another. Sanctity may be feigned; and [149] the visible felicities of this world, are most often the work of God by Naturall, and ordinary causes. And therefore no man can infallibly know by naturall reason, that another has had a supernaturall revelation of Gods will; but only a beliefe; every one (as the signs thereof shall appear greater, or lesser) a firmer, or a weaker belief.

But for the second, how he can be bound to obey them; it is not so hard. For if the Law declared, be not against the Law of Nature (which is undoubtedly Gods Law) and he undertake to obey it, he is bound by his own act; bound I say to obey it, but not bound to believe it: for mens beliefe, and interiour cogitations, are not subject to the commands, but only to the operation of God, ordinary, or extraordinary. Faith of Supernaturall Law, is not a fulfilling, but only an assenting to the same; and not a duty that we exhibite to God, but a gift which God freely giveth to whom he pleaseth; as also Unbelief is not a breach of any of his Lawes; but a rejection of them all, except the Laws Naturall. But this that I say, will be made yet cleerer, by the Examples, and Testimonies concerning this point in holy Scripture. The Covenant God made with *Abraham* (in a Supernaturall manner) was thus, *This*

Gen. 17.10. *is the Covenant which thou shalt observe between Me and Thee a and thy Seed after thee.* Abrahams Seed had not this revelation, nor were yet in being; yet they are a party to the Covenant, and bound to obey what *Abraham* should declare to them for Gods Law; which they could not be, but in vertue of the obedience they owed to their Parents; who (if they be Subject to no other earthly power, as here in the case of *Abraham*) have Soveraign power over their children, and servants. Againe, where God saith to *Abraham, In thee shall all Nations of the earth be blessed: For I know thou wilt command thy children, and thy house after thee to keep the way of the Lord, and to observe Righteousnesse and Judgement,* it is manifest, the obedience of his Family, who had no Revelation, depended on their former obligation to obey their Soveraign. At Mount *Sinai Moses* only went up to God; the people were forbidden to approach on paine of death; yet were they bound to obey all that *Moses* declared to them for Gods Law. Upon what ground, but on this submission of their own, *Speak thou to us, and we will heare thee; but let not God speak to us, lest we dye?* By which two places it sufficiently appeareth, that in a Common-wealth, a subject that has no certain and assured Revelation particularly to himself concerning the Will of God, is to obey for such, the Command of the Common-wealth: for if men were at liberty, to take for Gods Commandements, their own dreams, and fancies, or the dreams and fancies of private men; scarce two men would agree upon what is Gods Commandement; and yet in respect of them, every man would despise the Commandements of the Common-wealth. I conclude therefore, that in all things not contrary to the Morall Law, (that is to say, to the Law of Nature,) all Subjects are bound to obey that for divine Law, which is declared to be so, by the Lawes of the Common-wealth. Which also is evident to any mans reason; for whatsoever is not against the Law of Nature, may be made Law in the name of them that have the Soveraign power; and there is no reason men should be the lesse obliged by it, when tis propounded in the name of God. Besides, there is no place in the world where men are permitted to pretend other Commandements of God, than are declared for such by the Common-wealth. Christian States punish those that revolt from Christian Religion, and all other States, those that set up any Religion by them forbidden. For in whatsoever is not regulated by the Common-wealth, tis Equity (which is the Law of Nature, and therefore an eternall Law of God) that every man equally enjoy his liberty. [150]

There is also another distinction of Laws, into *Fundamentall*, and not *Fundamentall*: but I could never see in any Author, what a Fundamentall Law signifieth. Nevertchelesse one may very reasonably distinguish Laws in that manner.

Another division of Lawes.

For a Fundamentall Law in every Common-wealth is that, which being taken away, the Common-wealth faileth, and is utterly dissolved; as a building whose Foundation is destroyed. And therefore a Fundamentall Law is that, by which Subjects are bound to uphold whatsoever power is given to the Soveraign, whether a Monarch, or a Soveraign Assembly, without which the Common-wealth cannot stand; such as is the power of War and Peace, of Judicature, of Election of Officers, and of doing whatsoever he shall think necessary for the Publique good. Not Fundamentall is that, the abrogating whereof, draweth not with it the dissolution of the Common-Wealth; such as are the Lawes concerning Controversies between subject and subject. Thus much of the Division of Lawes.

A Fundamentall Law what.

I find the words *Lex Civilis*, and *Jus Civile*, that is to say, *Law* and *Right Civil*, promiscuously used for the same thing, even in the most learned Authors; which neverthelesse ought not to be so. For *Right* is *Liberty*, namely that Liberty which the Civil Law leaves us: But *Civill Law* is an *Obligation*; and takes from us the Liberty which the Law of Nature gave us. Nature gave a Right to every man to secure himselfe by his own strength, and to invade a suspected neighbour, by way of prevention: but the Civill Law takes away that Liberty, in all cases

Difference between Law and Right:

where the protection of the Law may be safely stayd for. Insomuch as *Lex* and *Jus*, are as different as *Obligation* and *Liberty*.

And between a Law and a Charter. Likewise *Lawes* and *Charters* are taken promiscuously for the same thing. Yet Charters are Donations of the Soveraign; and not Lawes, but exemptions from Law. The phrase of a Law is *Jubeo, Injungo, I command*, and *Enjoyn*: the phrase of a Charter is *Dedi, Concessi, I have Given, I have Granted*: but what is given or granted, to a man, is not forced upon him, by a Law. A Law may be made to bind All the Subjects of a Common-wealth: a Liberty, or Charter is only to One man, or some One part of the people. For to say all the people of a Common-wealth, have Liberty in any case whatsoever; is to say, that in such case, there hath been no Law made; or else having been made, is now abrogated.

[151]

Chap. XXVII.

Of Crimes, Excuses, *and* Extenuations.

Sinne what. A *Sinne*, is not onely a Transgression of a Law, but also any Contempt of the Legislator. For such Contempt, is a breach of all his Lawes at once. And therefore may consist, not onely in the *Commission* of a Fact, or in the Speaking of Words by the Lawes forbidden, or in the *Omission* of what the Law commandeth, but also in the *Intention*, or purpose to transgresse. For the purpose to breake the Law, is some degree of Contempt of him, to whom it belongeth to see it executed. To be delighted in the Imagination onely, of being possessed of another mans goods, servants, or wife, without any intention to take them from him by force, or fraud, is no breach of the Law, that sayth, *Thou shalt not covet*: nor is the pleasure a man may have in imagining, or dreaming of the death of him, from whose life he expecteth nothing but dammage, and displeasure, a Sinne; but the resolving to put some Act in execution, that tendeth thereto. For to be pleased in the fiction of that, which would please a man if it were reall, is a Passion so adhærent to the Nature both of man, and every other living creature, as to make it a Sinne, were to make Sinne of being a man. The consideration of this, has made me think them too severe, both to themselves, and others, that maintain, that the First motions of the mind, (though checked with the fear of God) be Sinnes. But I confesse it is safer to erre on that hand, than on the other.

A Crime what. A Crime, is a sinne, consisting in the Committing (by Deed, or Word) of that which the Law forbiddeth, or the Omission of what it hath commanded. So that every Crime is a sinne; but not every sinne a Crime. To intend to steale, or kill, is a sinne, though it never appeare in Word, or Fact: for God that seeth the thoughts of man, can lay it to his charge: but till it appear by some thing done, or said, by which the intention may be argued by a humane Judge, it hath not the name of Crime: which distinction the Greeks observed, in the word ἁμάρτημα, and ἔγκλημα, or ἀιτία[1]; whereof the former, (which is translated *Sinne*,) signifieth any swarving from the Law whatsoever; but the two later, (which are translated *Crime*,) signifie that sinne onely, whereof one man may accuse another. But of Intentions, which never appear by any outward act, there is no place for humane accusation. In like manner the Latines by *Peccatum*, which is *Sinne*, signifie all manner of deviation from the Law; but by *Crimen*, (which word they derive from *Cerno*, which signifies to perceive,) they mean onely such sinnes, as may be made appear before a Judge; and therefore are not meer Intentions.

From this relation of Sinne to the Law, and of Crime to the Civill Law, may be inferred, First, that where Law ceaseth, Sinne ceaseth. But because the Law of Nature is eternall, Violation of Covenants, Ingratitude, Arrogance, and all Facts contrary to any Morall vertue, can never cease to be Sinne. Secondly, that the Civill Law ceasing, Crimes cease: for there being no other Law remaining, but that of Nature, there is no place for Accusation; every man being his own Judge, and accused onely by his own Conscience, and cleared by the Uprightnesse of his own Intention. When therefore his Intention is Right, his fact is no Sinne: if otherwise, his fact is Sinne; but not Crime. Thirdly, That when the Soveraign Power ceaseth, Crime also ceaseth: for where there is no such Power, there is no protection to be had from the Law; and therefore every one may protect himself by his own power: for no man in the Institution of Soveraign Power can be supposed to give away the Right of preserving his own body; for the safety whereof all Soveraignty was ordained. But this is to be understood onely of those, that have not themselves contributed to the taking away of the Power that protected them: for that was a Crime from the beginning.

[152]

Where no Civ-ill Law is, there is no Crime.

The source of every Crime, is some defect of the Understanding; or some errour in Reasoning; or some sudden force of the Passions. Defect in the Understanding, is *Ignorance*; in Reasoning, *Erroneous Opinion*. Again, Ignorance is of three sorts; of the *Law*, and of the *Soveraign*, and of the *Penalty*. Ignorance of the Law of Nature Excuseth no man; because every man that hath attained to the use of Reason, is supposed to know, he ought not to do to another, what he would not have done to himselfe. Therefore into what place soever a man shall come, if he do any thing contrary to that Law, it is a Crime. If a man come from the *Indies* hither, and perswade men here to receive a new Religion, or teach them any thing that tendeth to disobedience of the Lawes of this Country, though he be never so well perswaded of the truth of what he teacheth, he commits a Crime, and may be justly punished for the same, not onely because his doctrine is false, but also because he does that which he would not approve in another, namely, that comming from hence, he should endeavour to alter the Religion there. But ignorance of the Civill Law, shall Excuse a man in a strange Coun-try, till it be declared to him; because, till then no Civill Law is binding.

In the like manner, if the Civill Law of a mans own Country, be

Ignorance of the Law of Nature excus-eth no man.

Ignorance of the Civill Law excuseth sometimes.

1. *Hamartena*, and *egklema*, or *aitia*.

not so sufficiently declared, as he may know it if he will; nor the Action against the Law of Nature; the Ignorance is a good Excuse: In other cases Ignorance of the Civill Law, Excuseth not.

Ignorance of the Soveraign excuseth not.

Ignorance of the Soveraign Power, in the place of a mans ordinary residence, Excuseth him not; because he ought to take notice of the Power, by which he hath been protected there.

Ignorance of the Penalty excuseth not.

Ignorance of the Penalty, where the Law is declared, Excuseth no man: For in breaking the Law, which without a fear of penalty to follow, were not a Law, but vain words, he undergoeth the penalty, though he know not what it is; because, whosoever voluntarily doth any action, accepteth all the known consequences of it; but Punishment is a known consequence of the violation of the Lawes, in every Common-wealth; which punishment, if it be determined already by the Law, he is subject to that; if not, then is he subject to Arbitrary punishment. For it is reason, that he which does Injury, without other limitation than that of his own Will, should suffer punishment without other limitation, than that of his Will whose Law is thereby violated.

[153]

Punishments declared before the Fact, excuse from greater punishments after it.

But when a penalty, is either annexed to the Crime in the Law it selfe, or hath been usually inflicted in the like cases; there the Delinquent is Excused from a greater penalty. For the punishment foreknown, if not great enough to deterre men from the action, is an invitement to it: because when men compare the benefit of their Injustice, with the harm of their punishment, by necessity of Nature they choose that which appeareth best for themselves: and therefore when they are punished more than the Law had formerly determined, or more than others were punished for the same Crime; it is the Law that tempted, and deceiveth them.

Nothing can be made a Crime by a Law made after the Fact.

No Law, made after a Fact done, can make it a Crime: because if the Fact be against the Law of Nature, the Law was before the Fact; and a Positive Law cannot be taken notice of, before it be made; and therefore cannot be Obligatory. But when the Law that forbiddeth a Fact, is made before the Fact be done; yet he that doth the Fact, is lyable to the Penalty ordained after, in case no lesser Penalty were made known before, neither by Writing, nor by Example, for the reason immediatly before alledged.

False Principles of Right and Wrong causes of Crime

From defect in Reasoning, (that is to say, from Errour,) men are prone to violate the Lawes, three wayes. First, by Presumption of false Principles: as when men from having observed how in all places, and in all ages, unjust Actions have been authorised, by the force, and victories of those who have committed them; and that potent men, breaking through the Cob-web Lawes of their Country, the weaker sort, and those that have failed in their Enterprises, have been esteemed the onely Criminals; have thereupon taken for Principles, and grounds of their Reasoning, *That Justice is but a vain word: That whatsoever a man can get by his own Industry, and hazard, is his own: That the Practice of all Nations cannot be unjust: That Examples of former times are good Arguments of doing the like again;* and many more of that kind: Which being granted, no Act in it selfe can be a Crime, but must be made so (not by the Law, but) by the success of them that commit it; and the

same Fact be vertuous, or vicious, as Fortune pleaseth; so that what
Marius[2] makes a Crime, *Sylla*[3] shall make meritorious, and *Cæsar* (the
same Lawes standing) turn again into a Crime, to the perpetuall disturbance of the Peace of the Common-wealth.

Secondly, by false Teachers, that either mis-interpret the Law of
Nature, making it thereby repugnant to the Law Civill; or by teaching
for Lawes, such Doctrines of their own, or Traditions of former times,
as are inconsistent with the duty of a Subject.

*False Teachers
mis-interpret-
ing the Law
of Nature,*

Thirdly, by Erroneous Inferences from True Principles; which happens commonly to men that are hasty, and præcipitate in concluding,
and resolving what to do; such as are they, that have both a great
opinion of their own understanding, and believe that things of this
nature require not time and study, but onely common experience, and
a good naturall wit; whereof no man thinks himselfe unprovided:
whereas the knowledge, of Right and Wrong, which is no lesse difficult,
there is no man will pretend to, without great and long study. And of
those defects in Reasoning, there is none that can Excuse (though some
of them may Extenuate) a Crime, in any man, that pretendeth to the
administration of his own private businesse; much lesse in them that
undertake a publique charge; because they pretend to the Reason, upon
the want whereof they would ground their Excuse.

[154]
*And false In-
ferences from
true Princi-
ples, by
Teachers.*

Of the Passions that most frequently are the causes of Crime, one,
is Vain-glory, or a foolish over-rating of their own worth; as if difference
of worth, were an effect of their wit, or riches, or bloud, or some other
naturall quality, not depending on the Will of those that have the Soveraign Authority. From whence proceedeth a Presumption that the
punishments ordained by the Lawes, and extended generally to all Subjects, ought not to be inflicted on them, with the same rigour they are
inflicted on poore, obscure, and simple men, comprehended under the
name of the *Vulgar.*

*By their Pas-
sions;*

Therefore it happeneth commonly, that such as value themselves by
the greatnesse of their wealth, adventure on Crimes, upon hope of
escaping punishment, by corrupting publique Justice, or obtaining Pardon by Mony, or other rewards.

*Presumption
of Riches,*

And that such as have multitude of Potent Kindred; and popular
men, that have gained reputation amongst the Multitude, take courage
to violate the Lawes, from a hope of oppressing[4] the Power, to whom
it belongeth to put them in execution.

And Friends;

And that such as have a great, and false opinion of their own Wisedome, take upon them to reprehend the actions, and call in question
the Authority of them that govern, and so to unsettle the Lawes with
their publique discourse, as that nothing shall be a Crime, but what
their own designes require should be so. It happeneth also to the same
men, to be prone to all such Crimes, as consist in Craft, and in deceiving of their Neighbours; because they think their designes are too

Wisedome.

2. Gaius Marius, a Roman general who staged a coup in 87 B.C. after a civil war.
3. Lucius Cornelius Sulla, a Roman general who opposed Marius and was dictator from 82 to
   79 B.C.
4. Overwhelming.

subtile to be perceived. These I say are effects of a false presumption of their own Wisdome. For of them that are the first movers in the disturbance of Common-wealth, (which can never happen without a Civill Warre,) very few are left alive long enough, to see their new Designes established: so that the benefit of their Crimes, redoundeth to Posterity, and such as would least have wished it: which argues they were not so wise, as they thought they were. And those that deceive upon hope of not being observed, do commonly deceive themselves, (the darknesse in which they believe they lye hidden, being nothing else but their own blindnesse;) and are no wiser than Children, that think all hid, by hiding their own eyes.

[155]   And generally all vain-glorious men, (unlesse they be withall timo-rous,) are subject to Anger; as being more prone than others to interpret for contempt, the ordinary liberty of conversation: And there are few Crimes that may not be produced by Anger.

Hatred, Lust, Ambition, Covetousnesse, causes of Crime.   As for the Passions, of Hate, Lust, Ambition, and Covetousnesse, what Crimes they are apt to produce, is so obvious to every mans experience and understanding, as there needeth nothing to be said of them, saving that they are infirmities, so annexed to the nature, both of man, and all other living creatures, as that their effects cannot be hindred, but by extraordinary use of Reason, or a constant severity in punishing them. For in those things men hate, they find a continuall, and unavoydable molestation; whereby either a mans patience must be everlasting, or he must be eased by removing the power of that which molesteth him: The former is difficult; the later is many times impossible, without some violation of the Law. Ambition, and Covetousnesse are Passions also that are perpetually incumbent,[5] and pressing; whereas Reason is not perpetually present, to resist them: and therefore whensoever the hope of impunity appears, their effects proceed. And for Lust, what it wants in the lasting, it hath in the vehemence, which sufficeth to weigh down the apprehension of all easie, or uncertain punishments.

Fear sometimes cause of Crime, as when the danger is neither present, nor corporeall.   Of all Passions, that which enclineth men least to break the Lawes, is Fear. Nay, (excepting some generous natures,) it is the onely thing, (when there is appearence of profit, or pleasure by breaking the Lawes,) that makes men keep them. And yet in many cases a Crime may be committed through Feare.

For not every Fear justifies the Action it produceth, but the fear onely of corporeall hurt, which we call *Bodily Fear*, and from which a man cannot see how to be delivered, but by the action. A man is assaulted, fears present death, from which he sees not how to escape, but by wounding him that assaulteth him; If he wound him to death, this is no Crime; because no man is supposed at the making of a Common-wealth, to have abandoned the defence of his life, or limbes, where the Law cannot arrive time enough to his assistance. But to kill a man, because from his actions, or his threatnings, I may argue he will kill me when he can, (seeing I have time, and means to demand protection, from the Soveraign Power,) is a Crime. Again, a man receives words

5. Weighing on (the mind).

of disgrace, or some little injuries (for which they that made the Lawes, had assigned no punishment, nor thought it worthy of a man that hath the use of Reason, to take notice of,) and is afraid, unlesse he revenge it, he shall fall into contempt, and consequently be obnoxious to the like injuries from others; and to avoyd this, breaks the Law, and protects himselfe for the future, by the terrour of his private revenge. This is a Crime: For the hurt is not Corporeall, but Phantasticall,[6] and (though in this corner of the world, made sensible by a custome not many years since begun, amongst young and vain men,) so light, as a gallant man, and one that is assured of his own courage, cannot take notice of. Also a man may stand in fear of Spirits, either through his own superstition, or through too much credit given to other men, that tell him of strange [156] Dreams and Visions; and thereby be made believe they will hurt him, for doing, or omitting divers things, which neverthelesse, to do or omit, is contrary to the Lawes; And that which is so done, or omitted, is not to be Excused by this fear; but is a Crime. For (as I have shewn before in the second Chapter) Dreams be naturally but the fancies remaining in sleep, after the impressions our Senses had formerly received waking; and when men are by any accident unassured they have slept, seem to be reall Visions; and therefore he that presumes to break the Law upon his own, or anothers Dream, or pretended Vision, or upon other Fancy of the power of Invisible Spirits, than is permitted by the Common-wealth, leaveth the Law of Nature, which is a certain offence, and followeth the imagery of his own, or another private mans brain, which he can never know whether it signifieth any thing, or nothing, nor whether he that tells his Dream, say true, or lye; which if every private man should have leave to do, (as they must by the Law of Nature, if any one have it) there could no Law be made to hold, and so all Common-wealth would be dissolved.

From these different sources of Crimes, it appeares already, that all Crimes are not (as the Stoicks of old time maintained) of the same allay.[7] There is place, not only for Excuse, by which that which seemed a Crime, is proved to be none at all; but also for Extenuation, by which the Crime, that seemed great, is made lesse. For though all Crimes doe equally deserve the name of Injustice, as all deviation from a strait line is equally crookednesse, which the Stoicks rightly observed; yet it does not follow that all Crimes are equally unjust, no more than that all crooked lines are equally crooked; which the Stoicks not observing, held it as great a Crime, to kill a Hen, against the Law, as to kill ones Father. *Crimes not equall.*

That which totally Excuseth a Fact, and takes away from it the nature of a Crime, can be none but that, which at the same time, taketh away the obligation of the Law. For the fact committed once against the Law, if he that committed it be obliged to the Law, can be no other than a Crime. *Totall Excuses.*

The want of means to know the Law, totally Excuseth: For the Law whereof a man has no means to enforme himself, is not obligatory. But

6. Mental or imaginary (rather than physical).
7. Quality; intrinsic character.

the want of diligence to enquire, shall not be considered as a want of means; Nor shall any man, that pretendeth to reason enough for the Government of his own affairs, be supposed to want means to know the Lawes of Nature· because they are known by the reason he pretends to: only Children, and Madmen are Excused from offences against the Law Naturall.

Where a man is captive, or in the power of the enemy, (and he is then in the power of the enemy, when his person, or his means of living, is so,) if it be without his own fault, the Obligation of the Law ceaseth; because he must obey the enemy, or dye; and consequently such obedience is no Crime: for no man is obliged (when the protection of the Law faileth,) not to protect himself, by the best means he can.

[157]   If a man by the terrour of present death, be compelled to doe a fact against the Law, he is totally Excused; because no Law can oblige a man to abandon his own preservation. And supposing such a Law were obligatory; yet a man would reason thus, *If I doe it not, I die presently; if I doe it, I die afterwards; therefore by doing it, there is time of life gained;* Nature therefore compells him to the fact.

When a man is destitute of food, or other thing necessary for his life, and cannot preserve himselfe any other way, but by some fact against the Law; as if in a great famine he take the food by force, or stealth, which he cannot obtaine for mony, nor charity; or in defence of his life, snatch away another mans Sword, he is totally Excused, for the reason next before alledged.

Excuses against the Author.   Again, Facts done against the Law, by the authority of another, are by that authority Excused against the Author; because no man ought to accuse his own fact in another, that is but his instrument: but it is not Excused against a third person thereby injured; because in the violation of the Law, both the Author, and Actor are Criminalls. From hence it followeth that when that Man, or Assembly, that hath the Soveraign Power, commandeth a man to do that which is contrary to a former Law, the doing of it is totally Excused: For he ought not to condemn it himselfe, because he is the Author; and what cannot justly be condemned by the Soveraign, cannot justly be punished by any other. Besides, when the Soveraign commandeth any thing to be done against his own former Law, the Command, as to that particular fact, is an abrogation of the Law.

If that Man, or Assembly, that hath the Soveraign Power, disclaime any Right essentiall to the Soveraignty, whereby there accrueth to the Subject, any liberty inconsistent with the Soveraign Power, that is to say, with the very being of a Common-wealth, if the Subject shall refuse to obey the Command in any thing, contrary to the liberty granted, this is neverthelesse a Sinne, and contrary to the duty of the Subject: for he ought to take notice of what is inconsistent with the Soveraignty, because it was erected by his own consent, and for his own defence; and that such liberty as is inconsistent with it, was granted through ignorance of the evill consequence thereof. But if he not onely disobey, but also resist a publique Minister in the execution of it, then it is a

Crime; because he might have been righted, (without any breach of the Peace,) upon complaint.

The Degrees of Crime are taken on divers Scales, and measured, First, by the malignity of the Source, or Cause: Secondly, by the contagion of the Example: Thirdly, by the mischiefe of the Effect; and Fourthly, by the concurrence of Times, Places, and Persons.

The same Fact done against the Law, if it proceed from Presumption of strength, riches, or friends to resist those that are to execute the Law, is a greater Crime, than if it proceed from hope of not being discovered, or of escape by flight: For Presumption of impunity by force, is a Root, from whence springeth, at all times, and upon all temptations, a contempt of all Lawes; whereas in the later case, the apprehension of danger, that makes a man fly, renders him more obedient for the future. A Crime which we know to be so, is greater than the same Crime proceeding from a false perswasion that it is lawfull: For he that committeth it against his own conscience, presumeth on his force, or other power, which encourages him to commit the same again: but he that doth it by errour, after the errour shewn him, is conformable to the Law. *Presumption of Power, aggravateth.*   [158]

Hee, whose errour proceeds from the authority of a Teacher, or an Interpreter of the Law publiquely authorised, is not so faulty, as he whose errour proceedeth from a peremptory pursute of his own principles, and reasoning: For what is taught by one that teacheth by publique Authority, the Common-wealth teacheth, and hath a resemblance of Law, till the same Authority controuleth it; and in all Crimes that contain not in them a denyall of the Soveraign Power, nor are against an evident Law, Excuseth totally: whereas he that groundeth his actions, on his private Judgement, ought according to the rectitude, or errour thereof, to stand, or fall. *Evill Teachers, Extenuate.*

The same Fact, if it have been constantly punished in other men, is a greater Crime, than if there have been many precedent Examples of impunity. For those Examples, are so many hopes of Impunity, given by the Soveraign himselfe: And because he which furnishes a man with such a hope, and presumption of mercy, as encourageth him to offend, hath his part in the offence; he cannot reasonably charge the offender with the whole. *Examples of Impunity, Extenuate.*

A Crime arising from a sudden Passion, is not so great, as when the same ariseth from long meditation: For in the former case there is a place for Extenuation, in the common infirmity of humane nature: but he that doth it with præmeditation, has used circumspection, and cast his eye, on the Law, on the punishment, and on the consequence thereof to humane society; all which in committing the Crime, hee hath contemned, and postposed[8] to his own appetite. But there is no suddennesse of Passion sufficient for a totall Excuse: For all the time between the first knowing of the Law, and the Commission of the Fact, shall be taken for a time of deliberation; because he ought by meditation of the Law, to rectifie the irregularity of his Passions. *Præmeditation, Aggravateth.*

8. Subordinated.

Where the Law is publiquely, and with assiduity, before all the people read, and interpreted; a fact done against it, is a greater Crime, than where men are left without such instruction, to enquire of it with difficulty, uncertainty, and interruption of their Callings, and be informed by private men: for in this case, part of the fault is discharged upon common infirmity; but in the former, there is apparent negligence, which is not without some contempt of the Soveraign Power.

Tacite appro-
bation of the
Soveraign,
Extenuates.

[159]

Those facts which the Law expresly condemneth, but the Law-maker by other manifest signes of his will tacitly approveth, are lesse Crimes, than the same facts, condemned both by the Law, and Law-maker. For seeing the will of the Law-maker is a Law, there appear in this case two contradictory Lawes; which would totally Excuse, if men were bound to take notice of the Soveraigns approbation, by other arguments, than are expressed by his command. But because there are punishments consequent, not onely to the transgression of his Law, but also to the observing of it, he is in part a cause of the transgression, and therefore cannot reasonably impute the whole Crime to the Delinquent. For example, the Law condemneth Duells; the punishment is made capitall: On the contrary part, he that refuseth Duell, is subject to contempt and scorne, without remedy; and sometimes by the Soveraign himselfe thought unworthy to have any charge, or preferment in Warre: If thereupon he accept Duell, considering all men lawfully endeavour to obtain the good opinion of them that have the Soveraign Power, he ought not in reason to be rigorously punished; seeing part of the fault may be discharged on the punisher: which I say, not as wishing liberty of private revenges, or any other kind of disobedience; but a care in Governours, not to countenance any thing obliquely, which directly they forbid. The examples of Princes, to those that see them, are, and ever have been, more potent to govern their actions, than the Lawes themselves. And though it be our duty to do, not what they do, but what they say; yet will that duty never be performed, till it please God to give men an extraordinary, and supernaturall grace to follow that Precept.

Comparison of
Crimes from
their Effects.

Again, if we compare Crimes by the mischiefe of their Effects, First, the same fact, when it redounds to the dammage of many, is greater, than when it redounds to the hurt of few. And therefore, when a fact hurteth, not onely in the present, but also, (by example) in the future, it is a greater Crime, than if it hurt onely in the present: for the former, is a fertile Crime, and multiplyes to the hurt of many; the later is barren. To maintain doctrines contrary to the Religion established in the Common-wealth, is a greater fault, in an authorised Preacher, than in a private person: So also is it, to live prophanely, incontinently, or do any irreligious act whatsoever. Likewise in a Professor of the Law, to maintain any point, or do any act, that tendeth to the weakning of the Soveraign Power, is a greater Crime, than in another man: Also in a man that hath such reputation for wisedome, as that his counsells are followed, or his actions imitated by many, his fact against the Law, is a greater Crime, than the same fact in another: For such men not onely commit Crime, but teach it for Law to all other men. And generally all Crimes are the greater, by the scandall they give; that is to say, by becomming stumbling-blocks to the weak, that look not so much upon the way they go in, as upon the light that other men carry before them.

Also Facts of hostility against the present state of the Common-wealth, are greater Crimes, than the same acts done to private men: For the dammage extends it selfe to all: Such are the betraying of the strengths, or revealing of the secrets of the Common-wealth to an Enemy; also all attempts upon the Representative of the Common-wealth, be it a Monarch, or an Assembly; and all endeavours by word, or deed to diminish the Authority of the same, either in the present time, or in succession: which Crimes the Latines understand by *Crimina læsæ Majestatis*, and consist in designe, or act, contrary to a Fundamentall Law. *Læsæ Majestas.* [160]

Likewise those Crimes, which render Judgements of no effect, are greater Crimes, than Injuries done to one, or a few persons; as to receive mony to give False judgement, or testimony, is a greater Crime, than otherwise to deceive a man of the like, or a greater summe; because not onely he has wrong, that falls by such judgements; but all Judgements are rendered uselesse, and occasion ministred to force,[9] and private revenges. *Bribery and False testimony.*

Also Robbery, and Depeculation[1] of the Publique treasure, or Revenues, is a greater Crime, than the robbing, or defrauding of a Private man; because to robbe the publique, is to robbe many at once. *Depeculation.*

Also the Counterfeit usurpation of publique Ministery, the Counterfeiting of publique Seales, or publique Coine, than counterfeiting of a private mans person, or his seale; because the fraud thereof, extendeth to the dammage of many. *Counterfeiting Authority*

Of facts against the Law, done to private men, the greater Crime, is that, where the dammage in the common opinion of men, is most sensible. And therefore *Crimes against private men compared.*

To kill against the Law, is a greater Crime, than any other injury, life preserved.

And to kill with Torment, greater, than simply to kill.

And Mutilation of a limbe, greater, than the spoyling a man of his goods.

And the spoyling a man of his goods, by Terrour of death, or wounds, than by clandestine surreption.[2]

And by clandestine Surreption, than by consent fraudulently obtained.

And the violation of chastity by Force, greater, than by flattery.

And of a woman Married, than of a woman not married.

For all these things are commonly so valued; though some men are more, and some lesse sensible of the same offence. But the Law regardeth not the particular, but the generall inclination of mankind.

And therefore the offence men take, from contumely, in words, or gesture, when they produce no other harme, than the present griefe of him that is reproached, hath been neglected in the Lawes of the Greeks,

9. Create opportunities for the use of force.
1. Embezzlement.
2. Theft.

Romans, and other both antient, and moderne Common-wealths; supposing the true cause of such griefe to consist, not in the contumely, (which takes no hold upon men conscious of their own vertue,) but in the Pusillanimity of him that is offended by it.

Also a Crime against a private man, is much aggravated by the person, time, and place. For to kill ones Parent, is a greater Crime, than to kill another: for the Parent ought to have the honour of a Soveraign, (though he have surrendred his Power to the Civill Law,) because he had it originally by Nature. And to Robbe a poore man, is a greater Crime, than to robbe a rich man; because 'tis to the poore a more sensible dammage.

[161]

And a Crime committed in the Time, or Place appointed for Devotion, is greater, than if committed at another time or place: for it proceeds from a greater contempt of the Law.

Many other cases of Aggravation, and Extenuation might be added: but by these I have set down, it is obvious to every man, to take the altitude of any other Crime proposed.

Publique
Crimes what.

Lastly, because in almost all Crimes there is an Injury done, not onely to some Private men, but also to the Common-wealth; the same Crime, when the accusation is in the name of the Common-wealth, is called Publique Crime; and when in the name of a Private man, a Private Crime; And the Pleas according thereunto called Publique, *Judicia Publica*, Pleas of the Crown; or Private Pleas. As in an Accusation of Murder, if the accuser be a Private man, the plea is a Private plea; if the accuser be the Soveraign, the plea is a Publique plea.

Chap. XXVIII.

Of Punishments, *and* Rewards.

The defini-
tion of
Punishment.

A Punishment, *is an Evill inflicted by publique Authority, on him that hath done, or omitted that which is Judged by the same Authority to be a Transgression of the Law; to the end that the will of men may thereby the better be disposed to obedience.*

Right to Pun-
ish whence
derived.

Before I inferre any thing from this definition, there is a question to be answered, of much importance; which is, by what door the Right, or Authority of Punishing in any case, came in. For by that which has been said before, no man is supposed bound by Covenant, not to resist violence; and consequently it cannot be intended,[1] that he gave any right to another to lay violent hands upon his person. In the making of a Common-wealth, every man giveth away the right of defending another; but not of defending himselfe. Also he obligeth himselfe, to assist him that hath the Soveraignty, in the Punishing of another; but of himselfe not. But to covenant to assist the Soveraign, in doing hurt to another, unlesse he that so covenanteth have a right to doe it himselfe, is not to give him a Right to Punish. It is manifest therefore that the

1. Understood.

Right which the Common-wealth (that is, he, or they that represent it) hath to Punish, is not grounded on any concession, or gift of the Subjects. But I have also shewed formerly, that before the Institution of Common-wealth, every man had a right to every thing, and to do whatsoever he thought necessary to his own preservation; subduing, hurting, or killing any man in order thereunto. And this is the foundation of that right of Punishing, which is exercised in every Common-wealth. For the Subjects did not give the Soveraign that right; but onely in laying down theirs, strengthned him to use his own, as he should think fit, for the preservation of them all: so that it was not given, but left to him, and to him onely; and (excepting the limits set him by naturall Law) as entire, as in the condition of meer Nature, and of warre of every one against his neighbour.

[162]

From the definition of Punishment, I inferre, First, that neither private revenges, nor injuries of private men, can properly be stiled Punishment; because they proceed not from publique Authority.

Private injuries, and revenges no Punishments:

Secondly, that to be neglected, and unpreferred by the publique favour, is not a Punishment; because no new evill is thereby on any man Inflicted; he is onely left in the estate he was in before.

Nor deny-all of preferment:

Thirdly, that the evill inflicted by publique Authority, without precedent publique condemnation,[2] is not to be stiled by the name of Punishment; but of an hostile act; because the fact for which a man is Punished, ought first to be Judged by publique Authority, to be a transgression of the Law.

Nor pain inflicted without publique hearing:

Fourthly, that the evill inflicted by usurped power, and Judges without Authority from the Soveraign, is not Punishment; but an act of hostility; because the acts of power usurped, have not for Author, the person condemned; and therefore are not acts of publique Authority.

Nor pain inflicted by Usurped power:

Fifthly, that all evill which is inflicted without intention, or possibility of disposing the Delinquent, or (by his example) other men, to obey the Lawes, is not Punishment; but an act of hostility; because without such an end, no hurt done is contained under that name.

Nor pain inflicted without respect to the future good.

Sixthly, whereas to certain actions, there be annexed by Nature, divers hurtfull consequences; as when a man in assaulting another, is himselfe slain, or wounded; or when he falleth into sicknesse by the doing of some unlawfull act; such hurt, though in respect of God, who is the author of Nature, it may be said to be inflicted, and therefore a Punishment divine; yet it is not contaned in the name of Punishment in respect of men, because it is not inflicted by the Authority of man.

Naturall evil consequences, no Punishments.

Seventhly, If the harm inflicted be lesse than the benefit, or contentment that naturally followeth the crime committed, that harm is not within the definition; and is rather the Price, or Redemption, than the Punishment of a Crime: Because it is of the nature of Punishment, to have for end, the disposing of men to obey the Law; which end (if it be lesse than the benefit of the transgression) it attaineth not, but worketh a contrary effect.

Hurt inflicted, if lesse than the benefit of transgressing, is not Punishment.

Eighthly, If a Punishment be determined and prescribed in the Law

Where the Punishment is

2. Conviction.

annexed to the Law, a greater hurt is not Punishment, but Hostility.

it selfe, and after the crime committed, there be a greater Punishment inflicted, the excesse is not Punishment, but an act of hostility. For seeing the aym of Punishment is not a revenge, but terrour; and the terrour of a great Punishment unknown, is taken away by the declaration of a lesse, the unexpected addition is no part of the Punishment.

[163] But where there is no Punishment at all determined by the Law, there whatsoever is inflicted, hath the nature of Punishment. For he that goes about the violation of a Law, wherein no penalty is determined, expecteth an indeterminate, that is to say, an arbitrary Punishment.

Hurt inflicted for a fact done before the Law, no Punishment.

Ninthly, Harme inflicted for a Fact done before there was a Law that forbad it, is not Punishment, but an act of Hostility: For before the Law, there is no transgression of the Law: But Punishment supposeth a fact judged, to have been a transgression of the Law; Therefore Harme inflicted before the Law made, is not Punishment, but an act of Hostility.

The Representative of the Common-wealth Unpunishable. Hurt to Revolted Subjects is done by right of War, not by way of Punishment.

Tenthly, Hurt inflicted on the Representative of the Commonwealth, is not Punishment, but an act of Hostility: Because it is of the nature of Punishment, to be inflicted by publique Authority, which is the Authority only of the Representative it self.

Lastly, Harme inflicted upon one that is a declared enemy, fals not under the name of Punishment: Because seeing they were either never subject to the Law, and therefore cannot transgresse it; or having been subject to it, and professing to be no longer so, by consequence deny they can transgresse it, all the Harmes that can be done them, must be taken as acts of Hostility. But in declared Hostility, all infliction of evill is lawfull. From whence it followeth, that if a subject shall by fact, or word, wittingly, and deliberatly deny the authority of the Representative of the Common-wealth, (whatsoever penalty hath been formerly ordained for Treason,) he may lawfully be made to suffer whatsoever the Representative will: For in denying subjection, he denyes such Punishment as by the Law hath been ordained; and therefore suffers as an enemy of the Common-wealth; that is, according to the will of the Representative. For the Punishments set down in the Law, are to Subjects, not to Enemies; such as are they, that having been by their own act Subjects, deliberately revolting, deny the Soveraign Power.

The first, and most generall distribution of Punishments, is into *Divine*, and *Humane*. Of the former I shall have occasion, to speak, in a more convenient place hereafter.

Humane, are those Punishments that be inflicted by the Commandement of Man; and are either *Corporall*, or *Pecuniary*, or *Ignominy*, or *Imprisonment*, or *Exile*, or mixt of these.

Punishments Corporall.

Corporall Punishment is that, which is inflicted on the body directly, and according to the intention of him that inflicteth it: such as are stripes, or wounds, or deprivation of such pleasures of the body, as were before lawfully enjoyed.

Capitall.

And of these, some be *Capitall*, some *Lesse* than *Capitall*. Capitall, is the Infliction of Death; and that either simply, or with torment. Lesse than Capitall, are Stripes, Wounds, Chains, and any other corporall Paine, not in its own nature mortall. For if upon the Infliction of a

Punishment death follow not in the intention of the Inflicter, the Punishment is not to bee esteemed Capitall, though the harme prove mortall by an accident not to be foreseen; in which case death is not [164] inflicted, but hastened.

Pecuniary Punishment, is that which consisteth not only in the deprivation of a Summe of Mony, but also of Lands, or any other goods which are usually bought and sold for mony. And in case the Law, that ordaineth such a punishment, be made with design to gather mony, from such as shall transgresse the same, it is not properly a Punishment, but the Price of priviledge, and exemption from the Law, which doth not absolutely forbid the fact, but only to those that are not able to pay the mony: except where the Law is Naturall, or part of Religion; for in that case it is not an exemption from the Law, but a transgression of it. As where a Law exacteth a Pecuniary mulct, of them that take the name of God in vaine, the payment of the mulct, is not the price of a dispensation to sweare, but the Punishment of the transgression of a Law undispensable. In like manner if the Law impose a Summe of Mony to be payd, to him that has been Injured; this is but a satisfaction for the hurt done him; and extinguisheth the accusation of the party injured, not the crime of the offender.

Ignominy, is the infliction of such Evill, as is made Dishonorable; or *Ignominy.* the deprivation of such Good, as is made Honourable by the Commonwealth. For there be some things Honorable by Nature; as the effects of Courage, Magna[ni]mity, Strength, Wisdome, and other abilities of body and mind: Others made Honorable by the Common-wealth; as Badges, Titles, Offices, or any other singular marke of the Soveraigns favour. The former, (though they may faile by nature, or accident,) cannot be taken away by a Law; and therefore the losse of them is not Punishment. But the later, may be taken away by the publique authority that made them Honorable, and are properly Punishments: Such are degrading men condemned, of their Badges, Titles, and Offices; or declaring them uncapable of the like in time to come.

Imprisonment, is when a man is by publique Authority deprived of *Imprisonment.* liberty; and may happen from two divers ends; whereof one is the safe custody of a man accused; the other is the inflicting of paine on a man condemned. The former is not Punishment; because no man is supposed to be Punisht, before he be Judicially heard, and declared guilty. And therefore whatsoever hurt a man is made to suffer by bonds, or restraint, before his cause be heard, over and above that which is necessary to assure his custody, is against the Law of Nature. But the later is Punishment, because Evill, and inflicted by publique Authority, for somewhat that has by the same Authority been Judged a Transgression of the Law. Under this word Impriso[n]ment, I comprehend all restraint of motion, caused by an externall obstacle, be it a House, which is called by the general name of a Prison; or an Iland, as when men are said to be confined to it; or a place where men are set to worke, as in old time men have been condemned to Quarries, and in these times to Gallies; or be it a Chaine, or any other such impediment.

Exile, (Banishment) is when a man is for a crime, condemned to *Exile*

[165] depart out of the dominion of the Common-wealth, or out of a certaine part thereof; and during a prefixed time, or for ever, not to return into it: and seemeth not in its own nature, without other circumstances, to be a Punishment; but rather an escape, or a publique commandement to avoid Punishment by flight. And *Cicero* sayes, there was never any such Punishment ordained in the City of *Rome*; but cals it a refuge of men in danger. For if a man banished, be neverthelesse permitted to enjoy his Goods, and the Revenue of his Lands, the meer change of ayr is no Punishment; nor does it tend to that benefit of the Common-wealth, for which all Punishments are ordained, (that is to say, to the forming of mens wils to the observation of the Law;) but many times to the dammage of the Common-wealth. For a Banished man, is a lawfull enemy of the Common-wealth that banished him; as being no more a Member of the same. But if he be withall deprived of his Lands, or Goods, then the Punishment lyeth not in the Exile, but is to be reckoned amongst Punishments Pecuniary.

The Punishment of Innocent Subjects is contrary to the Law of Nature.   All Punishments of Innocent subjects, be they great or little, are against the Law of Nature: For Punishment is only for Transgression of the Law, and therefore there can be no Punishment of the Innocent. It is therefore a violation, First, of that Law of Nature, which forbiddeth all men, in their Revenges, to look at any thing but some future good: For there can arrive no good to the Common-wealth, by Punishing the Innocent. Secondly, of that, which forbiddeth Ingratitude: For seeing all Soveraign Power, is originally given by the consent of every one of the Subjects, to the end they should as long as they are obedient, be protected thereby: the Punishment of the Innocent, is a rendring of Evill for Good. And thirdly, of the Law that commandeth Equity; that is to say, an equall distribution of Justice; which in Punishing the Innocent is not observed.

But the Harme done to Innocents in War, not so: But the Infliction of what evill soever, on an Innocent man, that is not a Subject, if it be for the benefit of the Common-wealth, and without violation of any former Covenant, is no breach of the Law of Nature. For all men that are not Subjects, are either Enemies, or else they have ceased from being so, by some precedent covenants. But against Enemies, whom the Commonwealth judgeth capable to do them hurt, it is lawfull by the originall Right of Nature to make warre; wherein the Sword Judgeth not, nor doth the Victor make distinction of Nocent,[3] and Innocent, as to the time past; nor has other respect of mercy, than as it conduceth to the good of his own People. And upon this ground it is, that also in Subjects, who deliberatly deny the Authority of the Common-wealth established, the vengeance is lawfully extended, not onely to the Fathers, but also to the third and fourth generation not yet in being, and consequently innocent of the fact, for which they are afflicted: because the nature of this offence, consisteth in the renouncing of subjection; which is a relapse into the condition of warre, commonly called Rebellion; and they that so offend, suffer not as Subjects, but as Enemies. For *Rebellion*, is but warre renewed.

Nor that which is done to declared Rebels.

[166]

3. Guilty.

REWARD, is either of *Gift*, or by *Contract*. When by Contract, it is called *Salary*, and *Wages*; which is benefit due for service performed, or promised. When of *Gift* it is benefit proceeding from the *grace* of them that bestow it, to encourage, or enable men to do them service. And therefore when the Soveraign of a Common wealth appointeth a Salary to any publique Office, he that receiveth it, is bound in Justice to performe his office; otherwise, he is bound onely in honour, to acknowledgement, and an endeavour of requitall. For though men have no lawfull remedy, when they be commanded to quit their private businesse, to serve the publique, without Reward, or Salary; yet they are not bound thereto, by the Law of Nature, nor by the Institution of the Common-wealth, unlesse the service cannot otherwise be done; because it is supposed the Soveraign may make use of all their means, insomuch as the most common Souldier, may demand the wages of his warrefare, as a debt.

Reward is either Salary, or Grace.

The benefits which a Soveraign bestoweth on a Subject, for fear of some power, and ability he hath to do hurt to the Common-wealth, are not properly Rewards; for they are not Salaryes; because there is in this case no contract supposed, every man being obliged already not to do the Common-wealth disservice: nor are they Graces; because they be extorted by fear, which ought not to be incident to the Soveraign Power: but are rather Sacrifices, which the Soveraign (considered in his naturall person, and not in the person of the Common-wealth) makes, for the appeasing the discontent of him he thinks more potent than himselfe; and encourage not to obedience, but on the contrary, to the continuance, and increasing of further extortion.

Benefits bestowed for fear, are not Rewards.

And whereas some Salaries are certain, and proceed from the publique Treasure; and others uncertain, and casuall, proceeding from the execution of the Office for which the Salary is ordained; the later is in some cases hurtfull to the Common-wealth; as in the case of Judicature. For where the benefit of the Judges, and Ministers of a Court of Justice, ariseth for the multitude of Causes that are brought to their cognisance, there must needs follow two Inconveniences: One, is the nourishing of sutes; for the more sutes, the greater benefit: and another that depends on that, which is contention about Jurisdiction; each Court drawing to it selfe, as many Causes as it can. But in offices of Execution there are not those Inconveniences; because their employment cannot be encreased by any endeavour of their own. And thus much shall suffice for the nature of Punishment, and Reward; which are, as it were, the Nerves and Tendons, that move the limbes and joynts of a Commonwealth.

Salaries Certain and Casuall.

Hitherto I have set forth the nature of Man, (whose Pride and other Passions have compelled him to submit himselfe to Government;) together with the great power of his Governour, whom I compared to *Leviathan*, taking that comparison out of the two last verses of the one and fortieth of *Job*; where God having set forth the great power of *Leviathan*, calleth him King of the Proud. *There is nothing*, saith he, *on earth, to be compared with him. He is made so as not to be afraid. Hee seeth every high thing below him; and is King of all the children of*

[167]

pride. But because he is mortall, and subject to decay, as all other Earthly creatures are; and because there is that in heaven, (though not on earth) that he should stand in fear of, and whose Lawes he ought to obey; I shall in the next following Chapters speak of his Diseases, and the causes of his Mortality; and of what Lawes of Nature he is bound to obey.

Chap. XXIX.

Of those things that Weaken, or tend to the DISSOLUTION *of a Common-wealth.*

Dissolution of Common-wealths proceedeth from their Imperfect Institution.

Though nothing can be immortall, which mortals make; yet, if men had the use of reason they pretend to, their Common-wealths might be secured, at least, from perishing by internall diseases. For by the nature of their Institution, they are designed to live, as long as Mankind, or as the Lawes of Nature, or as Justice it selfe, which gives them life. Therefore when they come to be dissolved, not by externall violence, but intestine disorder, the fault is not in men, as they are the *Matter*; but as they are the *Makers*, and orderers of them. For men, as they become at last weary of irregular[1] justling, and hewing one another, and desire with all their hearts, to conforme themselves into one firme and lasting edifice; so for want, both of the art of making fit Lawes, to square their actions by, and also of humility, and patience, to suffer the rude[2] and combersome points of their present greatnesse to be taken off, they cannot without the help of a very able Architect, be compiled, into any other than a crasie building, such as hardly lasting out their own time, must assuredly fall upon the heads of their posterity.

Amongst the *Infirmities* therefore of a Common-wealth, I will reckon in the first place, those that arise from an Imperfect Institution, and resemble the diseases of a naturall body, which proceed from a Defectuous[3] Procreation.

Want of Absolute power.

Of which, this is one, *That a man to obtain a Kingdome, is sometimes content with lesse Power, than to the Peace, and defence of the Commonwealth is necessarily required.* From whence it commeth to passe, that when the exercise of the Power layd by, is for the publique safety to be resumed, it hath the resemblance of an unjust act; which disposeth great numbers of men (when occasion is presented) to rebell; In the same manner as the bodies of children, gotten by diseased parents, are subject either to untimely death, or to purge the ill quality, derived from their vicious[4] conception, by breaking out into biles[5] and scabbs. And when Kings deny themselves some such necessary Power, it is not [168] alwayes (though sometimes) out of ignorance of what is necessary to

1. Disorderly.
2. Rough.
3. Defective.
4. Diseased or defective.
5. Boils.

the office they undertake; but many times out of a hope to recover the
same again at their pleasure: Wherein they reason not well; because
such as will hold them to their promises, shall be maintained against
them by forraign Common-wealths; who in order to the good of their
own Subjects let slip few occasions to *weaken* the estate of their Neighbours. So was *Thomas Becket* Archbishop of *Canterbury*, supported
against *Henry* the Second, by the Pope; the subjection of Ecclesiastiques to the Common-wealth, having been dispensed with by *William
the Conquerour* at his reception, when he took an Oath, not to infringe
the liberty of the Church. And so were the *Barons*, whose power was
by *William Rufus* (to have their help in transferring the Succession
from his Elder brother, to himselfe,) encreased to a degree, inconsistent
with the Soveraign Power, maintained in their Rebellion against King
John, by the French.

Nor does this happen in Monarchy onely. For whereas the stile of
the antient Roman Common-wealth, was, *The Senate, and People of
Rome*; neither Senate, nor People pretended to the whole Power; which
first caused the seditions, of *Tiberius Gracchus, Caius Gracchus, Lucius
Saturninus,*[6] and others; and afterwards the warres between the Senate
and the People, under *Marius* and *Sylla*; and again under *Pompey* and
Cæsar, to the Extinction of their Democraty, and the setting up of
Monarchy.

The people of *Athens* bound themselves but from one onely Action;
which was, that no man on pain of death should propound the renewing of the warre for the Island of *Salamis*; And yet thereby, if *Solon*
had not caused to be given out he was mad, and afterwards in gesture
and habit of a mad-man, and in verse, propounded it to the People that
flocked about him, they had had an enemy perpetually in readinesse,
even at the gates of their Citie; such dammage, or shifts, are all
Common-wealths forced to, that have their Power never so little
limited.

In the second place, I observe the *Diseases* of a Common-wealth, *Private Judge-*
that proceed from the poyson of seditious doctrines; whereof one is, *ment of Good*
That every private man is Judge of Good and Evill actions. This is true *and Evill.*
in the condition of meer Nature, where there are no Civill Lawes; and
also under Civill Government, in such cases as are not determined by
the Law. But otherwise, it is manifest, that the measure of Good and
Evill actions, is the Civill Law; and the Judge the Legislator, who is
alwayes Representative of the Common-wealth. From this false doctrine, men are disposed to debate with themselves, and dispute the
commands of the Common-wealth; and afterwards to obey, or disobey
them, as in their private judgements they shall think fit. Whereby the
Common-wealth is distracted and *Weakened.*

Another doctrine repugnant to Civill Society, is, that *whatsoever a* *Erroneous*
man does against his Conscience, is Sinne; and it dependeth on the *conscience.*
presumption of making himself judge of Good and Evill. For a mans
Conscience, and his Judgement is the same thing; and as the Judge-

6. Popular Roman politicians each of whom was elected tribune of the plebs in the first century
B.C., prior to the outbreak of civil war.

ment, so also the Conscience may be erroneous. Therefore, though he
[169] that is subject to no Civill Law, sinneth in all he does against his
Conscience, because he has no other rule to follow but his own reason;
yet it is not so with him that lives in a Common-wealth; because the
Law is the publique Conscience, by which he hath already undertaken
to be guided. Otherwise in such diversity, as there is of private Consciences, which are but private opinions, the Common-wealth must
needs be distracted, and no man dare to obey the Soveraign Power,
farther than it shall seem good in his own eyes.

Pretence of   It hath been also commonly taught, *That Faith and Sanctity, are not*
Inspiration. *to be attained by Study and Reason, but by supernaturall Inspiration,*
or Infusion, which granted, I see not why any man should render a
reason of his Faith; or why every Christian should not be also a Prophet;
or why any man should take the Law of his Country, rather than his
own Inspiration, for the rule of his action. And thus wee fall again into
the fault of taking upon us to Judge of Good and Evill; or to make
Judges of it, such private men as pretend to be super-naturally Inspired,
to the Dissolution of all Civill Government. Faith comes by hearing,
and hearing by those accidents, which guide us into the presence of
them that speak to us; which accidents are all contrived by God Almighty; and yet are not supernaturall, but onely, for the great number
of them that concurre to every effect, unobservable. Faith, and Sanctity,
are indeed not very frequent; but yet they are not Miracles, but brought
to passe by education, discipline, correction, and other naturall wayes,
by which God worketh them in his elect, at such time as he thinketh
fit. And these three opinions, pernicious to Peace and Government,
have in this part of the world, proceeded chiefly from the tongues, and
pens of unlearned Divines; who joyning the words of Holy Scripture
together, otherwise than is agreeable to reason, do what they can,
to make men think, that Sanctity and Naturall Reason, cannot stand
together.

Subjecting the   A fourth opinion, repugnant to the nature of a Common-wealth, is
Soveraign this, *That he that hath the Soveraign Power, is subject to the Civill*
Power to Civ- *Lawes.* It is true, that Soveraigns are all subject to the Lawes of Nature;
ill Lawes. because such lawes be Divine, and cannot by any man, or Common-
wealth be abrogated. But to those Lawes which the Soveraign himselfe,
that is, which the Common-wealth maketh, he is not subject. For to
be subject to Lawes, is to be subject to the Common-wealth, that is to
the Soveraign Representative, that is to himselfe; which is not subjection, but freedome from the Lawes. Which errour, because it setteth
the Lawes above the Soveraign, setteth also a Judge above him, and a
Power to punish him; which is to make a new Soveraign; and again
for the same reason a third, to punish the second; and so continually
without end, to the Confusion, and Dissolution of the Common-
wealth.

Attributing of   A Fifth doctrine, that tendeth to the Dissolution of a Common-
absolute Pro- wealth, is, *That every private man has an absolute Propriety in his*
priety to *Goods; such, as excludeth the Right of the Soveraign.* Every man has
Subjects. indeed a Propriety that excludes the Right of every other Subject: And

he has it onely from the Soveraign Power; without the protection
whereof, every other man should have equall Right to the same. But if   [170]
the Right of the Soveraign also be excluded, he cannot performe the
office they have put him into; which is, to defend them both from
forraign enemies, and from the injuries of one another; and consequently there is no longer a Common-wealth.

And if the Propriety of Subjects, exclude not the Right of the
Soveraign Representative to their Goods; much lesse to their offices
of Judicature, or Execution, in which they Represent the Soveraign
himselfe.

There is a Sixth doctrine, plainly, and directly against the essence of   *Dividing of*
a Common-wealth; and 'tis this, *That the Soveraign Power may be di-*   *the Soveraign*
vided. For what is it to divide the Power of a Common-wealth, but to   *Power.*
Dissolve it; for Powers divided mutually destroy each other. And for
these doctrines, men are chiefly beholding to some of those, that making profession of the Lawes, endeavour to make them depend upon
their own learning, and not upon the Legislative Power.

And as False Doctrine, so also often-times the Example of different   *Imitation of*
Government in a neighbouring Nation, disposeth men to alteration of   *Neighbour*
the forme already setled. So the people of the Jewes were stirred up to   *Nations.*
reject God, and to call upon the Prophet *Samuel*, for a King after the
manner of the Nations: So also the lesser Cities of *Greece*, were continually disturbed, with seditions of the Aristocraticall, and Democraticall factions; one part of almost every Common-wealth, desiring to
imitate the Lacedæmonians; the other, the Athenians. And I doubt not,
but many men, have been contented to see the late troubles in *Eng-*
land, out of an imitation of the Low Countries; supposing there needed
no more to grow rich, than to change, as they had done, the forme of
their Government. For the constitution of mans nature, is of it selfe
subject to desire novelty: When therefore they are provoked to the same,
by the neighbourhood also of those that have been enriched by it, it is
almost impossible for them, not to be content with those that solicite
them to change; and love the first beginnings, though they be grieved
with the continuance of disorder; like hot blouds, that having gotten
the itch, tear themselves with their own nayles, till they can endure the
smart no longer.

And as to Rebellion in particular against Monarchy; one of the most   *Imitation of*
frequent causes of it, is the Reading of the books of Policy, and Histories   *the Greeks,*
of the antient Greeks, and Romans; from which, young men, and all   *and Romans.*
others that are unprovided of the Antidote of solid Reason, receiving a
strong, and delightfull impression, of the great exploits of warre, at-
chieved by the Conductors of their Armies, receive withall a pleasing
Idea, of all they have done besides; and imagine their great prosperity,
not to have proceeded from the æmulation of particular men, but from
the vertue of their popular forme of government: Not considering the
frequent Seditions, and Civill warres, produced by the imperfection of
their Policy. From the reading, I say, of such books, men have undertaken to kill their Kings, because the Greek and Latine writers, in their   [171]
books, and discourses of Policy, make it lawfull, and laudable, for any

man so to do; provided before he do it, he call him Tyrant. For they say not *Regicide*, that is, killing of a King, but *Tyrannicide*, that is, killing of a Tyrant is lawfull. From the same books, they that live under a Monarch conceive an opinion, that the Subjects in a Popular Common-wealth enjoy Liberty; but that in a Monarchy they are all Slaves. I say, they that live under a Monarchy conceive such an opinion; not they that live under a Popular Government: for they find no such matter. In summe. I cannot imagine, how any thing can be more prejudiciall to a Monarchy, than the allowing of such books to be publikely read, without present applying such correctives of discreet Masters, as are fit to take away their Venime: Which Venime I will not doubt[7] to compare to the biting of a mad Dogge, which is a disease the Physicians call *Hydrophobia*, or *fear of Water*. For as he that is so bitten, has a continuall torment of thirst, and yet abhorreth water; and is in such an estate, as if the poyson endeavoured to convert him into a Dogge: So when a Monarchy is once bitten to the quick, by those Democraticall writers, that continually snarle at that estate; it wanteth[8] nothing more than a strong Monarch, which neverthelesse out of a certain *Tyrannophobia*, or feare of being strongly governed, when they have him, they abhorre.

As there have been Doctors, that hold there be three Soules in a man; so there be also that think there may be more Soules, (that is, more Soveraigns,) than one, in a Common-wealth; and set up a *Supremacy* against the *Soveraignty*; *Canons* against *Lawes*; and a *Ghostly Authority* against the *Civill*; working on mens minds, with words and distinctions, that of themselves signifie nothing, but bewray (by their obscurity) that there walketh (as some think invisibly) another Kingdome, as it were a Kingdome of Fayries, in the dark. Now seeing it is manifest, that the Civill Power, and the Power of the Common-wealth is the same thing; and that Supremacy, and the Power of making Canons, and granting Faculties, implyeth a Common-wealth; it followeth, that where one is Soveraign, another Supreme; where one can make Lawes, and another make Canons; there must needs be two Common-wealths, of one & the same Subjects; which is a Kingdome divided in it selfe, and cannot stand. For notwithstanding the insignificant distinction of *Temporall*, and *Ghostly*, they are still two Kingdomes, and every Subject is subject to two Masters. For seeing the *Ghostly* Power challengeth the Right to declare what is Sinne it challengeth by consequence to declare what is Law, (Sinne being nothing but the transgression of the Law;) and again, the Civill Power challenging to declare what is Law, every Subject must obey two Masters, who both will have their Commands be observed as Law; which is impossible. Or, if it be but one Kingdome, either the *Civill*, which is the Power of the Common-wealth, must be subordinate to the *Ghostly*, and then there is no Soveraignty but the *Ghostly*; or the *Ghostly* must be subordinate to the *Temporall*, and then there is no *Supremacy* but the *Temporall*. When therefore these two Powers oppose one another, the Common-wealth cannot but be in great danger of Civill warre, and Dissolution.

[172]

7. Hesitate.
8. Needs.

For the *Civill* Authority being more visible, and standing in the cleerer light of naturall reason, cannot choose but draw to it in all times a very considerable part of the people: And the *Spirituall*, though it stand in the darknesse of Schoole distinctions, and hard words; yet because the fear of Darknesse, and Ghosts, is greater than other fears, cannot want a party sufficient to Trouble, and sometimes to Destroy a Common-wealth, And this is a Disease which not unfitly may be compared to the Epilepsie, or Falling-sicknesse (which the Jewes took to be one kind of possession by Spirits) in the Body Naturall. For as in this Disease, there is an unnaturall spirit, or wind in the head that obstructeth the roots of the Nerves, and moving them violently, taketh away the motion which naturally they should have from the power of the Soule in the Brain, and thereby causeth violent, and irregular motions (which men call Convulsions) in the parts; insomuch as he that is seized therewith, falleth down sometimes into the water, and sometimes into the fire, as a man deprived of his senses; so also in the Body Politique, when the spirituall power, moveth the Members of a Common-wealth, by the terrour of punishments, and hope of rewards (which are the Nerves of it,) otherwise than by the Civill Power (which is the Soule of the Common-wealth) they ought to be moved; and by strange, and hard words suffocates their understanding, it must needs thereby Distract the people, and either Overwhelm the Common-wealth with Oppression, or cast it into the Fire of a Civill warre.

Sometimes also in the meerly Civill government, there be more than one Soule: As when the Power of levying mony, (which is the Nutritive faculty,) has depended on a generall Assembly; the Power of conduct and command, (which is the Motive faculty,) on one man; and the Power of making Lawes, (which is the Rationall faculty,) on the acci-dentall consent, not onely of those two, but also of a third; This en-dangereth the Common-wealth, somtimes for want of consent to good Lawes; but most often for want of such Nourishment, as is necessary to Life, and Motion. For although few perceive, that such government, is not government, but division of the Common-wealth into three Fac-tions, and call it mixt Monarchy; yet the truth is, that it is not one independent Common-wealth, but three independent Factions; nor one Representative Person, but three. In the Kingdome of God, there may be three Persons independent, without breach of unity in God that Reigneth; but where men Reigne, that be subject to diversity of opin-ions, it cannot be so. And therefore if the King bear the person of the People, and the generall Assembly bear also the person of the People, and another Assembly bear the person of a Part of the people, they are not one Person, nor one Soveraign, but three Persons, and three Soveraigns. *Mixt Government.*

To what Disease in the Naturall Body of man I may exactly compare this irregularity of a Common-wealth, I know not. But I have seen a man, that had another man growing out of his side, with an head, armes, breast, and stomach, of his own: If he had had another man growing out of his other side, the comparison might then have been exact. [173]

Hitherto I have named such Diseases of a Common-wealth, as are *Want of Mony.*

of the greatest, and most present danger. There be other, not so great; which neverthelesse are not unfit to be observed. At first, the difficulty of raising Mony, for the necessary uses of the Common-wealth; especially in the approach of warre. This difficulty ariseth from the opinion, that every Subject hath of a Propriety in his lands and goods, exclusive of the Soveraigns Right to the use of the same. From whence it commeth to passe, that the Soveraign Power, which foreseeth the necessities and dangers of the Commonwealth, (finding the passage of mony to the publique Treasure obstructed, by the tenacity of the people,) whereas it ought to extend it selfe, to encounter, and prevent such dangers in their beginnings, contracteth it selfe as long as it can, and when it cannot longer, struggles with the people by stratagems of Law, to obtain little summes, which not sufficing, he is fain at last violently to open the way for present supply, or Perish; and being put often to these extremities, at last reduceth the people to their due temper; or else the Common-wealth must perish. Insomuch as we may compare this Distemper very aptly to an Ague; wherein, the fleshy parts being congealed, or by venomous matter obstructed; the Veins which by their naturall course empty themselves into the Heart, are not (as they ought to be) supplyed from the Arteries, whereby there succeedeth at first a cold contraction, and trembling of the limbes; and afterwards a hot, and strong endeavour of the Heart, to force a passage for the Bloud; and before it can do that, contenteth it selfe with the small refreshments of such things as coole for a time, till (if Nature be strong enough) it break at last the contumacy of the parts obstructed, and dissipateth the venome into sweat; or (if Nature be too weak) the Patient dyeth.

Monopolies and abuses of Publicans.   Again, there is sometimes in a Common-wealth, a Disease, which resembleth the Pleurisie; and that is, when the Treasure of the Common-wealth, flowing out of its due course, is gathered together in too much abundance in one, or a few private men, by Monopolies, or by Farmes of the Publique Revenues; in the same manner as the Blood in a Pleurisie, getting into the Membrane of the breast, breedeth there an Inflammation, accompanied with a Fever, and painfull stitches.

Popular men.   Also, the Popularity of a potent Subject, (unlesse the Commonwealth have very good caution[9] of his fidelity,) is a dangerous Disease; because the people (which should receive their motion from the Authority of the Soveraign,) by the flattery, and by the reputation of an ambitious man, are drawn away from their obedience to the Lawes, to follow a man, of whose vertues, and designes they have no knowledge. And this is commonly of more danger in a Popular Government, than in a Monarchy; because an Army is of so great force, and multitude, as it

[174]   may easily be made believe, they are the People. By this means it was, that *Julius Cæsar*, who was set up by the People against the Senate, having won to himselfe the affections of his Army, made himselfe Master, both of Senate and People. And this proceeding of popular, and ambitious men, is plain Rebellion; and may be resembled to the effects of Witchcraft.

9. Assurance.

Another infirmity of a Common-wealth, is the immoderate greatnesse of a Town, when it is able to furnish out of its own Circuit, the
number, and expence of a great Army: As also the great number of
Corporations;[1] which are as it were many lesser Common-wealths in
the bowels of a greater, like wormes in the entrayles of a naturall man.
To which may be added, the Liberty of Disputing against absolute
Power, by pretenders to Politicall Prudence; which though bred for the
most part in the Lees[2] of the people; yet animated by False Doctrines,
are perpetually medling with the Fundamentall Lawes, to the molestation of the Common-wealth; like the little Wormes, which Physicians
call *Ascarides*.

*Excessive
greatnesse of a
Town, multi-
tude of
Corporations.*

*Liberty of dis-
puting against
Soveraign
Power.*

We may further adde, the insatiable appetite, or *Bulimia*, of enlarging
Dominion; with the incurable *Wounds* thereby many times received
from the enemy; And the *Wens*,[3] of ununited conquests, which are
many times a burthen, and with lesse danger lost, than kept; As also
the *Lethargy* of Ease, and *Consumption* of Riot and Vain Expence.

Lastly, when in a warre (forraign, or intestine,) the enemies get a
finall Victory; so as (the forces of the Common-wealth keeping the field
no longer) there is no farther protection of Subjects in their loyalty;
then is the Common-wealth DISSOLVED, and every man at liberty to
protect himselfe by such courses as his own discretion shall suggest
unto him. For the Soveraign, is the publique Soule, giving Life and
Motion to the Common-wealth; which expiring, the Members are governed by it no more, than the Carcasse of a man, by his departed
(though Immortall) Soule. For though the Right of a Soveraign Monarch cannot be extinguished by the act of another; yet the Obligation
of the members may. For he that wants protection, may seek it any
where; and when he hath it, is obliged (without fraudulent pretence of
having submitted himselfe out of feare,) to protect his Protection as
long as he is able. But when the Power of an Assembly is once suppressed, the Right of the same perisheth utterly; because the Assembly
it selfe is extinct; and consequently, there is no possibility for the Soveraignty to re-enter.

*Dissolution
of the
Common-
wealth.*

Chap. XXX.

Of the OFFICE *of the Soveraign Representative.*

The Office[1] of the Soveraign, (be it a Monarch, or an Assembly,)
consisteth in the end, for which he was trusted with the Soveraign
Power, namely the procuration of *the safety of the people*; to which he
is obliged by the Law of Nature, and to render an account thereof to
God, the Author of that Law, and to none but him. But by Safety here,
is not meant a bare Preservation, but also all other Contentments of

*The Procura-
tion of the
Good of the
People.*

1. Incorporated towns.
2. Dregs.
3. Warts.
1. Duty; function.

life, which every man by lawfull Industry, without danger, or hurt to the Commonwealth, shall acquire to himselfe.

By Instruction & Lawes.

And this is intended should be done, not by care applyed to Individualls, further than their protection from injuries, when they shall complain; but by a generall Providence, contained in publique Instruction, both of Doctrine, and Example; and in the making, and executing of good Lawes, to which individuall persons may apply their own cases.

Against the duty of a Soveraign to relinquish any Essentiall Right of Soveraignty:

And because, if the essentiall Rights of Soveraignty (specified before in the eighteenth Chapter) be taken away, the Common-wealth is thereby dissolved, and every man returneth into the condition, and calamity of a warre with every other man, (which is the greatest evill that can happen in this life;) it is the Office of the Soveraign, to maintain those Rights entire; and consequently against his duty, First, to transferre to another, or to lay from himselfe any of them. For he that deserteth the Means, deserteth the Ends; and he deserteth the Means, that being the Soveraign, acknowledgeth himselfe subject to the Civill Lawes; and renounceth the Power of Supreme Judicature; or of making Warre, or Peace by his own Authority; or of Judging of the Necessities of the Common-wealth; or of levying Mony, and Souldiers, when, and as much as in his own conscience he shall judge necessary; or of making Officers, and Ministers both of Warre, and Peace; or of appointing Teachers, and examining what Doctrines are conformable, or contrary to the Defence, Peace, and Good of the people. Secondly, it is against his Duty, to let the people be ignorant, or mis-informed of the grounds, and reasons of those his essentiall Rights; because thereby men are easie to be seduced, and drawn to resist him, when the Common-wealth shall require their use and exercise.

Or not to see the people taught the grounds of them.

And the grounds of these Rights, have the rather[2] need to be diligently, and truly taught; because they cannot be maintained by any Civill Law, or terrour of legall punishment. For a Civill Law, that shall forbid Rebellion (and such is all resistance to the essentiall Rights of Soveraignty,) is not (as a Civill Law) any obligation, but by vertue onely of the Law of Nature, that forbiddeth the violation of Faith; which naturall obligation if men know not, they cannot know the Right of any Law the Soveraign maketh. And for the Punishment, they take it but for an act of Hostility; which when they think they have strength enough, they will endeavour by acts of Hostility, to avoyd.

[176]

Objection of those that say there are no Principles of Reason for absolute Soveraignty.

As I have heard some say, that Justice is but a word, without substance; and that whatsoever a man can by force, or art, acquire to himselfe, (not onely in the condition of warre, but also in a Commonwealth,) is his own, which I have already shewed to be false: So there be also that maintain, that there are no grounds, nor Principles of Reason, to sustain those essentiall Rights, which make Soveraignty absolute. For if there were, they would have been found out in some place, or other; whereas we see, there has not hitherto been any Commonwealth, where those Rights have been acknowledged, or challenged.[3] Wherein they argue as ill, as if the Savage people of America, should

2. Prior; in advance.
3. Claimed.

deny there were any grounds, or Principles of Reason, so to build a house, as to last as long as the materials, because they never yet saw any so well built. Time, and Industry, produce every day new knowledge. And as the art of well building, is derived from Principles of Reason, observed by industrious men, that had long studied the nature of materials, and the divers effects of figure, and proportion, long after mankind began (though poorly) to build: So, long time after men have begun to constitute Common-wealths, imperfect, and apt to relapse into disorder, there may, Principles of Reason be found out, by industrious meditation, to make their constitution (excepting by externall violence) everlasting. And such are those which I have in this discourse set forth: Which whether they come not into the sight of those that have Power to make use of them, or be neglected by them, or not, concerneth my particular interest, at this day, very little. But supposing that these of mine are not such Principles of Reason; yet I am sure they are Principles from Authority of Scripture; as I shall make it appear, when I shall come to speak of the Kingdome of God, (administred by *Moses*,) over the Jewes, his peculiar[4] people by Covenant.

But they say again, that though the Principles be right, yet Common people are not of capacity enough to be made to understand them. I should be glad, that the Rich, and Potent Subjects of a Kingdome, or those that are accounted the most Learned, were no lesse incapable than they. But all men know, that the obstructions to this kind of doctrine, proceed not so much from the difficulty of the matter, as from the interest of them that are to learn. Potent men, digest hardly any thing that setteth up a Power to bridle their affections; and Learned men, any thing that discovereth their errours, and thereby lesseneth their Authority: whereas the Common-peoples minds, unlesse they be tainted with dependance on the Potent, or scribbled over with the opinions of their Doctors,[5] are like clean paper, fit to receive whatsoever by Publique Authority shall be imprinted in them. Shall whole Nations be brought to *acquiesce* in the great Mysteries of Christian Religion, which are above Reason; and millions of men be made believe, that the same Body may be in innumerable places, at one and the same time, which is against Reason; and shall not men be able, by their teaching, and preaching, protected by the Law, to make that received, which is so consonant to Reason, that any unprejudicated[6] man, needs no more to learn it, than to hear it? I conclude therefore, that in the instruction of the people in the Essentiall Rights (which are the Naturall, and Fundamentall Lawes) of Soveraignty, there is no difficulty, (whilest a Soveraign has his Power entire,) but what proceeds from his own fault, or the fault of those whom he trusteth in the administration of the Common-wealth; and consequently, it is his Duty, to cause them so to be instructed; and not onely his Duty, but his Benefit also, and Security, against the danger that may arrive to himselfe in his naturall Person, from Rebellion.

Objection from the Incapacity of the vulgar.

[177]

4. Special; chosen.
5. Teachers, authorities.
6. Unprejudiced.

And (to descend to particulars) the People are to be taught, First, that they ought not to be in love with any forme of Government they see in their neighbour Nations, more than with their own, nor (whatsoever present prosperity they behold in Nations that are otherwise governed than they,) to desire change. For the prosperity of a People ruled by an Aristocraticall, or Democraticall assembly, commeth not from Aristocracy, nor from Democracy, but from the Obedience, and Concord of the Subjects: nor do the people flourish in a Monarchy, because one man has the right to rule them, but because they obey him. Take away in any kind of State, the Obedience, (and consequently the Concord of the People,) and they shall not onely not flourish, but in short time be dissolved. And they that go about by disobedience, to doe no more than reforme the Common-wealth, shall find they do thereby destroy it; like the foolish daughters of *Peleus* (in the fable;) which desiring to renew the youth of their decrepit Father, did by the Counsell of *Medea*, cut him in pieces, and boyle him, together with strange herbs, but made not of him a new man. This desire of change, is like the breach of the first of Gods Commandements: For there God says, *Non habebis Deos alienos*; Thou shalt not have the Gods of other Nations; and in another place concerning *Kings*, that they are *Gods*.

Nor adhere (against the Soveraign) to Popular men,

Secondly, they are to be taught, that they ought not to be led with admiration of the vertue of any of their fellow Subjects, how high soever he stand, nor how conspicuously soever he shine in the Commonwealth; nor of any Assembly, (except the Soveraign Assembly,) so as to deferre to them any obedience, or honour, appropriate to the Soveraign onely, whom (in their particular stations) they represent; nor to receive any influence from them, but such as is conveighed by them from the Soveraign Authority. For that Soveraign, cannot be imagined to love his People as he ought, that is not Jealous of them, but suffers them by the flattery of Popular men, to be seduced from their loyalty, as they have often been, not onely secretly, but openly, so as to proclaime

[178]

Marriage with them *in facie Ecclesiæ*[7] by Preachers; and by publishing the same in the open streets: which may fitly be compared to the violation of the second of the ten Commandements.

Nor to Dispute the Soveraign Power:

Thirdly, in consequence to this, they ought to be informed, how great a fault it is, to speak evill of the Soveraign Representative, (whether One man, or an Assembly of men;) or to argue and dispute his Power, or any way to use his Name irreverently, whereby he may be brought into Contempt with his People, and their Obedience (in which the safety of the Common-wealth consisteth) slackened. Which doctrine the third Commandement by resemblance pointeth to.

And to have dayes set apart to learn their Duty:

Fourthly, seeing people cannot be taught this, nor when 'tis taught, remember it, nor after one generation past, so much as know in whom the Soveraign Power is placed, without setting a part from their ordinary labour, some certain times, in which they may attend those that are appointed to instruct them; It is necessary that some such times be determined, wherein they may assemble together, and (after prayers and praises given to God, the Soveraign of Soveraigns) hear those their

---

7. In the presence of the Church.

Duties told them, and the Positive Lawes, such as generally concern them all, read and expounded, and be put in mind of the Authority that maketh them Lawes. To this end had the *Jewes* every seventh day, a *Sabbath*, in which the Law was read and expounded; and in the solemnity whereof they were put in mind, that their King was God; that having created the world in six dayes, he rested the seventh day; and by their resting on it from their labour, that that God was their King, which redeemed them from their servile, and painfull labour in *Egypt*, and gave them a time, after they had rejoyced in God, to take joy also in themselves, by lawfull recreation. So that the first Table of the Commandements, is spent all, in setting down the summe of Gods absolute Power; not onely as God, but as King by pact, (in peculiar) of the Jewes; and may therefore give light, to those that have Soveraign Power conferred on them by the consent of men, to see what doctrine they Ought to teach their Subjects.

And because the first instruction of Children, dependeth on the care of their Parents; it is necessary that they should be obedient to them, whilest they are under their tuition; and not onely so, but that also afterwards (as gratitude requireth,) they acknowledge the benefit of their education, by externall signes of honour. To which end they are to be taught, that originally the Father of every man was also his Soveraign Lord, with power over him of life and death; and that the Fathers of families, when by instituting a Common-wealth, they resigned that absolute Power, yet it was never intended, they should lose the honour due unto them for their education. For to relinquish such right, was not necessary to the Institution of Soveraign Power; nor would there be any reason, why any man should desire to have children, or take the care to nourish, and instruct them, if they were afterwards to have no other benefit from them, than from other men. And this accordeth with the fifth Commandement. *And to Honour their Parents.*

Again, every Soveraign Ought to cause Justice to be taught, which (consisting in taking from no man what is his,) is as much as to say, to cause men to be taught not to deprive their Neighbours, by violence, or fraud, of any thing which by the Soveraign Authority is theirs. Of things held in propriety, those that are dearest to a man are his own life, & limbs; and in the next degree (in most men,) those that concern conjugall affection; and after them riches and means of living. Therefore the People are to be taught, to abstain from violence to one anothers person, by private revenges; from violation of conjugall honour; and from forcible rapine, and fraudulent surreption of one anothers goods. For which purpose also it is necessary they be shewed the evill consequences of false Judgement, by corruption either of Judges or Witnesses, whereby the distinction of propriety is taken away, and Justice becomes of no effect: all which things are intimated in the sixth, seventh, eighth, and ninth Commandements. [179] *And to avoyd doing of Injury.*

Lastly, they are to be taught, that not onely the unjust facts, but the designes and intentions to do them, (though by accident hundred,) are Injustice; which consisteth in the pravity[8] of the will, as well as in the *And to do all this sincerely from the heart.*

8. Depravity.

irregularity of the act. And this is the intention of the tenth Commandement, and the summe of the second Table; which is reduced all to this
one Commandement of mutuall Charity, *Thou shalt love they neighbour as they selfe*: as the summe of the first Table is reduced to *the love
of God*; whom they had then newly received as their King.

The use of   As for the Means, and Conduits, by which the people may receive
Universities.   this Instruction, wee are to search, by what means so many Opinions,
contrary to the peace of Mankind, upon weak and false Principles, have
neverthelesse been so deeply rooted in them. I mean those, which I
have in the precedent Chapter specified: as That men shall Judge of
what is lawfull and unlawfull, not by the Law it selfe, but by their own
Consciences; that is to say, by their own private Judgements: That Subjects sinne in obeying the Commands of the Common-wealth, unlesse
they themselves have first judged them to be lawfull: That their Propriety in their riches is such, as to exclude the Dominion, which the
Common-wealth hath over the same: That it is lawfull for Subjects to
kill such, as they call Tyrants: That the Soveraign Power may be divided, and the like; which come to be instilled into the People by this
means. They whom necessity, or covetousnesse keepeth attent on their
trades, and labour; and they, on the other side, whom superfluity,[9] or
sloth carrieth after their sensuall pleasures, (which two sorts of men
take up the greatest part of Man-kind,) being diverted from the deep
meditation, which the learning of truth, not onely in the matter of
Naturall Justice, but also of all other Sciences necessarily requireth,
receive the Notions of their duty, chiefly from Divines in the Pulpit,
and partly from such of their Neighbours, or familiar acquaintance, as
having the Faculty of discoursing readily, and plausibly, seem wiser and
better learned in cases of Law, and Conscience, than themselves. And
the Divines, and such others as make shew of Learning, derive their
[180] knowledge from the Universities, and from the Schooles of Law, or
from the Books, which by men eminent in those Schooles, and Universities have been published. It is therefore manifest, that the Instruction of the people, dependeth wholly, on the right teaching of Youth
in the Universities. But are not (may some man say) the Universities
of *England* learned enough already to do that? or is it you will undertake to teach the Universities? Hard questions. Yet to the first, I doubt
not to answer; that till towards the later end of *Henry the eighth*, the
Power of the Pope, was always upheld against the Power of the
Common-wealth, principally by the Universities; and that the doctrines
maintained by so many Preachers, against the Soveraign Power of the
King, and by so many Lawyers, and others, that had their education
there, is a sufficient argument, that though the Universities were not
authors of those false doctrines, yet they knew not how to plant the
true. For in such a contradiction of Opinions, it is most certain, that
they have not been sufficiently instructed; and 'tis no wonder, if they
yet retain a relish of that subtile liquor, wherewith they were first sea-
soned, against the Civill Authority. But to the later question, it is not

9. Overabundance.

fit, nor needfull for me to say either I, or No: for any man that sees what I am doing, may easily perceive what I think.

The safety of the People, requireth further, from him, or them that have the Soveraign Power, that Justice be equally administred to all degrees of People; that is, that as well the rich, and mighty, as poor and obscure persons, may be righted of the injuries done them; so as the great, may have no greater hope of impunity, when they doe violence, dishonour, or any Injury to the meaner sort, than when one of these, does the like to one of them: For in this consisteth Equity; to which, as being a Precept of the Law of Nature, a Soveraign is as much subject, as any of the meanest of his People. All breaches of the Law, are offences against the Common-wealth: but there be some, that are also against private Persons. Those that concern the Common-wealth onely, may without breach of Equity be pardoned; for every man may pardon what is done against himselfe, according to his own discretion. But an offence against a private man, cannot in Equity be pardoned, without the consent of him that is injured; or reasonable satisfaction.

The Inequality of Subjects, proceedeth from the Acts of Soveraign Power; and therefore has no more place in the presence of the Soveraign; that is to say, in a Court of Justice, then the Inequality between Kings, and their Subjects, in the presence of the King of Kings. The honour of great Persons, is to be valued for their beneficence, and the aydes they give to men of inferiour rank, or not at all. And the violences, oppressions, and injuries they do, are not extenuated, but aggravated by the greatnesse of their persons; because they have least need to commit them. The consequences of this partiality towards the great, proceed in this manner. Impunity maketh Insolence; Insolence Hatred; and Hatred, an Endeavour to pull down all oppressing and contumelious greatnesse, though with the ruine of the Common-wealth.

To Equall Justice, appertaineth also the Equall imposition of Taxes; the Equality whereof dependeth not on the Equality of riches, but on the Equality of the debt, that every man oweth to the Common-wealth for his defence. It is not enough, for a man to labour for the maintenance of his life; but also to fight, (if need be,) for the securing of his labour. They must either do as the Jewes did after their return from captivity, in re-edifying[1] the Temple, build with one hand, and hold the Sword in the other; or else they must hire others to fight for them. For the Impositions, that are layd on the People by the Soveraign Power, are nothing else but the Wages, due to them that hold the publique Sword, to defend private men in the exercise of severall Trades, and Callings. Seeing then the benefit that every one receiveth thereby, is the enjoyment of life, which is equally dear to poor, and rich; the debt which a poor man oweth them that defend his life, is the same which a rich man oweth for the defence of his; saving that the rich, who have the service of the poor, may be debtors not onely for their own persons, but for many more. Which considered, the Equality of Imposition, consisteth rather in the Equality of that which

[181]

Equall Taxes.

_____

1. Rebuilding.

is consumed, than of the riches of the persons that consume the same. For what reason is there, that he which laboureth much, and sparing the fruits of his labour, consumeth little, should be more charged, then he that living idly, getteth little, and spendeth all he gets; seeing the one hath no more protection from the Common-wealth, then the other? But when the Impositions, are layd upon those things which men consume, every man payeth Equally for what he useth: Nor is the Common-wealth defrauded, by the luxurious waste of private men.

Publique *Charity.*   And whereas many men, by accident unevitable, become unable to maintain themselves by their labour; they ought not to be left to the Charity of private persons; but to be provided for, (as far-forth as the necessities of Nature require) by the Lawes of the Common-wealth. For as it is Uncharitablenesse in any man, to neglect the impotent; so it is in the Soveraign of a Common-wealth, to expose them to the hazard of such uncertain Charity.

Prevention of *Idlenesse.*   But for such as have strong bodies, the case is otherwise: they are to be forced to work; and to avoyd the excuse of not finding employment, there ought to be such Lawes, as may encourage all manner of Arts; as Navigation, Agriculture, Fishing, and all manner of Manifacture that requires labour. The multitude of poor, and yet strong people still encreasing, they are to be transplanted into Countries not sufficiently inhabited: where neverthelesse, they are not to exterminate those they find there; but constrain them to inhabit closer together, and not range a great deal of ground, to snatch what they find; but to court each little Plot with art and labour, to give them their sustenance in due season. And when all the world is overcharged with Inhabitants, then the last remedy of all is Warre; which provideth for every man, by Victory, or Death.

[182] *Good Lawes* *what.*   To the care of the Soveraign, belongeth the making of Good Lawes. But what is a good Law? By a Good Law, I mean not a Just Law: for no Law can be Unjust. The Law is made by the Soveraign Power, and all that is done by such Power, is warranted,[2] and owned by every one of the people; and that which every man will have so, no man can say is unjust. It is in the Lawes of a Common-wealth, as in the Lawes of Gaming: whatsoever the Gamesters all agree on, is Injustice to none of them. A good Law is that, which is *Needfull*, for the *Good of the People*, and withall *Perspicuous*.

Such as are *Necessary.*   For the use of Lawes, (which are but Rules Authorised) is not to bind the People from all Voluntary actions; but to direct and keep them in such a motion, as not to hurt themselves by their own impetuous desires, rashnesse, or indiscretion; as Hedges are set, not to stop Travellers, but to keep them in the way. And therefore a Law that is not Needfull, having not the true End of a Law, is not Good. A Law may be conceived to be Good, when it is for the benefit of the Soveraign; though it be not Necessary for the People; but it is not so. For the good of the Soveraign and People, cannot be separated. It is a weak Soveraign, that has weak Subjects; and a weak People, whose Soveraign

2. Authorized.

wanteth Power to rule them at his will. Unnecessary Lawes are not good Lawes; but trapps for Mony: which where the right of Soveraign Power is acknowledged, are superfluous; and where it is not acknowledged, unsufficient to defend the People.

The Perspicuity, consisteth not so much in the words of the Law it selfe, as in a Declaration of the Causes, and Motives, for which it was made. That is it, that shewes us the meaning of the Legislator; and the meaning of the Legislator known, the Law is more easily understood by few, than many words. For all words, are subject to ambiguity; and therefore multiplication of words in the body of the Law, is multiplication of ambiguity: Besides it seems to imply, (by too much diligence,) that whosoever can evade the words, is without the compasse of the Law. And this is a cause of many unnecessary Processes.[3] For when I consider how short were the Lawes of antient times; and how they grew by degrees still longer; me thinks I see a contention between the Penners, and Pleaders of the Law; the former seeking to circumscribe the later; and the later to evade their circumscriptions; and that the Pleaders have got the Victory. It belongeth therefore to the Office of a Legislator, (such as is in all Common-wealths the Supreme Representative, be it one Man, or an Assembly,) to make the reason Perspicuous, why the Law was made; and the Body of the Law it selfe, as short, but in as proper, and significant termes, as may be. *Such as are Perspicuous.*

It belongeth also to the Office of the Soveraign, to make a right application of Punishments, and Rewards. And seeing the end of punishing is not revenge, and discharge of choler; but correction, either of the offender, or of others by his example; the severest Punishments are to be inflicted for those Crimes, that are of most Danger to the Publique; such as are those which proceed from malice to the Government established; those that spring from contempt of Justice; those that provoke Indignation in the Multitude; and those, which unpunished, seem Authorised, as when they are committed by Sonnes, Servants, or Favorites of men in Authority: For Indignation carrieth men, not onely against the Actors, and Authors of Injustice; but against all Power that is likely to protect them; as in the case of *Tarquin*;[4] when for the Insolent act of one of his Sonnes, he was driven out of *Rome*, and the Monarchy it selfe dissolved. But Crimes of Infirmity; such as are those which proceed from great provocation, from great fear, great need, or from ignorance whether the Fact be a great Crime, or not, there is place many times for Lenity, without prejudice to the Common-wealth; and Lenity when there is such place for it, is required by the Law of Nature. The Punishment of the Leaders, and teachers in a Commotion; not the poore seduced People, when they are punished, can profit the Common-wealth by their example. To be severe to the People, is to punish that ignorance, which may in great part be imputed to the Soveraign, whose fault it was, they were no better instructed. *Punishments.*

[183]

In like manner it belongeth to the Office, and Duty of the Soveraign, *Rewards.*

3. Legal proceedings.
4. Lucius Tarquinis Superbus, the legendary last king of Rome, who is said to have ruled from 534 to 510 B.C.

to apply his Rewards alwayes so, as there may arise from them benefit to the Common-wealth: wherein consisteth their Use, and End; and is then done, when they that have well served the Common-wealth, are with as little expence of the Common Treasure, as is possible, so well recompenced, as others thereby may be encouraged, both to serve the same as faithfully as they can, and to study the arts by which they may be enabled to do it better. To buy with Mony, or Preferment, from a Popular ambitious Subject, to be quiet, and desist from making ill impressions in the mindes of the People, has nothing of the nature of Reward; (which is ordained not for disservice, but for service past;) nor a signe of Gratitude, but of Fear: nor does it tend to the Benefit, but to the Dammage of the Publique. It is a contention with Ambition, like that of *Hercules* with the Monster *Hydra*, which having many heads, for every one that was vanquished, there grew up three. For in like manner, when the stubbornnesse of one Popular man, is overcome with Reward, there arise many more (by the Example) that do the same Mischiefe, in hope of like Benefit: and as all sorts of Manifacture, so also Malice encreaseth by being vendible.[5] And though sometimes a Civill warre, may be differred,[6] by such wayes as that, yet the danger growes still the greater, and the Publique ruine more assured. It is therefore against the Duty of the Soveraign, to whom the Publique Safety is committed, to Reward those that aspire to greatnesse by disturbing the Peace of their Country, and not rather to oppose the beginnings of such men, with a little danger, than after a longer time with greater.

Counsellours.   Another Businesse of the Soveraign, is to choose good Counsellours; I mean such, whose advice he is to take in the Government of the Common-wealth. For this word Counsell, *Consilium*, corrupted from *Considium*, is of a large signification, and comprehendeth all Assemblies of men that sit together, not onely to deliberate what is to be done [184] hereafter, but also to judge of Facts past, and of Law for the present. I take it here in the first sense onely: And in this sense, there is no choyce of Counsell, neither in a Democracy, nor Aristocracy; because the persons Counselling are members of the person Counselled. The choyce of Counsellours therefore is proper to Monarchy; In which, the Soveraign that endeavoureth not to make choyce of those, that in every kind are the most able, dischargeth not his Office as he ought to do. The most able Counsellours, are they that have least hope of benefit by giving evill Counsell, and most knowledge of those things that conduce to the Peace, and Defence of the Common-wealth. It is a hard matter to know who expecteth benefit from publique troubles; but the signes that guide to a just suspicion, is the soothing[7] of the people in their unreasonable, or irremediable grievances, by men whose estates are not sufficient to discharge their accustomed expences, and may easily be observed by any one whom it concerns to know it. But to know, who has most knowledge of the Publique affaires, is yet harder;

5. Saleable.
6. Deferred.
7. Encouraging.

and they that know them, need them a great deale the lesse. For to know, who knowes the Rules almost of any Art, is a great degree of the knowledge of the same Art; because no man can be assured of the truth of anothers Rules, but he that is first taught to understand them. But the best signes of Knowledge of any Art, are, much conversing in it, and constant good effects of it. Good Counsell comes not by Lot, nor by Inheritance; and therefore there is no more reason to expect good Advice from the rich, or noble, in matter of State, than in delineating the dimensions of a fortresse; unlesse we shall think there needs no method in the study of the Politiques, (as there does in the study of Geometry,) but onely to be lookers on; which is not so. For the Politiques is the harder study of the two. Whereas in these parts of *Europe*, it hath been taken for a Right of certain persons, to have place in the highest Councell of State by Inheritance; it is derived from the Conquests of the antient Germans; wherein many absolute Lords joyning together to conquer other Nations, would not enter in to the Confederacy, without such Priviledges, as might be marks of difference in time following, between their Posterity, and the Posterity of their Subjects; which Priviledges being inconsistent with the Soveraign Power, by the favour of the Soveraign, they may seem to keep; but contending for them as their Right, they must needs by degrees let them go, and have at last no further honour, then adhæreth naturally to their abilities.

And how able soever be the Counsellours in any affaire, the benefit of their Counsell is greater, when they give every one his Advice, and the reasons of it apart, than when they do it in an Assembly, by way of Orations; and when they have præmeditated, than when they speak on the sudden; both because they have more time, to survey the consequences of action; and are lesse subject to be carried away to contradiction, through Envy, Emulation, or other Passions arising from the difference of opinion.

The best Counsell, in those things that concern not other Nations, but onely the ease, and benefit the Subjects may enjoy, by Lawes that [185] look onely inward, is to be taken from the generall informations, and complaints of the people of each Province, who are best acquainted with their own wants, and ought therefore, when they demand nothing in derogation of[8] the essentiall Rights of Soveraignty, to be diligently taken notice of. For without those Essentiall Rights, (as I have often before said,) the Common-wealth cannot at all subsist.

A Commander of an Army in chiefe, if he be not Popular, shall not *Commanders.* be beloved, nor feared as he ought to be by his Army; and consequently cannot performe that office with good successe. He must therefore be Industrious, Valiant, Affable, Liberall and Fortunate, that he may gain an opinion both of sufficiency,[9] and of loving his Souldiers. This is Popularity, and breeds in the Souldiers both desire, and courage, to recommend themselves to his favour; and protects the severity of the Generall, in punishing (when need is) the Mutinous, or negligent Souldiers. But this love of Souldiers, (if caution be not given of the Com-

8. Detracting from.
9. Ability; competence.

manders fidelity,) is a dangerous thing to Soveraign Power; especially
when it is in the hands of an Assembly not popular. It belongeth therefore to the safety of the People, both that they be good Conductors,
and faithfull Subjects, to whom the Soveraign Commits his Armies.

But when the Soveraign himselfe is Popular; that is, reverenced and
beloved of his People, there is no danger at all from the Popularity of
a Subject. For Souldiers are never so generally unjust, as to side with
their Captain; though they love him, against their Soveraign, when they
love not onely his Person, but also his Cause. And therefore those, who
by violence have at any time suppressed the Power of their lawfull
Soveraign, before they could settle themselves in his place, have been
alwayes put to the trouble of contriving their Titles, to save the People
from the shame of receiving them. To have a known Right to Soveraign
Power, is so popular a quality, as he that has it needs no more, for his
own part, to turn the hearts of his Subjects to him, but that they see
him able absolutely to govern his own Family: Nor, on the part of his
enemies, but a disbanding of their Armies. For the greatest and most
active part of Mankind, has never hetherto been well contented with
the present.

Concerning the Offices of one Soveraign to another, which are comprehended in that Law, which is commonly called the *Law of Nations*,
I need not say any thing in this place; because the Law of Nations, and
the Law of Nature, is the same thing. And every Soveraign hath the
same Right, in procuring the safety of his People, that any particular
man can have, in procuring the safety of his own Body. And the same
Law, that dictateth to men that have no Civil Government, what they
ought to do, and what to avoyd in regard of one another, dictateth the
same to Common-wealths, that is, to the Consciences of Soveraign
Princes, and Soveraign Assemblies; there being no Court of Naturall
Justice, but in the Conscience onely; where not Man, but God raign-
eth; whose Lawes, (such of them as oblige all Mankind,) in respect of
God, as he is the Author of Nature, are *Naturall*; and in respect of the
[186]   same God, as he is King of Kings, are *Lawes*. But of the Kingdome of
God, as King of Kings, and as King also of a peculiar People, I shall
speak in the rest of this discourse.

Chap. XXXI.

Of the KINGDOME OF GOD BY NATURE.

The scope of   That the condition of meer Nature, that is to say, of absolute Liberty,
the following   such as is theirs, that neither are Soveraigns, nor Subjects, is Anarchy,
Chapters.   and the condition of Warre: That the Præcepts, by which men are
guided to avoyd that condition, are the Lawes of Nature: That a
Common-wealth, without Soveraign Power, is but a word, without substance, and cannot stand: That Subjects owe to Soveraigns, simple
Obedience, in all things, wherein their obedience is not repugnant to
the Lawes of God, I have sufficiently proved, in that which I have

already written. There wants onely, for the entire knowledge of Civill duty, to know what are those Lawes of God. For without that, a man knows not, when he is commanded any thing by the Civill Power, whether it be contrary to the Law of God, or not: and so, either by too much civill obedience, offends the Divine Majesty, or through feare of offending God, transgresses the commandements of the Common-wealth. To avoyd both these Rocks, it is necessary to know what are the Lawes Divine. And seeing the knowledge of all Law, dependeth on the knowledge of the Soveraign Power; I shall say something in that which followeth, of the KINGDOME OF GOD.

God is King, let the Earth rejoyce, saith the Psalmist. And again, God is King though the Nations be angry; and he that sitteth on the Cherubins, though the earth be moved. Whether men will or not, they must be subject alwayes to the Divine Power. By denying the Existence, or Providence of God, men may shake off their Ease, but not their Yoke. But to call this Power of God, which extendeth it selfe not onely to Man, but also to Beasts, and Plants, and Bodies inanimate, by the name of Kingdome, is but a metaphoricall use of the word. For he onely is properly said to Raigne, that governs his Subjects, by his Word, and by promise of Rewards to those that obey it, and by threatening them with Punishment that obey it not. Subjects therefore in the Kingdome of God, are not Bodies Inanimate, nor creatures Irrationall; because they understand no Precepts as his: Nor Atheists; nor they that believe not that God has any care of the actions of mankind; because they acknowledge no Word for his, nor have hope of his rewards, or fear of his threatnings. They therefore that believe there is a God that governeth the world, and hath given Præcepts, and propounded Rewards, and Punishments to Mankind, are Gods Subjects; all the rest, are to be understood as Enemies.

To rule by Words, requires that such Words be manifestly made known; for else they are no Lawes: For to the nature of Lawes belongeth a sufficient, and clear Promulgation, such as may take away the excuse of Ignorance; which in the Lawes of men is but of one onely kind, and that is, Proclamation, or Promulgation by the voyce of man. But God declareth his Lawes three wayes; by the Dictates of *Naturall Reason*, by *Revelation*, and by the *Voyce* of some *man*, to whom by the operation of Miracles, he procureth credit with the rest. From hence there ariseth a triple Word of God, *Rational, Sensible,* and *Prophetique*: to which Correspondeth a triple Hearing; *Right Reason, Sense Supernaturall,* and *Faith.* As for Sense Supernaturall, which consisteth in Revelation, or Inspiration, there have not been any Universall Lawes so given, because God speaketh not in that manner, but to particular persons, and to divers men divers things.

From the difference between the other two kinds of Gods Word, *Rationall,* and *Prophetique,* there may be attributed to God, a two-fold Kingdome, Naturall, and *Prophetique*: Naturall, wherein he governeth as many of Mankind as acknowledge his Providence, by the naturall Dictates of Right Reason; And Prophetique, wherein having chosen out one peculiar Nation (the Jewes) for his Subjects, he governed them,

Psal. 96.I.
Psal. 98.I.

Who are subjects in the kingdome of God.

[187]

A Threefold Word of God, Reason, Revelation, Prophecy.

A twofold Kingdome of God, Naturall and Prophetique.

and none but them, not onely by naturall Reason, but by Positive Lawes, which he gave them by the mouths of his holy Prophets. Of the Naturall Kingdome of God I intend to speak in this Chapter.

The Right of Gods Soveraignty is derived from his Omnipotence.

The Right of Nature, whereby God reigneth over men, and punisheth those that break his Lawes, is to be derived, not from his Creating them, as if he required obedience, as of Gratitude for his benefits; but from his *Irresistible Power.* I have formerly shewn, how the Soveraign Right ariseth from Pact: To shew how the same Right may arise from Nature, requires no more, but to shew in what case it is never taken away. Seeing all men by Nature had Right to All things, they had Right every one to reigne over all the rest. But because this Right could not be obtained by force, it concerned the safety of every one, laying by that Right, to set up men (with Soveraign Authority) by common consent, to rule and defend them: whereas if there had been any man of Power Irresistible; there had been no reason, why he should not by that Power have ruled, and defended both himselfe, and them, according to his own discretion. To those therefore whose Power is irresistible, the dominion of all men adhæreth naturally by their excellence of Power; and consequently it is from that Power, that the Kingdome over men, and the Right of afflicting men at his pleasure, belongeth Naturally to God Almighty; not as Creator, and Gracious; but as Omnipotent. And though Punishment be due for Sinne onely, because by that word is understood Affliction for Sinne; yet the Right of Afflicting, is not alwayes derived from mens Sinne, but from Gods Power.

[188]

Sinne not the cause of all Affliction.

This question, *Why Evill men often Prosper, and Good men suffer Adversity,* has been much disputed by the Antient, and is the same with this of ours, *by what Right God dispenseth the Prosperities and Adversities of this life;* and is of that difficulty, as it hath shaken the faith, not onely of the Vulgar, but of Philosophers, and which is more, of the Saints, concerning the Divine Providence. *How Good* (saith *David*) *is the God of Israel to those that are Upright in Heart; and yet my feet were almost gone, my treadings had well-nigh slipt; for I was grieved at the Wicked, when I saw the Ungodly in such Prosperity.* And *Job,* how earnestly does he expostulate with God, for the many Afflictions he suffered, notwithstanding his Righteousnesse? This question in the case of *Job,* is decided by God himselfe, not by arguments derived from *Job's* Sinne, but his own Power. For whereas the friends of *Job* drew their arguments from his Affliction to his Sinne, and he defended himselfe by the conscience of his Innocence, God himselfe taketh up the matter, and having justified the Affliction by arguments drawn from his Power, such as this, *Where wast thou when I layd the foundations of the earth,* and the like, both approved *Job's* Innocence, and reproved the Erroneous doctrine of his friends. Conformable to this doctrine is the sentence of our Saviour, concerning the man that was born Blind, in these words, *Neither hath this man sinned, nor his fathers; but that the works of God might be made manifest in him.* And though it be said, *That Death entred into the world by sinne,* (by which is meant that if *Adam* had never sinned, he had never dyed, that is, never suffered any separation of his soule from his body,) it follows not thence, that God could

Job 38. v. 4.

not justly have Afflicted him, though he had not Sinned, as well as he afflicteth other living creatures, that cannot sinne.

Having spoken of the Right of Gods Soveraignty, as grounded onely on Nature; we are to consider next, what are the Divine Lawes, or Dictates of Naturall Reason; which Lawes concern either the naturall Duties of one man to another, or the Honour naturally due to our Divine Soveraign. The first are the same Lawes of Nature, of which I have spoken already in the 14. and 15. Chapters of this Treatise; namely, Equity, Justice, Mercy, Humility, and the rest of the Morall Vertues. It remaineth therefore that we consider, what Præcepts are dictated to men, by their Naturall Reason onely, without other word of God, touching the Honour and Worship of the Divine Majesty. *Divine Lawes.*

Honour consisteth in the inward thought, and opinion of the Power, and Goodnesse of another: and therefore to Honour God, is to think as Highly of his Power and Goodnesse, as is possible. And of that opinion, the externall signes appearing in the Words, and Actions of men, are called *Worship*; which is one part of that which the Latines understand by the word *Cultus*: For *Cultus* signifieth properly, and constantly, that labour which a man bestowes on any thing, with a purpose to make benefit by it. Now those things whereof we make benefit, are either subject to us, and the profit they yeeld, followeth the labour we bestow upon them, as a naturall effect; or they are not subject to us, but answer our labour, according to their own Wills. In the first sense the labour bestowed on the Earth, is called *Culture*; and the education of Children a *Culture* of their mindes. In the second sense, where mens wills are to be wrought to our purpose, not by Force, but by Compleasance,[1] it signifieth as much as Courting, that is, a winning of favour by good offices; as by praises, by acknowledging their Power, and by whatsoever is pleasing to them from whom we look for any benefit. And this is properly *Worship*: in which sense *Publicola*, is understood for a Worshipper of the People; and *Cultus Dei*, for the Worship of God. *Honour and Worship what.*

[189]

From internall Honour, consisting in the opinion of Power and Goodnesse, arise three Passions; *Love*, which hath reference to Goodnesse; and *Hope*, and *Fear*, that relate to Power: And three parts of externall worship; *Praise*, *Magnifying*, and *Blessing*: The subject of Praise, being Goodnesse; the subject of Magnifying, and Blessing, being Power, and the effect thereof Felicity. Praise, and Magnifying are signified both by Words, and Actions: By Words, when we say a man is Good, or Great: By Actions, when we thank him for his Bounty, and obey his Power. The opinion of the Happinesse of another, can onely be expressed by words. *Severall signes of Honour.*

There be some signes of Honour, (both in Attributes and Actions,) that be Naturally so; as amongst Attributes, *Good, Just, Liberall*, and the like; and amongst Actions, *Prayers, Thanks*, and *Obedience*. Others are so by Institution, or Custome of men; and in some times and places are Honourable; in others Dishonourable; in others Indifferent: such *Worship Naturall and Arbitrary.*

1. Complaisance.

as are the Gestures in Salutation, Prayer, and Thanksgiving, in different times and places, differently used. The former is *Naturall*; the later *Arbitrary* Worship.

Worship Commanded and Free. And of Arbitrary Worship, there bee two differences: For sometimes it is a *Commanded*, sometimes *Voluntary* Worship: Commanded, when it is such as hee requireth, who is Worshipped: Free, when it is such as the Worshipper thinks fit. When it is Commanded, not the words, or gesture, but the obedience is the Worship. But when Free, the Worship consists in the opinion of the beholders: for if to them the words, or actions by which we intend honour, seem ridiculous, and tending to contumely; they are no Worship; because no signes of Honour; and no signes of Honour; because a signe is not a signe to him that giveth it, but to him to whom it is made; that is, to the spectator.

Worship Publique and Private. Again, there is a *Publique*, and a *Private* Worship. Publique, is the Worship that a Common-wealth performeth, as one Person. Private, is that which a Private person exhibiteth. Publique, in respect of the whole Common-wealth, is Free; but in respect of Particular men it is not so. Private, is in secret Free; but in the sight of the multitude, it is never without some Restraint, either from the Lawes, or from the Opinion of men; which is contrary to the nature of Liberty.

The end of Worship. [190] The End of Worship amongst men, is Power. For where a man seeth another worshipped, he supposeth him powerfull, and is the readier to obey him; which makes his Power greater. But God has no Ends: the worship we do him, proceeds from our duty, and is directed according to our capacity, by those rules of Honour, that Reason dictateth to be done by the weak to the more potent men, in hope of benefit, for fear of dammage, or in thankfulnesse for good already received from them.

Attributes of Divine Honour. That we may know what worship of God is taught us by the light of Nature, I will begin with his Attributes. Where, First, it is manifest, we ought to attribute to him *Existence*: For no man can have the will to honour that, which he thinks not to have any Beeing.

Secondly, that those Philosophers, who sayd the World, or the Soule of the World was God, spake unworthily of him; and denyed his Existence: For by God, is understood the cause of the World; and to say the World is God, is to say there is no cause of it, that is, no God.

Thirdly, to say the World was not Created, but Eternall, (seeing that which is Eternall has no cause,) is to deny there is a God.

Fourthly, that they who attributing (as they think) Ease to God, take from him the care of Man-kind; take from him his Honour: for it takes away mens love, and fear of him; which is the root of Honour.

Fifthly, in those things that signifie Greatnesse, and Power; to say he is *Finite*, is not to Honour him: For it is not a signe of the Will to Honour God, to attribute to him lesse than we can; and Finite, is lesse than we can; because to Finite, it is easie to adde more.

Therefore to attribute *Figure* to him, is not Honour; for all Figure is Finite:

Nor to say we conceive, and imagine, or have an *Idea* of him, in our mind: for whatsoever we conceive is Finite:

Nor to attribute to him *Parts*, or *Totality*; which are the Attributes onely of things Finite:

Nor to say he is in this, or that *Place*: for whatsoever is in Place, is bounded, and Finite:

Nor that he is *Moved*, or *Resteth*: for both these Attributes ascribe to him Place:

Nor that there be more Gods than one; because it implies them all Finite: for there cannot be more than one Infinite:

Nor to ascribe to him (unlesse Metaphorically, meaning not the Passion, but the Effect) Passions that partake of Griefe; as *Repentance*, *Anger, Mercy*: or of Want; as *Appetite, Hope, Desire*; or of any Passive faculty: For Passion, is Power limited by somewhat else.

And therefore when we ascribe to God a *Will*, it is not to be understood, as that of Man, for a *Rationall Appetite*; but as the Power, by which he effecteth every thing.

Likewise when we attribute to him *Sight*, and other acts of Sense; as also *Knowledge*, and *Understanding*; which in us is nothing else, but a tumult of the mind, raised by externall things that presse the organicall parts of mans body: For there is no such thing in God; and being things that depend on naturall causes, cannot be attributed to him.

Hee that will attribute to God, nothing but what is warranted by naturall Reason, must either use such Negative Attributes, as *Infinite*, *Eternall, Incomprehensible*; or Superlatives, as *Most High, most Great*, and the like; or Indefinite, as *Good, Just, Holy, Creator*; and in such sense, as if he meant not to declare what he is, (for that were to circumscribe him within the limits of our Fancy,) but how much wee admire him, and how ready we would be to obey him; which is a signe of Humility, and of a Will to honour him as much as we can: For there is but one Name to signifie our Conception of his Nature, and that is, I AM: and but one Name of his Relation to us, and that is *God*; in which is contained Father, King, and Lord. [191]

Concerning the actions of Divine Worship, it is a most generall Precept of Reason, that they be signes of the Intention to Honour God; such as are, First, *Prayers*: For not the Carvers, when they made Images, were thought to make them Gods; but the People that *Prayed* to them.

Secondly, *Thanksgiving*; which differeth from Prayer in Divine Worship, no otherwise, than that Prayers precede, and Thanks succeed the benefit; the end both of the one, and the other, being to acknowledge God, for Author of all benefits, as well past, as future.

Thirdly, *Gifts*; that is to say, *Sacrifices*, and *Oblations*, (if they be of the best,) are signes of Honour: for they are Thanksgivings.

Fourthly, *Not to swear by any but God*, is naturally a signe of Honour: for it is a confession that God onely knoweth the heart; and that no mans wit, or strength can protect a man against Gods vengeance on the perjured.

Fifthly, it is a part of Rationall Worship, to speak Considerately of God; for it argues a Fear of him, and Fear, is a confession of his Power. Hence followeth, That the name of God is not to be used rashly, and to no purpose; for that is as much, as in Vain: And it is to no purpose unlesse it be by way of Oath, and by order of the Common-wealth, to make Judgements certain; or between Common-wealths, to avoyd Warre. And that disputing of Gods nature is contrary to his Honour:

Actions that are signes of Divine Honour.

For it is supposed, that in this naturall Kingdome of God, there is no other way to know any thing, but by naturall Reason; that is, from the Principles of naturall Science; which are so farre from teaching us any thing of Gods nature, as they cannot teach us our own nature, nor the nature of the smallest creature living. And therefore, when men out of the Principles of naturall Reason, dispute of the Attributes of God, they but dishonour him: For in the Attributes which we give to God, we are not to consider the signification of Philosophicall Truth; but the signification of Pious Intention, to do him the greatest Honour we are able. From the want of which consideration, have proceeded the volumes of disputation about the nature of God, that tend not to his Honour, but to the honour of our own wits, and learning; and are nothing else but inconsiderate, and vain abuses of his Sacred Name.

[192]   Sixthly, in *Prayers, Thanksgiving, Offerings* and *Sacrifices*, it is a Dictate of naturall Reason, that they be every one in his kind the best, and most significant of Honour. As for example, that Prayers, and Thanksgiving, be made in Words and Phrases, not sudden, nor light, nor Plebeian; but beautifull, and well composed; For else we do not God as much honour as we can. And therefore the Heathens did absurdly, to worship Images for Gods: But their doing it in Verse, and with Musick, both of Voyce, and Instruments, was reasonable. Also that the Beasts they offered in sacrifice, and the Gifts they offered, and their actions in Worshipping, were full of submission, and commemorative of benefits received, was according to reason, as proceeding from an intention to honour him.

Seventhly, Reason directeth not onely to worship God in Secret; but also, and especially, in Publique, and in the sight of men: For without that, (that which in honour is most acceptable) the procuring others to honour him, is lost.

Lastly, Obedience to his Lawes (that is, in this case to the Lawes of Nature,) is the greatest worship of all. For as Obedience is more acceptable to God than Sacrifice; so also to set light by his Commandements, is the greatest of all contumelies. And these are the Lawes of that Divine Worship, which naturall Reason dictateth to private men.

Publique Worship consisteth in Uniformity.   But seeing a Common-wealth is but one Person, it ought also to exhibite to God but one Worship; which then it doth, when it commandeth it to be exhibited by Private men, Publiquely. And this is Publique Worship; the property whereof, is to be *Uniforme*: For those actions that are done differently, by different men, cannot be said to be a Publique Worship. And therefore, where many sorts of Worship be allowed, proceeding from different Religions of Private men, it cannot be said there is any Publique Worship, nor that the Common-wealth is of any Religion at all.

All Attributes depend on the Lawes Civill.   And because words (and consequently the Attributes of God) have their signification by agreement, and constitution of men; those Attributes are to be held significative of Honour, that men intend shall so be; and whatsoever may be done by the wills of particular men, where there is no Law but Reason, may be done by the will of the Common-wealth, by Lawes Civill. And because a Common-wealth hath no Will,

nor makes no Lawes, but those that are made by the Will of him, or
them that have the Soveraign Power; it followeth, that those Attributes
which the Soveraign ordaineth, in the Worship of God, for signes of
Honour, ought to be taken and used for such, by private men in their
publique Worship.

But because not all Actions are signes by Constitution; but some are *Not all*
Naturally signes of Honour, others of Contumely, these later (which *Actions.*
are those that men are ashamed to do in the sight of them they reverence) cannot be made by humane power a part of Divine worship; nor
the former (such as are decent, modest, humble Behaviour) ever be
separated from it. But whereas there be an infinite number of Actions,
and Gestures, of an indifferent nature; such of them as the Common-
wealth shall ordain to be Publiquely and Universally in use, as signes
of Honour, and part of Gods Worship, are to be taken and used for   [193]
such by the Subjects. And that which is said in the Scripture, *It is better
to obey God than men,* hath place in the kingdome of God by Pact,
and not by Nature.

Having thus briefly spoken of the Naturall Kingdome of God, and *Naturall*
his Naturall Lawes, I will adde onely to this Chapter a short declaration *Punishments.*
of his Naturall Punishments. There is no action of man in this life, that
is not the beginning of so long a chayn of Consequences, as no humane
Providence, is high enough, to give a man a prospect to the end. And
in this Chayn, there are linked together both pleasing and unpleasing
events; in such manner, as he that will do any thing for his pleasure,
must engage himselfe to suffer all the pains annexed to it; and these
pains, are the Naturall Punishments of those actions, which are the
beginning of more Harme than Good. And hereby it comes to passe,
that Intemperance, is naturally punished with Diseases; Rashnesse, with
Mischances; Injustice, with the Violence of Enemies; Pride, with
Ruine; Cowardise, with Oppression; Negligent government of Princes,
with Rebellion; and Rebellion, with Slaughter. For seeing Punishments
are consequent to the breach of Lawes; Naturall Punishments must be
naturally consequent to the breach of the Lawes of Nature; and therfore
follow them as their naturall, not arbitrary effects.

And thus farre concerning the Constitution, Nature, and Right of *The Conclu-*
Soveraigns; and concerning the Duty of Subjects, derived from the *sion of the*
Principles of Naturall Reason. And now, considering how different this *Second Part.*
Doctrine is, from the Practise of the greatest part of the world, especially
of these Western parts, that have received their Morall learning from
Rome, and *Athens;* and how much depth of Morall Philosophy is required, in them that have the Administration of the Soveraign Power;
I am at the point of believing this my labour, as uselesse, as the
Common-wealth of *Plato;* For he also is of opinion that it is impossible
for the disorders of State, and change of Governments by Civill Warre,
ever to be taken away, till Soveraigns be Philosophers. But when I
consider again, that the Science of Naturall Justice, is the onely Science
necessary for Soveraigns, and their principall Ministers; and that they
need not be charged with the Sciences Mathematicall, (as by *Plato* they
are,) further, than by good Lawes to encourage men to the study of

them; and that neither *Plato*, nor any other Philosopher hitherto, hath put into order, and sufficiently or probably proved all the Theoremes of Morall doctrine, that men may learn thereby, both how to govern, and how to obey; I recover some hope, that one time or other, this writing of mine, may fall into the hands of a Soveraign, who will consider it himselfe, (for it is short, and I think clear,) without the help of any interested, or envious Interpreter; and by the exercise of entire Soveraignty, in protecting the Publique teaching of it, convert this Truth of Speculation, into the Utility of Practice.

Chap. XXXII.

Of the Principles of CHRISTIAN POLITIQUES.

I have derived the Rights of Soveraigne Power, and the duty of Subjects hitherto, from the Principles of Nature onely; such as Experience has found true, or Consent (concerning the use of words) has made so; that is to say, from the nature of Men, known to us by Experience, and from Definitions (of such words as are Essentiall to all Politicall reasoning) universally agreed on. But in that I am next to handle, which is the Nature and Rights of a CHRISTIAN COMMON-WEALTH, whereof there dependeth much upon Supernaturall Revelations of the Will of God; the ground of my Discourse must be, not only the Naturall Word of God, but also the Propheticall. *The Word of God delivered by Prophets is the main principle of Christian Politiques.*

Neverthelesse, we are not to renounce our Senses, and Experience; nor (that which is the undoubted Word of God) our naturall Reason. For they are the talents which he hath put into our hands to negotiate,[1] till the coming again of our blessed Saviour; and therefore not to be folded up in the Napkin of an Implicite[2] Faith, but employed in the purchase of Justice, Peace, and true Religion. For though there be many things in Gods Word above Reason; that is to say, which cannot by naturall reason be either demonstrated, or confuted; yet there is nothing contrary to it; but when it seemeth so, the fault is either in our unskilfull Interpretation, or erroneous Ratiocination. *Yet is not naturall Reason to be renounced.*

Therefore, when any thing therein written is too hard for our examination, wee are bidden to captivate[3] our understanding to the Words; and not to labour in sifting out a Philosophicall truth by Logick, of such mysteries as are not comprehensible, nor fall under any rule of naturall science. For it is with the mysteries of our Religion, as with wholsome pills for the sick, which swallowed whole, have the vertue to cure; but chewed, are for the most part cast up again without effect.

But by the Captivity of our Understanding, is not meant a Submission of the Intellectuall faculty, to the Opinion of any other man; but of the Will to Obedience, where obedience is due. For Sense, Memory, Understanding, Reason, and Opinion are not in our power to change; but alwaies, and necessarily such, as the things we see, hear, and consider suggest unto us; and therefore are not effects of our Will, but our [196] *What it is to captivate the Understanding.*

1. To manage.
2. Unquestioning.
3. To subjugate, enthrall, or enchant.

Will of them. We then Captivate our Understanding and Reason, when we forbear contradiction; when we so speak, as (by lawfull Authority) we are commanded; and when we live accordingly; which in sum, is Trust, and Faith reposed in him that speaketh, though the mind be incapable of any Notion at all from the words spoken.

How God speaketh to men.

When God speaketh to man, it must be either immediately; or by mediation of another man, to whom he had formerly spoken by himself immediately. How God speaketh to a man immediately, may be understood by those well enough, to whom he hath so spoken; but how the same should be understood by another, is hard, if not impossible to know. For if a man pretend[4] to me, that God hath spoken to him supernaturally, and immediately, and I make doubt of it, I cannot easily perceive what argument he can produce, to oblige me to beleeve it. It is true, that if he be my Soveraign, he may oblige me to obedience, so, as not by act or word to declare I beleeve him not; but not to think any otherwise then my reason perswades me. But if one that hath not such authority over me, shall pretend the same, there is nothing that exacteth either beleefe, or obedience.

For to say that God hath spoken to him in the Holy Scripture, is not to say God hath spoken to him immediately, but by mediation of the Prophets, or of the Apostles, or of the Church, in such manner as he speaks to all other Christian men. To say he hath spoken to him in a Dream, is no more then to say he dreamed that God spake to him; which is not of force to win beleef from any man, that knows dreams are for the most part naturall, and may proceed from former thoughts; and such dreams as that, from selfe conceit, and foolish arrogance, and false opinion of a mans own godlinesse, or other vertue, by which he thinks he hath merited the favour of extraordinary Revelation. To say he hath seen a Vision, or heard a Voice, is to say, that he hath dreamed between sleeping and waking: for in such manner a man doth many times naturally take his dream for a vision, as not having well observed his own slumbering. To say he speaks by supernaturall Inspiration, is to say he finds an ardent desire to speak, or some strong opinion of himself, for which hee can alledge no naturall and sufficient reason. So that though God Almighty can speak to a man, by Dreams, Visions, Voice, and Inspiration; yet he obliges no man to beleeve he hath so done to him that pretends it; who (being a man) may erre, and (which is more) may lie.

By what marks Prophets are known.

1 Kings 22.

[197]

1 Kings 13.

How then can he, to whom God hath never revealed his Wil immediately (saving by the way of natural reason) know when he is to obey, or not to obey his Word, delivered by him, that says he is a Prophet? Of 400 Prophets, of whom the K. of *Israel* asked counsel, concerning the warre he made against *Ramoth Gilead*, only *Micaiah* was a true one. The Prophet that was sent to prophecy against the Altar set up by *Jeroboam*, though a true Prophet, and that by two miracles done in his presence appears to be a Prophet sent from God, was yet deceived by another old Prophet, that perswaded him as from the

---

4. Claim (not necessarily deceitfully).

mouth of God, to eat and drink with him. If one Prophet deceive another, what certainty is there of knowing the will of God, by other way than that of Reason? To which I answer out of the Holy Scripture, that there be two marks, by which together, not asunder, a true Prophet is to be known. One is the doing of miracles; the other is the not teaching any other Religion than that which is already established. Asunder (I say) neither of these is sufficient. *If a Prophet rise amongst you, or a Dreamer of dreams, and shall pretend the doing of a miracle, and the miracle come to passe; if he say, Let us follow strange Gods, which thou hast not known, thou shalt not hearken to him, &c.* But that *Prophet and Dreamer of dreams shall be put to death, because he hath spoken to you to Revolt from the Lord your God.* In which words two things are to be observed; First, that God wil not have miracles alone serve for arguments, to approve the Prophets calling; but (as it is in the third verse) for an experiment of the constancy of our adherence to himself. For the works of the *Egyptian* Sorcerers, though not so great as those of *Moses*, yet were great miracles. Secondly, that how great soever the miracle be, yet if it tend to stir up revolt against the King, or him that governeth by the Kings authority, he that doth such miracle, is not to be considered otherwise than as sent to make triall of their allegiance. For these words, *revolt from the Lord your God*, are in this place equivalent to *revolt from your King.* For they had made God their King by pact at the foot of Mount *Sinai*; who ruled them by *Moses* only; for he only spake with God, and from time to time declared Gods Commandements to the people. In like manner, after our Saviour Christ had made his Disciples acknowledge him for the *Messiah*, (that is to say, for Gods anointed, whom the nation of the *Jews* daily expected for their King, but refused when he came,) he omitted not to advertise[5] them of the danger of miracles. *There shall arise* (saith he) *false Christs, and false Prophets, and shall doe great wonders and miracles, even to the seducing (if it were possible) of the very Elect.* By which it appears, that false Prophets may have the power of miracles; yet are wee not to take their doctrin for Gods Word. St. *Paul* says further to the *Galatians*, that *if himself, or an Angell from heaven preach another Gospel to them, than he had preached, let him be accursed.* That Gospel was, that Christ was King; so that all preaching against the power of the King received, in consequence to these words, is by St. *Paul* accursed. For his speech is addressed to those, who by his preaching had already received *Jesus* for the *Christ*, that is to say, for King of the *Jews*.

And as Miracles, without preaching that Doctrine which God hath established; so preaching the true Doctrine, without the doing of Miracles, is an unsufficient argument of immediate Revelation. For if a man that teacheth not false Doctrine, should pretend to bee a Prophet without shewing any Miracle, he is never the more to bee regarded for his pretence, as is evident by *Deut. 18. v. 21, 22. If thou say in thy heart, How shall we know that the Word* (of the Prophet) *is not that which the Lord hath spoken. When the Prophet shall have spoken in the*

Deut. 13. v. 1, 2, 3, 4, 5.

Mat. 24. 24.

Gal. 1.8.

The marks of a Prophet in the old law, Miracles, and Doctrine conformable to the law.
[198]

5. To warn.

name of the Lord, that which shall not come to passe, that's the word which the Lord hath not spoken, but the Prophet has spoken it out of the pride of his own heart, fear him not. But a man may here again ask, When the Prophet hath foretold a thing, how shall we know whether it will come to passe or not? For he may foretel it as a thing to arrive after a certain long time, longer then the time of mans life; or indefinitely, that it will come to passe one time or other: in which case this mark of a Prophet is unusefull; and therefore the miracles that oblige us to beleeve a Prophet, ought to be confirmed by an immediate, or a not long deferr'd event. So that it is manifest, that the teaching of the Religion which God hath established, and the shewing of a present Miracle, joined together, were the only marks whereby the Scripture would have a true Prophet, that is to say, immediate Revelation to be acknowledged; neither of them being singly sufficient to oblige any other man to regard what he saith.

Miracles ceasing, Prophets cease, and the Scripture supplies their place. Seeing therefore Miracles now cease, we have no sign left, whereby to acknowledge the pretended Revelations, or Inspirations of any private man; nor obligation to give ear to any Doctrine, farther than it is conformable to the Holy Scriptures, which since the time of our Saviour, supply the place, and sufficiently recompense the want of all other Prophecy; and from which, by wise and learned interpretation, and carefull ratiocination, all rules and precepts necessary to the knowledge of our duty both to God and man, without Enthusiasme,[6] or supernaturall Inspiration, may easily be deduced. And this Scripture is it, out of which I am to take the Principles of my Discourse, concerning the Rights of those that are the Supream Governors on earth, of Christian Common-wealths; and of the duty of Christian Subjects towards their Soveraigns. And to that end, I shall speak in the next Chapter, of the Books, Writers, Scope and Authority of the Bible.

[199]

Chap. XXXIII.

Of the Number, Antiquity, Scope, Authority, and Interpreters of the Books of Holy SCRIPTURE.

Of the Books of Holy Scripture. By the Books of Holy SCRIPTURE, are understood those, which ought to be the *Canon*, that is to say, the Rules of Christian life. And because all Rules of life, which men are in conscience bound to observe, are Laws; the question of the Scripture, is the question of what is Law throughout all Christendome, both Naturall, and Civill. For though it be not determined in Scripture, what Laws every Christian King shall constitute in his own Dominions; yet it is determined what laws he shall not constitute. Seeing therefore I have already proved, that Soveraigns in their own Dominions are the sole Legislators; those Books only are Canonicall, that is, Law, in every nation, which are established for such by the Soveraign Authority. It is true, that God is the Soveraign of all Soveraigns; and therefore, when he speaks to any Subject, he

6. Prophetic frenzy.

ought to be obeyed, whatsoever any earthly Potentate command to the contrary. But the question is not of obedience to God, but of *when*, and *what* God hath said; which to Subjects that have no supernaturall revelation, cannot be known, but by that naturall reason, which guided them, for the obtaining of Peace and Justice, to obey the authority of their severall Common-wealths; that is to say, of their lawfull Soveraigns. According to this obligation, I can acknowledge no other Books of the Old Testament, to be Holy Scripture, but those which have been commanded to be acknowledged for such, by the Authority of the Church of *England*. What Books these are, is sufficiently known, without a Catalogue of them here; and they are the same that are acknowledged by St. *Jerome*,[1] who holdeth the rest, namely, the *Wisdome of Solomon, Ecclesiasticus, Judith, Tobias*, the first and the second of *Maccabees*, (though he had seen the first in *Hebrew*) and the third and fourth of *Esdras*, for *Apocrypha*. Of the Canonicall, *Josephus*[2] a learned *Jew*, that wrote in the time of the Emperour *Domitian*, reckoneth *twenty two*, making the number agree with the *Hebrew* Alphabet. St. *Jerome* does the same, though they reckon them in different manner. For *Josephus* numbers *five* Books of *Moses, thirteen* of *Prophets*, that writ the History of their own times (which how it agrees with the Prophets writings contained in the Bible wee shall see hereafter), and *four* of *Hymnes* and Morall Precepts. But St. *Jerome* reckons *five* Books of *Moses, eight* of *Prophets*, and *nine* of other Holy writ, which he calls of *Hagiographa*. The *Septuagint*, who were 70. learned men of the *Jews*, sent for by *Ptolemy* King of *Egypt*, to translate the *Jewish* law, out of the *Hebrew* into the *Greek*, have left us no other for holy Scripture in the *Greek* tongue, but the same that are received in the Church of *England*. [200]

As for the Books of the New Testament, they are equally acknowledged for Canon by all Christian Churches, and by all Sects of Christians, that admit any Books at all for Canonicall.

Who were the originall writers of the severall Books of Holy Scripture, has not been made evident by any sufficient testimony of other History, (which is the only proof of matter of fact); nor can be by any arguments of naturall Reason: for Reason serves only to convince the truth (not of fact, but) of consequence. The light therefore that must guide us in this question, must be that which is held out unto us from the Bookes themselves: And this light, though it shew us not the writer of every book, yet it is not unusefull to give us knowledge of the time, wherein they were written. *Their Antiquity.*

And first, for the *Pentateuch*, it is not argument enough that they were written by *Moses*, because they are called the five Books of *Moses*; no more than these titles, The Book of *Joshua*, the Book of *Judges*, the Book of *Ruth*, and the Books of the *Kings*, are arguments sufficient to prove, that they were written by *Joshua*, by the *Judges*, by *Ruth*, and by

---

1. An influential figure in the early Church (c. 342–420) who was responsible for producing the Vulgate (the authoritative translation of the Bible into Latin).
2. A Jewish historian (37–c. 101) who was appointed governor of Galilee by the Romans in A.D. 66.

the *Kings*. For in titles of Books, the subject is marked, as often as the writer. The *History of Livy*, denotes the Writer; but the *History of Scanderbeg*, is denominated from the subject. We read in the last Chapter of *Deuteronomie, ver.* 6. concerning the sepulcher of *Moses, that no man knoweth of his sepulcher to this day*, that is, to the day wherein those words were written. It is therefore manifest, that those words were written after his interrement. For it were a strange interpretation, to say *Moses* spake of his own sepulcher (though by Prophecy), that it was not found to that day, wherein he was yet living. But it may perhaps be alledged, that the last Chapter only, not the whole *Pentateuch*, was written by some other man, but the rest not: Let us therefore consider that which we find in the Book of *Genesis, chap.* 12. *ver.* 6. *And* Abraham *passed through the land to the place of* Sichem, *unto the plain of* Moreh, *and the* Canaanite *was then in the land*; which must needs bee the words of one that wrote when the *Canaanite* was not in the land; and consequently, not of *Moses*, who dyed before he came into it. Likewise *Numbers 21. ver. 14.* the Writer citeth another more ancient Book, Entituled, *The Book of the Warres of the Lord*, wherein were registred the Acts of *Moses*, at the Red-sea, and at the brook of *Arnon*. It is therefore sufficiently evident, that the five Books of *Moses* were written after his time, though how long after it be not so manifest.

But though *Moses* did not compile those Books entirely, and in the form we have them; yet he wrote all that which hee is there said to have written: as for example, the Volume of the Law, which is contained, as it seemeth, in the 11 of *Deuteronomie*, and the following Chapters to the 27. which was also commanded to be written on stones, in their entry into the land of *Canaan*. And this did *Moses* himself write, and deliver to the Priests and Elders of *Israel*, to be read every seventh year to all *Israel*, at their assembling in the feast of Tabernacles. And this is that Law which God commanded, that their Kings (when they should have established that form of Government) should take a copy of from the Priests and Levites; and which *Moses* commanded the Priests and Levites to lay in the side of the Arke; and the same which having been lost, was long time after found again by *Hilkiah*, and sent to King *Josias*, who causing it to be read to the People, renewed the Covenant between God and them.

That the Book of *Joshua* was also written long after the time of *Joshua*, may be gathered out of many places of the Book it self. *Joshua* had set up twelve stones in the middest of *Jordan*, for a monument of their passage; of which the Writer saith thus, *They are there unto this day*; for *unto this day*, is a phrase that signifieth a time past, beyond the memory of man. In like manner, upon the saying of the Lord, that he had rolled off from the people the Reproach of *Egypt*, the Writer saith, *The place is called* Gilgal *unto this day*; which to have said in the time of *Joshua* had been improper. So also the name of the Valley of *Achor*, from the trouble that *Achan* raised in the Camp, the Writer saith, *remaineth unto this day*; which must needs bee therefore long after the time of *Joshua*. Arguments of this kind there be many other; as *Josh.* 8.29. 13.13. 14.14. 15.63.

The Pentateuch not written by Moses.

Deut. 31.9.
[201]

Deut. 31.26.

*2 King. 22.8.
& 23.1, 2, 3.*

The Book of Joshua written after his time.

Josh. 4.9.

Josh. 5.9.

Josh. 7.26.

The same is manifest by like arguments of the Book of *Judges*, chap. 1.21,26. 6.24. 10.4. 15.19. 17.6. and *Ruth* 1.1. but especially *Judg.* 18.30. where it is said, that Jonathan *and his sonnes were Priests to the Tribe of* Dan, *untill the day of the captivity of the land.*

That the Books of *Samuel* were also written after his own time, there are the like arguments, 1 *Sam.* 5.5. 7.13, 15. 27.6. & 30.25. where, after *David* had adjudged equall part of the spoiles, to them that guarded the Ammunition, with them that fought, the Writer saith, *He made it a Statute and an Ordinance to* Israel *to this day.* Again, when *David* (displeased, that the Lord had slain *Uzzah*, for putting out his hand to sustain the Ark,) called the place *Perez-Uzzah*, the Writer saith, it is called so *to this day*: the time therefore of the writing of that Book, must be long after the time of the fact; that is, long after the time of *David*.

As for the two Books of the *Kings*, and the two Books of the *Chronicles*, besides the places which mention such monuments, as the Writer saith, remained till his own days; such as are 1 *Kings* 9.13. 9.21. 10.12. 12.19. 2 *Kings* 2.22. 8.22. 10.27. 14.7. 16.6. 17.23. 17.34. 17.41. 1 *Chron.* 4.41. 5.26. It is argument sufficient they were written after the captivity in *Babylon*, that the History of them is continued till that time. For the Facts Registred are alwaies more ancient than the Register; and much more ancient than such Books as make mention of, and quote the Register; as these Books doe in divers places, referring the Reader to the Chronicles of the Kings of *Juda*, to the Chronicles of the Kings of *Israel*, to the Books of the Prophet *Samuel*, of the Prophet *Nathan*, of the Prophet *Ahijah*; to the Vision of *Jehdo*, to the Books of the Prophet *Serveiah*, and of the Prophet *Addo*.

The Books of *Esdras* and *Nehemiah* were written certainly after their return from captivity; because their return, the re-edification of the walls and houses of *Jerusalem*, the renovation of the Covenant, and ordination of their policy are therein contained.

The History of Queen *Esther* is of the time of the Captivity; and therefore the Writer must have been of the same time, or after it.

The Book of *Job* hath no mark in it of the time wherein it was written: and though it appear sufficiently (*Ezekiel* 14.14. and *James* 5.11.) that he was no fained person; yet the Book it self seemeth not to be a History, but a Treatise concerning a question in ancient time much disputed, *why wicked men have often prospered in this world, and good men have been afflicted*; and it is the more probable, because from the beginning, to the third verse of the third chapter, where the complaint of *Job* beginneth, the *Hebrew* is (as St. *Jerome* testifies) in prose; and from thence to the sixt verse of the last chapter in Hexameter Verses; and the rest of that chapter again in prose. So that the dispute is all in verse; and the prose is added, but as a Preface in the beginning, and an Epilogue in the end. But Verse is no usuall stile of such, as either are themselves in great pain, as *Job*; or of such as come to comfort them, as his friends; but in Philosophy, especially morall Philosophy, in ancient time frequent.

The *Psalmes* were written the most part by David, for the use of the

The Booke of Judges and Ruth written long after the Captivity.

The like of the Bookes of Samuel.

2 Sam. 6.4.

The Books of the Kings, and the Chronicles.

[202]
Ezra and Nehemiah.

Esther.

Job.

The Psalter.

Quire.[3] To these are added some Songs of *Moses*, and other holy men; and some of them after the return from the Captivity, as the 137. and the 126. whereby it is manifest that the Psalter was compiled, and put into the form it now hath, after the return of the *Jews* from *Babylon*.

The Proverbs. The *Proverbs*, being a Collection of wise and godly Sayings, partly of *Solomon*, partly of *Agur* the son of *Jakeh*, and partly of the Mother of King *Lemuel*, cannot probably be thought to have been collected by *Solomon*, rather then by *Agur*, or the Mother of *Lemuel*; and that, though the sentences be theirs, yet the collection or compiling them into this one Book, was the work of some other godly man, that lived after them all.

Ecclesiastes and the Canticles. The Books of *Ecclesiastes* and the *Canticles* have nothing that was not *Solomons*, except it be the Titles, or Inscriptions. For *The Words of the Preacher, the Son of* David, *King in* Jerusalem; and, *The Song of Songs*, which is *Solomon's*, seem to have been made for distinctions sake, then, when the Books of Scripture were gathered into one body of the Law; to the end, that not the Doctrine only, but the Authors also might be extant.

The Prophets. Of the Prophets, the most ancient, are *Sophoniah, Jonas, Amos, Hosea, Isaiah* and *Michaiah*, who lived in the time of *Amaziah*, and *Azariah*, otherwise *Ozias*, Kings of *Judah*. But the Book of *Jonas* is not properly a Register of his Prophecy, (for that is contained in these few words, *Fourty dayes and* Ninivy *shall be destroyed*,) but a History or Narration of his frowardnesse and disputing Gods commandements; so that there is small probability he should be the Author, seeing he is the subject of it. But the Book of *Amos* is his Prophecy.

[203] *Jeremiah, Abdias, Nahum,* and *Habakkuk* prophecyed in the time of *Josiah.*

Ezekiel, Daniel, Aggeus, and *Zacharias,* in the Captivity.

When *Joel* and *Malachi* prophecyed, is not evident by their Writings. But considering the Inscriptions, or Titles of their Books, it is manifest enough, that the whole Scripture of the Old Testament, was set forth in the form we have it, after the return of the *Jews* from their Captivity in *Babylon*, and before the time of *Ptolemæus Philadelphus*, that caused it to bee translated into Greek by seventy men, which were sent him out of *Judea* for that purpose. And if the Books of *Apocrypha* (which are recommended to us by the Church, though not for Canonicall, yet for profitable Books for our instruction) may in this point be credited, the Scripture was set forth in the form wee have it in, by *Esdras*; as may appear by that which he himself saith, in the second book, chapt. 14. verse 21, 22, &c. where speaking to God, he saith thus, *Thy law is burnt; therefore no man knoweth the things which thou hast done, or the works that are to begin. But if I have found Grace before thee, send down the holy Spirit into me, and I shall write all that hath been done in the world, since the beginning, which were written in thy Law, that men may find thy path, and that they which will live in the later days, may live. And* verse 45. *And it came to passe when the forty dayes were*

3. Choir.

fulfilled, that the Highest spake, saying, The first that thou hast written, publish openly, that the worthy and unworthy may read it; but keep the seventy last, that thou mayst deliver them onely to such as be wise among the people. And thus much concerning the time of the writing of the Bookes of the Old Testament.

The Writers of the New Testament lived all in lesse then an age after Christs Ascension, and had all of them seen our Saviour, or been his Disciples, except St. *Paul,* and St. *Luke;* and consequently whatsoever was written by them, is as ancient as the time of the Apostles. But the time wherein the Books of the New Testament were received, and acknowledged by the Church to be of their writing, is not altogether so ancient. For, as the Bookes of the Old Testament are derived to us, from no higher time then that of *Esdras,*[4] who by the direction of Gods Spirit retrived them, when they were lost: Those of the New Testament, of which the copies were not many, nor could easily be all in any one private mans hand, cannot bee derived from a higher time, than that wherein the Governours of the Church collected, approved, and recommended them to us, as the writings of those Apostles and Disciples; under whose names they go. The first enumeration of all the Bookes, both of the Old, and New Testament, is in the Canons of the Apostles, supposed to be collected by *Clement* the first (after St. *Peter*) Bishop of *Rome.* But because that is but supposed, and by many questioned, the Councell of *Laodicea* is the first we know, that recommended the Bible to the then Christian Churches, for the Writings of the Prophets and Apostles: and this Councell was held in the 364. yeer after Christ. At which time, though ambition had so far prevailed on the great Doctors of the Church, as no more to esteem Emperours, though Christian, for the Shepherds of the people, but for Sheep; and Emperours not Christian, for Wolves; and endeavoured to passe their Doctrine, not for Counsell, and Information, as Preachers; but for Laws, as absolute Governours; and thought such frauds as tended to make the people the more obedient to Christian Doctrine, to be pious; yet I am perswaded they did not therefore falsifie the Scriptures, though the copies of the Books of the New Testament, were in the hands only of the Ecclesiasticks; because if they had had an intention so to doe, they would surely have made them more favorable to their power over Christian Princes, and Civill Soveraignty, than they are. I see not therefore any reason to doubt, but that the Old, and New Testament, as we have them now, are the true Registers of those things, which were done and said by the Prophets, and Apostles. And so perhaps are some of those Books which are called Apocrypha, if left out of the Canon, not for inconformity of Doctrine with the rest, but only because they are not found in the Hebrew. For after the conquest of Asia by Alexander the Great, there were few learned Jews, that were not perfect in the Greek tongue. For the seventy Interpreters that converted the Bible into Greek, were all of them Hebrews; and we have extant the works of *Philo*[5] and *Josephus* both Jews, written by them eloquently in Greek.

The New Testament.

[204]

4. Ezra.
5. A Jewish writer (c. 15 B.C.–?) on Greek philosophy and Judaism.

Their Scope.

But it is not the Writer, but the authority of the Church, that maketh a Book Canonicall. And although these Books were written by divers men, yet it is manifest the Writers were all indued with one and the same Spirit, in that they conspire[6] to one and the same end, which is the setting forth of the Rights of the Kingdome of *God*, the *Father, Son*, and *Holy Ghost*. For the Book of *Genesis*, deriveth the Genealogy of Gods people, from the creation of the World, to the going into Egypt: the other four Books of *Moses*, contain the Election of God for their King, and the Laws which hee prescribed for their Government: The Books of *Joshua, Judges, Ruth*, and *Samuel*, to the time of *Saul*, describe the acts of Gods people, till the time they cast off Gods yoke, and called for a King, after the manner of their neighbour nations: The rest of the History of the Old Testament, derives the succession of the line of *David*, to the Captivity, out of which line was to spring the restorer of the Kingdome of God, even our blessed Saviour *God the Son*, whose coming was foretold in the Bookes of the Prophets, after whom the Evangelists writt his life, and actions, and his claim to the Kingdome, whilst he lived on earth: and lastly, the Acts, and Epistles of the Apostles, declare the coming of God, the *Holy Ghost*, and the Authority he left with them, and their successors, for the direction of the Jews, and for the invitation of the Gentiles. In summe, the Histories and the Prophecies of the old Testament, and the Gospels and Epistles of the New Testament, have had one and the same scope, to convert men to the obedience of God; 1. in *Moses*, and the Priests; 2. in the man *Christ*; and 3. in the *Apostles* and the successors to Apostolicall power. For these three at several times did represent the person of God: *Moses*, and his successors the High Priests, and Kings of Judah, in the Old Testament: *Christ* himself, in the time he lived on earth: and the *Apostles*, and their successors, from the day of Pentecost (when the *Holy Ghost* descended on them) to this day.

[205]

The question of the Authority of the Scriptures stated.

It is a question much disputed between the divers sects of Christian Religion, *From whence the Scriptures derive their Authority*; which question is also propounded sometimes in other terms, as, *How wee know them to be the Word of God*, or, *Why we beleeve them to be so*: And the difficulty of resolving it, ariseth chiefly from the impropernesse of the words wherein the question it self is couched. For it is beleeved on all hands, that the first and originall *Author* of them is God; and consequently the question disputed, is not that. Again, it is manifest, that none can know they are Gods Word, (though all true Christians beleeve it,) but those to whom God himself hath revealed it supernaturally; and therefore the question is not rightly moved, of our *Knowledge* of it. Lastly, when the question is propounded of our *Beleefe*; because some are moved to beleeve for one, and others for other reasons, there can be rendred no one generall answer for them all. The question truly stated is, *By what Authority they are made Law*.

Their Authority and Interpretation.

As far as they differ not from the Laws of Nature, there is no doubt, but they are the Law of God, and carry their Authority with them,

6. Cooperate.

legible to all men that have the use of naturall reason: but this is no other Authority, then that of all other Morall Doctrine consonant to Reason; the Dictates whereof are Laws, not *made*, but *Eternall*.

If they be made Law by God himselfe, they are of the nature of written Law, which are Laws to them only to whom God hath so sufficiently published them, as no man can excuse himself, by saying, he knew not they were his.

He therefore, to whom God hath not supernaturally revealed, that they are his, nor that those that published them, were sent by him, is not obliged to obey them, by any Authority, but his, whose Commands have already the force of Laws; that is to say, by any other Authority, then that of the Common-wealth, residing in the Soveraign, who only has the Legislative power. Again, if it be not the Legislative Authority of the Common-wealth, that giveth them the force of Laws, it must bee some other Authority derived from God, either private, or publique: if private, it obliges onely him, to whom in particular God hath been pleased to reveale it. For if every man should be obliged, to take for Gods Law, what particular men, on pretence of private Inspiration, or Revelation, should obtrude upon him, (in such a number of men, that out of pride, and ignorance, take their own Dreams, and extravagant Fancies, and Madnesse, for testimonies of Gods Spirit; or out of ambition, pretend to such Divine testimonies, falsely, and contrary to their own consciences,) it were impossible that any Divine Law should be acknowledged. If publique, it is the Authority of the *Common-wealth*, or of the *Church*. But the Church, if it be one person, is the same thing with a Common-wealth of Christians; called a *Common-wealth*,   [206] because it consisteth of men united in one person, their Soveraign; and a *Church*, because it consisteth in Christian men, united in one Christian Soveraign. But if the Church be not one person, then it hath no authority at all; it can neither command, nor doe any action at all; nor is capable of having any power, or right to any thing; nor has any Will, Reason, nor Voice; for all these qualities are personall. Now if the whole number of Christians be not contained in one Common-wealth, they are not one person; nor is there an Universall Church that hath any authority over them; and therefore the Scriptures are not made Laws, by the Universall Church: or if it bee one Common-wealth, then all Christian Monarchs, and States are private persons, and subject to bee judged, deposed, and punished by an Universall Soveraigne of all Christendome. So that the question of the Authority of the Scriptures, is reduced to this, *Whether Christian Kings, and the Soveraigne Assemblies in Christian Common-wealths, be absolute in their own Territories, immediately under God; or subject to one Vicar of Christ, constituted over the Universall Church; to bee judged, condemned, deposed, and put to death, as hee shall think expedient, or necessary for the common good.*

Which question cannot bee resolved, without a more particular consideration of the Kingdome of God; from whence also, wee are to judge of the Authority of Interpreting the Scripture. For, whosoever hath a

lawfull power over any Writing, to make it Law, hath the power also
to approve, or disapprove the interpretation of the same.

* * *

[233]

Chap. XXXVII.

Of Miracles, and their Use.

A Miracle is a work that causeth Admiration.

By *Miracles* are signified the Admirable[1] works of God: & therefore
they are also called *Wonders.* And because they are for the most part,
done, for a signification of his commandement, in such occasions, as
without them, men are apt to doubt, (following their private naturall
reasoning,) what he hath commanded, and what not, they are commonly in Holy Scripture, called *Signes*, in the same sense, as they are
called by the Latines, *Ostenta*, and *Portenta*, from shewing, and fore-
signifying that, which the Almighty is about to bring to passe.

And must therefore be rare, and whereof there is no naturall cause known.

To understand therefore what is a Miracle, we must first understand
what works they are, which men wonder at, and call Admirable. And
there be but two things. which make men wonder at any event: The
one is, if it be strange, that is to say, such, as the like of it hath never,
or very rarely been produced: The other is, if when it is produced, we
cannot imagine it to have been done by naturall means, but onely by
the immediate hand of God. But when wee see some possible, naturall
cause of it, how rarely soever the like has been done; or if the like have
been often done, how impossible soever it be to imagine a naturall
means thereof, we no more wonder, nor esteem it for a Miracle.

Therefore, if a Horse, or Cow should speak, it were a Miracle; because both the thing is strange, & the naturall cause difficult to imagin:
So also were it, to see a strange deviation of nature, in the production
of some new shape of a living creature. But when a man, or other
Animal, engenders his like, though we know no more how this is done,
than the other; yet because 'tis usuall, it is no Miracle. In like manner,
if a man be metamorphosed into a stone, or into a pillar, it is a Miracle;
because strange: but if a peece of wood be so changed; because we see
it often, it is no Miracle: and yet we know no more, by what operation
of God, the one is brought to passe, than the other.

The first Rainbow that was seen in the world, was a Miracle, because
the first; and consequently strange; and served for a sign from God,
placed in heaven, to assure his people, there should be no more an
universall destruction of the world by Water. But at this day, because
they are frequent, they are not Miracles, neither to them that know
their naturall causes, nor to them who know them not. Again, there be
many rare works produced by the Art of man: yet when we know they
are done; because thereby wee know also the means how they are done,
we count them not for Miracles, because not wrought by the immediate
[234] hand of God, but by mediation of humane Industry.

1. Amazing, awe-inspiring.

Furthermore, seeing Admiration and Wonder, is consequent to the knowledge and experience, wherewith men are endued, some more, some lesse; it followeth, that the same thing, may be a Miracle to one, and not to another. And thence it is, that ignorant, and superstitious men make great Wonders of those works, which other men, knowing to proceed from Nature, (which is not the immediate, but the ordinary work of God,) admire not at all: As when Ecclipses of the Sun and Moon have been taken for supernaturall works, by the common people; when neverthelesse, there were others, could from their naturall causes, have foretold the very hour they should arrive: Or, as when a man, by confederacy, and secret intelligence, getting knowledge of the private actions of an ignorant, unwary man, thereby tells him, what he has done in former time; it seems to him a Miraculous thing; but amongst wise, and cautelous[2] men, such Miracles as those, cannot easily be done.

That which seemeth a Miracle to one man, may seem otherwise to another.

Again, it belongeth to the nature of a Miracle, that it be wrought for the procuring of credit to Gods Messengers, Ministers, and Prophets, that thereby men may know, they are called, sent, and employed by God, and thereby be the better inclined to obey them. And therefore, though the creation of the world, and after that the destruction of all living creatures in the universall deluge, were admirable works; yet because they were not done to procure credit to any Prophet, or other Minister of God, they use not to be called Miracles. For how admirable soever any work be, the Admiration consisteth not in that it could be done, because men naturally beleeve the Almighty can doe all things, but because he does it at the Prayer, or Word of a man. But the works of God in Egypt, by the hand of Moses, were properly Miracles; because they were done with intention to make the people of Israel beleeve, that Moses came unto them, not out of any design of his owne interest, but as sent from God. Therefore after God had commanded him to deliver the Israelites from the Egyptian bondage, when he said *They will not beleeve me, but will say, the Lord hath not appeared unto me*, God gave him power, to turn the Rod he had in his hand into a Serpent, and again to return it into a Rod; and by putting his hand into his bosome, to make it leprous; and again by pulling it out to make it whole, to make the Children of Israel beleeve (as it is verse 5.) that the God of their Fathers had appeared unto him: And if that were not enough, he gave him power to turn their waters into bloud. And when hee had done these Miracles before the people, it is said (verse 41.) that *they beleeved him*. Neverthelesse, for fear of Pharaoh, they durst not yet obey him. Therefore the other works which were done to plague Pharaoh, and the Egyptians, tended all to make the Israelites beleeve in Moses, and were properly Miracles. In like manner if we consider all the Miracles done by the hand of Moses, and all the rest of the Prophets, till the Captivity; and those of our Saviour, and his Apostles afterward; we shall find, their end was alwaies to beget, or confirm beleefe, that they came not of their own motion, but were sent by God.

The End of Miracles.

Exo. 4.1, &c.

[235]

2. Cautious.

Wee may further observe in Scripture, that the end of Miracles, was to beget beleef, not universally in all men, elect, and reprobate; but in the elect only; that is to say, in such as God had determined should become his Subjects. For those miraculous plagues of Egypt, had not for end, the conversion of Pharaoh; For God had told Moses before, that he would harden the heart of Pharaoh, that he should not let the people goe: And when he let them goe at last, not the Miracles perswaded him, but the plagues forced him to it. So also of our Saviour, it is written, (*Mat.* 13.58.) that he wrought not many Miracles in his own countrey, because of their unbeleef; and (in *Marke* 6.5.) in stead of, *he wrought not many*, it is, *he could work none*. It was not because he wanted power; which to say, were blasphemy against God; nor that the end of Miracles was not to convert incredulous men to Christ; for the end of all the Miracles of Moses, of the Prophets, of our Saviour, and of his Apostles was to adde men to the Church; but it was, because the end of their Miracles, was to adde to the Church (not all men, but) such as should be saved; that is to say, such as God had elected. Seeing therefore our Saviour was sent from his Father, hee could not use his power in the conversion of those, whom his Father had rejected. They that expounding this place of St. *Marke*, say, that this word, Hee could not, is put for, *He would not*, do it without example in the Greek tongue, (where *Would not*, is put sometimes for *Could not*, in things inanimate, that have no will; but *Could not*, for *Would not*, never,) and thereby lay a stumbling block before weak Christians; as if Christ could doe no Miracles, but amongst the credulous.

From that which I have here set down, of the nature, and use of a Miracle, we may define it thus, A MIRACLE, *is a work of God, (besides his operation by the way of Nature, ordained in the Creation,) done, for the making manifest to his elect, the mission of an extraordinary Minister for their salvation.*

The definition of a Miracle And from this definition, we may inferre; First, that in all Miracles, the work done, is not the effect of any vertue in the Prophet; because it is the effect of the immediate hand of God; that is to say, God hath done it, without using the Prophet therein, as a subordinate cause.

Secondly, that no Devil, Angel, or other created Spirit, can do a Miracle. For it must either be by vertue of some naturall science, or by Incantation, that is, [by][3] vertue of words. For if the Inchanters do it by their own power independent, there is some power that proceedeth not from God; which all men deny: and if they doe it by power given them, then is the work not from the immediate hand of God, but naturall, and consequently no Miracle.

There be some texts of Scripture, that seem to attribute the power of working wonders (equall to some of those immediate Miracles, wrought by God himself,) to certain Arts of Magick, and Incantation.

[236] As for example, when we read that after the Rod of Moses being cast
Exod. 7.11. on the ground became a Serpent, *the Magicians of Egypt did the like by their Enchantments*; and that after Moses had turned the waters of

---

3. Manuscript version.

the Egyptian Streams, Rivers, Ponds, and Pooles of water into blood,
the Magicians of Egypt did so likewise, with their Enchantments; and   *Exod. 7.22.*
that after Moses had by the power of God brought frogs upon the land,
the Magicians also did so with their Enchantments, and brought up   *Exod. 8.7.*
frogs upon the land of Egypt; will not a man be apt to attribute Miracles
to Enchantments; that is to say, to the efficacy of the sound of Words;
and think the same very well proved out of this, and other such places?
and yet there is no place of Scripture that telleth us what an Enchantment is. If therefore Enchantment be not, as many think it, a working
of strange effects by spells, and words; but Imposture, and delusion,
wrought by ordinary means; and so far from supernaturall, as the Im-
postors need not the study so much as of naturall causes, but the ordinary ignorance, stupidity, and superstition of mankind, to doe them;
those texts that seem to countenance the power of Magick, Witchcraft,
and Enchantment, must needs have another sense, than at first sight
they seem to bear.

For it is evident enough, that Words have no effect, but on those   *That men are*
that understand them; and then they have no other, but to signifie the   *apt to be de-*
intentions, or passions of them that speak; and thereby produce, hope,   *ceived by false*
fear, or other passions, or conceptions in the hearer. Therefore when a   *Miracles.*
Rod seemeth a Serpent, or the Waters Bloud, or any other Miracle
seemeth done by Enchantment; if it be not to the edification of Gods
people, not the Rod, nor the Water, nor any other thing is enchanted;
that is to say, wrought upon by the Words, but the Spectator. So that
all the Miracle consisteth in this, that the Enchanter has deceived a
man; which is no Miracle, but a very easie matter to doe.

For such is the ignorance, and aptitude to error generally of all men,
but especially of them that have not much knowledge of naturall
causes, and of the nature, and interests of men; as by innumerable and
easie tricks to be abused. What opinion[4] of miraculous power, before
it was known there was a Science of the course of the Stars, might a
man have gained, that should have told the people, This hour, or day
the Sun should be darkned? A Juggler by the handling of his goblets,
and other trinkets, if it were not now ordinarily practised, would be
thought to do his wonders by the power at least of the Devil. A man
that hath practised to speak by drawing in of his breath, (which kind
of men in antient time were called *Ventriloqui,*) and so make the weaknesse of his voice seem to proceed, not from the weak impulsion of the
organs of Speech, but from distance of place, is able to make very many
men beleeve it is a voice from Heaven, whatsoever he please to tell
them. And for a crafty man, that hath enquired into the secrets, and
familiar confessions that one man ordinarily maketh to another of his
actions and adventures past, to tell them him again is no hard matter;
and yet there be many, that by such means as that, obtain the reputation
of being Conjurers. But it is too long a businesse, to reckon up the   [237]
severall sorts of those men, which the Greeks called *Thaumaturgi,* that
is to say, workers of things wonderfull; and yet these do all they do, by

4. Reputation.

their own single dexterity. But if we looke upon the Impostures wrought by Confederacy, there is nothing how impossible soever to be done, that is impossible to bee beleeved. For two men conspiring, one to seem lame, the other to cure him with a charme, will deceive many: but many conspiring, one to seem lame, another so to cure him, and all the rest to bear witnesse; will deceive many more.

Cautions against the Imposture of Miracles. In this aptitude of mankind, to give too hasty beleefe to pretended Miracles, there can be no better, nor I think any other caution, then that which God hath prescribed, first by Moses, (as I have said before in the precedent chapter,) in the beginning of the 13. and end of the 18. of *Deuteronomy*; That wee take not any for Prophets, that teach any other Religion, then that which Gods Lieutenant, (which at that time was Moses,) hath established; nor any, (though he teach the same Religion,) whose Prædiction we doe not see come to passe. Moses therefore in his time, and Aaron, and his successors in their times, and the Soveraign Governour of Gods people, next under God himself, that is to say, the Head of the Church in all times, are to be consulted, what doctrine he hath established, before wee give credit to a pretended Miracle, or Prophet. And when that is done, the thing they pretend to be a Miracle, we must both see it done, and use all means possible to consider, whether it be really done; and not onely so, but whether it be such, as no man can do the like by his naturall power, but that it requires the immediate hand of God. And in this also we must have recourse to Gods Lieutenant; to whom in all doubtfull cases, wee have submitted our private judgments. For example; if a man pretend, that after certain words spoken over a peece of bread, that presently God hath made it not bread, but a God, or a man, or both, and neverthelesse it looketh still as like bread as ever it did; there is no reason for any man to think it really done; nor consequently to fear him, till he enquire of God, by his Vicar, or Lieutenant, whether it be done, or not. If he say not, then followeth that which Moses saith, (*Deut.* 18.22) *he hath spoken it presumptuously, thou shalt not fear him.* If he say 'tis done, then he is not to contradict it. So also if wee see not, but onely hear tell of a Miracle, we are to consult the Lawful Church; that is to say, the lawful Head thereof, how far we are to give credit to the relators of it. And this is chiefly the case of men, that in these days live under Christian Soveraigns. For in these times, I do not know one man, that ever saw any such wondrous work, done by the charm, or at the word, or prayer of a man, that a man endued but with a mediocrity[5] of reason, would think supernaturall: and the question is no more, whether what wee see done, be a Miracle; whether the Miracle we hear, or read of, were a reall work, and not the Act of a tongue, or pen; but in plain terms, whether the report be true, or a lye. In which question we are not every one, to make our own private Reason, or Conscience, but the Publique Reason, that is, the reason of Gods Supreme Lieutenant, Judge; and indeed we have made him Judge already, if wee have given

him a Soveraign power, to doe all that is necessary for our peace and

---

5. Moderate degree.

defence. A private man has alwaies the liberty, (because thought is free,) to beleeve, or not beleeve in his heart, those acts that have been given out for Miracles, according as he shall see, what benefit can accrew by mens belief, to those that pretend, or countenance them, and thereby conjecture, whether they be Miracles, or Lies. But when it comes to confession of that faith, the Private Reason must submit to the Publique; that is to say, to Gods Lieutenant. But who is this Lieutenant of God, and Head of the Church, shall be considered in its proper place hereafter.

* * *

Chap. XLIII.

Of what is NECESSARY *for a Mans Reception into the Kingdome of Heaven.*

The most frequent prætext of Sedition, and Civill Warre, in Christian Common-wealths hath a long time proceeded from a difficulty, not yet sufficiently resolved, of obeying at once, both God, and Man, then when their Commandements are one contrary to the other. It is manifest enough, that when a man receiveth two contrary Commands, and knows that one of them is Gods, he ought to obey that, and not the other, though it be the command even of his lawfull Soveraign (whether a Monarch, or a soveraign Assembly,) or the command of his Father. The difficulty therefore consisteth in this; that men when they are commanded in the name of God, know not in divers Cases, whether the command be from God, or whether he that commandeth, doe but abuse Gods name for some private ends of his own. For as there were in the Church of the Jews, many false Prophets, that sought reputation with the people, by feigned Dreams, and Visions; so there have been in all times in the Church of Christ, false Teachers, that seek reputation with the people, by phantasticall and false Doctrines; and by such reputation (as is the nature of Ambition,) to govern them for their private benefit.

The difficulty of obeying God and Man both at once,

But this difficulty of obeying both God, and the Civill Soveraign on earth, to those that can distinguish between what is *Necessary*, and what is not *Necessary* for their *Reception* into the *Kingdome of God*, is of no moment. For if the command of the Civill Soveraign bee such, as that it may be obeyed, without the forfeiture of life Eternall; not to obey it is unjust; and the precept of the Apostle takes place; *Servants obey your Masters in all things;* and, *Children obey your Parents in all things;* and the precept of our Saviour, *The Scribes and Pharisees sit in Moses Chaire, All therefore they shall say, that observe, and doe.* But if the command be such, as cannot be obeyed, without being damned to Eternall Death, then it were madnesse to obey it, and the Counsell of our Saviour takes place, (*Mat.* 10. 28.) *Fear not those that kill the body, but cannot kill the soule.* All men therefore that would avoid, both the punishments that are to be in this world inflicted, for disobedience to

Is none to them that distinguish between what is, and what is not Necessary to Salvation.

their earthly Soveraign, and those that shall be inflicted in the world to come for disobedience to God, have need be taught to distinguish well between what is, and what is not Necessary to Eternall Salvation.

[322]
All that is
Necessary to
Salvation is
contained in
Faith and
Obedience.

All that is NECESSARY to Salvation, is contained in two Vertues, Faith in Christ, and Obedience to Laws. The latter of these, if it were perfect, were enough to us. But because wee are all guilty of disobedience to Gods Law, not onely originally in Adam, but also actually by our own transgressions, there is required at our hands now, not onely Obedience for the rest of our time, but also a Remission of sins for the time past; which Remission is the reward of our Faith in Christ. That nothing else is Necessarily required to Salvation, is manifest from this, that the Kingdome of Heaven is shut to none but to Sinners; that is to say, to the disobedient, or transgressors of the Law; nor to them, in case they Repent, and Beleeve all the Articles of Christian Faith, Necessary to Salvation.

What Obedi-
ence is Neces-
sary;

The Obedience required at our hands by God, that accepteth in all our actions the Will for the Deed, is a serious Endeavour to Obey him; and is called also by all such names as signifie that Endeavour. And therefore Obedience, is sometimes called by the names of Charity, and Love, because they imply a Will to Obey; and our Saviour himself maketh our Love to God, and to one another, a Fulfilling of the whole Law: and sometimes by the name of Righteousnesse; for Righteousnesse is but the will to give to every one his owne, that is to say, the will to obey the Laws: and sometimes by the name of Repentance; because to Repent, implyeth a turning away from sinne, which is the same, with the return of the will to Obedience. Whosoever therefore unfeignedly desireth to fulfill the Commandements of God, or repenteth him truely of his transgressions, or that loveth God with all his heart, and his neighbor as himself, hath all the Obedience Necessary to his Reception into the Kingdom of God: For if God should require perfect Innocence, there could no flesh be saved.

And to what
Laws.

But what Commandements are those that God hath given us? Are all those Laws which were given to the Jews by the hand of Moses, the Commandements of God? If they bee, why are not Christians taught to Obey them? If they be not, what others are so, besides the Law of Nature? For our Saviour Christ hath not given us new Laws, but Counsell to observe those wee are subject to; that is to say, the Laws of Nature, and the Laws of our severall Soveraigns: Nor did he make any new Law to the Jews in his Sermon on the Mount, but onely expounded the Laws of Moses, to which they were subject before. The Laws of God therefore are none but the Laws of Nature, whereof the principall is, that we should not violate our Faith, that is, a commandement to obey our Civill Soveraigns, which wee constituted over us, by mutuall pact one with another. And this Law of God, that commandeth Obedience to the Law Civill, commandeth by consequence Obedience to all the Precepts of the Bible; which (as I have proved in the precedent Chapter) is there onely Law, where the Civill Soverain hath made it so; and in other places but Counsell; which a man at his own perill, may without injustice refuse to obey.

Knowing now what is the Obedience Necessary to Salvation, and to whom it is due; we are to consider next concerning Faith, whom, and why we beleeve; and what are the Articles, or Points necessarily to be beleeved by them that shall be saved. And first, for the Person whom we beleeve, because it is impossible to beleeve any Person, before we know what he saith, it is necessary he be one that wee have heard speak. The Person therefore, whom Abraham, Isaac, Jacob, Moses and the Prophets beleeved, was God himself, that spake unto them supernaturally: And the Person, whom the Apostles and Disciples that conversed with Christ beleeved, was our Saviour himself. But of them, to whom neither God the Father, nor our Saviour ever spake, it cannot be said, that the Person whom they beleeved, was God. They beleeved the Apostles, and after them the Pastors and Doctors of the Church, that recommended to their faith the History of the Old and New Testament: so that the Faith of Christians ever since our Saviours time, hath had for foundation, first, the reputation of their Pastors, and afterward, the authority of those that made the Old and New Testament to be received for the Rule of Faith; which none could do but Christian Soveraignes; who are therefore the Supreme Pastors, and the onely Persons, whom Christians now hear speak from God; except such as God speaketh to, in these days supernaturally. But because there be many false Prophets *gone out into the world,* other men are to examine such Spirits (as St. *John* adviseth us, 1 Epistle, Chap. 4. ver. 1.) *whether they be of God, or not.* And therefore, seeing the Examination of Doctrines belongeth to the Supreme Pastor, the Person which all they that have no speciall revelation are to beleeve, is (in every Common-wealth) the Supreme Pastor, that is to say, the Civill Soveraigne.

In the Faith of a Christian, who is the Person beleeved. [323]

The causes why men beleeve any Christian Doctrine, are various: For Faith is the gift of God; and he worketh it in each severall man, by such wayes, as it seemeth good unto himself. The most ordinary immediate cause of our beleef, concerning any point of Christian Faith, is, that wee beleeve the Bible to be the Word of God. But why wee beleeve the Bible to be the Word of God, is much disputed, as all questions must needs bee, that are not well stated. For they make not the question to be, *Why we Beleeve it,* but, *How wee Know it;* as if *Beleeving* and *Knowing* were all one. And thence while one side ground their Knowledge upon the Infallibility of the Church, and the other side, on the Testimony of the Private Spirit, neither side concludeth what it pretends. For how shall a man know the Infallibility of the Church, but by knowing first the Infallibility of the Scripture? Or how shall a man know his own Private spirit to be other than a beleef, grounded upon the Authority, and Arguments of his Teachers; or upon a Presumption of his own Gifts? Besides, there is nothing in the Scripture, from which can be inferred the Infallibility of the Church; much lesse, of any particular Church; and least of all, the Infallibility of any particular man.

The causes of Christian Faith.

It is manifest therefore, that Christian men doe not know, but onely beleeve the Scripture to be the Word of God; and that the means of making them beleeve which God is pleased to afford men ordinarily,

Faith comes by Hearing. [324]

is according to the way of Nature, that is to say, from their Teachers. It is the Doctrine of St. Paul concerning Christian Faith in generall, (*Rom.* 10. 17.) *Faith cometh by Hearing,* that is, by Hearing our lawfull Pastors. He saith also (ver. 14, 15. of the same Chapter) *How shall they beleeve in him of whom they have not heard? and how shall they hear without a Preacher? and how shall they Preach, except they be sent?* Whereby it is evident, that the ordinary cause of beleeving that the Scriptures are the Word of God, is the same with the cause of the beleeving of all other Articles of our Faith, namely, the Hearing of those that are by the Law allowed and appointed to Teach us, as our Parents in their Houses, and our Pastors in the Churches: Which also is made more manifest by experience. For what other cause can there bee assigned, why in Christian Common-wealths all men either beleeve, or at least professe the Scripture to bee the Word of God, and in other Common-wealths scarce any; but that in Christian Common-wealths they are taught it from their infancy; and in other places they are taught otherwise?

But if Teaching be the cause of Faith, why doe not all beleeve? It is certain therefore that Faith is the gift of God, and hee giveth it to whom he will. Nevertheless, because to them to whom he giveth it, he giveth it by the means of Teachers, the immediate cause of Faith is Hearing. In a School, where many are taught, and some profit, others profit not, the cause of learning in them that profit, is the Master; yet it cannot be thence inferred, that learning is not the gift of God. All good things proceed from God; yet cannot all that have them, say they are Inspired; for that implies a gift supernaturall, and the immediate hand of God; which he that pretends to, pretends to be a Prophet, and is subject to the examination of the Church.

But whether men *Know,* or *Beleeve,* or *Grant* the Scriptures to be the Word of God; if out of such places of them, as are without obscurity, I shall shew what Articles of Faith are necessary, and onely necessary for Salvation, those men must needs *Know, Beleeve,* or *Grant* the same.

The onely Necessary Article of Christian Faith;

The (*Unum Necessarium*) Onely Article of Faith, which the Scripture maketh simply Necessary to Salvation, is this, that JESUS IS THE CHRIST. By the name of *Christ,* is understood the King, which God had before promised by the Prophets of the Old Testament, to send into the world, to reign (over the Jews, and over such of other nations as should beleeve in him) under himself eternally; and to give them that eternall life, which was lost by the sin of Adam. Which when I have proved out of Scripture, I will further shew when, and in what sense some other Articles may bee also called *Necessary.*

[325]

Proved from the Scope of the Evan-gelists:

For Proof that the Beleef of this Article, *Jesus is the Christ,* is all the Faith required to Salvation, my first Argument shall bee from the Scope of the Evangelists; which was by the description of the life of our Saviour, to establish that one Article, *Jesus is the Christ.* The summe of St. Matthews Gospell is this, That Jesus was of the stock of David; Born of a Virgin; which are the Marks of the true Christ: That the *Magi* came to worship him as King of the Jews: That Herod for the same cause sought to kill him: That John Baptist proclaimed him: That he preached by himselfe, and his Apostles that he was that King: That he taught the Law, not as a Scribe, but as a man of Authority: That he cured diseases by his Word onely, and did many other Miracles, which were foretold the Christ should doe: That he was saluted King when hee entred into Jerusalem: That he fore-warned them to beware of all others that should pretend to be Christ: That he was taken, accused, and put to death, for saying, hee was King: That the cause of his condemnation written on the Crosse, was JESUS OF NAZARETH, THE KING OF THE JEWES. All which tend to no other end than this, that men should beleeve, that *Jesus is the Christ.* Such therefore was the Scope of St. Matthews Gospel. But the Scope of all the Evangelists (as may appear by reading them) was the same. Therefore the Scope of the whole Gospell, was the establishing of that onely Article. And St. John expressely makes it his conclusion, *John* 20. 31. *These things are written, that you may know that Jesus is the Christ, the Son of the living God.*

My second Argument is taken from the Subject of the Sermons of the Apostles, both whilest our Saviour lived on earth, and after his Ascension. The Apostles in our Saviours time were sent, *Luke* 9. 2. to Preach the Kingdome of God: For neither there, nor *Mat.* 10. 7. giveth he any Commission to them, other than this, *As ye go, Preach, saying, the Kingdome of Heaven is at hand*; that is, that *Jesus* is the *Messiah*, the *Christ*, the *King* which was to come. That their Preaching also after his ascension was the same, is manifest out of *Acts* 17. 6. *They drew* (saith St. Luke) *Jason and certain Brethren unto the Rulers of the City, crying, These that have turned the world upside down are come hither also, whom Jason hath received. And these all do contrary to the Decrees of Cæsar, saying, that there is another King, one Jesus:* And out of the 2. & 3. verses of the same Chapter, where it is said, that St. *Paul as his manner was, went in unto them; and three Sabbath dayes reasoned with them out of the Scriptures; opening*[1] *and alledging, that Christ must needs have suffered, and risen againe from the dead, and that this Jesus (whom hee preached) is Christ.* *From the Sermons of the Apostles:*

The third Argument is, from those places of Scripture, by which all the Faith required to Salvation is declared to be Easie. For if an inward assent of the mind to all the Doctrines concerning Christian Faith now taught, (whereof the greatest part are disputed,) were necessary to Salvation, there would be nothing in the world so hard, as to be a Christian. The Thief upon the Crosse though repenting, could not have been saved for saying, *Lord remember me when thou commest into thy Kingdome*; by which he testified no beleefe of any other Article, but this, That *Jesus was the King.* Nor could it bee said (as it is *Mat.* 11. 30.) that *Christs yoke is Easy, and his burthen Light:* Nor that *Little Children beleeve in him,* as it is *Matth.* 18. 6. Nor could St. Paul have said (1 *Cor.* 1. 21.) *It pleased God by the Foolishnesse of preaching, to save them that beleeve:* Nor could St. Paul himself have been saved, much lesse have been so great a Doctor of the Church so suddenly, that never perhaps thought of Transubstantiation, nor Purgatory, nor many other Articles now obtruded. *From the easinesse of the Doctrine:*

[326]

The fourth Argument is taken from places expresse, and such as *From formall and cleer texts.*

1. Explaining.

receive no controversie of Interpretation; as first, *John* 5. 39. *Search the Scriptures, for in them yee thinke yee have eternall life; and they are they that testifie of mee.* Our Saviour here speaketh of the Scriptures onely of the Old Testament; for the Jews at that time could not search the Scriptures of the New Testament, which were not written. But the Old Testament hath nothing of Christ, but the Markes by which men might know him when hee came; as that he should descend from David; be born at Bethlem, and of a Virgin; doe great Miracles, and the like. Therefore to beleeve that this Jesus was He, was sufficient to eternall life: but more than sufficient is not Necessary; and consequently no other Article is required. Again, (*John* 11. 26.) *Whosoever liveth and beleeveth in mee, shall not die eternally,* Therefore to beleeve in Christ, is faith sufficient to eternall life; and consequently no more faith than that is Necessary, But to beleeve in Jesus, and to beleeve that Jesus is the Christ, is all one, as appeareth in the verses immediately following. For when our Saviour (verse 26.) had said to Martha, *Beleevest thou this?* she answereth (verse 27.) *Yea Lord, I beleeve that thou art the Christ, the Son of God, which should come into the world:* Therefore this Article alone is faith sufficient to life eternall; and more than sufficient is not Necessary. Thirdly, *John* 20. 31. *These things are written that yee might beleeve, That Jesus is the Christ, the Son of God, and that beleeving yee might have life through his name.* There, to beleeve that *Jesus is the Christ,* is faith sufficient to the obtaining of life; and therefore no other Article is Necessary. Fourthly, 1 *John* 4. 2. *Every spirit that confesseth that Jesus Christ is come in the flesh, is of God.* And 1 *Joh.* 5. 1. *Whosoever beleeveth that Jesus is the Christ, is born of God.* And verse 5. *Who is hee that overcommeth the world, but he that beleeveth that Jesus is the Son of God?* Fiftly, *Act.* 8. ver. 36, 37. *See* (saith the Eunuch) *here is water, what doth hinder me to be baptized? And Philip said, If thou beleevest with all thy heart thou mayst. And hee answered and said, I beleeve that Jesus Christ is the Son of God.* Therefore this Article beleeved, *Jesus is the Christ,* is sufficient to Baptisme, that is to say, to our Reception into the Kingdome of God, and by consequence; onely Necessary. And generally in all places where our

[327]   Saviour saith to any man, *Thy faith hath saved thee,* the cause he saith it, is some Confession, which directly, or by consequence, implyeth a beleef, that *Jesus is the Christ.*

From that it is the Foundation of all other Articles.   The last Argument is from the places, where this Article is made the Foundation of Faith: For he that holdeth the Foundation shall bee saved. Which places are first, *Mat.* 24. 23. *If any man shall say unto you, Loe, here is Christ, or there, beleeve it not, for there shall arise false Christs, and false Prophets, and shall shew great signes and wonders, &c.* Here wee see, this Article *Jesus is the Christ,* must bee held, though hee that shall teach the contrary should doe great miracles. The second place is, *Gal.* 1. 8. *Though we, or an Angell from Heaven preach any other Gospell unto you, than that wee have preached unto you, let him bee accursed.* But the Gospell which Paul, and the other Apostles, preached, was onely this Article, that *Jesus is the Christ:* Therefore for the Beleef of this Article, we are to reject the Authority of an Angell from heaven; much more of any mortall man, if he teach the contrary. This is therefore the Fundamentall Article of Christian Faith. A third place is, 1 *Joh.* 4. 1. *Beloved, beleeve not every spirit. Hereby yee shall know the Spirit of God; every spirit that confesseth that Jesus Christ is come in the flesh, is of God.* By which it is evident, that this Article, is the measure, and rule, by which to estimate, and examine all other Articles; and is therefore onely Fundamentall. A fourth is, *Matt.* 16. 18. where after St. Peter had professed this Article, saying to our Saviour, *Thou art Christ the Son of the living God,* Our Saviour answered, *Thou art Peter, and upon this Rock I will build my Church:* from whence I inferre, that this Article is that, on which all other Doctrines of the Church are built, as on their Foundation. A fift is (1 *Cor.* 3. ver. 11, 12, &c.) *Other Foundation can no man lay, than that which is laid, Jesus is the Christ. Now if any man build upon this Foundation, Gold, Silver, pretious Stones, Wood, Hay, Stubble; Every mans work shall be made manifest; For the Day shall declare it, because it shall be revealed by fire, and the fire shall try every mans work, of what sort it is. If any mans work abide, which he hath built thereupon, he shall receive a reward: If any mans work shall bee burnt, he shall suffer losse; but he himself shall be saved, yet so as by fire.* Which words, being partly plain and easie to understand, and partly allegoricall and difficult; out of that which is plain, may be inferred, that Pastors that teach this Foundation, that *Jesus is the Christ,* though they draw from it false consequences, (which all men are sometimes subject to,) they may neverthelesse bee saved; much more that they may bee saved, who being no Pastors, but Hearers, beleeve that which is by their lawfull Pastors taught them. Therefore the beleef of this Article is sufficient; and by consequence, there is no other Article of Faith Necessarily required to Salvation.

Now for the part which is Allegoricall, as *That the fire shall try every mans work,* and that *They shall be saved, but so as by fire,* or *through fire,* (for the originall is διὰπυρὸς,[2]) it maketh nothing against this conclusion which I have drawn from the other words, that are plain. Neverthelesse, because upon this place there hath been an argument taken, to prove the fire of Purgatory, I will also here offer you my conjecture concerning the meaning of this triall of Doctrines, and saving of men as by Fire. The Apostle here seemeth to allude to the words of the Prophet Zachary, Ch. 13. 8, 9. who speaking of the Restauration of the Kingdome of God, saith thus, *Two parts therein shall be cut off, and die, but the third shall be left therein; And I will bring the third part through the Fire, and will refine them as Silver is refined, and will try them as Gold is tryed; they shall call on the name of the Lord, and I will hear them.* The day of Judgment, is the day of the Restauration of the Kingdome of God; and at that day it is, that St. Peter tells us * shall be the Conflagration of the world, wherein the wicked shall perish; but the remnant which God will save, shall passe through that Fire, unhurt, and be therein (as Silver and Gold are refined by the fire from their drosse) tryed, and refined from their Idolatry, and be made to call

[328]

2 *Pet.* 3. *v.* 7, 10, 12.

2. *Dia puros.*

upon the name of the true God. Alluding whereto St. Paul here saith, That *the Day* (that is, the Day of Judgment, the Great Day of our Saviours comming to restore the Kingdome of God in Israel) shall try every mans doctrine, by Judging, which are Gold, Silver, Pretious Stones, Wood, Hay, Stubble; And then they that have built false Consequences on the true Foundation, shall see their Doctrines condemned; neverthelesse they themselves shall be saved, and passe unhurt through this universall Fire, and live eternally, to call upon the name of the true and onely God. In which sense there is nothing that accordeth not with the rest of Holy Scripture, or any glimpse of the fire of Purgatory.

In what sense other Articles may be called Necessary.

But a man may here aske, whether it bee not as necessary to Salvation, to beleeve, that God is Omnipotent; Creator of the world; that Jesus Christ is risen; and that all men else shall rise again from the dead at the last day; as to beleeve, that *Jesus is the Christ.* To which I answer, they are; and so are many more Articles: but they are such, as are contained in this one, and may be deduced from it, with more, or lesse difficulty. For who is there that does not see, that they who beleeve Jesus to be the Son of the God of Israel, and that the Israelites had for God the Omnipotent Creator of all things, doe therein also beleeve, that God is the Omnipotent Creator of all things? Or how can a man beleeve, that Jesus is the King that shall reign eternally, unlesse hee beleeve him also risen again from the dead? For a dead man cannot exercise the Office of a King. In summe, he that holdeth this Foundation, *Jesus is the Christ,* holdeth Expressely all that hee seeth rightly deduced from it, and Implicitely all that is consequent thereunto, though he have not skill enough to discern the consequence. And there-

[329]

fore it holdeth still good, that the beleef of this one Article is sufficient faith to obtain remission of sinnes to the *Penitent,* and consequently to bring them into the Kingdome of Heaven.

That Faith, and Obedience are both of them Necessary to Salvation.

Now that I have shewn, that all the Obedience required to Salvation, consisteth in the will to obey the Law of God, that is to say, in Repentance; and all the Faith required to the same, is comprehended in the beleef of this Article *Jesus is the Christ;* I will further alledge those places of the Gospell, that prove, that all that is Necessary to Salvation is contained in both these joined together. The men to whom St. Peter preached on the day of Pentecost, next after the Ascension of our Saviour, asked him, and the rest of the Apostles, saying, (*Act.* 2. 37.) *Men and Brethren what shall we doe?* To whom St. Peter answered (in the next verse) *Repent, and be Baptized every one of you, for the remission of sins, and ye shall receive the gift of the Holy Ghost.* Therefore Repentance, and Baptisme, that is, beleeving that *Jesus is the Christ,* is all that is Necessary to Salvation. Again, our Saviour being asked by a certain Ruler, (*Luke* 18. 18.) *What shall I doe to inherit eternall life?* Answered (verse 20.) *Thou knowest the Commandements, Doe not commit Adultery, Doe not Kill, Doe not Steal, Doe not bear false witnesse, Honor thy Father, and thy Mother:* which when he said he had observed, our Saviour added, *Sell all thou hast, give it to the Poor, and come and follow me:* which was as much as to say, Relye on me that am the King: Therefore to fulfill the Law, and to beleeve that Jesus is the King, is all that is required to bring a man to eternall life. Thirdly,

St. Paul saith (*Rom.* 1. 17.) *The Just shall live by Faith;* not every one, but the *Just;* therefore *Faith* and *Justice* (that is, the *will to be Just,* or *Repentance*) are all that is Necessary to life eternall. And (*Mark* 1. 15.) our Saviour preached, saying, *The time is fulfilled, and the Kingdom of God is at hand, Repent and Beleeve the Evangile,* that is, the Good news that the Christ was come. Therefore to Repent, and to Beleeve that Jesus is the Christ, is all that is required to Salvation.

Seeing then it is Necessary that Faith, and Obedience (implyed in the word Repentance) do both concurre to our Salvation; the question by which of the two we are Justified, is impertinently disputed. Neverthelesse, it will not be impertinent,[3] to make manifest in what manner each of them contributes thereunto; and in what sense it is said, that we are to be Justified by the one, and by the other. And first, if by Righteousnesse be understood the Justice of the Works themselves, there is no man that can be saved; for there is none that hath not transgressed the Law of God. And therefore when wee are said to be Justified by Works, it is to be understood of the Will, which God doth alwaies accept for the Work it selfe, as well in good, as in evill men. And in this sense onely it is, that a man is called *Just,* or *Unjust;* and that his Justice Justifies him, that is, gives him the title, in Gods acceptation, of *Just;* and renders him capable of *living by his Faith,* which before he was not. So that Justice Justifies in that sense, in which to *Justifie,* is the same that to *Denominate a man Just;* and not in the signification of discharging the Law; whereby the punishment of his sins should be unjust.

But a man is then also said to be Justified, when his Plea, though in it selfe unsufficient, is accepted; as when we Plead our Will, our Endeavour to fulfill the Law, and Repent us of our failings, and God accepteth it for the Performance it selfe: And because God accepteth not the Will for the Deed, but onely in the Faithfull; it is therefore Faith that makes good our Plea; and in this sense it is, that Faith onely Justifies: So that *Faith* and *Obedience* are both Necessary to Salvation; yet in severall senses each of them is said to Justifie.

Having thus shewn what is Necessary to Salvation; it is not hard to reconcile our Obedience to God, with our Obedience to the Civill Soveraign; who is either Christian, or Infidel. If he bee a Christian, he alloweth the beleefe of this Article, that *Jesus is the Christ;* and of all the Articles that are contained in, or are by evident consequence deduced from it: which is all the Faith Necessary to Salvation. And because he is a Soveraign, he requireth Obedience to all his owne, that is, to all the Civill Laws; in which also are contained all the Laws of Nature, that is, all the Laws of God: for besides the Laws of Nature, and the Laws of the Church, which are part of the Civill Law, (for the Church that can make Laws is the Common-wealth,) there bee no other Laws Divine. Whosoever therefore obeyeth his Christian Soveraign, is not thereby hindred, neither from beleeving, nor from obeying God. But suppose that a Christian King should from this Foundation *Jesus is the Christ,* draw some false consequences, that is to say, make some superstructions[4] of Hay, or Stubble, and command the teaching

What each of them contributes thereunto.

[330]

Obedience to God and to the Civill Soveraign not inconsistent, whether Christian,

3. Inappropriate.
4. Superstructures.

of the same; yet seeing St. Paul says, he shal be saved; much more shall he be saved, that teacheth them by his command; and much more yet, he that teaches not, but onely beleeves his lawfull Teacher. And in case a Subject be forbidden by the Civill Soveraign to professe some of those his opinions, upon what just ground can he disobey? Christian Kings may erre in deducing a Consequence, but who shall Judge? Shall a private man Judge, when the question is of his own obedience? or shall any man Judg but he that is appointed thereto by the Church, that is, by the Civill Soveraign that representeth it? or if the Pope, or an Apostle Judge, may he not erre in deducing of a consequence? did not one of the two, St. Peter, or St. Paul erre in a superstructure, when St. Paul withstood St. Peter to his face? There can therefore be no contradiction between the Laws of God, and the Laws of a Christian Common-wealth.

Or Infidel.

And when the Civill Soveraign is an Infidel, every one of his own Subjects that resisteth him, sinneth against the Laws of God (for such as are the Laws of Nature,) and rejecteth the counsell of the Apostles, that admonisheth all Christians to obey their Princes, and all Children and Servants to obey their Parents, and Masters, in all things. And for their *Faith*, it is internall, and invisible; They have the licence that Naaman had, and need not put themselves into danger for it. But if they do, they ought to expect their reward in Heaven, and not complain of their Lawfull Soveraign; much lesse make warre upon him. For he that is not glad of any just occasion of Martyrdome, has not the faith he professeth, but pretends it onely, to set some colour upon his own contumacy. But what Infidel King is so unreasonable, as knowing he has a Subject, that waiteth for the second comming of Christ, after the present world shall bee burnt, and intendeth then to obey him (which is the intent of beleeving that Jesus is the Christ,) and in the mean time thinketh himself bound to obey the Laws of that Infidel King, (which all Christians are obliged in conscience to doe,) to put to death, or to persecute such a Subject?

[331]

And thus much shall suffice, concerning the Kingdome of God, and Policy Ecclesiasticall. Wherein I pretend not to advance any Position of my own, but onely to shew what are the Consequences that seem to me deducible from the Principles of Christian Politiques, (which are the holy Scriptures,) in confirmation of the Power of Civill Soveraigns, and the Duty of their Subjects. And in the allegation of Scripture, I have endeavoured to avoid such texts as are of obscure, or controverted Interpretation; and to alledge none, but in such sense as is most plain, and agreeable to the harmony and scope of the whole Bible; which was written for the reestablishment of the Kingdome of God in Christ. For it is not the bare Words, but the Scope of the writer that giveth the true light, by which any writing is to bee interpreted; and they that insist upon single Texts, without considering the main Designe, can derive no thing from them cleerly; but rather by casting atomes of Scripture, as dust before mens eyes, make every thing more obscure than it is; an ordinary artifice of those that seek not the truth, but their own advantage.

Chap. XLIV.

Of Spirituall Darknesse from MISINTERPRETATION of Scripture.

Besides these Soveraign Powers, *Divine*, and *Humane*, of which I have hitherto discoursed, there is mention in Scripture of another Power, namely, * that of *the Rulers of the Darknesse of this world*, * *the Kingdome of Satan*, and * *the Principality of Beelzebub over Dæmons*, that is to say, over Phantasmes that appear in the Air: For which cause Satan is also called * *the Prince of the Power of the Air*; and (because he ruleth in the darknesse of this world) * *The Prince of this world*: And in consequence hereunto, they who are under his Dominion, in opposition to the faithfull (who are the *Children of the Light*) are called the *Children of Darknesse*. For seeing Beelzebub is Prince of Phantasmes, Inhabitants of his Dominion of Air and Darknesse, the Children of Darknesse, and these Dæmons, Phantasmes, or Spirits of Illusion, signifie allegorically the same thing. This considered, the Kingdome of Darknesse, as it is set forth in these, and other places of the Scripture, is nothing else but a *Confederacy of Deceivers, that to obtain dominion over men in this present world, endeavour by dark, and erroneous Doctrines, to extinguish in them the Light, both of Nature, and of the Gospell; and so to dis-prepare them for the Kingdome of God to come.*

The Kingdom of Darknesse what.
* *Eph. 6. 12.*
* *Mat. 12. 26.*
* *Mat. 9. 34.*
* *Eph. 2. 2.*
* *Joh. 16. 11.*

As men that are utterly deprived from their Nativity, of the light of the bodily Eye, have no Idea at all, of any such light; and no man conceives in his imagination any greater light, than he hath at some time, or other, perceived by his outward Senses: so also is it of the light of the Gospel, and of the light of the Understanding, that no man can conceive there is any greater degree of it, than that which he hath already attained unto. And from hence it comes to passe, that men have no other means to acknowledge their owne Darknesse, but onely by reasoning from the un-foreseen mischances, that befall them in their ways; The Darkest part of the Kingdom of Satan, is that which is without the Church of God; that is to say, amongst them that beleeve not in Jesus Christ. But we cannot say, that therefore the Church enjoyeth (as the land of Goshen) all the light, which to the performance of the work enjoined us by God, is necessary. Whence comes it, that in Christendome there has been, almost from the time of the Apostles, such justling of one another out of their places, both by forraign, and Civill war? such stumbling at every little asperity of their own fortune, and

[334]

The Church not yet fully freed of Darknesse.

every little eminence of that of other men? and such diversity of ways in running to the same mark, *Felicity,* if it be not Night amongst us, or at least a Mist? wee are therefore yet in the Dark.

Four Causes of Spirituall Darknesse.

The Enemy has been here in the Night of our naturall Ignorance, and sown the tares of Spirituall Errors; and that, First, by abusing, and putting out the light of the Scriptures: For we erre, not knowing the Scriptures. Secondly, by introducing the Dæmonology of the Heathen Poets, that is to say, their fabulous Doctrine concerning Dæmons, which are but Idols, or Phantasms of the braine, without any reall nature of their own, distinct from humane fancy; such as are dead mens Ghosts, and Fairies, and other matter of old Wives tales. Thirdly, by mixing with the Scripture divers reliques of the Religion, and much of the vain and erroneous Philosophy of the Greeks, especially of Aristotle. Fourthly, by mingling with both these, false, or uncertain Traditions, and fained, or uncertain History. And so we come to erre, by *giving heed to seducing Spirits,* and the Dæmonology of such *as speak lies in Hypocrisie,* (or as it is in the Originall, 1 *Tim.* 4. 1, 2. *of those that play the part of lyars*) *with a seared conscience,* that is, contrary to their own knowledge. Concerning the first of these, which is the Seducing of men by abuse of Scripture, I intend to speak briefly in this Chapter.

Errors from misinterpreting the Scriptures, concerning the Kingdome of God.

The greatest, and main abuse of Scripture, and to which almost all the rest are either consequent, or subservient, is the wresting of it, to prove that the Kingdome of God, mentioned so often in the Scripture, is the present Church, or multitude of Christian men now living, or that being dead, are to rise again at the last day: whereas the Kingdome of God was first instituted by the Ministery of Moses, over the Jews onely; who were therefore called his Peculiar People; and ceased afterward, in the election of Saul, when they refused to be governed by God

[335]

any more, and demanded a King after the manner of the nations; which God himself consented unto, as I have more at large proved before, in the 35. Chapter. After that time, there was no other Kingdome of God in the world, by any Pact, or otherwise, than he ever was, is, and shall be King, of all men, and of all creatures, as governing according to his Will, by his infinite Power. Neverthelesse, he promised by his Prophets to restore this his Government to them again, when the time he hath in his secret counsell appointed for it shall bee fully come, and when they shall turn unto him by repentance, and amendment of life: and not onely so, but he invited also the Gentiles to come in, and enjoy the happinesse of his Reign, on the same conditions of conversion and repentance; and hee promised also to send his Son into the world, to expiate the sins of them all by his death, and to prepare them by his Doctrine, to receive him at his second coming: Which second coming not yet being, the Kingdome of God is not yet come, and wee are not now under any other Kings by Pact, but our Civill Soveraigns; saving onely, that Christian men are already in the Kingdome of Grace, in as much as they have already the Promise of being received at his comming againe.

As that the Kingdome

Consequent to this Errour, that the present Church is Christs Kingdome, there ought to be some one Man, or Assembly, by whose mouth

our Saviour (now in heaven) speaketh, giveth law, and which represent-   *of God is the*
eth his Person to all Christians, or divers Men, or divers Assemblies   *present*
that doe the same to divers parts of Christendome. This power Regal   *Church:*
under Christ, being challenged,[1] universally by the Pope, and in particular Common-wealths by Assemblies of the Pastors of the place,
(when the Scripture gives it to none but to Civill Soveraigns,) comes
to be so passionately disputed, that it putteth out the Light of Nature,
and causeth so great a Darknesse in mens understanding, that they see
not who it is to whom they have engaged their obedience.

Consequent to this claim of the Pope to Vicar Generall of Christ in   *And that the*
the present Church, (supposed to be that Kingdom of his, to which we   *Pope is his*
are addressed in the Gospel,) is the Doctrine, that it is necessary for a   *Vicar generall:*
Christian King, to receive his Crown by a Bishop; as if it were from
that Ceremony, that he derives the clause of *Dei gratia*[2] in his title;
and that then onely he is made King by the favour of God, when he
is crowned by the authority of Gods universall Vicegerent on earth; and
that every Bishop whosoever be his Soveraign, taketh at his Consecration an oath of absolute Obedience to the Pope. Consequent to the
same, is the Doctrine of the fourth Councell of Lateran, held under
Pope *Innocent* the third, (Chap. 3. *de Hæreticis.*) *That if a King at the*
Popes admonition, doe not purge his Kingdome of Hæresies, and being
excommunicate for the same, doe not give satisfaction within a year, his
Subjects are absolved of the bond of their obedience. Where, by Hæresies
are understood all opinions which the Church of Rome hath forbidden
to be maintained. And by this means, as often as there is any repug-   [336]
nancy between the Politicall designes of the Pope, and other Christian
Princes, as there is very often, there ariseth such a Mist amongst their
Subjects, that they know not a stranger that thrusteth himself into the
throne of their lawfull Prince, from him whom they had themselves
placed there; and in this Darknesse of mind, are made to fight one
against another, without discerning their enemies from their friends,
under the conduct of another mans ambition.

From the same opinion, that the present Church is the Kingdome   *And that the*
of God, it proceeds that Pastours, Deacons, and all other Ministers of   *Pastors are the*
the Church, take the name to themselves of the *Clergy;* giving to other   *Clergy.*
Christians the name of *Laity,* that is, simply *People.* For Clergy signifies
those, whose maintenance is that Revenue, which God having reserved
to himselfe during his Reign over the Israelites, assigned to the tribe of
Levi (who were to be his publique Ministers, and had no portion of
land set them out to live on, as their brethren) to be their inheritance.
The Pope therefore, (pretending the present Church to be, as the
Realme of Israel, the Kingdome of God) challenging to himselfe and
his subordinate Ministers, the like revenue, as the Inheritance of God,
the name of Clergy was sutable to that claime. And thence it is, that
Tithes, and other tributes paid to the Levites, as Gods Right, amongst
the Israelites, have a long time been demanded, and taken of Christians,
by Ecclesiastiques, *Jure divino,* that is, in Gods Right. By which meanes,

1. Claimed.
2. By the grace of God.

the people every where were obliged to a double tribute; one to the State, another to the Clergy; whereof, that to the Clergy, being the tenth of their revenue, is double to that which a King of Athens (and esteemed a Tyrant) exacted of his subjects for the defraying of all publique charges: For he demanded no more but the twentieth part; and yet abundantly maintained therewith the Commonwealth. And in the Kingdome of the Jewes, during the Sacerdotall Reigne of God, the Tithes and Offerings were the whole Publique Revenue.

From the same mistaking of the present Church for the Kingdom of God, came in the distinction betweene the *Civill* and the *Canon* Laws: The Civil Law being the Acts of *Soveraigns* in their own Dominions, and the Canon Law being the Acts of the *Pope* in the same Dominions. Which Canons, though they were but Canons, that is, *Rules Propounded*, and but voluntarily received by Christian Princes, till the translation of the Empire to *Charlemain*; yet afterwards, as the power of the Pope encreased, became *Rules Commanded*, and the Emperours themselves (to avoyd greater mischiefes, which the people blinded might be led into) were forced to let them passe for Laws.

From hence it is, that in all Dominions, where the Popes Ecclesiasticall power is entirely received, Jewes, Turkes, and Gentiles, are in the Roman Church tolerated in their Religion, as farre forth, as in the exercise and profession thereof they offend not against the civill power: whereas in a Christian, though a stranger, not to be of the Roman Religion, is Capitall; because the Pope pretendeth that all Christians are his Subjects. For otherwise it were as much against the law of Nations, to persecute a Christian stranger, for professing the Religion of his owne country, as an Infidell; or rather more, in as much as they that are not against Christ, are with him.

[337]

From the same it is, that in every Christian State there are certaine men, that are exempt, by Ecclesiasticall liberty, from the tributes, and from the tribunals of the Civil State; for so are the secular Clergy, besides Monks and Friars, which in many places, bear so great a proportion to the common people, as if need were, there might be raised out of them alone, an Army, sufficient for any warre the Church militant should imploy them in, against their owne, or other Princes.

Error from mistaking Consecration for Conjuration.

A second generall abuse of Scripture, is the turning of Consecration into Conjuration, or Enchantment. To *Consecrate*, is in Scripture, to Offer, Give, or Dedicate, in pious and decent language and gesture, a man, or any other thing to God, by separating of it from common use; that is to say, to Sanctifie, or make it Gods, and to be used only by those, whom God hath appointed to be his Publike Ministers, (as I have already proved at large in the 35. Chapter;) and thereby to change, not the thing Consecrated, but onely the use of it, from being Profane and common, to be Holy, and peculiar to Gods service. But when by such words, the nature or qualitie of the thing it selfe, is pretended to be changed, it is not Consecration, but either an extraordinary worke of God, or a vaine and impious Conjuration. But seeing (for the frequency of pretending the change of Nature in their Consecrations,) it cannot be esteemed a work extraordinary, it is no other than a *Conju-*

ration or *Incantation*, whereby they would have men to beleeve an alteration of Nature that is not, contrary to the testimony of mans Sight, and of all the rest of his Senses. As for example, when the Priest, in stead of Consecrating Bread and Wine to Gods peculiar service in the Sacrament of the Lords Supper, (which is but a separation of it from the common use, to signifie, that is, to put men in mind of their Redemption, by the Passion of Christ, whose body was broken, and blood shed upon the Crosse for our transgressions,) pretends, that by saying of the words of our Saviour, *This is my Body*, and *This is my Blood*, the nature of Bread is no more there, but his very Body; notwithstanding there appeareth not to the Sight, or other Sense of the Receiver, any thing that appeared not before the Consecration. The Egyptian Conjurers, that are said to have turned their Rods to Serpents, and the Water into Bloud, are thought but to have deluded the senses of the Spectators by a false shew of things, yet are esteemed Enchanters: But what should wee have thought of them, if there had appeared in their Rods nothing like a Serpent, and in the Water enchanted, nothing like Bloud, nor like any thing else but Water, but that they had faced down the King, that they were Serpents that looked like Rods, and that it was Bloud that seemed Water? That had been both Enchantment, and Lying. And yet in this daily act of the Priest, they doe the very same, by turning [338] the holy words into the manner of a Charme, which produceth nothing new to the Sense; but they face us down, that it hath turned the Bread into a Man; nay more, into a God; and require men to worship it, as if it were our Saviour himself present God and Man, and thereby to commit most grosse Idolatry. For if it bee enough to excuse it of Idolatry, to say it is no more Bread, but God; why should not the same excuse serve the Egyptians, in case they had the faces to say, the Leeks, and Onyons they worshipped, were not very Leeks, and Onyons, but a Divinity under their *species*, or likenesse. The words, *This is my Body*, are æquivalent to these, *This signifies, or represents my Body*; and it is an ordinary figure of Speech: but to take it literally, is an abuse; nor though so taken, can it extend any further, than to the Bread which Christ himself with his own hands Consecrated. For hee never said, that of what Bread soever, any Priest whatsoever, should say, *This is my body*, or, *This is Christs Body*, the same should presently be transubstantiated. Nor did the Church of Rome ever establish this Transubstantiation, till the time of *Innocent* the third; which was not above 500. years agoe, when the Power of Popes was at the Highest, and the Darknesse of the time grown so great, as men discerned not the Bread that was given them to eat, especially when it was stamped with the figure of Christ upon the Crosse, as if they would have men beleeve it were Transubstantiated, not onely into the Body of Christ, but also into the Wood of his Crosse, and that they did eat both together in the Sacrament.

The like Incantation, in stead of Consecration, is used also in the Sacrament of Baptisme: Where the abuse of Gods name in each severall Person, and in the whole Trinity, with the sign of the Crosse at each name, maketh up the Charm: As first, when they make the Holy

Incantation in the Ceremonies of Baptisme.

water, the Priest saith, *I Conjure thee, thou Creature of Water, in the name of God the Father Almighty, and in the name of Jesus Christ his onely Son our Lord, and in vertue of the Holy Ghost, that thou become Conjured water, to drive away all the Powers of the Enemy, and to eradicate, and supplant the Enemy, &c.* And the same in the Benediction of the Salt to be mingled with it; *That thou become Conjured Salt, that all Phantasmes, and Knavery of the Devills fraud may fly and depart from the place wherein thou art sprinkled; and every unclean Spirit bee Conjured by Him that shall come to judg the quicke and the dead.* The same in the Benediction of the Oyle, *That all the Power of the Enemy, all the Host of the Devill, all Assaults and Phantasmes of Satan, may be driven away by this Creature of Oyle.* And for the Infant that is to be Baptized, he is subject to many Charms: First, at the Church dore the Priest blows thrice in the Childs face, and sayes, *Goe out of him unclean Spirit, and give place to the Holy Ghost the Comforter.* As if all Children, till blown on by the Priest were Dæmoniaques: Again, before his entrance into the Church, he saith as before, *I Conjure thee,*

[339]   *&c. to goe out, and depart from this Servant of God:* And again the same Exorcisme is repeated once more before he be Baptized. These, and some other Incantations, are those that are used in stead of Benedictions, and Consecrations, in administration of the Sacraments of Baptisme, and the Lords Supper; wherein every thing that serveth to those holy uses (except the unhallowed Spittle of the Priest) hath some set form of Exorcisme.

And in Marriage, in Visitation of the Sick, and in Consecration of Places.

Nor are the other rites, as of Marriage, of Extreme Unction, of Visitation of the Sick, of Consecrating Churches, and Church-yards, and the like, exempt from Charms; in as much as there is in them the use of Enchanted Oyle, and Water, with the abuse of the Crosse, and of the holy word of David, *Asperges me Domine Hyssopo,*[3] as things of efficacy to drive away Phantasmes, and Imaginary Spirits.

Errors from mistaking Eternall Life, and Everlasting Death:

Another generall Error, is from the Misinterpretation of the words *Eternall Life, Everlasting Death,* and the *Second Death.* For though we read plainly in holy Scripture, that God created Adam in an estate of Living for Ever, which was conditionall, that is to say, if he disobeyed not his Commandement; which was not essentiall to Humane Nature, but consequent to the vertue of the Tree of Life; whereof hee had liberty to eat, as long as hee had not sinned; and that hee was thrust out of Paradise after he had sinned, lest hee should eate thereof, and live for ever; and that Christs Passion is a Discharge of sin to all that beleeve on him; and by consequence, a restitution of Eternall Life, to all the Faithfull, and to them onely: yet the Doctrine is now, and hath been a long time far otherwise; namely, that every man hath Eternity of Life by Nature, in as much as his Soul is Immortall: So that the flaming Sword at the entrance of Paradise, though it hinder a man from coming to the Tree of Life, hinders him not from the Immortality which God took from him for his Sin; nor makes him to need the sacrificing of Christ, for the recovering of the same; and consequently,

3. Sprinkle me, Lord, with hyssop (Psalms 51 7).

not onely the faithfull and righteous, but also the wicked, and the Heathen, shall enjoy Eternall Life, without any Death at all; much lesse a Second, and Everlasting Death. To salve this, it is said, that by *Second*, and *Everlasting Death*, is meant a Second, and Everlasting Life, but in Torments; a Figure never used, but in this very Case.

All which Doctrine is founded onely on some of the obscurer places of the New Testament; which neverthelesse, the whole scope of the Scripture considered, are cleer enough in a different sense, and unnecessary to the Christian Faith. For supposing that when a man dies, there remaineth-nothing of him but his carkasse; cannot God that raised inanimated dust and clay into a living creature by his Word, as easily raise a dead carkasse to life again, and continue him alive for Ever, or make him die again, by another Word? The *Soule* in Scripture, signifieth alwaies, either the Life, or the Living Creature; and the Body and Soule jointly, the *Body alive*. In the fift day of the Creation, God said, Let the waters produce *Reptile animæ viventis*, the creeping thing that hath in it a Living Soule; the English translate it, *that hath Life*: And again, God created Whales, & *omnem animam viventem*; which in the English is, *every Living Creature*: And likewise of Man, God made him of the dust of the earth, and breathed in his face the breath of Life, & *factus est Homo in animam viventem*, that is, *and Man was made a Living Creature*: And after *Noah* came out of the Arke, God saith, hee will no more smite *omnem animam viventem*, that is, *every Living Creature*: And Deut. 12. 23. *Eate not the Bloud, for the Bloud is the Soule*; that is, *the Life*. From which places, if by *Soule* were meant a *Substance Incorporeall*, with an existence separated from the Body, it might as well be inferred of any other living Creature, as of Man. But that the Souls of the Faithfull, are not of their own Nature, but by Gods speciall Grace, to remaine in their Bodies, from the Resurrection to all Eternity, I have already I think sufficiently proved out of the Scriptures, in the 38. Chapter. And for the places of the New Testament, where it is said that any man shall be cast Body and Soul into Hell fire, it is no more than Body and Life; that is to say, they shall be cast alive into the perpetuall fire of Gehenna.

[340]

This window it is, that gives entrance to the Dark Doctrine, first, of Eternall Torments; and afterwards of Purgatory, and consequently of the walking abroad, especially in places Consecrated, Solitary, or Dark, of the Ghosts of men deceased; and thereby to the pretences of Exorcisme and Conjuration of Phantasmes; as also of Invocation of men dead; and to the Doctrine of Indulgences; that is to say, of exemption for a time, or for ever, from the fire of Purgatory, wherein these Incorporeall Substances are pretended by burning to be cleansed, and made fit for Heaven. For men being generally possessed before the time of our Saviour, by contagion of the Dæmonology of the Greeks, of an opinion, that the Souls of men were substances distinct from their Bodies, and therefore that when the Body was dead, the Soule of every man, whether godly, or wicked, must subsist somewhere by vertue of its own nature, without acknowledging therein any supernaturall gift of Gods; the Doctors of the Church doubted a long time, what was the

As the Doctrine of Purgatory, and Exorcismes, and Invocation of Saints.

place, which they were to abide in, till they should be re-united to their Bodies in the Resurrection; supposing for a while, they lay under the Altars: but afterward the Church of Rome found it more profitable, to build for them this place of Purgatory; which by some other Churches in this later age, has been demolished.

The Texts al-
ledged for the
Doctrines
aforemen-
tioned have
[341]
been answered
before.

Let us now consider, what texts of Scripture seem most to confirm these three generall Errors, I have here touched. As for those which Cardinall Bellarmine[4] hath alledged, for the present Kingdome of God administred by the Pope, (than which there are none that make a better shew of proof,) I have already answered them; and made it evident, that the Kingdome of God, instituted by Moses, ended in the election of Saul: After which time the Priest of his own authority never deposed any King. That which the High Priest did to Athaliah, was not done in his owne right, but in the right of the young King Joash her Son: But Solomon in his own right deposed the High Priest Abiathar, and set up another in his place. The most difficult place to answer, of all those that can be brought, to prove the Kingdome of God by Christ is already in this world, is alledged, not by Bellarmine, nor any other of the Church of Rome; but by Beza;[5] that will have it to begin from the Resurrection of Christ. But whether hee intend thereby, to entitle the Presbytery to the Supreme Power Ecclesiasticall in the Common-wealth of Geneva, (and consequently to every Presbytery in every other Common-wealth,) or to Princes, and other Civill Soveraigns, I doe not know. For the Presbytery hath challenged the power to Excommunicate their owne Kings, and to bee the Supreme Moderators in Religion, in the places where they have that form of Church government, no lesse then the Pope challengeth it universally.

Answer to the
text on which
Beza inferreth
that the King-
dome of
Christ began
at the Resur-
rection.

The words are (Marke 9. 1.) *Verily I say unto you, that there be some of them that stand here, which shall not tast of death, till they have seene the Kingdome of God come with power.* Which words, if taken grammatically, make it certaine, that either some of those men that stood by Christ at that time, are yet alive; or else, that the Kingdome of God must be now in this present world. And then there is another place more difficult: For when the Apostles after our Saviours Resurrection, and immediately before his Ascension, asked our Saviour, saying, (Acts 1. 6.) *Wilt thou at this time restore again the Kingdome to Israel,* he answered them, *It is not for you to know the times and the seasons, which the Father hath put in his own power; But ye shall receive power by the comming of the Holy Ghost upon you, and yee shall be my (Martyrs) witnesses both in Jerusalem, & in all Judæa, and in Samaria, and unto the uttermost part of the Earth:* Which is as much as to say, My Kingdome is not yet come, nor shall you foreknow when it shall come; for it shall come as a theefe in the night; But I will send you the Holy Ghost, and by him you shall have power to beare witnesse to all the world (by your preaching) of my Resurrection, and the workes

4. Saint Robert Bellarmine (1542–1621), an Italian Jesuit who wrote an influential defense of the Catholic Church against the attacks of Protestants and who assailed King James of England for discriminating against Catholics. Ch. 42 of *Leviathan* (omitted from this edition) is a sustained critique of Bellarmine's arguments.
5. Theodore Beza (1519–1605), a leading Calvinist and Calvin's principal associate in Geneva.

I have done, and the doctrine I have taught, that they may beleeve in me, and expect eternall life, at my comming againe: How does this agree with the comming of Christs Kingdome at the Resurrection? And that which St. *Paul* saies (1 *Thessal.* 1. 9, 10.) *That they turned from Idols, to serve the living and true God, and to waite for his Sonne from Heaven;* Where to waite for his Sonne from Heaven, is to wait for his comming to be King in power; which were not necessary, if his King-dome had beene then present. Againe, if the Kingdome of God began (as *Beza* on that place (*Mark* 9. 1.) would have it) at the Resurrection; what reason is there for Christians ever since the Resurrection to say in their prayers, *Let thy Kingdom Come?* It is therefore manifest, that the words of St. *Mark* are not so to be interpreted. There be some of them that stand here (saith our Saviour) that shall not tast of death till they have seen the Kingdome of God come in power. If then this Kingdome were to come at the Resurrection of Christ, why is it said, *some of them,* rather than *all?* For they all lived till after Christ was risen.

[342]

But they that require an exact interpretation of this text, let them interpret first the like words of our Saviour to St. *Peter* concerning St. John, (chap. 21. 22.) *If I will that he tarry till I come, what is that to thee?* upon which was grounded a report that hee should not dye: Nev-erthelesse the truth of that report was neither confirmed, as well grounded; nor refuted, as ill grounded on those words; but left as a saying not understood. The same difficulty is also in the place of St. Marke. And if it be lawfull to conjecture at their meaning, by that which immediately followes, both here, and in St. Luke, where the same is againe repeated, it is not unprobable, to say they have relation to the Transfiguration, which is described in the verses immediately following; where it is said, that *After six dayes Jesus taketh with him Peter, and James, and John* (not all, but some of his Disciples) *and leadeth them up into an high mountaine apart by themselves, and was transfigured before them. And his rayment became shining, exceeding white as snow; so as no Fuller*[6] *on earth can white them. And there appeared unto them Elias with Moses, and they were talking with Jesus, &c.* So that they saw Christ in Glory and Majestie, as he is to come; insomuch as *They were sore afraid.* And thus the promise of our Saviour was accomplished by way of *Vision:* For it was a Vision, as may probably bee inferred out of St. Luke, that reciteth the same story (ch. 9. ve. 28.) and saith, that Peter and they that were with him, were heavy with sleep: But most certainly out of Matth. 17. 9. (where the same is again related;) for our Saviour charged them, saying, *Tell no man the Vision untill the Son of man be Risen from the dead.* Howsoever it be, yet there can from thence be taken no argument, to prove that the Kingdome of God taketh beginning till the day of Judgement.

Explication of the Place in Mark 9.

As for some other texts, to prove the Popes Power over civill Sover-aignes (besides those of *Bellarmine;*) as that the two Swords that Christ and his Apostles had amongst them, were the Spirituall and the Tem-

Abuse of some other texts in defence of the Power of the Pope.

6. Cleaner (of cloth).

porall Sword, which they say St. Peter had given him by Christ: And, that of the two Luminaries, the greater signifies the Pope, and the lesser the King; One might as well inferre out of the first verse of the Bible, that by Heaven is meant the Pope, and by Earth the King: Which is not arguing from Scripture, but a wanton insulting over[7] Princes, that came in fashion after the time the Popes were growne so secure of their greatnesse, as to contemne all Christian Kings; and Treading on the necks of Emperours, to mocke both them, and the Scripture, in the words of the 91. Psalm, *Thou shalt Tread upon the Lion and the Adder, the young Lion and the Dragon thou shalt Trample under thy feet.*

The manner of Consecrations [343] in the Scripture, was without Exorcisms.   As for the rites of Consecration, though they depend for the most part upon the discretion and judgement of the governors of the Church, and not upon the Scriptures; yet those governors are obliged to such direction, as the nature of the action it selfe requireth; as that the ceremonies, words, and gestures, be both decent, and significant, or at least conformable[8] to the action. When Moses consecrated the Tabernacle, the Altar, and the Vessels belonging to them, (*Exod.* 40.) he anointed them with the Oyle which God had commanded to bee made for that purpose; and they were holy: There was nothing Exorcized, to drive away Phantasmes. The same Moses (the civill Soveraigne of Israel) when he consecrated Aaron (the High Priest,) and his Sons, did wash them with Water, (not Exorcized water,) put their Garments upon them, and anointed them with Oyle; and they were sanctified, to minister unto the Lord in the Priests office; which was a simple and decent cleansing, and adorning them, before hee presented them to God, to be his servants. When King *Solomon*, (the civill Soveraigne of Israel) consecrated the Temple hee had built, (2 *Kings* 8.) he stood before all the Congregation of Israel; and having blessed them, he gave thanks to God, for putting into the heart of his father, to build it; and for giving to himselfe the grace to accomplish the same; and then prayed unto him, first, to accept that House, though it were not sutable to his infinite Greatnesse; and to hear the prayers of his Servants that should pray therein, or (if they were absent,) towards it; and lastly, he offered a sacrifice of Peace-offering, and the House was dedicated. Here was no Procession; the King stood still in his first place; no Exorcised Water; no *Asperges me*, nor other impertinent application of words spoken upon another occasion; but a decent, and rationall speech, and such as in making to God a present of his new built House, was most conformable to the occasion.

We read not that St. John did Exorcize the Water of Jordan; nor Philip the Water of the river wherein he baptized the Eunuch; nor that any Pastor in the time of the Apostles, did take his spittle, and put it to the nose of the person to be Baptized, and say, *In odorem suavitatis*, that is, *for a sweet savour unto the Lord*; wherein neither the Ceremony of Spittle, for the uncleannesse; nor the application of that Scripture for the levity, can by any authority of man be justified.

To prove that the Soule separated from the Body, liveth eternally,

7. Contemptuous abuse of.
8. Suitable.

not onely the Soules of the Elect, by especiall grace, and restauration *The immortal-* of the Eternall Life which Adam lost by Sinne, and our Saviour restored *ity of mans* by the Sacrifice of himself, to the Faithfull; but also the Soules of *Soule, not* Reprobates, as a property naturally consequent to the essence of man- *Scripture to be* kind, without other grace of God, but that which is universally given *of Nature, but* to all mankind; there are divers places, which at the first sight seem *of Grace.* sufficiently to serve the turn: but such, as when I compare them with that which I have before (Chapter 38.) alledged out of the 14 of *Job*, seem to mee much more subject to a divers interpretation, than the words of *Job*.

And first there are the words of Solomon (*Ecclesiastes* 12. 7.) *Then shall the Dust return to Dust, as it was, and the Spirit shall return to* [344] *God that gave it.* Which may bear well enough (if there be no other text directly against it) this interpretation, that God onely knows, (but Man not,) what becomes of a mans spirit, when he expireth; and the same Solomon, in the same Book, (Chap. 3. ver. 20, 21.) delivereth the same sentence in the sense I have given it: His words are, *All goe* (man and beast) *to the same place; all are of the dust, and all turn to dust again; who knoweth that the spirit of Man goeth upward, and that the spirit of the Beast goeth downward to the earth?* That is, none knows but God; Nor is it an unusuall phrase to say of things we understand not, *God Knows what*, and *God Knows where*. That of *Gen*. 5. 24. *Enoch walked with God, and he was not; for God took him*; which is expounded *Heb*. 13. 5. *He was translated, that he should not die; and was not found, because God had translated him. For before his Translation, he had this testimony, that he pleased God,* making as much for the Im- mortality of the Body, as of the Soule, proveth, that this his translation was peculiar to them that please God; not common to them with the wicked; and depending on Grace, not on Nature. But on the contrary, what interpretation shall we give, besides the literall sense of the words of Solomon (*Eccles.* 3. 19.) *That which befalleth the Sons of Men, befalleth Beasts, even one thing befalleth them; as the one dyeth, so doth the other; yea, they have all one breath* (one spirit;) *so that a Man hath no præeminence above a Beast, for all is vanity.* By the literall sense, here is no Naturall Immortality of the Soule; nor yet any repugnancy with the Life Eternall, which the Elect shall enjoy by Grace. And (chap. 4. ver. 3.) *Better is he that hath not yet been, than both they;* that is, than they that live, or have lived; which, if the Soule of all them that have lived, were Immortall, were a hard saying; for then to have an Immortall Soule, were worse than to have no Soule at all. And againe, (Chapt. 9. 5.) *The living know they shall die, but the dead know not any thing;* that is, Naturally, and before the resurrection of the body.

Another place which seems to make for a Naturall Immortality of the Soule, is that, where our Saviour saith, that Abraham, Isaac, and Jacob are living: but this is spoken of the promise of God, and of their certitude to rise again, not of a Life then actuall; and in the same sense that God said to Adam, that on the day hee should eate of the forbidden fruit, he should certainly die; from that time forward he was a dead man by sentence; but not by execution, till almost a thousand years after. So Abraham, Isaac, and Jacob were alive by promise, then, when Christ spake; but are not actually till the Resurrection. And the History of Dives and Lazarus, make nothing against this, if wee take it (as it is) for a Parable.

But there be other places of the New Testament, where an Immortality seemeth to be directly attributed to the wicked. For it is evident, that they shall all rise to Judgement. And it is said besides in many [345] places, that they shall goe into *Everlasting fire, Everlasting torments, Everlasting punishments; and that the worm of conscience never dyeth;* and all this is comprehended in the word *Everlasting Death,* which is ordinarily interpreted *Everlasting Life in torments:* And yet I can find no where that any man shall live in torments Everlastingly. Also, it seemeth hard, to say, that God who is the Father of Mercies, that doth in Heaven and Earth all that hee will; that hath the hearts of all men in his disposing; that worketh in men both to doe, and to will; and without whose free gift a man hath neither inclination to good, nor repentance of evill, should punish mens transgressions without any end of time, and with all the extremity of torture, that men can imagine, and more. We are therefore to consider, what the meaning is, of *Everlasting Fire,* and other the like phrases of Scripture.

I have shewed already, that the Kingdome of God by Christ beginneth at the day of Judgment: That in that day, the Faithfull shall rise again, with glorious, and spirituall Bodies, and bee his Subjects in that his Kingdome, which shall be Eternall: That they shall neither marry, nor be given in marriage, nor eate and drink, as they did in their naturall bodies; but live for ever in their individuall persons, without the specificall eternity of generation: And that the Reprobates also shall rise again, to receive punishments for their sins: As also, that those of the Elect, which shall be alive in their earthly bodies at that day, shall have their bodies suddenly changed, and made spirituall, and Immortall. But that the bodies of the Reprobate, who make the Kingdome of Satan, shall also be glorious, or spirituall bodies, or that they shall bee as the Angels of God, neither eating, nor drinking, nor engendring; or that their life shall be Eternall in their individuall persons, as the life of every faithfull man is, or as the life of Adam had been if hee had not sinned, there is no place of Scripture to prove it; save onely these places concerning Eternall Torments; which may otherwise be interpreted.

From whence may be inferred, that as the Elect after the Resurrection shall be restored to the estate, wherein Adam was before he had sinned; so the Reprobate shall be in the estate, that Adam, and his posterity were in after the sin committed; saving that God promised a Redeemer to Adam, and such of his seed as should trust in him, and repent; but not to them that should die in their sins, as do the Reprobate.

Eternall Torments what. These things considered, the texts that mention *Eternall Fire, Eternall Torments, or the Worm that never dieth,* contradict not the Doctrine of a Second, and Everlasting Death, in the proper and naturall sense of the word *Death.* The Fire, or Torments prepared for the wicked in

Gehenna, Tophet, or in what place soever, may continue for ever; and there may never want wicked men to be tormented in them; though not every, nor any one Eternally. For the wicked being left in the estate they were in after Adams sin, may at the Resurrection live as they did, marry, and give in marriage, and have grosse and corruptible bodies, as all mankind now have; and consequently may engender perpetually, after the Resurrection, as they did before: For there is no place of Scripture to the contrary. For St. Paul, speaking of the Resurrection (1 *Cor.* 15.) understandeth it onely of the Resurrection to Life Eternall; and not the Resurrection to Punishment. And of the first, he saith that the Body is *Sown in Corruption, raised in Incorruption; sown in Dishonour, raised in Honour; sown in Weaknesse, raised in Power; sown a Naturall body, raised a Spirituall body:* There is no such thing can be said of the bodies of them that rise to Punishment. So also our Saviour, when hee speaketh of the Nature of Man after the Resurrection, meaneth, the Resurrection to Life Eternall, not to Punishment. The text is *Luke* 20, verses 34, 35, 36. a fertile text. *The Children of this world marry, and are given in marriage; but they that shall be counted worthy to obtaine that world, and the Resurrection from the dead, neither marry, nor are given in marriage: Neither can they die any more; for they are equall to the Angells, and are the Children of God, being the Children of the Resurrection:* The Children of this world, that are in the estate which Adam left them in, shall marry, and be given in marriage; that is, corrupt, and generate successively; which is an Immortality of the Kind, but not of the Persons of men: They are not worthy to be counted amongst them that shall obtain the next world, and an absolute Resurrection from the dead; but onely a short time, as inmates of that world; and to the end onely to receive condign punishment for their contumacy. The Elect are the onely children of the Resurrection; that is to say, the sole heirs of Eternall Life: they only can die no more: it is they that are equall to the Angels, and that are the children of God; and not the Reprobate. To the Reprobate there remaineth after the Resurrection, a *Second,* and *Eternall* Death: between which Resurrection, and their Second, and Eternall death, is but a time of Punishment and Torment; and to last by succession of sinners thereunto, as long as the kind of Man by propagation shall endure; which is Eternally.

Upon this Doctrine of the Naturall Eternity of separated Soules, is founded (as I said) the Doctrine of Purgatory. For supposing Eternall Life by Grace onely, there is no Life, but the Life of the Body; and no Immortality till the Resurrection. The texts for Purgatory alledged by Bellarmine out of the Canonicall Scripture of the old Testament, are first, the Fasting of *David* for *Saul* and *Jonathan,* mentioned (2 *Kings,* 1. 12.); and againe, (2 *Sam.* 3. 35.) for the death of *Abner.* This Fasting of *David,* he saith, was for the obtaining of something for them at Gods hands, after their death; because after he had Fasted to procure the recovery of his owne child, assoone as he knew it was dead, he called for meate. Seeing then the Soule hath an existence separate from the Body, and nothing can be obtained by mens Fasting for the Soules that are already either in Heaven, or Hell, it followeth that there be some

[346]

Answer of the Texts alledged for Purgatory.

Soules of dead men, that are neither in Heaven, nor in Hell; and therefore they must bee in some third place, which must be Purgatory. [347] And thus with hard straining, hee has wrested those places to the proofe of a Purgatory: whereas it is manifest, that the ceremonies of Mourning, and Fasting, when they are used for the death of men, whose life was not profitable to the Mourners, they are used for honours sake to their persons; and when tis done for the death of them by whose life the Mourners had benefit, it proceeds from their particular dammage: And so *David* honoured *Saul*, and *Abner*, with his Fasting; and in the death of his owne child, recomforted himselfe, by receiving his ordinary food.

In the other places, which he alledgeth out of the old Testament, there is not so much as any shew, or colour of proofe. He brings in every text wherein there is the word *Anger*, or *Fire*, or *Burning*, or *Purging*, or *Clensing*, in case any of the Fathers have but in a Sermon rhetorically applied it to the Doctrine of Purgatory, already beleeved. The first verse of *Psalme*, 37. *O Lord rebuke me not in thy wrath, nor chasten me in thy hot displeasure:* What were this to Purgatory, if Augustine had not applied the *Wrath* to the fire of Hell, and the *Displeasure* to that of Purgatory? And what is it to Purgatory, that of *Psalme*, 66. 12. *Wee went through fire and water, and thou broughtest us to a moist place;* and other the like texts, (with which the Doctors of those times entended to adorne, or extend their Sermons, or Commentaries) haled to their purposes by force of wit?

Places of the New Testament for Purgatory answered.   But he alledgeth other places of the New Testament, that are not so easie to be answered: And first that of *Matth.* 12. 32. *Whosoever speaketh a word against the Sonne of man, it shall be forgiven him; but whosoever speaketh against the Holy Ghost, it shall not bee forgiven him neither in this world, nor in the world to come:* Where he will have Purgatory to be the World to come, wherein some sinnes may be forgiven, which in this World were not forgiven: notwithstanding that it is manifest, there are but three Worlds; one from the Creation to the Flood, which was destroyed by Water, and is called in Scripture *the Old World*; another from the Flood, to the day of Judgement, which is *the Present World*, and shall bee destroyed by Fire; and the third, which shall bee from the day of Judgement forward, everlasting, which is called *the World to come*; and in which it is agreed by all, there shall be no Purgatory: And therefore the World to come, and Purgatory, are inconsistent. But what then can bee the meaning of those our Saviours words? I confesse they are very hardly to bee reconciled with all the Doctrines now unanimously received: Nor is it any shame, to confesse the profoundnesse of the Scripture, to bee too great to be sounded by the shortnesse of humane understanding. Neverthelesse, I may propound such things to the consideration of more learned Divines, as the text it selfe suggesteth. And first, seeing to speake against the Holy Ghost, as being the third Person of the Trinity, is to speake against the Church, in which the Holy Ghost resideth; it seemeth the comparison is made, betweene the Easinesse of our Saviour, in bearing with offences done to him while hee himselfe taught the world, that is, when he was on earth, and the Severity of the Pastors after him, against those

which should deny their authority, which was from the Holy Ghost: As [348]
if he should say, You that deny my Power; nay you that shall crucifie
me, shall be pardoned by mee, as often as you turne unto mee by
Repentance: But if you deny the Power of them that teach you hereafter, by vertue of the Holy Ghost, they shall be inexorable, and shall
not forgive you, but persecute you in this World, and leave you without
absolution, (though you turn to me, unlesse you turn also to them,) to
the punishments (as much as lies in them) of the World to come: And
so the words may be taken as a Prophecy, or Prædiction concerning
the times, as they have along[9] been in the Christian Church: Or if this
be not the meaning, (for I am not peremptory in such difficult places,)
perhaps there may be place left after the Resurrection for the Repentance of some sinners: And there is also another place, that seemeth to
agree therewith. For considering the words of St. Paul (1 Cor. 15. 29.)
*What shall they doe which are Baptized for the dead, if the dead rise
not at all? why also are they Baptized for the dead?* a man may probably
inferre, as some have done, that in St. Pauls time, there was a custome
by receiving Baptisme for the dead, (as men that now beleeve, are
Sureties and Undertakers[1] for the Faith of Infants, that are not capable
of beleeving,) to undertake for the persons of their deceased friends,
that they should be ready to obey, and receive our Saviour for their
King, at his coming again; and then the forgivenesse of sins in the world
to come, has no need of a Purgatory. But in both these interpretations,
there is so much of paradox, that I trust not to them; but propound
them to those that are throughly versed in the Scripture, to inquire if
there be no clearer place that contradicts them. Onely of thus much,
I see evident Scripture, to perswade me, that there is neither the word,
nor the thing of Purgatory, neither in this, nor any other text; nor any
thing that can prove a necessity of a place for the Soule without the
Body; neither for the Soule of Lazarus during the four days he was
dead; nor for the Soules of them which the Romane Church pretend
to be tormented now in Purgatory. For God, that could give a life to a
peece of clay, hath the same power to give life again to a dead man,
and renew his inanimate, and rotten Carkasse, into a glorious, spirituall,
and immortall Body.

Another place is that of 1 Cor. 3. where it is said, that they which
built Stubble, Hay, &c. on the true Foundation, their work shall perish;
but *they themselves shall be saved; but as through Fire*: This Fire, he
will have to be the Fire of Purgatory. The words, as I have said before,
are an allusion to those of *Zach*. 13. 9. where he saith, *I will bring the
third part through the Fire, and refine them as Silver is refined, and will
try them as Gold is tryed*: Which is spoken of the comming of the
Messiah in Power and Glory; that is, at the day of Judgment, and Conflagration of the present world; wherein the Elect shall not be consumed, but be refined; that is, depose[2] their erroneous Doctrines, and
Traditions, and have them as it were sindged of; and shall afterwards

9. Manuscript version reads *long*.
1. Guarantors.
2. Renounce.

call upon the name of the true God. In like manner, the Apostle saith
[349] of them, that holding this Foundation *Jesus is the Christ*, shall build
thereon some other Doctrines that be erroneous, that they shall not be
consumed in that fire which reneweth the world, but shall passe
through it to Salvation; but so, as to see, and relinquish their former
Errours. The Builders, are the *Pastors*; the Foundation, that *Jesus is the
Christ*; the Stubble and Hay, *False Consequences drawn from it through
Ignorance, or Frailty*; the Gold, Silver, and pretious Stones, are their
True Doctrines; and their Refining or Purging, the *Relinquishing of their
Errors*. In all which there is no colour at all for the burning of Incor-
poreall, that is to say, Impatible[3] Souls.

Baptisme for   A third place is that of 1 *Cor*. 15. before mentioned, concerning
the Dead, how Baptisme for the Dead: out of which he concludeth, first, that Prayers
understood.   for the Dead are not unprofitable; and out of that, that there is a Fire
of Purgatory: But neither of them rightly. For of many interpretations
of the word Baptisme, he approveth this in the first place, that by Baptisme is meant (metaphorically) a Baptisme of Penance; and that men
are in this sense Baptized, when they Fast, and Pray, and give Almes:
And so Baptisme for the Dead, and Prayer for the Dead, is the same
thing. But this is a Metaphor, of which there is no example, neither in
the Scripture, nor in any other use of language; and which is also
discordant to the harmony, and scope of the Scripture. The word Baptisme is used (*Mar*. 10. 38. & *Luk*. 12. 50.) for being Dipped in ones
own bloud, as Christ was upon the Cross, and as most of the Apostles
were, for giving testimony of him. But it is hard to say, that Prayer,
Fasting, and Almes, have any similitude with Dipping. The same is
used also *Mat*. 3. 11. (which seemeth to make somewhat for Purgatory)
for a Purging with Fire. But it is evident the Fire and Purging here
mentioned, is the same whereof the Prophet *Zachary* speaketh (chap.
13. v. 9.) *I will bring the third part through the Fire, and will Refine
them, &c*. And St. Peter after him (1 *Epist*. 1. 7.) *That the triall of your
Faith, which is much more precious than of Gold that perisheth, though
it be tryed with Fire, might be found unto praise, and honour, and glory
at the Appearing of Jesus Christ*; and St. Paul (1 *Cor*. 3. 13.) *The Fire
shall trie every mans work of what sort it is*. But St. Peter, and St. Paul
speak of the Fire that shall be at the Second Appearing of Christ; and
the Prophet Zachary of the Day of Judgment: And therefore this place
of S. Mat. may be interpreted of the same; and then there will be no
necessity of the Fire of Purgatory.

Another interpretation of Baptisme for the Dead, is that which I have
before mentioned, which he preferreth to the second place of probability: And thence also he inferreth the utility of Prayer for the Dead.
For if after the Resurrection, such as have not heard of Christ, or not
beleeved in him, may be received into Christs Kingdome; it is not in
vain, after their death, that their friends should pray for them, till they
should be risen. But granting that God, at the prayers of the faithfull,
may convert unto him some of those that have not heard Christ

3. Invulnerable.

preached, and consequently cannot have rejected Christ, and that the
charity of men in that point, cannot be blamed; yet this concludeth
nothing for Purgatory, because to rise from Death to Life, is one thing;
to rise from Purgatory to Life is another; as being a rising from Life to   [350]
Life, from a Life in torments to a Life in joy.

A fourth place is that of *Mat. 5. 25. Agree with thine Adversary
quickly, whilest thou art in the way with him, lest at any time the Adversary deliver thee to the Judge, and the Judge deliver thee to the Officer,
and thou be cast into prison. Verily I say unto thee, thou shalt by no
means come out thence, till thou hast paid the uttermost farthing.* In
which Allegory, the Offender is the *Sinner*; both the Adversary and the
Judge is *God*; the Way is this *Life*; the Prison is the *Grave*; the Officer,
Death; from which, the sinner shall not rise again to life eternall, but
to a second Death, till he have paid the utmost farthing, or Christ pay
it for him by his Passion, which is a full Ransome for all manner of
sin, as well lesser sins, as greater crimes; both being made by the passion
of Christ equally veniall.

The fift place, is that of *Matth. 5. 22. Whosoever is angry with his
Brother without a cause, shall be guilty in Judgment. And whosoever
shall say to his Brother, RACHA, shall be guilty in the Councel. But
whosoever shall say, Thou Foole, shall be guilty to hell fire.* From which
words he inferreth three sorts of Sins, and three sorts of Punishments;
and that none of those sins, but the last, shall be punished with hell
fire; and consequently, that after this life, there is punishment of lesser
sins in Purgatory. Of which inference, there is no colour[4] in any interpretation that hath yet been given of them: Shall there be a distinction
after this life of Courts of Justice, as there was amongst the Jews in our
Saviours time, to hear, and determine divers sorts of Crimes; as the
Judges, and the Councell? Shall not all Judicature appertain to Christ,
and his Apostles? To understand therefore this text, we are not to consider it solitarily, but jointly with the words precedent, and subsequent.
Our Saviour in this Chapter interpreteth the Law of Moses; which the
Jews thought was then fulfilled, when they had not transgressed the
Grammaticall sense thereof, however they had transgressed against
the sentence, or meaning of the Legislator. Therefore whereas they
thought the Sixth Commandement was not broken, but by Killing a
man; nor the Seventh, but when a man lay with a woman, not his wife;
our Saviour tells them, the inward Anger of a man against his brother,
if it be without just cause, is Homicide: You have heard (saith hee) the
Law of Moses, *Thou shalt not Kill*, and that *Whosoever shall Kill, shall
bee condemned before the Judges*, or before the Session of the Seventy:
But I say unto you, to be Angry with ones Brother without cause; or to
say unto him *Racha*, or *Foole*, is Homicide, and shall be punished at
the day of Judgment, and Session of Christ, and his Apostles, with Hell
fire: so that those words were not used to distinguish between divers
Crimes, and divers Courts of Justice, and divers Punishments; but to
taxe the distinction between sin, and sin, which the Jews drew not from

4. Plausible basis or reason.

[351] the difference of the Will in Obeying God, but from the difference of their Temporall Courts of Justice; and to shew them that he that had the Will to hurt his Brother, though the effect appear but in Reviling, or not at all, shall be cast into hell fire, by the Judges, and by the Session, which shall be the same, not different Courts at the day of Judgment. This considered, what can be drawn from this text, to maintain Purgatory, I cannot imagine.

The sixth place is *Luke* 16. 9. *Make yee friends of the unrighteous Mammon, that when yee faile, they may receive you into Everlasting Tabernacles.* This he alledges to prove Invocation of Saints departed. But the sense is plain, That we should make friends with our Riches, of the Poore; and thereby obtain their Prayers whilest they live. *He that giveth to the Poore, lendeth to the Lord.*

The seventh is *Luke* 23. 42. *Lord remember me when thou commest into thy Kingdome:* Therefore, saith hee, there is Remission of sins after this life. But the consequence is not good. Our Saviour then forgave him; and at his comming againe in Glory, will remember to raise him againe to Life Eternall.

The Eight is *Acts* 2. 24. where St. Peter saith of Christ, *that God had raised him up, and loosed the Paines of Death, because it was not possible he should be holden of it:* Which hee interprets to bee a descent of Christ into Purgatory, to loose some Soules there from their torments: whereas it is manifest, that it was Christ that was loosed; it was hee that could not bee holden of[5] Death, or the Grave; and not the Souls in Purgatory. But if that which Beza sayes in his notes on this place be well observed, there is none that will not see, that in stead of *Paynes,* it should be *Bands;* and then there is no further cause to seek for Purgatory in this Text.

* * *

Chap. XLVI.

[367]   *Of* DARKNESSE *from* VAIN PHILOSOPHY, *and*
FABULOUS TRADITIONS.

What Philoso-   By PHILOSOPHY, is understood *the Knowledge acquired by Reasoning,*
phy is.   *from the Manner of the Generation of any thing, to the Properties; or from the Properties, to some possible Way of Generation of the same; to the end to bee able to produce, as far as matter, and humane force permit, such Effects, as humane life requireth.* So the Geometrician, from the Construction of Figures, findeth out many Properties thereof; and from the Properties, new Ways of their Construction, by Reasoning; to the end to be able to measure Land, and Water; and for infinite other uses. So the Astronomer, from the Rising, Setting, and Moving of the Sun, and Starres, in divers parts of the Heavens, findeth out the Causes of Day, and Night, and of the different Seasons of the Year; whereby he keepeth an account of Time: And the like of other Sciences.

5. Held (in restraint) by.

By which Definition it is evident, that we are not to account as any part thereof, that originall knowledge called Experience, in which consisteth Prudence: Because it is not attained by Reasoning, but found as well in Brute Beasts, as in Man; and is but a Memory of successions of events in times past, wherein the omission of every little circumstance altering the effect, frustrateth the expectation of the most Prudent: whereas nothing is produced by Reasoning aright, but generall, eternall, and immutable Truth. *Prudence no part of Philosophy.*

Nor are we therefore to give that name to any false Conclusions: For he that Reasoneth aright in words he understandeth, can never conclude an Error:

Nor to that which any man knows by supernaturall Revelation; because it is not acquired by Reasoning:

Nor that which is gotten by Reasoning from the Authority of Books; because it is not by Reasoning from the Cause to the Effect, nor from the Effect to the Cause; and is not Knowledg, but Faith. *No false Doctrine is part of Philosophy: No more is Revelation supernaturall: Nor learning taken upon credit of Authors.*

The faculty of Reasoning being consequent to the use of Speech, it was not possible, but that there should have been some generall Truthes found out by Reasoning, as ancient almost as Language it selfe. The Savages of America, are not without some good Morall Sentences; also they have a little Arithmetick, to adde, and divide in Numbers not too great: but they are not therefore Philosophers. For as there were Plants of Corn and Wine in small quantity dispersed in the Fields and Woods, before men knew their vertue, or made use of them for their nourishment, or planted them apart in Fields, and Vineyards; in which time they fed on Akorns, and drank Water: so also there have been divers true, generall, and profitable Speculations from the beginning; as being the naturall plants of humane Reason: But they were at first but few in number; men lived upon grosse Experience; there was no Method; that is to say, no Sowing, nor Planting of Knowledge by it self, apart from the Weeds, and common Plants of Errour and Conjecture: And the cause of it being the want of leasure from procuring the necessities of life, and defending themselves against their neighbors, it was impossible, till the erecting of great Common-wealths, it should be otherwise. *Leasure* is the mother of *Philosophy*; and *Common-wealth*, the mother of *Peace*, and *Leasure*: Where first were great and flourishing *Cities*, there was first the study of *Philosophy*. The *Gymnosophists* of *India*, the *Magi* of *Persia*, and the *Priests* of *Chaldæa* and *Egypt*, are counted the most ancient Philosophers; and those Countreys were the most ancient of Kingdomes. *Philosophy* was not risen to the *Græcians*, and other people of the West, whose *Common-wealths* (no greater perhaps then *Lucca*, or *Geneva*) had never *Peace*, but when their fears of one another were equall; nor the *Leasure* to observe any thing but one another. At length, when *Warre* had united many of these *Græcian* lesser Cities, into fewer, and greater; then began *Seven men*, of severall parts of *Greece*, to get the reputation of being *Wise*; some of them for *Morall* and *Politique* Sentences; and others for the learning of the *Chaldæans* and *Egyptians*, which was *Astronomy*, and *Geometry*. But we hear not yet of any *Schools* of *Philosophy*. *Of the Beginnings and Progresse of Philosophy.*

[368]

Of the Schools of Philosophy amongst the Athenians.   After the *Athenians* by the overthrow of the *Persian* Armies, had gotten the Dominion of the Sea; and thereby, of all the Islands, and Maritime Cities of the *Archipelago*, as well of *Asia* as *Europe*; and were grown wealthy; they that had no employment, neither at home, nor abroad, had little else to employ themselves in, but either (as St. *Luke* says, Acts 17. 21.) *in telling and hearing news*, or in discoursing of *Philosophy* publiquely to the youth of the City. Every Master took some place for that purpose. *Plato* in certain publique Walks called *Academia*, from one *Academus*: *Aristotle* in the Walk of the Temple of *Pan*, called *Lycæum*: others in the *Stoa*, or covered Walk, wherein the Merchants Goods were brought to land: others in other places; where they spent the time of their Leasure, in teaching or in disputing of their Opinions: and some in any place, where they could get the youth of the City together to hear them talk. And this was it which *Carneades*[1] also did at *Rome*, when he was Ambassadour: which caused *Cato*[2] to advise the Senate to dispatch him quickly, for feare of corrupting the manners of the young men that delighted to hear him speak (as they thought) fine things.

[369]   From this it was, that the place where any of them taught, and disputed, was called *Schola*, which in their Tongue signifieth *Leasure*; and their Disputations, *Diatribæ*, that is to say, *Passing of the time*. Also the Philosophers themselves had the name of their Sects, some of them from these their Schools: For they that followed *Plato's* Doctrine, were called *Academiques*; The followers of *Aristotle*, *Peripatetiques*, from the Walk hee taught in; and those that *Zeno* taught, *Stoiques*, from the *Stoa*: as if we should denominate men from *More-fields*, from *Pauls-Church*, and from the *Exchange*, because they meet there often, to prate and loyter.

Neverthelesse, men were so much taken with this custome, that in time it spread it selfe over all Europe, and the best part of Afrique; so as there were Schools publiquely erected, and maintained for Lectures, and Disputations, almost in every Common-wealth.

Of the Schools of the Jews.   There were also Schools, anciently, both before, and after the time of our Saviour, amongst the *Jews*: but they were Schools of their Law. For though they were called *Synagogues*, that is to say, Congregations of the People; yet in as much as the Law was every Sabbath day read, expounded, and disputed in them, they differed not in nature, but in name onely from Publique Schools; and were not onely in Jerusalem, but in every City of the Gentiles, where the Jews inhabited. There was such a Schoole at *Damascus*, whereinto *Paul* entred, to persecute. There were others at *Antioch*, *Iconium* and *Thessalonica*, whereinto he entred, to dispute: And such was the Synagogue of the *Libertines*, *Cyrenians*, *Alexandrians*, *Cilicians*, and those of *Asia*; that is to say, the Schoole of *Libertines*, and of *Jewes*, that were strangers in *Jerusalem*: And of this Schoole they were that disputed (*Act. 6. 9.*) with *Saint Steven*.

---

1. A Greek philosopher and skeptic (214–129 B.C.) who gave a set of lectures in Rome in 155 B.C., arguing that no adequate basis for a theory of justice exists.
2. A Roman leader (232–147 B.C.) who was prominent in the struggle against Carthage. In 155 B.C. he protested Caneades' lectures and had him expelled from Rome.

But what has been the Utility of those Schools? what Science is there at this day acquired by their Readings and Disputings? That wee have of Geometry, which is the Mother of all Naturall Science, wee are not indebted for it to the Schools. *Plato* that was the best Philosopher of the Greeks, forbad entrance into his Schoole, to all that were not already in some measure Geometricians. There were many that studied that Science to the great advantage of mankind: but there is no mention of their Schools; nor was there any Sect of Geometricians; nor did they then passe under the name of Philosophers. The naturall Philosophy of those Schools, was rather a Dream than Science, and set forth in senselesse and insignificant Language; which cannot be avoided by those that will teach Philosophy, without having first attained great knowledge in Geometry: For Nature worketh by Motion; the Wayes, and Degrees whereof cannot be known, without the knowledge of the Proportions and Properties of Lines, and Figures. Their Morall Philosophy is but a description of their own Passions. For the rule of Manners, without Civill Government, is the Law of Nature; and in it, the Law Civill; that determineth what is *Honest*, and *Dishonest*; what is *Just*, and *Unjust*; and generally what is *Good*, and *Evill*: whereas they make the Rules of *Good*, and *Bad*, by their own *Liking*, and *Disliking*: By which means, in so great diversity of taste, there is nothing generally agreed on; but every one doth (as far as he dares) whatsoever seemeth good in his owne eyes, to the subversion of Common-wealth. Their *Logique* which should bee the Method of Reasoning, is nothing else but Captions[3] of Words, and Inventions how to puzzle such as should goe about to pose them. To conclude, there is nothing so absurd, that the old Philosophers (as *Cicero* saith, who was one of them) have not some of them maintained. And I beleeve that scarce any thing can be more absurdly said in naturall Philosophy, than that which now is called *Aristotles Metaphysiques*; nor more repugnant to Government, than much of that hee hath said in his *Politiques*; nor more ignorantly, than a great part of his *Ethiques*.

The Schoole of the Græcians unprofitable.

[370]

The Schoole of the Jews, was originally a Schoole of the Law of Moses; who commanded (*Deut.* 31. 10.) that at the end of every seventh year, at the Feast of the Tabernacles, it should be read to all the people, that they might hear, and learn it: Therefore the reading of the Law (which was in use after the Captivity) every Sabbath day, ought to have had no other end, but the acquainting of the people with the Commandements which they were to obey, and to expound unto them the writings of the Prophets. But it is manifest, by the many reprehensions of them by our Saviour, that they corrupted the Text of the Law with their false Commentaries, and vain Traditions; and so little understood the Prophets, that they did neither acknowledge Christ, nor the works he did; of which the Prophets prophecyed. So that by their Lectures and Disputations in their Synagogues, they turned the Doctrine of their Law into a Phantasticall kind of Philosophy, concerning the incomprehensible nature of God, and of Spirits; which they compounded of the Vain Philosophy and Theology of the Græcians, mingled with their

The Schools of the Jews unprofitable.

3. Caviling, quibbling.

own fancies, drawn from the obscurer places of the Scripture, and which might most easily bee wrested to their purpose; and from the Fabulous Traditions of their Ancestors.

University what it is. That which is now called an *University*, is a Joyning together, and an Incorporation under one Government of many Publique Schools, in one and the same Town or City. In which, the principall Schools were ordained for the three Professions, that is to say, of the Romane Religion, of the Romane Law, and of the Art of Medicine. And for the study of Philosophy it hath no otherwise place, then as a handmaid to the Romane Religion: And since the Authority of Aristotle is onely current there, that study is not properly Philosophy, (the nature whereof dependeth not on Authors,) but Aristotelity. And for Geometry, till of very late times it had no place at all; as being subservient to nothing but rigide Truth. And if any man by the ingenuity of his owne nature, had attained to any degree of perfection therein, hee was commonly thought a Magician, and his Art Diabolicall.

[371]
Errors brought into Religion from Aristotles Metaphysiques. Now to descend to the particular Tenets of Vain Philosophy, derived[4] to the Universities, and thence into the Church, partly from Aristotle, partly from Blindnesse of understanding; I shall first consider their Principles. There is a certain *Philosophia prima*, on which all other Philosophy ought to depend; and consisteth principally, in right limiting of the significations of such Appellations, or Names, as are of all others the most Universall: Which Limitations serve to avoid ambiguity, and æquivocation in Reasoning; and are commonly called Definitions; such as are the Definitions of Body, Time, Place, Matter, Forme, Essence, Subject, Substance, Accident, Power, Act, Finite, Infinite, Quantity, Quality, Motion, Action, Passion, and divers others, necessary to the explaining of a mans Conceptions concerning the Nature and Generation of Bodies. The Explication (that is, the setling of the meaning) of which, and the like Terms, is commonly in the Schools called *Metaphysiques*; as being a part of the Philosophy of Aristotle, which hath that for title: but it is in another sense; for there it signifieth as much, as *Books written, or placed after his naturall Philosophy*: But the Schools take them for *Books of supernaturall Philosophy*: for the word *Metaphysiques* will bear both these senses. And indeed that which is there written, is for the most part so far from the possibility of being understood, and so repugnant to naturall Reason, that whosoever thinketh there is any thing to bee understood by it, must needs think it supernaturall.

Errors concerning Abstract Essences. From these Metaphysiques, which are mingled with the Scripture to make Schoole Divinity, wee are told, there be in the world certain Essences separated from Bodies, which they call *Abstract Essences, and Substantiall Formes*: For the Interpreting of which *Jargon*, there is need of somewhat more than ordinary attention in this place. Also I ask pardon of those that are not used to this kind of Discourse, for applying my selfe to those that are. The World, (I mean not the Earth onely, that denominates the Lovers of it *Worldly men*, but the *Universe*, that

4. Conveyed.

is, the whole masse of all things that are) is Corporeall, that is to say, Body; and hath the dimensions of Magnitude, namely, Length, Bredth, and Depth: also every part of Body, is likewise Body, and hath the like dimensions; and consequently every part of the Universe, is Body; and that which is not Body, is no part of the Universe: And because the Universe is All, that which is no part of it, is *Nothing*; and consequently *no where*. Nor does it follow from hence, that Spirits are *nothing*: for they have dimensions, and are therefore really *Bodies*; though that name in common Speech be given to such Bodies onely, as are visible, or palpable; that is, that have some degree of Opacity: But for Spirits, they call them Incorporeall; which is a name of more honour, and may therefore with more piety bee attributed to God himselfe; in whom wee consider not what Attribute expresseth best his Nature, which is Incomprehensible; but what best expresseth our desire to honour Him.

To know now upon what grounds they say there be *Essences Abstract*, [372] or *Substantiall Formes*, wee are to consider what those words do properly signifie. The use of Words, is to register to our selves, and make manifest to others the Thoughts and Conceptions of our Minds. Of which Words, some are the names of the Things conceived; as the names of all sorts of Bodies, that work upon the Senses, and leave an Impression in the Imagination: Others are the names of the Imaginations themselves; that is to say, of those Ideas, or mentall Images we have of all things wee see, or remember: And others againe are names of Names; or of different sorts of Speech: As *Universall, Plurall, Singular*, are the names of Names; and *Definition, Affirmation, Negation, True, False, Syllogisme, Interrogation, Promise, Covenant*, are the names of certain Forms of Speech. Others serve to shew the Consequence, or Repugnance[5] of one name to another; as when one saith, A *Man is a Body*, hee intendeth that the name of *Body* is necessarily consequent to the name of *Man*; as being but severall names of the same thing, *Man*; which Consequence is signified by coupling them together with the word *Is*. And as wee use the Verbe *Is*; so the Latines use their Verbe *Est*, and the Greeks their "Εστι[6] through all its Declinations. Whether all other Nations of the world have in their severall languages a word that answereth to it, or not, I cannot tell; but I am sure they have not need of it: For the placing of two names in order may serve to signifie their Consequence, if it were the custome, (for Custome is it, that give words their force,) as well as the words *Is*, or *Bee*, or *Are*, and the like.

And if it were so, that there were a Language without any Verb answerable to *Est*, or *Is*, or *Bee*; yet the men that used it would bee not a jot the lesse capable of Inferring, Concluding, and of all kind of Reasoning, than were the Greeks, and Latines. But what then would become of these Terms, of *Entity, Essence, Essentiall, Essentiality*, that are derived from it, and of many more that depend on these, applyed as most commonly they are? They are therefore no Names of Things; but Signes, by which wee make known, that wee conceive the Consequence of one name or Attribute to another: as when we say, a *Man*,

5. Inconsistency.
6. *Esti.*

is, *a living Body*, wee mean not that the *Man* is one thing, the *Living Body* another, and the *Is*, or *Beeing* a third: but that the *Man*, and the *Living Body*, is the same thing; because the Consequence, *If hee bee a Man, hee is a living Body*, is a true Consequence, signified by that word Is. Therefore, *to bee a Body, to Walke, to bee Speaking, to Live, to See*, and the like Infinitives; also *Corporeity, Walking, Speaking, Life, Sight*, and the like, that signifie just the same, are the names of *Nothing*; as I have elsewhere more amply expressed.

But to what purpose (may some man say) is such subtilty in a work of this nature, where I pretend to nothing but what is necessary to the doctrine of Government and Obedience? It is to this purpose, that men [373] may no longer suffer themselves to be abused, by them, that by this doctrine of *Separated Essences*, built on the Vain Philosophy of Aristotle, would fright them from Obeying the Laws of their Countrey, with empty names; as men fright Birds from the Corn with an empty doublet, a hat, and a crooked stick. For it is upon this ground, that when a Man is dead and buried, they say his Soule (that is his Life) can walk separated from his Body, and is seen by night amongst the graves. Upon the same ground they say, that the Figure, and Colour, and Tast of a peece of Bread, has a being, there, where they say there is no Bread: And upon the same ground they say, that Faith, and Wisdome, and other Vertues are sometimes *powred* into a man, sometimes *blown* into him from Heaven; as if the Vertuous, and their Vertues could be asunder; and a great many other things that serve to lessen the dependance of Subjects on the Soveraign Power of their Countrey. For who will endeavour to obey the Laws, if he expect Obedience to be Powred or Blown into him? Or who will not obey a Priest, that can make God, rather than his Soveraign; nay than God himselfe? Or who, that is in fear of Ghosts, will not bear great respect to those that can make the Holy Water, that drives them from him? And this shall suffice for an example of the Errors, which are brought into the Church, from the *Entities*, and *Essences* of Aristotle: which it may be he knew to be false Philosophy; but writ it as a thing consonant to, and corroborative of their Religion; and fearing the fate of Socrates.

Being once fallen into this Error of *Separated Essences*, they are thereby necessarily involved in many other absurdities that follow it. For seeing they will have these Forms to be reall, they are obliged to assign them *some place*. But because they hold them Incorporeall, without all dimension of Quantity, and all men know that Place is Dimension, and not to be filled, but by that which is Corporeall; they are driven to uphold their credit with a distinction, that they are not indeed any where *Circumscriptive*, but *Definitive*: Which Terms being meer Words, and in this occasion[7] insignificant, passe[8] onely in Latine, that the vanity[9] of them may bee concealed. For the Circumscription of a thing, is nothing else but the Determination, or Defining of its Place; and so both the Terms of the Distinction are the same. And in partic-

7. Case.
8. Sneak by.
9. Meaninglessness.

ular, of the Essence of a Man, which (they say) is his Soule, they affirm it, to be All of it in his little Finger, and All of it in every other Part (how small soever) of his Body; and yet no more Soule in the Whole Body, than in any one of those Parts. Can any man think that God is served with such absurdities? And yet all this is necessary to beleeve, to those that will beleeve the Existence of an Incorporeall Soule, Separated from the Body.

And when they come to give account, how an Incorporeall Substance can be capable of Pain, and be tormented in the fire of Hell, or Purgatory, they have nothing at all to answer, but that it cannot be known how fire can burn Soules.

Again, whereas Motion is change of Place, and Incorporeall Substances are not capable of Place, they are troubled to make it seem possible, how a Soule can goe hence, without the Body to Heaven, Hell, or Purgatory; and how the Ghosts of men (and I may adde of their clothes which they appear in) can walk by night in Churches, Church-yards, and other places of Sepulture. To which I know not what they can answer, unlesse they will say, they walke, *definitivè*, not *circumscriptivè*, or *spiritually*, not *temporally*: for such egregious distinctions are equally applicable to any difficulty whatsoever. [374]

For the meaning of *Eternity*, they will not have it to be an Endlesse Succession of Time; for then they should not be able to render a reason how Gods Will, and Præ-ordaining of things to come, should not be before his Præscience of the same, as the Efficient Cause before the Effect, or Agent before the Action; nor of many other their bold opinions concerning the Incomprehensible Nature of God. But they will teach us, that Eternity is the Standing still of the Present Time, a *Nunc-stans* (as the Schools call it;) which neither they, nor any else understand, no more than they would a *Hic-stans* for an Infinite greatnesse of Place. *Nunc-stans.*

And whereas men divide a Body in their thought, by numbring parts of it, and in numbring those parts, number also the parts of the Place it filled; it cannot be, but in making many parts, wee make also many places of those parts; whereby there cannot bee conceived in the mind of any man, more, or fewer parts, than there are places for: yet they will have us beleeve, that by the Almighty power of God, one body may be at one and the same time in many places; and many bodies at one and the same time in one place: As if it were an acknowledgment of the Divine Power, to say, that which is, is not; or that which has been, has not been. And these are but a small part of the Incongruities they are forced to, from their disputing Philosophically, in stead of admiring, and adoring of the Divine and Incomprehensible Nature; whose Attributes cannot signifie what he is, but ought to signifie our desire to honour him, with the best Appellations we can think on. But they that venture to reason of his Nature, from these Attributes of Honour, losing their understanding in the very first attempt, fall from one Inconvenience into another, without end, and without number; in the same manner, as when a man ignorant of the Ceremonies of Court, comming into the presence of a greater Person than he is used to speak *One Body in many places, and many Bodies in one place at once.*

to, and stumbling at his entrance, to save himselfe from falling, lets slip his Cloake; to recover his Cloake, lets fall his Hat; and with one disorder after another, discovers his astonishment and rusticity.

Absurdities in naturall Philosophy, as Gravity the Cause of Heavinesse.

[375]

Then for *Physiques*, that is, the knowledge of the subordinate, and secundary causes of naturall events; they render none at all, but empty words. If you desire to know why some kind of bodies sink naturally downwards toward the Earth, and others goe naturally from it; The Schools will tell you out of Aristotle, that the bodies that sink downwards, are *Heavy*; and that this Heavinesse is it that causes them to descend: But if you ask what they mean by *Heavinesse*, they will define it to bee an endeavour to goe to the center of the Earth: so that the cause why things sink downward, is an Endeavour to be below: which is as much as to say, that bodies descend, or ascend, because they doe. Or they will tell you the center of the Earth is the place of Rest, and Conservation for Heavy things; and therefore they endeavour to be there: As if Stones, and Metalls had a desire, or could discern the place they would bee at, as Man does; or loved Rest, as Man does not; or that a peece of Glasse were lesse safe in the Window, than falling into the Street.

Quantity put into Body already made.

If we would know why the same Body seems greater (without adding to it) one time, than another; they say, when it seems lesse, it is *Condensed*; when greater, *Rarefied*. What is that *Condensed*, and *Rarefied*? Condensed, is when there is in the very same Matter, lesse Quantity than before; and Rarefied, when more. As if there could be Matter, that had not some determined Quantity; when Quantity is nothing else but the Determination of Matter; that is to say of Body, by which we say one Body is greater, or lesser than another, by thus, or thus much. Or as if a Body were made without any Quantity at all, and that afterwards more, or lesse were put into it, according as it is intended the Body should be more, or lesse Dense.

Powring in of Soules.

For the cause of the Soule of Man, they say, *Creatur Infundendo*, and *Creando Infunditur*: that is, *It is Created by Powring it in*, and *Powred in by Creation.*

Ubiquity of Apparition.

For the Cause of Sense, an ubiquity of *Species*; that is, of the *Shews* or *Apparitions* of objects; which when they be Apparitions to the Eye, is *Sight*; when to the Eare, *Hearing*; to the Palate, *Tast*; to the Nostrill, *Smelling*; and to the rest of the Body, *Feeling.*

Will, the Cause of Willing.

For cause of the Will, to doe any particular action, which is called *Volitio*, they assign the Faculty, that is to say, the Capacity in generall, that men have, to will sometimes one thing, sometimes another, which is called *Voluntas*; making the *Power* the cause of the *Act*: As if one should assign for cause of the good or evill Acts of men, their Ability to doe them.

Ignorance an occult Cause.

And in many occasions they put for cause of Naturall events, their own Ignorance; but disguised in other words: As when they say, Fortune is the cause of things contingent; that is, of things whereof they know no cause: And as when they attribute many Effects to *occult qualities*; that is, qualities not known to them; and therefore also (as they thinke) to no Man else. And to *Sympathy, Antipathy, Antiperistasis, Specificall*

Qualities, and other like Termes, which signifie neither the Agent that produceth them, nor the Operation by which they are produced.

If such *Metaphysiques*, and *Physiques* as this, be not *Vain Philosophy*, there was never any; nor needed St. Paul to give us warning to avoid it.

[376]

And for their Morall, and Civill Philosophy, it hath the same, or greater absurdities. If a man doe an action of Injustice, that is to say, an action contrary to the Law, God they say is the prime cause of the Law, and also the prime cause of that, and all other Actions; but no cause at all of the Injustice; which is the Inconformity of the Action to the Law. This is Vain Philosophy. A man might as well say, that one man maketh both a streight line, and a crooked, and another maketh their Incongruity. And such is the Philosophy of all men that resolve of their Conclusions, before they know their Premises; pretending to comprehend, that which is Incomprehensible; and of Attributes of Honour to make Attributes of Nature; as this distinction was made to maintain the Doctrine of Free-Will, that is, of a Will of man, not subject to the Will of God.

One makes the things incongruent, another the Incongruity.

Aristotle, and other Heathen Philosophers define Good, and Evill, by the Appetite of men; and well enough, as long as we consider them governed every one by his own Law: For in the condition of men that have no other Law but their own Appetites, there can be no generall Rule of Good, and Evill Actions. But in a Common-wealth this measure is false: Not the Appetite of Private men, but the Law, which is the Will and Appetite of the State is the measure. And yet is this Doctrine still practised; and men judge the Goodnesse, or Wickednesse of their own, and of other mens actions, and of the actions of the Common-wealth it selfe, by their own Passions; and no man calleth Good or Evill, but that which is so in his own eyes, without any regard at all to the Publique Laws; except onely Monks, and Friers, that are bound by Vow to that simple obedience to their Superiour, to which every Subject ought to think himself bound by the Law of Nature to the Civill Soveraign. And this private measure of Good, is a Doctrine, not onely Vain, but also Pernicious to the Publique State.

Private Appetite the rule of Publique good:

It is also Vain and false Philosophy, to say the work of Marriage is repugnant to Chastity, or Continence, and by consequence to make them Morall Vices; as they doe, that pretend Chastity, and Continence, for the ground of denying Marriage to the Clergy. For they confesse it is no more, but a Constitution of the Church, that requireth in those holy Orders that continually attend the Altar, and administration of the Eucharist, a continuall Abstinence from women, under the name of continuall Chastity, Continence, and Purity. Therefore they call the lawfull use of Wives, want of Chastity, and Continence; and so make Marriage a Sin, or at least a thing so impure, and unclean, as to render a man unfit for the Altar. If the Law were made because the use of Wives is Incontinence, and contrary to Chastity, then all Marriage is vice: If because it is a thing too impure, and unclean for a man consecrated to God; much more should other naturall, necessary, and daily

And that lawfull Marriage is Unchastity:

[377]   works which all men doe, render men unworthy to bee Priests, because
they are more unclean.

But the secret foundation of this prohibition of Marriage of Priests,
is not likely to have been laid so slightly, as upon such errours in Morall
Philosophy; nor yet upon the preference of single life, to the estate of
Matrimony; which proceeded from the wisdome of St. Paul, who perceived how inconvenient a thing it was, for those that in those times
of persecution were Preachers of the Gospel, and forced to fly from
one countrey to another, to be clogged with the care of wife and children; but upon the designe of the Popes, and Priests of after times, to
make themselves the Clergy, that is to say, sole Heirs of the Kingdome
of God in this world; to which it was necessary to take from them the
use of Marriage, because our Saviour saith, that at the coming of his
Kingdome the Children of God *shall neither Marry, nor bee given in
Marriage, but shall bee as the Angels in heaven*; that is to say, Spirituall.
Seeing then they had taken on them the name of Spirituall, to have
allowed themselves (when there was no need) the propriety of Wives,
had been an Incongruity.

*And that all
Government
but Popular,
is Tyranny:*

From Aristotles Civill Philosophy, they have learned, to call all manner of Common-wealths but the Popular, (such as was at that time the
state of Athens,) *Tyranny*. All Kings they called Tyrants; and the Aristocracy of the thirty Governours set up there by the Lacedemonians
that subdued them, the thirty Tyrants: As also to call the condition of
the people under the Democracy, *Liberty*. A *Tyrant* originally signified
no more simply, but a *Monarch*: But when afterwards in most parts of
Greece that kind of government was abolished, the name began to
signifie, not onely the thing it did before, but with it, the hatred which
the Popular States bare towards it: As also the name of King became
odious after the deposing of the Kings in Rome, as being a thing naturall to all men, to conceive some great Fault to be signified in any
Attribute, that is given in despight, and to a great Enemy. And when
the same men shall be displeased with those that have the administration of the Democracy, or Aristocracy, they are not to seek for dis-
gracefull names to expresse their anger in; but call readily the one
Anarchy, and the other, *Oligarchy*, or the *Tyranny of a Few*. And that
which offendeth the People, is no other thing, but that they are governed, not as every one of them would himselfe, but as the Publique
Representant, be it one Man, or an Assembly of men thinks fit; that is,
by an Arbitrary government: for which they give evill names to their
Superiors; never knowing (till perhaps a little after a Civill warre) that
without such Arbitrary government, such Warre must be perpetuall;
and that it is Men, and Arms, not Words, and Promises, that make the
Force and Power of the Laws.

*That not
Men, but Law
governs.*

And therefore this is another Errour of Aristotles Politiques, that in
a wel ordered Common-wealth, not Men should govern, but the Laws.
What man, that has his naturall Senses, though he can neither write
nor read, does not find himself governed by them he fears, and beleeves
can kill or hurt him when he obeyeth not? or that beleeves the Law
can hurt him; that is, Words, and Paper, without the Hands, and Swords

[378]

of men? And this is of the number of pernicious Errors: for they induce
men, as oft as they like not their Governours, to adhære to those that
call them Tyrants, and to think it lawfull to raise warre against them:
And yet they are many times cherished from the Pulpit, by the Clergy.

There is another Errour in their Civill Philosophy(which they never   *Laws over the*
learned of Aristotle, nor Cicero, nor any other of the Heathen,) to   *Conscience.*
extend the power of the Law, which is the Rule of Actions onely, to
the very Thoughts, and Consciences of men, by Examination, and *In-
quisition* of what they Hold, notwithstanding the Conformity of their
Speech and Actions: By which, men are either punished for answering
the truth of their thoughts, or constrained to answer an untruth for fear
of punishment. It is true, that the Civill Magistrate, intending to employ
a Minister in the charge of Teaching, may enquire of him, if hee bee
content to Preach such, and such Doctrines; and in case of refusall,
may deny him the employment: But to force him to accuse himselfe
of Opinions, when his Actions are not by Law forbidden, is against the
Law of Nature; and especially in them, who teach, that a man shall
bee damned to Eternall and extream torments, if he die in a false
opinion concerning an Article of the Christian Faith. For who is there,
that knowing there is so great danger in an error, whom the naturall
care of himself, compelleth not to hazard his Soule upon his own
judgement, rather than that of any other man that is unconcerned in
his damnation?

For a Private man, without the Authority of the Common-wealth,   *Private Inter-*
that is to say, without permission from the Representant thereof, to   *pretation of*
Interpret the Law by his own Spirit, is another Error in the Politiques;   *Law.*
but not drawn from Aristotle, nor from any other of the Heathen Philosophers. For none of them deny, but that in the Power of making
Laws, is comprehended also the Power of Explaining them when there
is need. And are not the Scriptures, in all places where they are Law,
made Law by the Authority of the Common-wealth, and consequently,
a part of the Civill Law?

Of the same kind it is also, when any but the Soveraign restraineth
in any man that power which the Common-wealth hath not restrained;
as they do, that impropriate[1] the Preaching of the Gospell to one certain
Order of men, where the Laws have left it free. If the State give me
leave to preach, or teach; that is, if it forbid me not, no man can forbid
me. If I find my selfe amongst the Idolaters of America, shall I that am
a Christian, though not in Orders, think it a sin to preach Jesus Christ,
till I have received Orders from Rome? or when I have preached, shall
not I answer their doubts, and expound the Scriptures to them; that is,
shall I not Teach? But for this may some say, as also for administring
to them the Sacraments, the necessity shall be esteemed for a sufficient   [379]
Mission; which is true: But this is true also, that for whatsoever, a
dispensation is due for the necessity, for the same there needs no dispensation, when there is no Law that forbids it. Therefore to deny these
Functions to those, to whom the Civill Soveraigne hath not denied

1. Appropriate.

them, is a taking away of a lawfull Liberty, which is contrary to the Doctrine of Civill Government.

More examples of Vain Philosophy, brought into Religion by the Doctors of Schoole-Divinity, might be produced; but other men may if they please observe them of themselves. I shall onely adde this, that the Writings of Schoole-Divines, are nothing else for the most part, but insignificant Traines of strange and barbarous words, or words otherwise used, then in the common use of the Latine tongue; such as would pose[2] Cicero, and Varro,[3] and all the Grammarians of ancient Rome. Which if any man would see proved, let him (as I have said once before) see whether he can translate any Schoole-Divine into any of the Modern tongues, as French, English, or any other copious language: for that which cannot in most of these be made Intelligible, is not Intelligible in the Latine. Which Insignificancy of language, though I cannot note it for false Philosophy; yet it hath a quality, not onely to hide the Truth, but also to make men think they have it, and desist from further search.

Language of Schoole-Divines.

Lastly, for the Errors brought in from false, or uncertain History, what is all the Legend of fictitious Miracles, in the lives of the Saints; and all the Histories of Apparitions, and Ghosts, alledged by the Doctors of the Romane Church, to make good their Doctrines of Hell, and Purgatory, the power of Exorcisme, and other Doctrines which have no warrant, neither in Reason, nor Scripture; as also all those Traditions which they call the unwritten Word of God; but old Wives Fables? Whereof, though they find dispersed somewhat in the Writings of the ancient Fathers; yet those Fathers were men, that might too easily beleeve false reports; and the producing of their opinions for testimony of the truth of what they beleeved, hath no other force with them that (according to the Counsell of St. *John* 1 Epist. chap. 4. verse I.) examine Spirits, than in all things that concern the power of the Romane Church, (the abuse whereof either they suspected not, or had benefit by it,) to discredit their testimony, in respect of too rash beleef of reports; which the most sincere men, without great knowledge of naturall causes, (such as the Fathers were) are commonly the most subject to: For naturally, the best men are the least suspicious of fraudulent purposes. Gregory the Pope,[4] and S. Bernard[5] have somewhat of Apparitions of Ghosts, that said they were in Purgatory; and so has our Beda:[6] but no where, I beleeve, but by report from others. But if they, or any other, relate any such stories of their own knowledge, they shall not thereby confirm the more such vain reports; but discover their own Infirmity, or Fraud.

Errors from Tradition.

[380]   With the Introduction of False, we may joyn also the suppression of True Philosophy, by such men, as neither by lawfull authority, nor

---

2. Confuse.
3. Marcus Terentius Varro (116–27 B.C.) wrote a history of the Latin language.
4. Hobbes refers to the *Dialogorum Libri IV* of Pope Gregory I (c. 540–604).
5. An influential Cistercian monk (1090–1153).
6. The "Venerable" Bede (c. 673–735), a monk and the most prolific writer in Anglo-Saxon England, whose remarks on ghosts are contained in his *Ecclesiastical History of the English People*.

sufficient study, are competent Judges of the truth. Our own Naviga-
tions make manifest, and all men learned in humane Sciences, now
acknowledge there are Antipodes: And every day it appeareth more and
more, that Years, and Dayes are determined by Motions of the Earth.
Neverthelesse, men that have in their Writings but supposed such Doctrine, as an occasion to lay open the reasons for, and against it, have
been punished for it by Authority Ecclesiasticall.[7] But what reason is
there for it? Is it because such opinions are contrary to true Religion?
that cannot be, if they be true. Let therefore the truth be first examined
by competent Judges, or confuted by them that pretend to know the
contrary. Is it because they be contrary to the Religion established? Let
them be silenced by the Laws of those, to whom the Teachers of them
are subject; that is, by the Laws Civill: For disobedience may lawfully
be punished in them, that against the Laws teach even true Philosophy.
Is it because they tend to disorder in Government, as countenancing
Rebellion, or Sedition? then let them be silenced, and the Teachers
punished by vertue of his Power to whom the care of the Publique
quiet is committed; which is the Authority Civill. For whatsoever Power
Ecclesiastiques take upon themselves (in any place where they are subject to the State) in their own Right, though they call it Gods Right, is
but Usurpation.

Suppression of Reason.

Chap. XLVII.

[381]

Of the BENEFIT *that proceedeth from such Darknesse,
and to whom it accreweth.*

Cicero maketh honorable mention of one of the *Cassii*, a severe
Judge amongst the Romans, for a custome he had, in Criminall causes,
(when the testimony of the witnesses was not sufficient,) to ask the
Accusers, *Cui bono*; that is to say, what Profit, Honor, or other Contentment, the accused obtained, or expected by the Fact. For amongst
Præsumptions, there is none that so evidently declareth the Author, as
doth the BENEFIT of the Action. By the same rule I intend in this place
to examine, who they may be, that have possessed the People so long
in this part of Christendome, with these Doctrines, contrary to the
Peaceable Societies of Mankind.

*He that receiv-
eth Benefit by
a Fact, is pre-
sumed to be
the Author.*

And first, to this Error, *that the present Church now Militant on
Earth, is the Kingdome of God*, (that is, the Kingdome of Glory, or the
Land of Promise; not the Kingdome of Grace, which is but a Promise
of the Land,) are annexed these worldly Benefits; First, that the Pastors,
and Teachers of the Church, are entitled thereby, as Gods Publique
Ministers, to a Right of Governing the Church; and consequently (because the Church, and Common-wealth are the same Persons) to be
Rectors, and Governours of the Common-wealth. By this title it is, that
the Pope prevailed with the subjects of all Christian Princes, to beleeve,

*That the
Church Mili-
tant is the
Kingdome of
God, was first
taught by the
Church of
Rome.*

7. A reference to the persecution of Galileo after the publication of his *Dialogue Concerning
the Two Chief World Systems* in 1632.

that to disobey him, was to disobey Christ himselfe; and in all differences between him and other Princes, (charmed with the word *Power Spirituall,*) to abandon their lawfull Soveraigns; which is in effect an universall Monarchy over all Christendome. For though they were first invested in the right of being Supreme Teachers of Christian Doctrine, by, and under Christian Emperors, within the limits of the Romane Empire (as is acknowledged by themselves) by the title of *Pontifex Maximus,* who was an Officer subject to the Civill State; yet after the Empire was divided, and dissolved, it was not hard to obtrude upon the people already subject to them, another Title, namely, the Right of St. Peter; not onely to save entire their pretended Power; but also to extend the same over the same Christian Provinces, though no more united in the Empire of Rome. This Benefit of an Universall Monarchy, (considering the desire of men to bear Rule) is a sufficient Presumption, that the Popes that pretended to it, and for a long time enjoyed it, were the Authors of the Doctrine, by which it was obtained; namely, that the Church now on Earth, is the Kingdome of Christ. For that granted, it must be understood, that Christ hath some Lieutenant amongst us, by whom we are to be told what are his Commandements.

[382] After that certain Churches had renounced this universall Power of the Pope, one would expect in reason, that the Civill Soveraigns in all those Churches, should have recovered so much of it, as (before they had unadvisedly let it goe) was their own Right, and in their own hands. And in England it was so in effect; saving that they, by whom the Kings administred the Government of Religion, by maintaining their imployment to be in Gods Right, seemed to usurp, if not a Supremacy, yet an Independency on the Civill Power: and they but seemed to usurpe it, in as much as they acknowledged a Right in the King, to deprive them of the Exercise of their Functions at his pleasure.

And maintained also by the Presbytery. But in those places where the Presbytery took that Office, though many other Doctrines of the Church of Rome were forbidden to be taught; yet this Doctrine, that the Kingdome of Christ is already come, and that it began at the Resurrection of our Saviour, was still retained. But *cui bono?* What Profit did they expect from it? The same which the Popes expected: to have a Soveraign Power over the People. For what is it for men to excommunicate their lawful King, but to keep him from all places of Gods publique Service in his own Kingdom? and with force to resist him, when he with force endeavoureth to correct them? Or what is it, without Authority from the Civill Soveraign, to excommunicate any person, but to take from him his Lawfull Liberty, that is, to usurpe an unlawfull Power over their Brethren? The Authors therefore of this Darknesse in Religion, are the Romane, and the Presbyterian Clergy.

Infallibility. To this head, I referre also all those Doctrines, that serve them to keep the possession of this spirituall Soveraignty after it is gotten. As first, that the *Pope in his publique capacity cannot erre.* For who is there, that beleeving this to be true, will not readily obey him in whatsoever he commands?

Subjection of Bishops. Secondly, that all other Bishops, in what Common-wealth soever, have not their Right, neither immediately from God, nor mediately from their Civill Soveraigns, but from the Pope, is a Doctrine, by which there comes to be in every Christian Common-wealth many potent men, (for so are Bishops,) that have their dependance on the Pope, and owe obedience to him, though he be a forraign Prince; by which means he is able, (as he hath done many times) to raise a Civill War against the State that submits not it self to be governed according to his pleasure and Interest.

Thirdly, the exemption of these, and of all other Priests, and of all Monkes, and Fryers, from the Power of the Civill Laws. For by this means, there is a great part of every Common-wealth, that enjoy the benefit of the Laws, and are protected by the Power of the Civill State, which neverthelesse pay no part of the Publique expence; nor are lyable to the penalties, as other Subjects, due to their crimes; and consequently, stand not in fear of any man, but the Pope; and adhere to him onely, to uphold his universall Monarchy. *Exemptions of the Clergy.*

Fourthly, the giving to their Priests (which is no more in the New Testament but Presbyters, that is, Elders) the name of *Sacerdotes*, that is, Sacrificers, which was the title of the Civill Soveraign, and his publique Ministers, amongst the Jews, whilest God was their King. Also, the making the Lords Supper a Sacrifice, serveth to make the People beleeve the Pope hath the same power over all Christians, that Moses and Aaron had over the Jews; that is to say, all Power, both Civill and Ecclesiasticall, as the High Priest then had. *The names of Sacerdotes and Sacrifices.* [383]

Fiftly, the teaching that Matrimony is a Sacrament, giveth to the Clergy the Judging of the lawfulnesse of Marriages; and thereby, of what Children are Legitimate; and consequently, of the Right of Succession to hæreditary Kingdomes. *The Sacramentation of Marriage.*

Sixtly, the Deniall of Marriage to Priests, serveth to assure this Power of the Pope over Kings. For if a King be a Priest, he cannot Marry, and transmit his Kingdome to his Posterity; If he be not a Priest, then the Pope pretendeth this Authority Ecclesiasticall over him, and over his people. *The single life of Priests.*

Seventhly, from Auricular Confession, they obtain, for the assurance of their Power, better intelligence of the designs of Princes, and great persons in the Civill State, than these can have of the designs of the State Ecclesiasticall. *Auricular Confession.*

Eighthly, by the Canonization of Saints, and declaring who are Martyrs, they assure their Power, in that they induce simple men into an obstinacy against the Laws and Commands of their Civill Soveraigns even to death, if by the Popes excommunication, they be declared Heretiques or Enemies to the Church; that is, (as they interpret it,) to the Pope. *Canonization of Saints, and declaring of Martyrs.*

Ninthly, they assure the same, by the Power they ascribe to every Priest, of making Christ; and by the Power of ordaining Pennance; and of Remitting, and Retaining of sins. *Transubstantiation, Pennance, Absolution.*

Tenthly, by the Doctrine of Purgatory, of Justification by externall works, and of Indulgences, the Clergy is enriched. *Purgatory, Indulgences, Externall works.*

Eleventhly, by their Dæmonology, and the use of Exorcisme, and *Dæmonology and Exorcism.*

other things appertaining thereto, they keep (or thinke they keep) the People more in awe of their Power.

School-
Divinity.

Lastly, the Metaphysiques, Ethiques, and Politiques of Aristotle, the frivolous Distinctions, barbarous Terms, and obscure Language of the Schoolmen, taught in the Universities, (which have been all erected and regulated by the Popes Authority,) serve them to keep these Errors from being detected, and to make men mistake the *Ignis fatuus*[1] of Vain Philosophy, for the Light of the Gospell.

The Authors
of spirituall
Darknesse,
who they be.

To these, if they sufficed not, might be added other of their dark Doctrines, the profit whereof redoundeth manifestly, to the setting up of an unlawfull Power over the lawfull Soveraigns of Christian People; or for the sustaining of the same, when it is set up; or to the worldly Riches, Honour, and Authority of those that sustain it. And therefore by the aforesaid rule, of *Cui bono*, we may justly pronounce for the Authors of all this Spirituall Darknesse, the Pope, and Roman Clergy, and all those besides that endeavour to settle in the mindes of men this erroneous Doctrine, that the Church now on Earth, is that Kingdome of God mentioned in the Old and New Testament.

[384]

But the Emperours, and other Christian Soveraigns, under whose Government these Errours, and the like encroachments of Ecclesiastiques upon their Office, at first crept in, to the disturbance of their possessions, and of the tranquillity of their Subjects, though they suffered the same for want of foresight of the Sequel, and of insight into the designs of their Teachers, may neverthelesse bee esteemed accessaries to their own, and the Publique dammage: For without their Authority there could at first no seditious Doctrine have been publiquely preached. I say they might have hindred the same in the beginning: But when the people were once possessed by those spirituall men, there was no humane remedy to be applyed, that any man could invent: And for the remedies that God should provide, who never faileth in his good time to destroy all the Machinations of men against the Truth, wee are to attend his good pleasure, that suffereth many times the prosperity of his enemies, together with their ambition, to grow to such a height, as the violence thereof openeth the eyes, which the warinesse of their predecessours had before sealed up, and makes men by too much grasping let goe all, as Peters net was broken, by the struggling of too great a multitude of Fishes; whereas the Impatience of those, that strive to resist such encroachment, before their Subjects eyes were opened, did but encrease the power they resisted. I doe not therefore blame the Emperour Frederick for holding the stirrop to our countryman Pope Adrian;[2] for such was the disposition of his subjects then, as if hee had not done it, hee was not likely to have succeeded in the Empire: But I blame those, that in the beginning, when their power was entire, by suffering such Doctrines to be forged in the Universities of their own Dominions, have holden the Stirrop to all the succeeding Popes,

1. Fool's fire.
2. Adrian IV, pope from 1154 to 1159, was the only Englishman to be elected to the papacy. In 1155 Adrian compelled Emperor Frederick I to hold his stirrup while he mounted, thus causing the emperor to act as the pope's squire.

whilest they mounted into the Thrones of all Christian Soveraigns, to ride, and tire, both them, and their people, at their pleasure.

But as the Inventions of men are woven, so also are they ravelled out; the way is the same, but the order is inverted: The web begins at the first Elements of Power, which are Wisdom, Humility, Sincerity, and other vertues of the Apostles, whom the people converted, obeyed, out of Reverence, not by Obligation: Their Consciences were free, and their Words and Actions subject to none but the Civill Power. Afterwards the Presbyters (as the Flocks of Christ encreased) assembling to consider what they should teach, and thereby obliging themselves to teach nothing against the Decrees of their Assemblies, made it to be thought the people were thereby obliged to follow their Doctrine, and when they refused, refused to keep them company, (that was then called Excommunication,) not as being Infidels, but as being disobedient: And this was the first knot upon their Liberty. And the number of Presbyters encreasing, the Presbyters of the chief City or Province, got themselves an authority over the Parochiall Presbyters, and appropriated to themselves the names of Bishops: And this was a second knot [385] on Christian Liberty. Lastly, the Bishop of Rome, in regard of the Imperiall City, took upon him an Authority (partly by the wills of the Emperours themselves, and by the title of *Pontifex Maximus*, and at last when the Emperours were grown weak, by the priviledges of St. Peter) over all other Bishops of the Empire: Which was the third and last knot, and the whole *Synthesis* and *Construction* of the Pontificiall Power.

And therefore the *Analysis*, or *Resolution* is by the same way; but beginneth with the knot that was last tyed; as wee may see in the dissolution of the præter-politicall[3] Church Government in England. First, the Power of the Popes was dissolved totally by Queen Elizabeth; and the Bishops, who before exercised their Functions in Right of the Pope, did afterwards exercise the same in Right of the Queen and her Successours; though by retaining the phrase of *Jure Divino*,[4] they were thought to demand it by immediate Right from God: And so was untyed the first knot. After this, the Presbyterians lately in England obtained the putting down of Episcopacy: And so was the second knot dissolved: And almost at the same time, the Power was taken also from the Presbyterians: And so we are reduced to the Independency of the Primitive Christians to follow Paul, or Cephas, or Apollos, every man as he liketh best: Which, if it be without contention, and without measuring the Doctrine of Christ, by our affection to the Person of his Minister, (the fault which the Apostle reprehended in the Corinthians,) is perhaps the best: First, because there ought to be no Power over the Consciences of men, but of the Word it selfe, working Faith in every one, not alwayes according to the purpose of them that Plant and Water, but of God himself, that giveth the Increase: and secondly, because it is unreasonable in them, who teach there is such danger in every little Errour, to require of a man endued with Reason of his own, to follow

3. Extrapolitical.
4. Divine right.

the Reason of any other man, or of the most voices of many other men; Which is little better, then to venture his Salvation at crosse and pile.[5] Nor ought those Teachers to be displeased with this losse of their antient Authority: For there is none should know better then they, that power is preserved by the same Vertues by which it is acquired; that is to say, by Wisdome, Humility, Clearnesse of Doctrine, and sincerity of Conversation; and not by suppression of the Naturall Sciences, and of the Morality of Naturall Reason; nor by obscure Language; nor by Arrogating to themselves more Knowledge than they make appear; nor by Pious Frauds; nor by such other faults, as in the Pastors of Gods Church are not only Faults, but also scandalls, apt to make men stumble one time or other upon the suppression of their Authority.

Comparison of the Papacy with the Kingdome of Fayries.

[386]

But after this Doctrine, *that the Church now Militant, is the Kingdome of God spoken of in the Old and New Testament,* was received in the World; the ambition, and canvasing for the Offices that belong thereunto, and especially for that great Office of being Christs Lieutenant, and the Pompe of them that obtained therein the principall Publique Charges, became by degrees so evident, that they lost the inward Reverence due to the Pastorall Function: in so much as the Wisest men, of them that had any power in the Civill State, needed nothing but the authority of their Princes, to deny them any further Obedience. For, from the time that the Bishop of Rome had gotten to be acknowledged for Bishop Universall, by pretence of Succession to St. Peter, their whole Hierarchy, or Kingdome of Darknesse, may be compared not unfitly to the *Kingdome of Fairies*; that is, to the old wives *Fables* in England, concerning *Ghosts* and *Spirits,* and the feats they play in the night. And if a man consider the originall of this great Ecclesiasticall Dominion, he will easily perceive, that the *Papacy,* is no other, than the *Ghost* of the deceased *Romane Empire,* sitting crowned upon the grave thereof: For so did the Papacy start up on a Sudden out of the Ruines of that Heathen Power.

The *Language* also, which they use, both in the Churches, and in their Publique Acts, being *Latine,* which is not commonly used by any Nation now in the world, what is it but the *Ghost* of the Old *Romane Language?*

The *Fairies* in what Nation soever they converse, have but one Universall King, which some Poets of ours call King *Oberon*;[6] but the Scripture calls *Beelzebub,* Prince of *Dæmons.* The *Ecclesiastiques* likewise, in whose Dominions soever they be found, acknowledge but one Universall King, the *Pope.*

The *Ecclesiastiques* are *Spirituall* men, and *Ghostly* Fathers. The *Fairies* are *Spirits,* and *Ghosts. Fairies* and *Ghosts* inhabite Darknesse, Solitudes, and Graves. The *Ecclesiastiques* walke in Obscurity of Doctrine, in Monasteries, Churches, and Church-yards.

The *Ecclesiastiques* have their Cathedrall Churches; which, in what Towne soever they be erected, by vertue of Holy Water, and certain

---

5. By playing heads or tails, i.e., by the toss of a coin.
6. A king of the fairies in Frankish and German folklore who is also a figure in Shakespeare's *A Midsummer Night's Dream* and in Ben Jonson's *Oberon, the Faery Prince.*

Charmes called Exorcismes, have the power to make those Townes, Cities, that is to say, Seats of Empire. The *Fairies* also have their enchanted Castles, and certain Gigantique Ghosts, that domineer over the Regions round about them.

The *Fairies* are not to be seized on; and brought to answer for the hurt they do. So also the *Ecclesiastiques* vanish away from the Tribunals of Civill Justice.

The *Ecclesiastiques* take from young men, the use of Reason, by certain Charms compounded of Metaphysiques, and Miracles, and Traditions, and Abused Scripture, whereby they are good for nothing else, but to execute what they command them. The *Fairies* likewise are said to take young Children out of their Cradles, and to change them into Naturall Fools, which Common people do therefore call *Elves*, and are apt to mischief.

In what Shop, or Operatory[7] the Fairies make their Enchantment, the old Wives have not determined. But the Operatories of the *Clergy*, are well enough known to be the Universities, that received their Discipline from Authority Pontificiall.

When the *Fairies* are displeased with any body, they are said to send [387] their Elves, to pinch them. The *Ecclesiastiques*, when they are displeased with any Civill State, make also their Elves, that is, Superstitious, Enchanted Subjects, to pinch their Princes, by preaching Sedition; or one Prince enchanted with promises, to pinch another.

The *Fairies* marry not; but there be amongst them *Incubi*, that have copulation with flesh and bloud. The *Priests* also marry not.

The *Ecclesiastiques* take the Cream of the Land, by Donations of ignorant men, that stand in aw of them, and by Tythes: So also it is in the Fable of *Fairies*, that they enter into the Dairies, and Feast upon the Cream, which they skim from the Milk.

What kind of Money is currant in the Kingdome of *Fairies*, is not recorded in the Story. But the *Ecclesiastiques* in their Receipts accept of the same Money that we doe; though when they are to make any Payment, it is in Canonizations, Indulgences, and Masses.

To this, and such like resemblances between the *Papacy*, and the Kingdome of *Fairies*, may be added this, that as the *Fairies* have no existence, but in the Fancies of ignorant people, rising from the Traditions of old Wives, or old Poets: so the Spirituall Power of the *Pope* (without the bounds of his own Civill Dominion) consisteth onely in the Fear that Seduced people stand in, of their Excommunications; upon hearing of false Miracles, false Traditions, and false Interpretations of the Scripture.

It was not therefore a very difficult matter, for Henry 8. by his Exorcisme; nor for Qu. Elizabeth by hers, to cast them out. But who knows that this Spirit of Rome, now gone out, and walking by Missions through the dry places of China, Japan, and the Indies, that yeeld him little fruit, may not return, or rather an Assembly of Spirits worse than he, enter, and inhabite this clean swept house, and make the End

7. Workshop or laboratory.

thereof worse than the Beginning?[8] For it is not the Romane Clergy onely, that pretends the Kingdome of God to be of this World, and thereby to have a Power therein, distinct from that of the Civill State. And this is all I had a designe to say, concerning the Doctrine of the POLITIQUES. Which when I have reviewed, I shall willingly expose it to the censure of my Countrey.

8. A reference to Matthew 12.43; see above, p. 46.

A Review, and Conclusion

From the contrariety of some of the Naturall Faculties of the Mind, one to another, as also of one Passion to another, and from their reference to Conversation, there has been an argument taken, to inferre an impossibility that any one man should be sufficiently disposed to all sorts of Civill duty. The Severity of Judgment, they say, makes men Censorious, and unapt to pardon the Errours and Infirmities of other men: and on the other side, Celerity of Fancy, makes the thoughts lesse steddy than is necessary, to discern exactly between Right and Wrong. Again, in all Deliberations, and in all Pleadings, the faculty of solid Reasoning, is necessary: for without it, the Resolutions of men are rash, and their Sentences unjust: and yet if there be not powerfull Eloquence, which procureth attention and Consent, the effect of Reason will be little. But these are contrary Faculties; the former being grounded upon principles of Truth; the other upon Opinions already received, true, or false; and upon the Passions and Interests of men, which are different, and mutable.

And amongst the Passions, *Courage*, (by which I mean the Contempt of Wounds, and violent Death) enclineth men to private Revenges, and sometimes to endeavour the unsetling of the Publique Peace: And *Timorousnesse*, many times disposeth to the desertion of the Publique Defence. Both these they say cannot stand together in the same person.

And to consider the contrariety of mens Opinions, and Manners in generall, It is they say, impossible to entertain a constant Civill Amity with all those, with whom the Businesse of the world constrains us to converse: Which Businesse, consisteth almost in nothing else but a perpetuall contention for Honor, Riches, and Authority.

To which I answer, that these are indeed great difficulties, but not Impossibilities: For by Education, and Discipline, they may bee, and are sometimes reconciled. Judgment, and Fancy may have place in the same man; but by turnes; as the end which he aimeth at requireth. As the Israelites in Egypt, were sometimes fastened to their labour of making Bricks, and other times were ranging abroad to gather Straw: So also may the Judgement sometimes be fixed upon one certain Consideration, and the Fancy at another time wandring about the world. So also Reason, and Eloquence, (though not perhaps in the Naturall Sciences, yet in the Morall) may stand very well together. For wheresoever [390] there is place for adorning and preferring of Errour, there is much more place for adorning and preferring of Truth, if they have it to adorn. Nor is there any repugnancy between fearing the Laws, and not fearing a publique Enemy; nor between abstaining from Injury, and pardoning it in others. There is therefore no such Inconsistence of Humane Nature, with Civill Duties, as some think. I have known cleernesse of Judgment, and largenesse of Fancy; strength of Reason, and gracefull Elocution; a Courage for the Warre, and a Fear for the Laws, and all eminently in one man; and that was my most noble and honored friend Mr. *Sidney Godolphin*; who hating no man, nor hated of any, was unfortunately slain in the beginning of the late Civill warre, in the Publique quarrell, by an undiscerned, and an undiscerning hand.

To the Laws of Nature, declared in the 15. Chapter, I would have this added, *That every man is bound by Nature, as much as in him lieth, to protect in Warre, the Authority, by which he is himself protected in time of Peace.* For he that pretendeth a Right of Nature to preserve his owne body, cannot pretend a Right of Nature to destroy him, by whose strength he is preserved: It is a manifest contradiction of himselfe. And though this Law may bee drawn by consequence, from some of those that are there already mentioned; yet the Times require to have it inculcated, and remembred.

And because I find by divers English Books lately printed, that the Civill warres have not yet sufficiently taught men, in what point of time it is, that a Subject becomes obliged to the Conquerour; nor what is Conquest; nor how it comes about, that it obliges men to obey his Laws: Therefore for farther satisfaction of men therein, I say, the point of time, wherein a man becomes subject to a Conquerour, is that point, wherein having liberty to submit to him, he consenteth, either by expresse words, or by other sufficient sign, to be his Subject. When it is that a man hath the liberty to submit, I have shewed before in the end of the 21. Chapter; namely, that for him that hath no obligation to his former Soveraign but that of an ordinary Subject, it is then, when the means of his life is within the Guards and Garrisons of the Enemy; for it is then, that he hath no longer Protection from him, but is protected by the adverse party for his Contribution. Seeing therefore such contribution is every where, as a thing inevitable, (notwithstanding it be an assistance to the Enemy,) esteemed lawfull; a totall Submission, which is but an assistance to the Enemy, cannot be esteemed unlawful. Besides, if a man consider that they who submit, assist the Enemy but with part of their estates, whereas they that refuse, assist him with the whole, there is no reason to call their Submission, or Composition[1] an Assistance; but rather a Detriment to the Enemy. But if a man, besides the obligation of a Subject, hath taken upon him a new obligation of a Souldier, then he hath not the liberty to submit to a new Power, as long as the old one keeps the field, and giveth him means of subsistence, either in his Armies, or Garrisons: for in this case, he cannot [391] complain of want of Protection, and means to live as a Souldier: But when that also failes, a Souldier also may seek his Protection wheresoever he has most hope to have it; and may lawfully submit himself to his new Master. And so much for the Time when he may do it

---

1. Agreement to cease hostilities entered into in the 1640s by many royalist landowners in order to protect their holdings from confiscation; these included the earl of Devonshire (Hobbes's employer) and Francis Godolphin, to whom Hobbes dedicated *Leviathan*.

lawfully, if hee will. If therefore he doe it, he is undoubtedly bound to be a true Subject: For a Contract lawfully made, cannot lawfully be broken.

By this also a man may understand, when it is, that men may be said to be Conquered; and in what the nature of Conquest, and the Right of a Conquerour consisteth: For this Submission is it implyeth them all. Conquest, is not the Victory it self; but the Acquisition by Victory, of a Right, over the persons of men. He therefore that is slain, is Overcome, but not Conquered: He that is taken, and put into prison, or chaines, is not Conquered, though Overcome; for he is still an Enemy, and may save himself if hee can: But he that upon promise of Obedience, hath his Life and Liberty allowed him, is then Conquered, and a Subject; and not before. The Romanes used to say, that their Generall had *Pacified* such a *Province*, that is to say, in English, *Conquered* it; and that the Countrey was *Pacified* by Victory, when the people of it had promised *Imperata facere*, that is, *To doe what the Romane People commanded them*: this was to be Conquered. But this promise may be either expresse, or tacite: Expresse, by Promise: Tacite, by other signes. As for example, a man that hath not been called to make such an expresse Promise, (because he is one whose power perhaps is not considerable;) yet if he live under their Protection openly, hee is understood to submit himselfe to the Government: But if he live there secretly, he is lyable to any thing that may bee done to a Spie, and Enemy of the State. I say not, hee does any Injustice, (for acts of open Hostility bear not that name); but that he may be justly put to death. Likewise, if a man, when his Country is conquered, be out of it, he is not Conquered, nor Subject: but if at his return, he submit to the Government, he is bound to obey it. So that *Conquest* (to define it) is the Acquiring of the Right of Soveraignty by Victory. Which Right, is acquired, in the peoples Submission, by which they contract with the Victor, promising Obedience, for Life and Liberty.

In the 29. Chapter I have set down for one of the causes of the Dissolutions of Common-wealths, their Imperfect Generation, consisting in the want of an Absolute and Arbitrary Legislative Power; for want whereof, the Civill Soveraign is fain to handle the Sword of Justice unconstantly, and as if it were too hot for him to hold: One reason whereof (which I have not there mentioned) is this, That they will all of them justifie the War, by which their Power was at first gotten, and whereon (as they think) their Right dependeth, and not on the Possession. As if, for example, the Right of the Kings of England did depend on the goodnesse of the cause of *William* the Conquerour, and upon their lineall, and directest Descent from him; by which means, there would perhaps be no tie of the Subjects obedience to their Soveraign at this day in all the world: wherein whilest they needlessely think to justifie themselves, they justifie all the successefull Rebellions that Ambition shall at any time raise against them, and their Successors. Therefore I put down for one of the most effectuall seeds of the Death of any State, that the Conquerors require not onely a Submission of mens actions to them for the future, but also an Approbation of all their [392] actions past; when there is scarce a Common-wealth in the world, whose beginnings can in conscience be justified.

And because the name of Tyranny, signifieth nothing more, nor lesse, than the name of Soveraignty, be it in one, or many men, saving that they that use the former word, are understood to bee angry with them they call Tyrants; I think the toleration of a professed hatred of Tyranny, is a Toleration of hatred to Common-wealth in generall, and another evill seed, not differing much from the former. For to the Justification of the Cause of a Conqueror, the Reproach of the Cause of the Conquered, is for the most part necessary: but neither of them necessary for the Obligation of the Conquered. And thus much I have thought fit to say upon the Review of the first and second part of this Discourse.

In the 35. Chapter, I have sufficiently declared[2] out of the Scripture, that in the Common-wealth of the Jewes, God himselfe was made the Soveraign, by Pact with the People; who were therefore called his *Peculiar People,* to distinguish them from the rest of the world, over whom God reigned not by their Consent, but by his own Power: And that in this Kingdome Moses was Gods Lieutenant on Earth; and that it was he that told them what Laws God appointed them to be ruled by. But I have omitted to set down who were the Officers appointed to doe Execution; especially in Capitall Punishments; not then thinking it a matter of so necessary consideration, as I find it since. Wee know that generally in all Common-wealths, the Execution of Corporeall Punishments, was either put upon the Guards, or other Souldiers of the Soveraign Power; or given to those, in whom want of means, contempt of honour, and hardnesse of heart, concurred, to make them sue for such an Office. But amongst the Israelites it was a Positive Law of God their Soveraign, that he that was convicted of a capitall Crime, should be stoned to death by the People; and that the Witnesses should cast the first Stone, and after the Witnesses, then the rest of the People. This was a Law that designed[3] who were to be the Executioners; but not that any one should throw a Stone at him before Conviction and Sentence, where the Congregation was Judge. The Witnesses were neverthelesse to be heard before they proceeded to Execution, unlesse the Fact were committed in the presence of the Congregation it self, or in sight of the lawfull Judges; for then there needed no other Witnesses but the Judges themselves. Neverthelesse, this manner of proceeding being not throughly understood, hath given occasion to a dangerous opinion, that any man may kill another, in some cases, by a Right of Zeal; as if the Executions done upon Offenders in the Kingdome of [393] God in old time, proceeded not from the Soveraign Command, but from the Authority of Private Zeal: which, if we consider the texts that seem to favour it, is quite contrary.

First, where the Levites fell upon the People, that had made and worshipped the Golden Calfe, and slew three thousand of them; it was by the Commandement of Moses, from the mouth of God; as is man-

2. Demonstrated.
3. Designated.

ifest, *Exod.* 32. 27. And when the Son of a woman of Israel had blasphemed God, they that heard it, did not kill him, but brought him before Moses, who put him under custody, till God should give Sentence against him; as appears, *Levit.* 25. II, 12. Again, (*Numbers* 25. 6, 7.) when Phinehas killed Zimri and Cosbi, it was not by right of Private Zeale: Their Crime was committed in the sight of the Assembly; there needed no Witnesse; the Law was known, and he the heir apparent to the Soveraignty; and which is the principall point, the Lawfulnesse of his Act depended wholly upon a subsequent Ratification by Moses, whereof he had no cause to doubt. And this Presumption of a future Ratification, is sometimes necessary to the safety [of] a Commonwealth; as in a sudden Rebellion, any man that can suppresse it by his own Power in the Countrey where it begins, without expresse Law or Commission, may lawfully doe it, and provide to have it Ratified, or Pardoned, whilest it is in doing, or after it is done. Also *Numb.* 35. 30. it is expressely said, *Whosoever shall kill the Murtherer, shall kill him upon the word of Witnesses*: but Witnesses suppose a formall Judicature, and consequently condemn that pretence of *Jus Zelotarum*.[4] The Law of Moses concerning him that enticeth to Idolatry, (that is to say, in the Kingdome of God to a renouncing of his Allegiance (*Deut.* 13. 8.) forbids to conceal him, and commands the Accuser to cause him to be put to death, and to cast the first stone at him; but not to kill him before he be Condemned. And (*Deut.* 17. ver. 4, 5, 6.) the Processe against Idolatry is exactly set down: For God there speaketh to the People, as Judge, and commandeth them, when a man is Accused of Idolatry, to Enquire diligently of the Fact, and finding it true, then to Stone him; but still the hand of the Witnesse throweth the first stone. This is not Private Zeale, but Publique Condemnation. In like manner when a Father hath a rebellious Son, the Law is (*Deut.* 21. 18.) that he shall bring him before the Judges of the Town, and all the people of the Town shall Stone him. Lastly, by pretence of these Laws it was, that St. Steven was Stoned, and not by pretence of Private Zeal: for before hee was carried away to Execution, he had Pleaded his Cause before the High Priest. There is nothing in all this, nor in any other part of the Bible, to countenance Executions by Private Zeal; which being oftentimes but a conjunction of Ignorance and Passion, is against both the Justice and Peace of a Common-wealth.

In the 36. Chapter I have said, that it is not declared in what manner God spake supernaturally to Moses: Not that he spake not to him sometimes by Dreams and Visions, and by a supernaturall Voice, as to other Prophets: For the manner how he spake unto him from the Mercy-Seat, is expressely set down *Numbers* 7. 89. in these words, *From that time forward, when Moses entred into the Tabernacle of the Congregation to speak with God, he heard a Voice which spake unto him from over the Mercy-Seate, which is over the Arke of the Testimony, from between the Cherubins he spake unto him.* But it is not declared in what consisted the præeminence of the manner of Gods speaking to Moses, [394]

4. A right of zealotry.

above that of his speaking to other Prophets, as to Samuel, and to Abraham, to whom he also spake by a Voice, (that is, by Vision) Unlesse the difference consist in the cleernesse of the Vision. For *Face to Face*, and *Mouth to Mouth*, cannot be literally understood of the Infinitenesse, and Incomprehensibility of the Divine Nature.

And as to the whole Doctrine, I see not yet, but the Principles of it are true and proper; and the Ratiocination solid. For I ground the Civill Right of Soveraigns, and both the Duty and Liberty of Subjects, upon the known naturall Inclinations of Mankind, and upon the Articles of the Law of Nature; of which no man, that pretends but reason enough to govern his private family, ought to be ignorant. And for the Power Ecclesiasticall of the same Soveraigns, I ground it on such Texts, as are both evident in themselves, and consonant to the Scope of the whole Scripture. And therefore am perswaded, that he that shall read it with a purpose onely to be informed, shall be informed by it. But for those that by Writing, or Publique Discourse, or by their eminent actions, have already engaged themselves to the maintaining of contrary opinions, they will not bee so easily satisfied. For in such cases, it is naturall for men, at one and the same time, both to proceed in reading, and to lose their attention, in the search of objections to that they had read before: Of which, in a time wherein the interests of men are changed (seeing much of that Doctrine, which serveth to the establishing of a new Government, must needs be contrary to that which conduced to the dissolution of the old,) there cannot choose but be very many.

In that part which treateth of a Christian Common-wealth, there are some new Doctrines, which, it may be, in a State where the contrary were already fully determined, were a fault for a Subject without leave to divulge, as being an usurpation of the place of a Teacher. But in this time, that men call not onely for Peace, but also for Truth, to offer such Doctrines as I think True, and that manifestly tend to Peace and Loyalty, to the consideration of those that are yet in deliberation, is no more, but to offer New Wine, to bee put into New Cask, that both may be preserved together. And I suppose, that then, when Novelty can breed no trouble, nor disorder in a State, men are not generally so much inclined to the reverence of Antiquity, as to preferre Ancient Errors, before New and well proved Truth.

There is nothing I distrust more than my Elocution; which neverthelesse I am confident (excepting the Mischances of the Presse) is not obscure. That I have neglected the Ornament of quoting ancient Poets, Orators, and Philosophers, contrary to the custome of late time, (whether I have done well or ill in it,) proceedeth from my judgment, [395] grounded on many reasons. For first, all Truth of Doctrine dependeth either upon *Reason*, or upon *Scripture*; both which give credit to many, but never receive it from any Writer. Secondly, the matters in question are not of *Fact*, but of *Right*, wherein there is no place for *Witnesses*. There is scarce any of those old Writers, that contradicteth not sometimes both himself, and others; which makes their Testimonies insufficient. Fourthly, such Opinions as are taken onely upon Credit of Antiquity, are not intrinsecally the Judgment of those that cite them, but Words that passe (like gaping) from mouth to mouth. Fiftly, it is many times with a fraudulent Designe that men stick their corrupt Doctrine with the Cloves of other mens Wit. Sixtly, I find not that the Ancients they cite, took it for an Ornament, to doe the like with those that wrote before them. Seventhly, it is an argument of Indigestion; when Greek and Latine Sentences unchewed come up again, as they use to doe, unchanged. Lastly, though I reverence those men of Ancient time, that either have written Truth perspicuously, or set us in a better way to find it out our selves; yet to the Antiquity it self I think nothing due: For if we will reverence the Age, the Present is the Oldest. If the Antiquity of the Writer, I am not sure, that generally they to whom such honor is given, were more Ancient when they wrote, than I am that am Writing: But if it bee well considered, the praise of Ancient Authors, proceeds not from the reverence of the Dead, but from the competition, and mutuall envy of the Living.

To conclude, there is nothing in this whole Discourse, nor in that I writ before of the same Subject in Latine, as far as I can perceive, contrary either to the Word of God, or to good Manners; or [tending][5] to the disturbance of the Publique Tranquillity. Therefore I think it may be profitably printed, and more profitably taught in the Universities, in case they also think so, to whom the judgment of the same belongeth. For seeing the Universities are the Fountains of Civill, and Morall Doctrine, from whence the Preachers, and the Gentry, drawing such water as they find, use to sprinkle the same (both from the Pulpit, and in their Conversation) upon the People, there ought certainly to be great care taken, to have it pure, both from the Venime of Heathen Politicians, and from the Incantation of Deceiving Spirits. And by that means the most men, knowing their Duties, will be the less subject to serve the Ambition of a few discontented persons, in their purposes against the State; and be the lesse grieved with the Contributions necessary for their Peace, and Defence; and the Governours themselves have the lesse cause, to maintain at the Common charge any greater Army, than is necessary to make good the Publique Liberty, against the Invasions and Encroachments of forraign Enemies.

And thus I have brought to an end my Discourse of Civill and Ecclesiasticall Government, occasioned by the disorders of the present time, without partiality, without application,[6] and without other designe, than to set before mens eyes the mutuall Relation between Protection and Obedience; of which the condition of Humane Nature, and the Laws Divine, (both Naturall and Positive) require an inviolable observation. And though in the revolution of States, there can be no very good Constellation for Truths of this nature to be born under, (as having an angry aspect from the dissolvers of an old Government, and seeing but the backs of them that erect a new;) yet I cannot think it will be condemned at this time, either by the Publique Judge of Doctrine, or by any that desires the continuance of Publique Peace. And in this hope I return to my interrupted Speculation of Bodies Naturall; [396]

5. Manuscript version.
6. Obsequiousness.

wherein, (if God give me health to finish it,) I hope the Novelty will as much please, as in the Doctrine of this Artificiall Body it useth to offend. For such Truth, as opposeth no mans profit, nor pleasure, is to all men welcome.

BACKGROUNDS

Hobbes's Life

PIERRE BAYLE

[Pierre Bayle (1647–1706) was a French philosopher famous for his advo-
cacy of religious toleration, for his skepticism, and, above all, for his *Dictionnaire historique et critique,* in which he developed an oblique method
of subversive criticism that became popular in the eighteenth century. The
first edition of his *Dictionary* appeared in 1697. This selection on Hobbes
is from an English translation of the second edition, which appeared in
French in 1702; the translation was published in 1736.]

From the Dictionary Historical and Critical of Mr. Peter Bayle†

HOBBES, (Thomas) one of the greatest genius's of the XVIIth century,
was born at Malmesbury in England the fifth of April 1588. He had
made great progress in the languages, when at fourteen years of age he
was sent to Oxford, where he studied Aristotle's Philosophy five years.
Afterwards he went to William Cavendish, baron of Hardwic, who a
little after was made earl of Devonshire, in order to be governour to
his eldest son. He travelled into France and Italy with his pupil; and
finding that he remembered but little, either of his Greek or Latin, and
that Aristotle's Philosophy, in which he had made a great progress, was
despised by the wisest heads, he applied himself wholly to Literature
when he returned into his own country. Thucydides appearing to him
to be preferable to all the Greek historians, he translated him into
English, and published his translation in the year 1628, in order to
shew the English, in the history of the Athenians, the disorders and
confusions of a democratical government. In the year 1629, he travelled
into France with an English gentleman, in quality of his governour,
and applied himself to the study of the Mathematics during that journey. In the year 1631, he was invited by the countess of Devonshire,
to be tutor to her son, who was thirteen years of age, and three years
after he travelled with him into France and Italy. During his stay at
Paris, he applied himself to the study of Natural Philosophy, and especially to the inquiring into the causes of the sensitive operations of
animals. He daily discoursed with Father Mersennus, upon that subject.
He was recalled into England in the year 1637, but having foreseen

† *The Dictionary Historical and Critical of Mr. Peter Bayle,* second ed. (London: 1736), vol. 3,
   pp. 467–71.

the civil war from the time that he had observed what happened in the first session of the parliament in the year 1640, he sought out an agreeable retreat at Paris, where he might quietly philosophize with Father Mersennus, Gassendus, and some other great men. There he composed his treatise *de Cive*, of which he published only a few copies in the year 1642. He taught Mathematics to the prince of Wales, who was forced to retire into France; and he bestowed all his leisure hours in composing his Leviathan, which he caused to be printed in England in 1651, being still at Paris. Though he had given proofs of his faith according to the rites of the church of England, yet he was made odious to the episcopal party, and with such success as to be ordered to appear no more about the king. This occasioned his return into England, where considering his great merit, he lived but in an obscure manner with the earl of Devonshire. He drew this advantage from his obscure condition, that he had more leisure to compose his book *de Corpore*, and some others. He received great marks of esteem from Charles II at the restoration in 1660. From that time to his death, he applied himself to his studies, and to defend himself against his adversaries, who were very numerous. He retained the use of his understanding till his last sickness, though he had lived more than ninety one years. His long life was constantly that of a perfectly honest man; he loved his country, was faithful to his prince, a good friend, charitable, and obliging: notwithstanding all this, he has passed for an Atheist; but they who have written his life, maintain that he had very orthodox opinions about the nature of God. It has been said also, that he was afraid of apparition and spirits; but they maintain that this is a fable. They honestly confess, that in his youth he was a little given to wine and women; but that nevertheless, he lived a bachelor, that he might not be diverted from his study of Philosophy. He had meditated much more than he had read; and he never cared to collect a great library. He died the fourth of December, 1679, at the earl of Devonshire's, after a sickness of six weeks.

Hobbes's Self-Defense

Leviathan aroused much antagonism after its publication in 1651. Part of the reaction came from royalists who accused Hobbes of disloyalty to the Crown and of having written *Leviathan* in support of Oliver Cromwell's claims to supreme power. Hobbes was also criticized for his idiosyncratic interpretations of Scripture and his claims about religion and the proper relations between church and state. In 1662 John Wallis, professor of Mathematics at Oxford, published a satirical attack on Hobbes entitled *Hobbius heautontimoruminos*. Hobbes immediately replied in a letter about himself written in the third person to Wallis entitled *Considerations upon the Reputation, Loyalty and Manners of T. Hobbes*, which related Hobbes's own account of the motivations for some of his actions and writings. Hobbes was also attacked for some of the mathematical and scientific opinions in his major work of natural philosophy, *De Corpore* (which appeared in 1655), by Wallis and by Seth Ward, the Savilian Professor of Astronomy at Oxford. He replied to these attacks in *Six Lessons to the Savilian Professors of Mathematics*, which was published in 1656 as an appendix to the English translation of *De Corpore*.

From Considerations upon the Reputation, Loyalty and Manners of T. Hobbes†

* * *

When the Parliament sat, that began in April 1640, and was dissolved in May following, and in which many points of the regal power, which were necessary for the peace of the kingdom, and the safety of his Majesty's person, were disputed and denied, Mr. Hobbes wrote a little treatise in English, wherein he did set forth and demonstrate, that the said power and rights were inseparably annexed to the sovereignty; which sovereignty they did not then deny to be in the King; but it seems understood not, or would not understand that inseparability. Of this treatise, though not printed, many gentlemen had copies, which occasioned much talk of the author; and had not his Majesty dissolved the Parliament, it had brought him into danger of his life.

He was the first that had ventured to write in the King's defence; and one, amongst very few, that upon no other ground but knowledge of his duty and principles of equity, without special interest, was in all points perfectly loyal.

† From *The English Works of Thomas Hobbes of Malmesbury*, edited by Sir William Molesworth (London: John Bohn, 1839–45), vol. 4, pp. 414–15, 420–24.

The third of November following, there began a new Parliament, consisting for the greatest part of such men as the people had elected only for their averseness to the King's interest. These proceeded so fiercely in the very beginning, against those that had written or preached in the defence of any part of that power, which they also intended to take away, and in gracing those whom the King had disgraced for sedition, that Mr. Hobbes, doubting how they would use him, went over into France, the first of all that fled, and there continued eleven years, to his damage some thousands of pounds deep. * * *

Being at Paris, he wrote and published his book *De Cive*, in Latin, to the end that all nations which should hear what you and your Con-Covenanters were doing in England, might detest you, which I believe they do; for I know no book more magnified than this is beyond the seas.

When his Majesty, that now is, came to Paris, Mr. Hobbes had the honour to initiate him in the mathematics; but never was so impudent or ignorant as to call, or to think himself the King's tutor, as you, that understand not what that word, out of the University, signifies, do falsely charge him with; or ever to say, that he was one of his Majesty's domestic servants. While upon this occasion he staid about Paris, and had neither encouragement nor desire to return into England, he wrote and published his *Leviathan*, far from the intention either of disadvantage to his Majesty, or to flatter Oliver, who was not made Protector till three or four years after, on purpose to make way for his return. For there is scarce a page in it that does not upbraid both him, and you, and others such as you, with your abominable hypocrisy and villainy.

Nor did he desert his Majesty, as you falsely accuse him, as his Majesty himself knows. Nor was his Majesty, as you unmannerly term it, *in distress*. He had the title, right, and reverence of a King, and maintained his faithful servants with him. It is true that Mr. Hobbes came home, but it was because he would not trust his safety with the French clergy.

* * *

To that other charge, *that he writ his Leviathan in defence of Oliver's title*, he will say, that you in your own conscience know it is false. What was Oliver, when that book came forth? It was in 1650, and Mr. Hobbes returned before 1651. Oliver was then but General under your masters of the Parliament, nor had yet cheated them of their usurped power. For that was not done till two or three years after, in 1653, which neither he nor you could foresee. What title then of Oliver's could he pretend to justify? But you will say, he placed the right of government there, wheresoever should be the strength; and so by consequence he placed it in Oliver. Is that all? Then primarily his *Leviathan* was intended for your masters of the Parliament, because the strength was then in them. Why did they not thank him for it, both they and Oliver in their turns? There, Doctor, you deciphered ill. For it was written in the behalf of those many and faithful servants and subjects of his Majesty, that had taken his part in the war, or otherwise done their utmost endeavour to defend his Majesty's right and person against the rebels: whereby, having no other means of protection, nor, for the most part, of subsistence, they were forced to compound with your masters, and to promise obedience for the saving of their lives and fortunes; which in his book he hath affirmed they might lawfully do, and consequently not lawfully bear arms against the victors. They that had done their utmost endeavour to perform their obligation to the King, had done all that they could be obliged unto; and were consequently at liberty to seek the safety of their lives and livelihood wheresoever, and without treachery. But there is nothing in that book to justify the submission of you, or such as you, to the Parliament, after the King's being driven from them, or to Oliver; for you were the King's enemies, and cannot pretend want of that protection which you yourselves refused, denied, fought against, and destroyed. If a man owe you money, and you by robbing him, or other injury, disable him to pay you, the fault is your own; nor needs this exception, *unless the creditor rob him*, be put into the condition of the bond. Protection and obedience are relative. He that says a man may submit to an enemy for want of protection, can never be construed, but that he meant it of the obedient. But let us consider his words, when he puts for a law of nature, (vol. iii. p. 703) *that every man is bound, as much as in him lieth, to protect in war the authority by which he is himself protected in time of peace;* which I think is no ungodly or unreasonable principle. For confirmation of it, he defines in what point of time it is, that a subject becomes obliged to obey an unjust conqueror; and defines it thus: *it is that point wherein having liberty to submit to the conqueror, he consenteth either by express words, or by other sufficient signs, to be his subject.*

I cannot see, Doctor, how a man can be at liberty to submit to his new, that has not first done all he could for his old master: nor if he have done all he could, why that liberty should be refused him. If a man be taken by the Turk, and brought by terror to fight against his former master, I see how he may be killed for it as an enemy, but not as a criminal; nor can I see how he that hath liberty to submit, can at the same time be bound not to submit.

But you will say, perhaps, that he defines the time of that liberty to the advantage of Oliver, in that he says, that *for an ordinary subject, it is then, when the means of his life are within the guards and garrisons of the enemy; for it is then, that he hath no protection but from the enemy for his contribution.* It was not necessary for him to explain it to men of so great understanding, as you and other his enemies pretend to be, by putting in the exception, *unless they came into those guards and garrisons by their own treason.* Do you think that Oliver's party, for their submission to Oliver, could pretend the want of that protection?

The words therefore by themselves, without that exception, do signify no more than this; *that whosoever had done as much as in him did lie, to protect the King in war, had liberty afterwards to provide themselves of such protection as they could get;* which to those whose means of life were within the guards and garrisons of Oliver, was Oliver's protection.

Do you think, when a battle is lost, and you at the mercy of an enemy, it is unlawful to receive quarter with condition of obedience? Or if you receive it on that condition, do you think it honesty to break promise, and treacherously murder him that gave you your life? If that were good doctrine, he were a foolish enemy that would give quarter to any man.

You see, then, that this submission to Oliver, or to your then masters, is allowed by Mr. Hobbes his doctrine only to the King's faithful party, and not to any that fought against him, howsoever they coloured it, by saying they fought for the King and Parliament; nor to any that writ or preached against his cause, or encouraged his adversaries; nor to any that betrayed his counsels, or that intercepted or deciphered any letters of his, or of his officers, or of any of his party; nor to any that by any way had contributed to the diminution of his Majesty's power, ecclesiastical or civil; nor does it absolve any of them from their allegiance. You that make it so heinous a crime for a man to save himself from violent death, by a forced submission to a usurper, should have considered what crime it was to submit voluntarily to the usurping Parliament.

I can tell you besides, why those words were put into his last chapter, which he calls the review. It happened at that time that there were many honourable persons, that having been faithful and unblemished servants to the King, and soldiers in his army, had their estates then sequestered; of whom some were fled, but the fortunes of them all were at the mercy, not of Oliver, but of the Parliament. Some of these were admitted to composition, some not. They that compounded, though they helped the Parliament less by their composition, than they should have done, if they had stood out, by their confiscation, yet they were ill-spoken of, especially by those that had no estates to lose, nor hope to compound. And it was for this that he added to what he had written before, this caution, that if they would compound, they were to do it *bona fide,* without intention of treachery. Wherein he justified their submission by their former obedience, and present necessity; but condemned treachery.

*   *   *

From Six Lessons for the Savilian Professors in Oxford†

*   *   *

In your *Vindiciæ Academiarum,* you put for boasting, that in my *Leviathan,* page 331, I would have *that book by entire sovereignty imposed upon the Universities;* and in my *Review,* p. 713, that I say of my *Leviathan, "I think it may be profitably printed, and more profitably*

---

† From *The English Works of Thomas Hobbes of Malmesbury,* edited by Sir William Molesworth (London: John Bohn, 1839–45), vol. 7, pp. 335–36.

taught in the University." The cause of my writing that book, was the consideration of what the ministers before, and in the beginning of, the civil war, by their preaching and writing did contribute thereunto. Which I saw not only to tend to the abatement of the then civil power, but also to the gaining of as much thereof as they could (as did afterwards more plainly appear) unto themselves. I saw also that those ministers, and many other gentlemen who were of their opinion, brought their doctrines against the civil power from their studies in the Universities. Seeing therefore that so much as could be contributed to the peace of our country, and the settlement of sovereign power without any army, must proceed from teaching; I had reason to wish, that civil doctrine were truly taught in the Universities. And if I had not thought that mine was such, I had never written it. And having written it, if I had not recommended it to such as had the power to cause it to be taught, I had written it to no purpose. To me therefore that never did write anything in philosophy to show my wit, but, as I thought at least, to benefit some part or other of mankind, it was very necessary to commend my doctrine to such men as should have the power and right to regulate the Universities. I say my doctrine; I say not my *Leviathan.* For wiser men may so digest the same doctrine as to fit it better for a public teaching. But as it is, I believe it hath framed the minds of a thousand gentlemen to a conscientious obedience to present government, which otherwise would have wavered in that point. This therefore was no vaunting, but a necessary part of the business I took in hand.

*   *   *

Reactions to Hobbes

SIR ROBERT FILMER

[Filmer (1588–1653) was an English absolutist best known since the late seventeenth century for his *Patriarcha*, a defense of absolutism that was written long before *Leviathan* and probably before the beginnings of civil war in England in 1642, though the work was first published in 1680. His *Observations concerning the Originall of Government*, criticizing Hobbes, Milton, and Grotius was published in 1652.]

From Observations Concerning the Originall of Government, Upon Mr Hobs *Leviathan*†

The Preface

With no small content I read Mr Hobbes' book *De Cive*, and his *Leviathan*, about the rights of sovereignty, which no man, that I know, hath so amply and judiciously handled. I consent with him about the rights of exercising government, but I cannot agree to his means of acquiring it. It may seem strange I should praise his building and yet mislike his foundation, but so it is. His *jus naturae* [right of nature] and his *regnum institutivum* [kingdom by institution] will not down with me, they appear full of contradiction and impossibilities. A few short notes about them I here offer, wishing he would consider whether his building would not stand firmer upon the principles of *regnum patrimoniale* [a paternal kingdom], as he calls it, both according to Scripture and reason — since he confesseth the 'father being before the institution of a commonwealth' was originally an 'absolute sovereign' 'with power of life and death', and that 'a great family, as to the rights of sovereignty is a little monarchy'.[1] If, according to the order of nature, he had handled paternal government before that by institution, there would have been little liberty left in the subjects of the family to consent to institution of government.

In his pleading the cause of the people he arms them with a very large commission of array, which is a right in nature for every man to war against every man when he please, and also a right for all the people to govern. This latter point, although he affirm in words, yet by consequence he denies, as to me it seemeth.

---

† From *Patriarcha and Other Writings*, edited by Johann P. Sommerville (Cambridge: Cambridge UP, 1991), pp. 184–95. Reprinted with the permission of Cambridge University Press.
1. *Leviathan*, chs. 30, 20.

He saith a representative may be of all or but of a part of the people.[2] If it be of all, he terms it a democracy, which is the government of the people. But how can such a commonwealth be generated? For if every man covenant with every man, who shall be left to be the representative? If all must be representatives, who will remain to covenant? For he that is sovereign makes no covenant by his doctrine. It is not all that will come together that makes the democracy, but all that have power by covenant. Thus his democracy by institution fails.

The same may be said of a democracy by acquisition. For if all be conquerors, who shall covenant for life and liberty? And if all be not conquerors, how can it be a democracy by conquest?

A paternal democracy I am confident he will not affirm, so that in conclusion the poor people are deprived of their government, if there can be no democracy by his principles.

Next, if a representative aristocratical of a part of the people be free from covenanting, then that whole assembly (call it what you will) though it be never so great, is in the state of nature, and every one of that assembly hath a right not only to kill any of the subjects that they meet with in the streets, but also they all have a natural right to cut one another's throats even while they sit together in council, by his principles. In this miserable condition of war is his representative aristocratical by institution.

A commonwealth by conquest, he teacheth, 'is then acquired when the vanquished, to avoid present death, covenanteth that so long as his life and the liberty of his body is allowed him, the victor shall have the use of it at his pleasure'.[3] Here I would know how the liberty of the vanquished can be allowed if the victor have the use of it at pleasure, or how is it possible for the victor to perform his covenant, except he could always stand by every particular man to protect his life and liberty?

In his 'review and conclusion' he resolves that 'an ordinary subject hath liberty to submit when the means of his life is within the guards and garrisons of the enemy'.[4] It seems hereby that the rights of sovereignty by institution may be forfeited, for the subject cannot be at liberty to submit to a conqueror, except his former subjection be forfeited for want of protection.

If his conqueror be in the state of nature when he conquers, he hath a right without any covenant made with the conquered. If conquest be defined to be acquiring of right of sovereignty by victory, why is it said the right is acquired in the people's submission, by which they contract with the victor, promising obedience for life and liberty?[5] Hath not every one in the state of nature a right to sovereignty, before conquest, which only puts him in possession of his right?

If his conqueror be not in the state of nature, but a subject by covenant, how can he get a right of sovereignty by conquest when neither

2. *Leviathan*, ch. 18.
3. *Leviathan*, ch. 20.
4. *Leviathan*, "A Review, and Conclusion."
5. *Leviathan*, ch. 20.

he himself hath right to conquer, nor subjects a liberty to submit — since a former contract lawfully made cannot lawfully be broken by them?

I wish the title of the book had not been of a commonwealth, but of a weal public, or commonweal, which is the true word carefully observed by our translator of Bodin *De Republica* into English. Many ignorant men are apt by the name of commonwealth to understand a popular government, wherein wealth and all things shall be common, tending to the levelling community in the state of pure nature.

Observations on Mr Hobbes' Leviathan: or His Artificial Man a Commonwealth

I

If God created only Adam and of a piece of him made the woman, and if by generation from them two as parts of them all mankind be propagated; if also God gave to Adam not only the dominion over the woman and the children that should issue from them, but also over the whole earth to subdue it, and over all the creatures on it, so that as long as Adam lived no man could claim or enjoy anything but by donation, assignation or permission from him; I wonder how the *right of nature* can be imagined by Mr Hobbes, which, he saith, is a liberty for 'each man to use his own power as he will himself for preservation of his own life'; 'a condition of war of everyone against everyone'; 'a right of every man to everything, even to one another's body' (ch. 14), especially since himself affirms 'that originally the father of every man was also his sovereign lord with power over him of life and death' (ch. 30).

II

Mr Hobbes confesseth he believes 'it was never generally so', that there was such a *jus naturae* [right of nature] (ch. 13); and if not generally, then not at all, for one exception bars all if he mark it well. Whereas he imagines such a 'right of nature' may be now practised in America, he confesseth a government there of families, which government how 'small' or 'brutish' soever (as he calls it) is sufficient to destroy his *jus naturale*.

III

I cannot understand how this 'right of nature' can be conceived without imagining a company of men at the very first to have been all created together without any dependency one of another, or as 'mushrooms *(fungorum more)* they all on a sudden were sprung out of the earth without any obligation one to another' as Mr Hobbes' words are in his book *De Cive*, chapter 8, section 1; when the Scripture teacheth us otherwise, that all men came by succession and generation from one man. We must not deny the truth of the history of the creation.

IV

It is not to be thought that God would create man in a condition worse than any beasts, as if he made men to no other end by nature but to destroy one another. A right for the father to destroy his children or eat them, and for the children to do the like by their parents, is worse than cannibals. This horrid condition of mere nature when Mr Hobbes was charged with, his refuge was to answer 'that no son can be understood to be in the state of nature' (*De Cive* chapter 1, section 10) — which is all one with denying his own principle. For if men be not free-born, it is not possible for him to assign and prove any other time for them to claim a right of nature to liberty, if not at their birth.

V

But if it be allowed (which is yet most false) that a company of men were at first without a common power to keep them in awe, I do not see why such a condition must be called a state of war of all men against all men. Indeed if such a multitude of men should be created as the earth could not well nourish, there might be cause for men to destroy one another rather than perish for want of food. But God was no such niggard in the creation, and there being plenty of sustenance and room for all men, there is no cause or use of war till men be hindered in the preservation of life, so that there is no absolute necessity of war in the state of pure nature. It is the right of nature for every man to live in peace, that so he may tend the preservation of his life, which whilst he is in actual war he cannot do. War of itself as it is war preserves no man's life, it only helps to preserve and obtain the means to live. If every man tend the right of preserving life, which may be done in peace, there is no cause of war.

VI

But admit the state of nature were the state of war, let us see what help Mr Hobbes hath for it. It is a principle of his that 'the law of nature is a rule found out by reason' (I do think it is given by God), forbidding a man 'to do that which is destructive to his life, and to omit that by which he thinks it may be best preserved' (ch. 14). If the right of nature be a liberty for a man to do anything he thinks fit to preserve his life, then in the first place nature must teach him that life is to be preserved, and so consequently forbids to do that which may destroy or take away the means of life, or to omit that by which it may be preserved — and thus the right of nature and the law of nature will be all one. For I think Mr Hobbes will not say the right of nature is a liberty for a man to destroy his own life. The law of nature might better have been said to consist in a command to preserve or not to omit the means of preserving life, than in a prohibition to destroy, or to omit it.

VII

Another principle I meet with, 'If other men will not lay down their right as well as he, then there is no reason for any one to divest himself of his' (ch. 14). Hence it follows that if all the men in the world do not agree, no commonwealth can be established. It is a thing impossible for all the men in the world every man with every man to covenant to lay down their right. Nay it is not possible in the smallest kingdom, though all men should spend their whole lives in nothing else but in running up and down to covenant.

VIII

Right may be laid aside but not transferred: for 'he that renounceth or passeth away his right, giveth not to any other man a right which he had not before', and reserves a right in himself against all those with whom he doth not covenant (ch. 14).

IX

The only way to erect a common power, or a commonwealth, is for men to confer all their power and strength upon one man, or one assembly of men, that may reduce all their wills by plurality of voices to one will; which is to appoint one man or an assembly of men to bear their person, to submit their wills to his will. This is a real unity of them all in one person, made by covenant of every man with every man as if every man should say to every man, I authorise, and give up my right of governing myself to this man, or this assembly of men, on this condition, that thou give up thy right to him, and authorise all his actions. This done, the multitude so united in one person, is called a commonwealth. (ch. 17)

To authorise and give up his right of governing himself, to confer all his power and strength, and to submit his will to another, is to lay down his right of resisting. For if right of nature be a liberty to use power for preservation of life, laying down of that power must be a relinquishing of power to preserve or defend life, otherwise a man relinquisheth nothing.

To reduce all the wills of an assembly by plurality of voices to one will, is not a proper speech, for it is not a plurality but a totality of voices which makes an assembly be of one will — otherwise it is but the one will of a major part of the assembly. The negative voice of any one hinders the being of the one will of the assembly. There is nothing more destructive to the true nature of a lawful assembly than to allow a major part to prevail when the whole only hath right.

For a man to give up his right to one that never covenants to protect is great folly, since it is neither 'in consideration of some right reciprocally transferred to himself', nor can he hope for any other good by standing out of the way, that the other may enjoy his own original right without hindrance from him, by reason of so much diminution of impediments (ch. 14).

* * *

XIII

I cannot but wonder Mr Hobbes should say 'the consent of a subject to sovereign power is contained in these words, "I authorize and do take upon me all his actions", in which there is no restriction at all of his own former natural liberty' (ch. 21). Surely here Mr Hobbes forgot himself, for before he makes the resignation to go in these words also, I 'give up my right of governing myself to this man' (ch. 17). This is a restriction certainly of his own former natural liberty when he gives it away. And if a man allow his sovereign to kill him — which Mr Hobbes seems to confess — how can he reserve a right to defend himself? And if a man have a power and right to kill himself, he doth not authorise and give up his right to his sovereign, if he do not obey him when he commands him to kill himself.

XIV

Mr Hobbes saith 'No man is bound by the words' of his submission

> to kill himself or any other man, and consequently that the obligation a man may sometimes have upon the command of the sovereign to execute any dangerous or dishonourable office, dependeth not on the words of our submission but on the intention which is to be understood by the end thereof. When therefore our refusal to obey frustrates the end for which the sovereignty was ordained, then there is no liberty to refuse; otherwise there is. (ch. 21)

If no man be bound by the words of his subjection to kill any other man, then a sovereign may be denied the benefit of war, and be rendered unable to defend his people — and so the end of government frustrated. If the obligation upon the commands of a sovereign to execute a dangerous or dishonourable office dependeth not on the words of our submission but on the intention, which is to be understood by the end thereof, no man, by Mr Hobbes' rules, is bound but by the words of his *submission*; the intention of the *command* binds not, if the words do not. If the intention should bind, it is necessary the sovereign must discover it, and the people must dispute and judge it — which how well it may consist with the rights of sovereignty, Mr Hobbes may consider. Whereas Mr Hobbes saith the intention is to be understood by the ends, I take it he means the end by effect, for the end and the intention are one and the same thing. And if he mean the effect, the obedience must go before, and not depend on the understanding of the effect, which can never be if the obedience do not precede it. In fine, he resolves refusal to obey may depend upon the judging of what frustrates the end of sovereignty, and what not, of which he cannot mean any other judge but the people.

XV

Mr Hobbes puts a case by way of question:

> A great many men together have already resisted the sovereign power unjustly, or committed some capital crime, for which every one of them expecteth death: whether have they not the liberty then to join together and assist and defend one another? Certainly they have, for they but defend their lives, which the guilty man may as well do as the innocent. There was indeed injustice in the first breach of their duty. Their bearing of arms subsequent to it, though it be to maintain what they have done, is no new unjust act, and if it be only to defend their persons it is not unjust at all. (ch. 21)

The only reason here alleged for the bearing of arms is this, that it is no new unjust act—as if the beginning only of a rebellion were an unjust act, and the continuance of it none at all. No better answer can be given to this case than what the author himself hath delivered in the beginning of the same paragraph in these words: 'To resist the sword of the commonwealth in defense of another man, guilty or innocent, no man hath liberty, because such liberty takes away from the sovereign the means of protecting us, and is therefore destructive of the very essence of government'. Thus he first answers the question, and then afterwards makes it, and gives it a contrary answer. Other passages I meet with to the like purpose. He saith 'a man cannot lay down the right of resisting them that assault him by force to take away his life; the same may be said of wounds, chains and imprisonment' (ch. 14); 'A covenant [not] to defend myself from force by force is void'; right of defending life and means of living can never be abandoned (ch. 14).

These last doctrines are destructive to all government whatsoever, and even to the *Leviathan* itself. Hereby any rogue or villain may murder his sovereign, if the sovereign but offer by force to whip or lay him in the stocks, since whipping may be said to be a wounding, and putting in the stocks an imprisonment. So likewise every man's goods being a means of living, if a man cannot abandon them, no contract among men, be it never so just, can be observed. Thus we are at least in as miserable a condition of war as Mr Hobbes at first by nature found us.

*   *   *

JAMES HARRINGTON

[Harrington (1611–1677) was an English political philosopher best known for *The Commonwealth of Oceana*, a treatise first published in 1656, which contains many proposals that had an impact on the formation of the American republic. *The Prerogative of Popular Government* was published in 1658.]

From The Prerogative of Popular Government†

* * *

Nor, seeing I am gone so far, doth this at all imply free will, but (as is admirably observed by Mr Hobbes)[1] the freedom of that which naturally precedes will, namely deliberation or debate, in which, as the scale by the weight of reason or passion comes to be turned one way or other, the will is caused and, being caused, necessitated. When God cometh thus in upon the soul of man, he gives both the will and the deed; from which like office of the senate in a commonwealth — that is, from the excellency of their deliberation and debate which, prudently and faithfully unfolded unto the people, doth also frequently cause and necessitate both the will and the deed — God himself hath said of the senate that *they are gods*; an expression, though divine, yet not unknown to the heathens (*homo homini deus*; one man for the excellency of his aid may be a god unto another). * * *

For the things I have of this kind, as also for what I have said upon the words *chirotonia* and *ecclesia*, the Prevaricator is delighted to make me 'beholding underhand unto Mr Hobbes, notwithstanding the open enmity which he saith I profess to his politics.' * * * It is true I have opposed the politics of Mr Hobbes, to show him what he taught me, with as much disdain as he opposed those of the greatest authors, in whose wholesome fame and doctrine the good of mankind being concerned, my conscience bears me witness that I have done my duty. Nevertheless in most other things I firmly believe that Mr Hobbes is, and will in future ages be accounted, the best writer at this day in the world; and for his treatises of human nature, and of liberty and necessity, they are the greatest of new lights, and those which I have followed and shall follow.

BISHOP BRAMHALL

[John Bramhall (1594–1663) was made bishop of Derry, Ireland, in 1634. A royalist, he fled to England in 1641 and later spent years in exile in France, Germany, and the Netherlands before the Restoration in 1660. During this period he met Hobbes and argued with him about free will. In 1658 he published a lengthy attack on Hobbes's views about this subject, to which Hobbes replied with a lengthy treatise of his own. Bramhall's *The Catching of* Leviathan, *or the Great Whale* also appeared in 1658.]

---

† From *The Political Works of James Harrington,* edited by J. G. A. Pocock (Cambridge: Cambridge UP, 1977), pp. 422–23. Reprinted with the permission of Cambridge University Press.
1. *Leviathan,* chs. 6, 21.

From The Catching of *Leviathan*†

Thus destructive are his principles to the publick peace and tranquility of the World, but much more pernicious to the Commonwealth it self. He did prudently to deny that virtue did consist in a mean, for he himself doth never observe a mean. All his bolts fly over or under, but at the right mark it is in vain to expect him. Sometimes he fancieth an omnipotence in Kings, sometimes he strippeth them of their just rights. Perhaps he thinketh that it may fall out in politicks, as it doth sometimes in physick, *Bina venena invant*, Two contrary poysons may become a Cordial to the Common-wealth. I will begin with his defects, where he attributeth too little to Regal power.

First he teacheth, that no man is bound to go to warfare in person, except he do voluntarily undertake it. *A man that is commanded as a Souldier to fight against the enemy, may neverthelesse in many cases refuse without injustice.*[1] Of these many cases, he setteth down onely two. First, *when he substituteth a sufficient souldier in his place, for in this case he deserteth not the service of the Common-wealth.* Secondly, *there is allowance to be made for natural timorousnesse, or men of feminine courage.* This might passe as a municipal law, to exempt some persons at some time in some places. But to extend it to all persons, places and times, is absurd, and repugnant to his own grounds, who teacheth that *justice and injustice do depend upon the command of the Soveraign,* that *whatsoever he commandeth, he maketh lawful and just by commanding it.* His two cases are two great impertinencies, and belong to the Soveraign to do, or not to do as Graces, *who so is timerous or fearful, let him depart,* not to the Subjects as right. He forgetteth how often he hath denied all knowledge of good and evill to Subjects, and subjected their will absolutely to the will of the Soveraign, *The Soveraign may use every mans strength and wealth at his pleasure.* His acknowledgement that the Soveraign hath *right enough to punish his refusal with death,* is to no purpose. The question is not whether his refusal be punishable or not, but whether it be just or not. Upon his principles a Soveraign may *justly enough* put the most innocent Subject in the World to death, as we shall see presently. And his exception *when the defence of the Common-wealth requireth at once the help of all that are able to bear armes,* is no answer to the other case, and it self a case never like to happen. He must be *a mortall god* indeed, that can bring all the hands in a Kingdome to fight at one battle.

Another of his principles is this, *Security is the end for which men make themselves subjects to others, which if it be not enjoyed no man is understood to have subjected himself to others, or to have lost his right to defend himself at his own discretion. Neither is any man understood to have bound himself to any thing, or to have relinquished his right over all things, before his own security be provided for.* What ugly consequences do flow from this paradox, and what a large window it openeth

† From *The Catching of* Leviathan, *or the Great Whale* (London: John Crook, 1658), pp. 511–21, 542.
1. *Leviathan,* ch. 21.

to sedition and rebellion, I leave to the readers judgement. Either it must be left to the soveraign determination, whether the subjects security be sufficiently provided for, And then in vain is any mans sentence expected against himself, or to the discretion of the subject, (as the words themselves do seem to import,) and then there need no other bellowes to kindle the fire of a civill war, and put a whole commonwealth into a combustion, but this seditious Article.

We see the present condition of Europe what it is, that most soveraignes have subjects of a different communion from themselves, and are necessitated to tolerate different rites, for fear least whilst they are plucking up the tares, they should eradicate the wheat. And he that should advise them to do otherwise, did advise them to put all into fire and flame. Now hear this mercifull and peaceable Author, *It is manifest that they do against conscience, and with, as much as is in them, the eternall destruction of their subjects, who do not cause such doctrine and such worship, to be taught and exhibited to their subjects, as they themselves do believe to conduce to their eternall salvation, or tolerate the contrary to be taught and exhibited.* Did this man write waking or dreaming.

And howsoever in words he denie all resistance to the soveraign, yet indeed he admitteth it. *No man is bound by his pacts what soever they be, not to resist him, who bringeth upon him death or wounds, or other bodily dammage.* (by this learning the Scholler if he be able, may take the rod out of his masters hand, and whip him) It followeth: *Seeing therefore no man is bound to that which is impossible, they who are to suffer death or wounds or rather corporall dammage, and are not constant enough to endure them, are not obliged to suffer them.* And more fully: *In case a great many men together have already resisted the soveraign power unjustly, or committed some capitall crime, for which every one of them expecteth death, whether have they not the liberty to join together, and assist and defend one another? certainly they have, for they do but defend their lives, which the guilty man may as well do, as the innocent. There was indeed injustice in the first breach of their duty. Their bearing of armes subsequent to it, though it be to maintain what they have done, is no new unjust act.*[2] Why should we not change the name of *Leviathan* into the *Rebells catechism?* Observe the difference between the primitive spirit, and the Hobbian spirit. The Thebæan Legion of known valour in a good cause, when they were able to resist, did chuse rather to be cut in pieces to a man, than defend themselves against their Emperour by armes, because they would rather die innocent, than live nocent. But T. H. alloweth Rebells and conspirators to make good their unlawful attempts by armes: was there ever such a trumpetter of rebellion heard of before? perhaps he may say that he alloweth them not to justify their unlawfull acts, but to defend themselves. First this is contrary to himself, for he alloweth them *to maintain what they had unjustly done.* This is too much and too intolerable, but this is not all. Secondly, If they chance to win the field who must suffer for their faults? or who dare thenceforward call their Acts unlawfull?

2. *Leviathan*, ch. 21.

Will you hear what a casuist he is? *And for the other instance of attaining soveraignty by rebellion, it is manifest that though the event follow, yet because it cannot reasonably be expected; but rather the contrary, and because by gaining it so, others are taught to gain the same in like manner, the attempt thereof is against reason.*[3] And had he no other reasons indeed against horrid Rebellion but these two? It seemeth he accounteth conscience or the bird in the breast to be but an Idoll of the brain. And the Kingdome of heaven (as he hath made it) not valuable enough to be ballanced against an earthly Kingdome. And as for hell he hath expounded it and all the infernall fiends out of the nature of things, otherwise he could not have wanted better arguments against such a crying sin.

Another of his theorems is, that *no man is obliged by any pacts, to accuse himself.* Which in some cases is true, but in his sense, and in his latitude, and upon his grounds it is most untrue. When publick fame hath accused a man before hand, he may be called upon to purge himself or suffer. When the case is of publick concernment, and the circumstances pregnant, all nations do take the liberty to examine a man upon oath in his own cause, and where the safety and welfare of the commonwealth is concerned, as in cases of high treason, and for the more full discovery of conspiracies, upon the rack. Which they could not do lawfully if no man was bound in any case to discover himself. His reason is silly, *For in vain do we make him promise, who when he hath performed we know not whether he have performed or not.* And makes as much against all examination of witnesses as delinquents. *In vain do we make them give testimony, who when they have testified, we know not whether they have given right testimony or not.*

But his next conclusion will uncase him fully, and shew us what manner of man he is, *If the commonwealth come into the power of its enemies, so that they cannot be resisted, he who had the soveraignty before, is understood to have lost it.* What enemies he meaneth, such as have the just power of the sword, or such as have not, what he meaneth by the commonwealth the whole Kingdome, or any part of it, what he intendeth by *cannot be resisted,* whether a prevalence for want of forces to resist them, or a victory in a set battle, or a finall conquest, And what he meaneth by *losing the soveraignty,* losing it *de facto,* or *de jure,* losing the possession only, or losing the right also, he is silent. It may be because he knoweth not the difference, *Qui pauca confiderat facile pronuntiat,* He that considers little, giveth sentence more easily than truly, we must search out his sense some where else. *The obligation of subjects to the soveraign is understood to last as long, and no longer, than the power lasteth by which he is able to protect them, &c.* Wheresoever *a man seeth protection either in his own or in anothers sword, nature applieth his obedience to it, and his endeavour to maintain it.*[4] By his leave this is right dogs play, which alwais take part with the stronger side. But yet this is generall.

The next is more particular, *when in a war forreign or intestine the enemies get a final victory so as the forces of the commonwealth keeping*

---

3. *Leviathan*, ch. 15.
4. *Leviathan*, ch. 21.

the field no longer, there is no farther protection of subjects in their loyalty, then is the commonwealth dissolved, and every man at liberty to protect himself, by such courses as his own discretion shall suggest unto him. Yet these words final victory are doubtful. When Davids forces were chased out of the Kingdome, so that he was not able to protect his subjects in their loyalty, could this be called a final victory?

The next place is home, He who hath no obligation to his former soveraign, but that of an ordinary subject hath liberty to submit to a Conqueror, when the meanes of his life is within the guards and garrisons of the enemy, for it is then that he hath no longer protection from him, [his soveraign] but is protected by the adverse party for his contribution.[5] And he concludeth that a totall submission is as lawfull as a contribution. Which is contrary to the sense of all the world. If a lawful soveraign did give a generall release to his subject, as well as he giveth him licence to contribute, he said something. And to top up all these disloyall paradoxes he addeth, That they who live under the protection of a Conqueror openly, are understood to submit themselves to the government. And that in the very act of receiving protection openly, and not renouncing it openly, they do oblige themselves to obey the laws of their protector, to which in receiving protection they have assented.

Where these Principles prevaile, adieu honour, and honesty, and fidelity, and loyalty: all must give place to self-interest. What for a man to deserte his Soveraign upon the first prevalence of an enemy, or the first payment of a petty contribution, or the first apparence of a sword, that is more able to protect us for the present? Is this his great law of nature, pactis standum, to stand to what we have obliged ourselves? Then Kings from whom all mens right and property is derived, should not have so much right themselves in their own inheritance as the meanest subject. It seemeth T. H. did take his Soveraign for better, but not for worse. Faire fall those old Roman spirits who gave thanks to Terentius Varro, after he had lost the great battle of Cannæ by his own default, because he did not despair of the Common-wealth. And would not sell the ground that Hannibal was encamped upon, one farthing cheaper than if it had been in time of peace, which was one thing that discouraged that great Captain from continuing the siege of Rome.

His former discourse hath as many faults as lines. First all Soveraignty is not from the people. He himself acknowledgeth, That fatherly Empire or Power was instituted by God in the Creation, and was Monarchical. Secondly, where the application of Soveraign power to the person is from the people, yet there are other ends besides protection. Thirdly, protection is not a condition, though it be a duty. A failing in duty doth not cancel a right. Fourthly, protection ought to be mutual. The subject ought to defend his King, as well as the King his subject. If the King be disabled to protect his subject, by the subjects own fault, because he did not assist him as he ought, this doth not warrant the subject to seek protection elsewhere. Fifthly, he doth not distinguish beween a just Conqueror who hath the power of the sword, though he abuse it,

5. Leviathan, ch. 31.

and him that hath no power at all. I will try if he can remember whose words these are; *They that have already instituted a Common-wealth, being thereby bound by covenant to own the actions and judgements of one, cannot lawfully make a new covenant among themselves to be obedient to any other, in any thing whatsoever without his permission. And therefore they that are subjects to a Monarch, cannot without his leave cast off Monarchy, nor transfer their person from him that beareth it, to another man.*[6] This is home both for right and obligation.

Sixthly, there are other requisites to the extinction of the right of a Prince, and the obligation of a subject, than the present prevalence or conquest of an enemy. Seventhly, nature doth not dictate to a subject to violate his oaths and allegiance, by using his endeavours to maintain protection wheresoever he seeth it, either in his own sword or another mans. Eightly, total submission is not as lawful as contribution. Ninthly, actual submission doth not take away the Soveraigns right, or the subjects obligation. Tenthly, to live under the command or protection of a Conqueror doth not necessarily imply allegiance. Lastly, much lesse doth it imply an assent to all his laws, and an obligation to obey them.

*   *   *

Thus after the view of his Religion, we have likewise surveighed his Politicks, as full of black ugly dismal rocks as the former, dictated with the same magisteral authority; A man may judge them to be twins upon the fist cast of his eye. It was Solomons advise, *Remove not the ancient land-marks which thy fathers have set.* But T. H. taketh a pride in removing all ancient land-marks, between Prince and subject, Father and child, Husband and Wife, Master and servant, Man and Man. Nilus after a great overflowing, doth not leave such a confusion after it as he doth, nor an hog in a garden of herbs. I wish he would have turned probationer a while, and made trial of his new form of government first in his own house, before he had gone about to obtrude it upon the Commonwealth.

EDWARD HYDE

[Edward Hyde, 1st earl of Clarendon (1609–1674), was a statesman who, as lord chancellor under Charles II after the restoration of the Stuart monarchy in 1660, presided over the settlement of issues that had pervaded the political atmosphere in England during the previous twenty years of civil war and rule by Parliament and Cromwell. He was friendly with Hobbes, with whom, before the outbreak of civil war in 1642, he shared several friends; but the two became estranged after Hobbes's political writings began to appear. Clarendon fell from power in 1667 and, though he always professed loyalty to his king, spent the rest of his life in exile. His *Brief View and Survey of the Dangerous and Pernicious Errors to Church and States in Mr. Hobbes's Book, Entitled* Leviathan was written in the last years of his life and published posthumously in 1676.]

6. *Leviathan,* ch. 17.

From A Brief View and Survey of the Dangerous and Pernicious Errors to Church and State in . . . Leviathan†

Introduction

I have alwaies thought it a great excess in those who take upon them to answer other Mens Writings, to hold themselves oblig'd to find fault with every thing that they say, and to answer every clause, period, and proposition which he, to whom they have made themselves an adversary, hath laid down; by which, besides the voluminousness that it produces, which in it self is grievous to any Reader, they cannot but be guilty of many impertinences, and expose themselves to the just censures of others, and to the advantage of their Antagonists; since there are few Books which do not contain many things which are true, and cannot, or need not be contradicted. And considering withall, that those Books have in all times don most mischief, and scatter'd abroad, the most pernicious errors, in which the Authors, by the Ornament of their Style, and the pleasantness of their method, and subtlety of their Wit, have from specious premises, drawn their unskilful, and unwary Readers into unwarrantable opinions and conclusions, being intoxicated with terms and Allegorical expressions, which puzzel their understandings, and lead them into perplexities, from whence they cannot disentangle themselves; I have proposed to my self, to make some Animadversions upon such particulars, as may in my judgment produce much mischief in the World, in a Book of great Name, and which is entertain'd and celebrated (at least enough) in the World; a Book which contains in it good learning of all kinds, politely extracted, and very wittily and cunningly disgested, in a very commendable method, and in a vigorous and pleasant Style: which hath prevailed over too many, to swallow many new tenets as maximes without chewing; which manner of diet for the indisgestion of Mr *Hobbes* himself doth much dislike. The thorough novelty (to which the present age, if every any, is too much inclin'd) of the work receives great credit and authority from the known Name of the Author, a Man of excellent parts, of great wit, some reading, and somewhat more thinking; One who has spent many years in forreign parts and observation, understands the Learned as well as modern Languages, hath long had the reputation of a great Philosopher and Mathematician, and in his age hath had conversation with very many worthy and extraordinary Men, to which, it may be, if he had bin more indulgent in the more vigorous part of his life, it might have had a greater influence upon the temper of his mind, whereas age seldom submits to those questions, enquiries, and contradictions, which the Laws and liberty of conversation require: and it hath bin alwaies a lamentation amongst Mr *Hobbes* his Friends, that he spent too much time in thinking, and too little in exercising those thoughts in the com-

---

† From A *Brief View and Survey of the Dangerous and Pernicious Errors to Church and State in Mr. Hobbes's Book, Entitled* Leviathan (London, 1676), pp. 1–3, 5, 9–10, 26–41, 80–94, 195–99, 299–300, 316–17.

pany of other Men of the same, or of as good faculties; for want whereof his natural constitution, with age, contracted such a morosity, that doubting and contradicting Men were never grateful to him. In a word, Mr *Hobbes* is one of the most antient acquaintance I have in the World, and of whom I have alwaies had a great esteem, as a Man who besides his eminent parts of Learning and knowledg, hath bin alwaies looked upon as a Man of Probity, and a life free from scandal; and it may be there are few Men now alive, who have bin longer known to him then I have bin in a fair and friendly conversation and sociableness; and I had the honor to introduce those, in whose perfections he seemed to take much delight, and whose memory he seems most to extol, first into his acquaintance. * * * His Person is by many received with respect, and his Books continue still to be esteem'd, as well abroad as at home: which might very well have prevail'd, with those before mention'd arguments, to have diverted me from pretending to see farther into them then other Men had don, and to discover a malignity undiscerned that should make them odious. But then how prevalent soever these motives were with me; when I reflected upon the most mischievous Principles, and most destructive to the Peace both of Church and State, which are scatter'd throughout that Book of his *Leviathan*, (which I only take upon me to discover) and the unhappy impression they have made in the minds of too many; I thought my self the more oblig'd, and not the less competent for those animadversions, by the part I had acted for many years in the public administration of Justice, and in the Policy of the Kingdom. And the leasure to which God hath condemn'd me, seems an invitation, and obligation upon me, to give a testimony to the World, that my duty and affection for my King and Country, is not less then it hath ever bin, when it was better interpreted, by giving warning to both, of the danger they are in by the seditious Principles of this Book, that they may in time provide for their Security by their abolishing and extirpating those, and the like excesses.

*   *   *

I hope nothing hath fallen from my Pen, which implies the least undervaluing of Mr. *Hobbes* his Person, or his Parts. But if he, to advance his opinion in Policy, too imperiously reproches all men who do not consent to his Doctrine, it can hardly be avoided, to reprehend so great presumption, and to make his Doctrines appear as odious, as they ought to be esteemed: and when he shakes the Principles of Christian Religion, by his new and bold Interpretations of Scripture, a man can hardly avoid saying, He hath no Religion, or that He is no good Christian; and escape endeavouring to manifest, and expose the poison that lies hid and conceled. Yet I have chosen, rather to pass by many of his enormous sayings with light expressions, to make his Assertions ridiculous, then to make his Person odious, for infusing such destructive Doctrine into the minds of men, who are already too licentious in judging the Precepts, or observing the Practice of Christianity.

.   *   *   *

The Survey of Chapters 13, 14, 15, 16

The thirteenth, fourteenth, fifteenth, and sixteenth Chapters, will require a little more disquisition, since under the pretence of examining, or rather (according to his Prerogative) of determining what the natural condition of mankind is, he takes many things for granted which are not true; as (ch. 12) that *Nature hath made all men equal in the faculties of body and mind*, and imputes that to the Nature of Man in general, which is but the infirmity of some particular Men; and by a mist of words, under the notion of explaning common terms (the meaning whereof is understood by all Men, and which his explanation leaves less intelligible then they were before) he dazles Mens eies from discerning those Fallacies upon which he raises his Structure, and which he reserves for his second part. And whosoever looks narrowly to his preparatory Assertions, shall find such contradictions, as must destroy the foundation of all his new Doctrine in Government, of which some particulars shall be mentioned anon. So that if his Maxims of one kind were marshalled together, collected out of these four Chapters, and applied to his other Maxims which are to support his whole *Leviathan*, the one would be a sufficient answer to the other; and so many inconsistencies and absurdities would appear between them, that they could never be thought links of one chain; whereas he desires men should believe all the Propositions in his Book to be a chain of Consequences, without being in any degree wary to avoid palpable contradictions, upon the presumption of his Readers total resignation to his judgment. If it were not so, would any man imagine that a man of Mr. *Hobbes's* sagacity and provoking humor, should in his fourth Page so imperiously reproch the Scholes for absurdity in saying, That *heavy Bodies fall downwards out of an appetite to rest, thereby ascribing knowledg to things inanimate*; and himself should in his sixty second Page, describing the nature of foul weather, say, That *it lieth not in a shower or two of rain, but in an inclination thereto of many daies together*: as if foul weather were not as inaminate a thing as heavy Bodies, and inclination did not imply as much of knowledg as appetite doth. In truth, neither the one or the other word signifies in the before-mention'd instances, more then a natural tendency to motion and alteration.

When God vouchsafed to make man after his own Image, and in his own Likeness, and took so much delight in him, as to give him the command and dominion over all the Inhabitants of the Earth, the Air, and the Sea, it cannot be imagin'd but that at the same time he endued him with Reason, and all the other noble Faculties which were necessary for the administration of that Empire, and the preservation of the several Species which were to succeed the Creation: and therefore to uncreate him to such a baseness and villany in his nature, as to make Man such a Rascal, and more a Beast in his frame and constitution then those he is appointed to govern, is a power that God never gave to the Devil, nor hath any Body assume'd it, till Mr. *Hobbes* took it upon him. Nor can any thing be said more contrary to the Honor and Dignity of God Almighty, then that he should leave his master workmanship, Man, in a condition of War of every man against every man, in such a condition of confusion (ch. 14) *That every man hath a right to every thing, even to one anothers body*; inclin'd to all the malice, force and fraud that may promote his profit or his pleasure, and without any notions of, or instinct towards justice, honor, or good nature, which only makes man-kind superior to the Beasts of the Wilderness. Nor had Mr. *Hobbes* any other reason to degrade him to this degree of Bestiality, but that he may be fit to wear those Chains and Fetters which he hath provided for him. He deprives man of the greatest happiness and glory that can be attributed to him, who devests him of that gentleness and benevolence towards other men, by which he delights in the good fortune, and tranquility that they enjoy, and makes him so far prefer himself before all others, as to make the rest a prey to advance any commodity or conveniency of his own; which is a barbarity superior to what the most savage Beasts are guilty of,

> *— Quando leoni,*
> *Fortier eripuit vitam leo? Quo nemore unquam*
> *Expiravit per majoris dentibus apri?*

Man only, created in the likeness of God himself, is the only creature in the World, that out of the malignity of his own nature, and the base fear that is inseparable from it, is oblig'd for his own benefit, and for the defence of his own right, to worry and destroy all of his own kind, until they all become yoaked by a Covenant and Contract that Mr. *Hobbes* hath provided for them, and which was never yet entred into by any one man, and is in nature impossible to be entred into.

After such positive and magisterial Assertions against the dignity and probity of man-kind, and the honor and providence of God Almighty, the instances and arguments given by him are very unweighty and trivial to conclude the nature of man to be so full of jealousie and malignity, as he would have it believed to be, from that common practice of circumspection and providence, which custom and discretion hath introduced into human life. For men shut their Chests in which their mony is, as well that their servants or children may not know what they have, as that it may be preserved from Thieves; and they lock their doors that their Houses may not be common; and ride arm'd, and in company, because they know that there are ill men, who may be inclined to do injuries if they find an opportunity. Nor is a wariness to prevent the damage and injury that Thieves and Robbers may do to any man, an argument that Mankind is in that mans opinion inclin'd and disposed to commit those out-rages. If it be known that there is one Thief in a City, all men have reason to shut their doors and lock their chests: and if there be two or three Drunkards in a Town, all men have reason to go arm'd in the streets, to controul the violence or indignity they might receive from them. Princes are attended by their Guards in progress, and all their servants arm'd when they hunt, without any apprehension of being assaulted; custom having made it so necessary, that many men are not longer without their Swords then they are without their Doublets, who never were jealous that any man desir'd to hurt them. Nor will the instance he gives of the inhabitants in *America*, be more to his purpose then the rest, since, as far as we have any knowledg of them, the savage People there live under a most intire subjection and slavery to their several Princes; who indeed for the most part live in hostility towards each other, upon those contentions which engage all other Princes in War, and which Mr. *Hobbes* allows to be a just cause of War, jealousie of each others Power to do them harm. And these are the notable instances by which Mr. *Hobbes* hath by his painful disquisition and investigation, in the hidden and deep secrets of Nature, discover'd that unworthy fear and jealousie to be inherent in mankind, (ch. 13) *That the notions of right and wrong have no place, but Force and Fraud are the two cardinal Virtues; that there is no propriety, no dominion, no mine or thine distinct, but only that to be every mans that he can get, and for so long as he can keep it,* and this struggle to continue, till he submits to the servitude to which he hath design'd him for his comfort and security.

* * * He is very much offended with *Aristotle*, for saying in the first Book of his Politics, That by Nature some are fit to command and others to serve; which he saies, (ch. 15) is not only against reason, but also against experience, for *there are very few so foolish that had not rather govern themselves, then be governed by others.* Which Proposition doth not contradict any thing said by *Aristotle*, the Question being, Whether Nature hath made some men worthier, not whether it hath made all others so modest as to compose; and would have required a more serious Disquisition, since it is no more then is imputed to Horses, and other Beasts, whereof men find by experience, that some by nature are fitter for nobler uses, and others for vile, and to be only Beasts of burden. But indeed, he had the less need of reason to refute him, when he had a Law at hand to controul him, which he saies, is the Law of Nature, (ch. 15) *That every man must acknowledg every other man for his equal by nature;* which may be true as to the essentials of human Nature, and yet there may be inequality enough as to a capacity of Government. * * * And 'tis very true, that *Aristotle* did believe, that Divine Providence doth shew and demonstrate who are fit and proper for low and vile offices, not only by very notable defects in their understandings, incapable of any cultivation, but by some eminent deformity of the body (tho that doth not always hold) which makes them unfit to bear rule. And without doubt, the observation of all Ages since that time hath contributed very much to that Conclusion which Mr. *Hobbes* so much derides, of Inequality by nature, and that Nature it self hath a bounty which she extends to some men in a much superior degree then she doth to others. Which is not contradicted by seeing many great defects and indigencies of Nature in some men, wonderfully corrected and repair'd by industry, education, and above all, by conversation; nor by seeing some early blossoms in others, which raise a great expectation of rare perfection, that suddainly decay, and insensibly wither away by not being cherished and improved by diligence, or rather by being blasted by vice or supine laziness: those accidents may somtimes happen, do not very often, and are necessary to awaken men

out of the Lethargy of depending wholly upon the Wealth of Natures
store, without administring any supply to it, out of their industry and
observation. And every mans experience will afford him abundance of
examples in the number of his own acquaintance, in which, of those
who have alwaies had equal advantages of Education, Conversation,
Industry, and it may be of virtuous Inclinations, it is easie to observe
very different parts and faculties: some of quick apprehension, and as
steady comprehension, wit, judgment, and such a sagacity as discerns
at distance as well as at hand, concluding from what they see will fall
out, what is presently to be don; when others born, and bred with the
same care, wariness, and attention, and with all the visible advantages
and benefits which the other enjoied, remain still of a heavier and a
duller alloy, less discerning to contrive and fore-see, less vigorous to
execute, and in a word, of a very different Classis to all purposes; which
can proceed from no other cause, but the distinction that Nature her
self made between them, in the distribution of those Faculties to the
one with a more liberal hand then to the other.

*   *   *

But where are those Maxims to be found which Mr. *Hobbes* declares,
and publishes to be the Laws of Nature, in any other Author before
him? That is only properly call'd the Law of Nature, that is dictated to
the whole Species: as, to defend a mans self from violence, and to repel
force by force; not all that results upon prudential motives unto the
mind of such as have bin cultivated by Learning and Education, which
no doubt can compile such a Body of Laws, as would make all other
useless, except such as should provide for the execution of, and obedience to those. For under what other notion can that reasonable Conclusion, which is a necessary part of the Law of Nations, be call'd the
Law of Nature, which is his fifteenth Law, (ch. 15) *That all men that
mediate Peace be allow'd safe conduct?* And of this kind much of the
Body of his Law of Nature is compil'd; which I should not dislike, the
Style being in some sense not improper, but that I observe that from
some of these Conclusions which he pronounces to be (ch. 15) *immutable, and eternal as the Laws of Nature,* he makes deductions and
inferences to controul Opinions he dislikes, and to obtain Concessions
which are not right, by amuzing men with his method, and confound-
ing rather then informing their understandings, by a chime of words
in definitions and pleasant instances, which seem not easie to be contradicted, and yet infer much more then upon a review can be deduc'd
from them. And it is an unanswerable evidence of the irresistible force
and strength of Truth and Reason, that whil'st men are making war
against it with all their power and stratagems, somwhat doth still start
up out of the dictates and confessions of the Adversary that determines
the Controversie, and vindicates the Truth from the malice that would
oppress it. How should it else come to pass, that Mr. *Hobbes,* whil'st
he is demolishing the whole frame of Nature for want of order to support it, and makes it unavoidably necessary for every man to cut his
neighbors throat, to kill him who is weaker then himself, and to cir-

cumvent, and by any fraud destroy him who is stronger, in all which there is no injustice, because Nature hath not otherwise provided for every particular mans security; I say, how comes it to pass, that at the same time when he is possessed of this frenzy, he would in the same, and the next Chapter, set down such a Body of Laws prescribed by Nature it self, as are *immutable and eternal?* that there appears, by his own shewing, a full remedy against all that confusion, for avoiding whereof he hath devis'd all that unnatural and impossible Contract and Covenant? If the Law of the Gospel, *Whatsoever you require that others should do to you, that do ye to them,* be the Law, of all men, as he saies it is (ch. 14) that is, the Law of Nature; *Naturâ, id est jure gentium,* saies *Tully,* it being nothing else but *quod naturalis ratio inter omnes homines constituit;* If it be the Law of Nature that every man strive to accommodate himself to the rest, as he saies it is (ch. 15) and *that no man by deed, word, countenance or gesture, declare hatred or contemt of another;* If all men are bound by the Law of Nature, (ch. 15) *That they that are at controversie submit their right to the judgment of an arbitrator,* as he saies they are: If Nature hath thus providently provided for the Peace and Tranquillity of her Children, by Laws immutable & eternal, that are written in their hearts: how come they to fall into that condition of war, as to be every one against every one, and to be without any other cardinal Virtues, but of force and fraud? It is a wonderful thing, that a man should be so sharp-sighted, as to discern mankind so well inclosed and fortified by the wisdom of Nature, and so blind as to think him in a more secure estate by his transferring of right to another man, which yet he confesses is impossible intirely to transfer; and by Covenents and Contracts of his own devising, and which he acknowledges to be void in part, and in other parts impossible to be perform'd.

But I say, if in truth Nature hath dictated all those excellent Conclusions to every man, without which they cannot be called the Laws of Nature; and if it hath farther instituted all those Duties which are contain'd in the Second Table, all which he saies were the Laws of Nature: I know not what temtation or authority he could have, to pronounce mankind to be left by Nature in that distracted condition of war, except he prefer the authority of *Ovids Metamorphosis,* of the sowing of *Cadmus's* teeth, before any other Scripture, Divine or Humane. And it is as strange, that by his Covenants and Contracts which he is so wary in wording (as if he were the Secretary of Nature) that they may blind that man fast enough whom he pleases to assign to those Bonds; and as if he were the Plenipotentiary of Nature too, to bind and to loose all he thinks fit: he hath so ill provided for the Peace he would establish, that he hath left a door open for all the Confusion he would avoid, when, notwithstanding that he hath made them divest themselves of the liberty they have by Nature, and transfer all this into the hands of a single Person, who thereby is so absolute Soveraign, that he may take their Lives and their Estates from them without any act of Injustice, yet after all this transferring and devesting, every man reserves a right (as unalienable) to defend his own life, even against the sentence of Justice. What greater contradiction can there be to the Peace, which he would establish upon those unreasonable conditions, then this Liberty, which he saies can never be abandoned, and which yet may dissolve that peace every day? and yet he saies, (ch. 14) *This is granted to be true by all men, in that they lead Criminals to execution and prison with armed men, notwithstanding such Criminals have consented to the Law by which they are condemned.* Which indeed is an argument, that men had rather escape then be hanged; but no more an argument that they have a right to rescue themselves, then the fashion of wearing Swords is an argument that men are afraid of having their throats cut by the malice of their neighbors: both which, are arguments no man would urge to men, whose understandings he did not much undervalue. * * * I shall only conclude this, with an observation which the place seems to require, of the defect in Mr. *Hobbes's* Logic, which is a great presumption, that from very true Propositions he deduces very erroneous and absurd Conclusions. That no man hath power to transfer the right over his own life to the disposal of another man, is a very true Proposition, from whence he infers, that he hath reserved the power and disposal of it to himself, and therefore that he may defend it by force even against the judgment of Law and Justice: whereas the natural consequence of that Proposition is, That therefore such transferring and covenanting (being void) cannot provide for the peace and security of a Commonwealth. Without doubt, no man is *Dominus vitae suae*, and therefore cannot give that to another, which he hath not in himself. God only hath reserv'd that absolute Dominion and Power of life and death to Himself, and by his putting the Sword into the hand of the Supreme Magistrate, hath qualified and enabled him to execute that Justice which is necessary for the peace and preservation of his People, which may seem in a manner to be provided for by Mr. *Hobbes's* Law of Nature, if what he saies be true, (ch. 14) *That right to the end containeth right to the means.* And this sole Proposition, that men cannot dispose of their own lives, hath bin alwaies held as a manifest and undeniable Argument, that Soveraigns never had, nor can have their Power from the People.

* * *

The Survey of Chapter 21

Mr. *Hobbes* is so great an enemy to freedom, that he will not allow Man that which God hath given him, the Freedom of his Will; but he shall not entangle me in that Argument, which he hath enough exercis'd himself in with a more equal Adversary, who I think hath bin much too hard for him at his own weapon, Reason, the Learned Bishop of *Derry*, who was afterwards Arch-Bishop of *Armagh*, and by which he hath put him into greater choler then a Philosopher ought to subject himself to, the terrible strokes whereof I am not willing to undergo, and therefore shall keep my self close to that freedom and liberty only that is due to Subjects, and of which, his business in this Chapter, is to deprive them totally.

A man would have expected from Mr. *Hobbes's* Inventory of the several rights and powers of his Soveraign in his eighteenth Chapter, of which one was to prescribe Rules (ch. 18) *whereby every man might know what goods he may enjoy, and what actions he might do, without being molested by any of his fellow Subjects*, which he saies, *Men call Propriety*, that some such Rule should be established as might secure that Propriety, how little soever: but he hath now better explain'd himself, and finds, that Liberty and Property are only fences against the Invasion or force of fellow Subjects, but towards the Soveraign of no use or signification at all. No man hath a Propriety in any thing, that can restrain the King from taking it from him, and the liberty of a Subject (ch. 21) *lieth only in those things, which in regulating their actions, the Soveraign hath pretermitted such as is the liberty to buy and sell, and otherwise contract with one another; to chuse their own abode, their own diet, their own trade of life, and to institute their children as they think fit, and the like.* I wonder he did not insert the liberty to wear his Clothes of that fashion which he likes best, which is as important as most of his other Concessions. And yet he seems to be jealous, that even this liberty should make men imagine, that the Soveraign power should be in any degree limited, or than any thing he can do to a Subject, and upon what pretence soever, may be called injustice or injury, the contrary whereof he saies he hath shewed already; for he takes it as granted, that all that he hath said he hath proved * * * But I wonder more, that he doth not discern what every other man cannot but discern, that by his so liberal taking away, he hath not left the Subject any thing to enjoy even of those narrow concessions which he hath made to him. For how can any man believe that he hath liberty to buy and sell, when the Soveraign power can presently take away what he hath sold, from him who hath bought it, and consequently no man can sell or buy to any purpose? Who can say that he can chuse his own abode, or his own trade of life, or anything, when as soon as he hath chosen either, he shall be requir'd to go to a place where he hath no mind to go, and to do somwhat he would not chuse to do? for his person is no more at his own disposal then his goods are; so that he may as graciously retain to himself all that he hath granted.

Whether the Soveraign Power or the Liberty of the Subject receive the greater injury and prejudice by this brief state and description he makes of the no-liberty, that is, the portion he leaves to the Subject, would be a great question, if he had not bin pleas'd himself to determine, that his Subject (for God forbid that any other Prince should have such a Subject) is not capable of an injury; by which the whole mischief is like to fall upon the Soveraign. And what greater mischief and ruine can threaten the greatest Prince, then that their Subjects should believe, that all the liberty they have, consists only in those things which the Soveraign hath hitherto pretermitted, that is, which he hath not yet taken from them, but when he pleases in regulating their actions to determine the contrary, they shall then have neither liberty to buy or sell, nor to contract with each other, to chuse their own abode, their own diet, their own trade of life, or to breed their own children; and to make their misery compleat, and their life as little their own as the rest, that nothing the Soveraign can do to his subject, on what pretence soever, as well in order to the taking away his Life as his Estate, can be called injustice or injury; I say, what greater insecurity can any Prince be in or under, then to depend upon such Subjects? And alas! what security to himself or them can the Sword in his hand be, if no other hand be lift up on his behalf, or the Swords in all other hands be directed against him, that he may not cut off their heads when he hath a mind to it? And it is not Mr. *Hobbes's* autority that will make it believ'd, that he who desires more liberty, demands an exemtion from all Laws, by which all other men may be masters of their lives; and that every Subject is author of every act the Soveraign doth, upon the extravagant supposition of a consent that never was given; and if it were possible to have bin given, must have bin void at the instant it was given, by Mr. *Hobbes's* own rules, as shall be made out in its place. He himself confesses and saies it is evident to the meanest of capacities, that *mens actions are deriv'd from the opinions they have of the good and evil which from those actions redound unto themselves, and consequently men that are once possessed of an opinion that their obedience to the Soveraign power will be more hurtful to them then their disobedience, will disobey the Laws, and thereby over-throw the Common-wealth, and introduce confusion and civil War, for the avoiding whereof, all civil Government was ordained.* If this be true, (as there is no reason to believe it to be) is it possible that any man can believe, that the People, for we speak not of convincing the Philosophers and the Mathematicians, but of the general affections of the People, which must dispose them to obedience, that they can be perswaded by a long train of Consequences, from the nature of man, and the end of Government, and the institution thereof by Contracts and Covenants, of which they never heard, to believe that it is best for them to continue in the same nakedness in which they were created, for fear their clothes may be stoln from them, and that they have parted with their liberty to save their lives? There is no question, but of all calamities the calamity of War is greatest, and the rage and uncharitableness of civil War most formidable of all War. Indeed forreign War seldom destroies a Nation without domestic Combinations and Conspiracies, which makes a complication with civil War; and sure nothing can more inevitably produce that, then an universal opinion in the People, that their Soveraign can take from them all they have whenever he hath a mind to it, and their lives too, without any injustice, and consequently that their obedience to him will be more hurtful to them then their disobedience; so well hath he provided for the security of his Soveraign, if his doctrine were believ'd.

* * *

It is a very hard matter for an Architect in State and Policy, who doth despise all Precedents, and will not observe any Rules of practice, to make such a model of Government as will be in any degree pleasant to the Governor, or governed, or secure for either; which Mr. *Hobbes* finds, and tho he takes a liberty to raise his Model upon a supposition of a very formal Contract, that never was, or ever can be in nature, and hath the drawing and preparing his own form of Contract, is forc'd to allow such a latitude in obedience to his subject, as shakes the very pillars of his Government. And therefore, tho he be contented that by the words of his Contract, (ch. 21) *Kill me, and my fellow if you please,* the absolute power of all mens lives shall be submitted to the disposal of the Governors will and pleasure, without being oblig'd to observe any rules of Justice and Equity; yet he will not admit into his Contract the other words, (ch. 21) *I will kill my self, or my fellow,* and therefore that he is not bound by the command of his Soveraign to execute any dangerous or dishonorable office; but in such cases, men are not to resort so much to the words of the submission, as to the intention: which Distinction surely may be as applicable to all that monstrous autority which he gives his Governor to take away the Lives and Estates of his Subjects, without any cause or reason, upon an imaginary Contract, which if never so real, can never be supposed to be with the intention of the Contractor in such cases. And the subtle Distinctions he finds out to excuse Subjects from yielding obedience to their Soveraigns, and the Prerogative he grants to fear, for a whole Army to run away from the Enemy without the guilt of treachery or injustice, leaves us some hope, that he will at last allow such a liberty to Subjects, that they may not in an instant be swallowed up by the prodigious power which he pleases to grant to his Soveraign. And truly, he degrades him very dis-honorably, when he obliges him to be the Hang-man himself, of all those Malefactors, which by the Law are condemn'd to die; for he gives every man autority, without the violation of his duty, or swerving from the rules of Justice, absolutely to refuse to perform that office. Nor hath he provided much better for his security, then he hath for his honor, when he allows it lawful for any number of men, (ch. 21) *who have rebelled against the Soveraign, or committed some capital crime, for which every one of them expects death, then to join together, and defend each other, because they do but defend their lives, which the guilty man,* he saies, *may do as well as the innocent.* And surely, no man can legally take his life from him who may lawfully defend it; and then the murderer, or any other person gulty of a capital Crime, is more innocent, and in a better condition then the Executioner of Justice, who may be justly murdered in the just execution of his office. And it is a very childish security that he provides for his Soveraign against this Rebellion, and defence of themselves against the power of the Law, (ch. 21) that he declares *it to be lawful only for the defence of their lives, and that upon the offer of pardon for themselves, that self-defence is unlawful:* as if a body that is lawfully drawn together, with strength enough to defend their lives against the power of the Law, are like to disband and lay down their Arms, without other benefit and advantage then only of the saving of their lives. But tho he be so cruel as to devest his Subjects of all that liberty, which the best and most peaceable men desire to possess, yet he liberally and bountifully confers upon them such a liberty as no honest man can pretend to, and which is utterly inconsistent with the security of Prince and People; which unreasonable Indulgence of his cannot but be thought to proceed from an unlawful affection to those who he saw had power enough to defend the transcendent wickedness they had committed, tho they were without an Advocate to make it lawful for them to do so, till he took that office upon him in his *Leviathan*, as is evident by the instance he gives in the next Paragraph, that he thinks it lawful for every man to have as many wives as he pleases, if the King will break the silence of the Law, and declare that he may do so; which is a Prerogative he vouchsafes to grant to the Soveraign, to balance that liberty he gave to the Subject to defend himself and his companion against him, and is the only power that may inable him to be too hard for the other.

* * *

But that this Supreme Soveraign, whom he hath invested with the whole property and liberty of all his Subjects, and so invested him in it, that he hath not power to part with any of it by promise, or donation, or release, may not be too much exalted with his own greatness, he hath humbled him sufficiently, by giving his Subjects leave to withdraw their obedience from him when he hath most need of their assistance, for *the* (ch. 21) *obligation of Subjects to the Soveraign is understood (he saies) to last as long, and no longer, then the power lasts to protect them.* So that as soon as any Town, City, or Province of any Princes Dominions, is invaded by a Forreign Enemy, or possessed by a Rebellious Subject, that the Prince for the present cannot suppress the power of the one, or the other, the people may lawfully resort to those who are over them, and for their Protection perform all the Offices and duties of good Subjects to them, (ch. 21) *For the right men have by nature to protect themselves when none else can protect them, can by no covenant be relinquish'd, and the end of obedience is protection, which wherever a man seeth it either in his own, or in an others sword, nature applieth his obedience to it, and his endeavours to maintain it.* And truly it is no wonder if they do so, and that Subjects take the first opportunity to free themselves from such a Soveraign as he hath given them, and chuse a better for themselves. Whereas the duty of Subjects is, and all good Subjects believe they owe, another kind of duty and obedience to their Soveraign, then to withdraw their subjection because he is oppress'd; and will prefer poverty, and death it self, before they will renounce their obedience to their natural Prince, or do any thing that may advance the service of his Enemies. And since Mr. *Hobbes* gives so ill a testimony of his Government (which, by the severe conditions he would oblige mankind to submit to for the support of it, ought to be firm, and not to be shaken) (ch. 21) *that it is in its own nature not only subject to violent death by forreign war, but also from the ignorance, and passion of men, that it hath in it from the very institution many seeds of natural mortality by intestine discord,* worse then which he cannot say of any Government, we may very reasonably prefer the Government we have, and under which we have enjoi'd much happiness, before his which we do not know, nor any body hath had experience of, and which by his own confession is liable to all the accidents of mortality which any others have bin; and reject his that promises so ill, and exercises all the action of War in Peace, and when War comes, is liable to all the misfortunes which can possibly attend or invade it?

Whether the relation of Subjects be extinguisht in all those cases, which Mr. *Hobbes* takes upon him to prescribe, as Imprisonment, Banishment, and the like, I leave to those who can instruct him better in the Law of Nations, by which they must be judged, notwithstanding all his Appeals to the Law of Nature; and I presume if a banish'd Person (ch. 21) *during which,* he saies, *he is not subject,* shall join in an action under a Forreign power against his Country, wherein he shall with others be taken prisoner, the others shall be proceeded against as Prisoners of War, when he shall be judg'd as a Traitor and Rebel, which he could not be, if he were not a Subject: and this not only in the case of an hostile action, and open attemt, but of the most secret conspiracy that comes to be discover'd. And if this be true, we may conclude it would be very unsafe to conduct our selves by what Mr. *Hobbes* (ch. 20) *finds by speculation, and deduction of Soveraign rights from the nature, need, and designs of men.* Surely this woful desertion, and defection in the cases above mention'd, which hath bin alwaies held criminal by all Law that hath bin current in any part of the World, receiv'd so much countenance and justification by Mr. *Hobbes* his Book, and more by his conversation, that *Cromwel* found the submission to those principles produc'd a submission to him, and the imaginary relation between Protection and Allegiance so positively proclaim'd by him, prevail'd for many years to extinguish all visible fidelity to the King, whilst he perswaded many to take the Engagement as a thing lawful, and to become Subjects to the Usurper, as to their legitimate Soveraign; of which great service he could not abstain from bragging in a Pamphlet he set forth in that time, that he alone, and his doctrine had prevail'd with many to submit to the Government, who would otherwise have disturb'd the public Peace, that is, to renounce their fidelity to their true Soveraign, and to be faithful to the Usurper.

It appears at last, why by his institution he would have the power, and security of his Soveraign, wholy and only to depend upon the Contracts, and Covenants which the people make one with another, to transfer all their rights to a third person (who shall be Soveraign) without entring into any Covenant with the Soveraign himself, which would have devested them of that liberty to disobey him, which they have reserv'd to themselves; or receiving any Covenant from him, which might have obliged him to have kept his promise to them; by which they might have had somewhat left to them which they might have called their own, which his institution will not bear, all such promises being void. But if he be so tender hearted, as to think himself oblig'd to observe all the promises, and make good all the Grants he hath made, by which he may be disabled to provide for their safety, which is the ground that hath made all those Grants and promises to be void, he hath granted him power to remedy all this, by (ch. 21) *directly renouncing, or transferring the Soveraignty to another: and that he might openly, and in plain terms renounce, or transfer it, he makes no doubt;*

and then he saies, *if a Monarch shall relinquish the Soveraignty both for himself, and his heirs, his subjects return to the absolute liberty of nature. Because tho nature may declare who are his sons, and who are the neerest of his kin, yet it dependeth on his own will who shall be his Heir: and if he will have no Heir, There is no Soveraignty, or Subjection.* This seems the hardest condition for the poor Subject that he can be liable unto, that when he hath devested himself of all the right he had, only for his Soveraigns protection, that he may be redeem'd from the state of War and confusion that nature hath left him in, and hath paid so dear for that protection, it is left still in his Soveraigns power to withdraw that protection from him, to renounce his subjection, and without his consent to transfer the Soveraignty to another, to whom he hath no mind to be subject. One might have imagin'd that this new trick of transferring, and covenanting, had bin an universal remedy, that being once applied would for ever prevent the ill condition and confusion that nature hath left us in, and that such a right would have bin constituted by it, that Soveraignty would never have fail'd to the Worlds end: and that when the subject can never retract, or avoid the bargain he hath made, how ill soever he likes it, or improve it by acquiring any better conditions in it, it shall notwithstanding be in the Soveraigns power without his consent, and it may be without his privity, in an instant to leave him without any protection, without any security, and as a prey to all who are to strong for him. This indeed is the greatest Prerogative that he hath conferr'd upon his Soveraign, when he had given him all that belongs to his Subjects, that when he is weary of Governing, he can destroy them, by leaving them to destroy one another.

* * *

The Survey of Chapters 32, 33, 34

As we had no reason to expect a rational discourse of civil Government and Policy, when the opinion and judgment of all Lawyers were excluded, and all establish'd Laws contradicted, so we may well look for a worse of Christian Politics, when the advice of all Divines is positively protested against, and new notions of Divinity introduc'd, as rules to restrain our conceptions, and to regulate our understandings. And as he hath not deceiv'd us in the former, he will as little disappoint us in the latter. But having taken a brief survey of the dangerous opinions, and determinations in Mr. *Hobbes* his two first parts of his *Leviathan*, concerning the constitution, nature, and right of Soveraigns, and concerning the duty of Subjects, which he confesses *contains doctrine very different from the practice of the greatest part of the world*, and therefore ought to be watched with the more jealousy for the novelty of it; I shall not now accompany him through his remaining two parts in the same method, by taking a view of his presumtion in the interpretation of severall places of Scripture, and making very unnatural deductions from thence to the lessening the dignity of Scripture, and to the reproch of the highest actions don by the greatest Persons by the

immediate command of God himself. For if those marks, and conditions which he makes necessary to a true Prophet, and without which
he ought not to be believed, were necessary, *Moses* was no true Prophet,
nor had the Children of *Israel* any reason to believe, and follow him,
when he would carry them out of *Egypt*; for he concludes from the
Thirteenth Chapter of *Deuteronomy*, and the five first verses thereof,
(ch. 32) *that God will not have miracles alone serve for Argument to
prove the Prophets calling; for the works of the* Egyptian Sorcerers, *tho
not so great as those of* Moses, *yet were great miracles; and that how
great soever the miracles are, yet if the intent be to stir up revolt against
the King, or him that governeth by the Kings Autority, he that doth such
miracles is not to be consider'd otherwise, then as sent to make trial of
their Allegiance,* for he saies, those words in the text *revolt from the Lord
your God, are in this place equivalent to revolt from the King; for they
had made God their King by pact at the foot of Mount* Sinai: whereas
Moses had no other credit with the people, but by the miracles which
he wrought in their presence, and in their sight; and that which he did
perswade them to, was to revolt and withdraw themselves from the
obedience of *Pharaoh*, who was, during their abode in *Egypt*, the only
King they knew and acknowledged. So that in Mr. *Hobbes's* judgment
the people might very well have refused to believe him; and all those
Prophets afterwards who prophesied against several of the Kings, ought
to have bin put to death; and the Argumentation against the Prophet
Jeremy was very well founded, when the Princes said unto the King,
Jer. 38. 4. *We beseech thee let this man be put to death, for thus he
weakeneth the hands of the men of war,* when he declar'd that the City
should surely be given into the hands of the King of *Babylon.* But Mr.
Hobbes is much concern'd to weaken the credit of Prophets, and of all
who succeed in their places; and he makes great use of that Prophets
being deceiv'd by the old Prophet *in the first of Kings*, when he was
seduced to eat and drink with him. Whereas he might have known,
that that Prophet was not so much deceiv'd by an other, as by his own
willfulness, in closing with the temtation of refreshing himself by eating
and drinking; chusing rather to believe any man of what quality soever,
against the express command that he had received from God himself.

What his design was to make so unnecessary an enquiry into the
Authors of the several parts of Scripture, and the time when they were
written, and his more unnecessary inference, that *Moses* was not the
Author of the Five Books which the Christian world generally believe
to be written by him, tho the time of his death might be added afterwards very warrantably, and the like presumtion upon the other Books,
he best knows; but he cannot wonder that many men, who observe the
Novelty and positiveness of his assertions, do suspect, that he found it
necessary to his purpose, first to lessen the reverence that was accus-
tom'd to be paid to the Scriptures themselves, and the Autority thereof,
before he could hope to have his interpretation of them hearken'd unto,
and received; and in order to that, to allow them no other Autority but
what they receive from the Declaration of the King; so that in every
Kingdom there may be several, and contrary Books of Scripture; which

their Subjects must not look upon as Scripture, but as the Soveraign power declares it to be so; which is to shake or rather overthrow all the reverence, and submission which we pay unto it, as the undoubted word of God * * * This is a degree of impiety Mr. *Hobbes* was not arrived at when he first published his Book *de Cive*, where tho he allowed his Soveraign power to give what Religion it thought fit to its Subjects, he thought it necessary to provide it should be Christian, which was a caution too modest for his *Leviathan*. Nor can it be preserved, when the Scriptures, from whence Christianity can only be prov'd and taught to the people, are to depend only for the validity thereof, upon the will, understanding, and autority of the Prince, which (with all possible submission, reverence, and resignation to that Earthly power, and which I do with all my heart acknowledg to be instituted by God himself, for the good of mankind) hath much greater dignity in it self, and more reverence due to it, then it can receive from the united Testimony and Declaration of all the Kings and Princes of the world. With this bold Prologue of the uncertain Canon of Scripture, he takes upon him as the foundation of his true ratiocination *to determine out of the Bible the meaning of such words, as by their ambiguity may* (he saies) *render what he is to infer upon them obscure and disputable*. And with this licence he presumes to give such unnatural explanations, descriptions, and definitions to several words and terms, which in themselves have no difficulty, as disturbs the whole Analogy of Scripture, and exposes those expressions, which are dictated by the spirit of God, in his light and comical interpretations, to the mirth of those who are too much inclin'd to be merry with the Scripture, and to the scandal of all men who are piously affected, and look upon the Sacred Writings with that devotion that becomes them. And upon these foundations, with much more confidence then any of the Primitive Fathers of the Church assum'd to themselves, he proceeds to the interpretations of several Texts of Scripture, in a different sense from what those Fathers, and all other men but himself, have understood them to signify.

* * *

The Survey of Chapter 46

* * * And truly, it might be wished, that in this Chapter, he had either forborn to have asked that question, (ch. 46) *to what purpose such subtlety was in a discourse of that nature, where he pretends to nothing but what is necessary to the doctrine of Government and obedience;* or that he had given a clearer and more satisfactory answer, then by saying, that it is *to that purpose, that men may no longer suffer themselves to be abus'd by them, that by the doctrine of separated Essences, built on the vain Philosophy of* Aristotle, *would fright them from obeying the Laws of their Countries, as men fright Birds from the corn with an emty doublet, a hat, and a crooked stick.* It is not possible that Mr. *Hobbes* can believe that many of those who are most guilty of disobeying the Laws, or have openly and rebelliously opposed the Sov-

eraign power in his own Country, or in Foreign Kingdoms, have ever bin led into it by the *doctrine of separated Essences*, which very terms few of them have ever heard of. And if the Immortality of the Soul, which he thinks so great an absurdity, hath some dependance upon the opinion of separated Essences, it will still as little concern that Classis of Men, against whom he intends to inveigh, who rather believe they have no Souls at all, then that they are immortal, (the belief of which, would make them more consider what is like to become of them by their wicked and rebellious lives) to which they are most like to be induced by Mr. *Hobbes*'s Doctrine, that the Soul & Body die together, which would secure them from a world of troublesom apprehensions. He knew too well the Lord *Say*, Mr. *Pim*, and Mr. *Hambden*, who first promoted the Rebellion, and the Earl of *Essex* who conducted it, to suspect that they were corrupted to it by the Doctrine of separated Essences. And if *Cromwell*, and *Vane*, and *Ireton*, who carried it much farther then the others intended to do, and made it incapable of reconciliation, grew better inform'd of the mischiefs of that Doctrine, it was after the publication of the *Leviathan*; and yet they continued more of the opinion then most other men, in the literal sense, that Faith, and Wisdom, and other Virtues, were sometimes *pour'd into them*, and sometimes *blown into them from Heaven*, and yet were not more Rebels from that opinion then they were before: with which words Mr. *Hobbes* renews his mirth, more then he hath cause for, except it be for their sakes.

*   *   *

These, amongst others, are the Doctrines of Mr. *Hobbes* in his two last parts; which, I believe, in the judgment of most Christians, are as soon renounc'd as pronounc'd, and which indeed need little other confutation then the reciting them; yet I doubt not, many men will say, how scandalous soever the assertions seem to be, (since he appeals to the Scripture, and cites several Texts out of the same, for the making good the worst of his Opinions) it is pity that his ignorance, or perverseness in those Interpretations had not bin made appear, by manifesting that those places of Scripture could not admit that Interpretation, and what the genuine sense thereof is. Which consideration had bin more reasonable and necessary, if these Errors had bin publish'd, and those Glosses made and own'd by any National Church, or any Body of Learned men; but it may be thought too great a presumtion for a private man, a stranger to Divinity, to take upon him to put unnatural Interpretations upon several Texts of Scripture, the better to apply them, and make them subservient to his own corrupt purposes and opinions, contrary to the whole current of Scripture, and to the Doctrine thereof, and without the least autority or shadow, that the like Interpretation was ever made before by any other man: I say, such a person cannot reasonably expect, that any body should too seriously examine all his frivolous and light suggestions, and endeavor to vindicate those Texts from such impossible Interpretations. Yet if any man thinks it worth his pains, I am well content that he receive that honor, and will still hope that Mr. *Hobbes* may be so well instructed in the true sense and end of the Scripture, that he may better discern the eternity of the reward and punishment in the next World. And so we conclude our discourse upon his Book. * * *

GOTTFRIED WILHELM LEIBNIZ

[Leibniz (1646–1716) was a German mathematician who is distinguished for his systematic rationalist philosophy and for his independent discovery of differential and integral calculus. At an early age, he attempted to correspond with Hobbes, but Hobbes never bothered to respond to the much younger man's letters. For much of his life, Leibniz defended the ideas of a "universal" (European) empire and a reunification of Christendom. These ideas were at odds with Hobbes's strong interpretation of the concept of sovereignty, and Leibniz accordingly was led to a broad attack on Hobbes. In *Caesarinus Fürstenerius*, published in 1677, Leibniz's main aim was to weaken the idea of sovereignty to make it consistent with allegiance to a universal power such as the Holy Roman Empire.]

State-Sovereignty†

* * *

I know that these thoughts of mine on the nature of the state cannot be reconciled with the opinions of the sharp-witted Englishman Thomas Hobbes. But I also know that no people in civilized Europe is ruled by the laws that he has proposed; wherefore, if we listen to Hobbes, there will be nothing in our land but out-and-out anarchy. He says that by nature men have the right to do whatever seems to them to be useful; that from this their rights extend over all things. But from this, he goes on, arise internecine wars, causing the destruction of individuals, and therefore peace is necessary and this right of all men over all things must be taken away, as must be the individual judgment from which it flows. Each man must transfer his will to the state, i.e. to a monarchy or some assembly of the magnates or the people, or to some natural or civil person, so that each man is understood to will whatever the government or person which represents him wills. Furthermore, this civil person, the government, cannot be anything but unitary, and it is fruitless to divide the rights of supreme power among several persons or *collegia*. For if, for example, one should be given the right to propose laws, another that of imposing tributes, the state would be dissolved in the event of an angry disagreement. For without the power of managing affairs, which is money, nothing can be accomplished, and so it is clear that he who can deny the other the tributes can also deprive him of his remaining rights — which, Hobbes says, is

---

† From *Leibniz: Political Writings*, trans. and ed. by Patrick Riley (Cambridge: Cambridge UP, 1972), pp. 118–20. Reprinted with the permission of Cambridge University Press.

absurd.[1] Even more, it follows from his principles that every monarch (or he who is required to call no assembly of the people) can make arrangements for his successor at will. Nor does Hobbes deny this. And yet these theories would be exploded in France herself (which some people put forward as an example of an absolute kingdom).

Hobbes' fallacy lies in this, that he thinks things which can entail inconvenience should not be borne at all — which is foreign to the nature of human affairs. I would not deny that, when the supreme power is divided, many dissensions can arise; even wars, if everyone holds stubbornly to his own opinion. But experience has shown that men usually hold to some middle road, so as not to commit everything to hazard by their obstinacy. Prominent examples are Poland and the Netherlands: among the Poles, one territorial representative can dissolve the assembly by his obstinacy; in Holland, when something of great importance is being considered, such as peace, war or treaties, the disagreement of one town upsets everything. And yet, due to the prudence and moderation of those who preside over the whole, most matters are finished according to their wishes. In the German assemblies, too, not everything is transacted by majority vote, but some matters require unanimity, all of which cases would seem anarchy to Hobbes. Some others, who have expressed themselves a bit freely concerning our state, think them monstrous; but if this is true, I would venture to say that the same monsters are being maintained by the Dutch and the Poles and the English, even by the Spanish and the French. They know this who know what the noble orders of the kingdom of France, and those men otherwise selected from the kingdom (*les notables*), once said in public assembly concerning the fundamental laws of the kingdom and the limits of royal power. Nor is it unknown that aid is not obtained from the clergy, which is the third part of the kingdom, by mandates given from the plenitude of power (as they say), but by demands, negotiations, and discussions. Furthermore, half of France consists of provinces called *les pays des Etats*, like Lesser Brittany, Gallia Narbonensis, the county of Provence, the Dukedom of Burgundy, where the king certainly cannot exact extraordinary tributes with any more right than can the king of England in his realm. Anything further, exceeding custom or law, can have force only if it succeeds in the king's councils. Not even the emperor of Turkey is, in the minds of his subjects, above all laws, as can be seen from the form of the judiciary which condemned the Sultan Ibraim, the father of him who is now in power. The matter was not transacted by an uproar, as in the killing of Osman, but by careful deliberation of those holding the highest civilian offices. Following their decision, the chief priest, or mufti, sent a decree commanding the sultan to appear before the Char-Alla, or 'justice of God'. When he refused, he was informed that his subjects had been freed from their oath of fidelity. Although we should not approve this example of the barbarians, who err in whichever direction you might choose. Therefore Hobbesian empires, I think, exist neither among civ-

1. Hobbes, *De Cive* V–VII; *Leviathan*, chs. 13–18.

ilized peoples nor among barbarians, and I consider them neither possible nor desirable, unless those who must have supreme power are gifted with angelic virtues. For men will choose to follow their own will, and will consult their own welfare as seems best to them, as long as they are not persuaded of the supreme wisdom and capability of their rulers, which things are necessary for perfect resignation of the will. So that Hobbes' demonstrations have a place only in that state whose king is God, whom alone one can trust in all things.

CHARLES LOUIS DE SECONDAT, BARON DE LA BRÈDE ET DE MONTESQUIEU

[Montesquieu (1689–1755) was a French man of letters and philosopher from a family with a slight aristocratic background. He achieved great early success with his satirical *Persian Letters* (1721). His *Spirit of the Laws*, published in 1748, is one of the great works of modern political theory and was much admired — and envied — by Rousseau, among many others.]

Of the Laws of Nature†

Antecedent to the above-mentioned laws are those of nature, so called, because they derive their force entirely from our frame and existence. In order to have a perfect knowledge of these laws, we must consider man before the establishment of society: the laws received in such a state would be those of nature.

The law which, impressing on our minds the idea of a Creator, inclines us towards Him, is the first in importance, though not in order, of natural laws. Man in a state of nature would have the faculty of knowing, before he had acquired any knowledge. Plain it is that his first ideas would not be of a speculative nature; he would think of the preservation of his being, before he would investigate its origin. Such a man would feel nothing in himself at first but impotency and weakness; his fears and apprehensions would be excessive; as appears from instances (were there any necessity of proving it) of savages found in forests, trembling at the motion of a leaf, and flying from every shadow.

In this state every man, instead of being sensible of his equality, would fancy himself inferior. There would, therefore, be no danger of their attacking one another; peace would be the first law of nature.

The natural impulse or desire which Hobbes attributes to mankind of subduing one another is far from being well founded. The idea of empire and dominion is so complex, and depends on so many other notions, that it could never be the first which occurred to the human understanding.

Hobbes inquires, "For what reason go men armed, and have locks

---

† From *The Spirit of the Laws*, trans. by Thomas Nugent (New York: Hafner, 1949), pp. 3–5. Reprinted with the permission of Simon & Schuster, Inc. Copyright © 1949 by Macmillan Publishing Company.

and keys to fasten their doors, if they be not naturally in a state of war?" But is it not obvious that he attributes to mankind before the establishment of society what can happen but in consequence of this establishment, which furnishes them with motives for hostile attacks and self-defence?

Next to a sense of his weakness man would soon find that of his wants. Hence another law of nature would prompt him to seek for nourishment.

Fear, I have observed, would induce men to shun one another; but the marks of this fear being reciprocal, would soon engage them to associate. Besides, this association would quickly follow from the very pleasure one animal feels at the approach of another of the same species. Again, the attraction arising from the difference of sexes would enhance this pleasure, and the natural inclination they have for each other would form a third law.

Besides the sense or instinct which man possesses in common with brutes, he has the advantage of acquired knowledge; and thence arises a second tie, which brutes have not. Mankind have, therefore, a new motive of uniting; and a fourth law of nature results from the desire of living in society.

HENRY SIDGWICK

[Sidgwick (1838–1900) was an English philosopher in the utilitarian tradition who was a teacher and, in his later years, professor of moral philosophy at Cambridge University. His major work, *The Methods of Ethics* (first published in 1874), has been praised by John Rawls as "the first truly academic work in moral theory, modern in both method and spirit." *Outlines of the History of Ethics* was first published in 1886.]

Hobbes†

* * *

Hobbes's psychology is in the first place frankly materialistic; he holds that man's sensations, imaginations, thoughts, emotions, are all mere "appearances" of motions in the "interior parts" of his body. Accordingly he regards pleasure as essentially motion "helping vital action," and pain as motion "hindering" it. There is no logical connection between this theory and the doctrine that appetite or desire has always pleasure (or the absence of pain) for its object; but a materialist, framing a system of psychology, is likely to give special attention to the active impulses arising out of bodily wants, whose obvious end is the preservation of the agent's organism; and this, together with a philosophic wish to simplify, may lead him to the conclusion that all human impulses are similarly self-regarding. This, at any rate, is Hobbes's cardinal

† From *Outlines of the History of Ethics*, fifth ed. (London: Macmillan, 1902), pp. 163–70.

doctrine in moral psychology, that each man's appetites or desires are naturally directed either to the preservation of his life, or to that heightening of it which he feels as pleasure; including the aversions that are similarly directed "fromward" pain. Hobbes does not distinguish instinctive from deliberate pleasure-seeking; and he confidently resolves the most apparently unselfish emotions into phases of self-regard. Pity he finds to be grief for the calamity of others, arising from imagination of the like calamity befalling oneself; what we admire with seeming disinterestedness as beautiful (*pulchrum*) is really "pleasure in promise"; when men are not immediately seeking present pleasure, they desire power as a means to future pleasure, and thus have a derivative delight in the exercise of power which prompts to what we call benevolent action. The vaunted social inclinations of men, when we consider them narrowly, resolve themselves either into desire for personal benefit to be obtained from or through others, or desire for reputation; "all society is either for gain or glory." No doubt men naturally require mutual help: "infants have need of others to help them to live, and those of riper years to help them to live well"; but so far as this need is concerned, it is "dominion" rather than society that a man would naturally seek if all fear were removed: apart from mutual fear, men would have no natural tendency to enter into political union with their fellows, and to accept the restrictions and positive obligations which such union involves. If any one doubts this natural unsociality of man, Hobbes bids him consider what opinion of his fellows his own actions imply: "when taking a journey he arms himself; when going to sleep he locks his doors; when even in his house he locks his chests; and this when he knows there be laws and public officers, armed, to revenge all injuries that shall be done him."

What, then, is the conduct that ought to be adopted, the reasonable course of conduct, for this egoistic, naturally unsocial being, living side by side with similar beings? In the first place, since all the voluntary actions of men tend to their own preservation or pleasure, it cannot be reasonable to aim at anything else;[1] in fact, nature rather than reason fixes the end of human action, to which it is reason's function to show the means. Hence if we ask why it is reasonable for any individual to observe the rules of social behaviour that are commonly called moral, the answer is obvious that this is only indirectly reasonable, as a means to his own preservation or pleasure. It is not, however, in this, which is only the old Cyrenaic or Epicurean answer, that the distinctive point of Hobbism lies; but rather in the doctrine that even this indirect reasonableness of the most fundamental moral rules is entirely conditional on their general observance, which cannot be secured without the intervention of government. *E.g.* it is not reasonable for me to perform

---

1. There is, however, a noticeable — though perhaps unconscious — discrepancy between Hobbes's theory of the ends that men naturally seek and his standard for determining their natural rights. This latter is never Pleasure simply, but always Preservation — though on occasion he enlarges the notion of "preservation" into "preservation of life so as not to be weary of it." His view seems to be that in a state of nature most men would fight, rob, etc., "for delectation merely" or "for glory," and hence all men must be allowed an indefinite right to fight, rob, etc., "for preservation" [*Sidgwick's note*].

first my share of a contract, if I have "any reasonable suspicion" that the other party will not afterwards perform his; and such reasonable suspicion cannot be effectually excluded except in a state of society in which he is punished for non-performance. Thus the ordinary rules of social behaviour are only hypothetically obligatory until they are actualised by the erection of "a common power" that may "use the strength and means of all" to enforce on all the observance of rules tending to the common benefit. On the other hand, Hobbes yields to no one in maintaining the paramount importance of moral regulations. The rules prescribing justice or the performance of covenants, equity in judging between man and man, requital of benefits, sociability, forgiveness of wrong so far as security allows, the rules prohibiting contumely, pride, arrogance, and other subordinate precepts, — which may all be summed up in the simple formula, "Do not that to another which thou wouldest not have done to thyself," — he calls "immutable and eternal laws of nature"; meaning that though a man is not unconditionally bound to realise them in act, he is bound as a reasonable being to desire and aim at their realisation. For they must always be means to the attainment of peace, and the "first and fundamental law of nature" — so far as man's relations to his fellows are concerned — is to "seek peace and follow it"; though if peace cannot be obtained, he may reasonably "seek and use all helps and advantages of war." It is equally opposed to nature's end of self-preservation (1) that an individual should render unreciprocated obedience to moral rules in the interest of others, and so "make himself a prey to others," and (2) that he should refuse to observe such rules when he has sufficient security that they will be observed by others, and so "seek not peace but war." For the state of nature, in which men must be supposed to have existed before government was instituted, and into which they would relapse if it were abolished, is indeed a state free from moral restraints; but it is therefore utterly miserable. It is a state in which, owing to well-grounded mutual fear, every man has a right to everything, "even to one another's body," for it may conduce to his preservation; or, as Hobbes also expresses it, a state in which "right and wrong, justice and injustice, have no place";[2] but it is therefore also a state of war in which every man's hand is against his neighbour's, — a state so wretched and perilous that it is the first dictate of rational self-love to emerge from it into the peace of an ordered commonwealth. Such a commonwealth may arise either by "institution," through compact of the subjects with each other to obey as sovereign a defined individual or assembly acting as one, or by "acquisition" through force, followed by a surrender of the vanquished to the victor at discretion; but in either case the authority of the sovereign must be unquestioned and unlimited. The sovereign is itself bound by

---

2. Hobbes does not recognise any formal contradiction between the two statements; because he defines Right (substantive) = Liberty = absence of external impediments; but he practically means by "a right" what most people ordinarily mean by it, i.e. a rightful liberty, a liberty claimed and approved by the individual's reason. In any case the statement that "the notions of right and wrong have no place" in the state of nature is too wide for his real meaning; for he would admit that intemperance is prohibited by the Law of Nature in this state [Sidgwick's note].

the Law of Nature to seek the good of the people, which cannot be separated from its own good; but it is responsible to God alone for its fulfilment of this duty. Its commands are the final measure of right and wrong for the outward conduct of its subjects, and ought to be absolutely obeyed by every one, so long as it affords him protection, and does not threaten serious harm to him personally; since to dispute its dictates would be the first step towards anarchy, the one paramount peril outweighing all particular defects in legislation and administration.

It is easy to understand how, in the crisis of 1640, — when the ethico-political system of Hobbes first took written shape, — a peace-loving philosopher, weary of the din of warring sects, should regard the claims of individual conscience as essentially anarchical, and the most threatening danger to social wellbeing; but however strong might be men's yearning for order, a view of social duty, in which the only fixed positions were selfishness everywhere and unlimited power somewhere, could not but appear offensively paradoxical. Nevertheless, offensive or not, there was an originality, a force, an apparent coherence in Hobbism which rendered it undeniably impressive; in fact, we find that for two generations the efforts to construct morality on a philosophical basis take more or less the form of answers to Hobbes. From an ethical point of view Hobbism divides itself naturally into two parts, which are combined by Hobbes's peculiar political doctrines into a coherent whole, but are not otherwise necessarily connected. Its theoretical basis is the principle of egoism, — viz. that it is natural, and so reasonable, for each individual to aim solely at his own preservation or pleasure; while, for the practical determination of the particulars of duty it makes social morality entirely dependent on positive law and institution. It thus affirmed the relativity of good and evil in a double sense; — good and evil, for any individual citizen, may from one point of view be defined as the objects respectively of his desire and aversion; from another point of view, they may be said to be determined for him by his sovereign. It is the latter part or aspect of the system which is primarily attacked by the first generation of writers that replied to Hobbes. This attack, or rather the counter-exposition of orthodox doctrine, is conducted on different methods by the Cambridge moralists and by Cumberland respectively. The former, regarding morality primarily as a body of knowledge of right and wrong, good and evil, rather than a mere code of rules, insist on its absolute character, independent of any legislative will, and its intuitive certainty. The latter is content with the legal view of morality, but endeavours to establish the validity of the laws of nature by basing them on the single supreme principle of rational regard for the "common good of all," and showing them, as so based, to be adequately supported by Divine sanctions.

*　*　*

INTERPRETATIONS

MICHAEL OAKESHOTT

Introduction to *Leviathan*†

The System

In Hobbes's mind, his 'civil philosophy' belonged to a system of philosophy. Consequently, an enquiry into the character of this system is
not to be avoided by the interpreter of his politics. For, if the details of
the civil theory may not improperly be considered as elements in a
coherence of their own, the significance of the theory as a whole must
depend upon the system to which it belongs, and upon the place it
occupies in the system.

Two views, it appears, between them hold the field at the present
time. The first is the view that the foundation of Hobbes's philosophy
is a doctrine of materialism, that the intention of his system was the
progressive revelation of this doctrine in nature, in man and in society,
and that this revelation was achieved in his three most important philosophical works, *De Corpore*, *De Homine* and *De Cive*. These works,
it is suggested, constitute a continuous argument, part of which is re-
produced in *Leviathan*; and the novel project of the 'civil philosophy'
was the exposition of a politics based upon a 'natural philosophy', the
assimilation of politics to a materialistic doctrine of the world, or (it is
even suggested) to the view of the world as it appeared in the conclusions of the physical sciences. A mechanistic-materialist politics is made
to spring from a mechanistic-materialist universe. And, not improperly,
it is argued that the significance of what appears at the end is determined at least in part by what was proved or assumed at the beginning.
The second view is that this, no doubt, was the intention of Hobbes,
but that 'the attempt and not the deed confounds him'. The joints of
the system are ill-matched, and what should have been a continuous
argument, based upon a philosophy of materialism, collapses under its
own weight.

Both these views are, I think, misconceived. But they are the product
not merely of inattention to the words of Hobbes; it is to be feared that
they derive also from a graver fault of interpretation, a false expectation
with regard to the nature of a philosophical system. For what is expected
here is that a philosophical system should conform to an architectural
analogue, and consequently what is sought in Hobbes's system is a
foundation and a superstructure planned as a single whole, with civil
philosophy as the top storey. Now, it may be doubted whether any
philosophical system can properly be represented in the terms of ar-
chitecture, but what is certain is that the analogy does violence to the

† From "Introduction to *Leviathan*," in *Hobbes on Civil Association* (Berkeley and Los Angeles:
U of California P, 1975), pp. 15–28. Copyright © 1976 by Michael Oakeshott. Reprinted by
permission.

system of Hobbes. The coherence of his philosophy, the system of it, lies not in an architectonic structure, but in a single 'passionate thought' that pervades its parts.[1] The system is not the plan or key of the labyrinth of the philosophy; it is, rather, a guiding clue, like the thread of Ariadne.[2] It is like the music that gives meaning to the movement of dancers, or the law of evidence that gives coherence to the practice of a court. And the thread, the hidden thought, is the continuous application of a doctrine about the nature of philosophy. Hobbes's philosophy is the world reflected in the mirror of the philosophic eye, each image the representation of a fresh object, but each determined by the character of the mirror itself. In short, the civil philosophy belongs to a philosophical system, not because it is materialistic but because it is philosophical; and an enquiry into the character of the system and the place of politics in it resolves itself into an enquiry into what Hobbes considered to be the nature of philosophy.

For Hobbes, to think philosophically is to reason; philosophy is reasoning. To this all else is subordinate; from this all else derives. It is the character of reasoning that determines the range and the limits of philosophical enquiry; it is this character that gives coherence, system, to Hobbes's philosophy. Philosophy, for him, is the world as it appears in the mirror of reason; civil philosophy is the image of the civil order reflected in that mirror. In general, the world seen in this mirror is a world of causes and effects: cause and effect are its categories. And for Hobbes reason has two alternative ends: to determine the conditional causes of given effects, or to determine the conditional effects of given causes.[3] But to understand more exactly what he means by this identification of philosophy with reasoning, we must consider three contrasts that run through all his writing: the contrast between philosophy and theology (reason and faith), between philosophy and 'science' (reason and empiricism) and between philosophy and experience (reason and sense).

Reasoning is concerned solely with causes and effects. It follows, therefore, that its activity must lie within a world composed of things that are causes or the effects of causes. If there is another way of conceiving this world, it is not within the power of reasoning to follow it; if there are things by definition causeless or ingenerable, they belong to a world other than that of philosophy. This at once, for Hobbes, excludes from philosophy the consideration of the universe as a whole, things infinite, things eternal, final causes and things known only by divine grace or revelation: it excludes what Hobbes comprehensively calls *theology and faith*. He denies, not the existence of these things, but *their rationality*.[4] This method of circumscribing the concerns of philosophy is not, of course, original in Hobbes. It has roots that go back

---

1. Confucius said, 'T'zu, you probably think that I have learned many things and hold them in my mind.' 'Yes,' he replied, 'is that not true?' 'No,' said Confucius; 'I have one thing that permeates everything.' — Confucius, *Analects*, XV, 2. L., ch. 3.
2. *The English Works of Thomas Hobbes*. Ed. William Molesworth, 11 vols. (London: John Bohn, 1839–45), vol. II, p. vi. Hereafter *E.W.* plus vol. and page.
3. *E.W.*, I, 65–6, 387.
4. *L.*, ch. 11; *E.W.*, I, 10, 410.

to Augustine, if not further, and it was inherited by the seventeenth century (where one side of it was distinguished as the heresy of Fideism: both Montaigne and Pascal were Fideists) directly from its formulation in the Averroism of Scotus and Occam. Indeed, this doctrine is one of the seeds in scholasticism from which modern philosophy sprang. Philosophical explanation, then, is concerned with things caused. A world of such things is, necessarily, a world from which teleology is excluded; its internal movement comprises the impact of its parts upon one another, of attraction and repulsion, not of growth or development. It is a world conceived on the analogy of a machine, where to explain an effect we go to its immediate cause, and to seek the result of a cause we go only to its immediate effect.[5] In other words, the mechanistic element in Hobbes's philosophy is derived from his rationalism; its source and authority lie, not in observation, but in reasoning. He does not say that the natural world is a machine; he says only that the rational world is analogous to a machine. He is a scholastic, not a 'scientific' mechanist. This does not mean that the mechanistic element is unimportant in Hobbes; it means only that it is derivative. It is, indeed, of the greatest importance, for Hobbes's philosophy is, in all its parts, pre-eminently a philosophy of *power* precisely because philosophy is reasoning, reasoning the elucidation of mechanism and mechanism essentially the combination, transfer and resolution of forces. The end of philosophy itself is power — *scientia propter potentiam*.[6] Man is a complex of powers; desire is the desire for power, pride is illusion about power, honour opinion about power, life the unremitting exercise of power and death the absolute loss of power. And the civil order is conceived as a coherence of powers, not because politics is vulgarly observed to be a competition of powers, or because civil philosophy must take its conceptions from natural philosophy, but because to subject the civil order to rational enquiry unavoidably turns it into a mechanism.

In the writings of Hobbes, philosophy and science are not contrasted *eo nomine*. Such a contrast would have been impossible in the seventeenth century, with its absence of differentiation between the sciences and its still unshaken hold on the conception of the unity of human knowledge. Indeed, Hobbes normally uses the word science as a synonym for philosophy; rational knowledge is scientific knowledge. Nevertheless, Hobbes is near the beginning of a new view of the structure and parts of knowledge, a change of view which became clearer in the generation of Locke and was completed by Kant. Like Bacon and others before him, Hobbes has his own classification of the *genres* of knowledge,[7] and that it is a classification which involves a distinction between philosophy and what we have come to call 'science' is suggested by his ambiguous attitude to the work of contemporary scientists. He wrote with an unusually generous enthusiasm of the great advances made by

5. *E.W.*, II, xiv.
6. *E.W.*, I, xiv; Thomas Hobbes, *Opera Latina*, I. 6. Ed. William Molesworth, 5 vols. (London: John Bohn, 1839–45). Hereafter *O.L.*
7. *L.*, ch. 9.

Kepler, Galileo and Harvey; 'the beginning of astronomy', he says, 'is not to be derived from farther time than from Copernicus';[8] but he had neither sympathy nor even patience for the 'new or experimental philosophy', and he did not conceal his contempt for the work of the Royal Society, founded in his lifetime. But this ambiguity ceases to be paradoxical when we see what Hobbes was about, when we understand that one of the few internal tensions of his thought arose from an attempted but imperfectly achieved distinction between science and philosophy. The distinction, well known to us now, is that between knowledge of things as they appear and enquiry into the fact of their appearing, between a knowledge (with all the necessary assumptions) of the phenomenal world and a theory of knowledge itself. Hobbes appreciated this distinction, and his appreciation of it allies him with Locke and with Kant and separates him from Bacon and even Descartes. He perceived that his concern as a philosopher was with the second and not the first of these enquiries; yet the distinction remained imperfectly defined in his mind. But that philosophy meant for Hobbes something different from the enquiries of natural science is at once apparent when we consider the starting-place of his thought and the character of the questions he thinks it necessary to ask. He begins with sensation; and he begins there, not because there is no deceit or crookedness in the utterances of the senses, but because the fact of our having sensations seems to him the only thing of which we can be indubitably certain.[9] And the question he asks himself is, what *must* the world be like for us to have the sensations we undoubtedly experience? His enquiry is into the cause of sensation, an enquiry to be conducted, not by means of observation, but by means of reasoning. And if the answer he proposes owes something to the inspiration of the scientists, that does nothing to modify the distinction between science and philosophy inherent in the question itself. For the scientist of his day the world of nature was almost a machine, Kepler had proposed the substitution of the word *vis* for the word *anima* in physics; and Hobbes, whose concern was with the rational world (by definition also conceived as the analogy of a machine), discovered that some of the general ideas of the scientists could be turned to his own purposes. But these pardonable appropriations do nothing to approximate his enquiry to that of Galileo or Newton. Philosophy is reasoning, this time contrasted, not with theology, but with what we have come to know as natural science. And the question, What, in an age of science, is the task of philosophy? which was to concern the nineteenth century so deeply, was already familiar to Hobbes. And it is a false reading of his intention and his achievement which finds in his civil philosophy the beginning of sociology or a science of politics, the beginning of that movement of thought that came to regard 'the methods of physical science as the proper models for political'.[1]

But the contrast that finally distinguishes philosophy and reveals its

8. *E.W.*, I, viii.
9. It will be remembered that the brilliant and informal genius of Montaigne had perceived that our most certain knowledge is what we know about ourselves, and had made of this a philosophy of introspection.
1. J. S. Mill, *Autobiography*, p. 165.

full character is that between philosophy and what Hobbes calls experience. For in elucidating this distinction Hobbes shows us philosophy coming into being, shows it as a thing generated and relates it to its cause thereby establishing it as itself a proper subject of rational consideration. The mental history of a man begins with sensation, 'for there is no conception in a man's mind, which hath not at first, totally, or by parts, been begotten upon the organs of sense'.[2] Some sensations, perhaps, occupying but an instant, involve no reference to others and no sense of time. But commonly, sensations, requiring a minimum time of more than a single instant, and reaching a mind already stored with the relics of previous sensations, are impossible without that which gives a sense of time — memory.[3] Sensation involves recollection, and a man's experience is nothing but the recollected after-images of sensations. But from his power to remember man derives another power, imagination, which is the ability to recall and turn over in the mind the decayed relics of past sensation, the ability to experience even when the senses themselves have ceased to speak. Moreover imagination, though it depends on past sensations, is not an entirely servile faculty; it is capable of compounding together relics of sensations felt at different times. Indeed, in imagination we may have in our minds images not only of what we have never actually seen (as when we imagine a golden mountain though we have seen only gold and a mountain), but even of what we could never see, such as a chimera. But imagination remains servile in that 'we have no transition from one imagination to another whereof we never had the like before in our senses.'[4] Two things more belong to experience; the fruits of experience. The first is History, which is the ordered register of past experiences. The second is prudence, which is the power to anticipate experience by means of the recollection of what has gone before. 'Of our conceptions of the past, we make a future.'[5] A full, well-recollected experience gives the 'foresight' and 'wisdom' that belong to the prudent man, a wisdom that springs from the appreciation of those causes and effects that time and not reason teaches us. This is the end and crown of experience. In the mind of the prudent or sagacious man, experience appears as a kind of knowledge. Governed by sense, it is necessarily individual, a particular knowledge of particulars. But, within its limits, it is 'absolute knowledge';[6] there is no ground upon which it can be doubted, and the categories of truth and falsehood do not apply to it. It is mere, uncritical 'knowledge of fact': 'experience concludeth nothing universal'.[7] And in all its characteristics it is distinguished from philosophical knowledge, which (because it is reasoned) is general and not particular, a knowledge of consequences and not of facts, and conditional and not absolute.

Our task now is to follow Hobbes in his account of the generation of rational knowledge from experience. In principle, experience (except perhaps when it issues in history) is something man shares with animals

---

2. *L.*, ch. 1.
3. *E.W.*, I, 393.
4. *E.W.*, IV, 16.
5. *L.*, ch. 2.
6. *L.*, ch. 9.
7. *E.W.*, IV, 18.

and has only in a greater degree: memory and imagination are the unsought mechanical products of sensation, like the movements that continue on the surface of water after what disturbed it has sunk to rest. In order to surmount the limits of this sense-experience and achieve reasoned knowledge of our sensations, we require not only to have sensations, but to be conscious of having them; we require the power of introspection. But the cause of this power must lie in sense itself, if the power is to avoid the imputation of being an easy *deus ex machina*. Language satisfies both these conditions: it makes introspection possible, and springs from a power we share with animals, the physical power of making sounds. For, though language 'when disposed of in speech and pronounced to others'[8] is the means whereby men declare their thoughts to one another, it is primarily the only means by which a man may communicate his own thoughts to himself, may become conscious of the contents of his mind. The beginning of language is giving names to afterimages of sensations and thereby becoming conscious of them; the act of naming the image is the act of becoming conscious of it. For, 'a name is a word taken at pleasure to serve as a mark that may raise in our minds a thought like some thought we had before'.[9]

Language, the giving of names to images, is not itself reasonable, it is the arbitrary precondition of all reasoning:[1] the generation of rational knowledge is by words out of experience. The achievement of language is to 'register our thoughts', to fix what is essentially fleeting. And from this achievement follows the possibility of definition, the conjunction of general names, proposition and rational argument, all of which consist in the 'proper use of names in language'. But, though reasoning brings with it knowledge of the general and the possibility of truth and its opposite, absurdity,[2] it can never pass beyond the world of names. Reasoning is nothing else but the addition and subtraction of names, and 'gives us conclusions, not about the nature of things, but about the names of things. That is to say, by means of reason we discover only whether the connections we have established between names are in accordance with the arbitrary convention we have established concerning their meanings.'[3] This is at once a nominalist and a profoundly sceptical doctrine. Truth is of universals, but they are names, the names of images left over from sensations; and a true proposition is not an assertion about the real world. We can, then, surmount the limits of sense-experience and achieve rational knowledge; and it is this knowledge, with its own severe limitations, that is the concern of philosophy.

But philosophy is not only knowledge of the universal, it is a knowledge of causes. Informally, Hobbes describes it as 'the natural reason of man flying up and down among the creatures, and bringing back a true report of their order, causes and effects.'[4] We have seen already

8. E.W., I, 16.
9. E.W., I, 16.
1. This is why introspection that falls short of reasoning is possible. E.W., I, 73.
2. Since truth is of propositions, its opposite is a statement that is absurd or nonsensical. Error belongs to the world of experience and is a failure in foresight. L., ch. 5.
3. O.L., V, 257.
4. E.W., I, xiii.

how, by limiting philosophy to a knowledge of things caused (because reasoning itself must observe this limit) he separates it from theology. We have now to consider why he believed that the essential work of reasoning (and therefore of philosophy) was the demonstration of the cause of things caused. Cause for Hobbes is the means by which anything comes into being. Unlike any of the Aristotelian causes, it is essentially that which, previous in time, brings about the effect. A knowledge of cause is, then, a knowledge of how a thing is generated.[5] But why must philosophy be a knowledge of this sort? Hobbes's answer would appear to be, first, that this sort of knowledge can spring from reasoning while it is impossible to mere experience, and, secondly, that since, *ex hypothesi*, the data of philosophy are effects, the only possible enlargement of our knowledge of them must consist in a knowledge of their causes. If we add to the experience of an effect a knowledge of its generation, a knowledge of its 'constitutive cause';[6] we know everything that may be known. In short, a knowledge of causes is the pursuit in philosophy because philosophy is reasoning.[7]

The third characteristic of philosophical knowledge, as distinguished from experience, is that it is conditional, not absolute. Hobbes's doctrine is that when, in reasoning, we conclude that the cause of something is such and such, we can mean no more than that such and such is a possible efficient cause, and not that it is the actual cause. There are three criteria by which a suggested cause may be judged, and proof that the cause actually operated is not among them. For reasoning, a cause must be 'imaginable', the necessity of the effect must be shown to follow from the cause, and it must be shown that nothing false (that is, not present in the effect) can be derived.[8] And what satisfies these conditions may be described as an hypothetical efficient cause. That philosophy is limited to the demonstration of such causes is stated by Hobbes on many occasions; it applies not only to the detail of his philosophy, but also to the most general of all causes, to body and motion. For example, when he says that the cause or generation of a circle is 'the circumduction of a body where-of one end remains unmoved', he adds that this gives 'some generation [of the figure], though perhaps not that by which it was made, yet that by which it might have been made'.[9] And when he considers the general problem of the cause of sensations, he concludes, not with the categorical statement that body and motion are the only causal existents, but that body (that is, that which is independent of thought and which fills a portion of space) and motion are the hypothetical efficient causes of our having sensations. If there were no body there could be no motion, and if there were no motion of bodies there could be no sensation; *sentire semper idem et non sentire ad idem recidunt.*[1] From beginning to end there is

---

5. *E.W.*, VII, 78.
6. *E.W.*, II, xiv.
7. Hobbes gives the additional reason that a knowledge of causes is useful to mankind. *E.W.*, I, 7–10.
8. *Elements of Law*, Appendix II, § 1, 168.
9. *E.W.*, I, 6, 386–7.
1. *O.L.*, I, 321.

no suggestion in Hobbes that philosophy is anything other than conditional knowledge, knowledge of hypothetical generations and conclusions about the names of things, not about the nature of things.[2] With these philosophy must be satisfied, though they are but fictions. Indeed, philosophy may be defined as the establishment by reasoning of true fictions. And the ground of this limitation is, that the world being what it is, reasoning can go no further. 'There is no effect which the power of God cannot produce in many several ways,[3] verification *ad oculos* is impossible because these causes are rational not perceptible, and consequently the farthest reach of reason is the demonstration of causes which satisfy the three rational criteria.

My contention is, then, that the system of Hobbes's philosophy lies in his conception of the nature of philosophical knowledge, and not in any doctrine about the world. And the inspiration of his philosophy is the intention to be guided by reason and to reject all other guides: this is the thread, the hidden thought, that gives it coherence, distinguishing it from Faith, 'Science' and Experience. It remains to guard against a possible error. The lineage of Hobbes's rationalism lies, not (like that of Spinoza or even Descartes) in the great Platonic-Christian tradition, but in the sceptical, late scholastic tradition. He does not normally speak of Reason, the divine illumination of the mind that unites man with God; he speaks of reasoning. And he is not less persuaded of its fallibility and limitations than Montaigne himself.[4] By means of reasoning we certainly pass beyond mere sense-experience, but when imagination and prudence have generated rational knowledge, they do not, like drones, perish; they continue to perform in human life functions that reasoning itself cannot discharge. Nor, indeed, is man, in Hobbes's view, primarily a reasoning creature. This capacity for general hypothetical reasoning distinguishes him from the animal, but he remains fundamentally a creature of passion, and it is by passion not less than by reasoning that he achieves his salvation.[5]

We have considered Hobbes's view of philosophy because civil philosophy, whatever else it is, is philosophy. Civil philosophy, the subject of *Leviathan*, is precisely the application of this conception of philosophy to civil association. It is not the last chapter in a philosophy of materialism, but the reflection of civil association in the mirror of a rationalistic philosophy. But if the *genus* of civil philosophy is its character as philosophy, its *differentia* is derived from the matter to be considered. Civil philosophy is settling the generation or constitutive cause of civil association. And the kind of hypothetical efficient cause that civil philosophy may be expected to demonstrate is determined by the fact that civil association is an artifact: it is artificial, not natural. Now, to assert

2. *L.*, ch. 7.
3. *E.W.*, VII, 3. It may be observed that what is recognized here is the normally unstated presupposition of all seventeenth-century science: the Scotist belief that the natural world is the creation *ex nihilo* of an omnipotent God, and that therefore categorical knowledge of its detail is not deducible but (if it exists) must be the product of observation. Characteristically adhering to the tradition, Hobbes says that the only thing we can know of God is his omnipotence.
4. *L.*, ch. 5.
5. *L.*, ch. 13.

that civil association is an artifact is already to have settled the question of its generation, and Hobbes himself does not begin with any such assertion. His method is to establish the artificial character of civil association by considering its generation. But in order to avoid false expectations it will be wise for us to anticipate the argument and consider what he means by this distinction between art and nature.

Hobbes has given us no collected account of his philosophy of artifice; it is to be gathered only from scattered observations. But when these are put together, they compose a coherent view. A work of art is the product or effect of mental activity. But this in itself does not distinguish it securely from nature, because the universe itself must be regarded as the product of God's mental activity, and what we call 'nature' is to God an artifact;[6] and there are products of human mental activity which, having established themselves, become for the observer part of his natural world. More firmly defined, then, a work of art is the product of mental activity considered from the point of view of its cause. And, since what we have to consider are works of human art, our enquiry must be into the kind of natural human mental activity that may result in a work of art; for the cause of a work of art must lie in nature; that is, in experience. It would appear that the activities involved are willing and reasoning. But reasoning itself is artificial, not natural; it is an 'acquired' not a 'native' mental activity,[7] and therefore cannot be considered as part of the generation of a work of art.[8] We are left, then, with willing, which, belonging to experience and not reasoning, is undoubtedly a natural mental activity. The cause (hypothetical and efficient, of course) of a human work of art is the will of a man. And willing is 'the last desire in deliberating', deliberating being mental discourse in which the subject is desires and aversions.[9] It is a creative activity (not merely imitative), in the same way as imagination, working on sensations, creates a new world of hitherto separated parts. Both will and imagination are servile only in that their products must be like nature in respect of being mechanisms; that is, complexes of cause and effect.[1] Moreover, will creates not only when it is single and alone, but also in concert with other wills. The product of an agreement between wills is no less a work of art than the product of one will. And the peculiarity of civil association, as a work of art, is its generation from a number of wills. The word 'civil', in Hobbes, means artifice springing from more than one will. Civil history (as distinguished from natural history) is the register of events that have sprung from the voluntary actions of man in commonwealths.[2] Civil authority is authority arising out of an agreement of wills, while natural authority (that of the father in the family) has no such generation and is consequently

---

6. *L.*, Intro.
7. *L.*, ch. 4.
8. The expression 'natural reason' is not absent from Hobbes's writings, but it means the reasoning of individual men contrasted with the doubly artificial reasoning of the artificial man, the Leviathan. e.g. *L.*, Intro., chs. 6, 27, 28; *E.W.*, I, xiii.
9. *L.*, ch. 5.
1. *L.*, Intro.
2. *L.*, ch. 9.

of a different character.[3] And civil association is itself contrasted on this account with the appearance of it in mere natural gregariousness.[4]

Now, with this understanding of the meaning of both 'civil' and 'philosophical', we may determine what is to be expected for a civil philosophy. Two things may be expected from it. First, it will exhibit the internal mechanism of civil association as a system of cause and effect and settle the generation of the parts of civil association. And secondly, we may expect it to settle the generation, in terms of an hypothetical efficient cause, of the artifact as a whole; that is, to show this work of art springing from the specific nature of man. But it may be observed that two courses lie open to anyone, holding the views of Hobbes, who undertakes this project. Philosophy, we have seen, may argue from a given effect to its hypothetical efficient cause, or from a given cause to its possible effect. Often the second form of argument is excluded; this is so with sensations, when the given is an effect and the cause is to seek. But in civil philosophy, and in all reasoning concerned with artifacta, both courses are open; for the cause and the effect (human nature and civil association) are both given, and the task of philosophy is to unite the details of each to each in terms of cause and effect. Hobbes tells us[5] that his early thinking on the subject took the form of an argument from effect (civil association) to cause (human nature), from art to nature; but it is to be remarked that, not only in *Leviathan*, but also in all other accounts he gives of his civil philosophy, the form of the argument is from cause to effect, from nature to art. But, since the generation is rational and not physical, the direction from which it is considered is clearly a matter of indifference.

LEO STRAUSS

From Natural Right and History†

* * *

* * * Hobbes attempted to maintain the idea of natural law but to divorce it from the idea of man's perfection; only if natural law can be deduced from how men actually live, from the most powerful force that actually determines all men, or most men most of the time, can it be effectual or of practical value. The complete basis of natural law must be sought, not in the end of man, but in his beginnings,[1] in the *prima*

---

3. *L.*, ch. 20.
4. *L.*, ch. 17.
5. *E.W.*, II, vi, xiv.
† From *Natural Right and History* (Chicago: U of Chicago P, 1953), pp. 180–202. Reprinted by permission of The University of Chicago Press.
1. In the alternative title of the *Leviathan (The Matter, Form, and Power of a Commonwealth)* the end is not mentioned. See also what Hobbes says about his method in the Preface to *De cive*. He claims that he deduced the end from the beginning. In fact, however, he takes the end for granted; for he discovers the beginning by analyzing human nature and human affairs with that end (peace) in view (cf. *De cive*, I, 1, and *Leviathan*, chap. xi beginning). Similarly, in his analysis of right or justice, Hobbes takes for granted the generally accepted view of justice (*De cive*, Ep. ded.).

naturae or, rather, in the *primum naturae*. What is most powerful in most men most of the time is not reason but passion. Natural law will not be effectual if its principles are distrusted by passion or are not agreeable to passion.[2] Natural law must be deduced from the most powerful of all passion.

But the most powerful of all passions will be a natural fact, and we are not to assume that there is a natural support for justice or for what is human in man. Or is there a passion, or an object of passion, which is in a sense antinatural, which marks the point of indifference between the natural and the nonnatural, which is, as it were, the *status evanescendi* of nature and therefore a possible origin for the conquest of nature or for freedom? The most powerful of all passions is the fear of death and, more particularly, the fear of violent death at the hands of others: not nature but "that terrible enemy of nature, death," yet death insofar as man can do something about it, i.e., death insofar as it can be avoided or avenged, supplies the ultimate guidance.[3] Death takes the place of the *telos*. Or, to preserve the ambiguity of Hobbes's thought, let us say that the fear of violent death expresses most forcefully the most powerful and the most fundamental of all natural desires, the initial desire, the desire for self-preservation.

If, then, natural law must be deduced from the desire for self-preservation, if, in other words, the desire for self-preservation is the sole root of all justice and morality, the fundamental moral fact is not a duty but a right; all duties are derivative from the fundamental and inalienable right of self-preservation. There are, then, no absolute or unconditional duties; duties are binding only to the extent to which their performance does not endanger our self-preservation. Only the right of self-preservation is unconditional or absolute. By nature, there exists only a perfect right and no perfect duty. The law of nature, which formulates man's natural duties, is not a law, properly speaking. Since the fundamental and absolute moral fact is a right and not a duty, the function as well as the limits of civil society must be defined in terms of man's natural right and not in terms of his natural duty. The state has the function, not of producing or promoting a virtuous life, but of safeguarding the natural right of each. And the power of the state finds its absolute limit in that natural right and in no other moral fact.[4] If we may call liberalism that political doctrine which regards as the fundamental political fact the rights, as distinguished from the duties, of man and which identifies the function of the state with the protection or the safeguarding of those rights, we must say that the founder of liberalism was Hobbes.

By transplanting natural law on the plane of Machiavelli, Hobbes certainly originated an entirely new type of political doctrine. The premodern natural law doctrines taught the duties of man; if they paid any attention at all to his rights, they conceived of them as essentially derivative from his duties. As has frequently been observed, in the course of the seventeenth and eighteenth centuries a much greater emphasis was put on rights than ever had been done before. One may speak of

2. *Elements*, Ep. ded.
3. *Ibid*, I, 14, sec. 6; *De cive*, Ep. ded., I, 7, and III, 31; *Leviathan*, chaps. xiv and xxvii. One would have to start from here in order to understand the role of the detective story in present-day moral orientation.
4. *De cive*, II, III, VI, XIV; *Leviathan*, chaps. xiv, xxi, xxviii, and xxxii.

a shift of emphasis from natural duties to natural rights.[5] But quantitative changes of this character become intelligible only when they are seen against the background of a qualitative and fundamental change, not to say that such quantitative changes always become possible only by virtue of a qualitative and fundamental change. The fundamental change from an orientation by natural duties to an orientation by natural rights finds its clearest and most telling expression in the teaching of Hobbes, who squarely made an unconditional natural right the basis of all natural duties, the duties being therefore only conditional. He is the classic and the founder of the specifically modern natural law doctrine. The profound change under consideration can be traced directly to Hobbes's concern with a human guaranty for the actualization of the right social order or to his "realistic" intention. The actualization of a social order that is defined in terms of man's duties is necessarily uncertain and even improbable; such an order may well appear to be utopian. Quite different is the case of a social order that is defined in terms of the rights of man. For the rights in question express, and are meant to express, something that everyone actually desires anyway; they hallow everyone's self-interest as everyone sees it or can easily be brought to see it. Men can more safely be depended upon to fight for their rights than to fulfil their duties. In the words of Burke: "The little catechism of the rights of men is soon learned; and the inferences are in the passions."[6] With regard to Hobbes's classic formulation, we add that the premises already are in the passions. What is required to make modern natural right effective is enlightenment or propaganda rather than moral appeal. From this we may understand the frequently observed fact that during the modern period natural law became much more of a revolutionary force than it had been in the past. This fact is a direct consequence of the fundamental change in the character of the natural law doctrine itself.

The tradition which Hobbes opposed had assumed that man cannot reach the perfection of his nature except in and through civil society and, therefore, that civil society is prior to the individual. It was this assumption which led to the view that the primary moral fact is duty and not rights. One could not assert the primacy of natural rights without asserting that the individual is in every respect prior to civil society: all rights of civil society or of the sovereign are derivative from rights which originally belonged to the individual.[7] The individual as such, the individual regardless of his qualities — and not merely, as Aristotle had contended, the man who surpasses humanity — had to be conceived of as essentially complete independently of civil society. This conception is implied in the contention that there is a state of nature which antedates civil society. According to Rousseau, "the philosophers who have examined the foundations of civil society have all of them

5. Cf. Otto von Gierke, The Development of Political Theory (New York, 1939), pp. 108, 322, 352; and J. N. Figgis, The Divine Right of Kings (2d ed.; Cambridge: At the University Press, 1934), pp. 221–23. For Kant it is already a question why moral philosophy is called the doctrine of duties and not the doctrine of rights (see Metaphysik der Sitten, ed. Vorlaender, p. 45).
6. Thoughts on French Affairs, p. 367.
7. De cive, VI; Leviathan, chaps. xviii and xxviii.

felt the necessity to go back to the state of nature." It is true that the quest for the right social order is inseparable from reflection on the origins of civil society or on the prepolitical life of man. But the identification of the prepolitical life of man with "the state of nature" is a particular view, a view by no means held by "all" political philosophers. The state of nature became an essential topic of political philosophy only with Hobbes, who still almost apologized for employing that term. It is only since Hobbes that the philosophic doctrine of natural law has been essentially a doctrine of the state of nature. Prior to him, the term "state of nature" was at home in Christian theology rather than in political philosophy. The state of nature was distinguished especially from the state of grace, and it was subdivided into the state of pure nature and the state of fallen nature. Hobbes dropped the subdivision and replaced the state of grace by the state of civil society. He thus denied, if not the fact, at any rate the importance of the Fall and accordingly asserted that what is needed for remedying the deficiencies or the "inconveniences" of the state of nature is, not divine grace, but the right kind of human government. This antitheological implication of "the state of nature" can only with difficulty be separated from its intra-philosophic meaning, which is to make intelligible the primacy of rights as distinguished from duties: the state of nature is originally characterized by the fact that in it there are perfect rights but no perfect duties.[8]

---

8. *De cive*, praef.: "conditionem hominum extra societatem civilem (quam conditionem appellare liceat statum naturae)." Cf. Locke, *Treatises of Civil Government*, II, sect. 15. For the original meaning of the term, cf. Aristotle *Physics* 246ª10–17; Cicero *Offices* i. 67; *De finibus* iii. 16, 20; *Laws* iii. 3 (cf. also *De cive*, III, 25). According to the classics, the state of nature would be the life in a healthy civil society and not the life antedating civil society. The conventionalists assert, indeed, that civil society is conventional or artificial, but this implies a depreciation of civil society. Most conventionalists do not identify the life antedating civil society with the state of nature: they identify the life according to nature with the life of human fulfilment (be it the life of the philosopher or the life of the tyrant); the life according to nature is therefore impossible in the primeval condition that antedates civil society. On the other hand, those conventionalists who identify the life according to nature, or the state of nature, with the life antedating civil society, regard the state of nature as preferable to civil society (cf. Montaigne, *Essais*, II, 12, *Chronique des lettres françaises*, III, 311). Hobbes's notion of the state of nature presupposes the rejection of both the classic and the conventionalist view, for he denies the existence of a natural end, of a *summum bonum*. He identifies, therefore, the natural life with the "beginning," the life dominated by the most elementary wants; and at the same time he holds that this beginning is defective and that the deficiency is remedied by civil society. There is, then, according to Hobbes, no tension between civil society and what is natural, whereas, according to conventionalism, there is a tension between civil society and what is natural. Hence, according to conventionalism, the life according to nature is superior to civil society, whereas, according to Hobbes, it is inferior to it. We add that conventionalism is not necessarily egalitarian, whereas Hobbes's orientation necessitates egalitarianism. According to Thomas Aquinas, the *status legis naturae* is the condition in which man lived prior to the revelation of the Mosaic law (*Summa theologica* i. 2. qu. 102, *a*. 3 ad 12). It is the state in which the Gentiles live and therefore a condition of civil society (cf. Suarez, *Tr. de legibus*, I, 3, sec. 12; III, 11 ["in pura natura, vel in gentibus"]; III, 12 ["in statu purae naturae, si in illo esset respublica verum Deum naturaliter colens"]; also Grotius *De jure belli* ii. 5, sec. 15. 2 uses "status naturae" in contradistinction to the "status legis Christianae"; when Grotius [iii. 7, sec. 1] says: "citra factum humanum aut primaevo naturae statu," he shows, by the addition of "primaevo," that the state of nature as such is not "citra factum humanum" and hence does not essentially antedate civil society. However, if the human law is regarded as the outcome of human corruption, the *status legis naturae* becomes that condition in which man was subject to the law of nature alone, and not yet to any human laws (Wyclif, *De civili dominio*, II, 13, ed. Poole, p. 154). For the prehistory of Hobbes's notion of the state of nature cf. also Soto's doctrine as reported by Suarez, *op. cit.*, II, 17, sec. 9.

If everyone has by nature the right to preserve himself, he necessarily has the right to the means required for his self-preservation. At this point the question arises as to who is to be the judge of what means are required for a man's self-preservation or as to which means are proper or right. The classics would have answered that the natural judge is the man of practical wisdom, and this answer would finally lead back to the view that the simply best regime is the absolute rule of the wise and the best practicable regime is the rule of gentlemen. According to Hobbes, however, everyone is by nature the judge of what are the right means to his self-preservation. For, even granting that the wise man is, in principle, a better judge, he is much less concerned with the self-preservation of a given fool than is the fool himself. But if everyone, however foolish, is by nature the judge of what is required for his self-preservation, everything may legitimately be regarded as required for self-preservation: everything is by nature just.[9] We may speak of a natural right of folly. Furthermore, if everyone is by nature the judge of what is conducive to his self-preservation, consent takes precedence over wisdom. But consent is not effective if it does not transform itself into subjection to the sovereign. For the reason indicated, the sovereign is sovereign not because of his wisdom but because he has been made sovereign by the fundamental compact. This leads to the further conclusion that command or will, and not deliberation or reasoning, is the core of sovereignty or that laws are laws by virtue, not of truth or reasonableness, but of authority alone.[1] In Hobbes's teaching, the supremacy of authority as distinguished from reason follows from an extraordinary extension of the natural right of the individual.

The attempt to deduce the natural law or the moral law from the natural right of self-preservation or from the inescapable power of the fear of violent death led to far-reaching modifications of the content of the moral law. The modification amounted, in the first place, to a considerable simplification. Sixteenth- and seventeenth-century thought in general tended toward a simplification of moral doctrine. To say the least, that tendency easily lent itself to absorption in the broader concern with the guaranty for the actualization of the right social order. One tried to replace the "unsystematic" multiplicity of irreducible virtues by a single virtue, or by a single basic virtue from which all other virtues could be deduced. There existed two well-paved ways in which this reduction could be achieved. In the moral teaching of Aristotle, "whose opinions are at this day, and in these parts of greater authority than any other human writings" (Hobbes), there occur two virtues which comprise all other virtues or, as we may say, two "general" virtues: magnanimity, which comprises all other virtues in so far as they contribute to the excellence of the individual, and justice, which comprises all other virtues in so far as they contribute to man's serving others. Accordingly, one could simplify moral philosophy by reducing morality either to magnanimity or else to justice. The first was done by Descartes, the second by Hobbes. The latter's choice had the particular

9. *De cive*, I, III; *Leviathan*, chaps. xv and xlvi.
1. *De cive*, VI, XIV, and XVII; *Leviathan*, chap. xxvi; cf. also Sir Robert Filmer, *Observations concerning the Original of Government*, Preface.

advantage that it was favorable to a further simplification of moral doctrine: the unqualified identification of the doctrine of virtues with the doctrine of the moral or natural law. The moral law, in its turn, was to be greatly simplified by being deduced from the natural right of self-preservation. Self-preservation requires peace. The moral law became, therefore, the sum of rules which have to be obeyed if there is to be peace. Just as Machiavelli reduced virtue to the political virtue of patriotism, Hobbes reduced virtue to the social virtue of peaceableness. Those forms of human excellence which have no direct or unambiguous relation to peaceableness — courage, temperance, magnanimity, liberality, to say nothing of wisdom — cease to be virtues in the strict sense. Justice (in conjunction with equity and charity) does remain a virtue, but its meaning undergoes a radical change. If the only unconditional moral fact is the natural right of each to his self-preservation, and therefore all obligations to others arise from contract, justice becomes identical with the habit of fulfilling one's contracts. Justice no longer consists in complying with standards that are independent of human will. All material principles of justice — the rules of commutative and distributive justice or of the Second Table of the Decalogue — cease to have intrinsic validity. All material obligations arise from the agreement of the contractors, and therefore in practice from the will of the sovereign.[2] For the contract that makes possible all other contracts is the social contract or the contract of subjection to the sovereign.

If virtue is identified with peaceableness, vice will become identical with that habit or that passion which is per se incompatible with peace because it essentially and, as it were, of set purpose issues in offending others; vice becomes identical for all practical purposes with pride or vanity or *amour-propre* rather than with dissoluteness or weakness of the soul. In other words, if virtue is reduced to social virtue or to benevolence or kindness or "the liberal virtues," "the severe virtues" of self-restraint will lose their standing.[3] Here again we must have recourse to Burke's analysis of the spirit of the French Revolution; for Burke's polemical overstatements were and are indispensable for tearing away the disguises, both intentional and unintentional, in which "the new morality" introduced itself: "The Parisian philosophers . . . explode or render odious or contemptible, that class of virtues which restrain the appetite. . . . In the place of all this, they substitute a virtue which they call humanity or benevolence."[4] This substitution is the core of what we have called "political hedonism."

To establish the meaning of political hedonism in somewhat more precise terms, we must contrast Hobbes's teaching with the nonpolitical hedonism of Epicurus. The points in which Hobbes could agree with Epicurus, were these: the good is fundamentally identical with the pleasant; virtue is therefore not choiceworthy for its own sake but only with a view to the attainment of pleasure or the avoidance of pain; the

2. *Elements*, I, 17, sec. 1; *De cive*, Ep. ded., III, VI, XII, XIV, XVII, XVIII; *De homine*, XIII; *Leviathan*, chaps. xiv, xv, and xxvi.
3. "Temperantia privatio potius vitiorum quae oriuntur ab ingeniis cupidis (*quibus non laeditur civitas*, sed ipsi) quam virtus moralis (est)" (*De homine*, XIII, 9). The step from this view to "private vices, public benefits," is short.
4. Letter to Rivarol of June 1, 1791.

desire for honor and glory is utterly vain, i.e., sensual pleasures are, as such, preferable to honor or glory. Hobbes had to oppose Epicurus in two crucial points in order to make possible political hedonism. In the first place, he had to reject Epicurus' implicit denial of a state of nature in the strict sense, i.e., of a prepolitical condition of life in which man enjoys natural rights; for Hobbes agreed with the idealistic tradition in thinking that the claim of civil society stands or falls with the existence of natural right. Besides, he could not accept the implication of Epicurus' distinction between natural desires which are necessary and natural desires which are not necessary; for that distinction implied that happiness requires an "ascetic" style of life and that happiness consists in a state of repose. Epicurus' high demands on self-restraint were bound to be utopian as far as most men are concerned; they had therefore to be discarded by a "realistic" political teaching. The "realistic" approach to politics forced Hobbes to lift all restrictions on the striving for unnecessary sensual pleasures or, more precisely, for the *commoda bujus vitae*, or for power, with the exception of those restrictions that are required for the sake of peace. Since, as Epicurus said, "Nature has made [only] the necessary things easy to supply," the emancipation of the desire for comfort required that science be put into the service of the satisfaction of that desire. It required, above all, that the function of civil society be radically redefined: "the good life," for the sake of which men enter civil society, is no longer the life of human excellence but "commodious living" as the reward of hard work. And the sacred duty of the rulers is no longer "to make the citizens good and doers of noble things" but to "study, as much as by laws can be effected, to furnish the citizens abundantly with all good things . . . which are conducive to delectation."[5]

It is not necessary for our purpose to follow Hobbes's thought on its way from the natural right of everyone, or from the state of nature, to the establishment of civil society. This part of his doctrine is not meant to be more than the strict consequence from his premises. It culminates in the doctrine of sovereignty, of which he is generally recognized to be the classic exponent. The doctrine of sovereignty is a legal doctrine. Its gist is not that it is expedient to assign plenitude of power to the ruling authority but that that plenitude belongs to the ruling authority as of right. The rights of sovereignty are assigned to the supreme power on the basis not of positive law or of general custom but of natural law. The doctrine of sovereignty formulates natural public law.[6] Natural

---

5. *De cive*, I, XIII; *Leviathan*, chaps. xi and xiii; *De corpore*, I.

6. *Leviathan*, chap. xxx, the third and fourth paragraphs of the Latin version; *De cive*, IX, X, XI, XII, XIV; cf. also Malebranche, *Traité de morale*, ed. Joly, p. 214. There is this difference between natural law in the ordinary sense and natural public law, that natural public law and its subject matter (the commonwealth) are based on a fundamental fiction, on the fiction that the will of the sovereign is the will of all and of each or that the sovereign represents all and each (*De cive*, V, 6, 9, 11; VII, 14). The will of the sovereign has to be *regarded* as the will of all and of each, whereas, in fact, there is an essential discrepancy between the will of the sovereign and the wills of the individuals, the only wills that are natural: to obey the sovereign means precisely to do what the sovereign wills, not what I will. Even if my reason should habitually tell me to will what the sovereign wills, this rational will is not necessarily identical with my complete will, my actual or explicit will (cf. the reference to the "implicit wills" in *Elements*, II; cf. also *De cive*, XII). On the basis of Hobbes's premises, "representation" is then not a convenience but an essential necessity.

public law — *jus publicum universale seu naturale* — is a new discipline that emerged in the seventeenth century. It emerged in consequence of that radical change of orientation which we are trying to understand. Natural public law represents one of the two characteristically modern forms of political philosophy, the other form being "politics" in the sense of Machiavellian "reason of state." Both are fundamentally distinguished from classical political philosophy. In spite of their opposition to each other, they are motivated by fundamentally the same spirit.[7] Their origin is the concern with a right or sound order of society whose actualization is probable, if not certain, or does not depend on chance. Accordingly, they deliberately lower the goal of politics; they are no longer concerned with having a clear view of the highest political possibility with regard to which all actual political orders can be judged in a responsible manner. The "reason of state" school replaced "the best regime" by "efficient government." The "natural public law" school replaced "the best regime" by "legitimate government."

Classical political philosophy had recognized the difference between the best regime and legitimate regimes. It asserted, therefore, a variety of types of legitimate regimes; that is, what type of regime is legitimate in given circumstances depends on the circumstances. Natural public law, on the other hand, is concerned with that right social order whose actualization is possible under all circumstances. It therefore tries to delineate that social order that can claim to be legitimate or just in all cases, regardless of the circumstances. Natural public law, we may say, replaces the idea of the best regime, which does not supply, and is not meant to supply, an answer to the question of what is the just order here and now, by the idea of the just social order which answers the basic practical question once and for all, i.e., regardless of place and time.[8] Natural public law intends to give such a universally valid solution to the political problem as is meant to be universally applicable in practice. In other words, whereas, according to the classics, political theory proper is essentially in need of being supplemented by the practical wisdom of the statesman on the spot, the new type of political theory solves, as such, the crucial practical problem: the problem of what order is just here and now. In the decisive respect, then, there is no longer any need for statesmanship as distinguished from political theory. We may call this type of thinking "doctrinairism," and we shall say that doctrinairism made its first appearance within political philosophy — for lawyers are altogether in a class by themselves — in the seventeenth century. At that time the sensible flexibility of classical

7. Cf. Fr. J. Stahl, *Geschichte der Rechtsphilosophie* (2d ed.), p. 325: "Es ist eine Eigentümlichkeit der neuern Zeit, dass ihre Staatslehre (das Naturrecht) und ihre Staatskunst (die vorzugsweise sogenannte Politik) zwei völlig verschiedene Wissenschaften sind. Diese Trennung ist das Werk des Geistes, welcher in dieser Periode die Wissenschaft beherrscht. Das Ethos wird in der Vernunft gesucht, diese hat aber keine Macht über die Begebenheiten und den natürlichen Erfolg; was die äusserlichen Verhältnisse fordern und abnöthigen, stimmt gar nicht mit ihr überein, verhält sich feindlich gegen sie, die Rücksicht auf dasselbe kann daher nicht Sache der Ethik des Staates sein." Cf. Grotius *De jure belli*, Prolegomena, sec. 57.
8. Cf. *De cive*, praef. toward the end, on the entirely different status of the question of the best form of government, on the one hand, and the question of the rights of the sovereign, on the other.

political philosophy gave way to fanatical rigidity. The political philosopher became more and more indistinguishable from the partisan. The historical thought of the nineteenth century tried to recover for statesmanship that latitude which natural public law had so severely restricted. But since that historical thought was absolutely under the spell of modern "realism," it succeeded in destroying natural public law only by destroying in the process all moral principles of politics.

As regards Hobbes's teaching on sovereignty in particular, its doctrinaire character is shown most clearly by the denials which it implies. It implies the denial of the possibility of distinguishing between good and bad regimes (kingship and tyranny, aristocracy and oligarchy, democracy and ochlocracy) as well as of the possibility of mixed regimes and of "rule of law."[9] Since these denials are at variance with observed facts, the doctrine of sovereignty amounts in practice to a denial not of the existence, but of the legitimacy, of the possibilities mentioned: Hobbes's doctrine of sovereignty ascribes to the sovereign prince or to the sovereign people an unqualified right to disregard all legal and constitutional limitations according to their pleasure,[1] and it imposes even on sensible men a natural law prohibition against censuring the sovereign and his actions. But it would be wrong to overlook the fact that the basic deficiency of the doctrine of sovereignty is shared, if to different degrees, by all other forms of natural public law doctrines as well. We merely have to remind ourselves of the practical meaning of the doctrine that the only legitimate regime is democracy.

The classics had conceived of regimes (*politeiai*) not so much in terms of institutions as in terms of the aims actually pursued by the community or its authoritative part. Accordingly, they regarded the best regime as that regime whose aim is virtue, and they held that the right kind of institutions are indeed indispensable for establishing and securing the rule of the virtuous, but of only secondary importance in comparison with "education," i.e., the formation of character. From the point of view of natural public law, on the other hand, what is needed in order to establish the right social order is not so much the formation of character as the devising of the right kind of institutions. As Kant put it in rejecting the view that the establishment of the right social order requires a nation of angels: "Hard as it may sound, the problem of establishing the state [i.e., the just social order] is soluble even for a nation of devils, provided they have sense," i.e., provided that they are guided by enlightened selfishness; the fundamental political problem is simply one of "a good organization of the state, of which man is indeed capable." In the words of Hobbes, "when [commonwealths] come to be dissolved, not by external violence, but intestine

---

9. *De cive*, VII, XII; *Leviathan*, chap. xxix. See, *however*, the reference to legitimate kings and to illegitimate rulers in *De cive*, XII. *De cive*, VI and VII show that natural law, as Hobbes understands it, supplies a basis for objectively distinguishing between kingship and tyranny. Cf. also *ibid.*, XII with XIII.

1. As for the discrepancy between Hobbes's doctrine and the practice of mankind, see *Leviathan*, chaps. xx end, and xxxi end. As for the revolutionary consequences of Hobbes's doctrine of sovereignty, see *De cive*, VII as well as *Leviathan*, chaps. xix and xxix: there is no right of prescription; the sovereign is the present sovereign (see *Leviathan*, chap. xxvi).

disorder, the fault is not in men, as they are the *matter*, but as they are the *makers*, and orderers of them."[2] Man as the maker of civil society can solve once and for all the problem inherent in man as the matter of civil society. Man can guarantee the actualization of the right social order because he is able to conquer human nature by understanding and manipulating the mechanism of the passions.

There is a term that expresses in the most condensed form the result of the change which Hobbes has effected. That term is "power." It is in Hobbes's political doctrine that power becomes for the first time *eo nomine* a central theme. Considering the fact that, according to Hobbes, science as such exists for the sake of power, one may call Hobbes's whole philosophy the first philosophy of power. "Power" is an ambiguous term. It stands for *potentia*, on the one hand, and for *potestas* (or *jus* or *dominium*), on the other.[3] It means both "physical" power and "legal" power. The ambiguity is essential: only if *potentia* and *potestas* essentially belong together, can there be a guaranty of the actualization of the right social order. The state, as such, is both the greatest human force and the highest human authority. Legal power is irresistible force.[4] The necessary coincidence of the greatest human force and the highest human authority corresponds strictly to the necessary coincidence of the most powerful passion (fear of violent death) and the most sacred right (the right of self-preservation). *Potentia* and *potestas* have this in common, that they are both intelligible only in contradistinction, and in relation, to the *actus*: the *potentia* of a man is what a man *can* do, and the *potestas* or, more generally expressed, the right of a man, is what a man *may* do. The predominance of the concern with "power" is therefore only the reverse of a relative indifference to the *actus*, and this means to the purposes for which man's "physical" as well as his "legal" power is or ought to be used. This indifference can be traced directly to Hobbes's concern with an exact or scientific political teaching. The sound use of "physical" power as well as the sound exercise of rights depends on *prudentia*, and whatever falls within the province of *prudentia* is not susceptible of exactness. There are two kinds of exactness: mathematical and legal. From the point of view of mathematical exactness, the study of the *actus* and therewith of the ends is replaced by the study of *potentia*. "Physical" power as distinguished from the purposes for which it is used is morally neutral and therefore more amenable to mathematical strictness than is its use: power can be measured. This explains why Nietzsche, who went much beyond Hobbes and declared the will to power to be the essence of reality, conceived of power in terms of "quanta of power." From the point of view of legal exactness, the study of the ends is

---

2. *Leviathan*, chap. xxix; Kant, *Eternal Peace*, Definitive Articles, First Addition.
3. Cf., e.g., the headings of chap. x in the English and Latin versions of the *Leviathan*, and the headings of *Elements*, II, 3 and 4, with those of *De cive*, VIII and IX. For an example of the synonymous use of *potentia* and *potestas* see *De cive*, IX. A comparison of the title of the *Leviathan* with the Preface of *De cive* (beginning of the section on method) suggests that "power" is identical with "generation." Cf. *De corpore*, X, 1: *potentia* is the same as *causa*. In opposition to Bishop Bramhall, Hobbes insists on the identity of "power" with "potentiality" (*E.W.*, IV, 298).
4. *De cive*, XIV and XVI; *Leviathan*, chap. x.

replaced by the study of *potestas*. The rights of the sovereign, as distinguished from the exercise of these rights, permit of an exact definition without any regard to any unforeseeable circumstances, and this kind of exactness is again inseparable from moral neutrality: right declares what is permitted, as distinguished from what is honorable.[5] Power, as distinguished from the end for which power is used or ought to be used, becomes the central theme of political reflections by virtue of that limitation of horizon which is needed if there is to be a guaranty of the actualization of the right social order.

Hobbes's political doctrine is meant to be universally applicable and hence to be applicable also and especially in extreme cases. This indeed may be said to be the boast of the classic doctrine of sovereignty: that it gives its due to the extreme case, to what holds good in emergency situations, whereas those who question that doctrine are accused of not looking beyond the pale of normality. Accordingly, Hobbes built his whole moral and political doctrine on observations regarding the extreme case; for the experience on which his doctrine of the state of nature is based is the experience of civil war. It is in the extreme situation, when the social fabric has completely broken down, that there comes to sight the solid foundation on which every social order must ultimately rest: the fear of violent death, which is the strongest force in human life. Yet Hobbes was forced to concede that the fear of violent death is only "commonly" or in most cases the most powerful force. The principle which was supposed to make possible a political doctrine of universal applicability, then, is not universally valid and therefore is useless in what, from Hobbes's point of view, is the most important case — the extreme case. For how can one exclude the possibility that precisely in the extreme situation the exception will prevail?[6]

To speak in more specific terms, there are two politically important phenomena which would seem to show with particular clarity the limited validity of Hobbes's contention regarding the overwhelming power of the fear of violent death. In the first place, if the only unconditional moral fact is the individual's right of self-preservation, civil society can hardly demand from the individual that he resign that right both by going to war and by submitting to capital punishment. As regards capital punishment, Hobbes was consistent enough to grant that, by being justly and legally condemned to death, a man does not lose the right to defend his life by resisting "those that assault him": a justly condemned murderer retains — nay, he acquires — the right to kill his guards and everyone else who stands in his way to escape, in order to

---

5. *De cive*, X and VI annot. end. Cf. *Leviathan*, chap. xxi for the distinction between the permitted and the honorable (cf. Salmasius, *Defensio regia* [1649], pp. 40–45). Cf. *Leviathan*, chap. xi with Thomas Aquinas *Summa contra Gentiles* iii. 31.

6. *Leviathan*, chaps. xiii and xv. One may state this difficulty also as follows: In the spirit of the dogmatism based on skepticism, Hobbes identified what the skeptic Carneades apparently regarded as the conclusive refutation of the claims raised on behalf of justice, with the only possible justification of these claims: the extreme situation — the situation of the two shipwrecked men on a plank on which only one man can save himself — reveals, not the impossibility of justice, but the basis of justice. Yet Carneades did not contend that in such a situation one is compelled to kill one's competitor (Cicero *Republic* iii. 29–30): the extreme situation does not reveal a real necessity.

save dear life.[7] But, by granting this, Hobbes in fact admitted that there exists an insoluble conflict between the rights of the government and the natural right of the individual to self-preservation. This conflict was solved in the spirit, if against the letter, of Hobbes by Beccaria, who inferred from the absolute primacy of the right of self-preservation the necessity of abolishing capital punishment. As regards war, Hobbes, who proudly declared that he was "the first of all that fled" at the outbreak of the Civil War, was consistent enough to grant that "there is allowance to be made for natural timorousness." And as if he desired to make it perfectly clear to what lengths he was prepared to go in opposing the lupine spirit of Rome, he continues as follows: "When armies fight, there is on one side, or both, a running away: yet when they do it not out of treachery, but fear, they are not esteemed to do it unjustly, but dishonourably."[8] But, by granting this, he destroyed the moral basis of national defense. The only solution to this difficulty which preserves the spirit of Hobbes's political philosophy is the out-lawry of war or the establishment of a world state.

There was only one fundamental objection to Hobbes's basic as-sumption which he felt very keenly and which he made every effort to overcome. In many cases the fear of violent death proved to be a weaker force than the fear of hell fire or the fear of God. The difficulty is well illustrated by two widely separated passages of the Leviathan. In the first passage Hobbes says that the fear of the power of men (i.e., the fear of violent death) is "commonly" greater than the fear of the power of "spirits invisible," i.e., than religion. In the second passage he says that "the fear of darkness and ghosts is greater than other fears."[9] Hobbes saw his way to solve this contradiction: the fear of invisible powers is stronger than the fear of violent death as long as people believe in invisible powers, i.e., as long as they are under the spell of delusions about the true character of reality; the fear of violent death comes fully into its own as soon as people have become enlightened. This implies that the whole scheme suggested by Hobbes requires for its operation the weakening or, rather, the elimination of the fear of invisible powers. It requires such a radical change of orientation as can be brought about only by the disenchantment of the world, by the diffusion of scientific knowledge, or by popular enlightenment. Hobbes's is the first doctrine that necessarily and unmistakably points to a thoroughly "enlightened," i.e., a-religious or atheistic society as the solution of the social or political problem. This most important impli-cation of Hobbes's doctrine was made explicit not many years after his death by Pierre Bayle, who attempted to prove that an atheistic society is possible.[1]

7. Leviathan, chap. xxi; cf. also De cive, VIII.
8. Leviathan, chap. xxi; E.W., IV, 414. Cf. Leviathan, chap. xxx and De cive, 14, with Locke's chapter on conquest.
9. Leviathan, chaps. xiv and xxix; cf. also ibid., chap. xxxviii beginning; De cive, VI, XII, XVII.
1. A good reason for connecting Bayle's famous thesis with Hobbes's doctrine rather than with that of Faustus Socinus, e.g., is supplied by the following statement of Bayle (Dictionnaire, art. "Hobbes," rem. D): "Hobbes se fit beaucoup d'ennemis par cet ouvrage [De cive]; mais il fit avouer aux plus clairvoyants, qu'on n'avait jamais si bien pénétré les fondements de la politique." I cannot prove here that Hobbes was an atheist, even according to his own view

It is, then, only through the prospect of popular enlightenment that Hobbes's doctrine acquired such consistency as it possesses. The virtues which he ascribed to enlightenment are indeed extraordinary. The power of ambition and avarice, he says, rests on the false opinions of the vulgar regarding right and wrong; therefore, once the principles of justice are known with mathematical certainty, ambition and avarice will become powerless and the human race will enjoy lasting peace. For, obviously, mathematical knowledge of the principles of justice (i.e., the new doctrine of natural right and the new natural public law that is built on it) cannot destroy the wrong opinions of the vulgar, if the vulgar are not apprised of the results of that mathematical knowledge. Plato had said that evils will not cease from the cities if the philosophers do not become kings or if philosophy and political power do not coincide. He had expected such salvation for mortal nature as can reasonably be expected, from a coincidence over which philosophy has no control but for which one can only wish or pray. Hobbes, on the other hand, was certain that philosophy itself can bring about the coincidence of philosophy and political power by becoming popularized philosophy and thus public opinion. Chance will be conquered by systematic philosophy issuing in systematic enlightenment: *Paulatim eruditur vulgus*.[2] By devising the right kind of institutions and by enlightening the citizen body, philosophy guarantees the solution of the social problem, whose solution cannot be guaranteed by man if it is thought to depend on moral discipline.

Opposing the "utopianism" of the classics, Hobbes was concerned with a social order whose actualization is probable and even certain. The guaranty of its actualization might seem to be supplied by the fact

of atheism. I must limit myself to asking the reader to compare *De cive*, XV with *E.W.*, IV, 349. Many present-day scholars who write on subjects of this kind do not seem to have a sufficient notion of the degree of circumspection or of accommodation to the accepted views that was required, in former ages, of "deviationists" who desired to survive or to die in peace. Those scholars tacitly assume that the pages in Hobbes's writings devoted to religious subjects can be understood if they are read in the way in which one ought to read the corresponding utterances, say, of Lord Bertrand Russell. In other words, I am familiar with the fact that there are innumerable passages in Hobbes's writings which were used by Hobbes and which can be used by everyone else for proving that Hobbes was a theist and even a good Anglican. The prevalent procedure would merely lead to historical errors, if to grave historical errors, but for the fact that its results are employed for buttressing the dogma that the mind of the individual is incapable of liberating itself from the opinions which rule his society. Hobbes's last word on the question of public worship is that the commonwealth *may* establish public worship. If the commonwealth fails to establish public worship, i.e., if it allows "many sorts of worship," as it may, "it cannot be said . . . that the commonwealth is of any religion at all" (cf. *Leviathan*, chap. xxxi with the Latin version [p.m. 171]).

2. *De cive*, Ep. ded.; cf. *De corpore*, I, 7: the cause of civil war is ignorance of the causes of wars and of peace; hence the remedy is moral philosophy. Accordingly Hobbes, characteristically deviating from Aristotle (*Politics* 1302ª35 ff.), seeks the causes of rebellion chiefly in false doctrines (*De cive*, XII). The belief in the prospects of popular enlightenment — *De homine*, XIV, 13; *Leviathan*, chaps. xviii, xxx, and xxxi end — is based on the view that the natural inequality of human beings in regard to intellectual gifts is inconsiderable (*Leviathan*, chaps. xiii and xv; *De cive*, III). Hobbes's expectation from enlightenment seems to be contradicted by his belief in the power of pride or passion, and especially of pride or ambition. The contradiction is solved by the consideration that the ambition which endangers civil society is characteristic of a minority: of "the rich and potent subjects of a kingdom, or those that are accounted the most learned"; if "the common people," whom necessity "keepeth attent on their trades, and labour," are properly taught, the ambition and avarice of the few will become powerless. Cf. also *E.W.*, IV, 443–44.

that the sound social order is based on the most powerful passion and therewith on the most powerful force in man. But if the fear of violent death is truly the strongest force in man, one should expect the desired social order always, or almost always, to be in existence, because it will be produced by natural necessity, by the natural order. Hobbes overcomes this difficulty by assuming that men in their stupidity interfere with the natural order. The right social order does not normally come about by natural necessity on account of man's ignorance of that order. The "invisible hand" remains ineffectual if it is not supported by the *Leviathan* or, if you wish, by the *Wealth of Nations*.

There is a remarkable parallelism and an even more remarkable discrepancy between Hobbes's theoretical philosophy and his practical philosophy. In both parts of his philosophy, he teaches that reason is impotent and that it is omnipotent, or that reason is omnipotent because it is impotent. Reason is impotent because reason or humanity have no cosmic support: the universe is unintelligible, and nature "dissociates" men. But the very fact that the universe is unintelligible permits reason to rest satisfied with its free constructs, to establish through its constructs an Archimedean basis of operations, and to anticipate an unlimited progress in its conquest of nature. Reason is impotent against passion, but it can become omnipotent if it co-operates with the strongest passion or if it puts itself into the service of the strongest passion. Hobbes's rationalism, then, rests ultimately on the conviction that, thanks to nature's kindness, the strongest passion is the only passion which can be "the origin of large and lasting societies" or that the strongest passion is the most rational passion. In the case of human things, the foundation is not a free construct but the most powerful natural force in man. In the case of human things, we understand not merely what we make but also what makes our making and our makings. Whereas the philosophy or science of nature remains fundamentally hypothetical, political philosophy rests on a nonhypothetical knowledge of the nature of man. As long as Hobbes's approach prevails, "the philosophy concerned with the human things" will remain the last refuge of nature. For at some point nature succeeds in getting a hearing. The modern contention that man can "change the world" or "push back nature" is not unreasonable. One can even safely go much beyond it and say that man can expel nature with a hayfork. One ceases to be reasonable only if one forgets what the philosophic poet adds, *tamen usque recurret.*[3]

---

3. However, [nature] always returns [probably from Lucretius; *Editor*].

JOHANN P. SOMMERVILLE

[Hobbes on Political Obligation]†

Hobbes' moral and political opinions differed from those of most of his contemporaries on a number of details. They also differed in one important general respect. For Hobbes, all moral principles derive ultimately from individual self-preservation. For others, self-preservation was indeed important, but it was only one of a number of rules, each of which generated moral conclusions. The upshot of this is that it is doubtful whether it makes sense to describe Hobbes as having any genuine moral system at all. Normally, if we say that someone has a moral obligation to do something, we mean that he should do it whether or not it is in his interest. But for Hobbes, fulfilling a moral obligation means doing what leads to self-preservation, and self-preservation is in the individual's interest. Of course, other theorists gave people an incentive to carry out their moral obligations by claiming that if they failed to do so God would punish them either in this world or the next. 'Honesty is the best policy' was the claim, and this meant that it is always prudent to act honestly since the unpleasant consequences of dishonesty will inevitably outweigh any short-term benefits that it confers. But the usual attitude was that honesty is obligatory quite independently of any advantages that it brings. We have a moral obligation to obey the laws of nature, said theorists, and we also have a strong incentive to do so, since the consequences of disobedience will be very unfavourable for us. But though self-interest may provide a *motive* for obedience, it is not the ground of our obligation to obey.

Some commentators have argued that in Hobbes' system there is a similar distinction between the obligation to obey natural law and our motives for obedience. They claim that the obligation to obey is derived from the fact that the laws of nature are the commands of God. Self-preservation, so the argument runs, furnishes us only with a motive for obedience and not with the grounds of our obligation to obey. A major implication of this thesis is that Hobbes' theory is far closer than has usually been supposed to the orthodoxy of his contemporaries. This sort of argument was advanced by A. E. Taylor in 1938, and revised and extended by Howard Warrender in 1957. Warrender claimed that the ultimate source of obligation in Hobbes is God. Hobbes, he observed, distinguishes between two forms of 'natural obligation', both of which spring from God's power. The first of these forms might be called physical obligation, since it occurs 'when liberty is taken away by corporal impediments' (*De Cive*, ch. 15: 'ubi libertas impedimentis corporeis tollitur'). In other words, God has set down the physical rules according

---

† From *Thomas Hobbes: Political Ideas in Historical Context* by Johann P. Sommerville (New York: St. Martin's Press, 1992), pp. 74–79. Copyright © Johann P. Sommerville. Reprinted with permission of St. Martin's Press Incorporated.

Full citations to the works cited in notes 1–6, and to incomplete citations in subsequent selections, will be found in the Selected Bibliography (p. 377).

to which things operate. The second — and, from Warrender's point of view, crucial — type of obligation arises in people as a result of their consciousness of their own weakness and of God's irresistible power. Reason dictates that when we have no power to resist we are obliged to obey. Warrender calls this type of obligation 'moral obligation'.[1]

According to Warrender, the whole of Hobbes' theory of political obligation follows from our obligation to obey an irresistible God. Of course, we can have no such obligation if we are unaware of God's existence. So atheists — on Warrender's interpretation of Hobbes — have no obligation to obey natural law or the sovereign. All who do acknowledge God's existence, however, perceive that the laws of nature are God's laws and that obedience to them is morally obligatory. Political obligation, Warrender argued, follows from our duty to fulfil the laws of nature, including the law prescribing that we keep our covenants. The entire system of obligation is grounded, then, upon God's commands, or perhaps upon fear of the penalties for breaking these commands.[2]

Self-preservation, he continued, enters the picture only inasmuch as it gives us a *motive* for obeying natural law. According to Hobbes' psychological theory, he claimed, self-preservation is the supreme motive for people (except for salvation). Since it is rational for people to act in accordance with their best interests, and since these necessarily include self-preservation, they cannot rationally act in a way which is calculated not to preserve themselves. So we can have no adequate motive for obeying natural law if it does not in fact promote our preservation. But according to Warrender, all that follows from this is that congruence with self-preservation is a 'validating condition' of obedience to natural law — in that it makes such obedience psychologically possible. It does not at all follow that self-preservation is the *ground* of the obligation to obey.[3]

Warrender added two important contentions to his discussion of self-preservation, both of which are intended to demonstrate that individual self-preservation is not at the core of Hobbes' theory of obligation. The first is that natural law in Hobbes is concerned less with the preservation of the individual than with 'the conservation of men in multitudes'. 'The laws of nature', declared Warrender, 'are not strictly rules for personal preservation'; rather 'they are rules for the preservation of men in general'. The second, and connected claim is that individual self-preservation in Hobbes is described not as a duty but as a right (though Warrender added on the basis of some of Hobbes' other statements that even if it was a duty it would oblige us only because God has commanded it). The implication of both these claims is that the laws of

1. Warrender 1957, 8–10; Warrender held that Hobbes himself probably intended to ground obligation 'upon divine reward and punishment', but that he may have wished to ground it 'simply on the will of God' or 'upon a body of natural law having self-evident or intrinsic authority'; he asserted that the last option 'is the solution I would have preferred Hobbes to have taken': Warrender 1965, 90. A.E. Taylor's 'The ethical doctrine of Hobbes' was first published in *Philosophy* for 1938. It is reprinted (with small changes) in Taylor 1965. Brown 1965 contains much useful material on the controversy over the Taylor and Warrender theses.
2. Warrender 1957, 278–311.
3. Ibid., 92, 210–13.

nature and our duty to obey them are in no sense derived from individual self-preservation. If the laws are about 'the preservation of men in general' they cannot stem from a principle concerned only with the preservation of the individual. Again, if Hobbes had intended to ground a system of duties upon individual self-preservation, he would surely have made that principle itself a duty.[4]

According to Warrender, all obligations in Hobbes arise either through covenants or through laws.[5] Since the laws of nature are not covenants, it follows that it is as laws that they oblige — and not as theorems or dictates of reason. Hobbes tells us that it is in virtue of being commanded by God that natural laws are properly laws. Warrender drew the consequence that the laws of nature oblige us only because God has commanded them. There are a number of major problems with this highly ingenious argument. Firstly, as Quentin Skinner in particular has pointed out, if Warrender's account is correct Hobbes turns into a rather conventional exponent of natural law theory, and if this is so it is very surprising that his contemporaries failed to notice the fact. For those contemporaries believed that Hobbes *was* attempting to ground obligations upon the preservation of the individual.[6]

Secondly, the textual warrant for Warrender's thesis is dubious. Hobbes discusses the laws of nature extensively in the fifteenth chapter of *Leviathan* without mentioning God until the very end. There, indeed, he does state that if we consider the theorems of reason concerning self-preservation as they are 'delivered in the word of God, that by right commandeth all things; then are they properly called Lawes' (Lev 15: 111/80). But he places no weight at all upon this point. In the thirty-first chapter Hobbes addresses a similar topic, arguing that God rules by natural law over all who acknowledge his power (Lev 31: 246/ 187). Atheists, he here asserts, are not God's subjects because 'they acknowledge no Word for his, nor have hope of his rewards, or fear of his threatnings' (Lev 31: 246/186). He then proceeds to outline the duties towards God which believers in him may perceive by reason alone, and without any special revelation. Atheists, who do not believe in him, have no such duties. But Hobbes nowhere states that atheists lack obligations connected with their own preservation. If he had intended to base his whole theory of obligation upon God's commands, it is odd that he gave so little prominence to the point. Indeed, Filmer drew the conclusion that Hobbes did not really believe that the law of nature was 'given by God' at all.[7]

Warrender's thesis relies upon the claim that only laws and covenants oblige in Hobbes. In both the Roman and the common laws there was a close conceptual connection between obligation and agreements entered into by individuals — contracts or deeds.[8] The same association is to be found in Hobbes, though like many of his contemporaries he also

4. Ibid., 216, 213; 1965, 97; 1969, 153.
5. Warrender 1957, 28–9, 93–4.
6. Skinner 1972a, especially at 139–41.
7. Filmer 1991, 189.
8. Justinian 391–3 (III, 13), 476–84; Cowell 1607, sig.2Z1b-2a.

spoke of laws as creating obligations. But did Hobbes think that the laws of nature, considered merely as theorems of reason and not strictly as laws, impose obligations? The answer to this question is yes. 'The law of nature', he said, 'always and everywhere obliges' (*De Cive*, Ch. 3: 'legem naturae semper et ubique obligare'; cf. Lev 15: 110/79). There is not the slightest hint here or elsewhere in his discussion of natural law that atheists are under no obligation to obey it. Hobbes suggested that the existence of God can be proved by reason, but argued that the necessary proof was so difficult that men could easily be ignorant of it (*De Cive*, Ch. 14 Annot; see also Chapter 6, section 1 below). By contrast, he declared that no one could be ignorant of the laws of nature, for 'to leave all men unexcusable, they have been contracted into one easie sum, intelligible, even to the meanest capacity; and that is, *Do not that to another, which thou wouldest not have done to thy selfe*' (Lev 15: 109/79). Ignorance of the laws of nature cannot excuse anyone — even an atheist — from obeying them, since no one can in fact be ignorant of them. This makes no sense unless all are obliged to obey, even without knowledge of God. The primary sense in which the laws of nature oblige in Hobbes is as dictates or theorems of reason telling us how to preserve ourselves. Those who believe that the laws are also divine decrees or that God will punish us for infringing them — either here on earth by means of such natural punishments as disease for intemperance (Lev 31: 253–4/193), or by withholding eternal salvation from us in the afterlife — may have an additional incentive to obey them. But Hobbes shows little interest in such added incentives, and bases no point of importance upon them.

Warrender's contention that Hobbes' laws of nature are 'rules for the preservation of men in general' and not just for personal preservation is difficult to sustain. As we have seen, Hobbes' lists of the laws are singularly lacking in principles which provide for the propagation of the species, or which prefer the public good to private preservation. But the point is most decisively made simply by looking once again at Hobbes' definition of a law of nature. It is, he said, 'a Precept, or generall Rule, found out by Reason, by which a man is forbidden to do, that, which is destructive of his life, or taketh away the means of preserving the same; and to omit, that, by which he thinketh it may be best preserved' (Lev 14: 91/64). Plainly, the laws of nature *are* primarily rules for personal preservation, and only secondarily principles for the preservation of others. You should aim at peace, Hobbes is saying, because it will preserve you, though it is also incidentally true that it will benefit others.

As we have seen, Warrender argued that self-preservation in Hobbes' theory is a right not a duty, and therefore cannot be the basis of a system of duties. This argument is dubious. The right of nature in Hobbes is not simply a right to preserve yourself but rather a right to exercise your own judgement about the means most conducive to this end. It makes sense to call this a right because you can agree *not* to exercise your own judgement but instead to follow someone else's — and this is just what you do agree to when you enter the common-wealth. As we have just seen, Hobbes defines the laws of nature as deductions from the principle of individual self-preservation. They are, he said, 'derived from a single dictate of reason, exhorting us to seek our own preservation and safety' (*De Cive*, ch. 3: 'ab unico rationis, nos ad nostri conservationem & incolumitatem hortantis, dictamine derivata'). Since self-preservation is not deduced from itself, it does not qualify as a law of nature under Hobbes' definition of that term. But it is none the less the principle from which all the laws of nature — and not just the motive to obey them — are generated.

The idea that all obligation in Hobbes stems from God's will cannot be vindicated. His conception of morality is reducible to calculations of self-interest. It is sometimes asked whether Hobbes was a natural law theorist. As we have seen, there are a great many respects in which his theory coincides with those of natural law thinkers like Suarez and Grotius, and such perceptive contemporaries as Edward Gee and Sir Robert Filmer took him to be engaged in the same kind of activity as these writers. But by attempting to make moral philosophy an objective science grounded upon self-preservation, Hobbes altered the laws of nature in a vital respect, emptying them of any specifically moral as opposed to self-interested content. Provided these facts are recognised, it seems very much a matter of taste whether we style Hobbes a natural law theorist or not.

RICHARD TUCK

[Hobbes on Skepticism and Moral Conflict]†

*   *   *

Just as Hobbes's philosophy of science was in effect designed to validate and explain the traditional sceptical view that our observation of the world is radically contaminated by illusion, so his philosophy of ethics was intended to underwrite the traditional sceptic's moral relativism. It is important to stress here that Hobbes's writings on politics were intended to elucidate broadly *ethical* issues, and that he was not concerned (at least on the face of it) with explaining political behaviour in the supposedly 'value-free' manner of a modern political scientist. The dedicatory letters to both the *Elements of Law* and *De Cive* make this absolutely clear — particularly perhaps the latter, in which Hobbes remarked that 'what deals with figures, is called *Geometry*, with motion, *Physics*, and with natural right, *Morals*: all of them together are *Philosophy*'. The central problem with which he was concerned in the third section of his philosophy was thus not the explanation of human action (that belonged, if anywhere, in Section Two), but the problem of 'nat-

---

† From *Hobbes* by Richard Tuck (Oxford: Oxford UP, 1989), pp. 51–64. © Richard Tuck 1989. Reprinted by permission of Oxford University Press.

ural right' — the existence or non-existence of common ethical standards by which men should live their lives.

As we saw in Part I, the particular kind of humanism which had been fashionable in Hobbes's youth, and which was represented above all by the figures of Montaigne and Lipsius, stressed the sheer multiplicity of human beliefs and customs and threw up its hands in despair at the prospect of finding any common moral denominator. All that it was safe to say of human beings, these humanists came to believe, was that they are primarily concerned with preserving themselves in a dangerous world — and one made doubly dangerous by the presence of competing ideologies. This impulse to self-preservation, however, was not itself a moral matter. As we also saw in Part I, Hugo Grotius proposed what is in retrospect (like most good ideas) an obvious twist to this argument, namely that self-preservation *is* a moral principle: it is the foundational 'natural right' upon which all known moralities and codes of social behaviour must have been constructed. But it is balanced by a fundamental duty or 'natural law' to abstain from harming other people except where our own preservation is at stake.

Grotius's idea was that there must be a kind of equilibrium of permitted violence for any society to survive. If *too little* violence were permitted — that is, if people were not allowed to defend themselves when wantonly attacked — then a few aggressive individuals would destroy the rest. If *too much* violence were permitted — if people were allowed to attack other members of the society for whatever reasons they themselves thought fit — then this too would wreck the possibility of social life. So whatever the laws and customs of a society (and Grotius was as fully conscious as any earlier relativist of the enormous moral divergences between societies), they must in part be designed to protect this equilibrium of violence. Beyond this common core, however, societies could differ extravagantly in their laws, and anything which was accepted as law in a particular society would be immune to moral criticism coming from someone outside the society.

This was the most up-to-date and appealing moral theory on offer when Hobbes began to write the ethical section of his *Elements of Philsophy*, and it is not surprising that we constantly find echoes of Grotius in his works. It should be said that Grotius is virtually never referred to by *name*; but he shares that characteristic with almost all other philosophers, both past and contemporary — Hobbes being extremely reluctant to locate his own ideas in any familiar intellectual context. Hobbes's first task was to show that the relativist idea was correct, and could be explained by his own philosophy of science; he then had to show that something like the Grotian theory also followed from his fundamental principles — though he introduced into it a new sceptical twist, comparable perhaps to the hyperbolical doubt which Descartes had introduced in the course of his refutation of scepticism, and his answer to this new doubt pushed his political conclusions some way away from Grotius's.

The relativist idea was pungently expressed by Hobbes in the *Elements of Law*:

Every man, for his own part, calleth that which pleaseth, and is delightful to himself, GOOD; and that EVIL which displeaseth him: insomuch that while every man differeth from other in constitution, they differ also one from another concerning the common distinction of good and evil. Nor is there any such thing as ἀγαθὸν ἁπλῶ ζ [*agathon haplos*], that is to say, simply good. For even the goodness which we attribute to God Almighty, is his goodness to us. And as we call good and evil the things that please and displease us; so call we goodness and badness, the qualities of powers whereby they do it. (I.7.3)

Hobbes, in other words, treated *moral* terms in exactly the same way as he had treated colour terms: though common language and common sense might lead us to think that something is really and objectively good, in the same way as we might think something is really and objectively red, in fact such ideas are illusions or fantasies, features of the inside of our heads only. The sensation of colour is to be understood, as we have seen, as what it feels like to come under the influence of something in the external world which is not itself a colour, but a pulse of light impinging on our eyes; similarly, moral approval or disapproval are to be understood as feelings engendered by the impact of something external on the system of passions and wants which make up the human emotive psychology.

That there is such a system, Hobbes not unnaturally took for granted, regarding it as a matter of direct introspective observation. He equally took it for granted that the system must function in accordance with the general metaphysical principles he had laid down for all scientific explanation — that is, it must take the form of what we might call a *ballistical* system, in which moving bodies interact in various ways. But the specific theory he put forward was, like his optics, a *theory* only, though he claimed that it was superior to all other hypotheses available.

For it, he drew once again on Harvey's discovery of the circulation of the blood, and proposed that it was one part of a complicated system involving 'animal' and 'vital' spirits. To understand this, we have to remember that even schoolchildren nowadays are incomparably better equipped to talk about basic chemistry than the most highly educated intellectual of Stuart England. We possess, for example, the absolutely familiar and useful term 'gas' to describe a particular state in which matter can be found; but the word was only invented by a Flemish medical alchemist in Hobbes's lifetime, and was not in common usage for another hundred years. We also have the notion of electrical transmission through fibres, and an awareness that electricity and chemistry are intimately connected; again, no one in Hobbes's time could have had these ideas. So we must not think that he meant by 'spirit' anything particularly mysterious, and especially that he meant something *incorporeal* — Hobbes always insisted, as we have seen, that there could be no such thing.

What he meant was simply that there is some mechanical system in the body whereby sense-perceptions are transmitted to the brain, and that they there cause perturbations to the 'spirits' which link the brain and the heart, and that the consequent perturbations in the heart affect the circulation of the blood — and *in extremis* would cut it off altogether, killing the animal. The different physiological changes during this process are describable in terms of the familiar language of perception and emotion: thus the alterations in the make-up of the brain are *perceptions*, and the alterations in the behaviour of the blood are *passions*. Both kinds of alteration mistakenly lead people to attribute relevant properties to external objects, so that a spider, for example, can seem both 'black' and 'frightening', and perhaps also 'evil', though none of these terms really refers to anything.

Because moral judgements are a matter of feeling as well as perception, it was reasonable for Hobbes to say on the basis of this theory (as he always did) that the description of something as 'good' must be broadly the same as the description of it as 'pleasurable' — for the feeling of moral approbation is in a way a feeling of pleasure at the action in question. But it would also have been reasonable for him to have pointed out that the two feelings are not quite the same, and that the difference between them needs some explanation (a point made later, in effect, by Hume). That he never did, and persisted in holding that 'the good' and 'the pleasurable' were identical, is best seen as the consequence of his immersion in the scepticism of Montaigne's time, with its standard assumption that people take to be 'good' what is in their own interest (or, in the Latin terminology which they employed, and which went back to comparable arguments to be found in Cicero, that what was *honestum* was what was *utile*).

Having insinuated this identity, Hobbes had both stated and explained moral relativism: there were no objective moral properties, but what seemed good was what pleased any individual or was good *for him*. The implicit 'realism' of ordinary moral language, like that of the ordinary language of colour, was therefore a serious error. Hobbes indeed usually treated this error as the major difficulty in the way of a peaceful life, rather than (as is often supposed) viewing the clash of naked self-interest as the fundamental problem in human social existence.

The account of the passions which Hobbes gave, after all, treated them as broadly beneficial: what men feel strongly about or desire strongly is what helps them to survive, and they cannot for long want a state of affairs in which their survival is endangered. Such a view was common ground between Hobbes and many of his contemporaries, including Descartes: all argued that the traditional idea that reason should control the passions was an error, and that (properly understood) our emotions would guide us in the right direction. Men, on Hobbes's account, do not want to harm other men *for the sake of harming them*; they wish for power over them, it is true, but power only to secure their own preservation. The common idea that Hobbes was in some sense 'pessimistic' about human nature is wide of the mark, for his natural men (rather like Grotius's) were in principle stand-offish towards one another rather than inherently belligerent.

But Hobbes did believe that such creatures could not enjoy a decent social existence unless they were capable of using a common moral language to describe their activities. This is simply a deep-rooted assumption in his work, which is never fully justified, but which is constantly implied by the way in which he described the problem of human conflict. In *De Cive*, for example, he observed that

> the desires of men are different, as men differ among themselves in temperament, custom and opinion; we see this in sense-perceptions such as taste, touch or smell, but even more in the common business of life, where what one person *praises* — that is, calls *good* — another will *condemn* and call *evil*. Indeed, often the same man at different times will *praise* and *blame* the same thing. As long as this is the case there will necessarily arise discord and conflict. (III.31)

It was conflict over what to *praise*, or morally to approve, which Hobbes thus isolated as the cause of discord, rather than simple conflict over *wants*. What he was frightened of, it is reasonable to assume, were such things as the Wars of Religion, or other ideological wars; not (say) class wars, in which the clash of wants could more clearly be seen.

The malleability of opinion by outside forces was part of this problem: as he said in the passage just quoted, the same man could often believe quite different things, depending on the circumstances. In *Leviathan*, indeed, Hobbes describes the minds of 'the Common-people' as 'like clean paper, fit to receive whatsoever by Publique Authority shall be imprinted in them' unless they had already been 'scribbled over with the opinions of their Doctors' (ch. 30). Controlling or combating the pens which could write on this clean paper was crucial, and it was this which led him throughout his work bitterly to condemn the activities of rhetoricians: 'such is the power of eloquence, as many times a man is made to believe thereby, that he sensibly feeleth smart and damage, when he feeleth none, and to enter into rage and indignation, without any cause, than what is in the words and passion of the speaker' (*Elements of Law* II.8; see also *De Cive* XII). This was despite the fact that he himself, like all humanists, was both fascinated by and very skilled at rhetoric; indeed he wrote a couple of works on the subject to be read by his Cavendish pupils (one was published in 1637). But the power of rhetoric, and of other outside influences on opinion, made the resolution of conflict a doubly difficult affair.

Nevertheless, Hobbes believed that there was a solution to moral conflict. The traditional moralist's response to ethical disagreement had been to hope that sooner or later everyone would come to see the moral *facts* clearly and rationally, but Hobbes of course could not resort to pious hopes of this kind. Instead, he proposed that the route to agreement must lie through *politics*, and this must count as Hobbes's most distinctive contribution to political theory. He put his idea most clearly, and most sceptically, in a passage of the *Elements of Law* where he contrasted a 'state of nature' (by which he meant the condition of men without some proper political organization) with the state of men under a regime of civil laws — a state later writers standardly termed 'civil society', but which Hobbes (though he did sometimes use that expression) more commonly called a 'commonwealth' or, when he wrote in Latin, a *civitas* ('city' or 'state'). This passage contains, I believe, an accurate summary of the whole of Hobbes's theory, and is worth quoting at length.

> In the state of nature, where every man is his own judge, and differeth from other concerning the names and appellations of things, and from those differences arise quarrels, and breach of peace; it was necessary there should be a common measure of all things that might fall in controversy; as for example: of what is to be called right, what good, what virtue, what much, what little, what *meum* and *tuum*, what a pound, what a quart, &c. For in these things private judgements may differ and beget controversy. This common measure, some say, is right reason: with whom I should consent, if there were any such thing to be found or known *in rerum natura*. But commonly they that call for right reason to decide any controversy, do mean their own. But this is certain, seeing right reason is not existent, the reason of some man, or men, must supply the place thereof; and that man, or men, is he or they, that have the sovereign power . . . ; and consequently the civil laws are to all subjects the measures of their actions, whereby to determine, whether they be right or wrong, profitable or unprofitable, virtuous or vicious; and by them the use and definition of all names not agreed upon, and tending to controversy, shall be established. As for example, upon the occasion of some strange and deformed birth, it shall not be decided by Aristotle, or the philosophers, whether the same be a man or no, but by the laws. (II.10.)

This was the vision at the heart of Hobbes's moral and political philosophy, and whenever he had to summarize his theory (as, for example, in the *Critique of Thomas White* — see fo. 425v), he put some version of this idea in a central position.

But the obvious problem about it is this: if politics creates the moral consensus, how is political life possible in the first place? Surely the moral disagreements of the state of nature will overwhelm any attempt to set up a civil society or commonwealth? To answer this question, Hobbes (like Grotius) shifted from talking about 'the good', which had been the traditional subject for both ancient and Renaissance moralists, to talking instead about 'rights' — a subject which the ancient and Renaissance writers had barely tackled; indeed, there is arguably no word in classical Greek or Latin for a 'right'. It was much more the traditional material of medieval scholastic moralists, and its use in a central position by both Grotius and Hobbes marked a considerable break in appearances with the humanism of their youth, though the break in substance was much less striking. But within the language of rights, Hobbes first contrived a new sceptical doubt which seemed to render even the Grotian answer to relativism untenable, and which gave rise to the most famous aspect of Hobbes's theory: the picture of men as naturally and savagely at war with one another.

Put simply, Hobbes's argument begins in the following way. There is one thing on which even in a state of nature we can all agree, and that is that other people have a right to defend themselves against attack. We can also agree that if they wish to exercise that right, they will *have* to do certain things: they cannot, for example, exercise a right of self-preservation merely by sitting around and not responding when attacked. But we will also have to recognize that in a state of nature, there will be a larger number of cases where everyone must be their own judge of how and when to defend themselves.

The consequence of this last fact is that, despite our initial agreement about the general right of self-preservation, there will in practice still be a radical instability in the state of nature. There is not much point in my saying that I agree with you in principle about your right to preserve yourself, if I disagree about whether this is the moment for you to *implement* that right. Suppose I see you walking peacefully through the primitive savannah, whistling and swinging your club: are you a danger to me? You may well think not: you have an entirely pacific disposition. But I may think you are, and the exercise of my natural right of self-preservation depends only on *my* assessment of the situation. So if I attack you, I must be justified in doing so. We have all the instability of a wholly relativist world back again, despite our agreement that people are in general justified in protecting themselves. The state of nature thus becomes a state of war, savagery, and degradation — of which, Hobbes remarked, 'present-day Americans give us an example' (*De Cive* I.).

As I said, this is Hobbes's argument put in a simple form. Before discussing how he proposed to get from the state of nature to civil society, it is worth enlarging on the details of the argument, all of which have proved contentious for generations of Hobbes's readers.

First, what is involved in the claim that we can all agree that each of us possesses a right to defend ourselves? Hobbes expressed the claim in the following way in the *Elements of Law*:

> forasmuch as necessity of nature maketh men to will and desire *bonum sibi*, that which is good for themselves, and to avoid that which is hurtful; but most of all that terrible enemy of nature, death . . . ; it is not against reason that a man doth all he can to preserve his own body and limbs, both from death and pain. And that which is not against reason, men call RIGHT, or *jus*, or blameless liberty of using our own natural power and ability. It is therefore a *right of nature*: that every man may preserve his own life and limbs, with all the power he hath. (I.14.6)

In both *De Cive* and *Leviathan* we find almost identical formulations. On the face of it, this passage might suggest that whatever we do, we must have the right to do it, since, according to Hobbes's general theory of action, we always act in such a way as to secure what we take to be good for us; so that the right to preserve ourselves is merely a special case of this general right. A philosopher later in the seventeenth century who did in fact say just this was the Dutchman Benedict de Spinoza, who drew in many respects on Hobbes's ideas. But Hobbes did not himself ever argue such a thing; indeed, on a number of occasions he specifically said that it is possible in a state of nature to do things, and to want to do things, which we have *no* right to do. In one of the explanatory footnotes to the second edition of *De Cive*, for example, he observed that it would be impossible ever to justify drunkenness or cruelty ('that is, revenge which does not look to some future good'), since they could never be seen as conducing to our preservation (III). It is clear that he believed that our only natural right is the right barely to preserve ourselves, and to use whatever means we take to be necessary for that purpose.

His reasons for thinking this are not set out straightforwardly anywhere, but the limitation of our 'natural' rights to self-preservation alone is something which makes very good sense against the background of Hobbes's pessimism about human mental and emotional malleability. If we are skilled at persuasion, for example, then for our own purposes we can get other people to believe and want almost anything; the one thing we will *not* be able to persuade them is that they want their own death. At that point their fundamental nature will rebel against us. Everyone, in turn, will have to recognize this fact about other people, and thus to accept that the one common and unmalleable belief to be found among men is the belief that their own preservation is a good. Beyond that, any belief is possible. Seen in this light, Hobbes's reasons for limiting our natural rights to the special case of self-preservation were precisely the same as Grotius's: the fact that whatever else people might believe, they will have to acknowledge that all men will always, whatever the circumstances, want to preserve themselves — and that this is the *one* thing which they will always want to do. If there is to be agreement among men, it will have to be on such a basis; if we were to acknowledge other people's right to do whatever they wanted, we would have no hope of leaving the world of moral conflict.

It should be said that Hobbes took seriously one possible exception to the universality of self-preservation, the case of martyrdom for religious reasons (see *Elements of Law* II.6, *De Cive* XVIII, and *Leviathan* ch. 43). However, as we shall see later in the section on religion, Hobbes's attitude to martyrdom altered during his life as his views about the Christian religion changed. In the earlier works he had a good reason for supposing that Christian martyrdom was a special case; in *Leviathan* he no longer had such a reason, and the discussion of martyrdom in that work is appropriately muted: Christians, he now argued, have for their faith 'the licence that Naaman had, and need not put themselves into danger for it'.

The second claim which Hobbes made, and which has proved puzzling to many readers, was the one which I summarized earlier by saying that men in a state of nature can agree that if they wish to exercise their natural right to self-preservation, they will *have* to do certain things: they cannot, for example, exercise this right merely by sitting around and not responding when attacked. Hobbes expressed this claim by talking about the *law of nature*. In the *Elements of Law* he argued as follows:

> Forasmuch as all men, carried away by the violence of their pas-
> sion, and by evil custom, do those things which are commonly
> said to be against the law of nature; it is not the consent of passion,
> or consent in some error gotten by custom, that makes the law of
> nature. Reason is no less of the nature of man than passion, and
> is the same in all men, because all men agree in the will to be
> directed and governed in the way to that which they desire to
> attain, namely their own good, which is the work of reason. There
> can therefore be no other law of nature than reason, nor no other
> precepts of NATURAL LAW, than those which declare unto us
> the ways of peace, where the same may be obtained, and of de-
> fence where it may not. (I.15)

Once again, we find virtually identical formulations in *De Cive* and
Leviathan.

What Hobbes meant was that if you wish to preserve yourself, then
it is absurd — a logical error — to suppose that you could better preserve
yourself in a situation of war than one of peace. The exercise of the
right of nature requires as a matter of logic that men do whatever the
law of nature requires. He did not mean that men *will* always follow
the precepts of the law — as he said in *De Cive* (III), passions and
perturbations of the mind can prevent people from apprehending the
truth of the precepts; 'but there is no one who is not sometimes in a
quiet mind', and when in that condition they will see clearly what they
must do.

The puzzle which has sometimes arisen about this argument is, what
is the point of differentiating between a *right* of nature and a *law* of
nature, if the general theory is that we *have* to defend ourselves and
have to follow certain rules in order to do so? The puzzle is made
particularly teasing because Hobbes actually took some care to distinguish between rights and laws: in *Leviathan* he remarked that 'RIGHT,
consisteth in liberty to do, or to forbeare; Whereas LAW, determineth,
and bindeth to one of them: so that Law, and Right, differ as much,
as Obligation, and Liberty; which in one and the same matter are
inconsistent' (ch. 14; cf. *Elements of Law* II.10 and *De Cive* XIV).
Hobbes's first readers, friendly and hostile alike, were struck by this
point. As Sir Robert Filmer, one of the hostile ones, said,

> If the right of nature be a liberty for a man to do anything he
> thinks fit to preserve his life, then in the first place nature must
> teach him that life is to be preserved, and so consequently forbids
> to do that which may destroy or take away the means of life . . . :
> and thus the right of nature and the law of nature will be all one:
> for I think Mr. Hobbes will not say the right of nature is a liberty
> for a man to destroy his own life . . .

But this objection, and the similar ones made by more recent writers
(see Part III), miss the point of Hobbes's definition of the right of nature. In the *Elements of Law*, he said that the right was for a man to
'preserve his own life and limbs, *with all the power he hath*' (my italics),
and in *Leviathan* he said (even more clearly) that the right 'is the

Liberty each man hath to use his own power, *as he will himselfe*, for the preservation of his own Nature' (ch. 14; again, my italics). The thing which Hobbes was interested in, and which made this a *right* or a *liberty* and not a duty, was that in nature we are each to do what *we* want in order to preserve ourselves. It is this openendedness, this dependence solely upon the will of the individual agent, which is important about a right, and it was this which Hobbes captured by describing our natural capacity to make our own decisions about how to protect ourselves as a right. The 'law' of nature tells us what we *ought* to decide if we are thinking rationally, but the 'right' tells us that it is we who have to decide, and that we are naturally and psychologically free to go any way we choose towards the necessary goal of our survival.

It is this fact, that it is each individual in the state of nature who decides on the route to take for his own preservation, which is captured in the third claim which I summarized above: that in the state of nature 'there will be a large number of cases where everyone must be their own judge of how and when to defend themselves'. This was the claim which split Hobbes off from Grotius (and which the Dutchman recognized as the issue between them when he read *De Cive* in 1643; Mersenne and Hobbes may even have sent him a copy). Hobbes expressed it by saying (in the words of the *Elements of Law*) that 'every man by right of nature is judge himself of the necessity of the means, and of the greatness of the danger'. This too is repeated in *De Cive* and *Leviathan*, and it was a point upon which Sir Charles Cavendish, otherwise a very friendly reader of Hobbes's work, fastened critically when he first read *De Cive* (along with the point about the relationship between the right and the law of nature). He was right to do so, since virtually the whole of what is distinctive about Hobbes's political theory follows from this simple proposition.

For if men are to be their own judges of what conduces to their preservation, all the anti-sceptical advantages of the Grotian theory are immediately lost, since by virtue of Hobbes's general philosophy, it has to be the case that there is no clear and objective truth about the external world, and that all men will make different decisions about what counts as a danger to them. But if that is so, then there will still be no agreement about what should be done, and everyone will act on the basis of their own different assessments of the situation. Conflict will arise despite the apparent solution to the relativist problem contained in the idea of a natural and universal right of self-defence. The grimmest version of sceptical relativism seems after all to be the only possible ethical vision; and for ethics taken independently of politics, this is indeed Hobbes's conclusion.

*   *   *

JEAN HAMPTON

The Failure of Hobbes's Social Contract Argument†

A good sign that Hobbes's justification of sovereignty fails is that it is rare to see someone walk away from a reading of *Leviathan* a convinced absolutist. Ever since they were first published, Hobbes's political writings, though often evoking admiration (Skinner 1972), have generally aroused intense opposition from conservative and liberal thinkers alike. As one scholar of the seventeenth century notes, Hobbes was regarded as the "Monster of Malmesbury," the "bug-bear of the nation" (Mintz 1969, vii), and another scholar of the period relates that when Clarendon decided to spend his time during his banishment in France refuting *Leviathan*, he was embarking upon a "reputable and well-thought-of task" (Bowle 1951, 33). Twentieth-century readers, although intrigued by the power of Hobbes's argument, are even more opposed to instituting any of Hobbes's ideas than his contemporaries. What these attitudes indicate is that Hobbes's argument, compelling and sophisticated though it is, fails to justify its conclusion, and in this chapter we will explore exactly where and how it fails.

*　*　*

In this section, I want to discuss a problem with Hobbes's argument that has been little recognized in recent years by Hobbes scholars but that was appreciated by a number of Hobbes's important contemporary critics, including Clarendon, Bramhall, and Filmer. This problem is so serious that it renders the entire Hobbesian justification for absolute sovereignty invalid. Although, as we saw in the last section, Hobbes's argument does not fail because he cannot establish the rationality of creating an absolute sovereign, nonetheless it fails because he cannot establish, given his psychology, that men and women are *able* to do what is required to create a ruler satisfying his definition of an absolute sovereign. That is, if we assume Hobbes's shortsightedness account of conflict, his regress argument, and especially his psychological theories of human nature, we will see that the result of the only kind of "authorization" action they are able to perform will not be the institution of an absolute sovereign. Indeed, whenever Hobbes argues that people can create an absolute sovereign and that it is rational for them to do so, he has subtly but importantly changed his conception of what an absolute sovereign is and what submission to such a ruler entails. It is extremely important to appreciate that Hobbes equivocates at this crucial point in his argument in order to avoid being straightforwardly inconsistent. The purpose of this section is to expose that equivocation so as to reveal this inconsistency.

In Chapter 4 we presented Hobbes's regress argument and the con-

† From *Hobbes and the Social Contract Tradition* (Cambridge: Cambridge UP, 1986), pp. 189, 197–206. Reprinted with the permission of Cambridge University Press.

ception of absolute sovereignty that his argument supports. To review: The regress argument holds that in a civil society there must be some decision and enforcement entity that limits other such entities in society but that itself has no limits, and because this entity cannot be a law or set of laws, it must be a person. (Recall also that we argued against Hobbes's claim that this entity could be a set of persons.) Hence, the result of this argument is that civil society must have a person with *unlimited* decision and enforcement powers at its helm: That person is called the sovereign, and he has the power to decide *all* questions in the commonwealth, holding power permanently insofar as he has the power to decide the most important question in the commonwealth, that is, whether or not he should remain in power.

However, can such a sovereign really be created by Hobbesian people? In Chapter 5 we explored Hobbes's contention that a sovereign is created when a person is "authorized" by his subjects, where this means that they "surrender their right to all things" to him. And in Chapter 6 we attempted to cash out this metaphorical language consistent with Hobbesian psychology; in particular, we argued that one authorizes a sovereign when one obeys his commands to punish others and, in general, when one does nothing to frustrate his enforcement powers. We found, however, that there had to be one big exception to any person's willingness to support the sovereign's punishment efforts in the commonwealth: One could never willingly obey the sovereign's command to punish oneself, insofar as doing so would endanger one's self-preservation rather than preserve it. Given a human being's inevitable commitment to self-preservation, Hobbes must grant that each human being will "surrender" her punishment powers to the sovereign only insofar as doing so will not endanger her life. Thus, according to Hobbes, each human being carries with her into the commonwealth a "self-defense" right. But if she does, is the resulting ruler a genuine sovereign? Does he still have the power to decide all questions in the commonwealth? Does he still reign permanently? In order to answer these questions, we need to know precisely what this self-defense right is and how extensive it is. It clearly precludes obeying a sovereign's commands to punish oneself, but what else does it preclude?

Hobbes does not clearly define this self-defense right. Indeed, its name suggests that it is only a negative description of the fundamental right of self-preservation. However, Hobbes has to take the position that the self-defense right is only a small part of the larger self-preservation right, distinguishable from the "right to all things" that is surrendered to the ruler so that he is made sovereign. If Hobbes does not, then obviously nothing is surrendered to the sovereign. So let us begin by defining the right very narrowly as the privilege or liberty to defend one's body if it is attacked, or to do what is necessary to procure the means (e.g., food and shelter) to assure bodily survival. On our supposition, Hobbes must expect a subject to disobey *any* command by the sovereign when obedience likely would threaten that subject's bodily survival more than would disobedience.

But if we accept this very natural interpretation of the self-defense

right, then isn't this granting the subjects the right of private judgment
concerning whether or not their lives have been endangered? Why
doesn't it make their obedience to him conditional on his commands
not threatening their lives, where *they* are the judges of this question?
And because empowerment comes about only from obedience, why
doesn't this make the sovereign's empowerment conditional on people's
determination that such obedience is rational? Yet, insofar as it does,
they do not really empower a truly absolute sovereign at all, because
there is no single permanent power to decide all questions and hence
ensure peace among men. Conservative readers of *Leviathan* in the
seventeenth century were quick to notice these subversive implications
of the self-defense right. Filmer correctly perceived that by granting that
the subjects had a right to defend themselves, even when the right is
very limited in scope, Hobbes makes the subjects the judges of whether
or not the sovereign has endangered their survival, and hence allows
the subjects to decide whether or not they will disobey certain of the
sovereign's commands (1652, 4). This means that the sovereign is not
the only authority in a commonwealth and that he will have to reckon
with disobedience or rebellion on the part of some or all of his subjects
if they decide that his laws or actions jeopardize their lives.

In fact, one of the consequences of allowing the subjects this self-
defense right was Hobbes's very peculiar position on the legitimacy of
rebellion in a commonwealth, a position that made all royalists who
had lived through the events of the 1640s furious. Hobbes says that one
is never justified in initiating a rebellion, because no man will be better
off if the sovereign is deposed and the state of nature returns. However,

> in case a great many men together, have already resisted the Sov-
> eraign Power unjustly, or committed some Capitall crime, for
> which every one of them expecteth death, whether have they not
> the Liberty then to joyn together, and assist, and defend one an-
> other? Certainly they have: For they but defend their lives, which
> the Guilty man may as well do, as the Innocent. There was indeed
> injustice in the first breach of their duty; Their bearing of Arms
> subsequent to it, though it be to maintain what they have done,
> is no new unjust act. And if it be onely to defend their persons, it
> is not unjust at all. [*Lev*, chs. 21, 17]

After quoting this passage, Bishop Bramhall asks: "Why should we not
change the Name of *Leviathan* into *Rebells catechism?*" (1658, 515)[1]
What is upsetting Bramhall and others[2] is that in this passage Hobbes
is partially condoning as right certain rebel activity in a commonwealth.
He even uses the phrase 'not unjust' to describe rebellion if it is done
to preserve the rebels' lives, and this usage is quite shocking, because
he has defined injustice simply as disobedience to the sovereign's laws,
which the rebellious subject is surely committing. But probably Hobbes

---

1. And see Clarendon (1676, 87): "[Hobbes] devest(s) his Subjects of all that liberty, which the
   best and most peaceable men desire to possess, yet he literally and bountifully confers upon
   them such a liberty as no honest man can pretend to, and which is utterly inconsistent with
   the security of Prince and People. . . ."
2. See also Filmer (1652, 8–9).

simply misspoke here, and really meant by "not unjust" the concept "is a prudent course of action." Indeed, it seems plausible that in this passage Hobbes is contending that although people who start a rebellion are not behaving prudently, nevertheless if they know that they will be killed by the sovereign's forces on their surrender, then their continuation of the attack and the bearing of arms becomes prudent. And clearly Hobbes makes this point, because he maintains that the rebels retain a self-defense right and hence cannot refuse to defend their lives when they are under attack. But by taking this position, Hobbes is committed to advocating the continuation of rebel activity in a commonwealth once it has begun, and hence sanctioning the internal warfare and civil strife that the creation of an absolute sovereign was supposed to end. In defense, Hobbes would, of course, stress that he argues against the legitimacy of initiating a rebellion, but his conservative critics angrily appreciate that he also condones (and must condone) as rational the continuation of rebellious activity once it has begun.[3] And not only did these critics find this condoning of rebellious activity offensive; more important, they found it inconsistent with the idea that when one subjugates oneself to a sovereign, one makes him the judge of all questions in the commonwealth and the master of every area of one's life.

However, what upset the conservatives even more was that Hobbes did not limit the scope of the self-defense right to mere bodily survival. In Chapter 21, on the liberties of the subjects, Hobbes uses a very broad notion of this right, that is, that one can rightfully resist or defend onself against anything that *might lead* not only to death but also to mere injury of one's body, as a foundation for a number of subject liberties that would seriously undermine the supposedly limitless and absolute power of the sovereign. For example, he says that "If a man be interrogated by the Soveraign, or his Authority, concerning a crime done by himselfe, he is not bound (without assurance of Pardon) to confesse it; because no man (as I have shewn . . .) can be obliged by Covenant to accuse himselfe." (*Lev*, ch. 21) Given that such interrogation is not a direct attack on the subject's bodily survival, and given that the subject is supposed to have made the sovereign his master and hence obliged himself to obey the commands of the sovereign, how can he refuse to disobey the sovereign's orders here? Is this "owning all the Actions (without exception) of the Man, or Assembly we make our Soveraign?" (*Lev*, ch. 21, 10, 111) And what about the passage in which Hobbes says

> No man is bound . . . either to kill himselfe, or any other man; and consequently . . . the Obligation a man may sometimes have, upon the Command of the Soveraign to execute any *dangerous*, or *dishonourable* Office, dependeth not on the Words of our Submission; but on the Intention; which is to be understood by the End thereof. [*Lev*, ch. 21; emphasis added]

3. It was because of passages like this that Clarendon thought Hobbes was offering in *Leviathan* a justification of de facto power in general, and Cromwell's rule in particular. See Chapter 6, note 14.

What? Is Hobbes saying that people have a right to *lie* to their sovereign, that they can refuse not only to kill other men but also to commit those actions that are dangerous or *dishonorable*? Clarendon was shocked that Hobbes would suggest that the right to defend oneself could include defending not only one's body but also one's reputation (1676, 135). In addition, Hobbes says in this paragraph that men have a right to choose not to obey a sovereign's command to kill another. But if all or many of the sovereign's subjects choose to exercise this "right" (believing their disobedience to be prudent), what coercive power does the sovereign have left? How can he amass an army to quell internal rebellion? How can he even create a police force that will pursue criminals, or carry out executions? The self-defense right has now been interpreted so broadly that it is essentially equivalent to the *entire* right to preserve oneself.

However, there is an important reason why Hobbes *must* broaden the self-defense right in this way. Remember that Hobbes's entire justification of the state, as we saw in Chapter 6, rests on its being conducive to a person's self-preservation. But according to Hobbesian psychology, the pursuit of this goal is central to a person's life not only outside but also inside a commonwealth. Hobbesian people do not simply forget their ultimate desire to preserve themselves when they enter the commonwealth; it remains their premier goal. But insofar as it does, each of them will determine the rationality of performing any action in the commonwealth by determining to what extent it will further this goal. So Hobbes's psychological views force him to admit that the goal of self-preservation (not merely some limited concern for "self-defense") provides the criterion for determining whether or not to obey *any* of the laws of the commonwealth. And this means that such people are incapable of letting the sovereign determining their every action; their psychology is such that they will obey a sovereign command only when, in their eyes, it will further their lives to do so.

Perhaps even more remarkably, there are two passages in *Leviathan* in which Hobbes actually admits this is so. One of them occurs in Chapter 21 in the midst of Hobbes's attempt to define the self-defense right:

> When . . . our refusall to obey, frustrates the End for which the Soveraignty was ordained; then there is no Liberty to refuse: otherwise there is. [*Lev*, ch. 21]

It appears from this passage that the subjects are supposed to perform some kind of expected-utility calculation about the relative benefits of obeying or disobeying the sovereign's commands, taking into consideration not only the dangers of disobedience but also the effect the action of disobedience will have on the stability and final purposes of government. But if these calculations dictate disobedience, the subject is "right" (i.e., rational) to disobey. So, by taking this position, Hobbes essentially is admitting that the self-defense right retained by each subject in the commonwealth is equivalent to the *entire* right of self-preservation and hence makes the subjects the judges of whether or not they will obey *any* of the sovereign's laws.

The second passage in *Leviathan* in which Hobbes admits that the subjects must be the ones who finally decide whether or not to obey the ruler occurs later in Chapter 21. In this passage, Hobbes contends that the ability of the sovereign to protect his subjects and make their lives secure defines the extent and limits of the subjects' rightful obedience to the sovereign:

> The Obligation of Subjects to the Soveraign, is understood to last as long, and no longer, than [sic] the power lasteth, by which he is able to protect them. . . . The end of Obedience is Protection. [*Lev*, ch. 21; see also DC, EW ii, 6]

The interesting question one is left with on reading this passage is, *Who decides* whether or not the sovereign is adequately protecting his subjects? If a ruler is absolute sovereign, then he should have final say over what his subjects should and should not do, and hence he should be the judge of whether or not they should continue to obey his laws; but because it follows (as Filmer recognized[4]) from Hobbes's psychology that human beings will always judge any course of action on the basis of how well it furthers their self-preservation, he is committed to saying that the subjects will decide whether or not submission to the sovereign is furthering their lives. Indeed, given that psychology, we can expect them to do nothing else — whether the sovereign likes it or not. But this means Hobbes is forced to say that an *"absolute sovereign" reigns at his subjects' pleasure*, for it is they who decide whether or not obedience will secure them protection! When commenting on this passage, Bishop Bramhall appreciates not only how difficult it is for Hobbes to say anything else but also how disastrous this position is for Hobbes's political argument:

> Either it must be left to the soveraign determination, whether the subjects security be sufficiently provided for, And then in vain is any mans sentence expected against himself, or to the discretion of the subject, (as the words themselves do seem to import,) and then there need no other bellowes to kindle the fire of a civill war, and put a whole commonwealth into a combustion, but this seditious Article. [1658, 513]

Bramhall's point is that insofar as Hobbes is forced to admit that the subjects decide whether or not to continue their obedience to the sovereign, the commonwealth will inevitably degenerate into chaos and civil war.

But is Bramhall right to say this? Insofar as the self-defense right retained by the subject must be understood by Hobbes, given his psychology, as the entire right to preserve oneself, exactly why does this spell disaster for his political argument? That is, why does it mean that Hobbe's argument for absolute sovereignty is *invalid*?

Consider that an absolute sovereign is defined by Hobbes to be someone who is the *final decider* of *all* questions in a commonwealth, and

4. See Filmer (1652, 8): "[Hobbes] resolves refusal to obey, may depend upon the judging of what frustrates the end of Soveraignty and what not, of which he cannot meane any other Judge but the people."

whose subjects are literally enslaved to him. But if the subjects retain a right to determine whether or not to obey the sovereign's laws, then the sovereign not only fails to be the ultimate decider of every issue but also is not the decider of the most important question in the commonwealth, whether or not he will continue to receive power from his subjects. The sovereign's empowerment comes about only when the subjects obey his punishment commands. But now we see that *they decide* whether or not it is advantageous for them to obey these commands on the basis of whether or not doing so will further their self-preservation. So these "slaves" are continually deciding whether or not to let their master have the whip! Clearly this is not genuine enslavement at all, and the ruler with the whip is not someone who has absolute power to do what he wishes, but only the power to do what his subjects will *let* him do.

Indeed, as long as the subjects retain the right to preserve themselves in a commonwealth, they cannot be said to have surrendered *anything* to the sovereign. Whatever power he has been granted by the subjects for the purpose of furthering their self-preservation can and will be taken back by the subjects when they determine that doing so will further their self-preservation. And insofar as any sovereign will lose his punishment power if his subjects decide it is no longer advantageous for them to obey his punishment commands, the sovereign's power *must* be understood to be a "loan" from the people, not a permanent grant. The power he wields not only comes from them but also returns to them if *they* decide his use of it will do more to hurt them than to help them, and this is exactly the relationship that prevails between any principal and his agent. In fact, the same process of making agreements in order to institute the sovereign can also be used by the subjects to take back the power they lent to him, and used instead to reach agreement on lending that power to a different ruler who these subjects believe will be better able to further their self-preservation. If the "protection agency" hired by the people is perceived by them to be doing a poor job of furthering their self-preservation, they may find it in their best interest to "fire" that agency and "hire" another. But this means that as long as people retain the right to preserve themselves in the commonwealth, Hobbes is also forced to admit that there is really an *agency relationship* between people and ruler, and this is exactly what he did *not* want to conclude in *Leviathan*.

But readers might question the idea that this conclusion is a disastrous one for Hobbes. Couldn't he contend that the less-than-absolute ruler-agent that Hobbesian people can create is still powerful enough to achieve peace among them? Perhaps he can, but the fact remains that in *Leviathan* he explicitly contends in his regress argument that nothing less than a ruler who reigns permanently and has the power to decide all questions in the commonwealth can end the warfare among human beings. Thus, if we accept the truth of the regress argument, we are forced to accept that the kind of ruler Hobbesian people are able to create is not good enough to secure peace. Indeed, it is useful to review components of Hobbes's regress argument in order to see exactly how, given this argument, the "agency commonwealth" forced on Hobbes by his psychological views is doomed to fail. Or, to put it more crudely, it is useful to see the way in which Hobbes is skewered with his own sword.

Consider that as long as subjects retain the right to preserve themselves, and hence the right to decide whether or not to obey any of their ruler's commands, *private judgment* has not been destroyed in the commonwealth, and Hobbes himself contends, using his ethical and psychological views, that any commonwealth in which private judgment exists will be destroyed from within:

> I observe the *Diseases* of a Common-wealth, that proceed from the poyson of seditious doctrines; whereof one is, *That every private man is Judge of Good and Evill actions.* . . . From this false doctrine, men are disposed to debate with themselves, and dispute the commands of the Common-wealth; and afterwards to obey, or disobey them, as in their private judgements they shall think fit. Whereby the Common-wealth is distracted and *Weakened.* [*Lev,* ch. 29]

What we have discovered is that Hobbesian people are incapable of giving up their power of private judgment in a commonwealth because they will always retain the ability in a commonwealth to determine whether any action—including the action of obeying the sovereign's commands—is more conducive to their self-preservation than any available alternative. And given what Hobbes says in the foregoing passage, he would believe that the results of each subject retaining this right will be, first, debates whether or not to obey the ruler's commands that cannot be resolved in any way except by violence, followed by seditious actions by dissatisfied subjects fanning this violence, leading eventually to full-scale civil war. And as we see from their remarks cited earlier, Hobbes's contemporary critics, including Cumberland, Filmer, and Bramhall, agree with this general point. So Hobbes's regress argument in *Leviathan* (based on his psychology) against any political union in which subjects retain the right to make private judgments (and so the right to judge their ruler's performance) is also an argument against the political union Hobbes himself is forced to espouse given that same psychology.

Consider another aspect of the regress argument against agency commonwealths made in Chapter 18 of *Leviathan* involving the existence of a contract between ruler and people in these regimes. Hobbes insists (*Lev,* ch. 18) that any contract-created commonwealth is doomed to fail. Because there can be no legal judge to decide any controversy about how well the ruler is living up to the agency contract, each subject will judge this question on the basis of how well the ruler is advancing her self-preservation. But such individual assessments are bound to conflict, and Hobbes believes that it will be only a short period of time before this sort of contract-created commonwealth will degenerate into a state of war as the subjects turn to violence (just as they did in England during the 1640s) to resolve their disagreements over how well the ruler is performing. But, as we have seen, in a Hobbesian commonwealth the subjects retain, by virtue of their psychological makeup, the right to decide whether or not to obey the sovereign's commands. This means that the sovereign is essentially empowered by them for as long as they believe that following his commands will be conducive to their interests, so that there is, at the very least, an *implicit agreement* between him and the subjects specifying what he must do to retain the power given to him by the subject's obedience. It follows that this "implicit agency-contract" commonwealth is doomed to fail.

The third and perhaps most significant problem introduced into Hobbes's commonwealth by the subjects' retention of the right to preserve themselves is the loss of the permanence and continuity of sovereign rule. Because the subjects "surrender their right to all things" to the sovereign, they give him a property right in them, so that if they try to take back the right they previously surrendered from either him or his successor (who has been willed that property right), "they take from him that which is his own, and so again it is injustice." (*Lev.* ch. 18) There is a peculiar and intriguing moral tone to this passage that, given Hobbes's subjectivist ethical position, ought not to be there. We tried to "explain away" this moral tone in Chapter 5 by interpreting the wrongfulness of rebellion prudentially: Deposing the sovereign or refusing to obey his hand-picked successor is wrong, not because it violates some deontologically valid moral law but because it will precipitate violence and civil strife, endangering not only the lives of other members of the commonwealth but also one's own life.

But note what this prudential explanation of the wrongfulness of rebellion takes for granted! It assumes that *the subjects* can and will judge whether it is prudent for them to remain in the commonwealth or work to depose it. And we can expect that they will (rationally) choose not to obey these commands whenever doing so will threaten their self-preservation. This means that a sovereign holds power because most or all of his subjects have chosen to obey him — that is, have chosen to let him have power, which means that, in the end, he rules because *they let him rule.* But a sovereign cannot be permanently authorized when the subjects are not only able but also "prudentially obliged" to secede from his rule when their lives are, in *their* eyes, endangered. Such a ruler holds power conditionally, not permanently. And no successor of a sovereign can be assured of his property right over the subjects if these subjects are not only able but also "prudentially obliged" to rethink the advisability of their allegiance after the reins of power have been passed on. In the end, this successor receives power not when the previous sovereign bequeaths it to him, but only when the subjects decide to let him have it by obeying his punishment commands. And that decision might go against him, destroying the continuity of rule in this political society.

I believe that it is because Hobbes *cannot* permanently and absolutely bind people, as he has described them, to any ruler or ruler-successor by arguing for the prudence of their allegiance to that ruler that Hobbes's remarks on a subject's obligation to the ruler continually have a moral tone. Because his argument is critically weak at this point, he "cheats," either consciously or unconsciously, by invoking moral ideas that not only have no place in his argument but also have already been rejected in the course of making that argument. Consider his remarks in Chapter 18 on why "The subjects cannot change the forme of government." He starts out by saying that

> they that have already Instituted a Commonwealth, being thereby bound by Covenant, to own the Actions, and Judgements of one, cannot lawfully make a new Covenant, amongst themselves, to be obedient to any other, in any thing whatsoever, without his permission. [*Lev*, ch. 18]

Why do they need his permission? Perhaps because it is prudent for them to ask for it? But if they think another individual would make a better sovereign because he would further their preservation more effectively than the original sovereign, why doesn't prudence dictate *not* asking the original sovereign's permission and simply making the switch? But, Hobbes might contend, switching sovereigns likely will bring forth a time of bloodshed and chaos, so that it is not in one's best interest to try it. However, what if the subjects believe that the switch can be made with little loss of life, or believe that the switch is so desirable that an expected-utility calculation tells them it is worth the risk of bloodshed? Hobbes cannot rule out the possibility that situations like this could exist. And it is probably because he cannot preserve permanence of rule by appealing to prudence to block rebellion on all occasions that he suggests that the action is wrong in some objectively moral sense.

That moral tone surfaces a few sentences later when he says, as we noted earlier, that deposing the sovereign is taking from him "that which is his own," an act that is "injustice." In Chapter 5 we gave a prudential interpretation of this passage, but perhaps the more natural interpretation is a moral one, that is, that it is morally wrong to take the sovereign's power from him because that would be stealing. But where do these scruples against stealing come from? From the laws of nature, whose dictates are not even supposed to be followed if doing so will endanger one's preservation? No, these laws contain nothing that would rule out theft in *all* circumstances. Indeed, stealing (i.e., seizing an object that another has claimed) would seem to be (prudentially) right and rational if the object is necessary for one's preservation and if taking it does not endanger one's life. Hence, far from laying a moral foundation for the *complete* condemnation of stealing, Hobbes's laws of nature and his psychology lay the groundwork for explaining when it is rational and (prudentially) correct to be a thief—even a "rebellious" thief of the sovereign's power.

So the moral tone in these passages seems to be Hobbes's attempt to circumvent deep trouble in his argument—a way to try to make the sovereign's rule permanent and his successor's rule secure, when no such permanence or continuity of rule follows from his argument. Critics such as Warrender have been rightfully sensitive to the moral tone of Hobbes's discussion of a subject's obligation to her sovereign, although missing the way in which, given Hobbes's subjectivist metaethics and his analysis of the validity of the laws of nature, that moral tone is completely out of place in his argument, and actually signals that argument's failure.

So, we now see that Hobbes's social contract argument is invalid: That argument cannot show that people, as he has described them, can institute what Hobbes defines as an absolute sovereign. Indeed, let us spell out this invalidity precisely:

1. In order for peace to be secured, an absolute sovereign must be created, and an absolute sovereign is defined as one who is master of all his subject-slaves; this absolute sovereign is the final decider of all questions in the commonwealth, including the question whether or not he will continue to hold power, and in virtue of deciding this last question, he holds power permanently.

2. Hobbesian people empower a ruler by obeying his punishment commands, and they do so whenever *they decide* such obedience is conducive to their best interests.

3. But from (2), it follows that the ruler created by Hobbesian people does not decide *all* questions; in particular, he does not decide for his subjects the question whether or not they will obey his commands — including his punishment commands.

4. It follows from (3) that insofar as a ruler holds power only as long as his subjects obey his punishment commands, the subjects determine (by their decision whether or not to obey these commands) whether or not he will continue to hold power.

5. Hence, from (3) and (4), Hobbesian people cannot create a ruler who meets the definition of a sovereign in (1) (i.e., a ruler who decides all questions in the commonwealth and whose reign is permanent), which, from (1), means that they cannot secure peace.

So there is no successful geometric deduction of absolute sovereignty in *Leviathan*, although Hobbes certainly tried mightily to construct one. Although most twentieth-century critics have commonly assumed that Hobbes's political conclusions can be dismissed because they rest on false premises, they have not appreciated the more important fact that the conclusions themselves do not follow from those premisses. Indeed, we see that Hobbes's dilemma in *Leviathan* is identical with that of Philip Hunton. Recall the discussion in Chapter 4 of Hunton's difficulty in explaining how people who "elected" their sovereign in an original contract were not superior to their ruler even though they were his creators. Hunton ends up maintaining that the subjects *surrender* some or all of their rights to their ruler, thereby enslaving themselves to him, but Hunton also insists that they retain a "moral" power to evaluate his conduct. In the end, it turns out that Hobbes tries to hold a similar sort of contradictory position.

But we really should have appreciated that Hobbes's argument was in trouble by the end of Chapter 6. In that chapter we relied on Hobbes's psychology to specify precisely the concrete actions that Hobbesian people would take to institute a ruler. And the actions we specified *presupposed* that people always retained the right to determine if the performance of any of those actions was in their interest. Indeed, this right was at the heart of my attempt to explain how Hobbesian people could create a commonwealth, because at every stage of the creation process I was concerned to show that these people would (or could) find the actions required at that stage advantageous to them. So, in setting out to define 'authorization' consistent with Hobbesian psychology, I ended up by cashing out the metaphor not of "surrendering power" but of "loaning power" to the ruler.

Indeed, the fact that I so naturally cashed out the notion of authorization consistent with Hobbes's psychology but inconsistent with his definition of absolute sovereignty suggests why so many critics have not realized that his political argument in *Leviathan* is invalid. Hobbes equivocates: He gives only a metaphoric definition of the notion of authorization, characterizing it as a surrender, such that it appears consistent with his official definition of absolute sovereignty; but when he actually uses the notion of authorization in his argument, he implicitly uses it in the way I defined in Chapter 6 — assuming that it involves obedience to the ruler *for self-interested reasons* — and linking it with a self-defense right. The fact that this use does *not* cash out the surrender metaphor and is actually inconsistent with the official definition of absolute sovereignty is therefore very difficult to see.

DAVID JOHNSTON

Theory and Transformation:
The Politics of Enlightenment†

Apart from the vigor and vividness of its language, the feature of *Leviathan* that distinguishes it most clearly from Hobbes's earlier political works is the great extent and detail of the attention it devotes to Scriptural exegesis and theological argumentation. In *The Elements of Law*, a work of twenty-nine chapters, Hobbes had devoted two chapters to a discussion of potential conflicts between religious and political authority. In *De Cive* he expanded this discussion considerably, creating a new division of four chapters on religious subjects, which he placed at the end of his book. Even with this expansion of their role, however, Scriptural and religious questions remained a distinctly subordinate subject in Hobbes's work. Their status in *Leviathan* is very different from that which they had held in these earlier compositions. *Leviathan* includes a new chapter on religion in general, placed in a pivotal po-

† From *The Rhetoric of* Leviathan: *Thomas Hobbes and the Politics of Cultural Transformation* by David Johnston (Princeton: Princeton UP, 1986), pp. 114–20, 128–33. Reprinted by permission of Princeton University Press.

sition at the end of Hobbes's account of human nature and immediately before the portrait of the state of nature with which his theory of the generation of a commonwealth begins. Of four parts into which he now divided his treatise, the third and longest is devoted almost entirely to Scriptural interpretation, while the fourth is concerned mainly with the diagnosis of spiritual errors. In short, Scriptural and religious questions occupy more space in *Leviathan* than any other topic discussed in the work, including Hobbes's theory of the commonwealth itself.

What is the significance of Hobbes's introduction of these new arguments into the body of his work? What bearing do they have upon the political argument detailed in parts I and II of his book? Until very recently these questions received scant attention in the critical literature. The traditional interpretation has been that the theological views developed in parts III and IV of *Leviathan*, however interesting they may be in themselves, are of no real significance for his political philosophy. The foundation of that philosophy, according to this interpretation, is entirely naturalistic. Hobbes develops his political argument out of an analysis of human nature, especially the passions, and its consequences for social interaction. He does not derive it from a set of theological presuppositions, as political philosophers had customarily done since early medieval times. From this viewpoint, then, the theological arguments adumbrated in *Leviathan* appear to be mere appendages to the true work. They are addressed to concerns that are local and transitory, by contrast with the more enduring concerns of Hobbes's political philosophy in the proper sense.[1] While many adherents to this interpretation regard these theological arguments as mere trappings, designed to make Hobbes's doctrines palatable to a nation of Christian believers, it has also been maintained by critics who have taken them to be an elaboration of his sincere religious beliefs.[2] Raymond Polin has expressed the essence of this interpretation clearly and forcefully by arguing that Hobbes's theology is "superimposed" upon his political philosophy, and should in no sense be regarded as an integral part of that philosophy.[3]

This interpretation was strongly challenged some years ago, mainly as a result of Howard Warrender's thorough and carefully argued study of Hobbes's theory of obligation. Warrender argued that the pivotal concept in Hobbes's theory of obligation was that of natural law. The laws of nature are the basis upon which men acquire all their obligations, including those toward their civil sovereign. In this sense they provide the foundation for all commonwealths and all civil laws. But these laws of nature, he suggested, are intelligible only as expressions of divine will. Furthermore, the obligation to obey them, which must

---

1. Polin, *Politique et Philosophie chez Hobbes*; Strauss, *Political Philosophy of Hobbes* (Chicago: U of Chicago P, 1952), Oakeshott, *Hobbes on Civil Association* (Paris: Presses Universitaires de France, 1953), p. 48. Strauss adopts a somewhat different view in his later essay, "On the Basis of Hobbes's Political Philosophy," in *What Is Political Philosophy?* (Glencoe, Ill.: The Free Press, 1959), pp. 170–196.
2. Paul J. Johnson, "Hobbes's Anglican Doctrine of Salvation," in Ralph Ross, Herbert W. Schneider, and Theodore Waldman, eds., *Thomas Hobbes in His Time* (Minneapolis: University of Minnesota Press, 1974), pp. 102–125.
3. *Hobbes, Dieu, et les hommes* (Paris: Presses Universitaires de France, 1981), p. 61.

exist prior to and independently of all acquired obligations, cannot be understood without reference to divine sanctions. No obligation can be operative or valid unless those obliged by it have a sufficient motive to obey. The only motive sufficient to validate men's obligation to obey the laws of nature is provided by the divine sanction of salvation. Hence the theological concepts of divine will and divine sanctions are basic to Hobbes's entire political philosophy, the foundations of which are in this sense essentially theological rather than naturalistic.[4]

Warrender and others who have advocated this revisionist interpretation have provided many new insights into the structure of Hobbes's political argument, and some of these have proven themselves to be valuable correctives to the traditional view of Hobbes. But their thesis that the foundation of that argument is religious or theological rather than naturalistic is unconvincing. The general source of the confusion is not difficult to identify. Advocates of this revisionist interpretation have focused their attention sharply upon the juridical concepts and language of Hobbes's political philosophy. By so doing they have forced defenders of the traditional, naturalistic view to take this language much more seriously than they have sometimes done in the past. At the same time, however, the revisionists have tended to neglect the behavioral and causal language that is also an integral component of Hobbes's political argument, and have thus underestimated the importance of this entire dimension of his political philosophy, which is encapsulated, among many other places, in his characterization of the laws of nature as "dictates of Reason, . . . or Theoremes *concerning what conduceth to the conservation and defence of themselves.*"[5]

The most curious thing about this revisionist interpretation, however, is that its advocates have made almost no effort to draw upon the voluminous evidence of Hobbes's own theological argumentation in parts III and IV of *Leviathan*. In spite of their claims about the importance of Hobbes's theological concepts or religious beliefs to his political philosophy, these revisionists seem to have accepted, either tacitly or expressly, the traditional view that those portions of *Leviathan* are of no very great or enduring interest.[6] While postulating that his theological views are integral to, or indeed the very foundation of, his political philosophy as a whole, these revisionist critics have actually had little more to say about Hobbes's own theological argumentation than their traditionalist adversaries.

Only very recently has a new cohort of scholars, more interested in and sensitive to the historical context and concreteness of Hobbes's political philosophy than earlier generations of critics, begun to rectify this omission. The seminal work on this point was an essay on Hobbes's religious and historical views by J.G.A. Pocock. Analyzing Hobbes's argument in the latter half of *Leviathan* more closely than any previous critic in recent times, Pocock was led to conclude that

---

4. *The Political Philosophy of Hobbes: His Theory of Obligation* (Oxford: Clarendon Press, 1957), esp. pp. 99–100, 272–277.
5. *Leviathan*, ch. 15, emphasis added.
6. In addition to Warrender, cf. on this point F. C. Hood, *The Divine Politics of Thomas Hobbes* (Oxford: Clarendon Press, 1964), esp. p. 252.

this second half of the work is neither strictly subordinate to the political argument of its first half, as most defenders of the traditional interpretation have asserted, nor an elaboration of views that form the theoretical foundation of that political argument, as advocates of the revisionist view have claimed. Instead, he argues, Hobbes simply "embarks on a new course" at the midpoint of *Leviathan*. The first half of that work deals with the domain of nature and reason, while its second half deals with the historical domain of prophecy and faith; and this latter domain is not, in spite of the usual opinion to the contrary, "reabsorbed" into the former. For Pocock, then, *Leviathan* is in effect two separate works, composed in two distinct languages, which stand side by side, neither being subordinate to the other.[7]

Perhaps the greatest virtue of Pocock's work is that it demonstrates emphatically the importance of taking Hobbes's words in the latter half of *Leviathan* seriously. But taking his words seriously is not the same thing as taking him at his word, as Pocock also tends to do. Thus, for example, he argues that Hobbes would never have written "chapter after chapter of exegesis with the proclaimed intention of arriving at the truth about it" had he not believed that the Christian Scriptures constitute the true prophetic word of God.[8] This argument from bulk is unconvincing, if only because it underestimates Hobbes's capacity for political wile. Pocock is absolutely right to chastise most previous scholars for ignoring what Hobbes actually wrote about the Scriptures and sacred history,[9] but his own methodological dictum that critics should concern themselves less with Hobbes's sincerity of conviction than with the effects his words seem designed to produce does not lead to the conclusions he reaches in his essay.

From a strictly logical point of view, the traditional interpretation, according to which parts III and IV of *Leviathan* are a mere appendage to the "real" political argument of that work, is substantially correct. The theological argumentation of Hobbes's work is neither the foundation nor in any other sense an integral part of his political philosophy, if we understand that philosophy to be an abstract, timeless scheme for the organization of political society. That scheme is constructed by interweaving a set of observations about human behavior and interaction, formulated as theoretical propositions, with a set of legalistic or juridical propositions about the grounds, origins, and distribution of rights and obligations. In no essential way does it involve or rest upon theological concepts or religious beliefs. From this point of view, then, the second half of the book is indeed a superimposition, which can be explained only by going outside the bounds of its central argument.

But this conclusion flows from the adoption of assumptions about the nature of Hobbes's work that are different from those held by Hobbes himself. For him, as I have sought to suggest, *Leviathan* was not simply and exclusively a work of "science" or abstract speculation

---

7. "Time, History, and Eschatology in the Thought of Thomas Hobbes," in J.G.A. Pocock, *Politics, Language, and Time* (New York: Atheneum, 1973), pp. 148–201, esp. pp. 159, 167, 191.
8. "Time, History, and Eschatology," pp. 167–168.
9. "Time, History, and Eschatology," pp. 160–162.

about the causes and organization of political society. It was above all else a work of political persuasion and engagement, which sought to shape popular opinion in ways designed to benefit the cause of peace.

Considered as a political act, the metaphysical, theological, and historical argumentation of parts III and IV of *Leviathan* are integral to the design of Hobbes's book as a whole. Indeed, from this practical point of view it can be argued that they constitute the core of, and lay the foundation for, his project in *Leviathan*. If, in other words, we focus upon the effects Hobbes's words seem designed to produce, we find that (Pocock's investigations notwithstanding) there is a close, even intimate, relationship between the argumentation of the second half of the book and that of its first half. The second half of *Leviathan* is designed to shape the thoughts and opinions of its readers in ways that will make the argumentation of the first half persuasive and compelling. In this sense, parts III and IV lay the groundwork upon which the practical effects envisaged in parts I and II of the work are to arise.[1] The balance of this chapter will sketch the reasoning behind my interpretation, while the chapters that follow will attempt to demonstrate its validity by examining the content and implications of Hobbes's metaphysical, theological, and historical argumentation.

*   *   *

By becoming linked with the historic struggle for "enlightenment," as he conceived it—a struggle he might easily have traced back to Erasmus and other representatives of earlier Renaissance humanism—Hobbes's political philosophy acquired a temporal dimension that had not been present in its initial formulation. In *The Elements of Law*, he had analyzed the commonwealth and the distribution of rights and obligations within it in essentially ahistorical and abstract terms. He had based a timeless theory of government and politics upon an equally timeless model of human nature. In *Leviathan* he clung to all the essential features of that theory. But the discrepancy between that model of human nature and his portrait of man as an irrational being gives *Leviathan* an historical dimension that had been lacking from Hobbes's earlier works. His theory of the commonwealth still had an abstract, timeless quality about it, but the model of man upon which it rested was now linked to a specific historical moment. Hobbes's theory would not achieve practical realization until men became the rational actors they had always had the potential to be. This would not occur until knowledge had triumphed over ignorance, reason had driven out superstition, and enlightenment had vanquished the forces of darkness. The practical realization of Hobbes's political philosophy

---

1. The nearest approach to this interpretation in the existing literature is that offered by Eisenach in *Two Worlds of Liberalism*. Like Pocock, however, Eisenach greatly exaggerates the disjunction between the two halves of *Leviathan*, going so far as to argue that the work "contains two separate languages, logics, psychologies, and politics" (p. 70). This claim arises out of his acceptance of Pocock's assumption that faith and prophecy constitute a form and realm of knowledge for Hobbes, whereas in fact Hobbes treats faith as a form of mere opinion, not as knowledge, and seeks to undermine the entire concept of prophecy. * * * For another attempt to revise Pocock's interpretation in a similar direction, see Patricia Springborg, "*Leviathan* and the Problem of Ecclesiastical Authority," *Political Theory* 3 (1975), pp. 289–303.

had become linked to a possible event in future time: the transformation of human beings into the relatively enlightened, rational creatures that had always been the inhabitants of his vision of political society.

This possible future transformation of man became, for Hobbes, the crucial event in human history. The prospects for a commonwealth as he envisaged it were vitally dependent upon the outcome of the struggle between superstition and enlightenment. His theory of the state could not fully be put into practice before the movement toward enlightenment had triumphed. Yet there was no certainty that this triumph would take place. Hence Hobbes was led by what seemed to be inexorable necessity to a basic reformulation of the design of his political theory. His original aim had been to demonstrate the proper distribution of rights and obligations in a commonwealth. This demonstration, he hoped, would help convince men of the need for absolute sovereignty. Now, however, Hobbes saw that he would have to take on aims much broader than these original ones. To promote enlightenment itself, an entire outlook and approach to life, became an integral part of Hobbes's political purpose. His original theory was now encapsulated within a project of even grander design. The cultivation of rational modes of thought and action was an essential step toward the realization of his political aims. It became an aim in itself, distinct from, but inseparably wedded to, the original purposes of Hobbes's political theory.

This new aim generated a stratum of argument that was new in *Leviathan*. Hobbes had touched upon certain religious themes and used Scriptural arguments in both of the earlier versions of his political theory. But in each of these previous works the religious and Scriptural argumentation had been strictly subordinated to his central political aims. Its purpose had been to show that there could be little or no conflict between a man's duties to God and his obligations to his earthly sovereign, and thereby to remove one important potential obstacle to civil obedience. Though Hobbes reproduces many of the arguments of these earlier works in *Leviathan*, the theological argumentation in that work as a whole has a very different character from that which it had before. The doctrines of Christianity, as he portrays them, have been infiltrated over the centuries by many superstitious and magical traditions. As taught by some of the established churches, Christianity has become a carrier of superstition and spiritual darkness. The struggle for enlightenment is, in very large measure, a struggle against these tendencies within established Christian doctrine. The theological argumentation of *Leviathan* is essentially different from that of Hobbes's earlier works because the central aim of that argumentation is new. That new aim was to expose the superstitious and magical elements in Christianity so that these could be expelled from Christian doctrine. Ultimately, it was to lay the groundwork for a fundamental change in the habits of thought and action that had prevailed throughout most of the Christian era — amounting almost to a transformation of the human psyche that would prepare men and women to be assembled, for the first time in history, into a truly lasting political society.

The formulation of this new aim was the pivotal event in the development of Hobbes's political philosophy. It stands behind all the alter-

ations that distinguish *Leviathan* from his earlier works. The new ambition to appeal to a large, public audience and thus shape popular
opinion directly; the vividness of language, designed to leave a deep
and lasting impression upon his readers; the new stratum of theological
argumentation, so vastly more developed than it had been in his previous works—all these changes were linked to this one great shift in
Hobbes's aims. The philosophical treatise that was designed to show
the need for absolute sovereignty by means of logical demonstration,
and that had constituted the main content of *The Elements of Law*, is
contained in *Leviathan* as well. But in *Leviathan* that treatise is merely
one part of a work of much larger extent and scope. The opposition
between reason and rhetoric had been Hobbes's basic theme in *The
Elements of Law*. In *Leviathan*, it was replaced by a new theme, that
of the struggle between enlightenment and superstition, between the
forces of light and the forces of darkness. And the form in which he
presents this theme is less that of a philosophical argument in the ordinary sense than that of an epic, with all the grandeur of conception
that term implies.[2]

The fact that Hobbes presents this theme in a new form is intimately
related to the reorientation of his aims. "The Sciences," he points out,
"are small Power. . . . For Science is of that nature, as none can
understand it to be, but such as in a good measure have attayned it."[3]
This observation is especially applicable when the aim is not so much
to demonstrate the truth of a scientific conclusion from principles that
are already accepted as to establish the validity of those principles themselves. For the principles of science, as Hobbes often remarks, cannot
be demonstrated by scientific methods. They are self-evident truths, and
must simply be presented to the reader in the hope that he or she will
recognize them as such: "For this kind of Doctrine, admitteth no other
Demonstration."[4] Science cannot prove that the principles upon which
it rests are true. But this limitation inherent in the nature of science
need not prevent its advocates from using other means to persuade their
readers to accept those principles as truths. The vigor and vividness of
Hobbes's language in *Leviathan*, as well as the extremely polemical cast
of his theological argumentation, are designed to accomplish just this
aim. The language of *Leviathan* was necessarily rhetorical, in a deeper
sense than the language of his earlier works of political philosophy had
been, because the aim of that work was not merely to demonstrate the
truth of Hobbes's political argument. That aim, rather, was to establish
the authority of science, and through it to promote rational modes of
thought and action, with a superstitious people. The form in which
Hobbes presents his argument was a consequence of his adoption of
this new and extra-scientific aim. In this sense *Leviathan* is at least as
much a polemic *for* science and enlightenment as it is an instance of
scientific or philosophical argument.

By recasting his argument into this new form, Hobbes effected a

---

2. Cf. Sheldon Wolin, *Hobbes and the Epic Tradition of Political Theory* (Los Angeles: Clark
   Memorial Library, 1970), which argues a thesis similar to that of this and the following
   paragraph.
3. *Leviathan*, ch. 10.
4. *Leviathan*, Introduction, p. 83; cf. *De Corpore* I.6.5, 13, 15.

synthesis between some of the possibilities inherent in his own idea of science, on the one hand, and the rhetorical lessons he had imbibed during the years before he had conceived that idea, on the other. From the beginning, his idea of science had left open the question of what was to be done to reconcile discrepancies between scientific theory and empirical reality. In fact, the geometrical archetype implied that such discrepancies should be interpreted as signs of the imperfection of reality, not evidence of defective theory. The analogy with geometry did not immunize the theorems of science from empirical criticism entirely, of course, since for Hobbes any science should be capable of proving its mettle through its usefulness in changing and controlling reality. Until an opportunity to apply its theorems had been seized, however, empirical criticism of science would remain meaningless. Recasting the argument of *Leviathan* was a way of helping to create such an opportunity for his political theory. By drawing upon the lessons of the rhetorical tradition, which emphasized the power of the visual image or "speaking picture" in contrast to the weakness of merely conceptual discourse for creating mental impressions, Hobbes was attempting to create conditions under which the validity of his own theory of government and politics could be confirmed through its practical realization.

Hence the change in form and methods that distinguishes the argumentation of *Leviathan* from that of his earlier works of political philosophy represents neither an abandonment nor in any essential sense a modification of his original purposes. The truth is that this change is a sign and consequence of Hobbes's increased determination to achieve those purposes. The final aim — to bring into being a commonwealth based upon firmer, more rational foundations than any that had ever existed before — remained unchanged. But attainment of this aim now seemed to be contingent upon a prior cultural transformation. The polemical defense of science and enlightenment against magic and superstition was designed to help bring about this transformation, to implant those (in Hobbes's view, rational) habits of thought and action which were required if his scheme for the organization of political society was to work. This defense led Hobbes to offer interpretations of the metaphysical, prophetic, and historical dimensions of human existence as well as the assessment of man's political situation already expressed in earlier versions of his political philosophy.

GEORGE KATEB

Hobbes and the Irrationality of Politics†

* * *

Hobbes introduces a concept that is not a mere mitigation of his commitment to the war-state, but actually opens up a radical critique

† From *Political Theory* 17.3 (August 1989): 383–88. Reprinted by permission.

of it. I refer to Hobbes's contention, present in both *De Cive* and *Leviathan*, that each individual has an unrenounceable right to life. One can never be thought obliged to risk or sacrifice one's life for any purpose, though of course one may have to risk or will even lose it in the effort to save it. If, as we have seen, the idea of the duty of self-preservation is a device to dissuade people from embarking on civil war or activities that threaten it, the idea of an unrenounceable right to life is crucially a device that works with the effect of psychologically strengthening each individual against the claims of any government, including, or perhaps especially, *Leviathan*. Moreover, the duty to preserve oneself can reinforce the psychological effect of the right to do so, and thus become another device against the claims of government.

Hobbes says:

> And therefore there be some Rights, which no man can be understood by any words, or other signes, to have abandoned or transferred. As first a man cannot lay down the right of resisting them, that assault him by force, to take away his life; because he cannot be understood to ayme thereby, at any Good to himselfe. The same may be said of Wounds, and Chains, and Imprisonment.[1]

The right by nature to do anything whatever to preserve oneself is a right each of us has equally with all others. It exists not only where there is no government (or other protector) or where its protection has temporarily lapsed, but also where there is a government and one is threatened by it. No matter what one does, no matter what obligation one owes, no matter what wrong one has done, no matter what the cost to innocent others, one can never owe or forfeit one's life. We must notice, however, that the unrenounceable right establishes no corresponding duty in others to respect it. When government is impotent or in abeyance, I have a right to do what I must to save my life, inside or outside society, and so does everyone else, even at my expense. Similarly, a functioning government may have lawful designs on my life (or bodily integrity or freedom); but I have the right to elude or resist those designs. One may always "without Injustice, refuse" to cooperate with one's own hurt or ruin at the hands of Leviathan itself.[2]

Hobbes's theory teaches that in the most important respect, therefore, every human being under every government always lives in a state of nature. If nations exist in a state of nature because there is no government above them all, the most important illustration of the state of nature between individuals is a settled society. The reason is not so much because the passions are (by their very nature) irritable and transgressive, but much more because every society always has some life-threatening purposes or projects, which every individual has the right to avoid or resist for himself. The other side of the coin is that the ruler, no matter his origins, is always a conqueror, and the state his personal property. He is always in a kind of state of nature with his subjects, as they are with him. The idea of society as a state of nature is a brutal but demystifying and hence emancipatory notion.

1. Hobbes, *Leviathan*, chs. 14, 15, and 21.
2. Ch. 21.

Now, Hobbes takes no steps to guarantee his radical idea institutionally, although a conception of society that was even less naturalistic than Hobbes's own would require guarantees. In Hobbes's theory, the ruler will use and treat individuals as he sees fit by right or by strength. He will overpower them and their unrenounceable right to life. I do not think, however, the idea is thereby eviscerated. It is possible to think, rather, that even in the absence of institutionalized guarantees, a climate more favorable to individual integrity would develop if a ruler and the people alike accepted Hobbes's teaching on this matter. Clearly, however, institutionalized guarantees best suit (some manifestations of) the unrenounceable right to life.

It may be asked, what is the source of this unrenounceable right? The answer is not clear. There is no answer in Hobbes's answer: "Nature gave a right to every man to secure himselfe by his own strength, and to invade a suspected neighbour, by way of prevention."[3] Hobbes leaves no natural teleology standing: "the universe, as one aggregate of things natural, hath no intention."[4] In addition, Hobbes has theoretically disabled himself from appealing to an overriding instinct in human beings to self-preservation and thus from somehow deriving a right from an instinct. Spinoza's apparently similar teaching in his two tractatuses is even more obscure to me than Hobbes's. In Hobbes the true ground is, I think, a feeling: Hobbes's passionate tenderness toward all human beings, especially vulnerable ones. With what right, with what possible authority, could anyone require a fellow creature not to try to preserve itself?

In any case, the unrenounceable right to life is made by Hobbes to yield a number of important consequences. A seemingly narrow idea has immense explosive power. It shakes Hobbes's own theory; it should shake any theory, and any practice. Hobbes himself draws the following consequences. The general failure of authority revokes one's allegiance. Prisoners of war may change allegiance. Those engaged in the very activity that Hobbes dreads most — namely, civil war — may rightfully resist their capture. One may lie under torture. The ruler is wrong to compel a person to bear witness against himself in a criminal proceeding. One may try to elude or resist one's legal punishment. Indeed, at one point Hobbes even says that the ruler's right to punish is his personal natural right to overcome hostility; it cannot be a right understood as inhering in sovereignty precisely because no subject has the right to authorize his own hurt or ruin.[5] (There is kinship between the right to life and the rule of law, and Hobbes briliantly expounds and extols the rule of law in chapters 26 through 28 of Leviathan.)

All these ideas tend to erode the mystique of political authority. Insofar as they do so, they give evidence of Hobbes's emancipatory power. We must now bring the matter home to the issue of Hobbes's commitment to the personified nation and thus to the inevitability of war. Hobbes tries to deal with the fact that wars can sometimes be fought only if the ruler conscripts able-bodied men. He does his best to estab-

3. Ch. 26.
4. Hobbes, Questions, 237.
5. Hobbes, Leviathan, chs. 14 and 21.

lish the ruler's *covenantally based* right to conscript, not merely his natural *power-based* right to overcome impediments to his will. Thus, he is unwilling to conceptualize conscription in the way that he (sometimes) does punishment. His unpurged patriotism blocks the move. Yet his readers may make the move for him.

How can one be obliged to conscription and yet have an unrenounceable right to life? Assume that a given war is not a war directed at the enslavement or massacre of the population. Also take into account all that Hobbes says or suggests concerning the inferiority of the value of all things in life in comparison to (unenslaved) life itself. One should conclude that though Hobbes may prefer able-bodied men to forget both their duty and their right to stay alive, and to lend themselves to the patriotic endeavor to defend the life of the personified nation at the expense of their literal lives. Hobbes's most distinctive concept teaches that they should not. They should be ready to accept surrender, provided they do not anticipate enslavement or massacre.

Hobbes is, to be sure, equivocal. This shows itself in the fact that he formulates the social contract in two different ways. Initially and at least twice thereafter, he wants us to conceive that we are held together in society solely by the pledge not to harm each other. Yet elsewhere he includes the provision that we pledge our "mutuall ayd against . . . enemies abroad"; that we oblige ourselves to "join together against a common Enemy"; and that we oblige ourselves "to assist him that hath the Sovereignty, in the Punishing of another."[6] He thus gives both a minimal and an expanded version of the social contract. The minimal contract is a drastic departure from traditional thought because it conceives of a population as contingently thrown into life in the same place and time and held together by rational good sense (abetted by fear of punishment). The expanded one re-establishes traditional thought on a new basis by continuing to see a population as a people that have ties that are more profound and more ancient than the ties of rational good sense and that antedate the very idea of a social contract and may very well outlive it. Further, the expanded contract in itself creates an artificial reason to die and kill; the minimal version truly seeks peace.

I do not see how the expanded contractual understanding is compatible with the idea of an unrenounceable right to life. I therefore do not see how Hobbes can succeed in the perhaps frightened effort he makes at the very end of *Leviathan*[7] to stabilize the rather erratic discource on conscription that appears in chapter 21. He awkwardly adds a law of nature to those he had already listed in chapter 15. The addition comes as a belated discovery. The awkwardness is disarming, but it is also a sign of his own doubts. He says that "every man is bound by Nature, as much as in him lieth, to protect in Warre, the Authority, by which he is himself protected in time of Peace."[8] That seems to seal able-bodied men into a system of conscription. The matter is not so simple, however. The phrase "as much as in him lieth" may be the key. In chapter 21, Hobbes says that some men have "naturall timor-

6. Chs. 14, 15, 18, 22, 26.
7. In "A Review, and Conclusion."
8. Ch. 29.

ousnesse" or "feminine courage."[9] Allowance should be made for them: they should be let off or permitted to buy their way out. Even though the sovereign may punish with death their refusal to fight, they are not guilty of injustice (that is, a breach of covenant), but of cowardice, of acting dishonorably. But Hobbes has already taught us how cheap a thing honor is. He is even prepared to say that it is good if most subjects lack fortitude, which is necessary for soldiers, "yet, for other men, the less they dare, the better it is both for the commonwealth and for themselves."[1] The implication is that the ruler can always put together an adequate volunteer army — provided people do not resist paying their taxes. Finally, the best that Hobbes can do is to give conscription a shaky theoretical defense. Maybe that is all that he wants to do.

Hobbes cannot bring himself to reject conscription outright. He does not follow through on his sentence, "for it can never be that Warre shall preserve life, and Peace destroy it."[2] His patriotic sentiments obstruct the logical unfolding of his theory, which is properly completed by Kant in *Perpetual Peace*. The essence of any self-consistent contract theory is the preservation of all human lives, or as many as possible, and on minimally decent terms. Yet his theory emanates from his deepest philosophical self, not from his patriotic feelings. Though he seems to try to construct a sufficient argument to discourage civil war, and anything that may help bring it on, by invoking the dangers of the international state of nature, the most distinctive element in his political theory defeats his strategy. His real passion, we may then say, is probably on the side of the fragile individual, on the side of the ordinary person, not on the side of all those (in power or aspiring to it) who gain from the mystifications that crush him. For that reason, even when in behalf of civil peace for the sake of life rather than foreign wars, he crudely discredits or insufficiently esteems the aims and motives that instigate civil war; he is still an emancipator. The notion of the fragile individual can also be used in spite of Hobbes's intentions, but in line with his real passion, to defend the necessity for constitutional democracy, as well as to defend resistance to it when its heightened sense of legitimacy encourages its adventurism abroad. His most general power, however, consists in getting us to wonder whether any value can ever justify losing and taking life, even if we choose some other way of valuing life than by reference to an unrenounceable right. At the same time, on our own but perhaps fortified by him, we can reject the common contention that only those willing to die and kill for political and civil freedom deserve to have it. If I am told that what I cherish and benefit from depends on the willingness of others to risk death and to die, all I can say is that I must admit to living exploitatively.

In sum, one can say that Hobbes is radical in the intensity of his wish to subdue people to obedience and that he therefore gives too little to political freedom and too much to the alleged necessity of war. But he is even more radical in his ability to set them free because his analysis exposes the vanity of elites and imparts a reverence for mere

9. Ch. 21.
1. Hobbes, *Behemoth*, 45.
2. Hobbes, *Leviathan*, ch. 15.

being. Free of absolutism, people can still be freed some more by Hobbes. The individualism that is centered in the sense of individual fragility is always able to engender radical results. Though one must heed him selectively, he is, in truth, an emancipator.

RICHARD E. FLATHMAN

Of Making and Unmaking†

Thomas Hobbes is first and foremost a theorist of individual human beings as the *Makers* of themselves and their worlds. He is also and equally a theorist of failed attempts at makings, of mismakings, and of unmakings or destroyings. Himself the maker of an elaborately constructed system of ideas, Hobbes's writings depict a densely material universe pulsating with energy and movement but largely lacking in humanly intelligible or serviceable order or purpose. Into this universe he thrusts individuals and loose and fluctuating groups who struggle to give shape and impart direction to themselves, their environment, and one another. Often futile or worse, occasionally partly successful, these efforts cease only at death and largely constitute the human experience.

The most famous such making is that with which Hobbes opens his masterwork, the devising of an "artificial animal," "that great LEVIA-THAN called a COMMONWEALTH." Hobbes likens this act to no less than the "**fiat, or let us make man,** pronounced by God in the creation" and goes so far as to say that it begets a "mortall God." This astonishing figure is the emblem of his reputation as an uncompromising proponent of absolutist and authoritarian government.

Surrounding, informing and — I argue — finally subordinating the making of the Leviathan are a plethora of images of individual human beings each of whom he invites us to regard as at least God-*like* in their capacities to construct, out of their own passions and desires, beliefs and purposes, themselves and their worlds. The omnipotent God of the various Judeo-Christian mythologies made Adam out of dust and Eve out of a bone. In what we and perhaps Hobbes himself might regard as his transposition and transvaluation of this tale, Hobbesian human beings impose form and purpose upon the matter that is themselves — their own bodies and minds — and their universe.

The thematic of human beings as God-like makers of themselves stands in a never fully relieved, often sharply drawn, tension with other pronounced tendencies in Hobbes's thinking. Hobbes was for the most part scornful of prevailing conceptions of humankind as Knowers of or Believers in something apart from themselves, as active or passive instrumentalities of Reason or Truth. At the same time, he insisted upon respects in which human beings are Sufferers from forces they did not produce and could little alter, respects in which they are captives of a Fate. Whereas Hobbes credits the omnipotent God with having created

† From *Thomas Hobbes: Skepticism, Individuality and Chastened Politics* by Richard E. Flathman (Newbury Park: Sage, 1993), pp. 1–9. Reprinted by permission of Sage Publications, Inc.

the universe ex nihilo or out of nothing but Herself, the comparable task confronting human beings is the more difficult one of crafting their selves and things serviceable to those selves out of materials that they know to have certain unalterable characteristics but about which there is otherwise much that they do not and cannot comprehend.

Hobbes thought that the universe consisted of whirling atoms of matter and believed that the motions of these particles formed an unbroken and unbreakable network of strictly causal relationships. Along with his metaphysical materialism and determinism, he thought that there are quite narrow limitations on what human beings can know about and do with and to their world. An opponent of the various doctrinaire or programmatic skepticisms with which he was familiar, he nevertheless contested the soaring religious, philosophical and scientific claims and aspirations of his own and previous ages and he repeatedly drew attention to the defects and liabilities of perception, reason, language and the other sources and resources on which his own most affirmative arguments and conclusions relied.

For these and related reasons, the "givens" bequeathed to humankind by God and Nature, while necessary to the possibility of human "being" and potentially contributive to human well-being, are insufficient for the former, radically so for the latter, and often recalcitrant to human purposes. In order to so much as identify and perpetuate themselves, and more emphatically in order to achieve a degree of "felicity" and "commodious living," women, men and some difficult to classify figures who make brief but intriguing appearances in Hobbes's works, must themselves give form and course to the opaque and often resistant materials that are their experiences and their lives.

It is a daunting task.

The most fundamental artifice of all is inventing names and assigning them to nameless and largely incomprehensible things. This is done quite arbitrarily in that initially it is by their choosing alone that individual human beings invent names and stipulate their meanings. By performing acts of naming they endeavor to impart a degree of stability and intelligibility to themselves and their world. As they cumulate names into languages and form them into conceptions, further thinking and acting become possible, in particular those modes of thought and action that produce the vastly more complex makings that are the sciences and the arts, moral and legal rules, the institutions of government.

If only because of its extraordinary prominence in *Leviathan*, this feature of Hobbes's thinking is familiar to his most casual readers. Partly because Hobbes's influence has extended well beyond his considerable readership, this bracing, invigorating, but apparently also deeply disturbing conception of humankind has become a main though never dominant element in the thinking ("modern," "antimodern," "postmodern," and other) that he did much to inaugurate; a chief albeit never triumphant competitor for the intellectual and spiritual allegiances of the women and men of the ages that he has influenced. In ways that we sometimes find inspiriting and gratifying but that often leave us anxious and fearful, in much of our thinking we conceive of ourselves as Hobbesian creatures.

A self-esteeming and cheerful, certainly a buoyant if only intermittently optimistic man. Hobbes was not one to regret what might be regarded as the insouciance or even malice of God, the fact that the "Author of Nature" had written human beings into largely unfriendly circumstances and left them to cope as best they could by their own inventings and devisings. If God or Nature had done more *for* human beings (as much more, for example, as She or It had done for subhuman animals) they would thereby also have done much more *to* them; certainly they would have diminished the challenge and the zest that Hobbes savored as unique to the human estate. Hobbes did not stint in detailing the difficult, troubled character of human affairs. He nevertheless believed that there are a number of respects in which human beings have done quite well in and with their makings, yet other respects in which by his time they were positioned to do markedly better for themselves than their predecessors had managed.

The clearest case of successful making is what we would call mathematics and its application to the natural sciences and through them to "arts" such as navigation and engineering, agriculture and medicine. Hobbes thought that the set of human inventions that he called geometry had been brought to the status of a genuine science. He describes geometry as an extensive (albeit incomplete and presumably uncompletable), unambiguous, and internally consistent body of propositions (definitions, axioms and deductions therefrom) that are beyond cogent dispute. He was also convinced that the conclusions of geometry and applications of the geometric method in science more generally had imposed substantial intelligibility on the matter of nature. If not deflected or corrupted by the misconceived "experimental science" that was burgeoning around him and that he fiercely combated, science could progressively tame nature's motions and forces, could harness them to human purposes. If as a practical matter there remained far more to lament than to celebrate in politics, morals, and the other modes in which human beings attempt the inveterately difficult task of "keeping company" with one another, Hobbes believed that implementation of his own civil philosophy would set things as straight as there is any reason to want them to be.

In short, Hobbes thought that artificing has sometimes been and in appropriate respects can increasingly be efficacious and durable. Despite their radically subjective character, the stipulations that create language, and the inferences drawn from and actions taken on the basis of those stipulations, could be additive and hence progressive, could diminish the necessity and the desirability of further makings or later re-makings. Along with insisting, often vehemently, that many of the "fabrications"[1] inherited from previous generations had been ill-made and needed remaking and even eradication, he thought that some among them had been skillfully constructed and could and should be

---

1. Because artifacts such as words, conceptions, and theories make rather than present or represent "things," for Hobbes they themselves cannot be fabrications in the sense of lies or deceits (albeit he was intensely aware that language enables lying and that lies are often told and deceptions frequently perpetrated concerning artifacts). For the same reason, that they are "made up" by their creators, for those who oppose this Hobbesian view they will be fabrications in the pejorative sense and will never be without a taint of falsification.

received and used rather than forgotten, destroyed, or refashioned by those who come later. Hobbes was nearly Heraclitian in his conception of a natural universe pervaded by a flux that defied human comprehension; as regards the humanly made world he resisted the despairing pessimism commonly associated with such cosmologies and seemingly impelled by his own deeply skeptical temperament.

It is arguable that this refusal on Hobbes's part was no better than the desperate act of a man who had thought himself into an untenable position. Certainly it has often been argued, against Hobbes and recognizably Hobbesian views, that the combination of positions thus far sketched is incoherent and hence self-invalidating. A "world" constructed out of nothing more substantial than the arbitrary wills and artifices of radically particularized individual beings could hardly be orderly, stable or durable. Worse, because by Hobbes's own insistence each of these "beings" is by nature nothing more than a swirling, fluctuating concatenation of particles, the notion that "they" could be God-like makers is altogether incredible. How could such beings produce and use language; how could they form, elaborate, and employ conceptions and theories; construct and operate elaborate machines; devise and maintain effective institutions? By denying the humanly knowable divine, natural or rational order posited by his main theological and philosophical opponents, by claiming to liberate human beings to devise an order of their own making and liking, Hobbes cast humankind into an abyss of self- and mutual unintelligibility. Insofar as the women and men of later centuries have followed Hobbes, that is where their self-conceptions and self-understandings leave them.

Hobbes did sometimes understate and perhaps underestimate the difficulties implied by his most general philosophical positions, did exaggerate the possibility of making good the enormous deficits left in the human condition by God, nature and thus far by human history. Of course this judgment does not itself invalidate his biting critiques of opposing and apparently more encouraging views, critiques that do much to expose the illusory or rather delusory character of the strong assurances of order and intelligibility that others have offered themselves and us. Accordingly, we should show our gratitude for the lessons Hobbes has taught us by bringing them to bear on the more affirmative aspects of his thinking. We should subject his own proposals and prescriptions to the same skeptical attack that he launched against the too sanguine and overly zealous religious, philosophical and political dogmatists of his time.

Unquestionably a part of the present task, Hobbes has done much of this critical work for us. He sometimes understated or diminished the skeptical and other circumscribing implications and complications of his cosmological and theological, metaphysical and epistemological views; but his works also contain extended discussions that are more than candid in insisting on the limitations on and obstacles to our knowing and understanding, our thinking and acting. Hobbes is not a dogmatic skeptic or passive nihilist who asserts the impossibility of warranted beliefs or efficacious purposeful action. No attentive reader can miss the powerfully skeptical tendency of his thinking concerning the divine and its relation to the human, language and the possibilities of communication and mutual understanding, reasoning and knowing, science and the understanding and control of nature.

There is a related point that is yet more important for present purposes. Hobbes sometimes indulged himself in overstatement as to the possibility and desirability of achieving political and moral order through contract, covenant and the rule of the Leviathan. But we have to consider the possibility that the common or public order he thought possible and desirable would encompass no more than limited aspects of human life, was neither meant nor expected to impose any very extensive controls on the thinking and acting of individual human beings. The view that he is first and foremost a theorist of individual makings and unmakings suggests that public order is for the sake of the multiplicity of partial, personal, and internally conflicted orders that each of us makes and remakes for ourselves.

Hobbes puts substantial difficulties in the way of entertaining this possibility. Leaving for later discussion a certain ambivalence that he betrays concerning the desirable scope and purposes of the form of association that he called a commonwealth, the most serious among these difficulties reside in his infamous description of the state of nature. Taken at face value, this frightening and often decried account teaches that human relations governed by nothing but individual self-command and self-control ineluctably deteriorate into a destructive "war of all against all." If this is the case, the notion that individual persons should for the most part be left to their own self-making and self-governance is no better than a reckless fantasy. The human beings he describes had better be governed, rigorously and perhaps entirely so, by someone or something else. It seems that if we credit Hobbes's analysis of the state of nature we must also take at face value his argument for a sovereign with the authority and power not only to rule but substantially to remake its subjects. Or rather we could resist this conclusion only by taking the deeply pessimistic view that Hobbesian human beings are ungovernable, fated to misery if not to mutual annihilation. On this familiar and understandable view of his thinking, Hobbes reduces us to a choice between two equally repugnant options: peace, order and a measure of commodious living at the price of docile submission to authoritarian government; assertive self-making and self-direction at the cost of disorder, conflict, and mutual destruction. Because, if these exhaust and are the mutually exclusive alternatives, Hobbes has an unmistakable preference for the first, it is absurd to think of him as a theorist of robust individuality and abundant diversity, of minimal governmental control and discipline.

I contest this reading. By way of preparation, I here mention a consideration that is partly available in the discussion thus far and that has often been advanced by critics who think that Hobbes's position, whether evaluated as appealing or repulsive, is untenable because internally contradictory or incoherent. The line of criticism to which I refer goes as follows: For all of Hobbes's talk about the absolute authority and fear-inspiring power of the Sovereign, his Leviathan is and on his premises can only be a paper tiger, is and must be incapable of cogently demanding or effectively compelling more than minimal obedience from its subjects. His Leviathan couldn't begin to impose the order and control he wanted.

This critique of the most specifically political aspects of Hobbes's thinking is a particular version of the objection that, quite generally, his views cannot account for regularity or order sufficient to intelligible experience. If human beings as he depicts them cannot so much as make sense of themselves, one another, and their world, they can hardly construct and maintain a politically organized society. As with the more general formulation of this objection, it may be that those who advance it are governed — whether knowingly — by assumptions that Hobbes has good reason to reject. As Hobbes most often deploys them, concepts such as regular-erratic, order-disorder, intelligible-incomprehensible/ mysterious (and therefore also peace, security, stability, felicity and their opposite, obverse, and contrasting terms) operate over ranges or along continua. They do not form binaries or dichotomies, are matters of more and less, not all or none. There are real difficulties with his epistemology and his philosophies of language and science, but he should not be castigated for failing to meet criteria of knowledge, meaning and explanation that he repudiated and that, partly for reasons he brought against them, have not fared notably well in subsequent discussions. Most pertinent here, acknowledging the objections against his theory of making and maintaining a politically organized society does not excuse us from asking whether some of those objections proceed from conceptions of the character and proper purposes of governance and politics that deserve the scorn that (remarkably few lapses aside) he heaped on them.

· Hobbes was, as we might put it in this preliminary discussion, a pretty smart fellow. If it is obvious to us (from his descriptions of and prescriptions for it!) that the gimcrack contraption that he calls Leviathan could have little effective authority and even less power over its subjects, it might not be unreasonable to assume that he wanted it that way. We will see that he gives us more definite reasons for this inference. (And thereby gives us reasons for preferring a state and a politics something like the one he proposes to the vastly more potent and hence immeasurably more dangerous varieties that had begun to emerge in his time and that now threaten our very existence.)

Hobbes is a spirited participant in debates that are alive and urgent here and now. If we attack or defend his ideas we had better be prepared to support our own.

My claim is that the primary unit of Hobbes's thinking is the individual person and her makings, unmakings and remakings of herself and her worlds, the primary objective of his political and moral thinking is to promote and protect each person's pursuit of her own felicity as she herself sees it.

Selected Bibliography

I. MAJOR WORKS, IN ADDITION TO *LEVIATHAN*, BY THOMAS HOBBES

The Answer of MR Hobbes to SR William D'Avenant's Preface before Gondibert. In William D'Avenant, *Gondibert 1651*. Menston, England: Scolar Press Limited, 1970.

Aristotle's Treatise on Rhetoric. Literally Translated [by Thomas Hobbes] with Hobbes's Analysis. London: George Bell and Sons, 1958.

The Autobiography of Thomas Hobbes. Translated by Benjamin Farrington. *The Rationalist Annual*, 1958.

Behemoth, or The Long Parliament. Edited by Ferdinand Tonnies. With an Introduction by Stephen Holmes. Chicago: U of Chicago P, 1990.

Decameron Physiologicum. In *The English Works of Thomas Hobbes of Malmesbury*, vol. VII. Edited by Sir William Molesworth. Reprint of the edition of 1845. London: Scientia Aalen, 1962.

De Cive, or The Citizen. In Bernard Gert, ed., *Man and Citizen: Thomas Hobbes*. New York: Humanities Press, 1972.

De Corpore. In Richard S. Peters, ed., *Body, Man, and Citizen: Selections from Hobbes's Writings*. London: Collier Books, 1962.

De Homine. In Bernard Gert, ed., *Man and Citizen: Thomas Hobbes*. New York: Humanities Press, 1972.

A Dialogue between a Philosopher and a Student of the Common Laws of England. Edited and with an Introduction by Joseph Cropsey. Chicago: U of Chicago P, 1971.

Elements of Law. In Richard S. Peters, ed., *Body, Man, and Citizen: Selections from Hobbes's Writings*. London: Collier Books, 1962.

Hobbes's Thucydides. Edited and with an Introduction by Richard Schlatter. New Brunswick: Rutgers UP, 1975.

The Iliads and Odysses of Homer. Translated . . . by Tho: Hobbes. . . . With a large PREFACE concerning the Vertues of an Heroick Poem; written by the Translator. First published 1676. The Second Edition. New York: AMS Press, 1979.

Of Liberty and Necessity. In Richard S. Peters, ed., *Body, Man, and Citizen: Selections from Hobbes's Writings*. London: Collier Books, 1962.

A Physical Dialogue of the Nature of the Air. "Appendix" in Stevin Shapin and Simon Schaffer, *Leviathan and the Air-Pump: Hobbes, Boyle, and the Experimental Life*. Princeton: Princeton UP, 1985.

Six Lessons to the Professor of the Mathematics. In *The English Works of Thomas Hobbes of Malmesbury*, vol. VII. Edited by Sir William Molesworth. Reprint of the edition of 1845. London: Scientia Aalen, 1962.

"Third Set of Objections [to Descartes's *Meditations*] With the Author's [Descartes's] Replies." *The Philosophical Writings of Descartes*, vol. II, pp. 121–37. Translated by John Cottingham, Robert Stoothoff, and Dugdald Murdoch. Cambridge: Cambridge UP, 1984.

Thomas White's De Mundo Examined. Translated by Harold Whitmore Jones. London: Bradford UP, 1976.

II. BIBLIOGRAPHIES AND SELECTED WORKS CONCERNING HOBBES'S THOUGHT

Aubrey, John. *Aubrey's Brief Lives*. Edited by Oliver Lawson Dick. Ann Arbor: The U of Michigan P, 1957.

Baumgold, Deborah. *Hobbes's Political Theory*. New York: Cambridge UP, 1988.

Bertram, Martin. *Hobbes: The Natural and the Artifacted Good*. Bern: Peter Lange, 1981.

Bowle, John. *Hobbes and His Critics: A Study in Seventeenth-Century Constitutionalism*. London: Jonathan Cape, 1951.

Brandt, Frithiof. *Thomas Hobbes' Mechanical Conception of Nature*. Copenhagen: Levin and Munksgaard, 1928.

Brown, Keith C., ed. *Hobbes Studies*. Oxford: Basil Blackwell, 1965.

Child, Arthur C. *Making and Knowing in Hobbes, Vico, and Dewey*. Berkeley: U of California P, 1953.

Connolly, William C. *Political Theory and Modernity*. Oxford: Basil Blackwell, 1988.

Eisenach, Eldon. *Two Worlds of Liberalism: Religion and Politics in Hobbes, Locke, and Mill.* Chicago: U of Chicago P, 1981.

Gauthier, David. *The Logic of Leviathan.* Oxford: Clarendon Press, 1969.

Goldsmith, M. M. *Hobbes's Science of Politics.* New York: Columbia UP, 1966.

Herzog, Don. *Happy Slaves.* Chicago: U of Chicago P, 1989.

Hood, F. C. *The Divine Politics of Thomas Hobbes.* Oxford: Clarendon Press, 1964.

International Hobbes Association Newsletter. Colorado Springs, CO.

Jacobson, Norman. *Pride and Solace.* New York: Methuen, 1986.

Kavka, Gregory S. *Hobbesian Moral and Political Theory.* Princeton: Princeton UP, 1986.

Macpherson, C. B. A. *The Political Theory of Possessive Individualism.* Oxford: Clarendon Press, 1962.

Mintz, Samuel, *The Hunting of Leviathan.* Cambridge: Cambridge University Press, 1962.

Peters, Richard. *Hobbes.* Harmondsworth: Penguin, 1956.

Pocock, J. G. A. "Time, History and Eschatology in the Thought of Thomas Hobbes." In Pocock's *Politics, Language and Time.* New York: Atheneum, 1971.

Rapaczynski, Andrzey. *Nature and Politics: Liberalism in the Philosophies of Hobbes, Locke and Rousseau.* Ithaca: Cornell UP, 1987.

Raphael, D. D. *Hobbes: Morals and Politics.* London: Allen and Unwin, 1977.

Reik, Miriam, M. *The Golden Lands of Thomas Hobbes.* Detroit: Wayne State UP, 1977.

Rogow, Arnold. *Thomas Hobbes.* New York: W. W. Norton, 1986.

Ryan, Alan. "Hobbes on Individualism." In G. A. G. Rogers and Alan Ryan, eds., *Perspectives on Thomas Hobbes.* Oxford: Clarendon Press, 1988.

———. "A More Tolerant Hobbes?" In Susan Mendus, ed., *Justifying Toleration.* New York: Cambridge UP, 1988.

Sacksteder, William. *Hobbes Studies (1879–1979): A Bibliography.* Bowling Green: Philosophy Documentation Center, 1982.

Skinner, Quentin. "Conquest and Consent: Thomas Hobbes and the Engagement Controversy." In G. E. Aylmer, ed., *The Interregnum: The Quest for Settlement, 1646–1660.* Hamden, CT: Archon Books, 1972.

———. "The Ideological Context of Hobbes's Political Thought." In Maurice Cranston and Richard Peters, eds., *Hobbes and Rousseau: A Collection of Critical Essays.* Garden City: Anchor Doubleday, 1972.

Sorell, Tom. *Hobbes.* London: Routledge & Kegan Paul, 1986.

Strauss, Leo. *The Political Philosophy of Hobbes: Its Basis and Its Genesis.* Oxford: Clarendon Press, 1936.

Taylor, A. E. "The Ethical Doctrine of Hobbes." In Keith C. Brown, ed., *Hobbes Studies.* Oxford: Basil Blackwell, 1965.

Thomas, Keith. "The Social Origins of Hobbes's Political Thought." In Keith C. Brown, ed., *Hobbes Studies.* Oxford: Basil Blackwell, 1965.

Tuck, Richard. "Grotius, Carneades, and Hobbes." *Grotiana* n.s. 4 (1983): 43–62.

———. *Hobbes.* Oxford: Oxford UP, 1989.

———. *Natural Rights Theories.* Cambridge: Cambridge UP, 1979.

———. "Optics and Skeptics: The Philosophical Foundations of Hobbes's Political Thought." In E. Leites, ed., *Conscience and Casuistry in Early Modern Europe.* Cambridge: Cambridge UP, 1987.

Warrander, Howard. *The Political Philosophy of Hobbes.* Oxford: Oxford University Press, 1957.

Watkins, J. W. *Hobbes's System of Ideas.* London: Hutchinson University Library, 1965.

Wolin, Sheldon. *Hobbes and the Epic Tradition of Political Theory.* Los Angeles: Clark Memorial Library, 1970.

Zagorin, Perez. "Hobbes on Our Mind." *Journal of the History of Ideas* 51 (1990): 317–35.

Selected Glossary

admirable   amazing, awe-inspiring
arbitrary   discretionary (see n. 6, p. 37)
bewray   reveal
challenge   claim
conscience   consciousness
consent   agree, agreement
constitution   decree, establishment, the way a thing is constituted
contumacy   obstinacy
conversation   behavior, dealings with others
dominion   right of governing or possession
emulation   rivalry
enthusiasm   prophetic frenzy
feign   contrive or imagine (not necessarily in a deceptive or fanciful sense)
froward   perverse, difficult to deal with
impertinent   inappropriate
industry   diligence
intend   understand
invention   discovery
mediocrity   moderation
office   duty, function
perfect   complete
pretend   claim (not necessarily with intent to deceive)
propriety   property
rude   uneducated, rough
scope   purpose
sentence   conclusion, judgment

Index of Authorities
Cited in *Leviathan*